Bank Credit Extension and Real Economic Activity in South Africa

Nombulelo Gumata • Eliphas Ndou

Bank Credit Extension and Real Economic Activity in South Africa

The Impact of Capital Flow Dynamics, Bank Regulation and Selected Macro-prudential Tools

palgrave
macmillan

Nombulelo Gumata
Economist
South African Reserve Bank, South Africa

Eliphas Ndou
Economist
South African Reserve Bank, South Africa

ISBN 978-3-319-43550-3 ISBN 978-3-319-43551-0 (eBook)
DOI 10.1007/978-3-319-43551-0

Library of Congress Control Number: 2016958293

Printed on acid-free paper

This Palgrave Macmillan imprint is published by Springer Nature
The registered company is Springer International Publishing AG
The registered company address is: Gewerbestrasse 11, 6330 Cham, Switzerland

Preface

The four parts of this book examine a variety of issues. Among them are establishing the strength of links between credit supply dynamics and the real economy and determining if they are responsible for fragile economic growth recovery. We also assess the impacts of financial regulation uncertainty, regulator excesses and bank risk-taking channels in South Africa. We use simple scatterplot analysis cross-correlation to examine the lead-lag relationship and then apply advanced econometric analysis to show linkages that could not be shown using simple basic statistical techniques.

Unconventional Monetary Policies Since the onset of the US subprime crisis, which translated into global financial crisis and recession followed by serious economic uncertainties, the South African economy has experienced a fragile recovery. To deal with domestically weak economic growth recoveries in the USA, UK and the Eurozone, monetary policy-makers embarked on quantitative easing, which injected liquidity using various instruments. It is undeniable that prevailing low interest rates in these economies led to capital flows into emerging markets, including in South Africa. Thus increased demand for assets in these economies may lead to high asset prices and a reversal of capital flows through disposing of these assets may lower their prices.

Recent Policy Changes Currently, as policymakers are implementing prudential polices, we give new insights into what policymakers infer from the role of existing macro-prudential tools which were implemented by financial institutions themselves for the residential sector on economic activity. These macro-prudential policies coincide with different monetary policy phases; hence we give new insights into the extent of the interaction between macro-prudential policies and monetary policy and show that prudential policies also spill over into price stability and inflation expectation. In addition, inflationary pressures and expected inflation rates may lead to undesirablly tight prudential tools. We fill these gaps by showing the strength of spill over linkage.

Part I: Global Liquidity, Capital Flows, Asset Prices and Credit Dynamics in South Africa

Subsequent to the 2007 global financial crisis, key central banks in advanced economies embarked on conventional and unconventional accommodative monetary policies. The policy rates were lowered to very low levels and bank balance sheet expanded considerably. While large amounts of global liquidity may be desirable, there are mixed views on the extent to which South Africa (SA) has benefited from abundant global liquidity during this period of low interest, made possible through increased capital inflows which impact the real economy. Amidst this expectation, the debate is captured via the views of the *"initiator countries vs the recipient countries"*. First, the tapering of asset purchases can be interpreted as an indication that the US economy is recovering, and this can be seen as good news for the South African economy to the extent that, with positive growth impulses from the USA, global growth and demand benefit South African exporters. The thesis is that an improvement in world output (global demand) will lead to increased demand for South African exports. Thus, spill-over to foreign economies could occur via exports growth amongst other key channels of transmission. While income effects encompassed within the trade channel and tend to dominate the development, this is not the only channel that fully reflects the spill-over effects of foreign demand. The exchange rate appreciation linked to G3 central bank liquidity injection could lead to undesirable outcomes.

Global liquidity can operate via different channels, hence we investigate its effects through assessing different aspects. Is there any evidence of the inverse transmission of global liquidity shocks into the domestic economy? We apply counterfactual analysis to see what would happen to selected variables in the absence of G3 liquidity. Are there any differential effects on gross domestic product (GDP) growth between US and European Central Bank (ECB) liquidity? We extend the analysis and quantify the undesirable effects of capital flow uncertainty by providing a systematic analysis of how large capital inflows, capital inflow reversals and net portfolio flow volatility affect economic performance, and show there exists an understated sectoral reallocations transmission channel. To give further insights, we perform a counterfactual analysis to assess how economic growth, changes in the Real Effective Exchange Rate (REER) and growth in credit extension would have evolved in the absence of the contributions of capital flows. While credit market indicators may exhibit divergences, to overcome this and enable proper indication of prevailing conditions, we construct a credit conditions index (CCI) for South Africa. This matters as we examine the extent to which tighter credit conditions impact real economic activity. We use the constructed CCI to examine the extent to which the massive policy rate reduction since 2009 impacted credit conditions. Are the repo rate contributions during the recession similar to those in other periods when the repo rate was lower before the tightening phase in 2007? Given that equity markets are impacted by capital flows dynamics, we identify episodes of real stock price busts and the associated economic costs, the behavior of selected macroeconomic variables and the possible existence of financial imbalances prior, during and after episodes of costly booms, especially before the unwinding of unconventional policy measures and the imminent normalization of monetary policy settings. We demonstrate how economic growth would have likely evolved in the absence of stock returns and volatility as well as their propagation.

Part II: Credit Supply Dynamics and Economy

The second part of the book focuses on credit supply dynamics and real economic activity. Theory suggests that credit and GDP growth are linked. As shown in Fig. 1, neither credit nor GDP levels have returned to pre-recession trends and have remained fairly subdued. Some quarters use this to explain the fact that the economy has been plagued by two negative gaps in the credit markets and the real economy.

The close movement between GDP and credit could indicate that credit supply dynamics matter for the real economy such that the adverse credit supply shock may be responsible for weak economic growth recovery and elevated credit interest rate spreads. Certain chapters in Part II of the book disentangle the adverse credit supply shock effects from those of tighter monetary policy and adverse credit demand shocks. It is only the demand and supply side effect of credit that matters, so it is possible that regulatory changes which require banks to hold liquid government securities play a big role. In this context, we determine the relationship between government credit supply contributions to growth in (i)

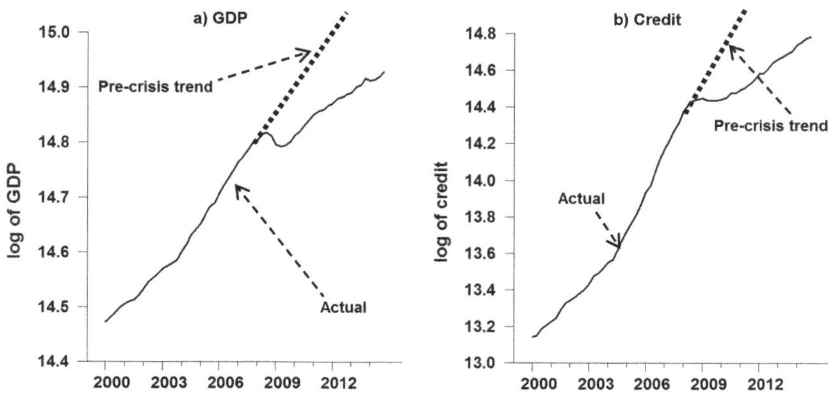

Fig. 1 Credit and GDP trends pre- and post-global financial crisis and recession (*Source*: South African Reserve Bank and authors' calculations)

GDP and (ii) gross fixed capital formation and bond yields and credit risk. Apart from influencing GDP growth, we show policymakers that credit market frictions introduce nonlinear effects with implications for the direction and magnitudes of the repo rate adjustment and inflation dynamics, paths and magnitudes of the policy rate adjustments in any way towards the primary mandate of curbing inflationary pressures. We establish thresholds and show that nonlinearities in credit market dynamics are relevant for monetary policy and financial stability, and that this an under-researched area. The nonlinearities may reveal if negative credit shocks lead to larger declines in output under a low credit regime relative to the high credit regime. In addition, the nonlinearities may reveal whether positive economic growth shocks lead to higher credit growth in a lower credit relative to the higher credit regime.

Part III: Financial Regulatory Uncertainty and Bank Risk-Taking

The third part of the book focuses on financial regulation uncertainty, regulators excesses and interest rate spreads and the bank risk-taking channel. In Fig. 2 the capital adequacy ratio (CAR) has exceeded the minimum required ratio over the long horizons. The liquidity asset holdings of banks have exceeded the minimum required levels since 2009.

In addition to regulatory amounts or quantities, the National Credit Act (NCA) was passed into legislation in 2005 and implemented in June 2007. Empirically, little is known about this macro-prudential tool's effectiveness and how it interacts with monetary policy. So to what extent did the NCA, holding excess Capital Adequacy Ratio (CAR) and Liquid Asset Holdings (LAH), impact credit dynamics? In view of the costs involved, did these excesses induce any frictions in credit markets by raising lending spreads? How do the effects of these excesses differ from those associated with the NCA and Basel III shocks? We also show that the NCA does propagate the effects of monetary policy on credit and output, which may be indicative of an economic case for these tools to be coordinated. Regulatory uncertainty may also be a significant player which impacts the interdependence between growth in credit and lending spreads before and after the financial

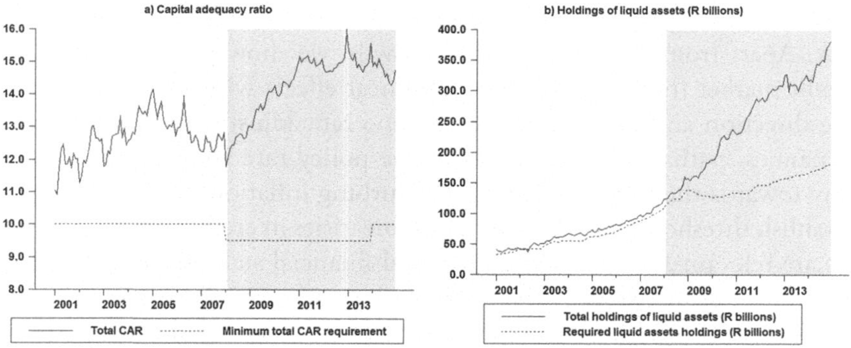

Fig. 2 Capital adequacy ratio and the holding of liquid assets (*Source*: South African Reserve Bank and authors' calculations)

crisis in August 2007, inflation and the repo rate shocks. We apply the financial regulatory policy uncertainty as constructed by Nodari (2015) to show the extent that regulatory uncertainty could be responsible for anemic macroeconomic performance

Part IV: Macro-prudential Tools and Monetary Policy

Little is known about the effects of macro-prudential tools in South Africa, and Part IV of the book focuses on the effects of selected tools. The macro-prudential policies for residential mortgage lending tools include the repayment-to-income (RTI) ratio shock and unexpected tightening in loan-to-value (LTV) ratio. Credit provisions tend to move together with the repo rate; however, this has changed since 2010. This change in the relationship may have unintended policy consequences (Fig. 3).

We rely on the literature on the interaction of monetary and financial policy, which argues that some features of the housing market explain differences in the transmission of monetary policy and can amplify swings in the real economy and can be sources of financial instability. The interaction of macro-prudential policies for residential mortgage lending and monetary policy can induce macroeconomic fluctuations, particularly if

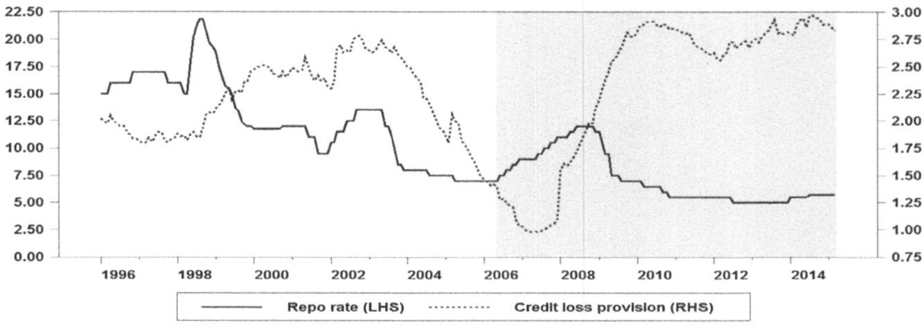

Fig. 3 Credit loss provisions as a percentage of total loans and advances and the repo rate (*Note*: The variables are expressed in percentages; *Source*: South African Reserve Bank and authors' calculations)

they move in the same direction as other shocks that amplify or dampen collateral constraints. Based on this we reveal what the data tell us about the nature of the interaction between LTVs and the repo rate since 2001 as well show the extent to which tight (loose) LTVs reinforce (neutralize) the contractionary (accommodative) monetary policy stance. Does LTV and inflation move in the same direction in most periods? If so, does high inflation expectation pose risks to financial stability via the LTV channel? In addition, we identify when LTV tightening shocks uplift and drag down inflation outcomes and expectations. The role of inflation in influencing LTV and RTI standards has been not clearly articulated in policy circles and its spill-over effects into financial stability issues. Hence, we show policymakers whether evidence indicates that price stability benefits or not from an LTV and RTI tightening shock.

Acknowledgments

We are grateful to our colleagues at the South African Reserve Bank for responding in a timely manner to data requests and areas that needed clarification. We thank our colleagues at the South African private banks for providing us with micro-level data and responding to numerous requests for additional granular data and clarity. Their cooperation has greatly enriched the analysis and policy recommendations contained in the book. We thank the Rats software support service for helping us with troubling shooting.

Contents

List of Figures

List of Tables

1

Introduction

The United States mortgages subprime crisis is acknowledged as the start of what became the global financial crisis in 2007. This period was followed by global recession and the Euro Area sovereign debt crisis. South Africa went into a brief but sharp recession in 2009. The subsequent period was characterized by elevated economic uncertainties and fragile recovery. In response to the financial crisis, central banks in advanced economies lowered key policy rates to almost zero percent and embarked on various unconventional monetary policy interventions, injecting liquidity in global financial markets. The central assumption underlying this approach by central banks was not solely to normalize the functioning of interbank markets but to improve global output and demand conditions. The transmission of quantitive easing (QE) was supposed to stimulate economic growth, investment and expenditure, primarily by encouraging risk-taking by firms and households via the so called "real risk-taking (Casterns, 2015)."

The policy interventions addressing the fundamental sources of the financial crisis attended to what most commentators attributed as the weak link—the financial regulatory and supervisory environment. The global financial crisis demonstrated clearly to policymakers and financial regulators that the mandates of price and financial stability are not

N. Gumata, E. Ndou, *Bank Credit Extension and Real Economic Activity in South Africa*, DOI 10.1007/978-3-319-43551-0_1

mutually exclusive. Subsequently, policymakers have rigorously reviewed and tightened financial regulation and supervision. In addition, micro- and macro-prudential policy tools have returned to the core of the interaction between price and financial stability. To put it another way, the interaction between monetary and financial stability policies across the financial (credit) and business cycles has become a pertinent policy issue.

This book uses a combination of statistical tools and advanced econometric analysis to show linkages between various measures of global liquidity conditions, capital flows, financial regulation and selected macro-prudential tools with real economic activity. These analytical tools assist in the empirical and related policy implications.

The first part of the book explores the role of excess global liquidity and various aspects of capital flows and asset prices in real economic activity. It is an undeniable fact that low interest rates and the liquidity injections by advanced economies led to capital inflow surges into emerging markets (EMs), including South Africa. We establish that, in the main, the effects of large-scale global liquidity injections on the South African economy were mostly transmitted via the exchange, bond market and equity prices channels. Using various approaches, the results converge and confirm that global liquidity and capital flow shocks following the financial crisis were inversely transmitted into the South African economy, mainly via the financial channel. The exchange rate made much of the adjustments and worsened the domestic competitiveness. This inverse adjustment to the international financial shock resulted in the slowdown in gross domestic product (GDP) growth via the effects of global liquidity and capital flows on the appreciation of the real effective exchange rate (REER) and the trade balance relative to the current account. Furthermore, the results confirm the potency of US Fed balance sheet and US dollar liquidity changes on the South African economy. The impact of the US Fed balance sheet policy intervention on SA variables surpasses that of the ECB balance sheet. This happens despite the fact that the Euro Area is the country's major trading partner.

Of significance to policy is the adjustment of the REER via the trade balance that calls for a serious consideration of the drivers of growth. The adjustments of the REER imply that a policy strategy to pursue investment-led growth versus exports-led growth should be seriously considered. There is a need to fully appreciate and understand the role of the balance sheet channel. The results suggest that the balance sheet channel is a drag on investment following depreciation. Implied in this finding is a serious reassessment of exchange rate policy. Real exchange rate depreciations lead to a significant slowdown in investment via the balance sheet channel and in most cases it dominates the exports competitiveness channel.

Within the financial channel, the inverse transmission of global liquidity was also evident in the extraordinary increase in domestic equity prices. This book dedicates a chapter to this matter, assessing whether the domestic equity markets are in a boom phase and what the potential costs of a bust would mean. We establish that that not all equity price booms are similar and that their ensuing busts need not necessarily result in costly economic downturns.

Furthermore, we show that net portfolio volatility, sudden stop and surge episodes shocks are sources of macroeconomic fluctuation and amplify negative shocks. Net portfolio flow volatility shock has large adverse effects on GDP growth. We then put forward the hypothesis that the adverse effects are not confined to output deterioration; there are other transmission channels linked to shifts in the sectoral allocation of investment. We do in fact find that net portfolio flow volatility shock significantly reduces the gross value added by the manufacturing, agriculture and construction sectors. Private sector employment and, in particular, the financial and construction sectors are more responsive to surge shocks. On the other hand, mining and manufacturing sector employment shares decline in response to a capital flow surge.

These reactions seem to be partly related to the responses of the REER. It is possible that appreciation in the REER due to the capital flow surge results in the loss of competitiveness. Furthermore, an increase in access to foreign capital tends to lead to reallocations out of sectors that produce tradable goods into sectors that produce non-tradable goods. The policy implication is that the major recipient and sector that gains the most during episodes of capital flow surges is the financial sector, followed by the construction sector. The financial and construction sector growth disproportionately benefits from high collateral projects which are in turn very low productivity projects. This pattern of sectorial shifts can be detrimental to aggregate productivity growth and may have adverse effects on real growth (Benigno, 2015). In light of the empirical evidence gathered in these chapters, we conclude that policymakers in South Africa have to seriously engage on the exchange rate policy that will serve the growth objectives set out in the country's National Development Plan.

Furthermore, the evidence fails to establish a significantly strong link between global liquidity, the associated surge in capital flows, exchange rate appreciation and credit growth in South Africa. The evidence suggests that the REER lags credit by about twelve quarters. This therefore means that even though capital flow shocks resulted in appreciation in the REER this does not necessarily impact credit growth. This implies that global liquidity and capital flow surges have little impact on domestic credit growth. It is corroborated by the findings that capital inflows shock post-2009 did not stimulate economic credit growth. Similarly, the credit conditions index has been neutral during this period and annual credit growth has averaged 7 percent, which is well below the estimated credit threshold of 9.5 percent. This credit threshold can play an important role as a complementary indicator to the credit gaps to calibrate a countercyclical capital buffer for regulatory purposes.

Collectively, the evidence in part two of the book shows that credit conditions are largely determined by domestic factors. We fail to find a strong direct link between capital flows to domestic credit growth and house prices. South Africa is therefore different in this relative to most emerging markets that have experienced a feedback loop between capital flows into the banking sector and overheating credit markets. But we know that this evidence is completely silent vis-à-vis the role of credit demand and supply factors and what they mean for policy. Since demand and supply shocks often occur at the same time, they need to be correctly identified to better inform policymakers. Economic fundamentals suggest that aggregate supply moves output and prices in different directions. Meanwhile, aggregate demand shock moves output and prices in the same direction.

We therefore disaggregate demand and supply of credit factors and assess their impact on lending rate spreads and the macroeconomy. We establish that credit supply shock raises lending spreads. Shocks to loan spreads exert negative effects on credit and economic growth. This means that monetary policy affects the price of credit as lending spreads decline. Loosened policy settings for a prolonged period can help to alleviate the adverse effects of the loan supply shock and spreads.

Nonetheless, our evidence establishes that monetary policy is not the only policy intervention that can deal with adverse credit supply shock and compress spreads. Improved economic growth can compresses loan spreads, support GDP and credit growth. Furthermore, for financial stability purposes we also establish that if lending spreads capture risk taking by banks, the fact that spreads tend to fall when the policy rate tightens augers well for the impact of policy aimed at reducing risk behavior. Similarly, we find that all bank funding risk measures respond negatively to tightening in monetary policy. This suggests that monetary policy is not neutral from a financial stability perspective. Therefore, monetary policy is a potential tool that can alleviate the burden on macro-prudential tools should such a need arise.

Lending rate spreads increased at the same time that the policy rate declined to historic lows. This implies a disconnect between monetary policy and lending rate spreads. The effects of accommodative monetary policy were not passed through to the real economy. We therefore estimated threshold levels of loan spreads above which they exert negative effects on economic growth. The estimates show that the thresholds occur at levels lower than 7.5 percent. The policy implication is that while monetary policy can lower the policy rate to mitigate the adverse effects of loan spreads there is a need for supplementary tools which may also lower spreads. This is particularly important, as excessive levels of lending spreads can weaken the desired effects of monetary policy easing and are detrimental to financial stability.

The evidence brings us to a conclusion that the estimated threshold levels for spreads can be used as a guide to assessing the harmful effects of certain levels of spreads to credit supply and economic growth. At the same time, the evidence established a strong feedback loop between macroeconomic performance and bank lending risk. Growth matters for the lending or asset side of the bank risk-taking channel. The thresholds for lending spreads can help the design of mechanisms to address the stickiness of spreads. In addition, such thresholds for lending spreads can serve as guides of spread levels that support monetary policy and serve financial stability well. However, policy interventions should not lose sight of maintaining the profitability of the banking system.

Currently, policymakers are operationalizing the financial stability mandate and implementing a range of prudential policies. Lessons learned from the global financial crisis showed that, in part, prolonged periods of low interest rates and expansionary monetary policy affect bank risk-taking behavior. However, most of the tools in the prudential toolkit are largely untested. Section three of the book introduces a comprehensive coverage of active macro-prudential tools in South Africa. Because these tools operate in the same space as monetary policy, it is possible that they interact, propagate or neutralize the effects of monetary policy on credit and output. This can lead to sub-optimal policy outcomes. Hence, based on the findings, we infer policy implications on whether there is a case for coordination of policies or not.

The book dedicates a number of chapters to providing empirical evidence on the bank risk-taking channel and the interaction of selected bank regulatory tools, macro-prudential tools and monetary policy in South Africa. We quantify and demonstrate the extent to which a contractionary policy stance affects the bank risk-taking channel and the implications for macroeconomic performance. In addition, we show that prudential policies spill-over into the price stability mandate and affect inflation expectations. Elevated inflationary pressures and expected inflation may lead to undesirable tightening in prudential tools.

First, we establish a credit growth threshold which can be used as a complementary indicator to the credit gaps that are proposed to be used to calibrate a countercyclical capital buffer for regulatory purposes. The Basel Committee on Banking Supervision (2010b) uses the Hodrick–Prescott (HP) filter to set a threshold level. However, there are a number of drawbacks associated with this approach. It is for this reason that we estimate the threshold for credit growth and contribute to efforts that use different approaches and quantitative techniques in this area.

The modified Balke (2000) threshold technique establishes a threshold value of around 9.5 percent for credit growth. The credit gap based on the threshold converges with the information we receive from the credit conditions index (CCI). The credit gap based on the threshold and the CCI suggests that credit conditions are neutral and are not as tight as suggested by, for example, the credit gap based on the HP filter. The empirical analysis based on this credit growth threshold shows that inflation is bad for economic growth, irrespective of credit regimes. It indicates the negative effects of inflation are not constrained by credit regimes. Meaning that even in low credit regimes, high inflation exerts disproportionately negative effects on growth. This supports the assertions that credit shocks are important drivers of inflation in high credit regimes. Inflation shocks explain higher fluctuations in economic growth in the higher credit regime. Between periods of high credit and GDP growth regimes, additional accommodative monetary policy simply adds to inflationary pressures.

When inflation is very low in a high GDP growth regime, credit market frictions are non-binding. This is because in a low inflationary environment, credit rationing might not emerge at all and the negative link between inflation and capital accumulation disappears. However, this does not mean that there are no risks that can emerge in low inflation environments. The recent global financial crisis demonstrated that periods of robust growth and well-contained inflation can mask significantly large financial excesses and imbalances, undermining financial instability. Hence, there is a role for regulatory, supervisory and macro-prudential policies.

For the interaction of monetary policy with regulatory tools and macro-prudential tools we find that contractionary monetary policy reinforces the bank risks. If lending spreads capture risk taking by banks, raising the policy rate reduces risk taking and this may lessen the burden on the use of macro-prudential tools. Therefore, monetary policy is not neutral from a financial stability perspective.

The Basel III regulatory framework introduced the liquidity coverage ratio (LCR) and the net stable funding ratio (NSFR). Under these regulations banks are required to hold sufficient liquid assets to accommodate the withdrawal of deposits at different horizons. Evidence in the book shows that the regulatory reforms imposed costs on banks and exerted adverse effects on bank credit supply and the pricing of loans. Banks' excess liquid asset holdings and capital adequacy ratio reinforce each other and exert negative effects on credit and GDP growth. Furthermore, credit loss provisions have a procyclical relationship with credit growth and real economic activity.

We consider three macro-prudential tools aimed at the household sector and aspects of housing. We find that the National Credit Act, loan-to-value (LTV) ratios and the repayment-to-income (RTI) ratio reinforce the effects of the repo rate. But a positive repo rate shock leads to bigger contractions in output and credit aggregates than the LTV tightening shock. In addition, although these prudential tools are designed mainly for financial stability purposes we find that they have beneficial spill-overs to price stability. Banks tighten LTVs and RTIs in response to an unexpected positive current inflation expectations shock.

For policy, the evidence we have gathered from regulatory and macroprudential tools implies that efforts to gradually integrate financial stability into monetary policy decisions should be accompanied by the recognition of the potential "trade-offs" in instruments. There is a greater need for coordination as this will assist in achieving the desired effects on their own targets.

1.1 The Role of Global Liquidity, Capital Flows, Assets Prices and Credit Dynamics in South Africa

The first part of the book deals with global liquidity, capital flows and the domestic economy. Subsequent to the 2007 global financial crisis, key central banks in advanced economies embarked on conventional and unconventional accommodative monetary policies. These show policy rates and bank balance sheets moving in same direction in Fig. 1.1a, b.

There are mixed views on the extent to which South Africa has benefited from abundant global liquidity during this period of low interest, possible through capital inflows which impact the real economy. The debate about the unintended consequences of unconventional accommodative monetary policies is captured via the views of the "initiator countries vs the recipient countries." The unconventional monetary policy as depicted by expanding balance sheets in Fig. 1.1 was supposed to support the global economic recovery and spill-over to the South African economy. This is premised on the foreign repercussion process which suggests that economies are interdependent. Therefore, economies' outputs are positively related and incomes are altered when autonomous spending in one country changes (that is, from YF_0 to YF_1), as shown in Fig. 1.2.

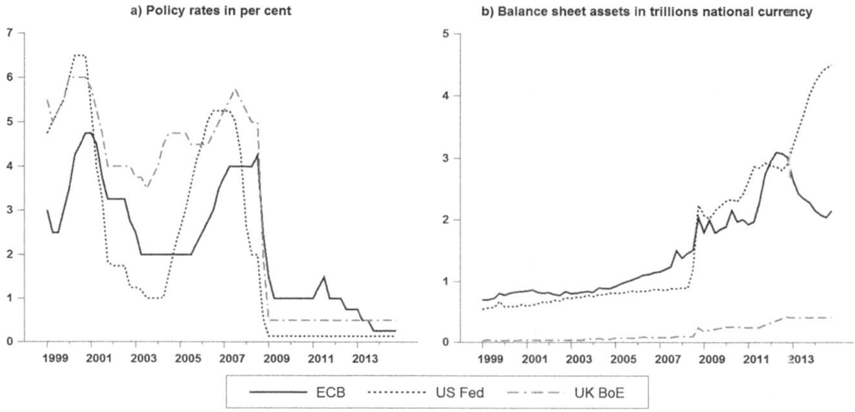

Fig. 1.1 Advanced economies' central bank balance sheet and policy rates (*Source*: IMF IFS database)

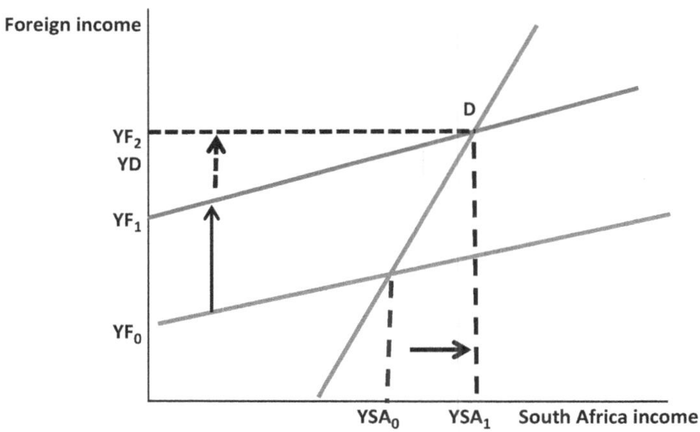

Fig. 1.2 The depiction of foreign repercussions effects (*Source*: Adapted from Appleyard et al. (2008) and authors' drawing)

The rise in foreign income should lead to increased imports from South African, leading to income increases from YSA_0 to YSA_1. That is, a boom in the foreign economy is transmitted into South Africa and will then feedback into the originating country via trade channels, raising both economies' incomes.

We find evidence of the inverse transmission of global liquidity shocks into the domestic economy. The exchange rate appreciation-linked G3 central bank liquidity injections lead to undesirable outcomes. For instance, the responses of the current account (exports less imports) and GDP growth to a capital flows shock in Fig. 1.3 show that capital flows contributions to the trade balance and economic growth tend to be negative. This evidence indicates that capital flows make the domestic economy be more outward orientated, as imports rise more than both exports and growth in output.

The fact is that imports tend to rise more than both GDP and exports because the REER makes the bulk of the adjustment and appreciates. These findings present evidence that contributes to providing facts that can help in shaping the thinking about possible policy interventions to address these imbalances.

1.2 Asset Price Booms and Costly Asset Busts

The transmission of excess global liquidity and capital flows resulted in a massive increase in domestic equity prices shown in Fig. 1.4. We address a topical policy issue of identifying equity price booms and costly equity busts.

Firstly, we define stock price busts as periods when the four-quarter moving average of the annual growth rate of stock prices falls below a threshold of −15 percent set by Borgy et al. (2009), below −20 percent set by Bordo and Jeanne (2002) and when the Christiano–Fitzgerald band-pass filter falls below zero by more than one standard deviation. Fig. 1.5 shows that methodologies point to the same bust episodes that occurred in 1974–1975, 1983, 1992 and 2008.

For policy what matters most are the costs associated with asset price busts. Because of this we explored what happens during the identified bust episodes. How severe are the economic costs? For this analysis we define a costly asset price boom as a boom that is followed by a widening of the output gap of at least 3 percentage points .within three years following the end of the boom. The identified economic costs associated with identified bust episodes are shown in Fig. 1.6.

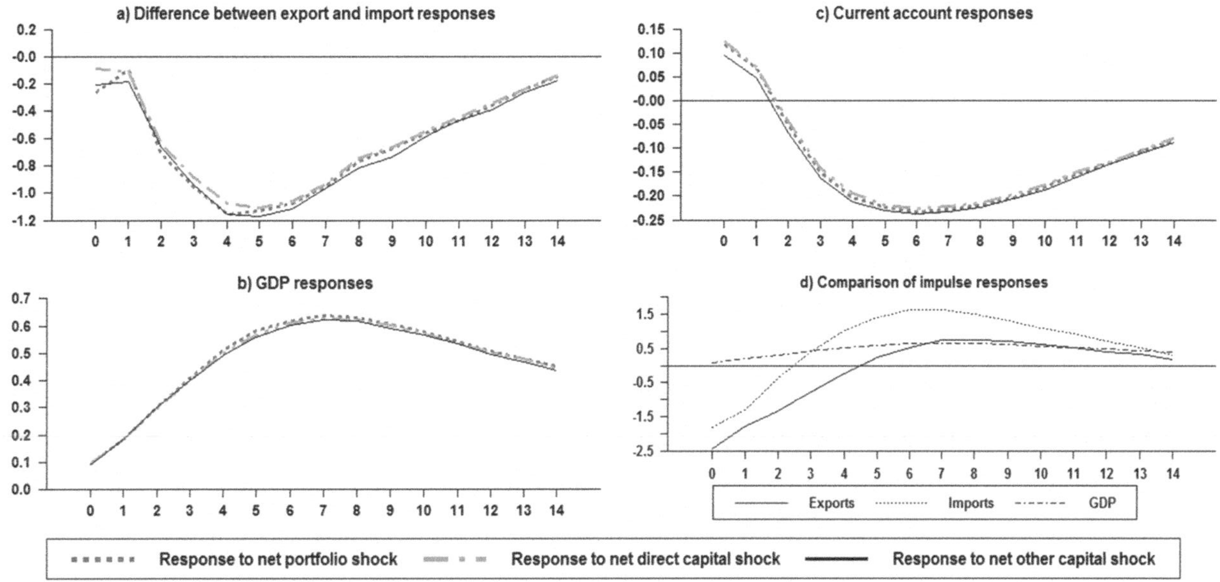

Fig. 1.3 The responses of GDP, current account and net exports to a one-standard deviation increase net capital flow shock (*Source*: Authors' calculations)

Fig. 1.4 The Johannesburg Stock Exchange (JSE) All Share price index (*Source*: South African Reserve Bank)

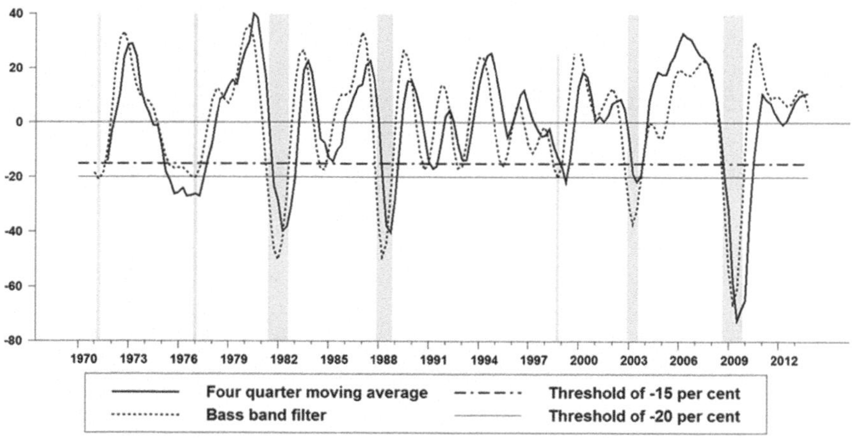

Fig. 1.5 Comparison of stock busts identified by two methods (*Note*: The *light shaded portions* refer to those busts identified by the band-pass filter approach. *Source*: Authors' calculations)

Indeed, the evidence points to economic costs during stock bust episodes. However, does it mean that all booms result in severe economic costs, hence the concerns of policymakers?

In Table 1.1 we show that the average stock price busts are estimated to last nearly seven quarters. The mean real stock price growth declined by between 14 and 38 percent and the mean decline in output below its trend output was the most severe at 1.6 percent for the 2008Q2–2010Q2 period.

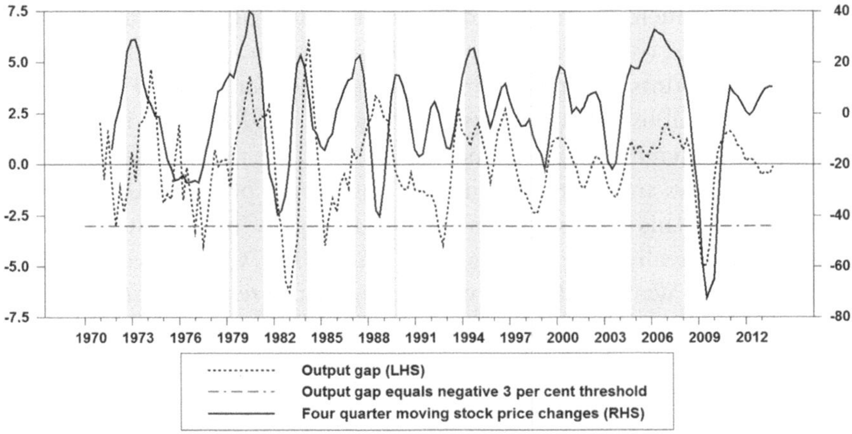

Fig. 1.6 Identified periods of stock price booms and associated output losses (*Source*: Authors' calculations)

Table 1.1 Estimated stock prices busts and the output gap

Period	Duration in quarters	Mean GDP gap (%)	Mean real stock price changes (%)
1974Q3–1977Q3	13	−0.33	−22.01
1981Q1–1983Q1	9	−0.79	−22.84
1987Q3–1989Q1	7	2.11	−19.53
1990Q3–1991Q3	5	−1.07	−14.08
1998Q2–1999Q2	5	−1.90	−16.45
2002Q3–2003Q3	6	−0.55	−14.12
2008Q3–2010Q2	10	−1.60	−37.03

Note: The cumulative widening in the output gap is measured as the accumulated deviation from a one-sided Hodrick–Prescott filter, while a smoothness parameter of 1600 for the duration of the bust is used to identify costly stock price booms over the period
Source: Authors' calculations

1.3 Changing Relationships Between GDP and Capital Flows

We contribute to the South African discussions on capital flows by introducing the classification of capital flow episodes shock according to (1) the *sudden stops* that occur when foreign capital inflows suddenly slow or stop, (2) *surges* which happen when foreign capital inflows increase rapidly, (3) *retrenchment* which occurs when domestic investors liquidate their foreign investments and (iv) *capital flight*, which occurs when domestic investors send large amounts of capital abroad (Forbes and Warnock 2011).

First, we establish that net capital flows and GDP growth in SA have varied over different policy regimes in Fig. 1.7. The relationship between net capital flows and economic growth was steeper prior to 2000 relative to post-2000. This relationship is very flat in Fig. 1.7b, suggesting capital flows did not really raise GDP growth after 20007Q3. However, based on Forbes and Warnock (2011) we investigate the relevance and costs of capital flow episodes on credit dynamics.

We explored the significance of economic costs exerted by surges, sudden stops and capital flight and retrenchments. Furthermore, global risk appetite affects and drives capital flow dynamics. We assessed the effects of global risk on capital flows, episodes of capital flow surges, sudden stops, capital flight and retrenchments, the exchange rate, GDP and credit growth. In Fig. 1.8 we find that sudden stops contributed to a pronounced economic growth contraction, more so than other categories, around 1999, 2001, 2009 and slightly in 2011.

Capital flight coincides with periods of calm and uplifted economic growth during the 2003–2007 and 2009Q4–2011Q2 but was a drag on economic growth for most of the period thereafter. Capital flow surges display a similar pattern of contributions.

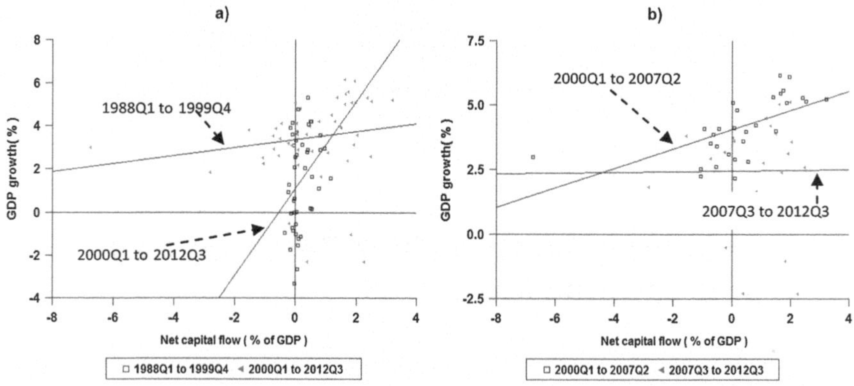

Fig. 1.7 Relationship between GDP and net capital flows relationship over time (*Source*: Authors' calculations)

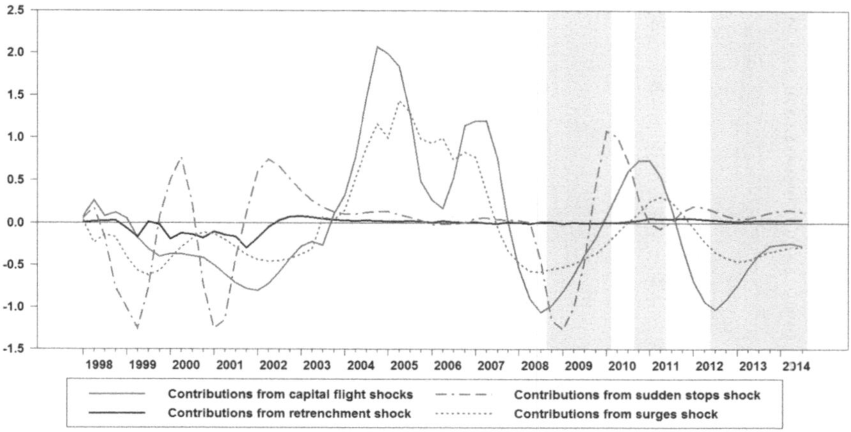

Fig. 1.8 Contributions of capital flow episodes to economic growth (*Note*: The *light shaded areas* denote QE1, QE2 and QE3, respectively. *Source*: Authors' calculations)

We extend the analysis and quantify the undesirable effects of capital flow uncertainty. We provide a systematic analysis of how large capital inflows, capital inflow reversals and net portfolio flow volatility affect economic performance and sectorial reallocations. In Fig. 1.9 we find that when GDP growth rises, the REER appreciates significantly and partly results in a decline in inflation. But the capital flow surges shock is also transmitted via sector employment shifts. Private sector employment and, in particular, the financial and construction sectors are more responsive to surge shocks. The employment shares in finance and construction increase in response to capital inflow surge shocks.

The mining and manufacturing sectors' employment shares decline in response to the capital flows surge. This response seems to be partly related to the responses of the REER. It is possible that the appreciation in the REER due to the capital flow surge results in the loss of competitiveness. Benigno et al. (2015) also establish that capital inflow increases tend to lead to reallocations out of sectors that produce tradable goods into sectors that produce non-tradable goods. Cecchetti and Kharroubi (2015) show that during periods of high capital flow episodes the financial sector growth disproportionately benefits from high collateral projects which are in turn very low productivity projects. In addition, under

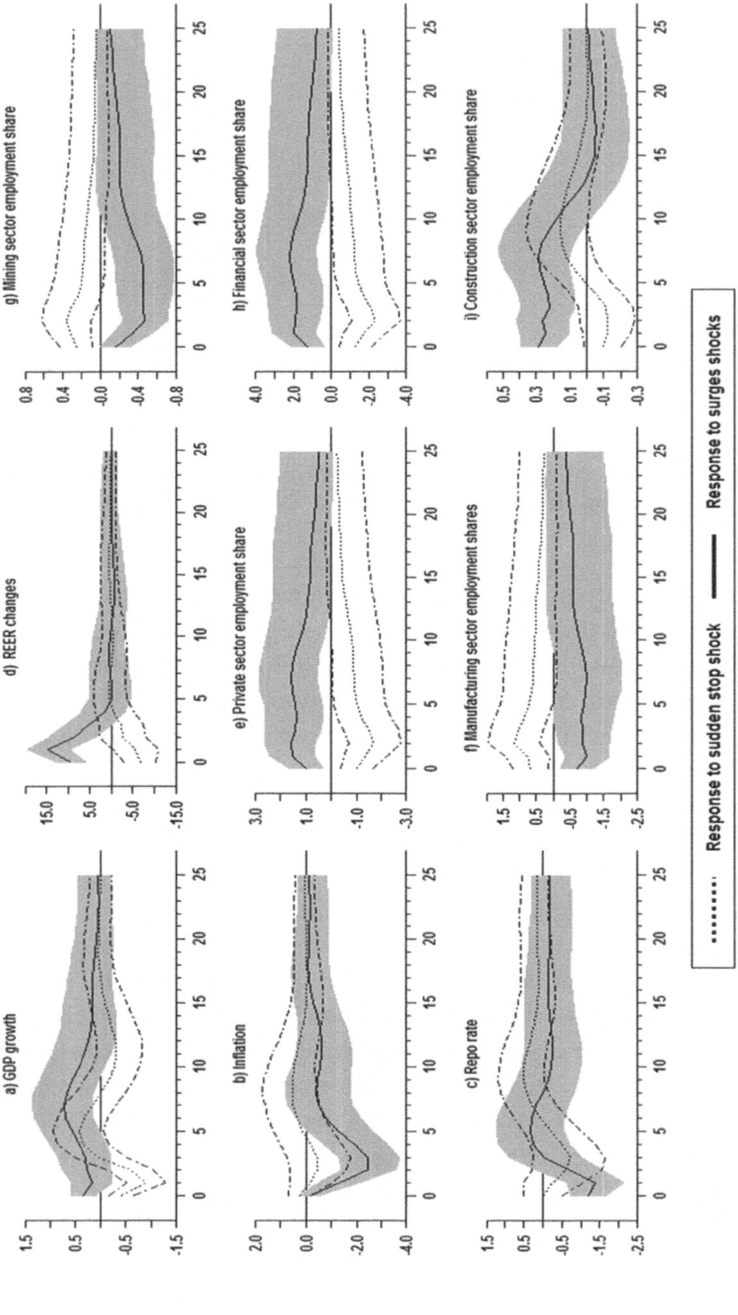

Fig. 1.9 Responses of various macroeconomic variables to capital flow surge and sudden stop shocks (*Note*: The *light grey shaded areas* and dashed lines denote the 16th and 84th percentiles. *Source*: Authors' calculations)

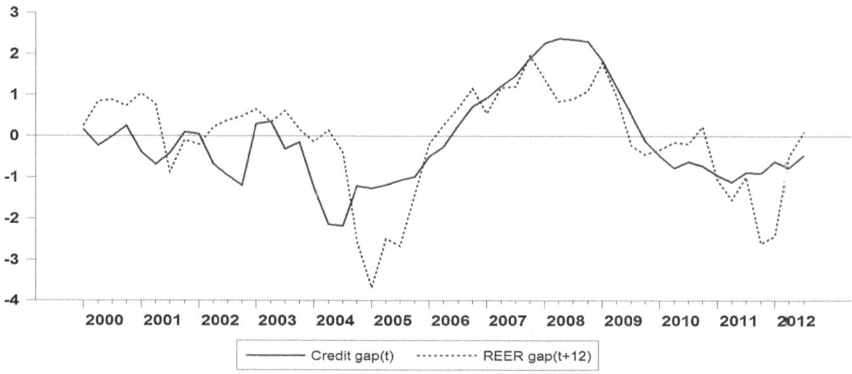

Fig. 1.10 The credit and real effective exchange rate cycles (*Note*: These are standardized HP filter gaps in percent deviation)

certain conditions a fast-growing financial sector is detrimental to aggregate productivity growth and industries that compete for resources with the financial sector are adversely affected by financial booms.

1.4 The Relationship Between Capital Flows and Domestic Credit Growth

Bruno and Shin (2013) refer to a popular narrative suggesting that low interest rates in advanced economies act as a driver of cross-border capital flows and result in excessive credit growth and inflation in the recipient economies. In light of evidence showing a strong feedback loop between capital flows into the banking sector and overheating credit markets that affects most emerging markets, we examine whether this is the case for South Africa. First, we explore the domestic interaction between credit extension and REER in Fig. 1.10.

The literature shows that capital inflows initially lead to currency appreciation and a boost to domestic demand as the relative prices of durable and capital goods falls. The improved external financing conditions are then followed by easy access to credit. In the presence of excessive risk taking and lending appetites this can feed into rapid credit growth and systemic risk. Kara (2013) shows that for Turkey the REER is a leading indicator for credit growth. This is in contrast to the relationship in Fig. 1.10, where the REER significantly lags credit growth by almost three years (12 quarters). Therefore, even though the REER and credit gaps are highly correlated, this happens with a significantly long lag. This evidence indirectly suggests that global liquidity and capital flow surges have little impact on domestic credit growth.

In addition, in Fig. 1.11 we find that capital flows lead to credit growth but the magnitudes of these results suggest that credit is not highly responsive to capital flows. The counterfactual analysis between actual and counterfactual in credit shows that capital flow shocks play a very small and limited role in credit extension.

This means that other domestic factors played a much more significant role in stimulating growth in credit. If that is the case, how have credit conditions evolved during the period of massive liquidity injections? For this analysis we construct a CCI for South Africa. The CCI allows us to examine the extent to which tighter credit conditions impact real economic activity. In addition, we use the CCI to examine the extent to which the massive policy rate reduction since 2009 impacted credit conditions.

Based on the constructed CCI in Fig. 1.12 credit conditions were tighter prior to 2004 and 2008–2010. Thereafter, credit conditions have more or less fluctuated around the zero level, suggesting neutral conditions with a loose bias.

We establish that the CCI and coincident business cycle indicator move in opposite directions. This relationship is consistent with theoretical assertions that looser credit conditions tend to be associated with the period of the expansionary business cycle phase, whereas tighter credit conditions tend to correspond to contractionary or subdued business cycle phases. There is co-movement between the CCI and the Ernst & Young Bureau for Economic Research (EY/BER) lending standards for retail and investment banks. We establish a positive relationship between the credit conditions index and the EY/BER lending standards.

Furthermore, in Fig. 1.13 the repo rate contributed to looser credit conditions, suggesting that the prolonged period of easier monetary policy helped in loosening credit conditions. Although the CCI and the credit gaps are important indicators of credit conditions and are informative

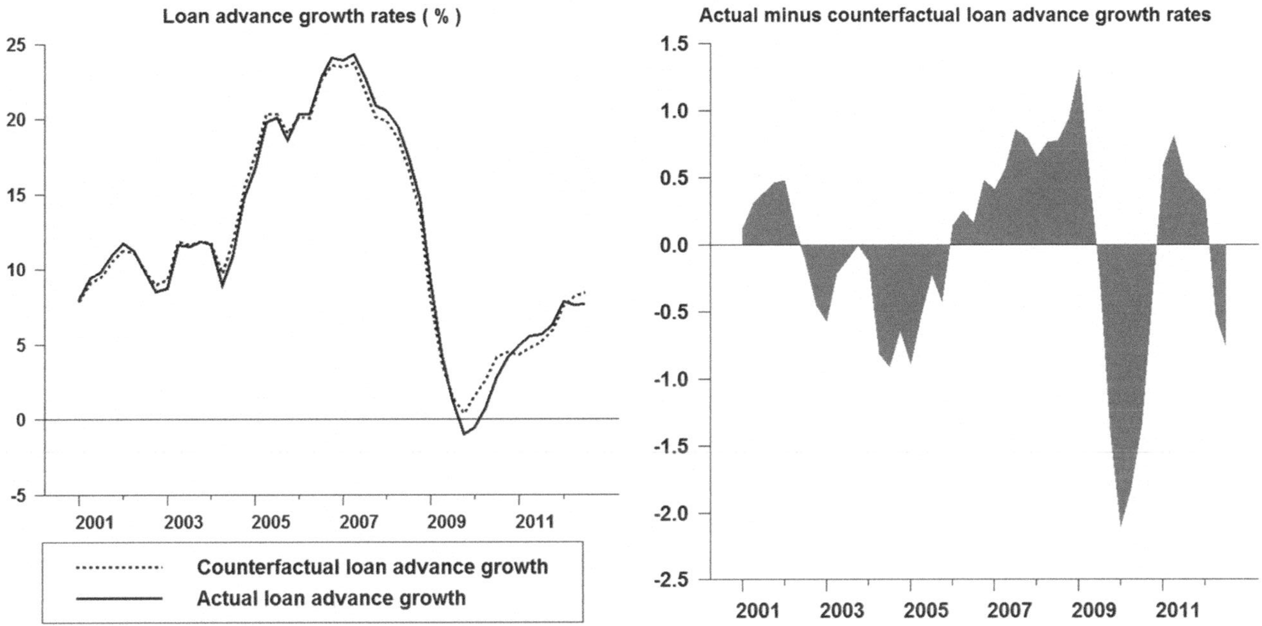

Fig. 1.11 Actual and counterfactual scenarios for credit growth (*Source*: Authors' calculations)

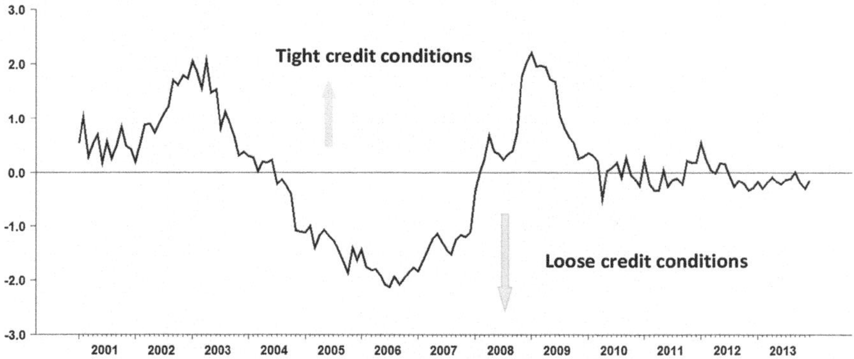

Fig. 1.12 The credit conditions index (*Source*: Authors' calculations)

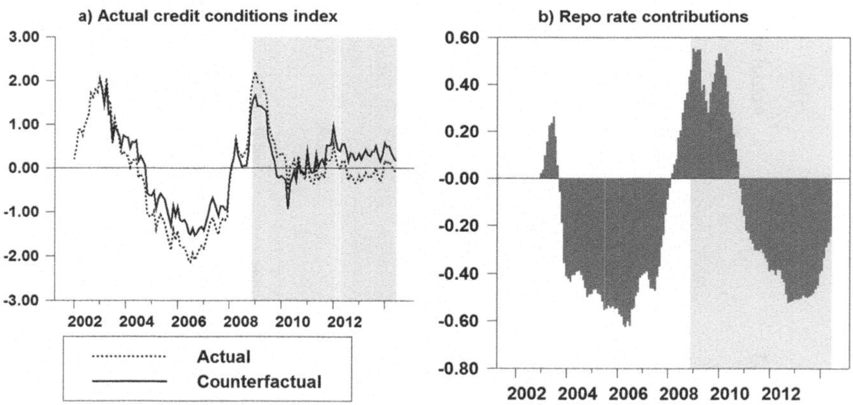

Fig. 1.13 Actual and counterfactual credit conditions index and repo rate contributions (*Source*: Authors' calculations)

to policymakers, they are unable to show whether it is credit demand or supply factors that require policy interventions. As a result, the separation of supply and demand factors is important and reveals whether an adverse credit demand or supply shock is the problem. The separation is relevant to the policy discussions as it enables policymakers to design appropriate intervention tools in dealing with credit market dynamics.

At the same time that the policy rate declined and made positive contributions to credit, lending rate margins increased. In Fig. 1.14 is evi-

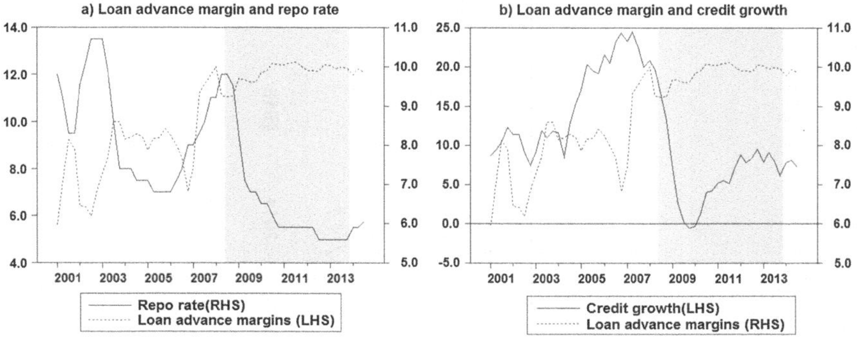

Fig. 1.14 The repo rate, margins and credit growth (*Note*: The *shaded portion* shows the period when the repo rate started to decline until the recent policy tightening phase. *Source*: SARB and authors' calculations)

dent that the lending margins did not respond to the decline in the policy rate, as they stayed constant at elevated levels. The increase in spreads coincided with a steep deceleration in credit growth. Therefore, the slowing credit extension was accompanied by a rise in loan spreads at the same time that the policy rate was reduced to historic low levels, which is consistent with the predictions of a credit supply shock.

So it is evident in Fig. 1.14 that a decline in the quantity of credit was accompanied by an increase in lending margins. This suggests that there is evidence pointing to the dominance of a supply shock impacting developments in the quantity of loans. We assessed the impact of credit supply shocks on credit growth, GDP growth and capital formation. Fig. 1.15 shows that sluggish growth in credit and weak growth in gross capital formation is largely due to the depressing contributions of the credit supply shocks.

The evidence therefore indicates that policymakers had an impact on the price of credit by lowering the repo rate. However, growth in credit volumes remained depressed due to an adverse credit supply shock. This suggests the quantity component was not stimulated enough and that additional policy measures were needed to stimulate the credit quantities and to complement the policy effects on the price of credit. Elevated levels of loan spreads are among the factors. We determine the threshold levels of loan spreads that are less harmful to economic growth and credit growth.

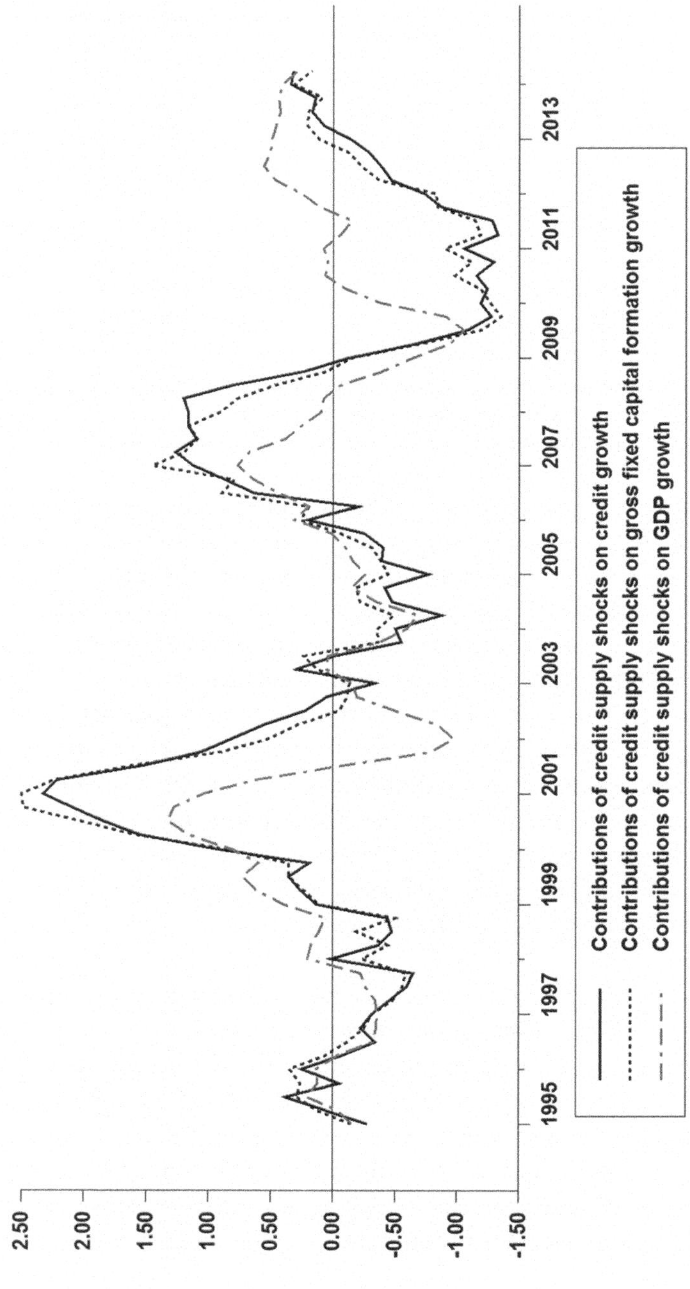

Fig. 1.15 Comparisons of contributions of credit supply shock on selected economic variables (*Source*: Authors' calculations)

1.5 How Strong Is the Link Between Credit Supply Dynamics and the Real Economy?

We have presented evidence that credit supply shocks matter and their adverse effects were reinforced by elevated interest rate spreads. What is also evident is that GDP and credit growth have not recovered and remain below trend. Fig. 1.16 shows that the domestic economy has been weighed down by two negative gaps in the credit markets and the real economy.

The concurrence and widening of the two gaps is of concern to policymakers, especially in light of the evidence shown in Fig. 1.17. Credit and GDP growth are positively related and the cross-correlation relationship suggests that the association is much stronger when GDP growth leads credit growth. This means that robust and sustainable credit growth requires strong GDP growth. A high credit regime on its own does not lead to a prolonged credit growth.

But the trends in Fig. 1.16 assume linearity and yet the period following the global financial crisis is characterized by unconventional policy interventions and zero (even negative) policy rates, which represent nonlinearity. As a result, we establish credit growth thresholds and assess the nonlinearities they introduce and their relevance for monetary policy

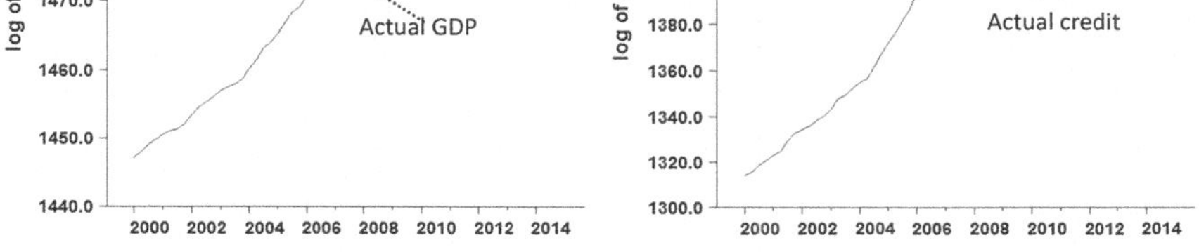

Fig. 1.16 Credit and GDP trends pre- and post-global financial crisis and recession

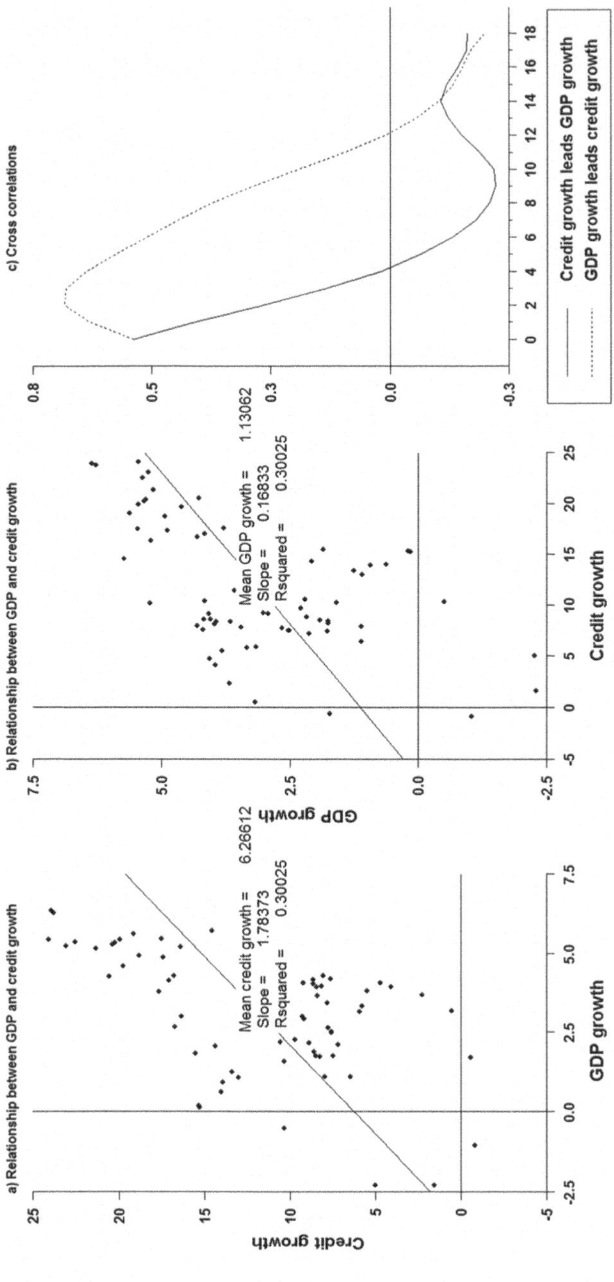

Fig. 1.17 Relationship between credit and GDP growth (*Source*: Authors' calculations)

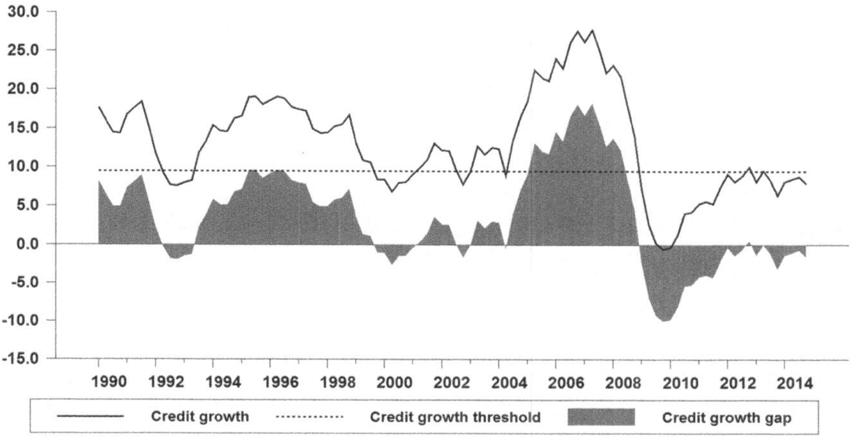

Fig. 1.18 Credit growth, credit gap and the estimated threshold (*Source*: Authors' calculations)

and financial stability. We establish a threshold of 9.5 percent for credit growth as shown in Fig. 1.18.

First, for financial stability considerations the estimated credit gap based on the credit threshold is not as negative and wide as other measures estimate. The credit gap suggests that credit conditions are neutral. The information conveyed by the credit gap corroborates this for the CCI in Fig. 1.12. Within the context of the interaction of price and financial stability it seems that the credit growth threshold complemented by the CCI can serve as one of the benchmarks to assess the build-up of potential threats to both policy objectives. It can assist within the financial regulatory framework as one of the reference points to activate tools aimed at restricting credit-driven demand pressures and overheating in credit markets.

For monetary policy considerations, we find that the credit growth threshold introduces nonlinearities within the credit growth regimes. In the higher credit growth regime, a rise in inflation lowers economic growth and a positive credit growth shock raises inflation for a longer period. The repo rate increases steeply and persists at elevated levels in response to persistent inflationary pressures. In addition, we find that inflation is bad for economic growth, irrespective of credit regimes. High inflation exerts disproportionately negative effects on growth. The findings provide evidence that policymakers should distinguish between credit regimes. High credit growth regimes imply a more aggressive policy stance relative to low credit regimes.

1.6 Financial Regulation, Bank Risk Channels, Credit Supply Shocks and the Macroeconomy

Regulators embarked on extensive regulatory reforms after the financial crisis. The regulatory reforms are also motivated by restoring the appropriate and prudent levels of credit growth to limit future episodes of costly credit and asset price booms and busts. Part three of the book deals with a variety of aspects associated with the changing financial regulatory landscape. First, we explore whether elevated financial regulation policy uncertainty (FRPU) explained part of the widening in lending rate margins, credit risk and the sluggish recovery in credit growth in South Africa.

We examine the impact of the FRPU because the uncertainty surrounding these reforms can result in adverse economic effects.[1] In addition, FRPU shocks are similar to demand shocks and exert depressing effects on output and other macroeconomic variables. However, similar to other measures of uncertainty, FRPU cannot be directly observed but must be deduced from others (Bloom et al. 2013).

For empirical analysis we focus on (1) financial regulatory policy uncertainty and (2) own changes in lending spreads, which may be due to changes in risk aversion or risk bearing, risk repricing, changes that arise from within banking products themselves and other bank or credit market specific factors. The own factors are captured by how much own movements in lending rate margins contribute to the evolution of spreads, based on the historical decompositions approach. In Fig. 1.19 we find that the actual margins exceed the counterfactual margins, suggesting

[1] We approximate financial regulatory policy uncertainty in South Africa by using the index constructed in Nodari (2014). It is an appropriate benchmark because financial regulation measures tend to be coordinated across the globe and there are spill-overs of such regulatory changes.

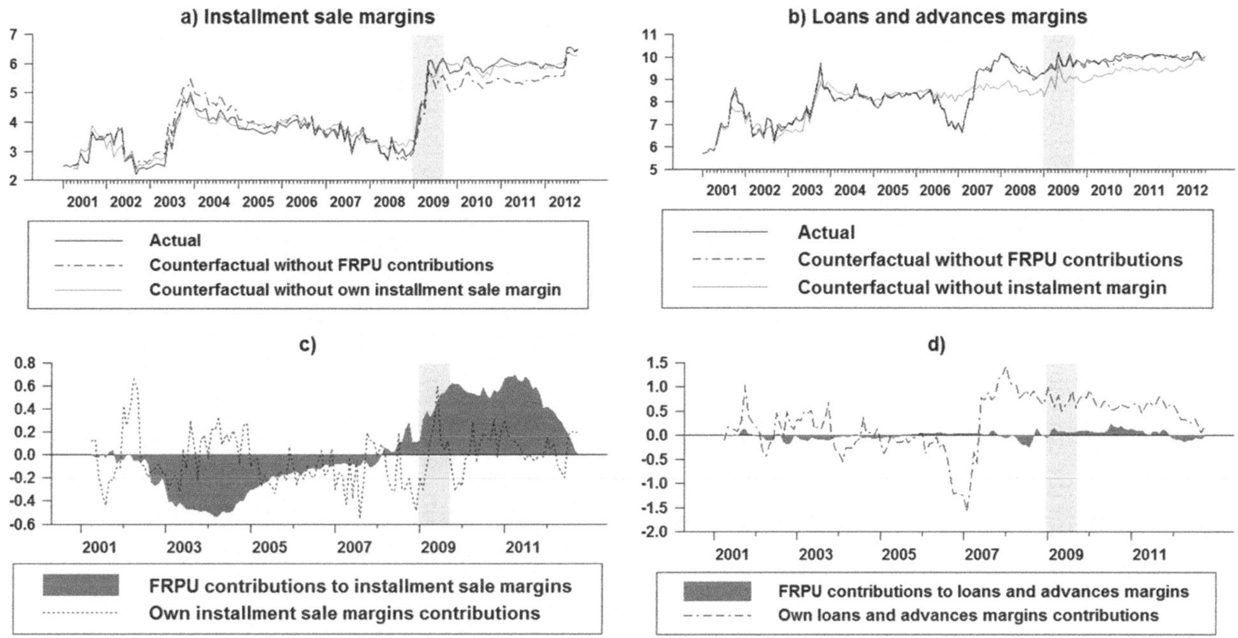

Fig. 1.19 The roles of the FRPU and own margins in the evolution of spreads (*Note*: The *light shaded ports* denote the recession in 2009. *Source*: Authors' calculations)

that the FRPU contributed to a higher level of interest rate margins. In the absence of the FRPU, lending rate margins would have been lower.

The own movements in the lending rate margins indicate the possible role of the effects of the repricing of risk and products consistent with the realignment of banks' internal strategies, as postulated by Walentin (2014). A comparison of the contributions of the FRPU and own factors to the widening of the lending rate margins shows that the FRPU contributions exceeded the own contributions for the installment sale lending rate margins in Fig. 1.19e, in contrast to the contributions of own factors in Fig. 1.19h for other loans lending rate margins. This suggests that own movements played a bigger role in the structural level shift in the other loans lending rate margin.

The financial regulatory reforms and the explicit mandates of financial stability for central banks have implications for the interaction of financial regulation, macro-prudential tools and monetary policy. Studies show that monetary policy is a poor tool to deal with excess leverage, bank risk taking, or the apparent deviations of asset prices from fundamentals. Furthermore, the policy rate is a blunt tool. A higher policy rate does reduce some excessively high asset prices, but it comes at a cost of a larger output gap (IMF 2013). In addition, the literature shows that there is no single tool that influences all financial behavior and stability consistently, so a variety of tools is used. In the banking sector, tools range from countercyclical capital buffers, dynamic provisioning, reserve requirements and levies on short-term borrowing. Whereas, for the household sector, loan-to-value (LTV) caps for mortgage loans and debt-to-income (DTI) limits or lending standards are employed.

We dedicate a number of chapters in part three of the book to analyzing the interaction of active bank regulatory and macro-prudential tools with monetary policy. We start with identifying the bank risk-taking channel in South Africa. The risk-taking channel occurs when expansionary monetary policy lasts for extended periods, therefore impacting risk perceptions, attitudes and incentives of banks to take on more risk in their portfolios. The channels of transmission involved are no longer just the increase in the volume of loans but also an increase in the risk aspect of lending aligned with the deterioration in the quality of portfolios (Angeloni et al. 2013).

We tested for the existence of the bank risk-taking channel in South Africa by considering both sides of the banks' balance sheets. We examined the responses of funding risk, bank risk and lending risk to a contractionary monetary policy shock. In addition, we assessed whether contractionary monetary policy reinforces these bank risks. We find evidence of the bank risk-taking channel of monetary policy through the funding risk channel. Furthermore, the evidence confirms that a rise in funding and bank risk lowers output significantly. In Fig. 1.20 we show that the contributions of the repo rate and the combined bank risks on GDP growth have reinforced each other during and post-recession in 2009.

Furthermore, the relationship between lending rate spreads and the repo rate in Fig. 1.21 suggests that monetary policy has a bearing on bank risk attitudes and risk taking. A negative relationship between the repo rate and lending rate margins suggests that when the policy rate tightens the spreads should fall.

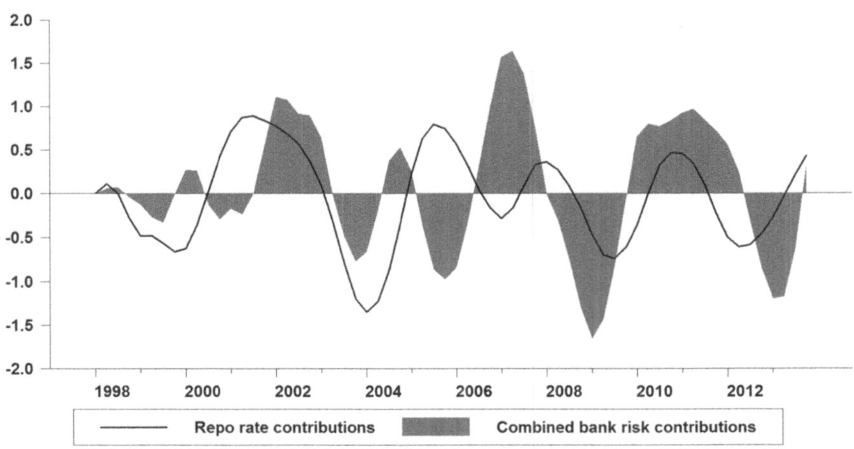

Fig. 1.20 Combined bank risk versus repo rate contributions to GDP growth (*Note*: The recession in 2009Q1–Q3 is *lightly shaded*. The header of each graph show the measure of funding risk used in calculation of combined risk measure. The four graphs show that four different risk measures were used. *Source*: Authors' calculations)

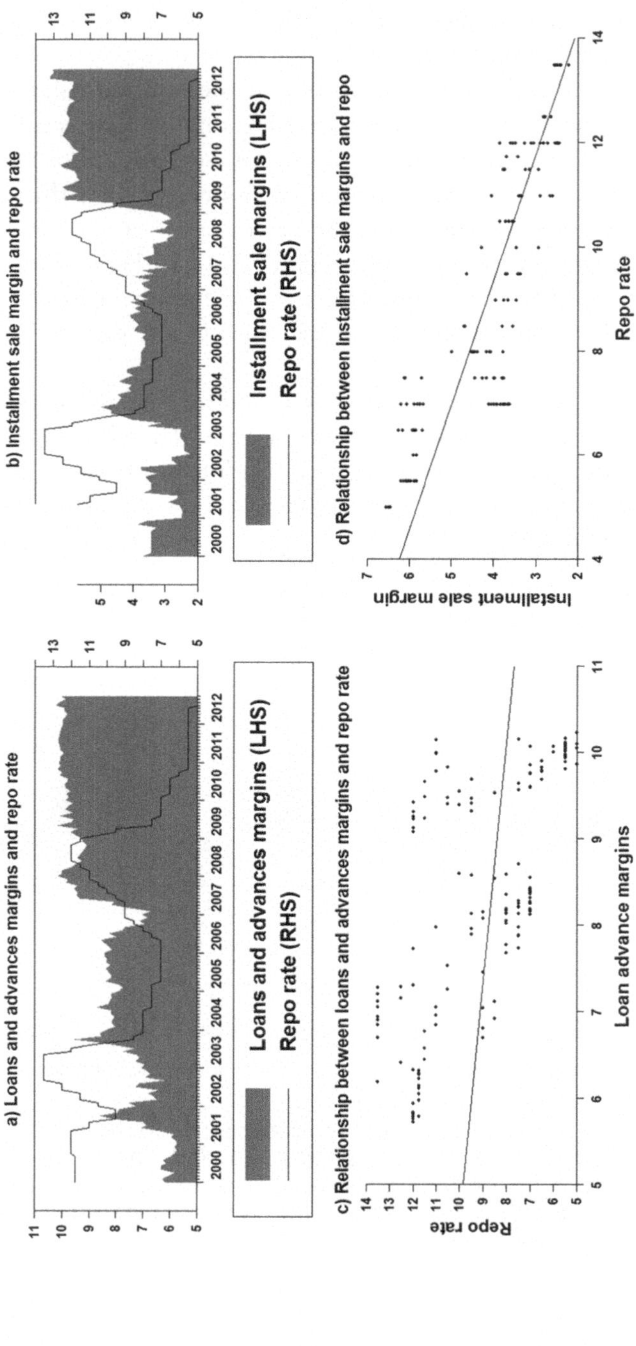

Fig. 1.21 The relationship between lending spreads and repo rate (*Source*: Authors' calculations)

If lending spreads capture risk taking by banks, this means raising rates reduces risk taking and this may lessen the burden on the use of macro-prudential tools. Therefore, monetary policy is not neutral from a financial stability perspective. Although monetary policy is not exactly the right tool for the task of financial stability, it can be used to dampen risk taking when necessary.

The Basel III regulatory framework introduced the liquidity coverage ratio (LCR) and the net stable funding ratio (NSFR). Under these regulations, banks are required to hold sufficient liquid assets to accommodate the withdrawal of deposits at different horizons. These regulations also interact with previously existing regulations such as Capital Adequacy Ratios (CAR).

It is an undisputable fact in Fig. 1.22 that CAR has exceeded the minimum required ratio over the long horizons. The liquid asset holdings (LAH) of banks exceeded the minimum required levels since 2009. Furthermore, these regulations interact with previously existing regulations such as the National Credit Act (NCA) which was passed into legislation in 2005 and implemented in June 2007. Hence, we assess the macroeconomic impact of the excess holdings of CAR and LAH. How do the effects of these excesses differ from those associated with the NCA and the Basel III shocks?

We find in Fig. 1.23a that the biggest contraction in growth in credit is due to the NCA shock followed by the Basel III shock. Excess CAR shock has a bigger effect and the excess LAH shock has the least effect. These effects probably attest to the fact that these regulatory tools are directed at different aspects of the banks' balance sheets. In contrast, the effects due to the NCA and LAH shocks are felt fairly quickly, within one month.

Fig. 1.23c shows that credit takes the longest time to recover following an NCA shock at 27 months. This is followed by the Basel III shock at 22 months. Growth in credit takes nearly the same amount of time (one and half years) to recover following excess LAH and excess CAR shocks. It is surprising that the Basel III shock had pronounced effects before its full implementation. Furthermore, the NCA does propagate the effects of monetary policy on credit and output, suggesting an economic case for these tools to be coordinated.

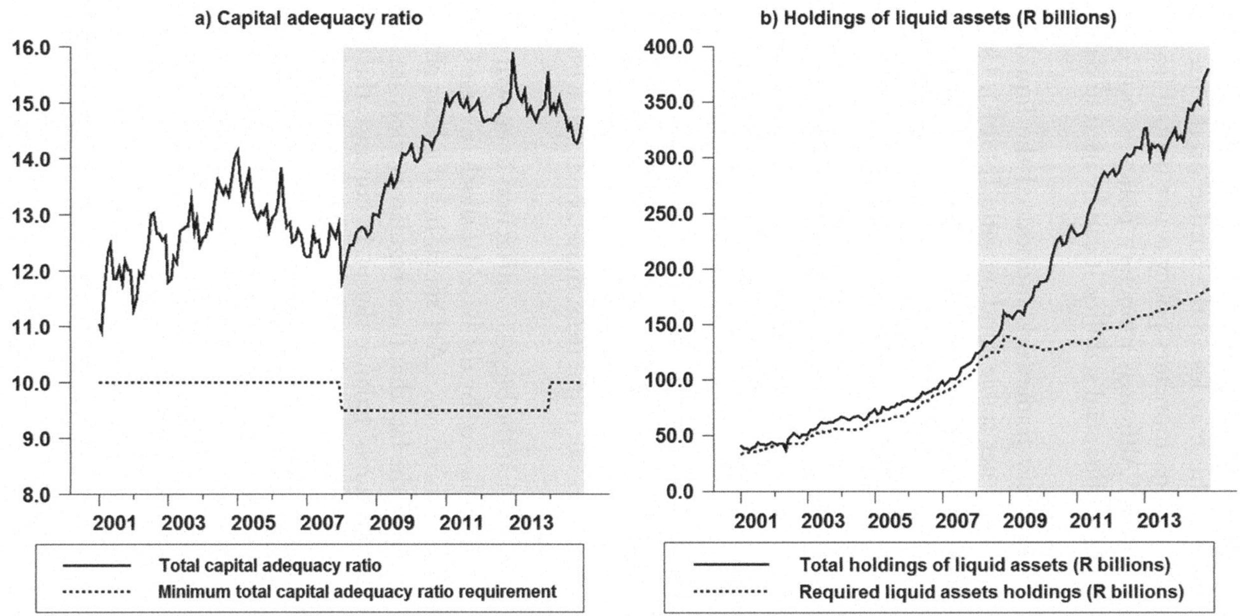

Fig. 1.22 Banks' capital adequacy ratio and holding of liquid assets (*Source*: South African Reserve Bank and authors' calculations)

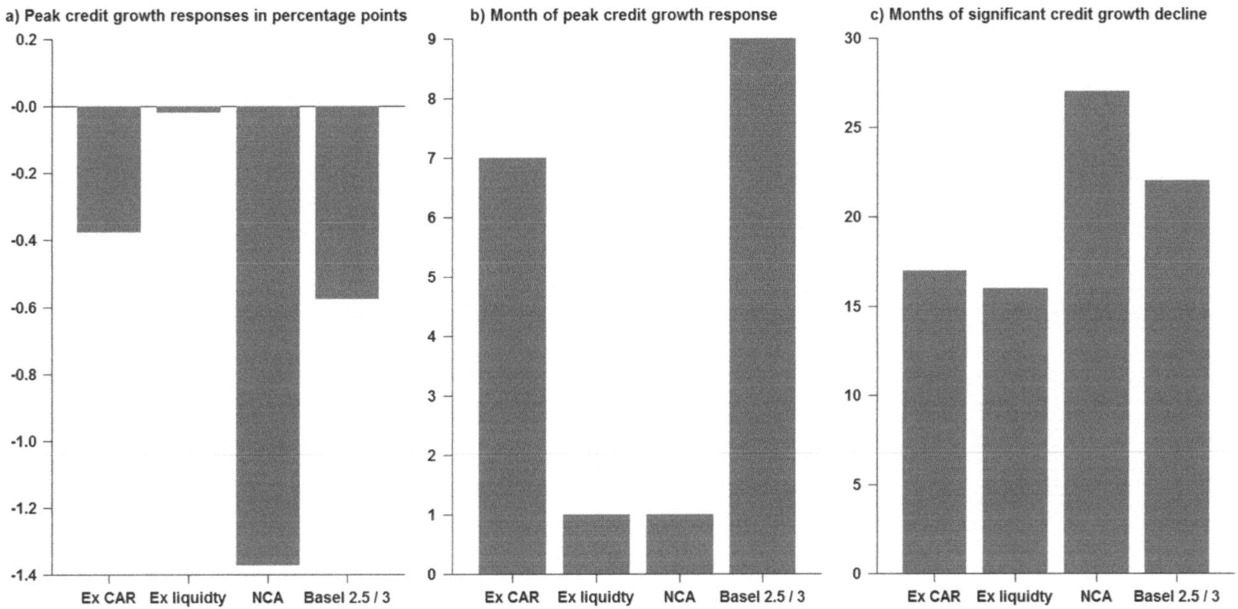

Fig. 1.23 Comparison of responses in growth in credit to various regulatory shocks (*Source*: Authors' calculation)

Even though such liquidity requirements are meant to reduce the likelihood of bank runs and financial crises, they come at a cost and may exert adverse effects on bank credit supply and the pricing of loans. In view of the costs involved, did excesses induce any frictions in credit markets by raising lending spreads? The financial reforms require banks to hold liquid government securities. To assess for the impact of these regulatory changes we determine whether there is a strong link in the evolution of credit supply shocks and government bond yields. We assess two relationships, between (1) credit supply shock contributions to GDP growth and sovereign bond yields and (2) credit supply shock contributions to gross capital formation and sovereign bond yields.

We find in Fig. 1.24b that government bond yields had a positive relationship with credit supply shock contributions to GDP before the financial crisis in 2007Q2. The relationship became negative in 2007Q3–2008Q4, as in Fig. 1.24c. The large negative effects during the recession in 2009Q1 to the 2014Q2 period in Fig. 1.24d suggest a worsened relationship then.

High sovereign bond yields are likely to have an impact on credit supply conditions as they reflect increased risk of funding for governments. This happens when banks include large amounts of government bonds on their balance sheets. The results suggest that this may be the case in South Africa and that sovereign risk partly influenced bank credit supply via the bank lending channel.

Furthermore, in Fig. 1.25 we show that government bond yields impacted the credit supply contributions to gross fixed capital formation. We find an increased negative relationship after the recession in 2009Q1 until 2014Q2. This suggests that high bond yields reduced the contribution of credit supply shocks to growth in fixed capital formation.

We conclude that credit supply shocks are an important factor in the evolution of credit supply dynamics. High government bond yields possibly had an impact on credit supply conditions. It is possible that they increased risk and funding costs.

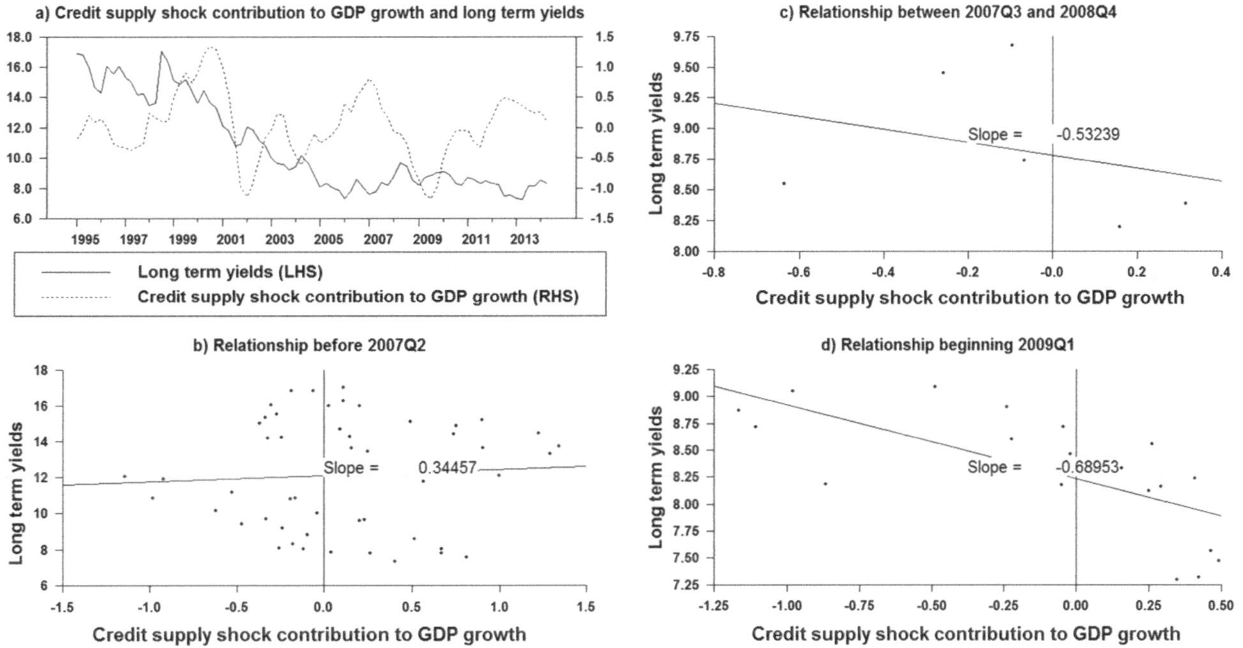

Fig. 1.24 Relationship between bond yields and credit supply shock contributions to GDP growth (*Source*: Authors' calculations)

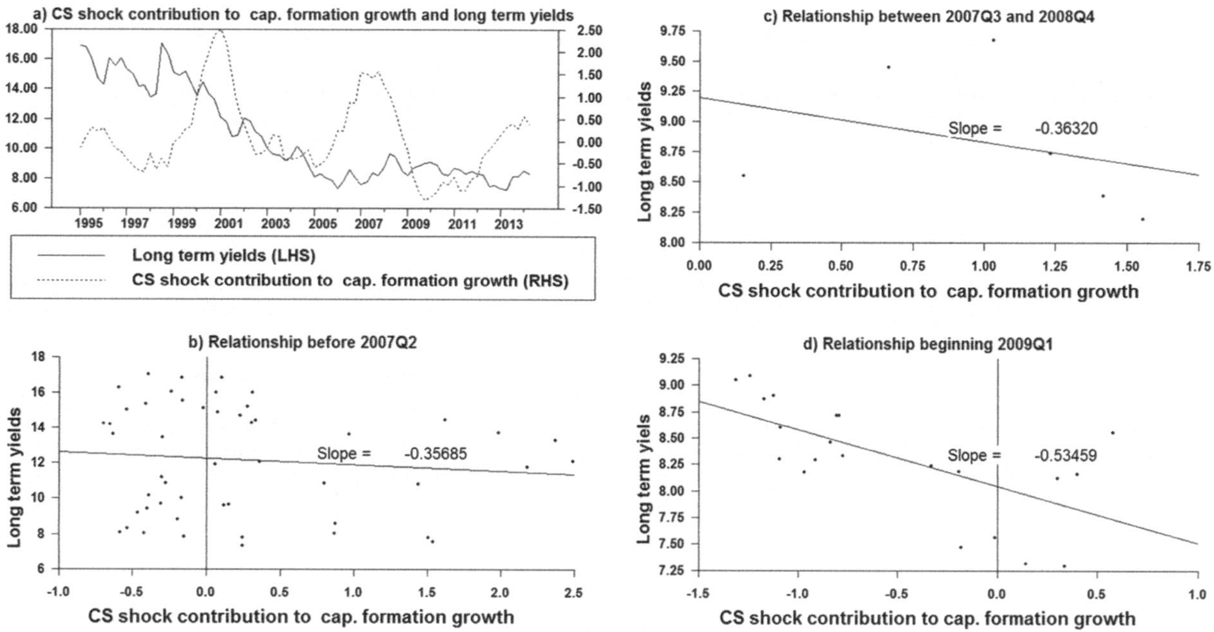

Fig. 1.25 Relationship between bond yields and credit supply shock contributions to capital formation growth (*Note*: Cap refers to capital. *Source*: Authors' calculations)

1.7 Does a Tit for Tat Exchange Exist Between NCA and Monetary Policy Shocks?

Earlier we stated that the NCA does propagate the effects of monetary policy on credit and output, suggesting an economic case for these tools to be coordinated. We dedicated a chapter to assess for the robustness of these results. Despite the NCA having been implemented for some time now, empirically, little is known about this macro-prudential tool's effectiveness and how it interacts with monetary policy. We therefore assess the macroeconomic performance of the interaction of the NCA and the repo rate. We find in Fig. 1.26 that the policy rate and the NCA propagate each other. Following the crisis and recession, both policies had a constraining effect and dragged down the growth in credit.

1.8 Credit Loss Provisions as a Macro-prudential Tool

Credit loss provisions are part of the macro-prudential toolkit. We assessed whether the weak growth in credit can be linked to credit loss provisions as macro-prudential tool. How have provisions been a driver of business cycle fluctuations in South Africa? Furthermore, how do tight provisions for credit losses impact monetary policy? Are there nonlinear effects? To contextualize these questions, we show credit loss provisions and the repo rate in Fig. 1.27. The trends show that these policy tools are moving in different directions.

We found that credit loss provisions play an important role in influencing business cycle fluctuations. There is a procyclical relationship between provisions, credit growth and real economic activity. An unexpected increase in provisions significantly lowers credit growth, retail sales and manufacturing production growth in Fig. 1.28.

Banks decrease provisions when the economic outlook is positive, leading to growth in credit. A similar pattern of inverse relationships and responses

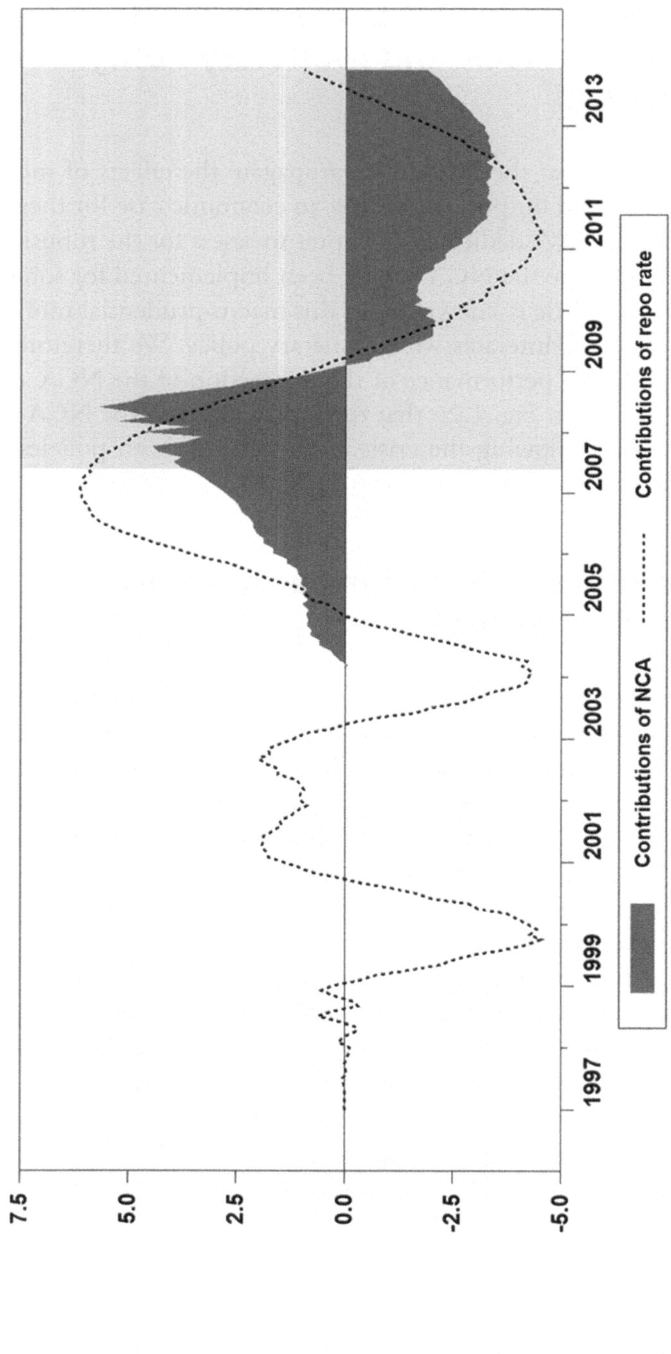

Fig. 1.26 Contributions from NCA and repo rate on credit growth (*Source*: Authors' calculations)

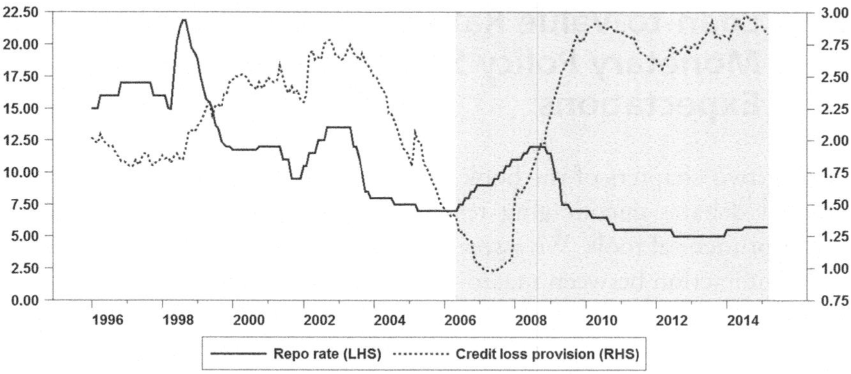

Fig. 1.27 Credit loss provisions as a percentage of total loans and advances and the repo rate (*Note*: The variables are expressed in percent. *Source*: South African Reserve Bank and authors' calculations)

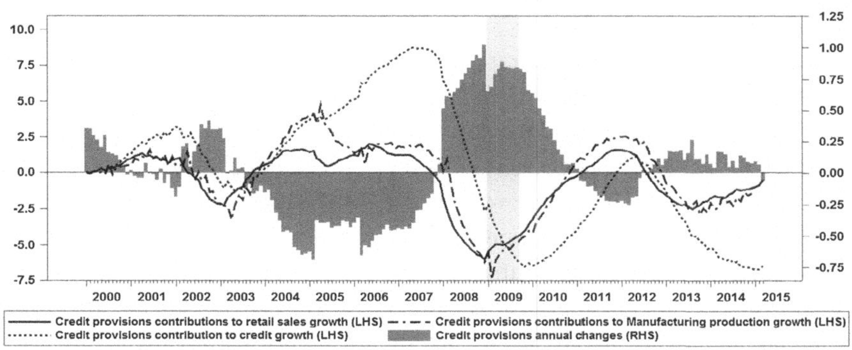

Fig. 1.28 Credit provision contributions to real economic activity (*Source*: Authors' calculations)

is found when using the provisions threshold to distinguish between high and low provisions regimes. The results imply that banks take up more risk during upswings and make less provisions. In contrast, banks increase provisions during growth downswings. Historical decompositions confirm that this backward-looking approach to provisions amplifies fluctuations in credit growth, retail sales and manufacturing production.

1.9 Loan-to-Value Ratios, the Contractionary Monetary Policy Stance and Inflation Expectations

The last two chapters of the book take their cue from the ongoing international debates encouraging researchers to gather empirical data on macro-prudential tools. We assess what the data tells us about the nature of the interaction between macro-prudential tools for housing and monetary policy since 2001. First we assess the extent to which tight (loose) LTVs reinforce (neutralize) the contractionary (accommodative) monetary policy stance. Does the transmission of the LTV shock occur through the same channels that are impacted by a tight (accommodative) monetary policy shock? Price stability is the primary mandate of the monetary policy authorities. Therefore, we ask whether there is a spill-over impact of a macro-prudential tool such as the LTV tightening shock on inflation and inflation expectations.

Fig. 1.29 shows the repo rate, LTVs and headline inflation. Between 2011 and 2013 the tightening in LTVs was accompanied by a historically low policy rate. This is in stark contrast to the massive loosening in LTVs prior to 2007, which coincided with the repo rate tightening.

Furthermore, inflation moved in the same direction as LTVs before 2011 but after 2011 the decline in LTVs was not accompanied by a similar declining trend in the inflation rate. Inflation expectations impact economic activity and inflation outcomes. In Fig. 1.30a, b, the plot between LTVs and the BER, all current inflation expectations show that when LTVs lead current inflation expectations, the latter tends to rise for a prolonged period. Meaning that periods of loose LTVs tend to be associated with inflationary episodes. On the other hand, when current inflation expectations lead the LTVs, the latter is tightened. The implication is that banks associate periods of heightened inflationary pressures with tight policy, hence they tighten LTVs.

The evidence indicates that the repo rate and LTV tightening shock effects reinforce each other. In addition, the transmission of the LTV shock occurs through the same channels as those that are impacted by tight monetary policy shock. But a positive repo rate shock leads to bigger contractions in output and credit aggregates than the LTV tightening

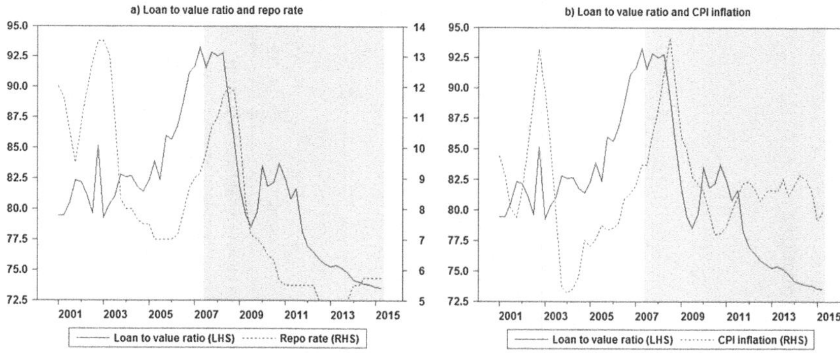

Fig. 1.29 Repo rate, LTV ratio and headline inflation (*Note*: The *grey highlighted area* in all the graphs shows the period of the National Credit Act and the National Credit Act Amendments. *Source*: South African Reserve Bank and authors' calculations)

shock. For policy, this implies that efforts to gradually integrate financial stability into monetary policy decisions should be accompanied by the recognition of the potential "trade-offs" in instruments. This will assist in achieving the desired effects on their own targets.

Furthermore, in Fig. 1.31 we find that inflation expectation shocks lead to LTV tightening. To bring the discussion of the macro-prudential tools closer to price stability, we went further, asking: Does a positive inflation expectations shock impact LTVs? We establish that indeed LTVs do decline significantly in response to an unexpected positive current inflation expectations shock. The deterioration in the inflation outlook leads to the LTV tightening. In this response, LTVs assist in weakening credit-driven inflationary pressures and can help monetary policy to maintain price stability via its impact on inflation.

1.10 Repayment-to-Income and Loan-to-Value Ratios Shocks on the Housing Market

The last chapter looks at repayment-to-income (RTI) as a macro-prudential tool for housing. Income is a major determinant of housing consumption and the RTI as a prudential tool is targeted at risks associ-

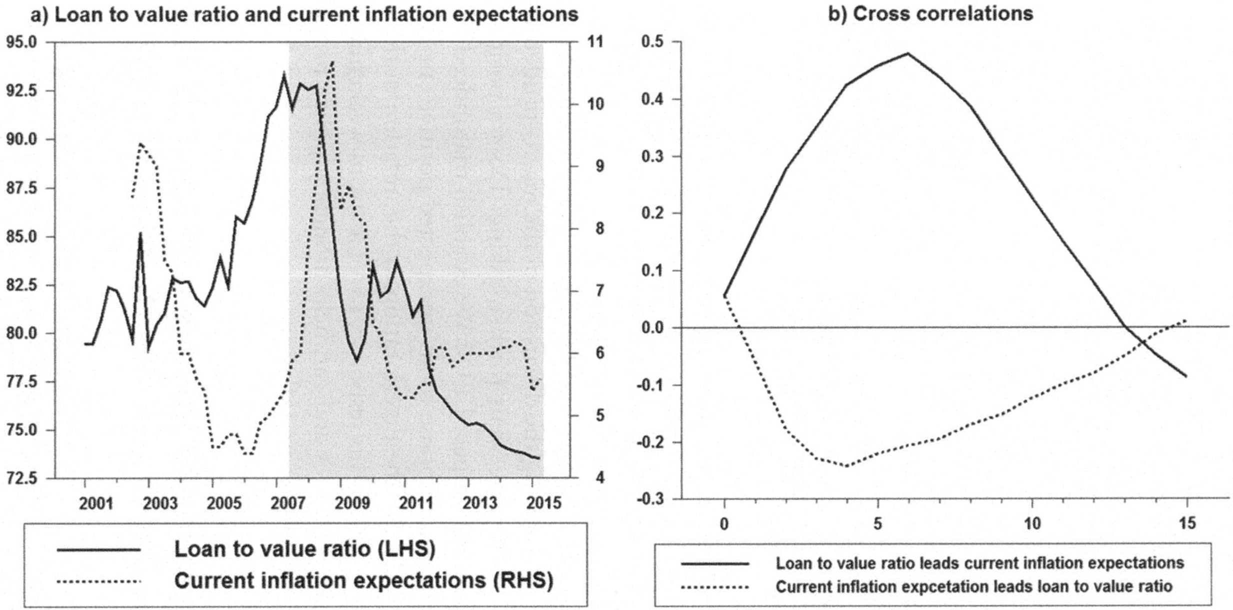

Fig. 1.30 Relationship between LTV and inflation expectation (*Note*: The *grey highlighted area* in all the graphs shows the period of the National Credit Act and the National Credit Act Amendments. *Source*: South African Reserve Bank and authors' calculations)

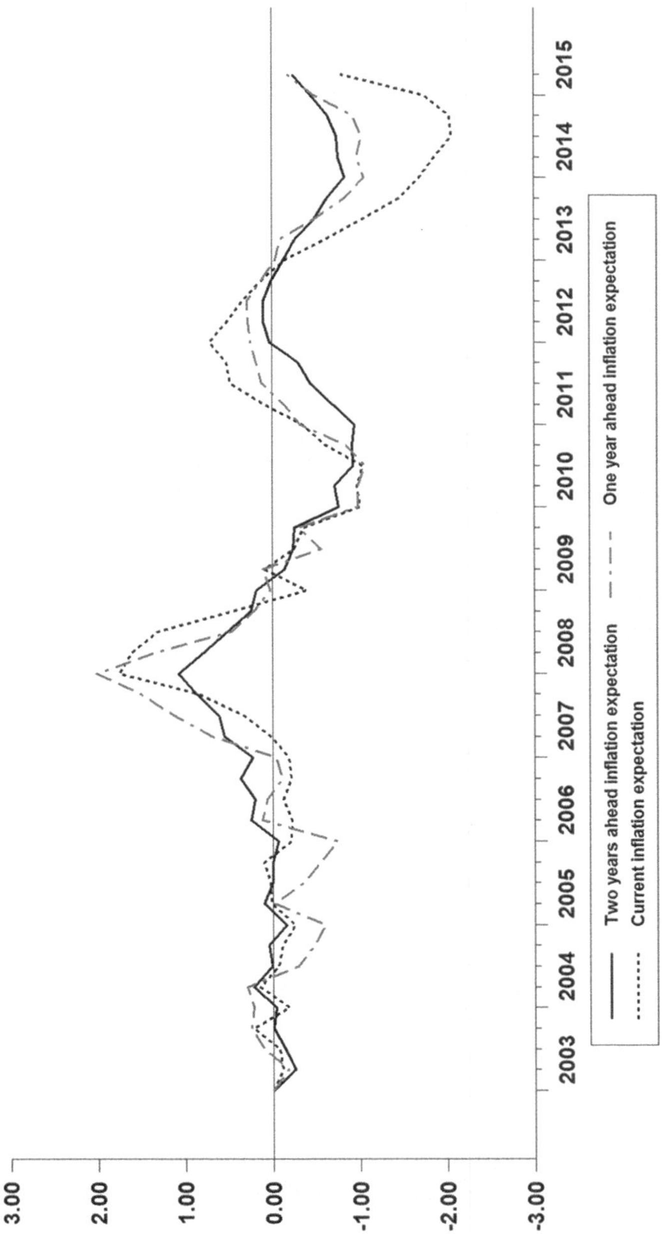

Fig. 1.31 Contributions of positive inflation expectations shock to LTV (*Source*: Authors calculations)

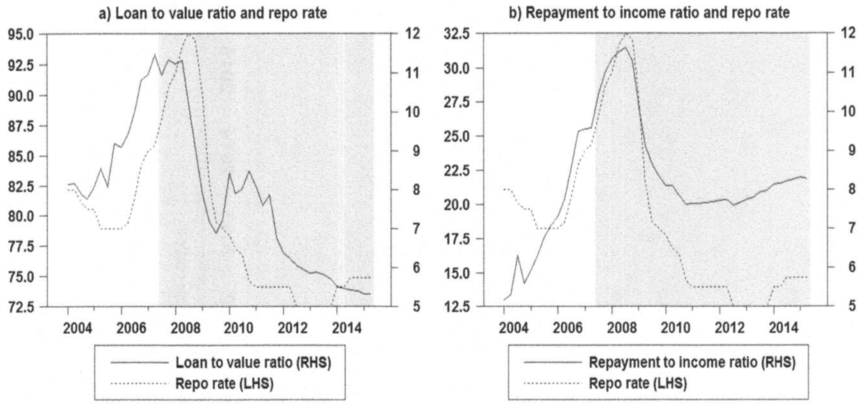

Fig. 1.32 The evolution of the LTV ratio, RTI and repo rate (*Note*: The *grey highlighted area* in all the graphs shows the period of the National Credit Act and the National Credit Act Amendments. *Source*: South African Reserve Bank and authors' calculations)

ated with the debt repayment channel. But the RTI does not operate in isolation. It is an outcome of the interactions with the NCA, repo rate and LTVs. We therefore assess the extent to which the RTI and LTV shocks impact the economy, inflation and repo rate dynamics. Are LTV tightening shocks and the unexpected reduction in the RTI shocks complementary or supplementary tools? In Fig. 1.32 the RTI and LTVs tend to move with the repo rate.

The evidence in Fig. 1.33 shows that the RTI and LTV move together, but not perfectly—there has been divergence after 2011. The signs of relationship between RTI and LTV indicate that there is complementarity between these tools.

We establish that the RTIs and LTVs, via demand and supply factors, equilibrate house prices. The loosening of LTV leads to an increase in housing demand and raises house prices. However, this is in contrast to the negative effects loose LTVs have on the housing supply. Nonetheless, the decline in housing supply depresses house price growth. So, the LTV shock moves residential property demand and supply in different directions. In turn, this has implications for house price dynamics and possibly wealth and collateral effects for consumers.

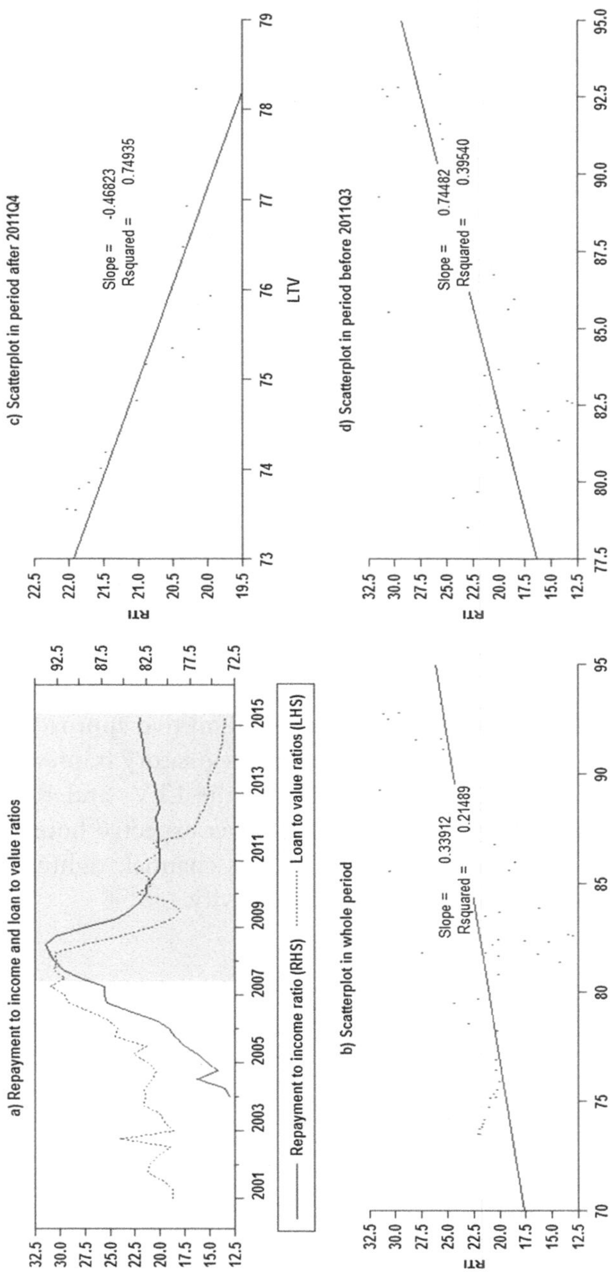

Fig. 1.33 Relationship between RTI and LTV over different periods (*Note*: The *grey highlighted area* in all the graphs shows the period of the National Credit Act and the National Credit Act Amendments. *Source*: South African Reserve Bank and authors' calculations)

The loosening of LTVs via demand and supply also possibly equilibrates house prices, but this is accompanied by an increase in the house price-income ratio and worsens the affordability matrices. However, the beneficial effects last for a year and start to dissipate, suggesting that although LTVs do indeed help in equilibrating demand and supply factors in the housing market, other factors play a role for longer durations. An unexpected increase in house prices leads to a significant loosening of the LTV. This implies that an increase in wealth and collateral effects associated with house price appreciation enables the creditors to loosen lending standards based on the LTV. At the same time, banks increase the RTI, suggesting that the increase in house prices impacts affordability metrics. In order to supply mortgage credit, banks accommodate positive house price shocks by increasing the income gearing or repayment burden and the limit on the mandatory down payment.

It is of policy relevance in this relationship that, during the sample period, house price increases in most instances preceded the loosening of the LTVs and increases in the RTIs. This implies that as tools at the discretion of banks, LTVs and RTIs help to reinforce the momentum in house prices. As a result, if the intention is to use these tools to avoid overheating or dampen mortgage credit and house price growth, the RTIs and LTVs should be adjusted in a proactive or pre-emptive approach. This approach probably requires a macro-prudential regulatory framework. It can potentially exploit the house price link to the LTVs and RTIs via the expectations channel, as agents gradually lower expected house price increases. In addition, through the expectations channel, tighter LTVs and lower RTIs can also dampen speculative activity.

Part I

Global Liquidity, Capital Flows, Asset Prices and Credit Dynamics in South Africa

2

The Inverse Transmission of Positive Global Liquidity Shocks into the South African Economy

Learning Objectives

- Understand how the foreign repercussion process occurs as envisaged by the use of global liquidity injections
- Ascertain what evidence is available regarding the inverse transmission of global liquidity shocks into the South African economy
- Determine the differences in the impact of various rounds of G3 central bank liquidity injections via quantity and price measures on domestic credit, inflation and the policy rate
- Examine the role of domestic labor markets in the adjustments to external shocks
- Compare how the impact of the US Fed and ECB bank balance sheet shocks exert inverse transmission effects on the domestic economy
- Apply counterfactual scenarios to assess the impact of the inverse transmission and the role of commodity price dynamics

N. Gumata, E. Ndou, *Bank Credit Extension and Real Economic Activity in South Africa*, DOI 10.1007/978-3-319-43551-0_2

2.1 Introduction

Subsequent to the 2007 global financial crisis central banks in advanced economies embarked on conventional and unconventional accommodative monetary policies. These policies injected sizeable liquidity into financial markets and some of the liquidity was channelled to emerging market economies (EMEs) via capital flow surges. The size of capital flows to EMEs was much larger than the capacity they could absorb without having distortionary effects. For instance, Carstens (2015) argues that excess global liquidity associated with the conduct of unconventional monetary policies in advanced economies resulted in substantial distortions, particularly in EMEs.

At a global level, the dialogue about the unintended consequences of unconventional accommodative monetary policies was captured via the views of the "initiator countries vs the recipient countries." This chapter explores the extent to which G3 central bank liquidity injections impacted domestic credit, financial and real economic variables.[1] In particular, is there any evidence of the inverse transmission of positive global liquidity shocks into the South African economy? Do commodity prices impact the response of credit growth and the repo rate to US and ECB liquidity injection shocks?

The foreign repercussion process depicted in Fig. 2.1 suggests that economies are interdependent with respect to macroeconomic activity. Therefore, output in different economies is positively related and incomes are altered when autonomous spending in one country changes from YF_0 to YF_1 in Fig. 2.1. If South African income did not rise following an autonomous increase in foreign income, the latter would be at YD which corresponds to point D. Furthermore, if foreign income rises from YD to YF_2 by exporting to South Africa as the latter's income rises, the feedback mechanism means that South African income rises from YSA_0 to YSA_1. That is, a boom in the foreign economy is transmitted to South Africa and will then feed back into the originating country via the trade channel, raising incomes in both countries. So, it is a "win-win" outcome.

[1] Throughout the chapter, and elsewhere in the book, we refer to the US Federal Reserve, Bank of England and the European Central Bank as the G3 central banks.

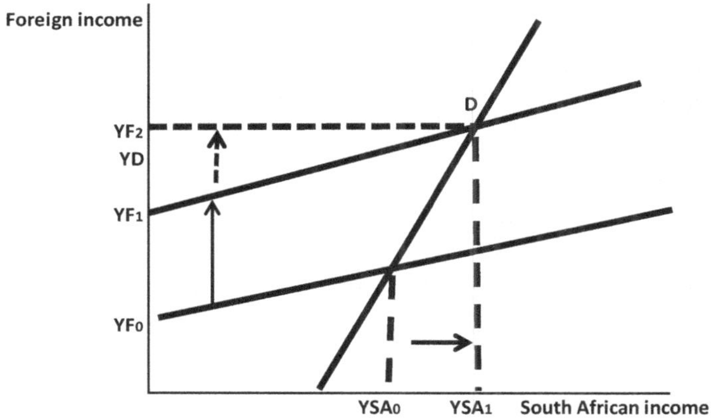

Fig. 2.1 The depiction of foreign repercussions effects (*Source*: Adapted from Appleyard et al. (2008) and authors' drawing)

The central assumption of this idea is that an improvement in world output and global demand will lead to increased demand for South African exports. This was part of the core motivation of embarking on quantitive easing (QE). The transmission of QE was supposed to stimulate economic growth, investment and expenditure primarily by encouraging risk taking by firms and households via the so called "real risk-taking." This would spill-over to foreign economies via exports growth amongst other key channels of transmission. This view emphasized the trade channel as responsive to foreign income improvements. In its simple form, the exports function shown in Eq. (2.1) suggests that exports depend positively on foreign income (demand) and negatively on the exchange rate.

$$\text{Exports} = \text{f}\left(\text{foreign income, exchange rate}\right) \tag{2.1}$$

Did this foreign repercussion process occur as envisaged by the use of QE? If not, what then happened? To answer these questions, this chapter explores the inverse transmission effects of QE on aggregate demand, supply and labor markets in South Africa.[2] The next section discusses this mechanism.

[2] It is possible that other domestic factors might have contributed to the observed trends in various macroeconomic variables. However, the assessment in this chapter is only geared towards exploring the role of various rounds of QE.

2.2 How Does the Inverse Transmission of Global Financial Shocks such as QE Arise?

Fig. 2.2 shows that theoretically a positive global liquidity shock can be inversely transmitted into South Africa by impacting aggregate demand, supply and labor markets. Fig 2.2 shows the interaction between aggregate demand (AD) and aggregate supply (AS) and distinguishes between the short-run (AS_{sr}) and the long-run (AS_{lr}) aggregate supply curves. In

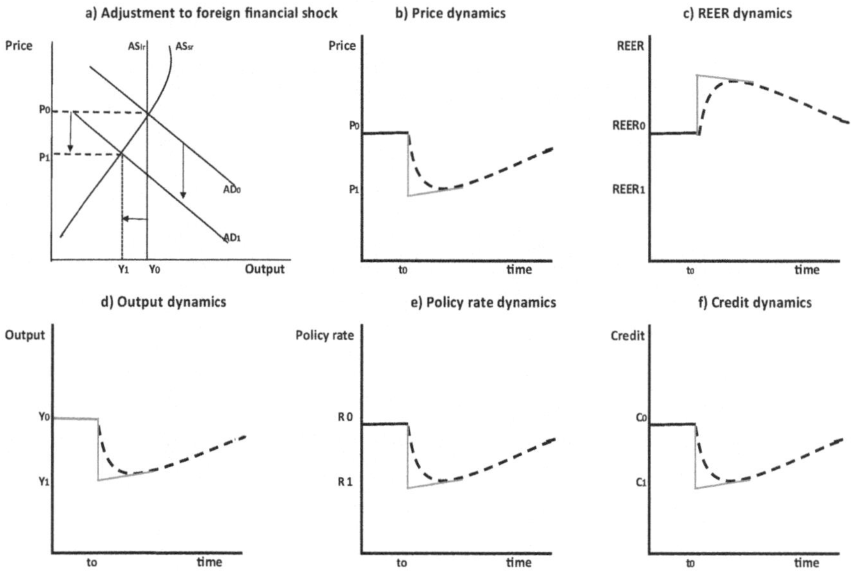

Fig. 2.2 Theoretical predictions of inverse transmission of global financial shocks such as QE to South Africa (*Note*: AD refers to aggregate demand curve. AD_0 and AD_1 refer to initial and final aggregate demand curve, respectively. AS refers to the aggregate supply curve. Ass_{r0} to Ass_{r1} refer to initial and final short-run aggregate supply curve. AS_{lr} refers to long-run aggregate supply. AD_0 and AD_1 refer to initial and final aggregate demand curve, respectively. Y_0 and Y_1 are initial and final outputs, respectively. R_0 and R_1 are the initial and final repo rate levels, respectively. C_0 and C_1 are the initial and final credit levels, respectively. *Source*: Adapted from Appleyard et al. (2008) and authors' drawing)

addition, it also differentiates between instantaneous (fast) by the solid line and sluggish (slow) by the dotted line macroeconomic adjustments.

In Fig. 2.2 the global financial shock through the portfolio rebalancing channel leads to a surge in capital inflows or the "search for yield." This appreciates the recipient country's exchange rate as foreigners exchange their currency for the domestic currency to buy domestic assets. In Fig. 2.2a evidence shows the inversely transmitted effects of a financial shock on domestic aggregate demand. The real effective exchange rate (REER) dynamics in Fig. 2.2c indicate the appreciation which in turn makes domestic goods less competitive and therefore expensive to the rest of the world. The appreciation leads to a price reduction from P_0 to P_1 in Fig. 2.2b. Similarly, in Fig. 2.2a the aggregate demand curve shifts downwards, leading to price and output declines. The policy rate also adjusts downwards in response to the decline in prices and output.

All the macroeconomic variables depicted in Fig. 2.2 can adjust instantaneously or sluggishly in returning to pre-shock levels. The instantaneous adjustment is shown by the solid line. Alternatively, they can adjust sluggishly as shown by the dotted lines. The inverse transmission mainly occurs via the decline in output and a stronger exchange rate. These effects are in contrast to those assumed under the foreign repercussion framework shown in Fig. 2.1.

What is the role of labor markets in the adjustment process? The adjustment of the labor markets is needed to return to equilibrium. This happens via a reduction in nominal wages as labor markets realize that actual prices are now lower than expected. This shifts the short-run aggregate supply from Ass_{r0} to Ass_{r1} such that the initial output equilibrium is restored.

2.3 Developments in Policy Rates and Central Bank Balance Sheets

This chapter uses quarterly data starting in 1999Q1 to 2014Q4. Fig. 2.3 shows the evolution of the data used to derive the global factors for price and quantity measures of global liquidity used in the empirical estimations. The trends in the G3 policy rates in Fig. 2.3a and the balance sheets in Fig. 2.3b provide good measures of global liquidity con-

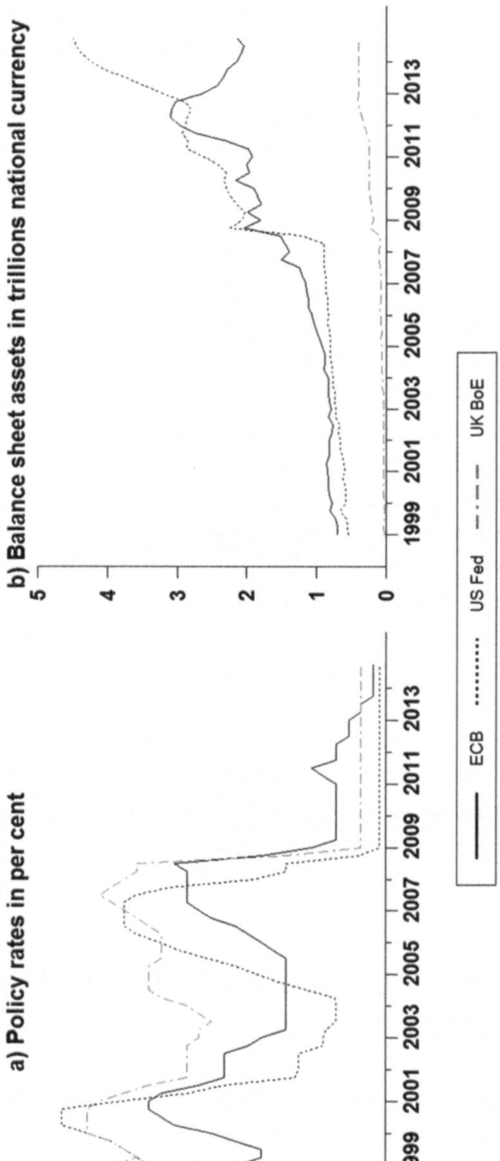

Fig. 2.3 Prices and quantity measures of G3 liquidity (*Source*: IMF IFS database and authors' calculations)

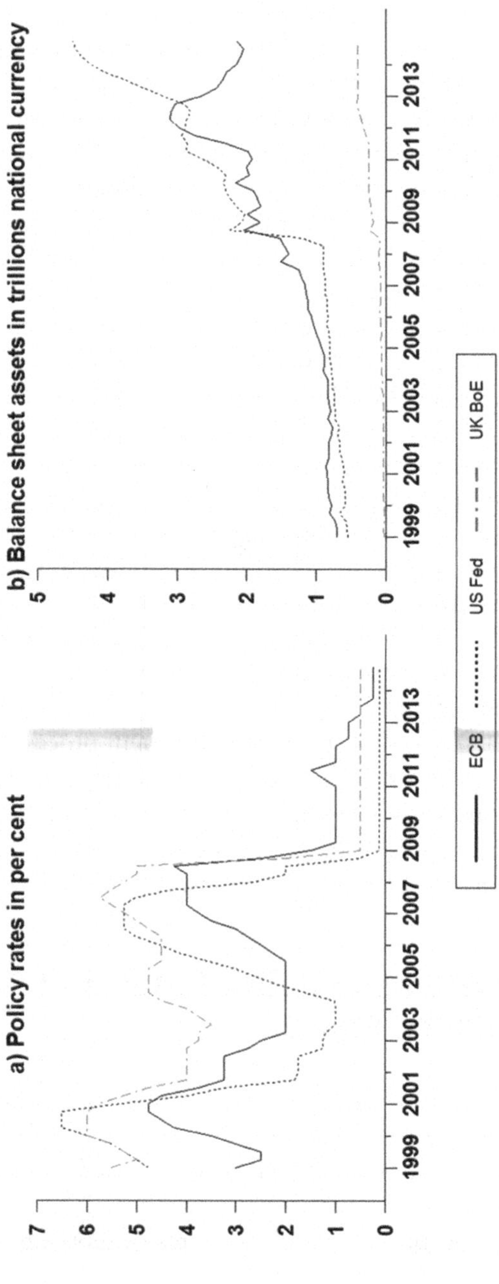

ditions.[3] Policy rates determined by central banks influence interbank interest rates and other short-term interest and are an important determinant of financing costs and financial conditions. Through expectations for growth and inflation, they also exert pressure on the yield curve. As the policy rates hit the zero lower bound, central banks engaged in asset purchases (QE), hence the growth in their balance sheets as shown in Fig. 2.3b.

Fig. 2.4a, b show the correlation coefficients between the central bank policy rates and the asset purchases. All the correlation coefficients are high and above the minimum 30 percent co-movement required between variables in order to construct a factor. The observed high correlation coefficients also point to high levels of synchronicity in policy actions. The global liquidity indicators are constructed by using the principal components analysis (PCA). In this step, the principal component methodology extracts a common factor that captures the greatest common variation in a group of variables. The PCA method has the advantages in that it allows for summarizing a large information set into a single indicator.[4]

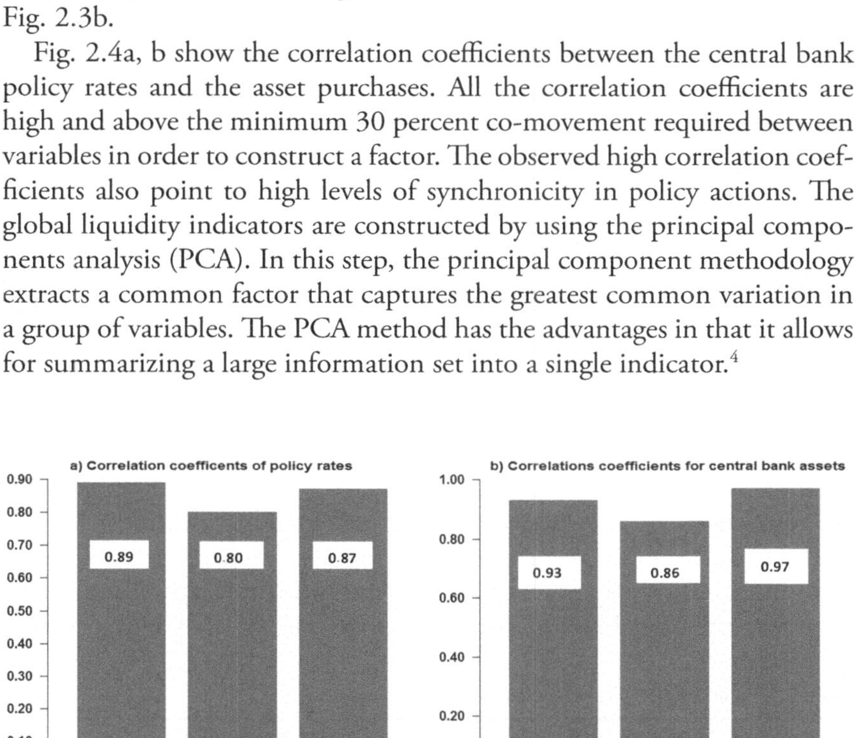

Fig. 2.4 Correlations between price and quantity measures of global liquidity (*Source*: Authors' calculations)

[3] For further reading on other quantity and price measures of global liquidity see Eickmeier et al. (2014), Djigbenou (2014) and Choi et al. (2014).

[4] For extensive discussion on the PCA see Johnson and Wichern (1992).

The quantity measure of global liquidity is derived from the central bank balance sheets data and the price measure is derived from the policy rates. Prior to constructing the global liquidity factors using the PCA approach, the data is de-trended and then purged of any macroeconomic effects.[5]

2.4 Are There Any Differences in the Impact of Quantity and Price Measures of Global Liquidity Shocks on the South African Economy?

This section distinguishes between the effects related to quantity and price measures of global liquidity shock using a Bayesian sign-restricted factor-augmented vector autoregression (FAVAR). The Uhlig (2005) pure sign restriction approach in a FAVAR is used to identify multiple shocks, as done in Eickmeier et al. (2014).[6] The identification scheme adopted in the empirical estimations is shown in Table 2.1. No sign restrictions are imposed on the variables of interest, namely GDP and credit. These are left unconstrained and the data is allowed to determine their responses. The restrictions are only placed on the global liquidity measures.

The quantity measure of the global liquidity shock is identified by imposing a positive sign on the quantity measure, a negative sign on the price measure of global liquidity, a negative sign on The Chicago Board

Table 2.1 Identifying sign restrictions

	Global variables		South African variables					
Shocks	Global liquidity	VIX	GDP	Credit	Repo rate	CPI	REER	Equity prices
Quantity	+	–	?	?	?	?	?	+
Price	–	–	?	?	?	?	?	+

[5] In this case, because global liquidity conditions are aligned to economic activity, they are purged of the macroeconomic effects by regressing the financial data on GDP growth.

[6] For further reading on the technical aspects see Helbing et al. (2011), Mumtaz and Surico (2009), and Choi and Lee (2010) among others.

Volatility Index (VIX). A decline in the price measures of global liquidity results in lower levels of global risk perception as proxied by VIX. A similar response is imposed on the increase in the quantity measure of global liquidity. This is consistent with theoretical motivations that suggest that the easing of the policy stance by the central bank should result in a decline in the policy rates and this should lower risk aversion or increase risk appetite. In addition, literature shows that periods of ample global liquidity and capital flows to EMEs are associated with changes in global risk appetite and aversion. Both quantity and price shocks increase equity prices.

The specification of the FAVAR model estimated in the empirical section is shown in Eq. (2.2).

$$Y_t = \begin{Bmatrix} \text{Gliq}, VIX, GDP, \text{credit, repo}, CPI, \\ \text{REER, equity prices} \end{Bmatrix} \tag{2.2}$$

The model includes external variables captured in the price and quantity factors of global liquidity and VIX for global investor risk perception. The rest of the variables are domestic, namely GDP, inflation, repo rate, JSE annual changes and the REER. All the variables enter the VAR in growth rates except for the global factors and the repo rate. In other models estimated in later sections, the REER is substituted with credit growth, exports growth, the trade balance and the current account as a percentage of GDP, in separate estimations.

In addition, in the estimations that compare the effects of quantity and price measures of global liquidity, a negative sign is imposed on the price measure of global liquidity shock and VIX and a positive sign on equity prices. In these estimations, the quantity measure of global liquidity is left unrestricted. The VAR models are estimated using one lag, as chosen by the Akaike Information Criterion (AIC). Only 1,000 impulses that satisfy the imposed conditions are kept and those that disobey restrictions are discarded. The imposed restrictions of the shocks last for at least two quarters.

Evidence in Fig. 2.5 shows similarities in the direction of the responses to price and quantity shocks of global liquidity but the magnitudes differ noticeably. It is evident that the quantity measure of global liquidity

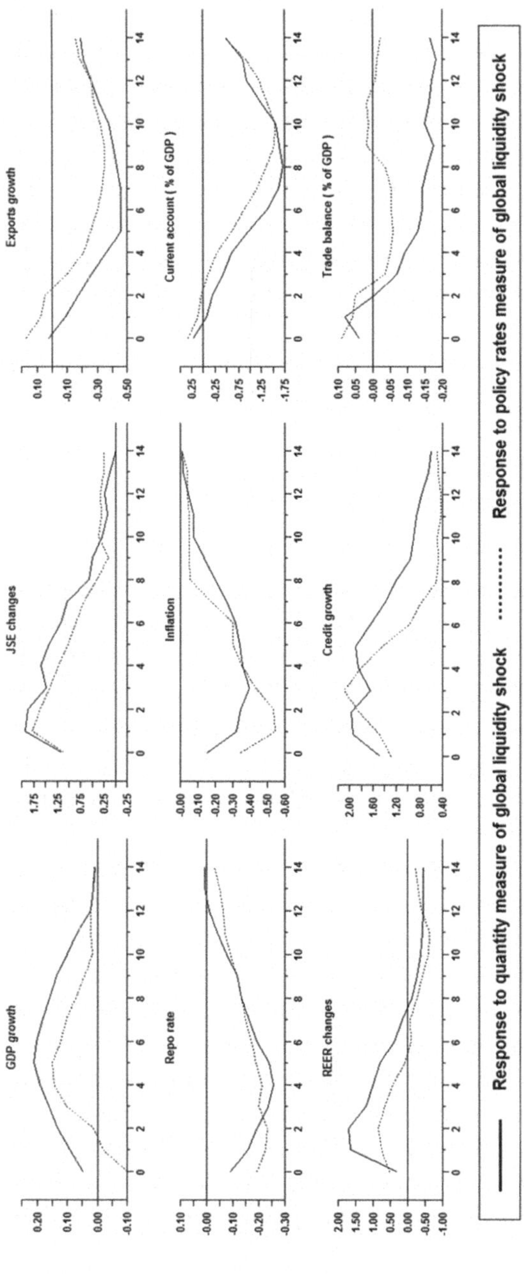

Fig. 2.5 A comparison of responses to quantity and price measures of global liquidity shocks (*Source:* Authors' calculations)

shock raises GDP growth, stock prices and credit growth more than the price measure of global liquidity shock. The current account, trade balance, repo rate and exports growth decline significantly in response to the quantity measure of global liquidity when compared to the responses to the price measure.

The REER appreciates very much in response to the quantity measure of global liquidity. The decline in inflation is more pronounced in response to the price measure of global liquidity. Thereafter, the impulse responses of the REER and inflation due to the two shocks move together. The responses of the repo rate differ on impact and peak in the fourth quarter. The repo rate declines by a big magnitude in response to the quantity measure of global liquidity. Overall, the results imply that the quantity-based measure of global liquidity has a significantly pronounced and, in some cases, persistent impact compared to those due to the price measure.

2.4.1 Is There an Inverse Transmission Relationship Between Global Liquidity Shocks and Selected Macroeconomic Variables Before and After 2008Q4?

This section of the chapter examines whether the sensitivity of South African macroeconomic variables changed in response to the implementation of the first round of QE (QE1) in 2008Q4. The start of QE is used as a reference point to break up the sample into pre- and post-QE periods, namely 2000Q1–2008Q3 and 2008Q4–2014Q4.[7] The global liquidity shocks are extracted from the FAVAR model and, thereafter, the scatter plots assess changes in the sensitivity of the macroeconomic variables. The results of the sensitivities are presented in Fig. 2.6 and show that the slopes in the bilateral relationships during the two subsamples have changed. For instance, in Fig. 2.6a the relationship between exports

[7] The sample is split in line with results that show that time-varying parameter models with slowly evolving coefficients might be partially affected by the pre-crisis period data (Weale and Wieladek 2014).

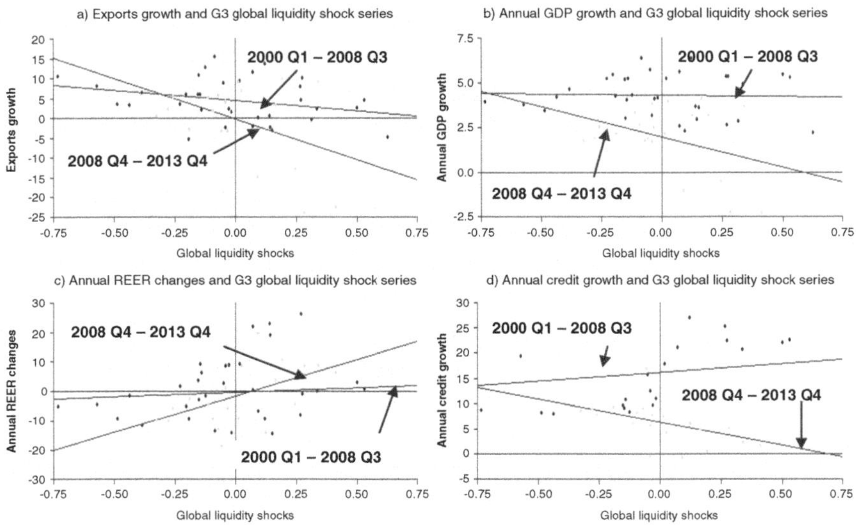

Fig. 2.6 The relationship between the global liquidity shock series and selected macroeconomic variables (*Source*: Authors' calculations)

growth and the global liquidity shocks became steeper and negative during 2008Q4 to 2014Q3 period. Why did the exports decline?

One possible channel is via the appreciation of the REER and the loss of competitiveness, as shown in Fig. 2.6b. The REER appreciated very much during the period of QE1 relative to the pre-QE period. The relationship between GDP and credit growth and the global liquidity shock in Fig. 2.6b, d became negative in 2008Q4–2014Q3. This suggests that the period of further rounds of QE did not lead to improved GDP and credit growth. In fact, the relationship is negative, suggesting possible adverse effects. We conclude that although global liquidity is not entirely bad, an inverse transmission occurred after 2008Q4.

Is the evidence of the inverse transmission based only on one approach? No, the cross correlations when global liquidity shocks lead the REER changes, GDP and credit growth shown in Fig. 2.7 indicate further evidence of the inverse transmission of global liquidity shocks into the South African economy.

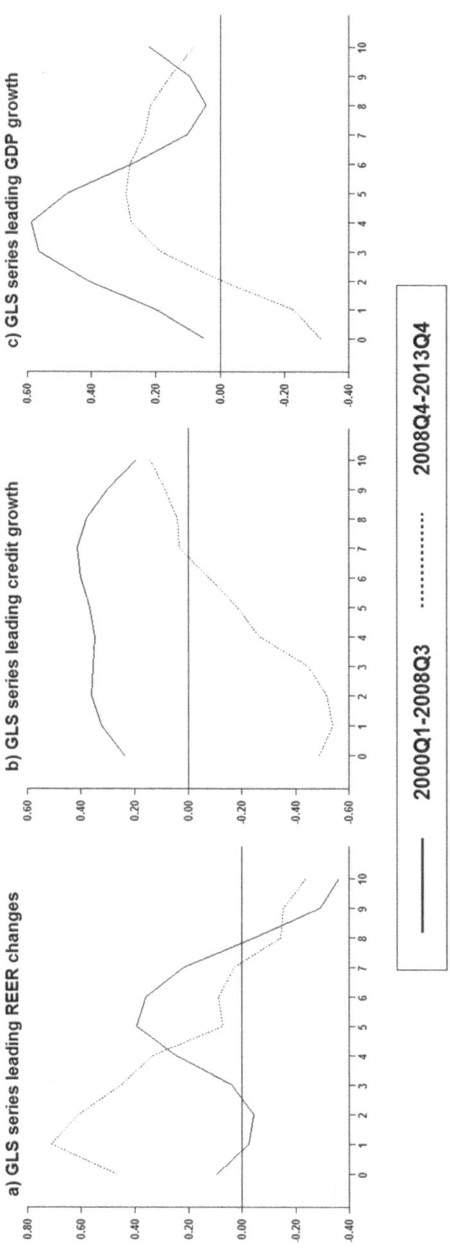

Fig. 2.7 Cross correlations between global liquidity shock and selected macroeconomic variables before 2008Q3 and post-2008Q4 (*Source*: Authors' calculations)

Evidence indicates significantly large differences in the dynamics of the variables in both subsamples. Fig. 2.7a shows a very strong positive relationship, suggesting that increased global liquidity from 2008Q4 was linked to the strong REER appreciation. In Fig. 2.7b an increase in the global liquidity shock is positively related to economic growth in 2000Q–2008Q3. This is in contrast to the negative relationship in first quarters in the 2008Q4–2013Q4 period. Fig. 2.7c shows that credit growth is positively correlated to the global liquidity shock series before 2008Q3, but thereafter it is negatively correlated to global liquidity shocks. The evidence concludes that the period of quantitative easing lead to inverse transmission effects.

The third approach to determine plausibility of the inverse transmission of global liquidity shocks is to explore the three QE episodes as exogenous variables in the FAVAR model. This implies using the dummy variable approach in which the dummy variable is set to equal one in each QE episode and zero otherwise. A dummy variable for the financial crisis is constructed and included in the model to facilitate the comparison of the responses of the domestic variables. The financial crisis dummy is set to one for the period when the crisis started and zero otherwise. The results of the three rounds of QE on credit growth are shown in Fig. 2.8. Similar to earlier results, credit growth declines very much following each episode of QE.

Furthermore, it is evident that the responses of credit growth are different during the various rounds of QE. The responses of credit growth to the financial crisis dummy and QE2 shock are the most severe compared to the other rounds of QE. However, with the exception of the initial responses to QE3 in the first two quarters, the response of credit is negative to all shocks. This is further evidence that QE had inverse transmission effects on credit growth.

2.4.2 What Do the Counterfactual Scenarios Say About Inverse Transmission?

Based on the preceding model, the analysis now goes further and shows inferences from the counterfactual scenarios. The counterfactual scenarios look at how the variables being investigated would have evolved in

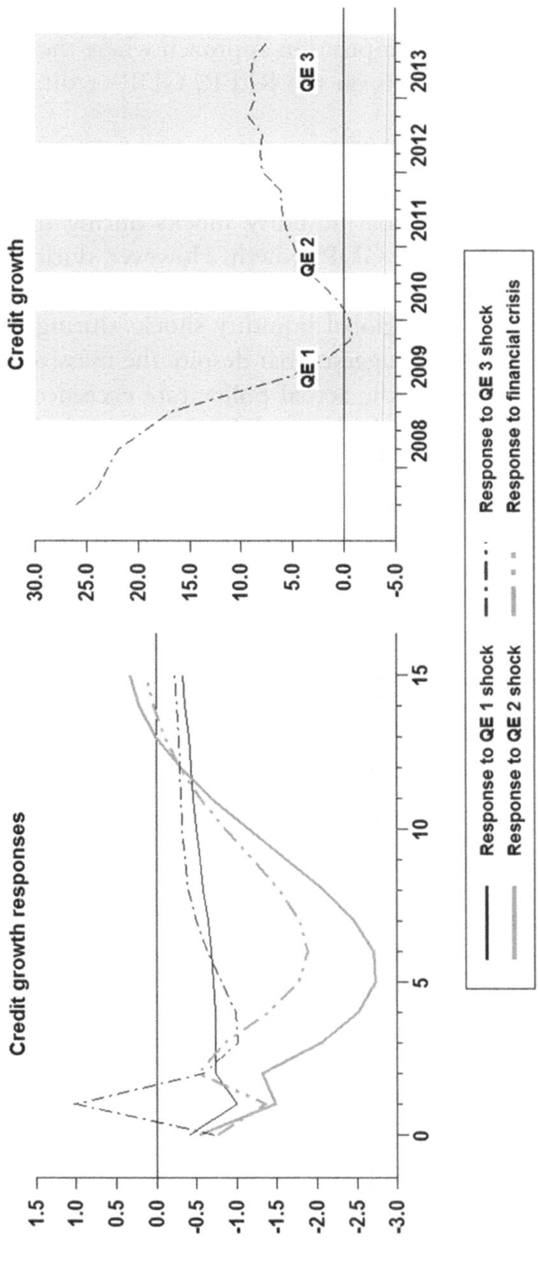

Fig. 2.8 Credit growth responses to various QE shocks (*Source*: Authors' calculations)

the absence of global liquidity shocks. The counterfactual scenarios are based on the historical decomposition approach where the contributions of the global liquidity shocks on the REER, GDP, credit, inflation and repo rate are removed.

Fig. 2.9 shows that actual GDP growth declined more than the counterfactual, suggesting that global liquidity worsened during QE1 and QE3. This implies that global liquidity shocks during these phases of QE worsened the decline in GDP growth. However, during QE2 actual GDP growth was above the counterfactual meaning that there were positive effects associated with global liquidity shocks during this phase of QE. In addition, Fig. 2.9c suggests that despite the massive reduction in the repo rate during QE1, the actual policy rate exceeded the counterfactual in Fig. 2.9d. It was only during QE2 that the actual repo rate was lower than the counterfactual.

The higher actual repo rate than the counterfactual may be due to anticipated inflationary pressures from the depreciated exchange rate in Fig. 2.10a, b. In contrast to the appreciation of almost 20 percentage points during 2009 and 2010, which coincided with QE1, the REER depreciated on average by nearly 10 percentage points between 2011 and 2013, coinciding with QE3. The changes in the inflationary pressures associated with the REER are clearly visible in Fig. 2.10d. During the period of QE3 the depreciation in the REER limited the benefits of global liquidity shocks on inflation. Actual inflation was higher than the counterfactual scenario and this possibly explains why the repo rate did not decline further.

Fig. 2.11 shows inverse transmission of QE1, QE2 and QE3 on GDP and REER changes. The REER appreciated very much during QE1 whilst GDP growth contracted. Even depreciations of REER in 2011 onwards did not have stimulatory effects on GDP growth, as it remained subdued.

Thus, evidence from the historical decompositions and various episodes of QE points to the inverse transmission effects.

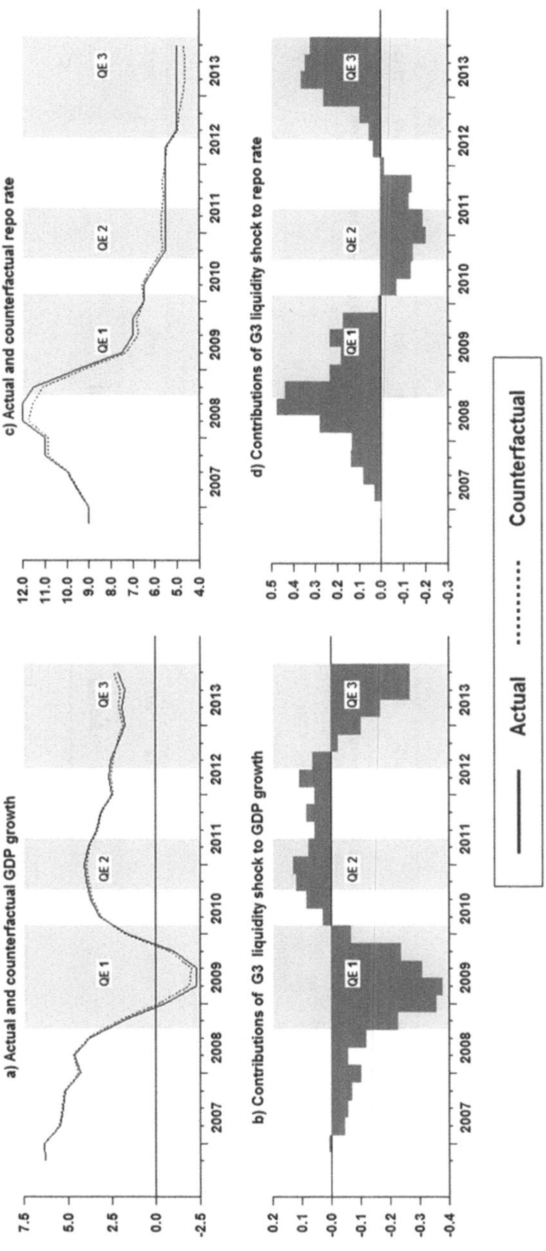

Fig. 2.9 Actual and counterfactual variables and historical contributions (*Source*: Authors' calculations)

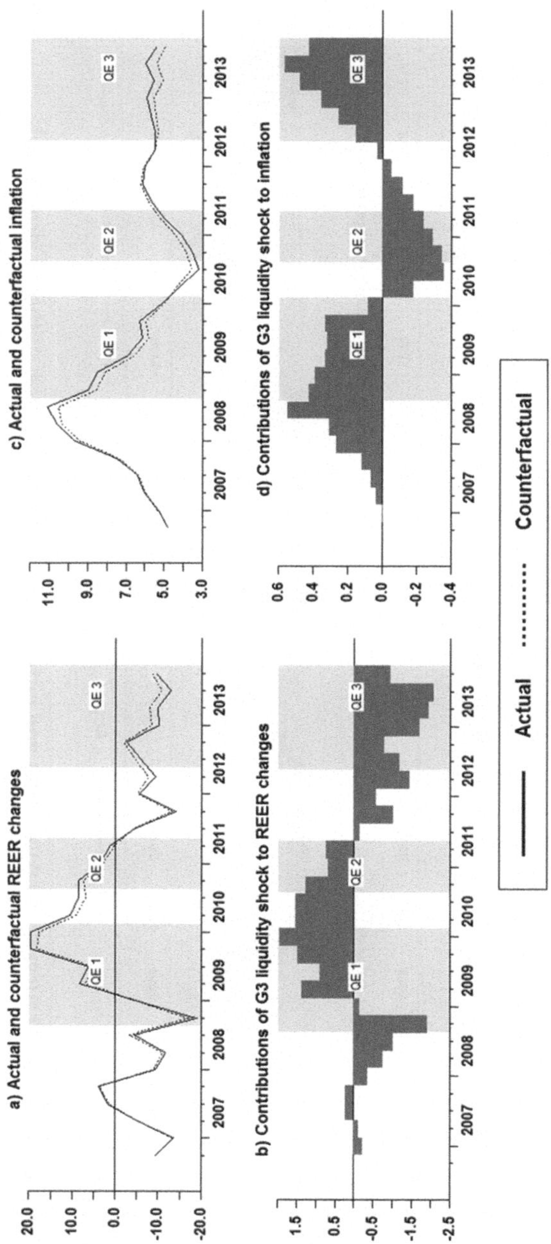

Fig. 2.10 Actual and counterfactual variables and historical contributions (*Source*: Authors' calculations)

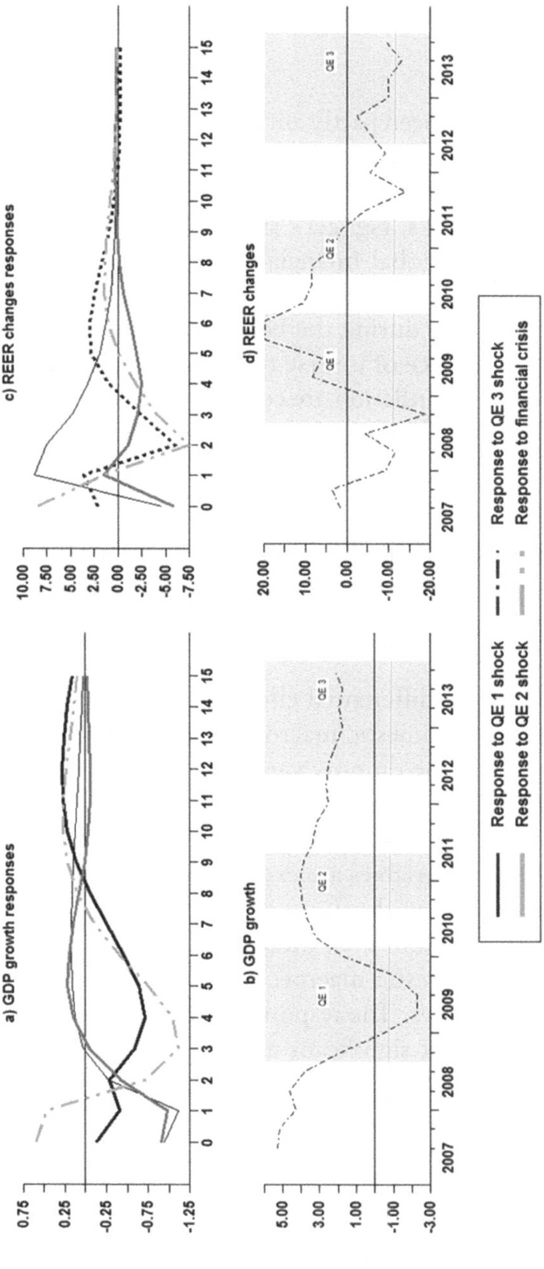

Fig. 2.11 QE effects on GDP growth and REER changes (*Source*: Authors' calculations)

2.4.3 Policy Rate and Inflation Responses to Various Phases of QE

The QE shocks may have been partly anticipated, as they were announced. But it is possible that the magnitudes may not have been correctly foreseen. This suggests that there may have been heterogeneous policy rate adjustments to these shocks. Fig. 2.12 shows that domestic policymakers did not respond to the global financial crisis by immediately reducing the policy rate. It was only by the time of QE1 that the policy rate was lowered, and then further during the beginning phase of QE3. There is, therefore, a lack of evidence of inverse transmission on the repo rate.

The initial reactions of inflation are contrary to theoretical predictions. It was only during QE1 that inflation declined. The capital inflows and the REER appreciation channels did not lower inflation quickly.

2.4.4 Did the US Fed and ECB Bank Balance Sheet Shocks Exert Inverse Transmission Effects on the South African Economy?

This section analyzes the differential effects of the US Fed and ECB balance sheets changes on domestic macroeconomic variables. For the estimations in this section, the dummy variables are set to equal one for the period 2008Q4–2014Q4 for the US Fed balance sheet changes and the period 2009Q2–2014Q4 for the ECB balance sheet changes, and zero otherwise. The dummy variables are exogenous in the model. The specification of the model is kept the unchanged.

Evidence in Figs. 2.13 and 2.14 indicates that there are differences in the responses of the domestic macroeconomic variables to the US and ECB balance sheet changes. The responses to shocks related to the ECB balance sheet do not exert significant effects on South African variables when compared to the US Fed balance sheet changes. This is consistent with expectations that the ECB balance sheet will not have significant effects on the South African economy, despite the Euro Area being a major trading partner.

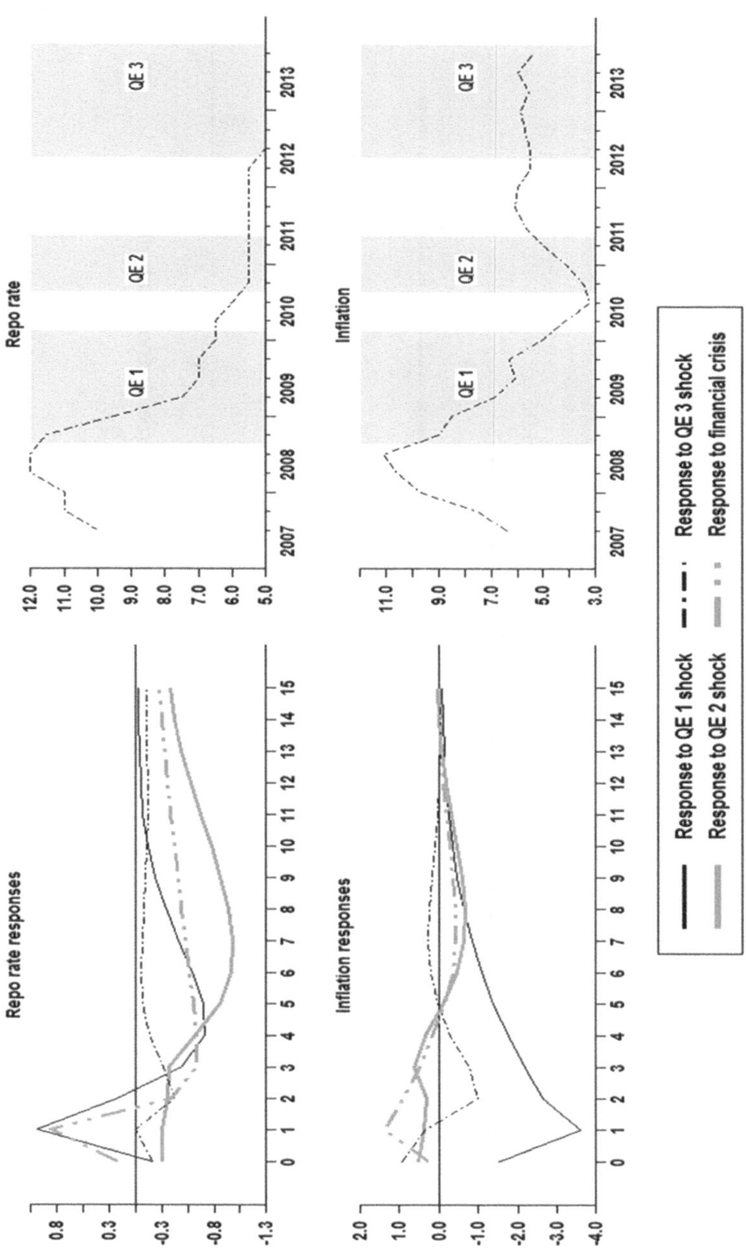

Fig. 2.12 Comparison of the repo rate responses to various US quantitative easing episodes (*Source*: Authors' calculations)

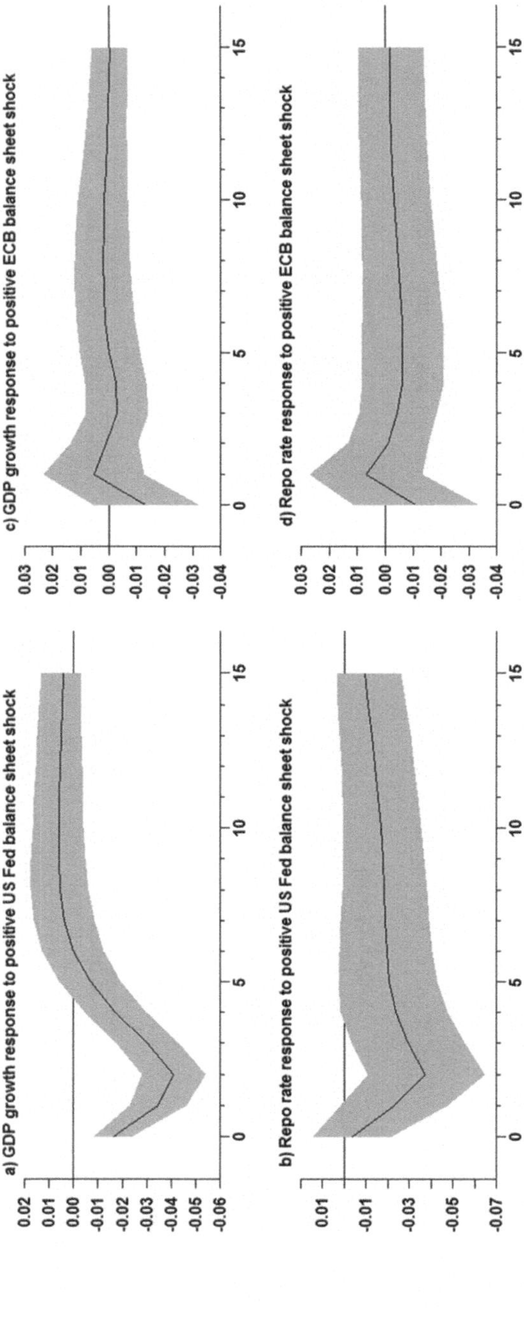

Fig. 2.13 Selected responses to US Fed and ECB balance sheet shocks (*Source*: Authors' calculations)

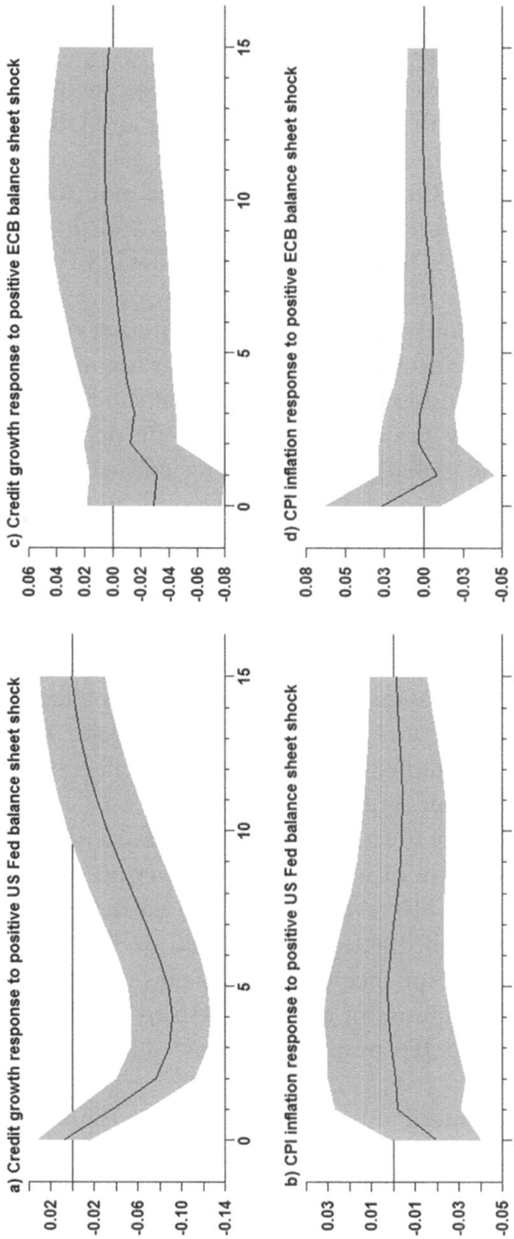

Fig. 2.14 Selected responses to US Fed and ECB balance sheet shocks (*Source*: Authors' calculations)

The US Fed balance sheet shock leads to a significant reduction in GDP and credit growth in Figs. 2.13 and 2.14. This is accompanied by a significant, albeit transitory, reduction in the repo rate in Fig. 2.14. This confirms the potency of the US Fed balance sheet and US dollar liquidity changes on the South African economy.

It is, however, surprising that inflation does not respond to these shocks. This perhaps indicates that inflation is mostly determined by domestic factors and the effects associated with the US Fed and ECB balance sheet changes only play a very small role.

These findings are similar to Vergara (2015), in that the inflation experience by most EMEs during the QE period was not aligned to the large negative output gaps and low demand. External shocks resulted in large declines in commodity prices and exchange rate depreciations. Jordan (2015) notes that the global effects have affected Swiss imported goods' inflation but the volatility and persistence was not significantly affected.

2.4.5 The Role of Commodity Prices: Inferences from the Counterfactual Analysis

Would the presence or absence of commodity prices affect the direction of responses of credit growth to global liquidity shocks? Fig. 2.15 shows that a positive global liquidity shock has a positive effect on credit growth whether commodity prices are included or not.

Both the ECB balance sheet and QE shocks have a negative impact on credit growth, irrespective of whether commodity prices are included or excluded in the model. However, the US Fed balance sheet shocks and various rounds of QE shocks lead to a muted decline in credit growth when commodity prices are included. This means that commodity prices tend to cushion the response of credit growth to shocks due to the US Fed balance sheet and QE compared to those due to the ECB balance sheet.

So how should domestic monetary policy have responded to external shocks? Do commodity price developments constrain monetary policy responses? The repo rate responses and the counterfactual in Fig. 2.16 show that shocks emanating from the US balance sheet lead to big-

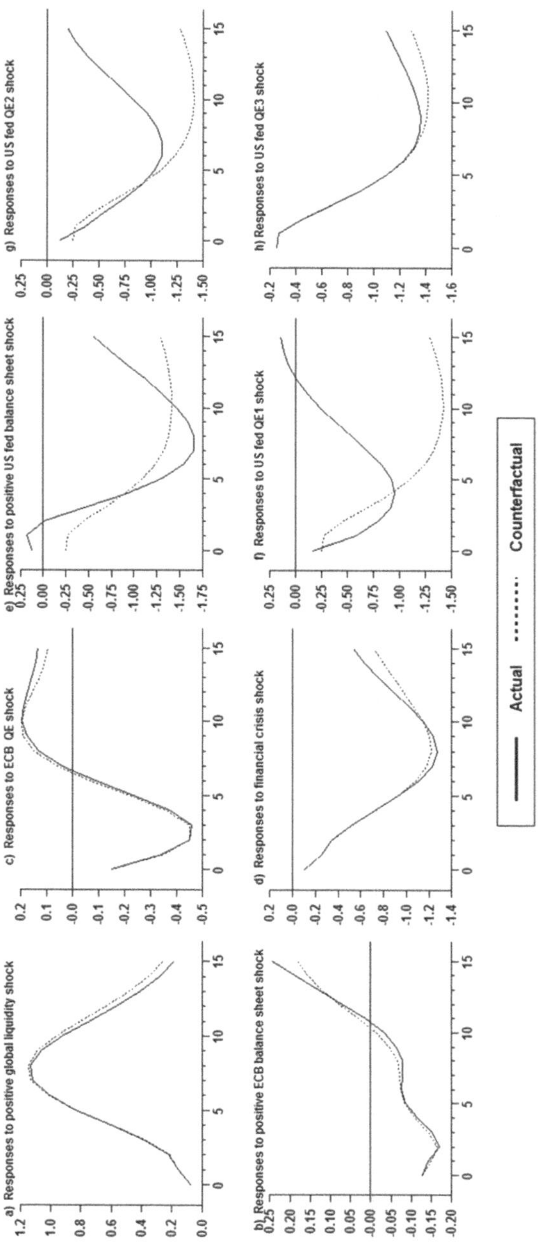

Fig. 2.15 Credit responses to various shocks and the role of commodity prices (*Source*: Authors' calculations)

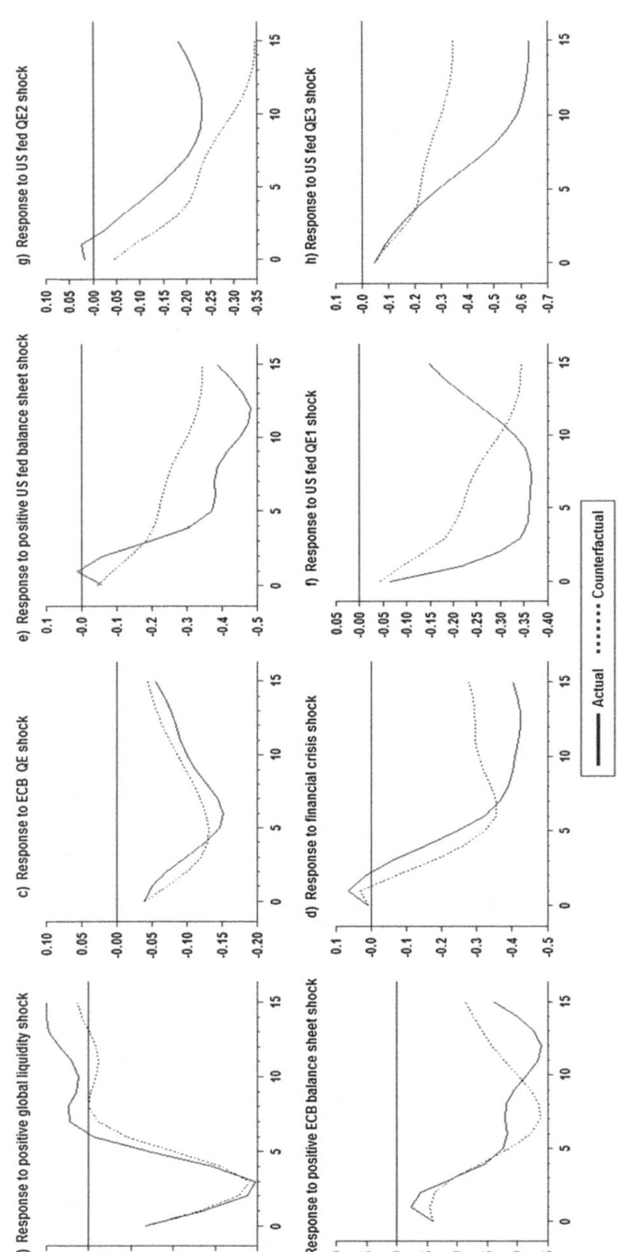

Fig. 2.16 Repo rate responses to various shocks and the role of commodity prices (*Source*: Authors' calculations)

ger reductions in the repo rate compared to those emanating from the ECB balance sheet, irrespective of whether or not commodity prices are included in the estimations. In most cases, the repo rate is loosened more in the presence of commodity prices than in their absence.

2.5 Conclusion and Policy Implications

The chapter set out to investigate whether the South African data supports the inverse transmission of excess global liquidity associated with asset purchases by central banks in advanced economies. The most significant policy implications emanating from the study relate to the responses of domestic variables to price and quantity measures of global liquidity. Evidence shows that there are similarities in the direction of the responses but the magnitudes differ noticeably. Quantity measure of global liquidity shock raises GDP growth, stock prices, credit growth more than shocks due to price measure. The REER appreciates due to positive global liquidity shocks but does not necessarily result in a persistently low inflation rate. This suggests that domestic factors play a much bigger role in determining the trajectory and persistence of inflation. Furthermore, the appreciation in the REER results in a decline in exports growth.

On financial stability, there is no evidence that excess global liquidity plays a significant role in domestic credit growth. It is possible that the results indicate limited intermediation of capital flows via the banking sector. This means that regulators and policymakers have to contend with these findings when designing domestic policies aimed at dealing with capital flows. In addition, Carstens (2015) shows that macro-prudential policies tend to be far less effective when capital flows are not channelled through the banking system and rather are intermediated via market-based financing mechanisms.

Summary of Main Findings

- Evidence supports the theoretical predictions of the inverse transmission effects of global liquidity shocks. The effects are more prevalent on the REER, exports, credit and GDP growth.

- There are distinct differences in responses of domestic variables to price and quantity measures of global liquidity. These findings indicate the dominant effects of the quantity measures of global liquidity relative to those of price policy measures.
- Evidence indicates that the US Fed balance sheet and by association US dollar liquidity plays a dominant role in South African variables. The impact of shocks to the US balance surpasses those due to the ECB balance sheet. This happens despite the fact that the Euro Area is South Africa's major trading partner.
- Commodity prices cushion the responses of credit growth to US Fed balance sheet shocks compared to those emanating from the ECB balance sheet.

3

The Impact of Capital Flows on Credit Extension: The Counterfactual Approach

Learning Objectives

- See the effects of capital flow shocks on credit growth, economic growth and the real effective exchange rate.
- Use the counterfactual analysis to show the extent to which credit growth, economic growth and changes in the REER would have evolved in the absence of capital flows.
- Show the importance of amplification effects of commodity prices on the responses of credit growth to capital flow shocks.

3.1 Introduction

What are the effects of positive capital flow shocks on credit growth? To what extent do the commodity prices amplify the responses of credit growth to net capital and banking flow shocks? What does the counterfactual analysis suggest credit growth is when capital flows are shut off? Various rounds of quantitative easing (QE) in advanced economies injected liquidity in financial markets and triggered a surge of capital

N. Gumata, E. Ndou, *Bank Credit Extension and Real Economic Activity in South Africa*, DOI 10.1007/978-3-319-43551-0_3

inflows into emerging market economies (EMEs). This chapter specifically explores the impact of net capital flows on credit growth, the extent to which economic growth (GDP) and competitiveness is measured by the performance of the real effective exchange rate (REER).

3.2 The Relationship Between GDP and Net Capital Flows Over Time

The relationship between net capital flows to and GDP growth has varied over different policy regimes. Fig. 3.1a shows that the relationship between net capital flows and economic growth was most steep prior to 2000 relative to post-2000. Fig. 3.1b shows GDP growth was strongly and positively correlated to net capital flows before the financial crisis and from 20007Q3 this relationship is very flat, suggesting capital flows did not raise GDP growth much. Theoretically, the balance of payment can be decomposed into the capital account and the current account balance as in Eq. (3.1).

$$\text{Balance of payments} = \text{Current account} + \text{capital account} + \text{changes in foreign reserves} \tag{3.1}$$

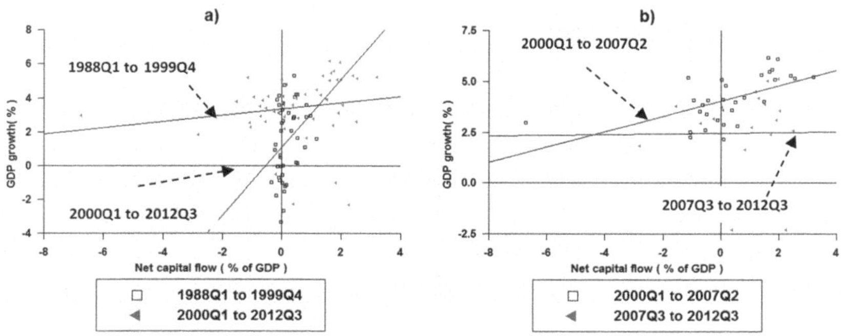

Fig. 3.1 GDP and net capital flow relationship (*Source*: SARB and authors' calculations)

The capital account (or net flow of funds) is determined by the interest rate differential between domestic and foreign rates. A rise in domestic interest rates, which raises the interest rate differential, is expected to trigger capital inflows domestically. The opposite policy action is expected to trigger capital outflows.

Theoretically, these capital flow dynamics are expected to impact the exchange rate. An increase (decrease) in capital inflow is expected to appreciate (depreciate) the exchange rate. Therefore, through the impact on the exchange rate, net capital flows are expected to affect the trade balance and the current account. Equation (3.2) shows that the trade balance is made up of exports and imports. The exchange rate is important to both key variables of the equation.

$$\begin{aligned}\text{Trade balance} = \text{Exports}\left(\text{foreign income, exchange rate}\right) - \\ \text{Imports}\left(\text{domestic income, exchange rate}\right)\end{aligned} \quad (3.2)$$

The exchange rate appreciation is expected to depress exports and boost imports. In addition, a rise in domestic income is expected to lead to higher imports and worsen the trade balance. A rise in foreign income is expected to support demand for domestic exports. This means that there are a number of channels through which net capital flow shocks are transmitted into the components of the balance of payments.

3.3 How Are Capital Flow Shocks Transmitted Through the Balance of Payments Components?

What are the effects of capital flow shocks on GDP, the components of trade balance and the current account? To answer this question, the Tillman (2013) approach is adopted and adjusted to include the components of the trade balance and the current account.[1] The data spans 1988Q1 to 2012Q3. The intention is to show the trajectories of

[1] See Tillman (2013) for details.

the variables over 14 quarters in response to a one standard deviation shock in net capital flows.

Fig. 3.2 shows that the responses are more negative for the difference between the exports and imports compared to those for GDP growth. The trajectories of the current account and the difference between exports and imports stay below the zero line, indicating that these variables remain negative but at a decreasing rate over time. On the contrary, GDP tends to increase, and this is the case over all horizons depicted in Fig. 3.2. This indicates that at longer lags net exports tend to be a drag on economic growth.

The difference in exports and imports (exports less imports) trajectories is negative throughout the horizons and reaches a peak decline of 1 percentage point. This confirms that when imports rise more than exports in response to a capital flows shocks, the contributions of the trade balance to economic growth tend to adversely impact real economic growth. Thus, the evidence indicates that capital flows make the domestic economy more outward orientated, as imports rise more than both exports and growth in output.

The fact that imports tend to rise more than both GDP and exports remains of concern for policymakers. So, evidence presented in this section contributes to providing facts on the long-term relationships. It may help in shaping the thinking about possible policy interventions aimed at addressing these imbalances, although the analysis of such policy interventions is beyond the scope of this chapter.

3.4 The Counterfactual Analysis of Capital Flows and GDP

What would GDP growth be in the absence of capital flows? The counterfactual analysis based on the historical decompositions of GDP growth into the base forecast and contributions made by the net capital flow shock are used to answer this question. The counterfactual GDP is obtained by subtracting the contribution of the capital flow shocks to actual GDP. Thereafter, the annual counterfactual economic growth is

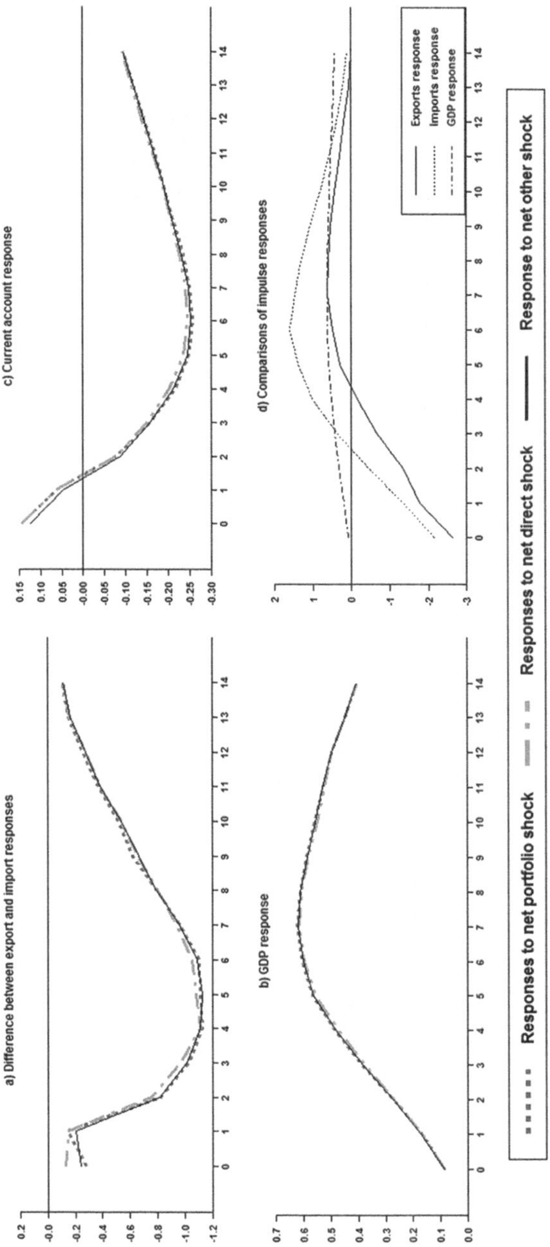

Fig. 3.2 Net exports, current account and GDP responses to a positive net capital flow shock (*Source*: Authors' calculations)

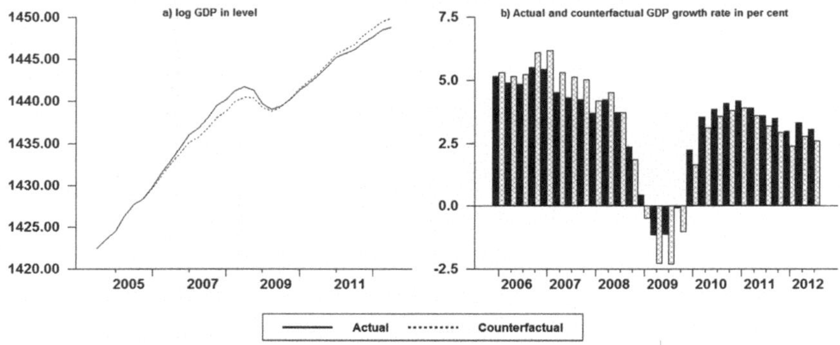

Fig. 3.3 Actual and counterfactual GDP levels and growth rates (*Note*: Numbers in the vertical axis for GDP levels represent GDP log multiplied by 100. *Source*: Authors' calculations)

calculated and compared to actual GDP growth. The difference between the counterfactual and actual GDP growth rates indicates the role which the model attributes to a capital flow shock. The trends of actual and counterfactual GDP in levels and growth rates are shown in Fig. 3.3.

Fig. 3.3a shows that actual GDP contracted more than the counterfactual GDP growth in 2009, and there was little difference in 2010. These results suggest that the slowdown in economic activity during the recession was in part a reflection of the adverse effects of net capital flows, possibly transmitted through the trade balance shown in Fig. 3.2a relative to the current account in Fig. 3.2c. At the same time, this may reflect the sensitivity of imports to the capital inflow shocks as shown in Fig. 3.2d, which rise more than exports across horizons.

A comparison of the counterfactual and actual REER dynamics can shed light on other channels of transmission and adjustment. The impact of capital flows on the REER is given by the gap between the estimated counterfactual and actual REER in Fig. 3.4.

The positive difference such as seen in 2009 implies that capital flows contributed to the worsening of the country's competitiveness relative to its trading partners as the currency appreciated more than it would have in the absence of capital flows. This implies that the surge in capital inflows resulted in an overvalued REER and increased the pace of erosion of domestic competitiveness relative to trading partners.

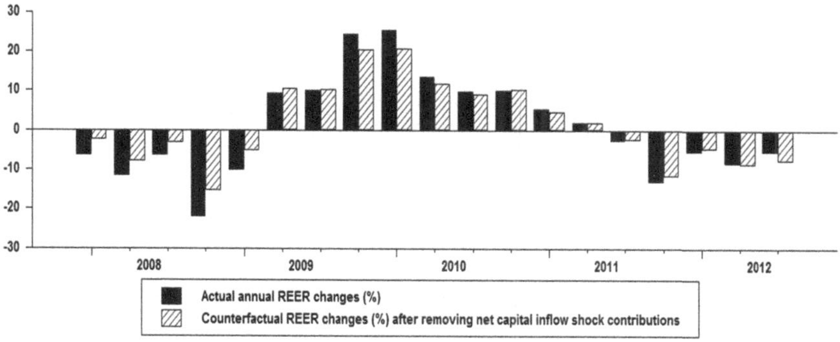

Fig. 3.4 Actual and counterfactual REER (*Source*: Authors' calculations)

3.5 To What Extent Did Capital Flows Drive Credit Growth, if at All?

The literature and empirical studies investigating the effects of capital flows in other EMEs suggest that capital flows can lead to credit booms. Bruno and Shin (2013) refer to a popular narrative suggesting that low interest rates in advanced economies act as a driver of cross-border capital flows and result in overheating, excessive credit growth and consequent inflation in the recipient economies. It is argued that for small open economies, capital flows affect macroeconomic and financial stability through the risk-taking channel, fluctuations in domestic credit and exchange rates and ultimately output and inflation. The interaction between credit extension and the exchange rate suggests a mechanism in which capital inflows initially lead to currency appreciation. The appreciated exchange rate in turn leads to a temporary boost in domestic demand through a fall in the relative prices of durable and capital goods and improved external financing conditions, followed by easy access to credit. This may lead to an excessive risk-taking and lending appetite and thus feed into rapid credit growth and systemic risk. The feedback loop between the exchange rate and credit growth may turn into a spiral, which may eventually end up with a sudden reversal of the cycle, disrupting macroeconomic and financial stability (Kara 2013).

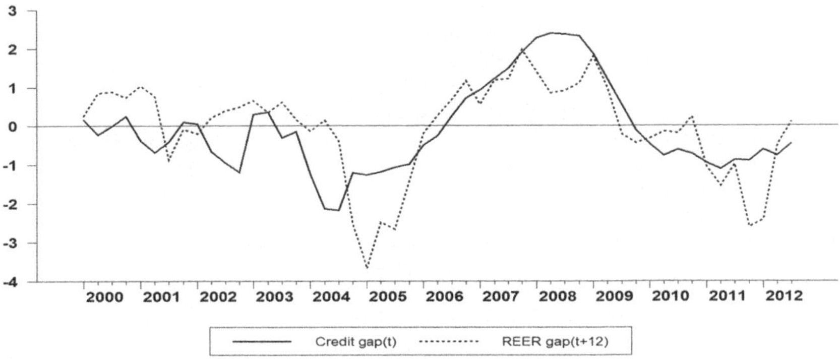

Fig. 3.5 The credit and real effective exchange rate cycles (The gaps were estimated using data spanning 1985Q1 to 2012Q3 but the graph presented here only focuses on the inflation targeting framework period. *Note*: These are standardized HP filter gaps in percent deviation. *Source*: Authors' calculations)

As a precursor to the analysis, Fig. 3.5 plots cycles in domestic credit and exchange rates to assess how these variables interact overtime. The trends in Fig. 3.5 suggest that there is a correlation between the current credit gap and the REER gap of about 12 quarters lag. This is in stark contrast to the Turkish estimates that show that the REER gap leads the loans gap by three quarters.[2]

The implication of the twelve quarters lag is that even though the earlier section established that capital flow shocks result in the REER appreciation and are inversely transmitted to GDP growth via the adjustment of the trade balance relative to the current account, this does not necessarily impact credit growth. In contrast with it being one of the leading indicators of credit growth as established by Kara 2013 in Turkey, evidence indicates that the REER significantly lags credit growth by almost three years (12 quarters). Therefore, even though the REER and credit gaps are highly correlated, this happens with a significantly long lag. This evidence indirectly suggests that global liquidity and capital flow surges may have little impact on domestic credit growth.

But what does the empirical evidence suggest the impact of capital flows on credit growth is in South Africa? To answer this question, the specification in

[2] See Kara (2013) and Aysan et al. (2014) for further details.

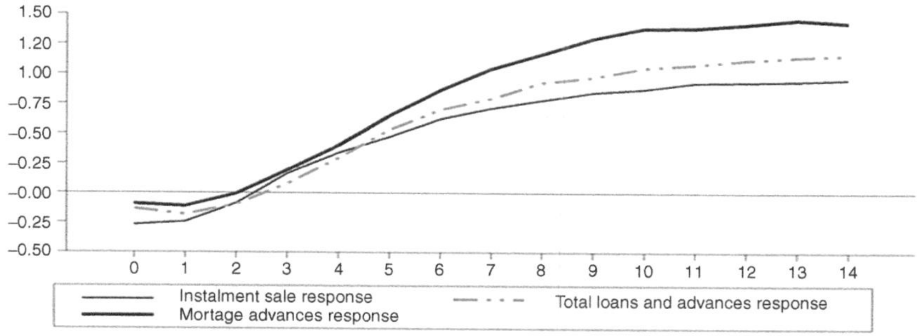

Fig. 3.6 The responses of credit growth and components to capital flows shocks (*Source*: Authors' calculations)

the earlier sections is adjusted to include credit. The data sample spans 1988Q1 to 2012Q3. The impulse responses in Fig. 3.6 show that capital flows lead to increases in credit growth and the components of credit. At peak magnitudes, total credit rises by 1 percentage points mortgage advances growth peak at 1.5 percentage points and installment sales credit rises by just below 1 percentage points after ten quarters. The magnitudes of these results suggest that credit growth and the key components are not highly responsive to capital flows.

3.5.1 What Do the Counterfactual Scenarios Suggest the Role of Capital Flows on Credit Growth Is?

The counterfactual analysis is applied to investigate the impact of capital flows on credit growth. The gap between actual and counterfactual credit growth indicates the influence of capital inflows. Evidence presented in Fig. 3.7 indicates that actual credit growth was higher than the counterfactual scenario for the large part of the time between 2005 and 2009, and in 2011. This means that other domestic factors played a much more significant role in stimulating credit growth than capital flows. Capital flow shocks played a very small and limited role in credit growth, the most significant drivers of credit may be primarily domestically generated, rather than highly dependent on foreign capital flows.

Similarly, Fig. 3.8 shows that growth in total credit extended to the private sector remains below its counterfactual growth rate, suggesting that capital flows did not improve the extension of credit.

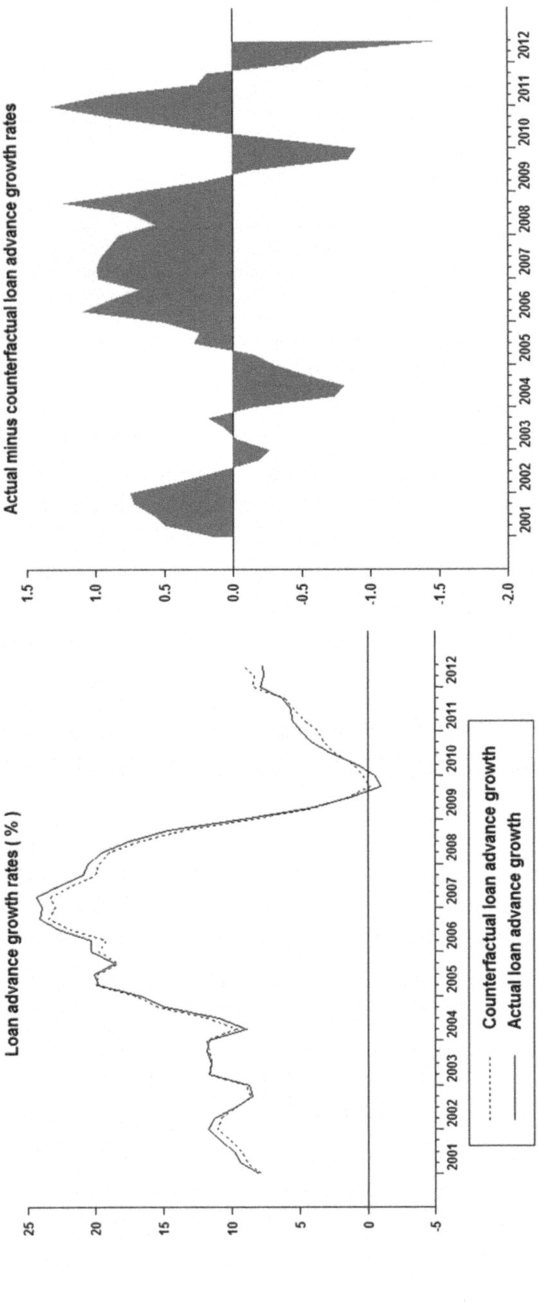

Fig. 3.7 Actual and counterfactual total loans and advances growth (*Source*: Authors' calculations)

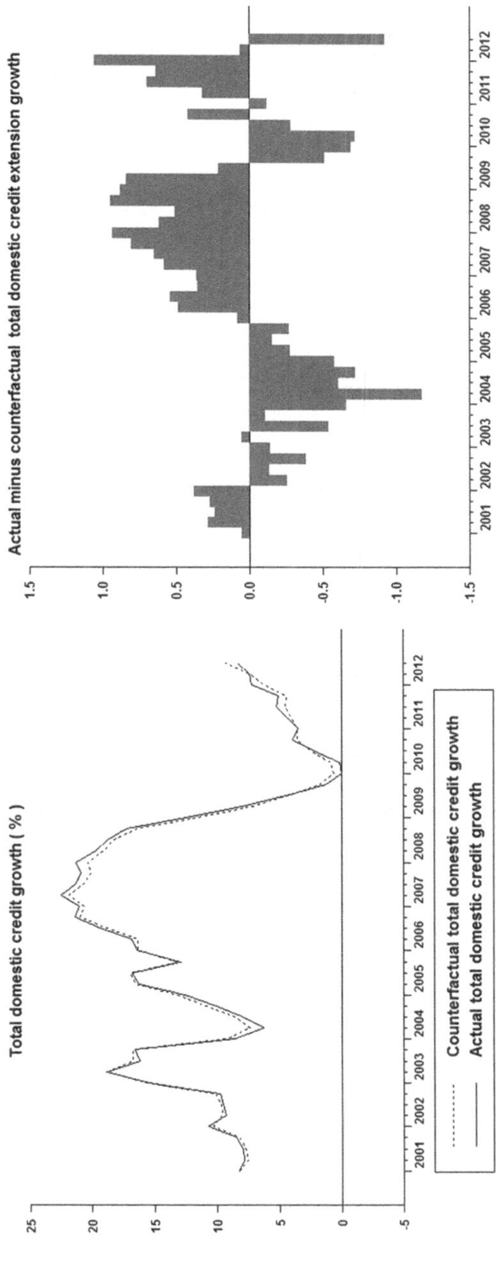

Fig. 3.8 Actual and counterfactual scenarios for total private sector credit growth (*Source*: Authors' calculations)

This suggests that domestic credit extension is mostly determined by domestic factors. The overall conclusion is that credit extension in its various broad definitions is not primarily driven by capital flows but rather by domestic factors.

3.5.2 What About Commodity Prices, Do They Play Any Meaningful Role?

The vector autoregression (VAR) specifications used in the previous sections are adjusted to include South African commodity prices including gold (in rand terms). The actual and counterfactual credit growth responses and the amplification role of commodity prices are shown in Fig. 3.9.

The credit responses to positive capital flow shocks suggest that actual credit growth remains above the counterfactual throughout the entire forecast, two quarters after the shock. In addition, the results suggest that the commodities price channel plays a meaningful role in amplifying the impact of capital flows on credit growth. Nonetheless, the magnitudes of the amplifications remain fairly small and below 1 percentage point.

3.5.3 Does the Composition of Capital Flows Change the Role of Commodity Prices on Credit?

Is the direction of the response of credit growth different in the presence (absence) of commodity prices in a model that includes banking flows? The specification of the VAR model estimated in this section is adjusted to include banking flow shocks, which refer to the sum of portfolio and foreign direct investment (FDI) banking flows. Fig. 3.10 shows that a positive banking flow shock leads to an increase in credit and the commodity prices channel propagates the impact. This implies that commodity prices amplify credit responses to positive banking flow shocks.

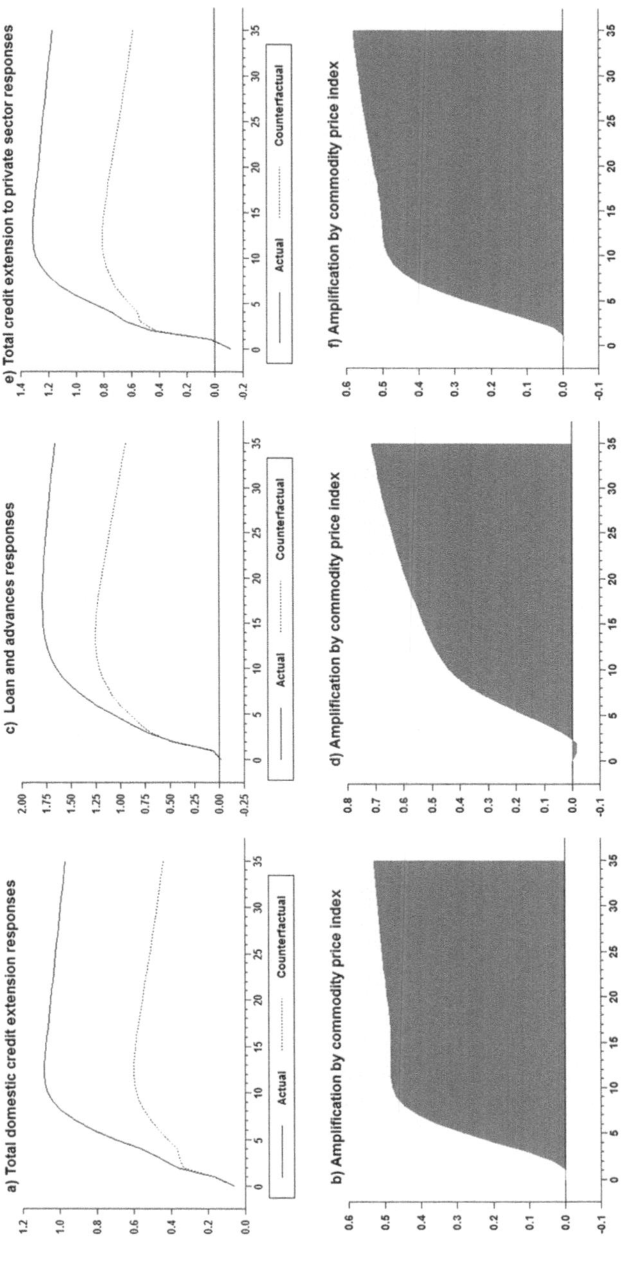

Fig. 3.9 Credit responses to a positive net capital flow shock (*Source*: Authors' calculations)

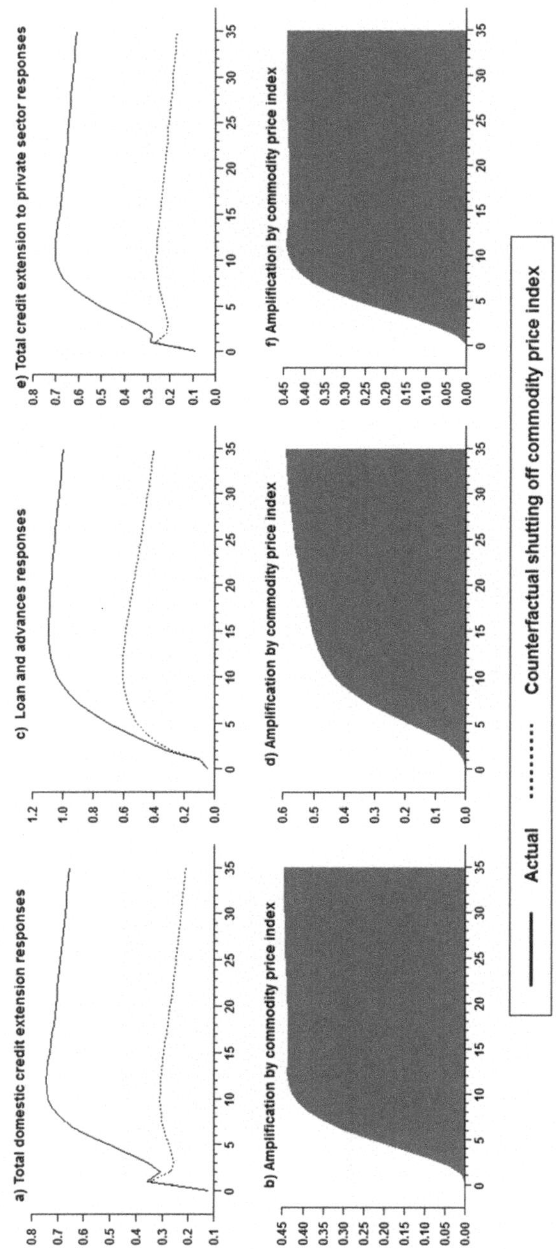

Fig. 3.10 Responses to credit to bank flows (*Source*: Authors' calculations)

3.6 Conclusion and Policy Implications

The analysis in this chapter looked at the effects of net capital flows against the backdrop of various rounds of quantitative easing episodes in advanced economies that triggered a surge of capital inflows into EMEs such as South Africa. The results show that capital flows affect and explain part of economic growth but this is predominantly the case during periods of relative stable economic growth. The same analysis shows that the exchange rate was overvalued for the major part of 2009, suggesting that the movements in the REER could have also contributed to the domestic loss of competitiveness relative to South Africa's trading partners. In addition, imports rise more than exports and GDP growth in response to a capital flow shocks, making the domestic economy be more outward orientated.

Capital flow shocks (including banking flows) lead to an increase in credit growth and the commodity price channel propagates the impact. However, capital flow shocks and commodity prices play a very small and limited role in credit extension. This indicates that the most significant drivers of credit may be primarily domestically generated and domestically oriented, rather than highly dependent on a foreign capital flow shocks.

Summary of Findings

- Evidence shows imports rise more than exports and GDP growth, making the domestic economy more outward orientated.
- The counterfactual scenarios show that the REER was overvalued for the major part of 2009 and eroded domestic competitiveness relative to trading partners.
- The REER changes lag credit growth almost three years. This implies that the REER changes do not necessarily impact credit growth, even though they are transmitted into the domestic economy via the trade channel. This is in stark contrast to other EMEs, where REER changes are leading indicators of domestic credit growth.

- Positive net capital flows and banking shocks increase credit and the commodities price channel plays a propagating role. However, the magnitudes are limited, meaning that other domestic factors played a much more significant role in stimulating credit growth than capital flow shocks and commodity prices.

4

Capital Flow Episodes Shocks, Global Investor Risk and Credit Growth

Learning Objectives

- Show the importance of classifying capital flow episodes, separating between foreign and domestic investor activities
- Understand the channels of transmission of capital flow waves and how they impact real economic activity and credit growth
- Show how changes in global risk shocks impact capital flow surges, sudden stop episodes, credit growth and real activity
- Demonstrate the significance of economic costs exerted by capital flow surges, sudden stops and capital flight and retrenchments
- Show costs associated with capital flows driven by domestic and foreign investor behavior.
- Examine the role of commodity prices and the exchange rate in amplifying credit growth based on the counterfactual scenarios
- Establish whether capital flow surges and sudden stop shocks lead to the reallocation of sectorial credit shares

N. Gumata, E. Ndou, *Bank Credit Extension and Real Economic Activity in South Africa*, DOI 10.1007/978-3-319-43551-0_4

4.1 Introduction

This chapter extends the analysis of the impact of capital flows and credit growth by investigating the relevance and costs of capital flow episodes on credit dynamics. The capital flow episodes are based on the Forbes and Warnock (2011) classification of capital flow episodes shocks. Do capital flow surges and sudden stops have different effects on credit growth and real economic activity? Forbes and Warnock (2011) classify capital flows as either (1) sudden stops or surges, or (2) decompose capital flows into foreigners' and domestic investor activity. This classification is used to estimate the economic costs of capital flow episodes. Furthermore, the chapter analyses the role of commodity prices and the exchange rate in amplifying or exacerbating the responses of credit growth to changes in global investor risk perceptions as proxied by The Chicago Board Options Exchange (CBOE) Volatility Index (VIX), capital flow surges and sudden stop shocks.

Forbes and Warnock (2011) state that capital flows volatility can amplify economic cycles and increase the vulnerability of the financial system.[1] How significant are the economic costs exerted by surges, sudden stops, capital flight and retrenchments? What can the findings in this chapter tell researchers and policymakers about such episodes?

4.2 The Classification of Capital Flow Episodes and the Importance of Separating Between Foreign and Domestic Investor Activity

Forbes and Warnock (2011) show that the reference definition of the data used in classifying capital flow episodes really matters. There is a difference between using gross capital flows versus net capital flows in defining capital flow episodes. It is noted in the literature that the shortcoming of using net capital flows to define capital flow episodes is (1) the

[1] Despite increasing financial vulnerability, they established that during episodes of global liquidity contraction, economies benefitted from capital inflows driven by domestic investors as they liquidated their foreign investments.

failure to differentiate between changes in foreign and domestic investor behavior, (2) the size and volatility of gross flows can increase while net capital flows have become more stable, (3) domestic investor flows can become increasingly important. Therefore, the change in net capital flows can no longer be driven by foreign investors alone. This is particularly important when considering the relaxation of exchange controls on residents in recent years while, finally, another shortcoming is (4) the increased incidence of sudden stops and retrenchment resulting from investors liquidating their foreign investment positions.

In addition, it is important that South African discussions on capital flows should discern capital flow waves according to (1) the *sudden stops* that occur when foreign capital inflows suddenly slow or stop, (2) *surges* which happen when foreign capital inflows increase rapidly, (3) *retrenchment* which occurs when domestic investors liquidate their foreign investments and (4) *capital flight* which occurs when domestic investors send large amounts of capital abroad. This also means that domestic investors are not cut off from global capital markets. Domestic investors have ample access to these markets and utilize them by moving their domestic funds abroad (Forbes and Warnock 2011).

What can trigger a capital flight episode of capital flows? This might happen if domestic investors with superior information foresee a negative shock to the local market or see an investment opportunity abroad. These motives imply that in anticipation of a shock, economic agents shift their money to global markets. This leads to a net capital inflows decline. However, the difference is that this decline is not prompted by foreign investors (Rothenberg and Warnock 2011).

4.3 How Do Capital Flows Wave Categories Impact Real Economic Activity and Credit Growth?

The empirical approach adopted in this chapter uses episodes identified by Forbes and Warnock (2011) for four capital flow wave categories to investigate the effects of capital flow dynamics on economic growth. To this end, dummy variables that capture these episodes separately are generated. The dummy variables for each capital flow wave episode are equal to one for the period identified by Forbes and Warnock and zero otherwise. This is done for each capital flow category.

Various bivariate vector autoregression (VAR) models are estimated in light of South African macroeconomic variables; these include dummy variables for capital wave episodes, namely (1) a sudden stop episode, (2) capital inflow surge episodes, (3) capital flight episodes and (4) capital retrenchment episodes. The sample spans 1995Q1 to 2014Q3. To capture the impact of structural and policy changes during this period, the two dummy variables are constructed: for (1) inflation targeting which is equal to one for the period beginning 2000Q1 to the end of the sample and zero otherwise; and (2) the recession, which is equal to one for the 2009Q1–Q3 and zero otherwise.

The VAR models have two lags as selected by AIC and include a constant. The identification scheme follows the Choleski decomposition approach. Each capital flows episode dummy variable is placed before the South African macroeconomic variables. This suggests that the capital flow episode is independent of the South African variables. For robustness analysis, the VAR models are estimated using different orderings.

In the estimations, credit, GDP and VIX growth, inflation and the rand exchange rate are expressed as log annual changes. The sections that estimate the sectorial shifts in credit extension use the shares of households and companies in total loans and advances. The capital flow shocks are a one-standard deviation shock in each capital flows episode. The standard deviations are based on 1,000 Monte Carlo draws. The error bonds denote the 16th and 84th percentiles.

4.3.1 How Do Capital Flows Episodes Shocks Affect GDP Growth?

What are the effects of sudden stops on the South Africa real economy? How do these differ from those of capital flow surges? What is the role of the stock and money markets, and exchange rate channels? It is true that sudden stops and capital flow surges have real effects, as shown by the accumulated responses in Fig. 4.1. Capital inflow surge episode shocks

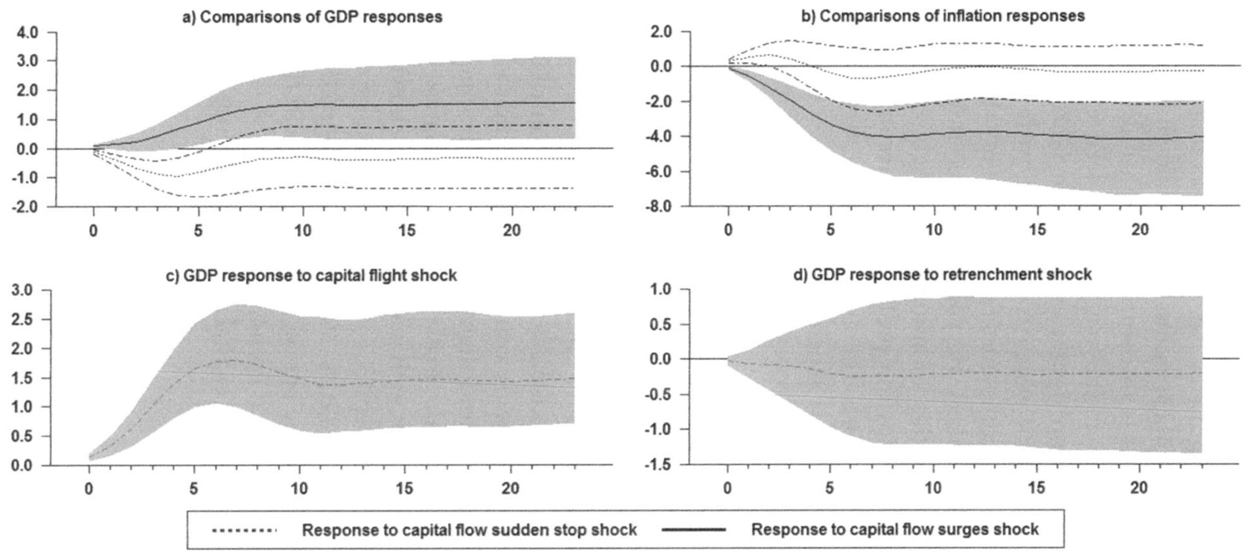

Fig. 4.1 Accumulated responses of economic growth, rand dollar exchange rate changes and inflation to capital flow episodes (*Note*: The *light shaded areas* denote the 16th and 84th percentiles error bonds. *Source*: Authors' calculations)

raise economic growth significantly after a year in Fig. 4.1a and the sudden stop shock lowers GDP growth. Fig. 4.1b shows that inflation declines by a cumulative 4 percentage points a year following a capital inflow surge episode shock. This is in contrast to the sudden stop shock that raises inflation transitorily in the first year. Fig. 4.1d shows that a capital retrenchment shock has no significant effect on GDP growth. In contrast, a capital flight shock which is consistent with investment made abroad by South African companies raises GDP growth significantly.

Why should policymakers be concerned about episodes of capital waves? Fig. 4.1 show that lumping capital flight episodes with sudden stop episodes increases the probability of recommending policies that impede global investors. These two episodes may reflect changing domestic investors' behavior, which requires a review of domestic policies. Distinguishing between these episodes presents a clearer analysis and view to policymakers.

What are the implications of capital flow episodes for economic growth? How have the four classifications of capital flow episodes contributed to economic growth during the period 1998 and 2014? Moreover, how do the results in this chapter relate to the Forbes and Warnock (2011) argument that capital flow volatility can amplify economic cycles?

Evidence indicates that sudden stops in Fig. 4.2 contributed to a more pronounced economic growth contraction than did other categories around 1999, 2001, 2009 and slightly in 2011. These periods coincide with the East Asian crisis, the massive rand depreciation and the recession. Capital flight coincides with periods of calm as shown in Fig. 4.2 by the black dotted line.[2] This episode uplifted economic growth during the 2003–2007 period and 2009Q4–2011Q2 but dragged down economic growth around 2008 and the period after 2011Q4, and this period coincided with elevated global and domestic uncertainty. A similar pattern of contributions is displayed by capital flow surges, denoted by the dotted line.

[2] Refers to periods when domestic investors increased their flows abroad.

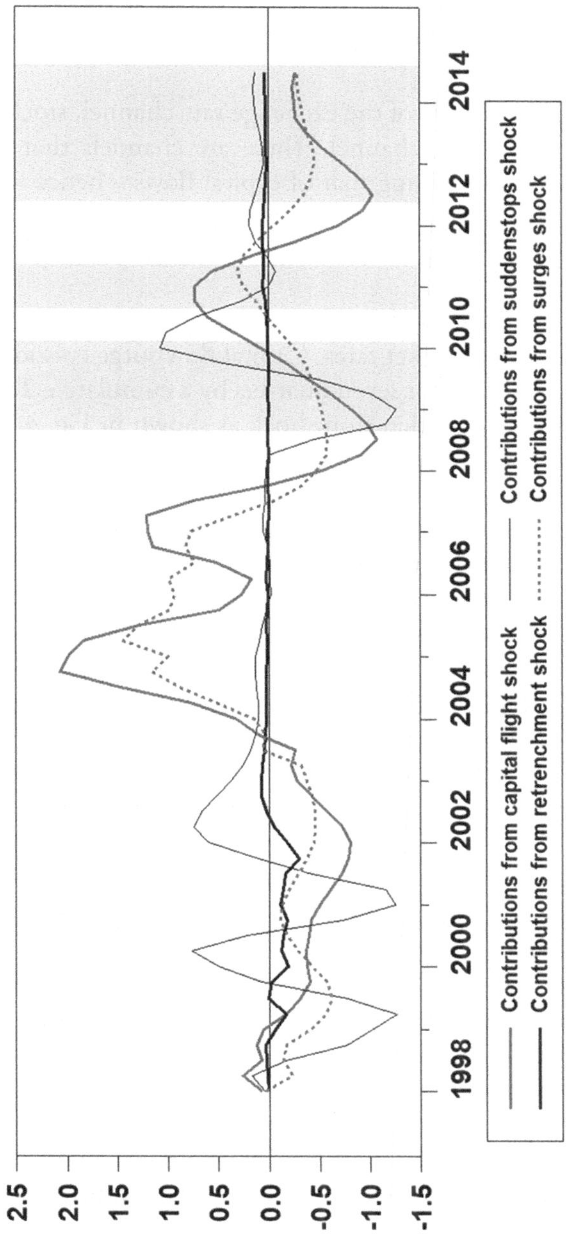

Fig. 4.2 The contributions of capital flow episodes to economic growth (The *light shaded areas* denote QE1, QE2 and QE3, respectively. *Source*: Authors' calculations)

4.3.2 Through Which Channels Are Capital Flows Wave Episodes Transmitted?

This section examines the role of the exchange rate channel, stock market channel and money market channel. These are channels that respond quickly to information including that of capital flows—hence we determine how these respond to capital flow episodes classification. The cumulative exchange rate appreciation shown in Fig. 4.3a is 10 percentage points in the fifth quarter.

Fig. 4.3c shows effects of capital inflows surge episode shock and a sudden stop shock to money market rates. Capital flow surge episode shocks depress money market rates for seven quarters by a cumulative 2 percentage points. In contrast, a sudden stop shock as shown in Fig. 4.3c raises money markets for two quarters by less than cumulative 1 percent. In Fig. 4.3b the sudden stop shock decreases stock market growth by nearly a cumulative 15 percent at the end of the year. In contrast, the capital inflow surge episode shock raises stock market growth by more than a cumulative 20 percentage points after six quarters.

The evidence concludes that the direction of all the impulse responses is as expected and consistent with economic predictions. However, in most cases the evidence shows that capital flow surge episodes effects tend to last longer than those induced by sudden stop episodes. Indeed, sudden stops are associated with a significant slowdown in economic growth and currency depreciation. In contrast, capital flight by domestic investors stimulates economic activity. Hence, the bunching of these episodes using net capital flows can lead to the misidentification of sudden stop episodes, thereby leading to a possibly misinformed policy response (Rothenberg and Warnock 2011).

Overall, this analysis reveals the significant effects of capital flow episodes on the domestic economy. This validates the South African policymakers' concerns that distortions caused by sudden stops and that capital flow volatility can have substantial economic costs. The results presented here suggest that there is a need for a clear identification of these episodes and their causes. This is important for the design of policies aimed at reducing external vulnerabilities and mitigating negative economic outcomes.

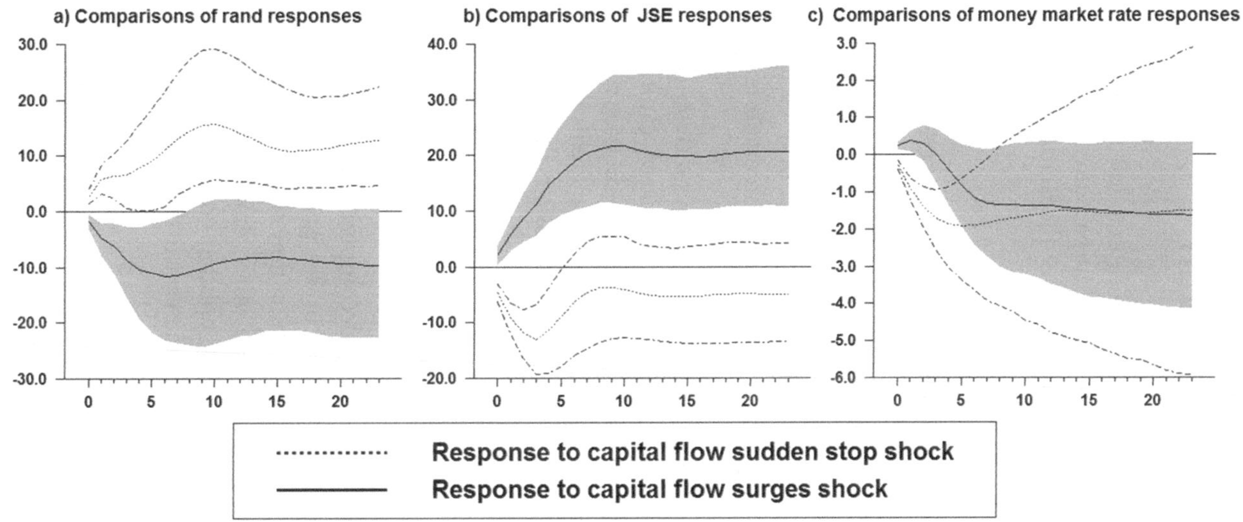

Fig. 4.3 Selected comparisons of cumulative responses to capital flow surges and sudden stops (*Source*: Authors' calculations)

4.4 How Do Capital Flows Wave Categories Impact Credit Growth?

This section examines three aspects of capital flow waves on credit growth which include (1) how these shocks impact credit growth, (2) historical contributions and (3) proportions of fluctuations in credit dynamics induced by these shocks.

4.4.1 Evidence from Impulse Responses

Fig. 4.4a shows that credit growth responses vary between capital flow surges and sudden stop episodes shocks. Surges raise credit growth with a peak effect of 1.5 percentage points for around 10 quarters. In contrast, sudden stop shock leads to contraction in credit growth which lasts nearly 6 quarters.

Fig. 4.4b shows that credit growth responds differently to capital flow retrenchment shocks and capital flight shock. A capital flow retrenchment shock leads to a significant decline in credit growth. However, capital flight shock leads to significant increase in credit growth comparable to that exerted by capital flow surges, although the trajectories and persistence effects of shocks differ.

4.4.2 Evidence from Historical Decompositions

This section applies a historical decomposition approach to determine which capital flows shock uplifted or dragged credit. In Fig. 4.5, prior to 2004Q1 and after 2009Q3 the capital flow surges shock for most periods dragged credit growth more than other shocks. Between 2004Q2 and 2009Q1 the capital surges shock uplifted credit growth more than others. Capital flow surges contributed very little to credit growth evolution.

4.4.3 Evidence from Variance Decompositions

Do capital flow shocks episodes induce similar movements in credit growth? Fig. 4.6 shows a comparison in the fluctuations in credit growth

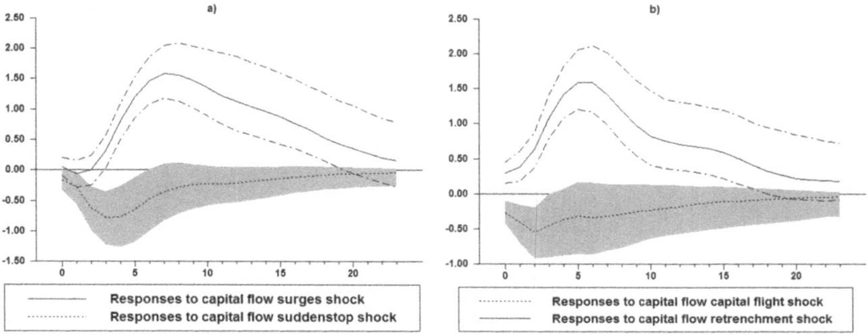

Fig. 4.4 The effects of capital flow episodes on credit growth (*Source*: Authors' calculations)

induced by capital flow episode shocks. Capital flight shock induces more movements in credit growth than other shocks. On the other hand, capital flow surges explain relatively large fluctuations in credit growth than do sudden stops shocks.

4.5 Does Global Risk Aversion Shock Impact Capital Flow Surges, Sudden Stop Episodes and Credit Growth?

One global element that features prominently in policy discussions is the presence or absence of risk appetite by foreign investors and its effects on domestic factors. How does global risk aversion interact with domestic real activities? Fig. 4.7 shows the trends and scatter plots relationships between VIX with GDP growth, non-resident activity in the domestic bond and equities markets and the rand/US dollar exchange rate.

Elevated levels of risk tend to be associated with a decline in non-resident activity in the South African financial market, as shown in Fig. 4.7f, g. This was the case in 2008 and 2009. The exchange rate is also sensitive to changes in global risk, although this has not been the case since 2012. Fig. 4.7a reveals a weak relationship between VIX and economic growth.

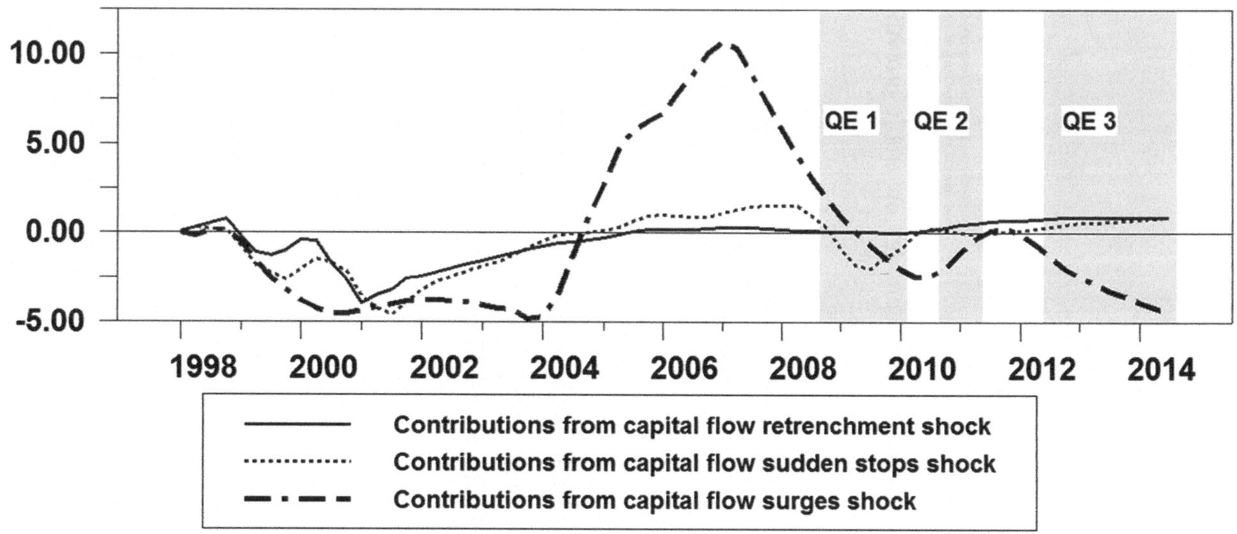

Fig. 4.5 Contributions of different capital flow episode shocks over time (The *light shaded areas* denote QE1, QE2 and QE3, respectively. *Source*: Authors' calculations)

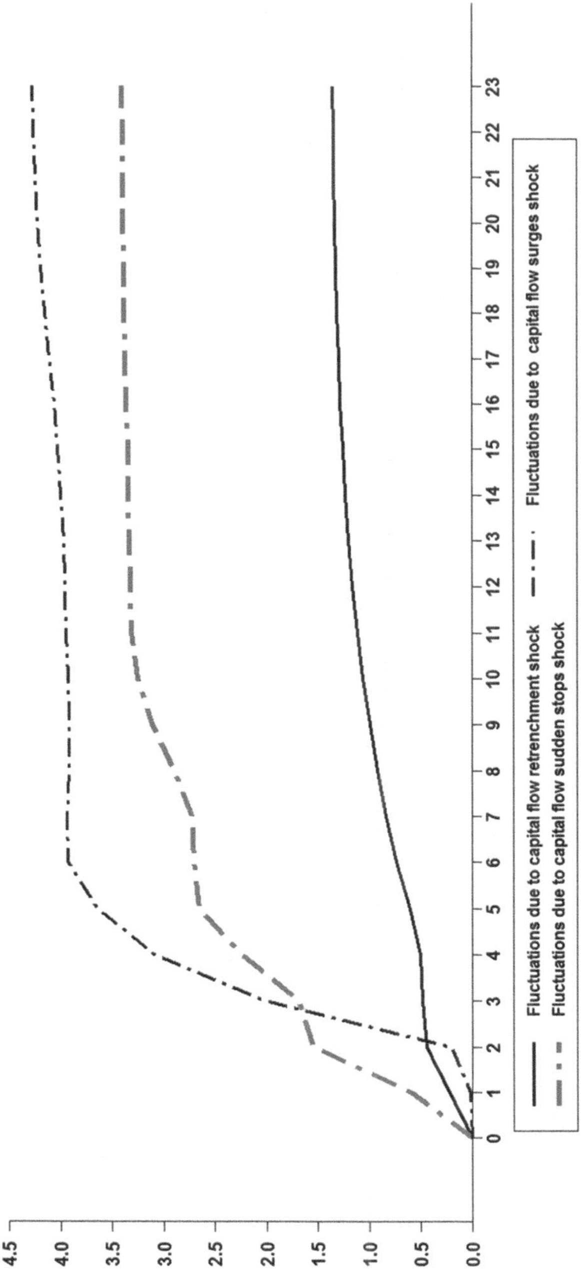

Fig. 4.6 Fluctuations explained by shocks to capital flow episodes (*Source*: Authors' calculations)

As shown in Fig. 4.8, VIX shock significantly raises the sudden stops episodes in Fig. 4.8a, lowers capital inflow surge episodes in Fig. 4.8b and lead to exchange rate depreciation for nearly a year in Fig. 4.8d.

What happens to GDP and credit growth in response to an unexpected positive one standard deviation VIX shock? Fig. 4.8c, d confirm that GDP and credit growth decline for nearly six and more than six quarters, respectively. However, Fig. 4.8f shows that credit growth declines very much due to the global risk shock and this holds irrespective of whether surges or sudden stop episodes are included in the model.

4.6 Counterfactual Scenarios and the Propagation Effects of Commodity Prices and the Exchange Rate

What is the role of commodity prices and the exchange rate in propagating the responses of credit growth to VIX, capital flow surges and sudden stop shocks? Would the direction of responses of credit growth be different in the presence and absence of commodity prices? Fig. 4.9 shows that capital flow surges and bank flow shocks raise credit growth more than the counterfactual suggests. This indicates that commodity prices magnify the impact of changes in risk perceptions and capital flows on credit growth. In contrast, sudden stop shocks depress credit growth very much in the presence of commodity prices. This implies that commodity prices tend to worsen the responses of credit growth to sudden stop episodes.

What about the role of the exchange rate in amplifying the credit responses to capital flow surges and VIX shocks? Are there any discernible effects on the share of credit to households and companies? Fig. 4.10 shows that credit to companies increases more than the counterfactual, indicating that the exchange rate amplifies the responses. In contrast, the VIX shocks reduce share of credit to companies but raise credit to

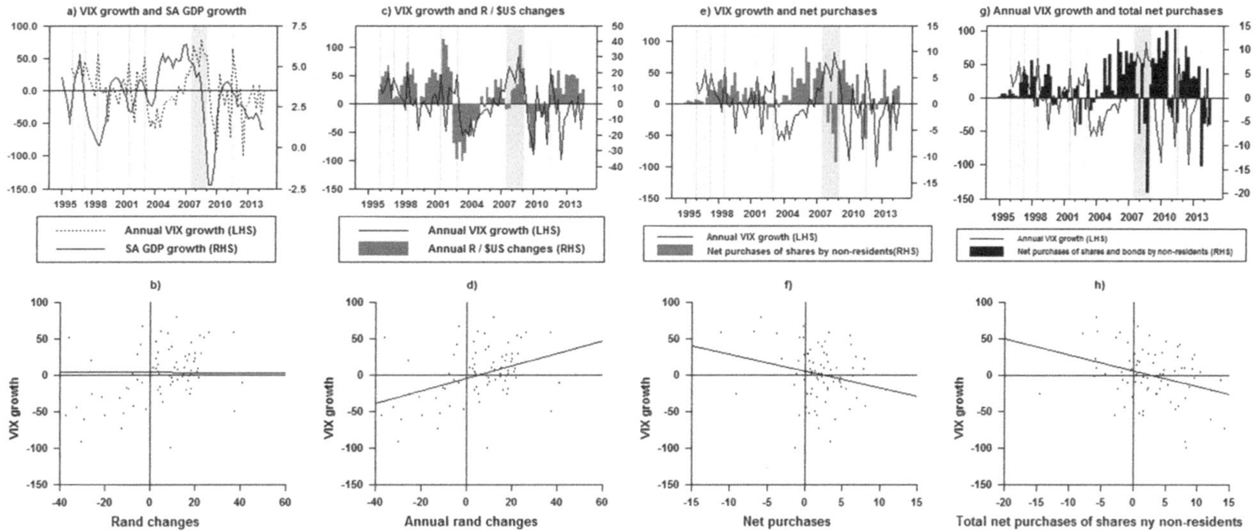

Fig. 4.7 VIX, GDP growth, non-resident capital flow activity and the exchange rate (The *light grey shaded areas* denote periods when VIX was equal to 31 percent, which is equal to a one positive standard deviation VIX shock used to generate the impulse responses in the empirical analysis. *Source*: Authors' calculations)

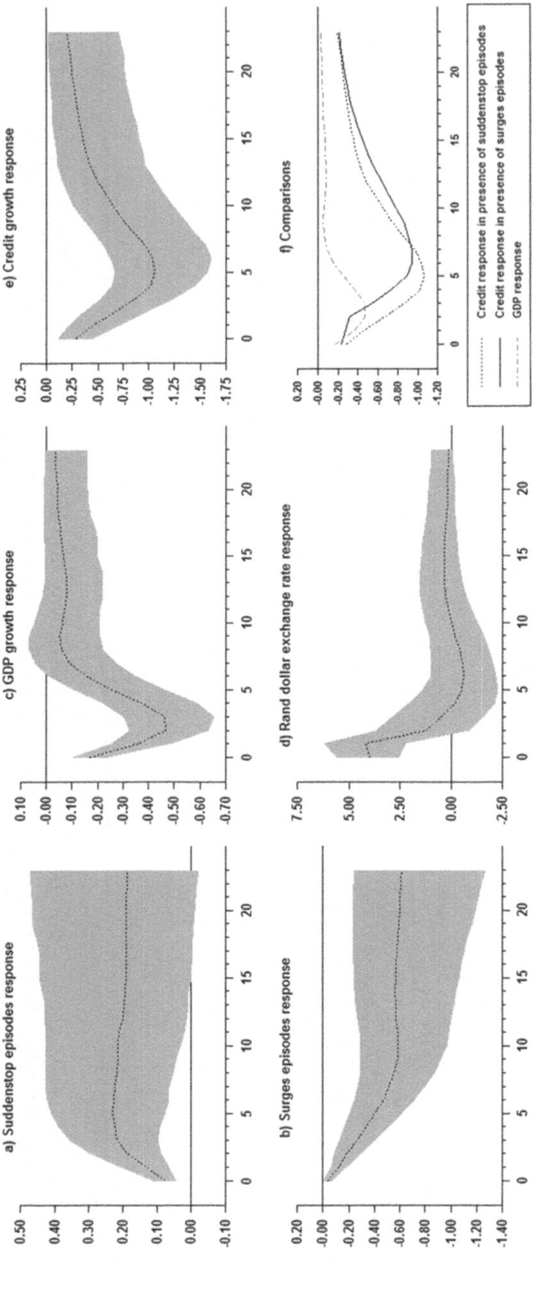

Fig. 4.8 The accumulated impulse responses to an unexpected positive one standard deviation VIX shock (*Source:* Authors' calculations)

households. Capital flow surges and VIX shocks lead to sectorial credit reallocations.

In contrast, Fig. 4.11 shows that a sudden stop shock leads to a decline in credit to households, suggesting that the exchange rate tightens financial conditions and lowers credit to households. Overall, the evidence indicates the occurrence of reallocation of credit following a sudden stop shocks.

4.7 Conclusion and Policy Implications

Evidence in this chapter corroborates Forbes and Warnock (2011) and establishes that global risk is a driver of capital flow volatility. Elevated levels of risk tend to be associated with a decline in non-resident activity in the South African financial market. Global risk shocks significantly increase sudden stops episodes, lower capital inflow surge episodes and lead to exchange rate depreciation. Furthermore, episodes of capital waves may reflect changing domestic investors' behavior.

Commodity prices and the exchange rate propagate and magnify the responses of credit growth to global risk shocks, capital flow surges and sudden stop shocks. Sudden stop shocks result in depressed credit growth in the presence of commodity prices. The exchange rate amplifies the responses of credit to companies due to capital flow surges and VIX shocks. Capital flow surges and global risk shocks lead to sectorial credit reallocations. However, changes in global risk are outside the control of domestic policymakers and may pose policy dilemmas. In line with Forbes and Warnock (2011), this implies that policymakers concerned about effects of capital flow volatility should prioritize strengthening the country's ability to withstand volatility.

Evidence indicates that sudden stops contributed more to a pronounced economic growth contraction than did other categories around 1999, 2001, 2009 and slightly in 2011. Capital flow surge episodes effects tend to last longer than those induced by sudden stop episodes. However, sudden stops are associated with a significant slowdown in economic growth and currency depreciation. Capital flight by domestic investors stimulates economic activity and coincides with periods of calm. This means

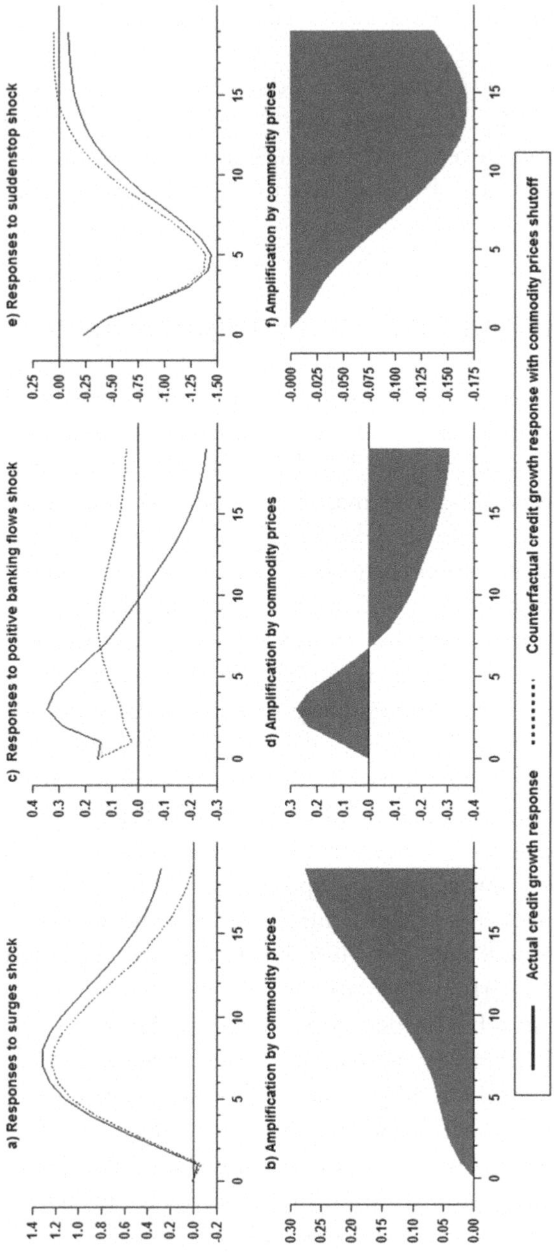

Fig. 4.9 Credit growth responses and role of commodity prices (*Source*: Authors' calculations)

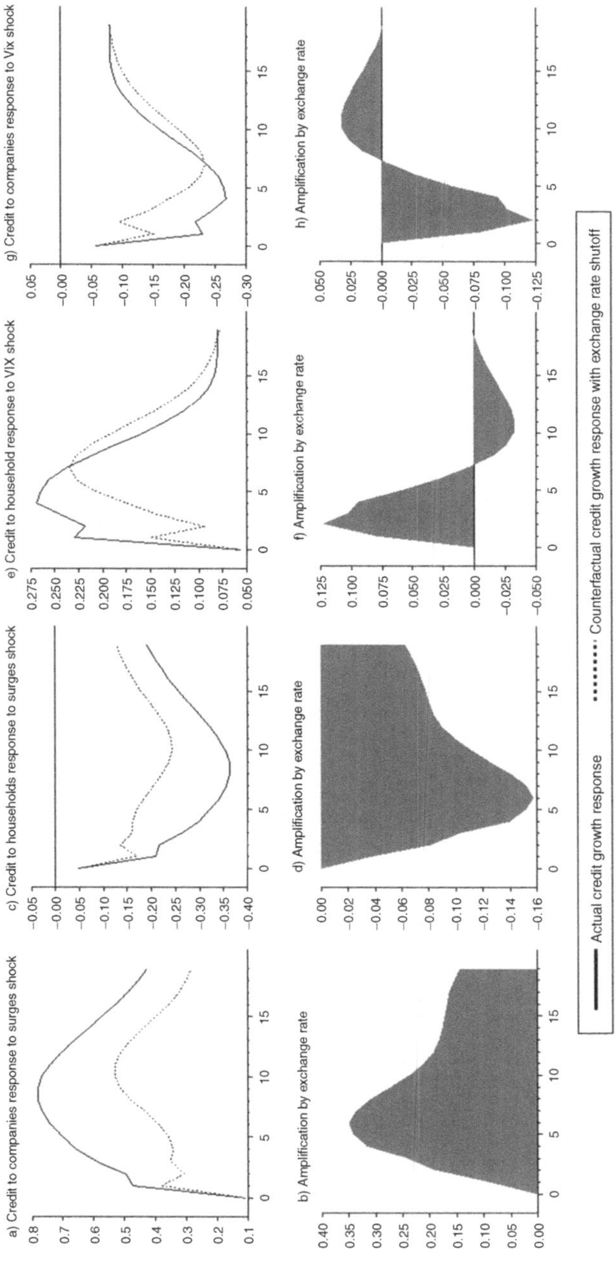

Fig. 4.10 Responses of sectorial credit shares to surges and VIX shocks and the role of the exchange rate (*Source:* Authors' calculations)

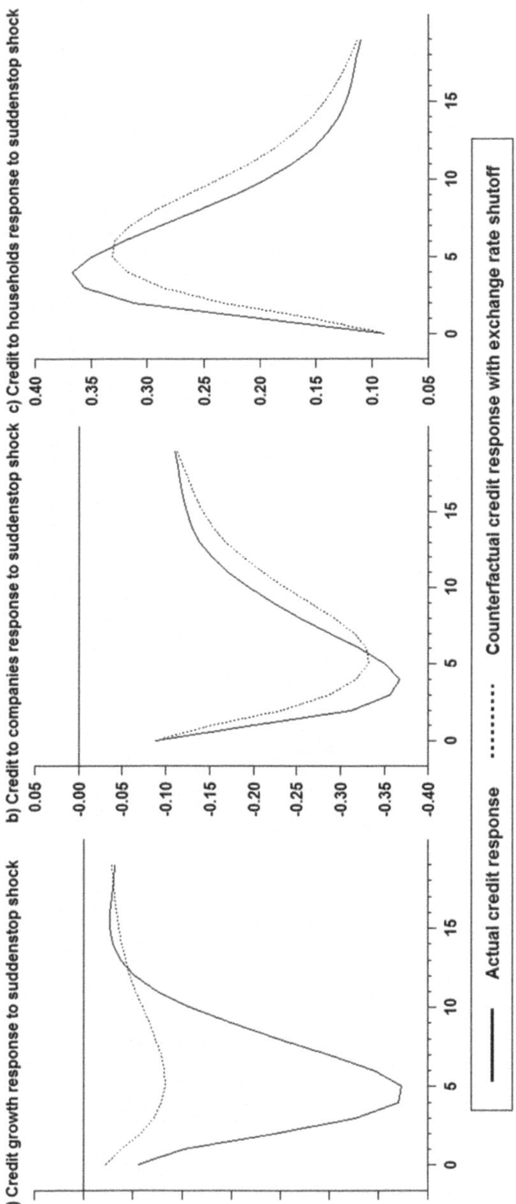

Fig. 4.11 Responses of sectorial credit shares to sudden stops and role of exchange rate (*Source*: Authors' calculations)

that it is necessary to distinguish between different capital flows episodes as this presents a clearer analysis and allows for policy recommendations and responses. Policymakers should be aware that foreign and domestic investors can be motivated by different factors and react differently to various policies and other shocks.

Summary of Main Findings

- Elevated global risk as proxied by VIX is associated with a decline in non-resident activity in the South African financial market and significantly raises the likelihood of sudden stops episodes.
- Sudden stop episodes are associated with a significant slowdown in economic growth, as well as stock market and currency depreciation.
- Capital inflow surge episodes raise economic growth, appreciate the exchange rate, lower inflation and raise the stock market.
- Commodity prices and the exchange rate propagate and magnify the responses of credit growth to global risk shocks, capital flow surges and sudden stop shocks. Evidence shows that capital flow surges and global risk shocks lead to sectorial credit reallocations.

5

Bank, Non-bank Capital Flows and Household Sector Credit Reallocation

Learning Objectives

- Establish the impact of the composition of capital flows on the sectorial credit shares to assess the potential financial stability risks involved
- Use the findings to assist in shaping policy responses and design of macro-prudential tools

5.1 Introduction

The relationship between capital flows, domestic credit and the real economy remains at the center of policy discussions. Excess global liquidity and funding conditions spill-over to emerging market economies via cross-border bank lending activity and are expected to lead to overheating credit markets. Samarina and Bezemer (2016) argue that since the 1990s, foreign capital inflows resulted in the sectorial reallocation of credit from non-financial businesses to households. Their study established evidence that foreign capital inflows into the non-bank sectors are associated with lower shares of business lending in domestic bank portfolios.

N. Gumata, E. Ndou, *Bank Credit Extension and Real Economic Activity in South Africa*, DOI 10.1007/978-3-319-43551-0_5

Against this background, this chapter extends the analysis on the role of global liquidity and capital flows play on domestic credit markets by considering the role of the composition of capital flows in bank and non-bank capital flows. Formally, the chapter tests the hypothesis stated below.

Hypothesis 1 Capital inflows into non-banks and banks are associated with a decrease in the share of domestic bank loans to households.

Testing this hypothesis has implications for the interaction of monetary policy and financial stability objectives. The monetary policy stance through triggering a favorable interest rate differential can attract capital flows. This may inadvertently facilitate for the sectorial credit shifts and possibly lead to overheating in credit markets. These effects have a bearing on financial stability considerations and the design of macro-prudential tools.

5.1.1 Does the Sectorial Reallocation of Credit Extension Matter?

Indeed it does. Empirical literature indicates the presence of the substitution effect between domestic bank loans and foreign capital. The substitution is attributed to limited profitable investment opportunities at a time when capital is abundant and highly mobile. This causes competition between domestic and foreign finances for investment opportunities and may result in a substitution effect. However, this substitution effect does not imply that total bank lending falls. Rather that it induces a sectorial reallocation of credit.

In addition, the abundant and—in many cases—cheap capital allows domestic banks to fund domestic lending from international capital rather than from domestic bank deposits only. Hence, access to foreign sources of funding loosens banks' financing constraints. On the other hand, domestic non-financial businesses may demand less credit from banks as they can access funding from non-banks. So, banks can respond to the decline in demand by non-financial businesses by expanding lending to households. As a result, the share of non-financial business loans in the banks' portfolio declines.

Fig. 5.1 shows the evolution of bank credit to households and companies in South Africa. It is evident that there have been large sectorial

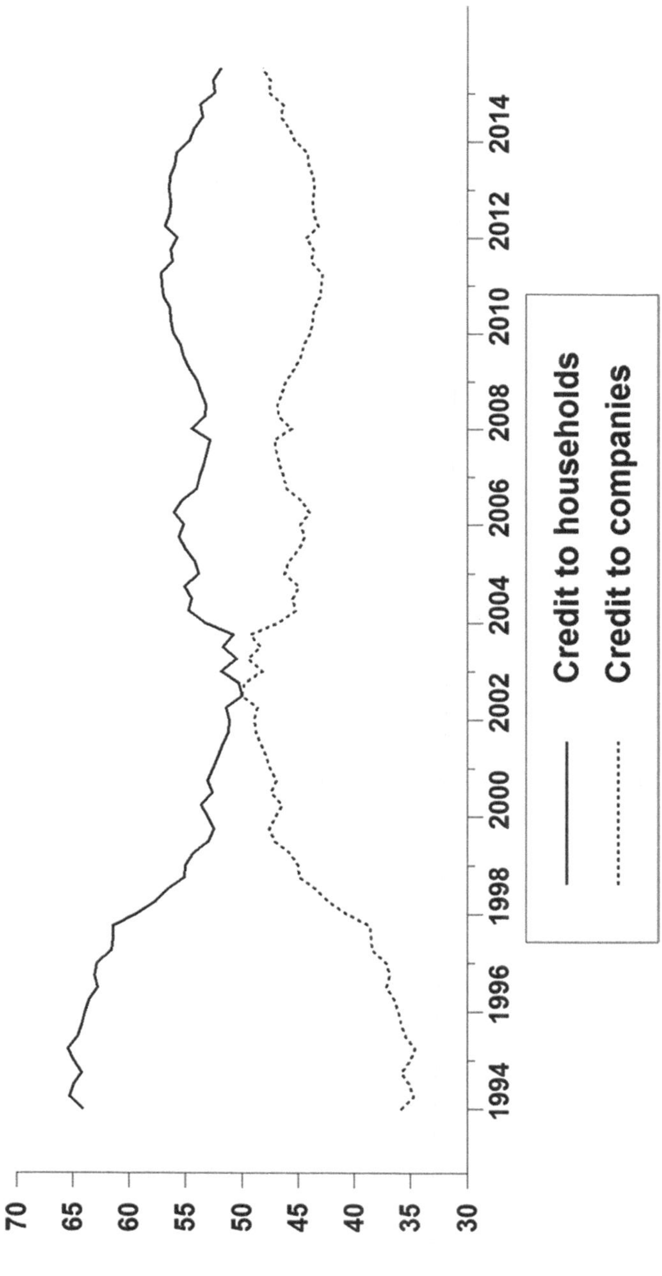

Fig. 5.1 The shares of credit to households and companies (*Source*: SARB and authors' calculations)

shifts in credit over time. However, in contrast to the theories mentioned above, this chapter assesses whether capital inflows lead to a reduction in lending to households as a share of domestic banks' loan portfolios.

5.2 Relationship Between Credit to Households, Bank and Non-bank Capital Flows

Fig. 5.2a, b show a negative relationship between credit to households and foreign direct investment (FDI) flows. The relationship between total portfolio flows and credit to households is flat in Fig. 5.2c, d. However, does the relationship depend on the definition of capital flows?

The bilateral relationship using scatterplots in Fig. 5.3 establishes a negative relationship which suggests that an increase in capital inflow leads to a reduction in the share of credit to households. This is the case for portfolio and FDI bank and non-bank flows.

The robust evidence of the negative relationship between the share of credit to the household sector, FDI and portfolio bank and non-bank flows is visible in Fig. 5.4. This holds true for flows. Does the relationship vary between bank and non-bank flows? Yes, it does. Fig. 5.4a, b show that the steepness of the slope varies between the bank and non-bank flows in the FDI and portfolio flows categories. The relationship is steeper between credit to households and banks' portfolio flows.

Furthermore, the cross-correlations approach in Fig. 5.5 establishes a negative relationship for most periods in the early horizons. This suggests that credit to households tends to decline for some time when preceded by elevated banking and non-banking flows. However, the correlations tend to be negative in the first 12 quarters in Fig. 5.5a, c and become positive afterwards.

This means that elevated capital flows of all categories do not result in a strong increase in credit to households on impact. The positive impact comes at a considerable lag. Even then it is very weak. The negative relationship between capital flows and credit to households is indicative of credit reallocation dynamics but it is very possible that they are very weak.

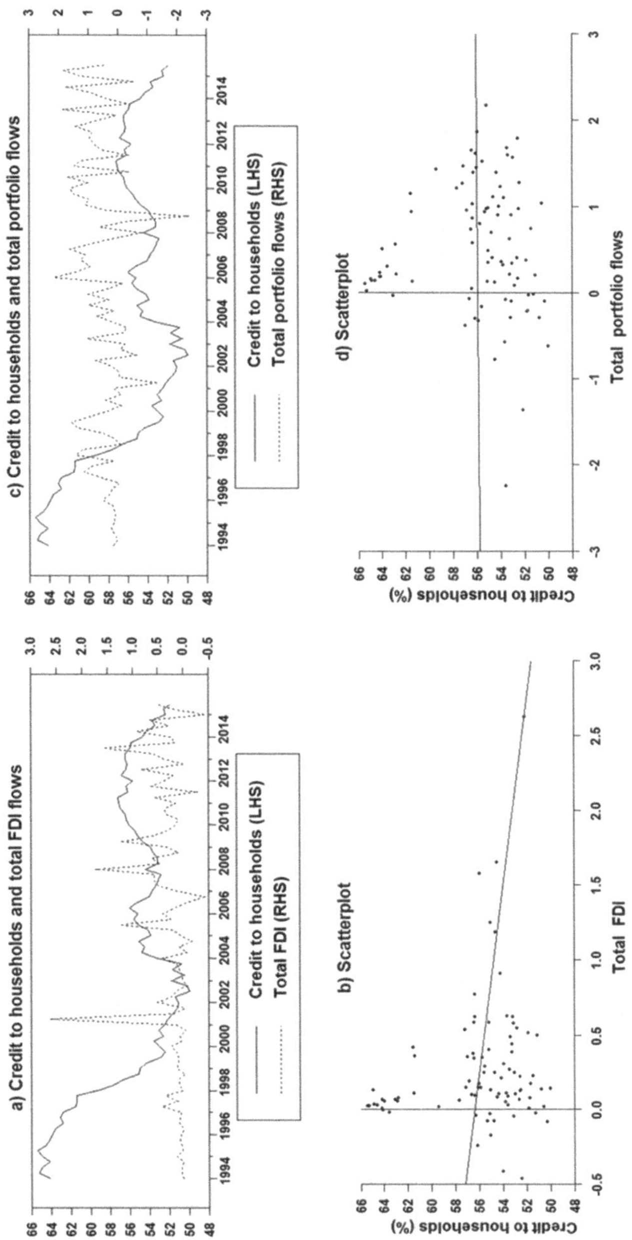

Fig. 5.2 Relationship between credit to households, FDI and total portfolio capital flows (Credit to households is expressed as percentage of total loans and advances. *Source*: SARB and authors' calculations)

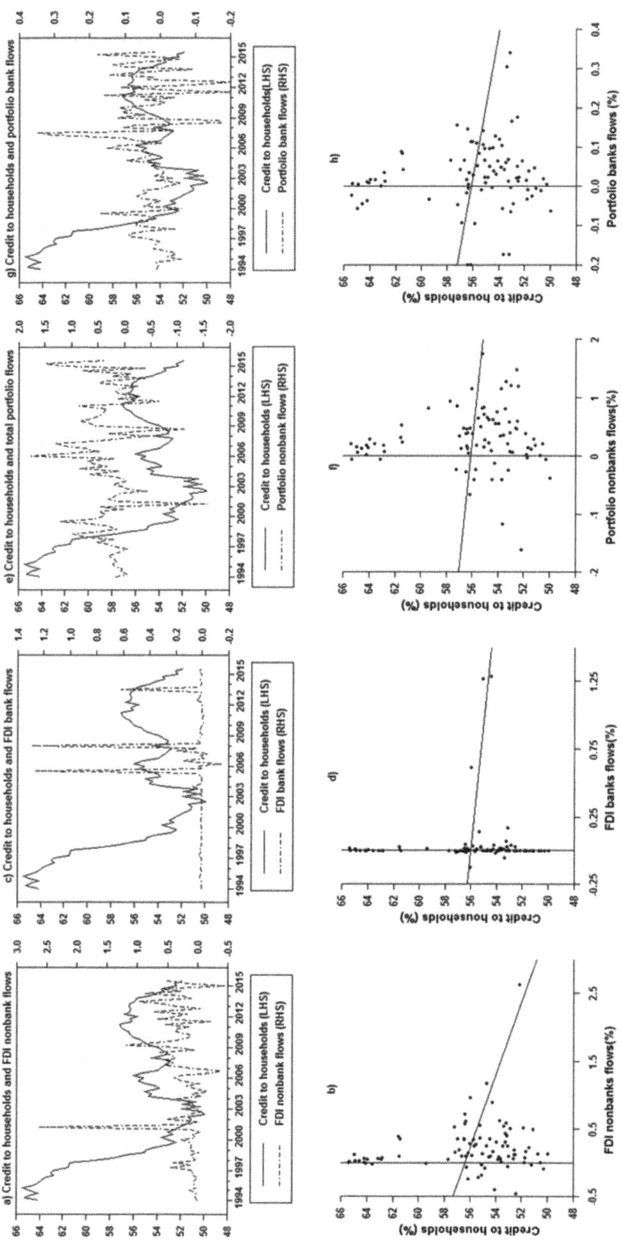

Fig. 5.3 Bilateral relationships between credit to households and capital flows (*Source*: SARB and authors' calculations)

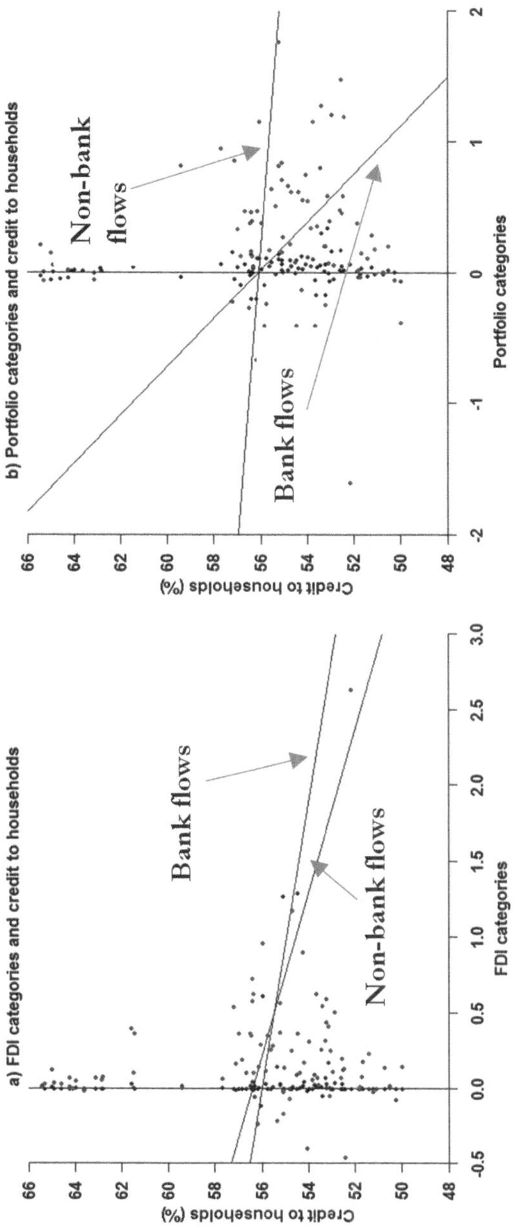

Fig. 5.4 The sensitivity of the credit to households relationship to disaggregated capital flows (*Source*: SARB and authors' calculations)

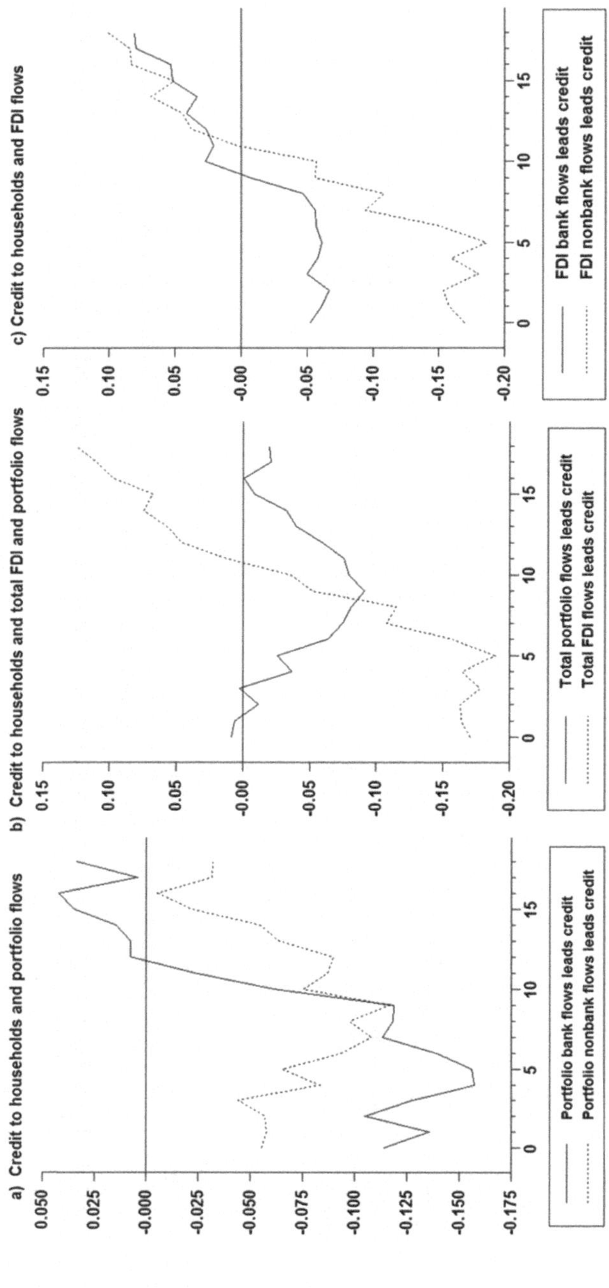

Fig. 5.5 Cross-correlations between credit to households, banking and non-banking flows (*Source*: SARB and authors' calculations)

5.3 VAR Results

The empirical analysis uses a vector autoregression (VAR) approach to determine periods at which the effects of capital flows have significant effects on credit to households and the magnitudes of the peak effects. A VAR model includes four variables: annual GDP growth, annual inflation rate, credit to household as percentage of total credit and different capital flow categories. The capital flow categories include: (1) total FDI flows, (2) FDI bank flows, (3) FDI non-bank flows, (4) total portfolio flows, (5) portfolio bank flows and (6) portfolio non-bank flows. All the capital flow categories are expressed as percentage of GDP. The sample spans 1994Q1–2015Q3. The capital flow categories are included individually in the model. The models are estimated with three lags chosen by the the Akaike Information Criterion (AIC) and 10,000 bootstrap draws. The error bands are shown by the shaded area and denote the 16th and 84th percentiles

Similar to the findings in stylized sections, Fig. 5.6 establishes negative responses to various capital inflow shocks. This indicates that banking and non-banking flows lead to sectorial credit reallocations from the household sector.

However, the statistical significance of the responses differs. Based on the 16th and 84th percentiles, there is significant reallocation of credit to households due to FDI bank and non-bank flow shock in Fig. 5.6a, b, as well as to portfolio bank flow shock in (f). Amongst all the shocks, the decline in credit to household does not exceed 0.25 total credit percent at peak response, which indicates that when the reallocations occur, they are very small.

5.3.1 Fluctuations in Credit to Households Explained by Bank and Non-bank Capital Flows

What proportion of fluctuations in credit to households is induced by capital flows? Fig. 5.7a shows that non-bank flows explain more movements in credit to households than bank flows. Amongst the FDI flows

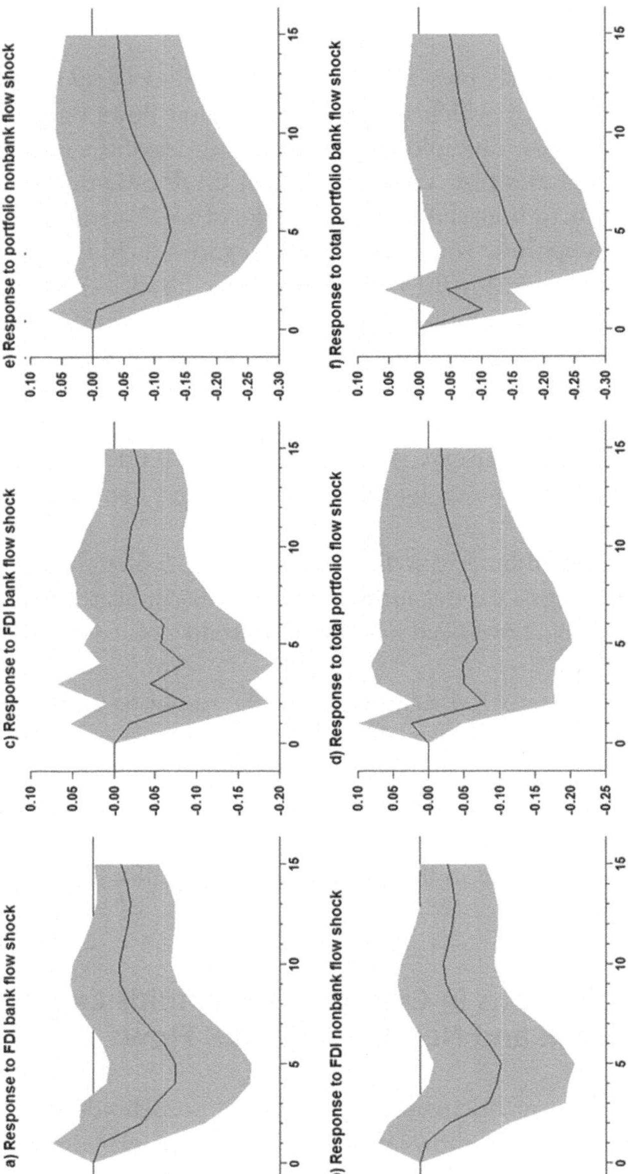

Fig. 5.6 Responses of credit to households to capital flow shock (*Source*: SARB and authors' calculations)

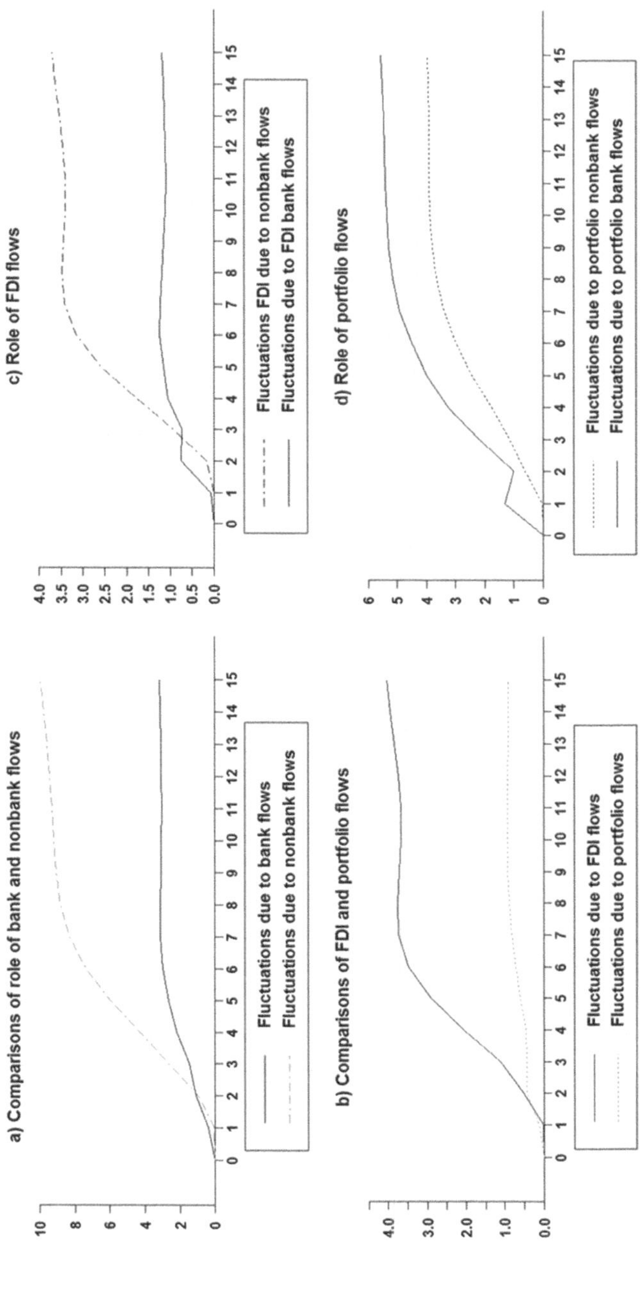

Fig. 5.7 Fluctuations in credit to households as percentages of total loans and advances (*Source*: SARB and authors' calculations)

categories in Fig. 5.7c, the non-bank flows induce more fluctuations in credit to households than bank flows. In contrast, portfolio bank flows explain more credit fluctuations than portfolio non-bank flows in Fig. 5.7d.

5.3.2 The Counterfactual Contributions

To derive the counterfactual scenarios and periods in which bank and non-bank flows uplifted and were a drag on credit to households, a historical decomposition approach is used. The historical contributions approach decomposes the share of credit to households into own contributions and those from other variables. To calculate the counterfactual share of credit to households, the responses of household credit are purged of the contributions of bank and non-bank flows, respectively. Thereafter, the counterfactual share of credit to households is calculated as the difference between responses purged of and those that are not purged of the effects of bank and non-bank flows.

Figs. 5.8a and 5.9a show the actual and counterfactual credit to households. The contributions from bank and non-bank flows are shown in Figs. 5.8b and 5.9b. In Fig. 5.8a, the difference between actual and counterfactual credit to household is very slight, suggesting that bank flow contributions only play a small role in credit to household dynamics. This is confirmed by a magnitude of less than 1 percent at the peak contributions in Fig. 5.8b during the recent credit and house price boom of 2004–2007. During the period of the financial crisis and recession, bank flows only contributed a maximum of 1 percent in the decline in credit to households.

The non-bank flows made positive contributions to credit to households in Fig. 5.9a in 2002–2005 and after 2014. The contributions were negative between 2006 and 2013. In terms of magnitudes, the peak increase contribution is nearly 1.5 percent and peak decline remains below 1.5 percent. These magnitudes indicate that non-bank flow contributions play but a small role in driving credit to household dynamics.

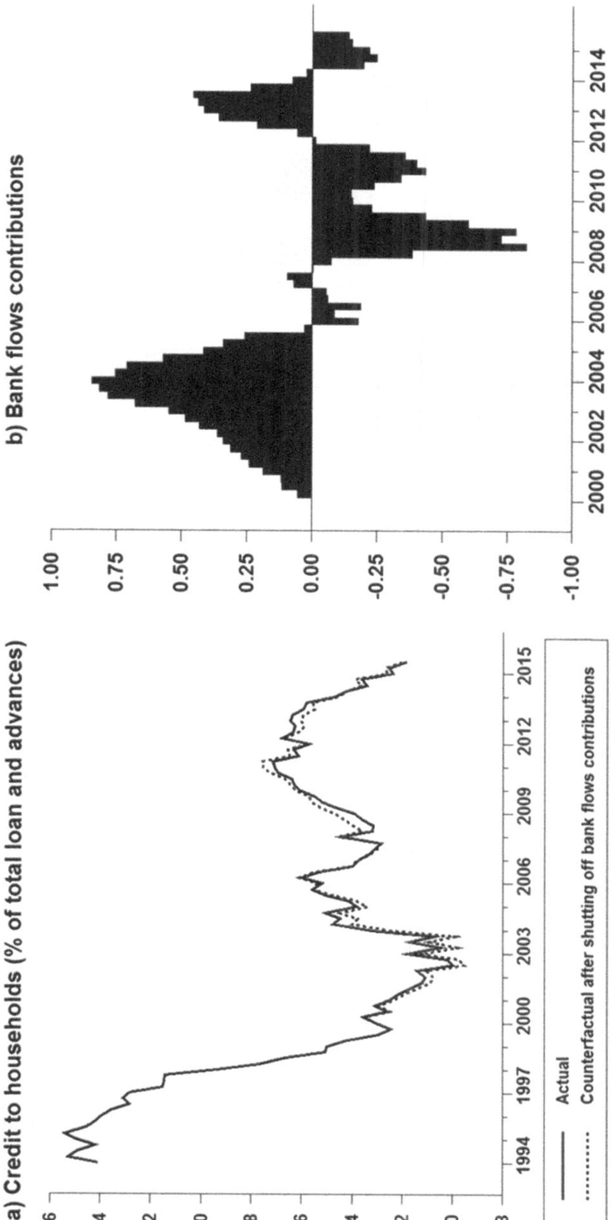

Fig. 5.8 The contributions of bank flows shocks to credit to households (*Source*: SARB and authors' calculations)

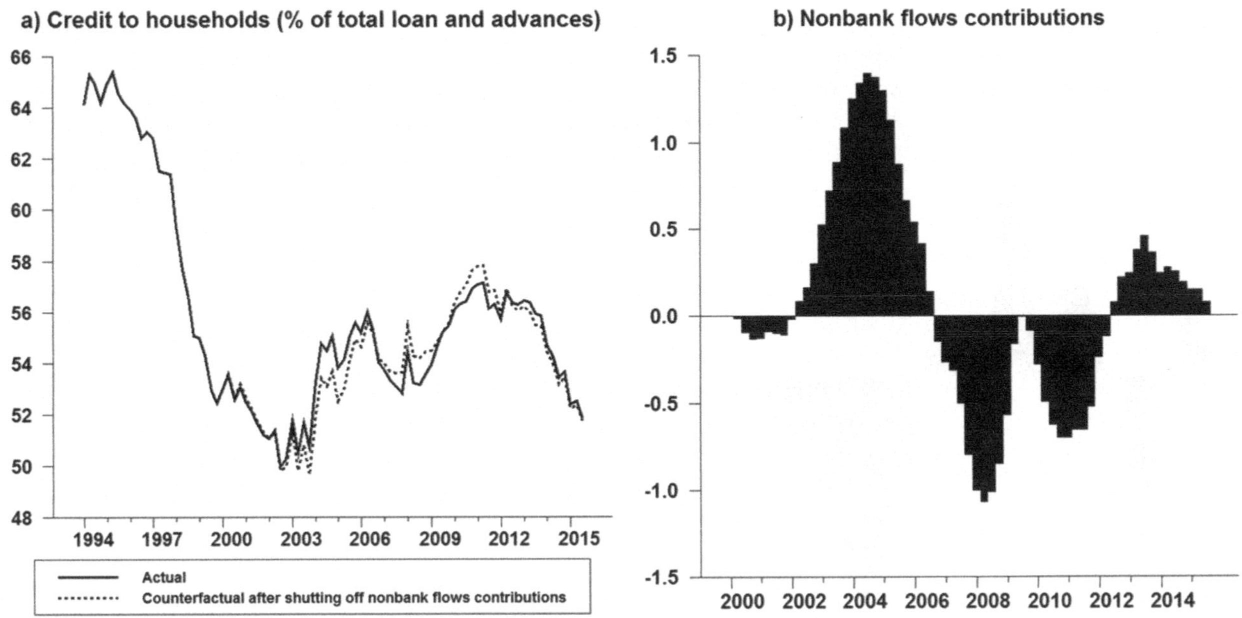

Fig. 5.9 The contributions of non-bank flows shocks to credit to households (*Source*: SARB and authors' calculations)

5.4 Conclusion and Policy Recommendations

The chapter searched for evidence of sectorial reallocation of the share of household credit due to bank and non-bank capital flow shocks. The findings establish a negative relationship between credit to households' share of credit and all categories of capital flows. The magnitudes of the negative effects, though statistically significant, are small—suggesting that this is not a big problem in South Africa. Although the magnitudes are small, the results suggest that capital mobility has detrimental effects on the domestic allocation of bank credit. The negative effects are particularly evident when capital is flowing into the non-bank sector. Despite small magnitudes, if the negative effects occur over a prolonged period this means that they can crowd out domestic credit to households. This can create a significant change in the banks' loan portfolios.

However, from a financial stability and macro-prudential regulation perspective, the small magnitude probably offers no sense of comfort. Regulators are well aware that small and localized financial practices can mask severe threats to financial stability. Although small, the impact of bank and non-bank capital flows on the reallocation of credit suggests that close monitoring and regulation of these sectorial patterns is necessary so that policymakers are not caught off guard. In addition, these findings imply that prudential targeted regulations, as opposed to broad regulations, may be more effective.

Summary of Main Findings

- Household credit is negatively related to all categories of capital flows.
- Bank and non-bank capital flow shocks result in the sectorial reallocation of credit and a decline in the share of credit to households.
- The impact of the negative effects is small, meaning that the sectorial credit reallocation induced by capital flows is not a big problem in South Africa.

6

Capital Flows and the Reallocation of Credit from Companies

Learning Objectives

- Establish whether the substitution effects induced by the composition of capital flows benefits credit to companies
- Examine the potential financial stability risks involved and how regulatory and macro-prudential tools can respond to mitigate these risks
- Look at whether the composition of capital flows amplifies the responses of the repo rate to positive inflation shocks

6.1 Introduction

The previous chapter showed that bank and non-bank capital flows are negatively related to the households' share of total credit. The negative effects are small, suggesting that capital flows do not induce large sectorial reallocations in bank credit. However, companies and households respond differently to changes in credit and financial conditions. To what

N. Gumata, E. Ndou, *Bank Credit Extension and Real Economic Activity in South Africa*, DOI 10.1007/978-3-319-43551-0_6

extent do foreign capital flows result in domestic bank lending being dominated by credit to companies? We test the relevance of the hypothesis stated below.

Hypothesis Are capital inflows into banks and non-banks associated with a decrease in the share of domestic bank loans to companies?

Empirical literature establishes a link from larger capital inflows to more fragile bank loan portfolios which runs via foreign capital into the non-bank sector. This link is stronger when investment opportunities are fewer. In addition, the substitution effect matters because financial openness tends to cause domestic lending credit booms. It allows domestic banks to fund domestic lending from international capital rather than from domestic bank deposits only. Hence, access to foreign sources of funding loosens banks' financing constraints. In addition, banks can experience a decline in the demand for their loans by domestic non-financial business as other sources of funding become competitive. It can then happen that banks respond to this by reducing lending to households and increase the companies' loan share in the domestic bank portfolios. This has implications for macro-prudential policy and the regulation of capital flows.

6.2 Does the Relationship Between Credit to Companies Depend on the Definition of the Capital Flow Category?

The bilateral relationships in Figs. 6.1 and 6.2 establish a positive relationship which suggests that increased capital inflows in the form of bank and non-bank flows lead to an increase in the share of credit to companies.

The positive relationship between credit to companies, bank and non-banking flows is robust evidence as it holds for both foreign direct investment (FDI) and portfolio flows in Fig. 6.3a, b. This is different to findings in relation to credit to the household sector. Robust evidence of a negative relationship between credit to the household sector and FDI and portfolio bank and non-banking flows was established.

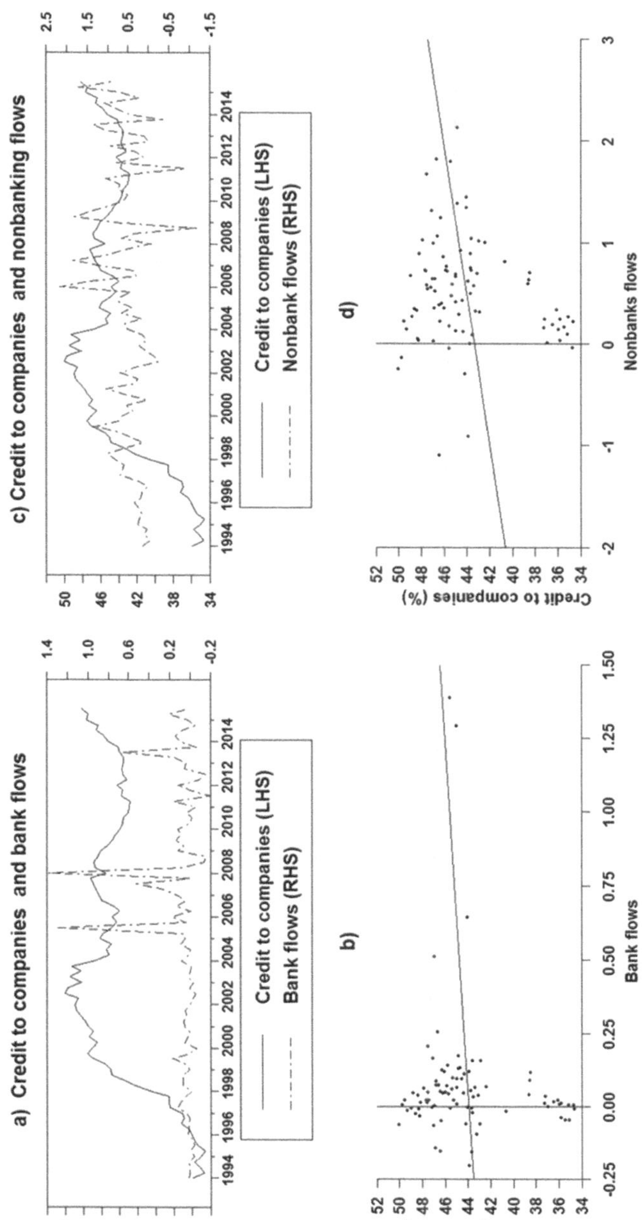

Fig. 6.1 Relationship between credit to companies and bank and non-bank capital flows (*Source*: SARB and Authors' calculations)

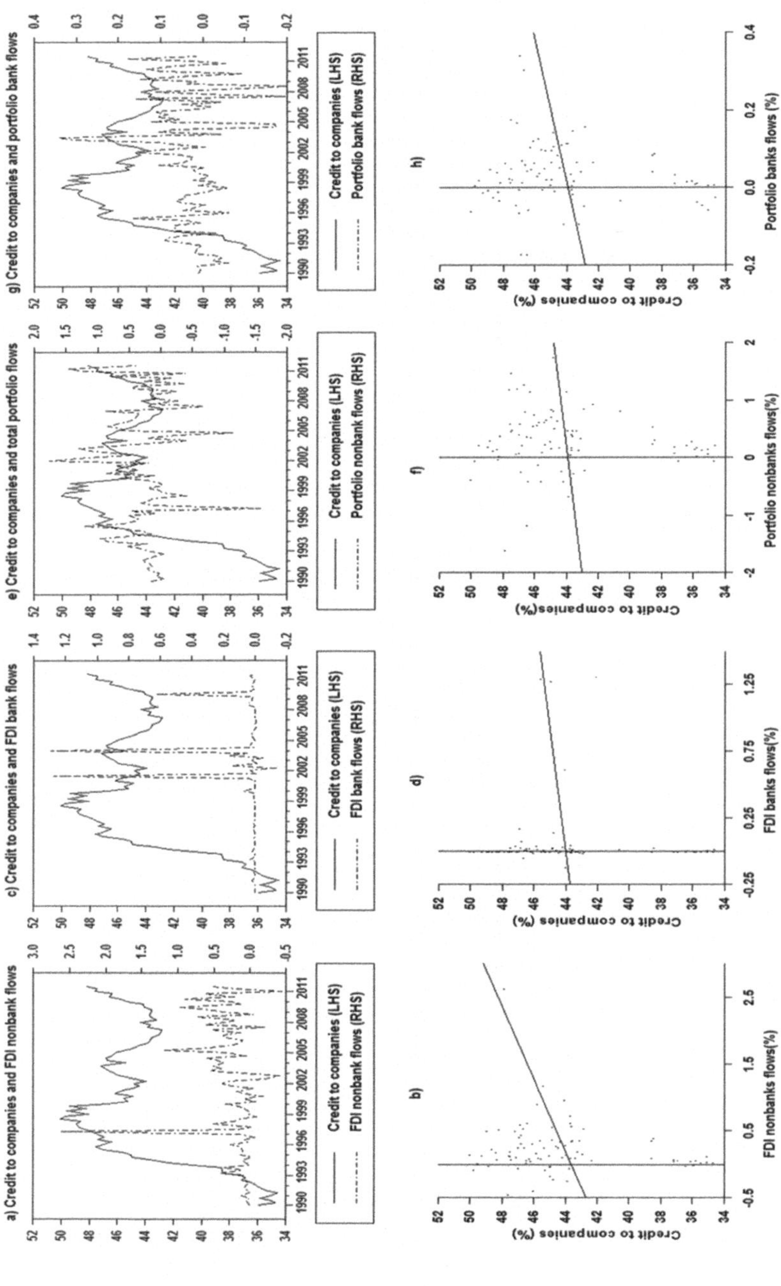

Fig. 6.2 Bilateral relationships between credit to companies and capital flows (*Source:* SARB and Authors' calculations)

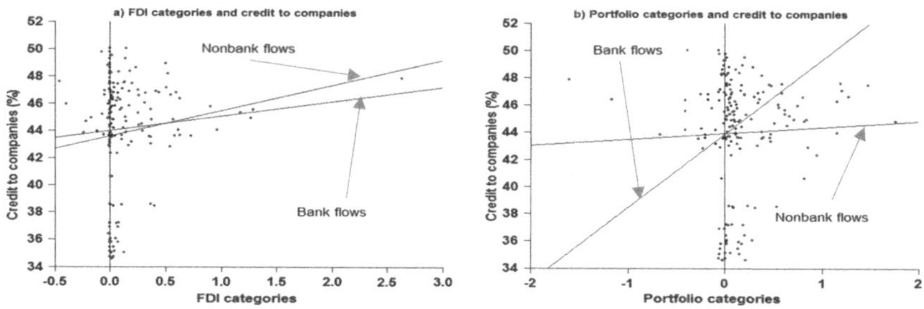

Fig. 6.3 Sensitivity of credit to companies to disaggregated capital flows (*Source*: SARB and authors' calculations)

Does the relationship vary between bank and non-bank flows? Yes, it does. Fig. 6.3a, b show that the steepness of the slope varies between the bank and non-bank flows in the FDI and portfolio flows categories. Credit to companies is more sensitive to the bank portfolio inflows compared to the non-bank category.

These results indicate that there is a positive relationship between capital flows and credit to companies. This evidence supports the theory of the prevalence of credit reallocation dynamics towards companies.

6.3 The VAR Results

This section estimates a vector autoregression (VAR) model with four variables from 1994Q1 to 2015Q3. The four variables are annual GDP growth, annual inflation rate, credit to companies as percentage of total loans and advances and capital flow categories. The capital flow categories refer to (1) total FDI or FDI bank flow or non-bank flows and (2) total portfolio or portfolio bank or non-bank flows. The flow categories are expressed as percentage of GDP. The capital flow categories are included separately in the model. The VAR model has three lags selected by AIC and 10,000 Monte Carlo draws. The impulse responses are the 16th and 84th percentiles and are shaded in grey. Similar to the findings in the stylized sections, Fig. 6.4 shows positive impulse responses of credit to

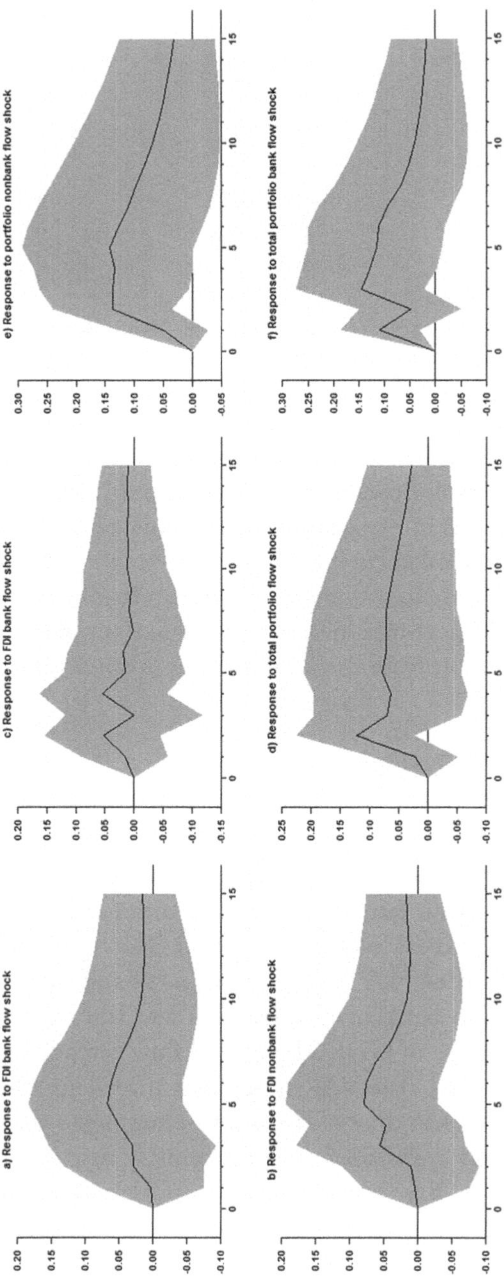

Fig. 6.4 The responses of credit to companies to capital flow shocks (*Source*: Authors' calculations)

companies to different categories of capital flows shocks. This indicates that banking and non-banking flows lead to sectorial credit reallocations towards companies.

There is a significant increase in the reallocation of credit to companies due to portfolio flows, portfolio bank flows and non-bank flow shock in Fig. 6.4d, e and (d), respectively. However, amongst all the capital flow shocks, the increase in credit to companies does not exceed 0.3 percentage points. This indicates that although the reallocation of credit toward companies occurs, it is in very small magnitudes. However, this positive impact is much higher compared to the negative (decline) impact of 0.25 percentage points at peak response of these capital flow categories on the household sector credit share shown in the previous chapter.

Does the aggregation of FDI and portfolio flows into banking and non-banking flows impact the relationship between credit to companies and capital flows? Fig. 6.5a, b show that credit to companies increases due to a positive bank and non-bank flow shock. However, the increase is significant towards non-bank flows shocks in Fig. 6.5c. Credit to companies rises for nearly 10 quarters.

6.4 Fluctuations in Credit to Companies Explained by Bank and Non-bank Shocks

To determine the proportion of fluctuations in credit to companies that is induced by capital flow shocks, variance decompositions are used. Fig. 6.6a shows that non-bank flows explain more movements in credit to companies than bank flows. Fig. 6.6b shows that portfolio flow shocks induce more fluctuations in credit to companies than FDI flow shocks.

This is in contrast to evidence that non-bank flows explain more movements in credit to households than bank flows, in particular FDI non-bank than bank flows. On the other hand, portfolio bank flows explain more household credit fluctuations than portfolio non-bank flows.

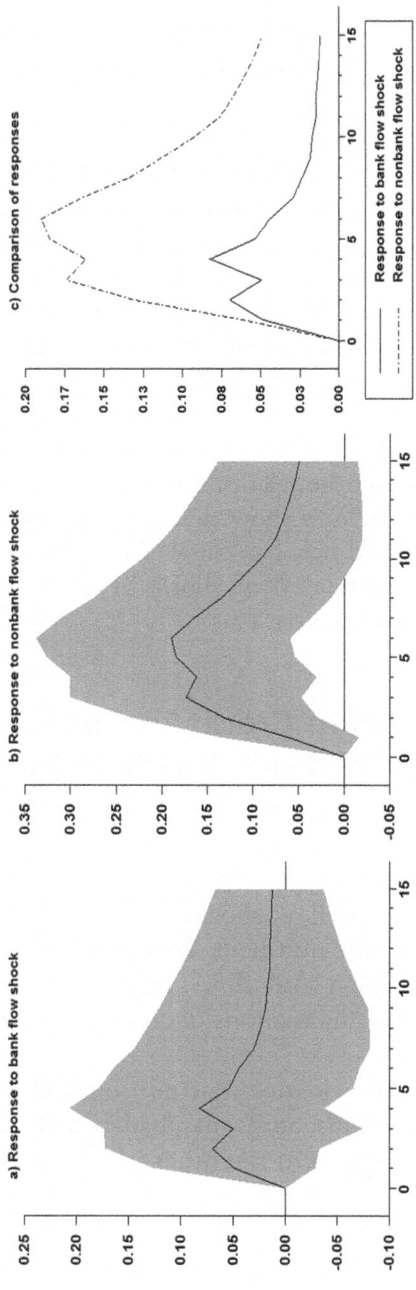

Fig. 6.5 Credit to companies' responses to bank and non-bank flows (*Source*: Authors' calculations)

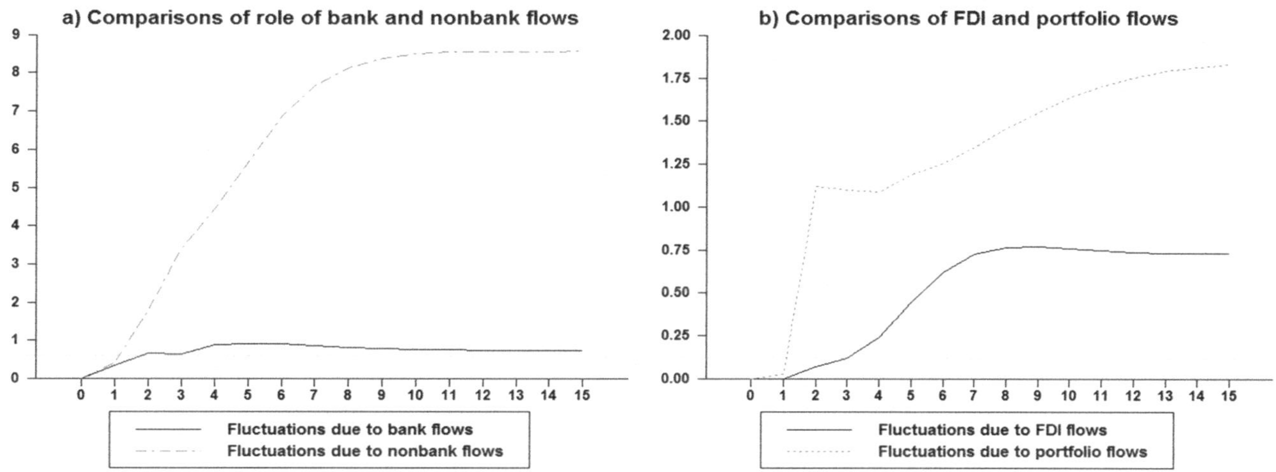

Fig. 6.6 Fluctuations in credit to companies as percentage of total loans and advances (*Source*: Authors' calculations)

6.5 Do Capital Flows Amplify the Responses of the Repo Rate to Positive Inflation Shocks? Evidence from the Counterfactual Contributions

So far we have established some important aspects. First, portfolio flows matter very much for credit reallocation towards companies. Second, portfolio flows induce slightly higher variability in credit to companies than FDI flows. Third, non-bank flows explain more fluctuations in credit to companies than bank flows. But, do capital flows amplify the responses of the repo rate to positive inflation shocks? That is, is the repo rate response different in the presence of the capital flows channel than when it is shut off in the model?

Fig. 6.7 shows that credit to companies is positively related to inflation. Fig. A6.2 in the appendix shows that the positive relationship between credit to companies and inflation is robust to measurement, that is, as a share of total credit and the growth rate in the level of credit to companies. In contrast, Fig. A6.1 in the appendix shows that household credit share is negatively related to inflation. This relationship holds even for the level of credit growth to households in Fig. A6.2.

At the same time, Fig. 6.7 shows that portfolio flows reduce inflation and the repo rate. The magnitude in the decline in inflation due to portfolio flows is larger than the size of the inflation increase due to credit to companies. This means that increased capital flows tend to neutralize the inflationary pressures associated with increased credit to companies. The repo rate declines due to increased portfolio flows.

However, to determine the actual and counterfactual repo rate response to positive inflation shocks each capital flow category is shut off. The gap between the actual repo rate in the presence of various capital flow categories and the counterfactual responses when these capital flow channels are shut off establish their amplification or dampening role and magnitudes.

Fig. 6.8 shows the response of the repo rate to positive inflation shocks in the presence of portfolio flow channels and when they are shut off. These are cumulative repo rate responses following a 1 percentage points positive inflation shock. When the counterfactual repo rate

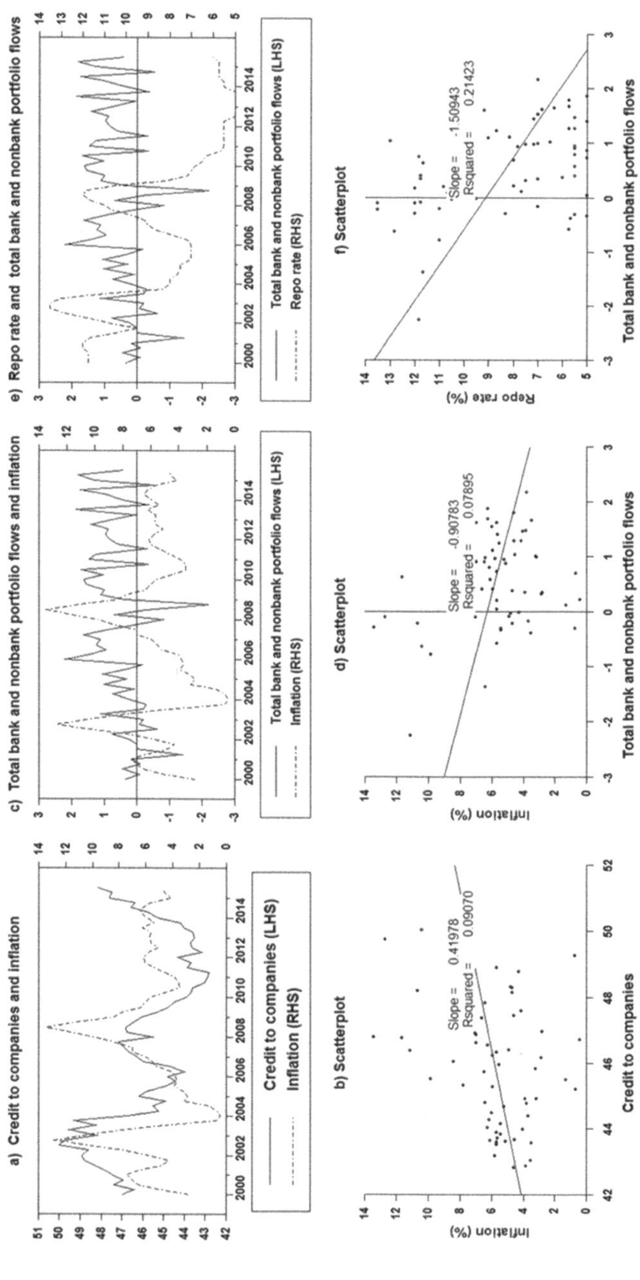

Fig. 6.7 Credit to companies and selected macroeconomic indicators (*Source*: Authors' calculations)

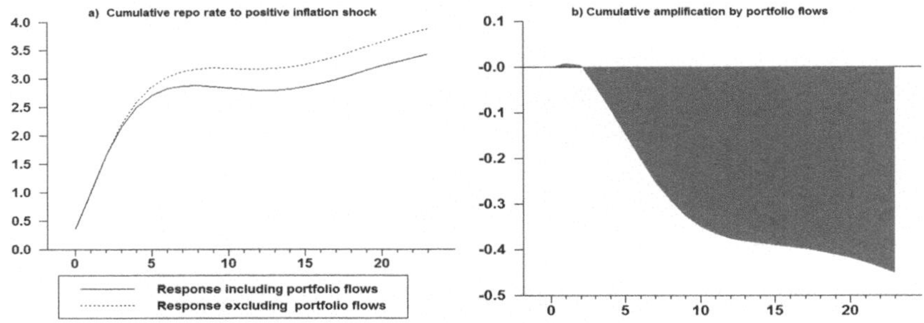

Fig. 6.8 Cumulative repo rate response to positive inflation shocks and amplification by portfolio flows (*Source*: Authors' calculations)

responses exceed the actual repo rate response, the implication is that increased portfolio flows induce lower magnitudes of repo rate increase than when capital flows are shut off. In cumulative terms, the repo rate responses indicate that it may lower by 0.4 percentage points over long horizons.

The responses to portfolio bank and non-bank flows, FDI bank and non-bank flows in Fig. 6.9 arrive at similar conclusions. The counterfactual repo rate exceeds the actual repo rate, meaning that increased capital flow activity induces lower increases in repo rate due to positive inflation shocks. This is possibly linked to the appreciation in the exchange rate that is usually associated with an increase in capital flows. Nonetheless, the results reveal that the repo rate responds to positive inflation shocks, irrespective of capital flow activity.

6.6 The Historical Decompositions and Counterfactual Scenarios

Fig. 6.10 shows that banks flow uplifted credit to companies between 2005 and 2012 as well as the beginning again in mid-2014 and thereafter.

On the other hand, the contributions of both non-bank and bank flows in Fig. 6.11 were largely negative in between 2000 and 2007 due to the contribution of non-bank flows. It also seems to be the case currently that non-bank flows are neutralizing the positive impact of bank flows shown in Fig. 6.10.

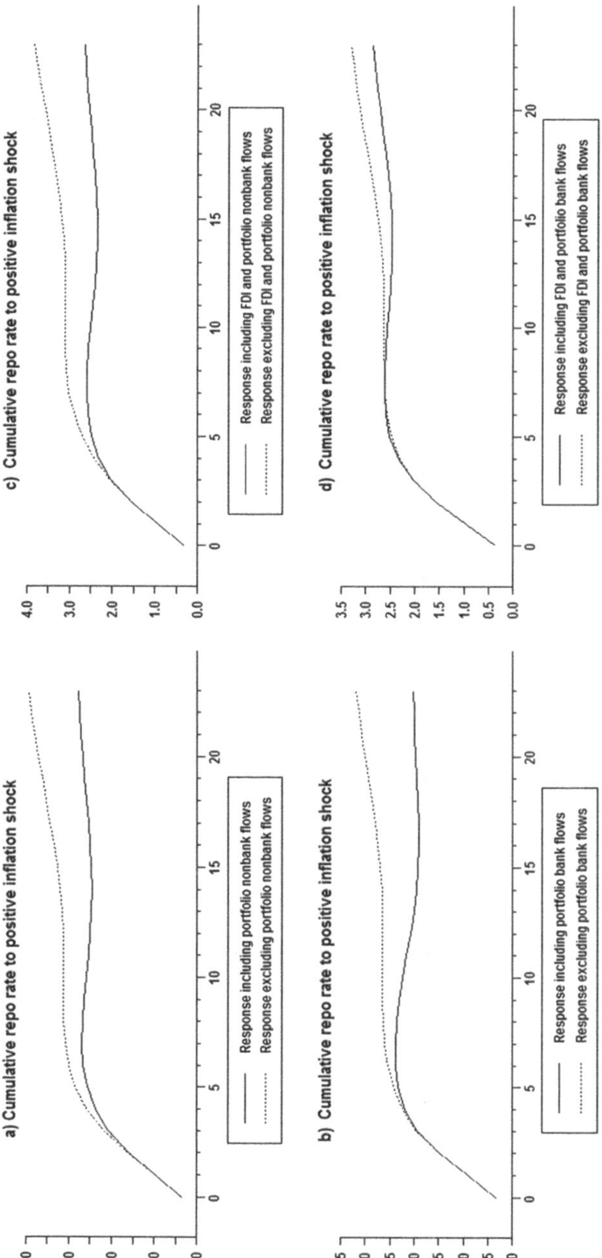

Fig. 6.9 Cumulative repo rate responses to positive inflation shocks and amplification by various capital flow categories (*Source*: Authors' calculations)

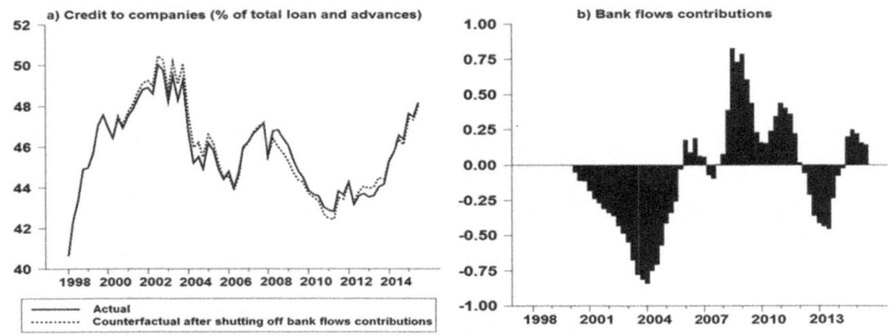

Fig. 6.10 Actual and counterfactual credit to companies and contributions of bank flows (*Source*: Authors' calculations)

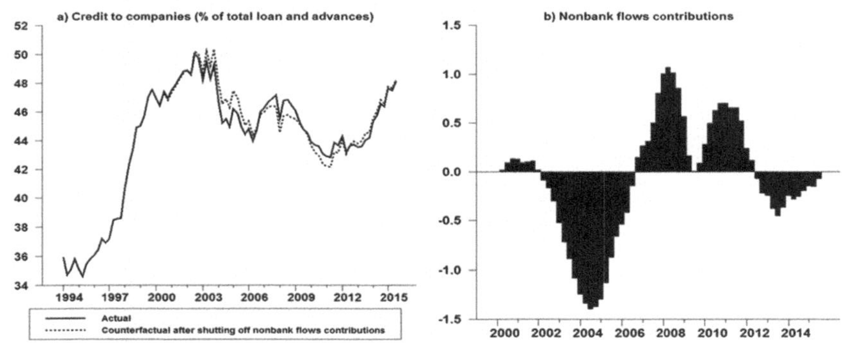

Fig. 6.11 Actual and counterfactual credit to companies and contributions of bank and non-bank flows (*Source*: Authors' calculations)

6.7 Conclusion and Policy Implications

The results in this chapter suggest that capital mobility may lead to an increase in the domestic allocation of bank credit towards companies. In addition, portfolio flow shocks induce more fluctuations in credit to companies than FDI flow shock. This is in contrast to the findings that non-bank flows explain more movements in credit to households than bank flows. This evidence supports the theory of the prevalence of credit reallocation dynamics towards companies.

The counterfactual exercises show that the repo rate does increase to curb inflationary pressures. However, the policy tightening is larger in the absence of increased capital flow activity. This means that increased capital flow activity induces muted repo rate increases in response to inflationary pressures. This is linked to the exchange rate appreciation response to capital flows that tends to dampen inflation pressures. The results imply that the inflation target mandate is binding and policymakers respond to inflationary pressures irrespective of the sources.

For regulatory and prudential policy, the evidence of the prevalence of credit reallocation towards companies means that capital flows can result in excesses in some market segments. To mitigate the build-up of such imbalances and the potential negative spill-over effects requires targeted regulatory tools instead of broad regulation.

Summary of Main Findings

- There is a positive relationship between credit to companies, bank and non-banking flows.
- Credit to companies is more sensitive to bank portfolio inflows compared to non-bank inflows.
- Capital flows induce credit reallocation towards companies.
- The share of credit to companies and growth rates are positively related to inflation.
- Increased capital flow activity via the exchange rate channel induces lower increases in repo rate due to positive inflation shocks.

Appendix

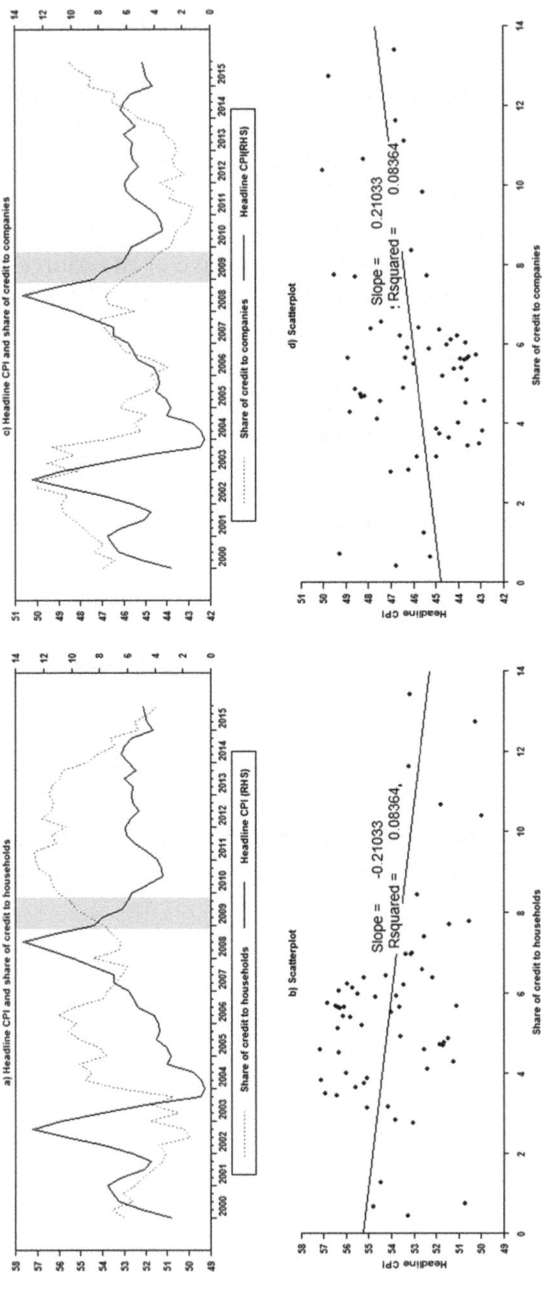

Fig. A6.1 Relationships between credit shares to companies and households with inflation (*Source*: SARB and Authors' calculations)

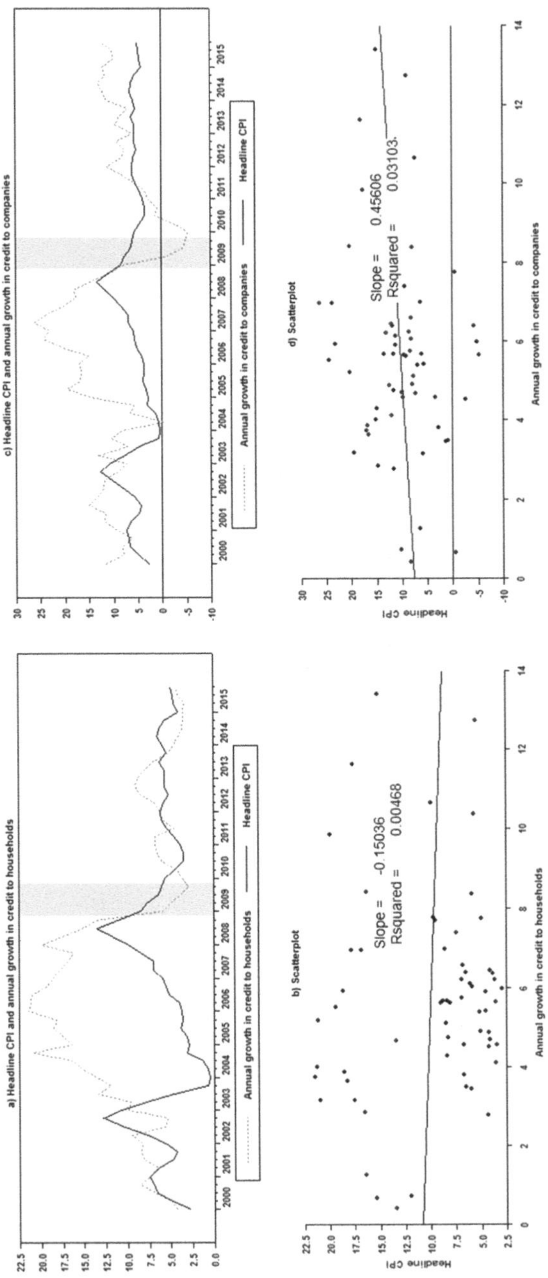

Fig. A6.2 Relationships between growth in credit to companies and households with inflation (*Source*: SARB and Authors' calculations)

7

Stock Price Returns, Volatility and Costly Asset Price Boom–Bust Episodes

Learning Objectives

- Understand how stock market price returns and volatility exert different impacts on macroeconomic variables.
- Distinguish between the adverse effects of stock price volatility shocks and those exerted by a positive monetary policy shock.
- Assess the impact of unexpected stock returns shocks on inflation and economic growth.
- Establish how the contributions of stock price returns and volatility reinforce each other.
- Understand in which periods different techniques identify asset price booms and busts.
- Learn what the Taylor rule suggests about monetary policy settings during asset price booms.
- Assess whether all booms in South Africa are followed by costly busts. In cases where they are, determine the cumulative output costs and the severity of equity price and house price busts.

N. Gumata, E. Ndou, *Bank Credit Extension and Real Economic Activity in South Africa*, DOI 10.1007/978-3-319-43551-0_7

7.1 Introduction

The Johannesburg Stock Exchange (JSE) index price more than doubled from a low of 19,657.9 to 53,741.7 points between March 2009 and April 2015, as illustrated in Fig. 7.1. Policymakers have raised concerns about the sustainability of the price boom and what the impact of a sharp correction would be. However, it is not necessarily undesirable to have asset price rises, but the problem arises when the asset prices decline and the impact spills over into economic activity.

The literature provides evidence that busts following asset price cycle booms tend to be associated with significant real economic contractions and slow recoveries. This is because of the feedback loop linked to costly busts of asset price booms, lending and leveraging against these asset prices.

Have there been episodes of non-costly asset price booms and busts in South Africa? The literature is clear that not all asset price booms are alike. For example, the boom in technology stocks in the late 1990s was not fueled by a feedback loop between bank lending and rising equity values. In addition, stock market bubbles are much harder to identify given that they are not primarily driven by credit booms. Hence, literature argues that it is this distinguishing

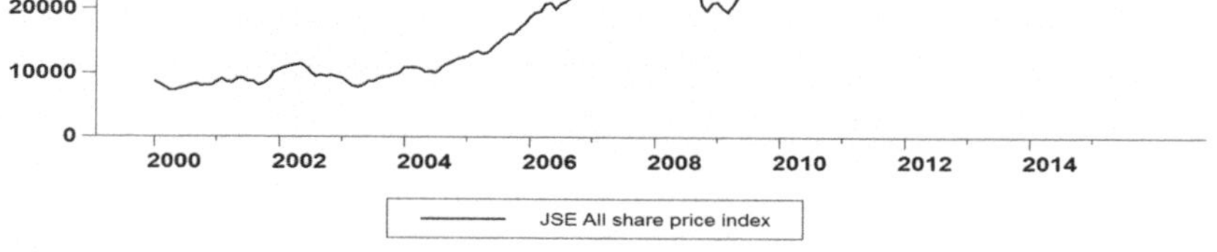

Fig. 7.1 The JSE All share price index (*Source*: SARB)

characteristic that also makes them less harmful. Their collapse is less likely to lead to financial instability. However, in extreme cases, as evidenced by the recent financial crisis, the collapse of asset price booms can compromise the functioning of the financial system as a whole (Mishkin 2008).

Why care about these stock price booms and busts if they are hard to identify? First, when stock price booms collapse and the positive feedback loop between credit and stock prices is reversed, it means policymakers have to manage the costs involved. Second, departures of asset prices from levels implied by economic fundamentals as evidenced by asset price bubbles have additional implications for economic efficiency. They can lead to inappropriate investments that decrease the efficiency of the economy by diverting resources towards economic activities that are only supported by the bubble.

The literature is fraught with evidence showing that discussions of booms and busts have to distinguish between equity and property prices, for several reasons related to: (1) the efficient markets hypothesis most likely to apply to equity markets relative to property markets; (2) concentration of the ownership of stock among households and their consumption decisions; (3) the relative leverage of housing purchases and its impact on the balance sheets of both households and financial intermediaries.[1]

This chapter pays particular attention to equity price busts and their associated economic costs. The effects of various dynamics of equity booms and busts are quantified and the role of stock price returns and volatility on economic growth is illustrated. The movements induced by portfolio outflows on economic growth, stock price returns and volatility are examined. Furthermore, episodes of real stock price busts and the associated economic costs are identified. The analysis focuses on the behavior of selected macroeconomic variables and the possible existence of financial imbalances prior to, during and after episodes of costly booms.

---

[1] See IMF (2003), Cecchetti (2012, 2006), Yavas (2013), Xiong (2013), amongst others

7.2 Stylized Facts in the Relationship Between Economic Growth and Stock Market Dynamics

Fig. 7.1 showed that, having fallen to record low levels in 2009 subsequent to the financial crisis and the ensuing recession, equity prices have performed extraordinarily well. So, what is (1) the relationship between stock returns and economic growth and (2) the relationship between economic growth and volatility in stock price returns? The time series for stock price volatility is based on average monthly stock price volatility for the period January 1988 to September 2012 using a Garch (1,1) model. The volatility estimate is obtained by regressing monthly stock returns on constant and lagged monthly stock price returns. Fig. 7.2 shows the GDP growth, the stock price returns and volatility.

The data shows that stock price returns tend to move closely with economic growth and that peaks in stock price volatility tend to coincide with the slowdown in GDP. On the other hand, there is a negative relationship between GDP and stock price volatility.

7.3 Differential Effects Between Stock Price Returns and Volatility on Economic Growth

This chapter assesses the differential effects of stock price returns and volatility from four perspectives: (1) how economic growth responds to unexpected stock price returns and volatility shocks of the same magnitude; (2) how stock price returns and volatility impact inflationary pressures and economic growth; (3) quantifying the fluctuations in economic growth induced by stock price returns and volatility, and how movements induced by these shocks compare to those of other economic shocks; and (4) the extent to which these shocks transmit portfolio outflow shocks into the economy and the proportion of movements due to portfolio outflow shocks. The empirical analysis applies vector autoregression (VAR) models that include portfolio inflows and outflows as they are amongst

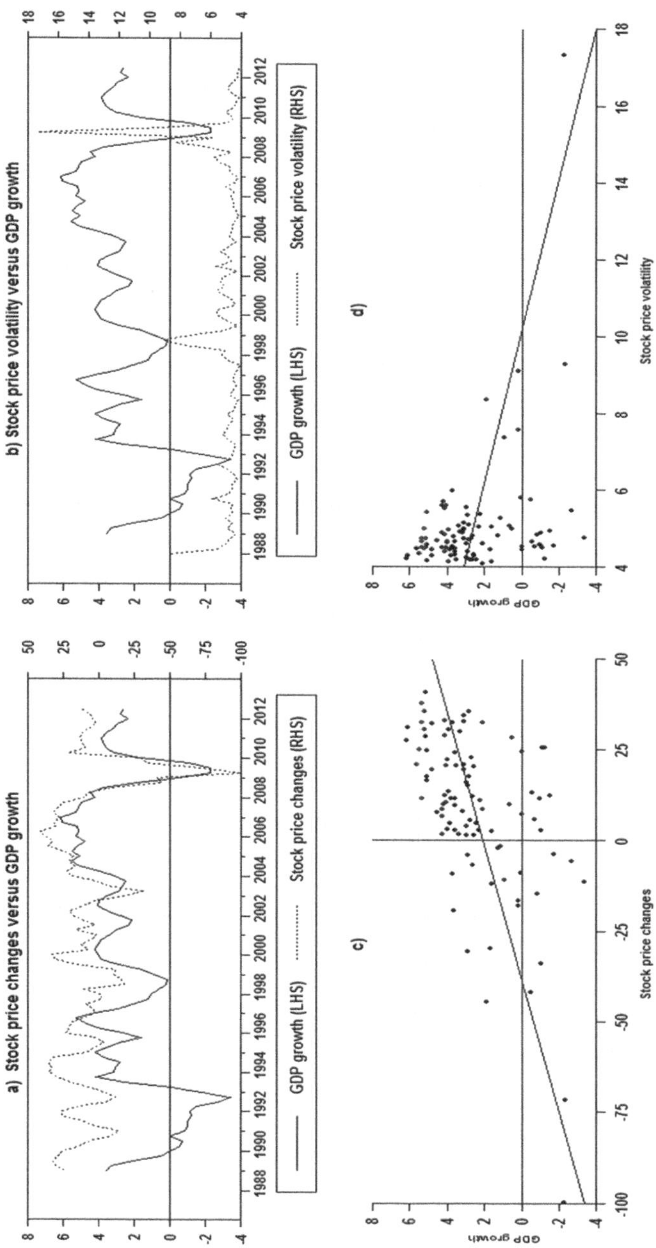

Fig. 7.2 Stock market prices returns, volatility and economic growth (*Source*: SARB and authors' calculations)

the key drivers of developments in asset prices. Different models are estimated where portfolio inflows and outflows are used interchangeably to assess the impact of a unit shock in both stock price returns and volatility.[2]

Fig. 7.3d shows that unexpected positive stock price volatility shock lowers inflation. This might be a result of uncertainty and postponement of planned decisions, which in turn may reduce the demand for investment and lower aggregate demand. An unexpected positive unit shock in stock price volatility depresses economic growth significantly and slows inflation.

In Fig. 7.3a a positive unexpected rise in stock price returns raises economic growth in the first three quarters and leads to a slowdown in economic growth after four quarters. Why is this the case? It can be explained by the different sensitivities of the variables included in the model. Given that the mandate of the South African Reserve Bank is price stability, Fig. 7.4a compares the sensitivities of economic growth and inflation to an unexpected shock in stock returns. Inflation is relatively more sensitive to unexpected increase in stock price returns than to economic growth. The inflation rise is consistent with evidence reported in literature operating through wealth effects, which tend to raise investment and aggregate demand, and ultimately results in a rise in inflation.

So does it matter which stock price component is used in assessing the impact of inflation on economic growth? Fig. 7.4c shows that the choice of the stock price component does matter. Inflation leads to relatively larger contractions in economic growth when considering stock price volatility, as opposed to when considering stock price returns only.

7.3.1 Do Stock Price Dynamics and Fluctuations on Economic Growth Relative to Other Shocks

How do stock price returns and volatility shocks impact fluctuations in economic growth compared to those attributed to movements in economic growth, inflation, policy rate, portfolio inflows and outflows? Fig. 7.5a, b show that own movements in GDP account for a higher proportion of

---

[2] See Kim and Yang (2009) for further details on dealing with the issue of simultaneity between capital inflows and asset prices.

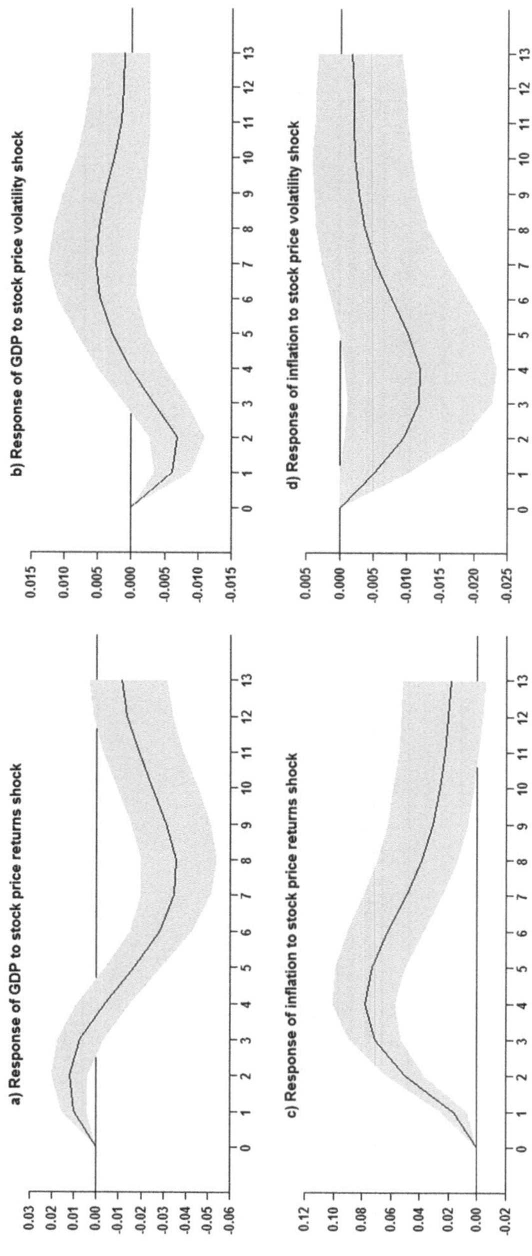

Fig. 7.3 Effects of stock market dynamics on economic growth and inflation (*Source*: Authors' calculations)

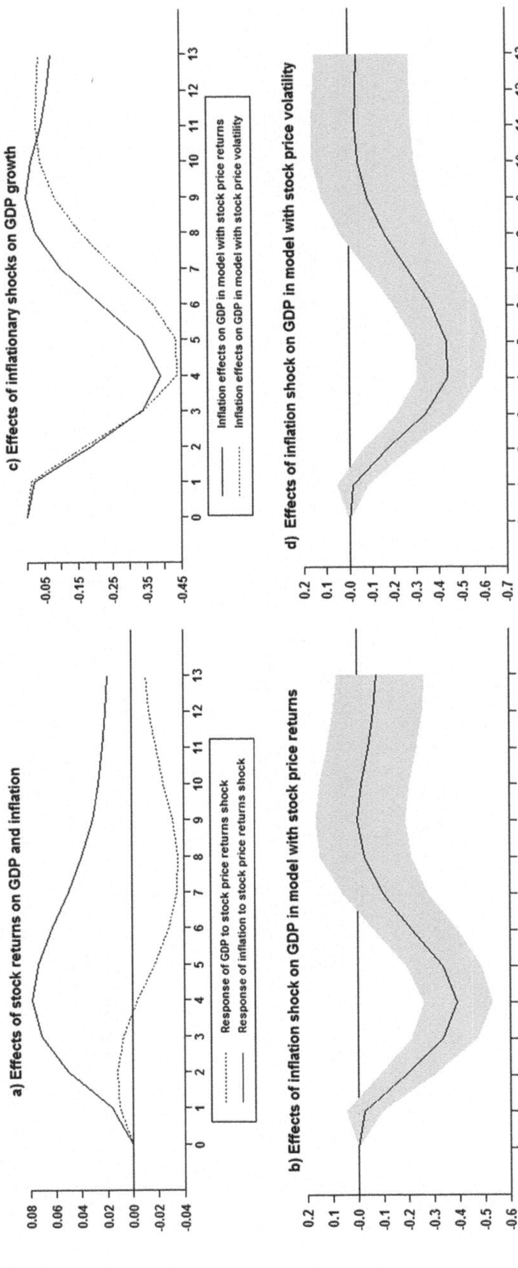

Fig. 7.4 Assessing the effects of stock returns, inflation and economic growth (*Source*: Authors' calculations)

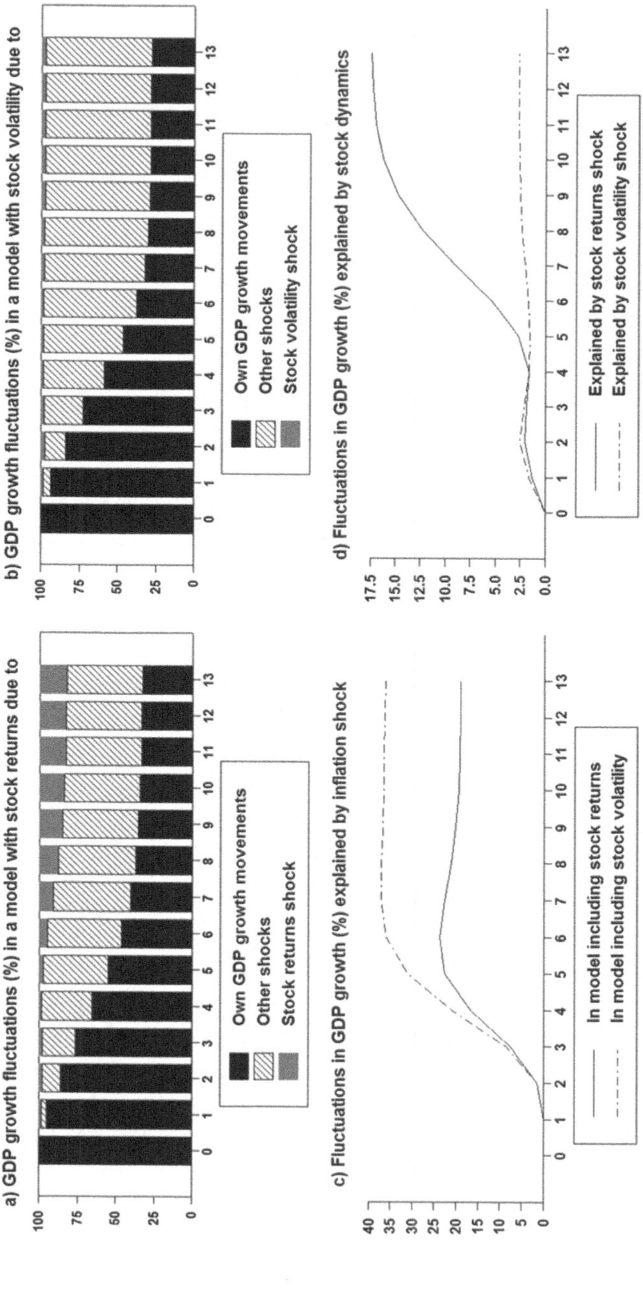

Fig. 7.5 The drivers of fluctuations in economic growth (*Source*: Authors' calculations)

economic growth in the first six quarters. Inflation accounts for a relatively high percentage of fluctuations in economic growth after four quarters in Fig. 7.5c, but the effect is large in the presence of stock volatility. However, it is noticeable in Fig. 7.5d that stock price returns induce greater movements in GDP relative to stock price volatility shocks.

These findings show that stock price returns have a positive effect on economic growth but they raise inflation and this has a dampening effect on their simulative effects. Inflation tends to depress economic growth more in the presence of stock price volatility relative to the presence of stock price returns in Fig. 7.5c

7.3.2 Stock Price Returns and Volatility Transmit Portfolio Outflow Shocks

Is there a transmission channel of portfolio outflows shocks in South Africa operating via stock price returns and volatility and how significant are the channels? Fig. 7.6 shows that stock price returns decline significantly in response to an unexpected portfolio outflow shock while stock price volatility rises significantly.

The evidence shows that portfolio outflow shocks are transmitted via stock returns and their accompanying volatility. What about the effects of portfolio outflows on economic growth? Evidence presented in Fig. 7.6c, d confirms that portfolio outflows are destabilizing. An unexpected positive portfolio outflow shock depresses economic growth significantly, irrespective of the returns and the volatility variables. Why is there a differential response in the magnitudes and the duration of portfolio outflow effects between stock price returns and volatility? This can be explained in two ways: (1) by examining fluctuations in economic growth in the presence of returns and volatility and (2) by examining how portfolio outflows impact fluctuations in stock price returns and volatility. Fig. 7.7a shows that economic growth fluctuates relatively more due to portfolio outflow shocks in the presence of stock volatility than stock price returns.

Whereas, in Fig. 7.7b portfolio outflows induce relatively higher fluctuations in stock price volatility than in stock price returns.

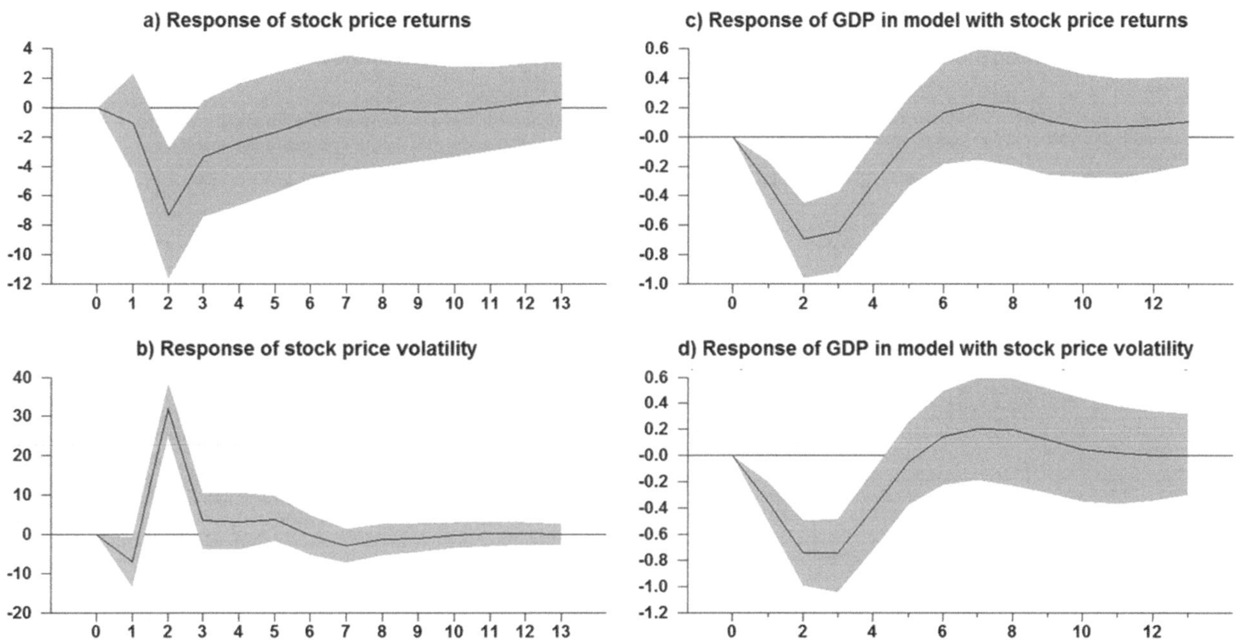

Fig. 7.6 Effects of an unexpected portfolio outflow shock on GDP growth, stock price returns and volatility (*Source*: Authors' calculations)

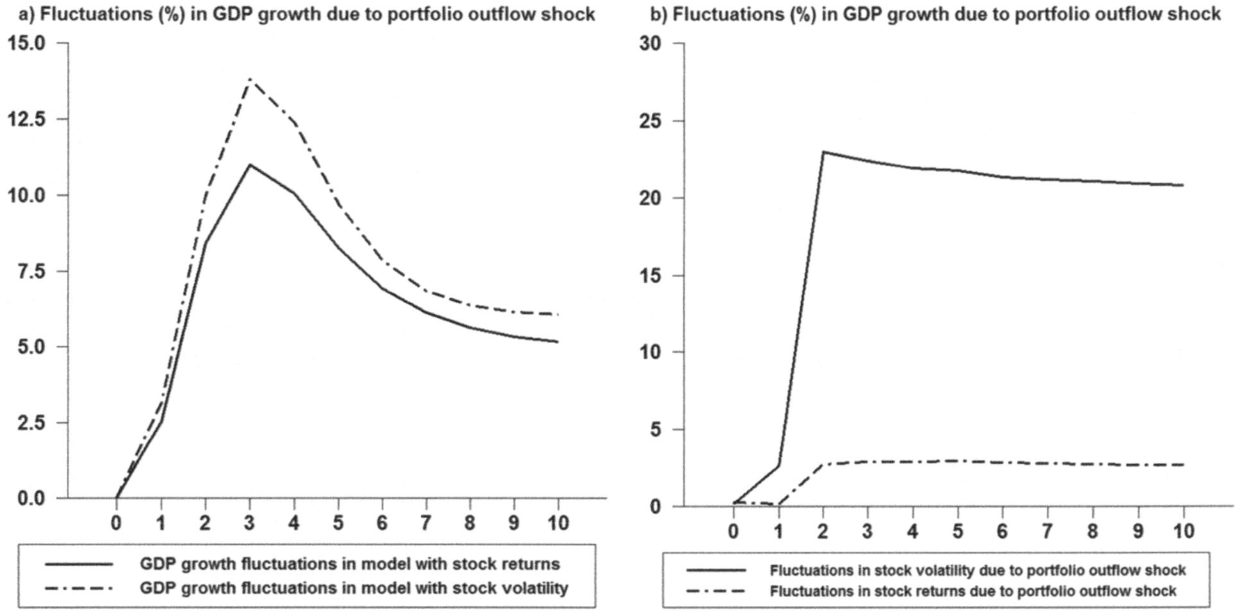

Fig. 7.7 The proportion of movements in economic growth and the role of portfolio outflows (*Source*: Authors' calculations)

7.3.3 Volatility and Monetary Policy Tightening Shocks Impacts on Economic Growth

Evidence shows that unexpected stock price volatility depresses economic growth. However, between an unexpected stock price volatility and unexpected tightening in monetary policy shocks which one exerts more depressing effects? Fig. 7.8 shows that the response of GDP growth to stock price volatility and interest rates is negative. However, the depressing effects of stock price volatility tend to be smaller when compared to those exerted by a positive monetary policy shock. Inflation has depressing effects on GDP growth that are far more severe compared to those of stock price volatility and interest rates.

7.3.4 Economic Growth Evolution and the Role of Stock Returns and Volatility

In Fig. 7.9a, c actual and counterfactual economic growth rate show the contributions of stock price returns and volatility. Post-2009 actual economic growth exceeded the counterfactual growth, indicating that stock price returns and low volatility contributed to uplifting economic activity in the beginning of 2010 and in later periods. However, during the domestic recession both the stock market returns and high volatility aggravated the recessionary effects. In contrast, low volatility in the post-recession period was linked to positive contributions towards economic growth.

Furthermore, the comparison of the contributions of stock price returns and volatility in Fig. 7.10 for the period 2000–2012 shows that the contributions of stock price returns and volatility tend to move in the same direction and reinforce each other. The reinforcing effects are magnified in the presence of stock price returns.

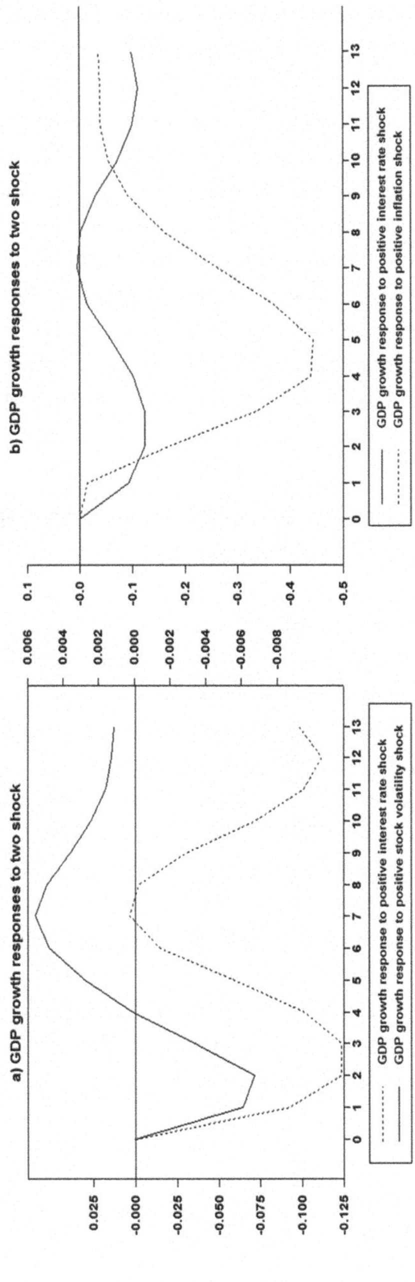

Fig. 7.8 The responses of GDP to stock price volatility and monetary policy shocks (*Source*: Authors' calculations)

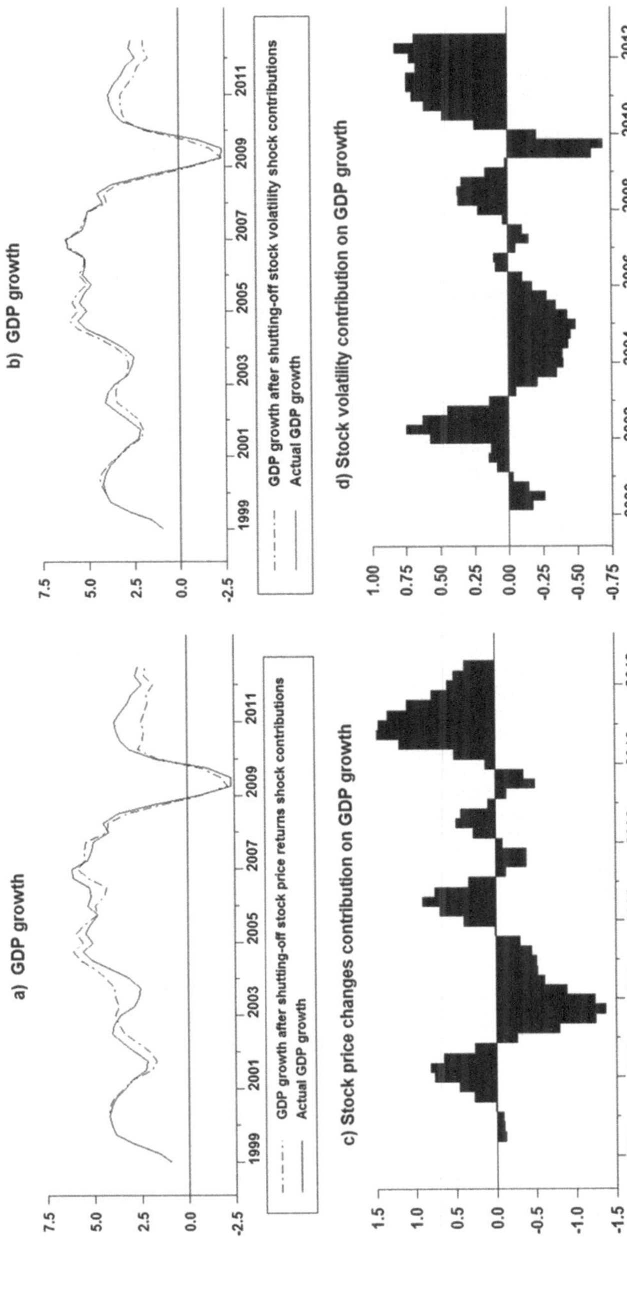

Fig. 7.9 Propagation effects of stock returns and volatility on economic growth (*Source*: Authors' calculations)

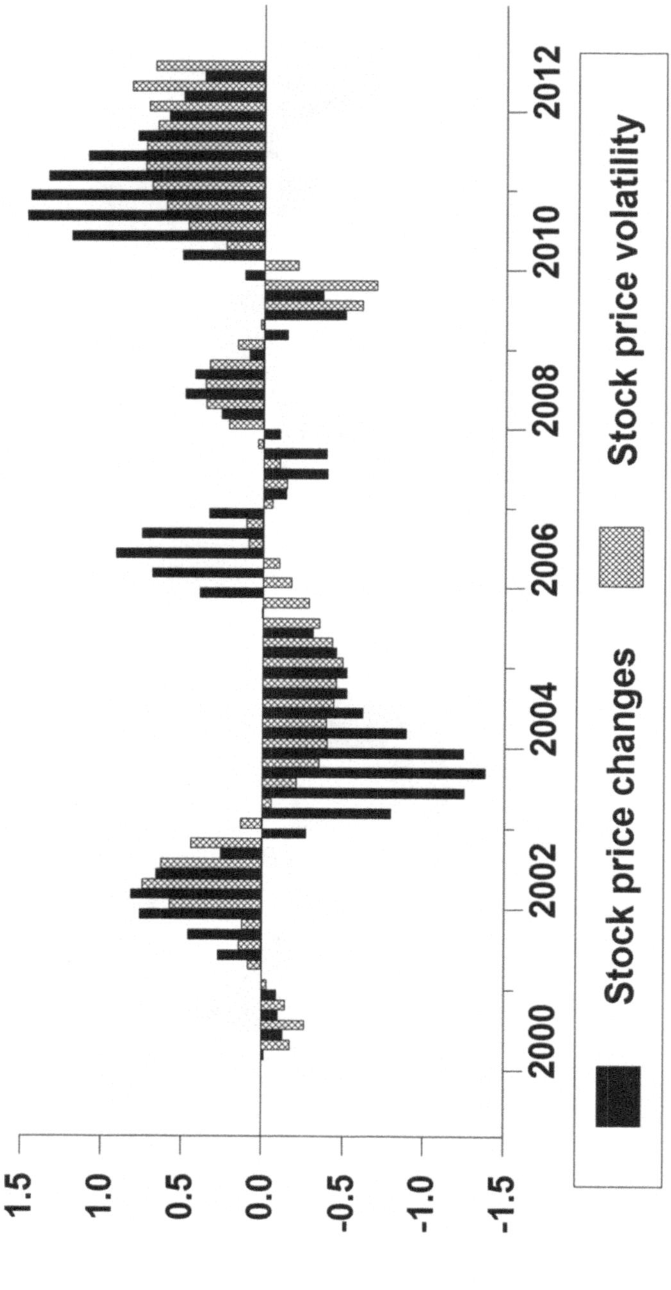

Fig. 7.10 Contributions of stock returns and volatility to economic growth (*Source*: Authors' calculations)

7.4 Asset Price Booms and Busts: Inferences from Various Measures

So far, the evidence has established the macroeconomic effects of stock price returns and stock price volatility shock, and the responses of economic activity to a contractionary monetary policy shock and stock price developments. But how costly are equity price booms and busts?

First, to identify stock price booms and busts the approach in Fatas et al. (2009) and Borgy et al. (2009) is used. The authors define stock busts as periods when the four quarter moving average of the annual growth rate of stock prices falls below a specific threshold. Borgy et al. (2009) set the threshold at −15 percent, whereas Bordo and Jeanne (2002) set it at −20 percent. Both thresholds are used in this analysis. This methodology has been applied consistently across countries and the thresholds are able to pick up the major well-known asset price busts.

Second, the stock price busts (booms) are identified using the band-pass filter. The threshold occurs when the Christiano–Fitzgerald band-pass filter falls (rises) below (above) zero by more than one standard deviation. The results of these approaches are shown in Fig. 7.11. Bust periods are shaded by the light grey color. In part (a) these are identified by cut-offs of negative −15 percent and negative −20 percent. In part (b) these are determined by a negative one standard deviation, that is, approximately a negative −20 percent based on band-pass filter.

In Fig. 7.11 the results from both methodologies are highly comparable and both are able to identify busts based on the −15 percent and −20 percent thresholds. These findings based on light shaded portions of busts using the band-pass filter approach identify the same episodes and turning points. What differs is the duration of the identified bust periods. The band-pass filter identifies turning points earlier, as shown in Fig. 7.12, when compared to the moving average series. The bust episodes identified in 1974–75, 1983, 1992 and 2008 concur with evidence in other international studies.

We further show what happens during the identified bust episodes and the severity of the economic costs? Table 7.1 shows the economic costs associated with bust episodes, the duration of stock price busts, the average real stock price declines and the size of the output gaps. These calculations

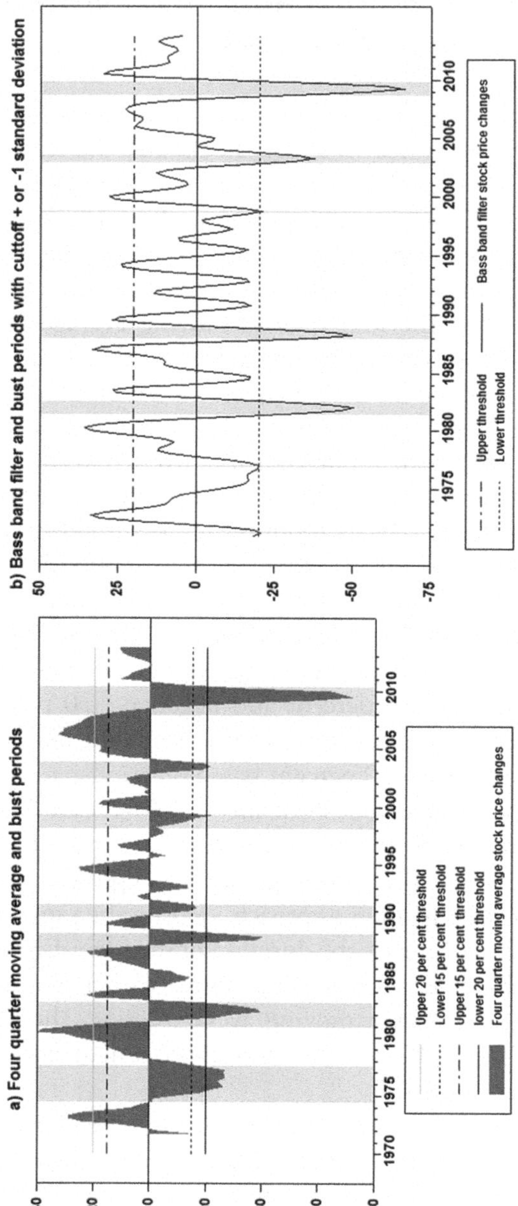

Fig. 7.11 Comparison of stock busts and booms identified by two methods (*Source*: Authors' calculations)

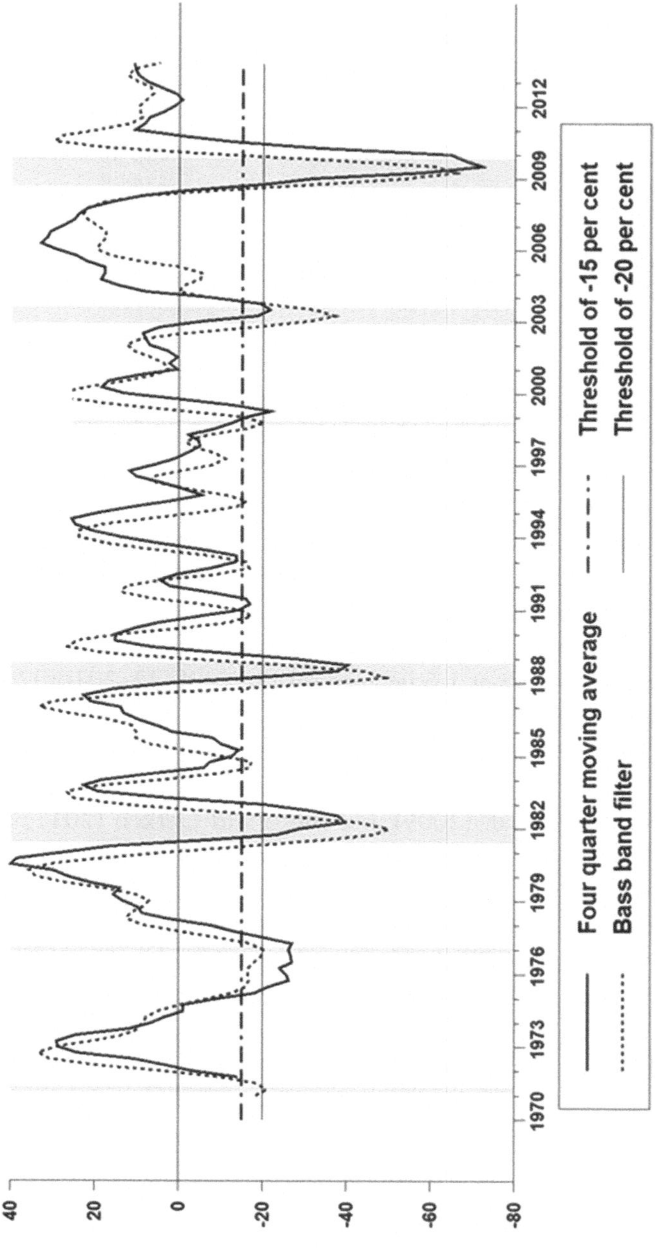

Fig. 7.12 Comparison of stock busts identified by two methods (*Source*: Authors' calculations)

Table 7.1 Estimated stock prices busts and the output-gap

Period	Duration in quarters	Mean GDP gap (%)	Mean real stock price changes (%)
1974Q3–1977Q3	13	−0.33	−22.01
1981Q1–1983Q1	9	−0.79	−22.84
1987Q3–1989Q1	7	2.11	−19.53
1990Q3–1991Q3	5	−1.07	−14.08
1998Q2–1999Q2	5	−1.90	−16.45
2002Q3–2003Q3	6	−0.55	−14.12
2008Q3–2010Q2	10	−1.60	−37.03

Source: Authors' calculations

are based on the estimated periods when the bust occurred based on the four-quarter moving average and the deviations of output from its potential trend based on the Hodrick–Prescott filter.[3] The cumulative widening in the output gap is measured as the accumulated deviation from a one-sided Hodrick–Prescott filter with a smoothness parameter of 1,600.

In Table 7.1 the average stock price busts are estimated to last nearly seven quarters. The mean real stock price growth declined by between 14 and 38 percent; and the mean decline in output below its trend output was the most severe at 1.6 percent for the 2008Q2–2010Q2 period. Indeed, the evidence points to serious economic costs during stock bust episodes. However, does it mean that all booms result in severe economic costs?

Following Borgy et al. (2009) and Alessi and Detken (2011) a costly asset price boom is defined as a costly boom that is followed by a widening of the output gap of at least 3 percentage points within three years following the end of the boom. The equity boom episodes using this criterion and those identified as less costly are shown in Fig. 7.13.

Fig. 7.13 corroborates the findings that not all stock price booms are followed by costly economic episodes. However, the literature provides evidence showing that discussions of booms and busts have to distinguish between equity and property prices. Fig. 7.14a shows the real house price busts (booms) determined using the four-quarter moving average

[3] See Fatas et al. (Fatas et al. 2009) for further details.

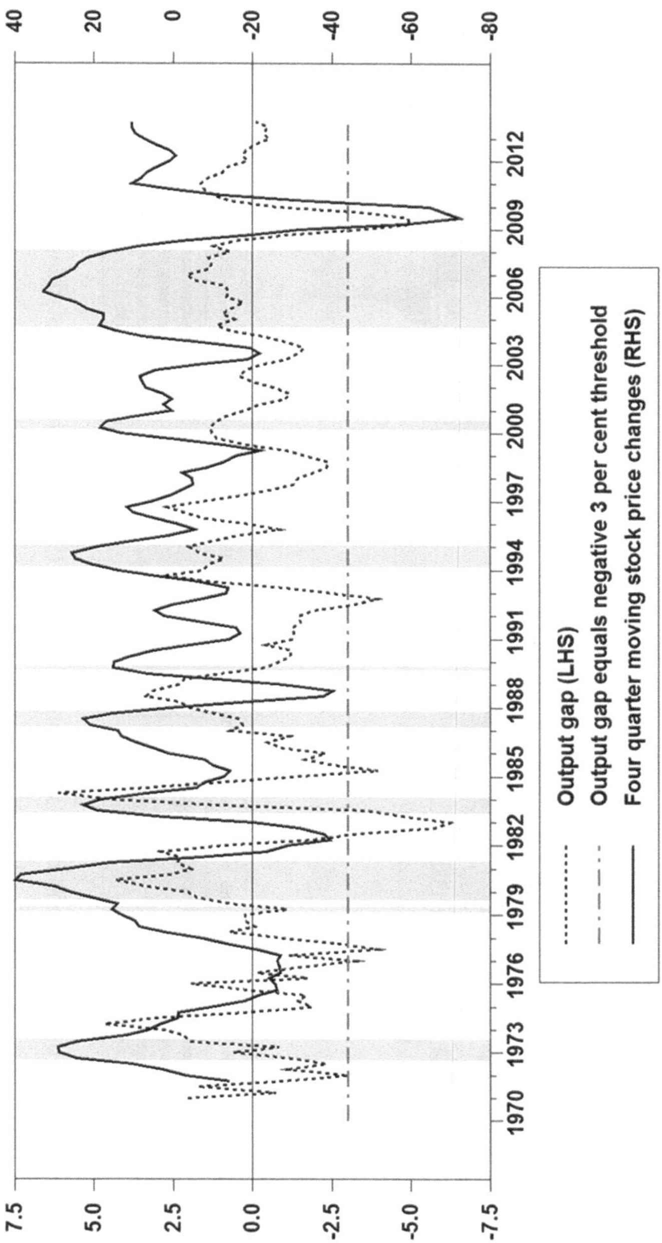

Fig. 7.13 Identified periods of stock price booms and associated output losses (*Source*: Authors' calculations)

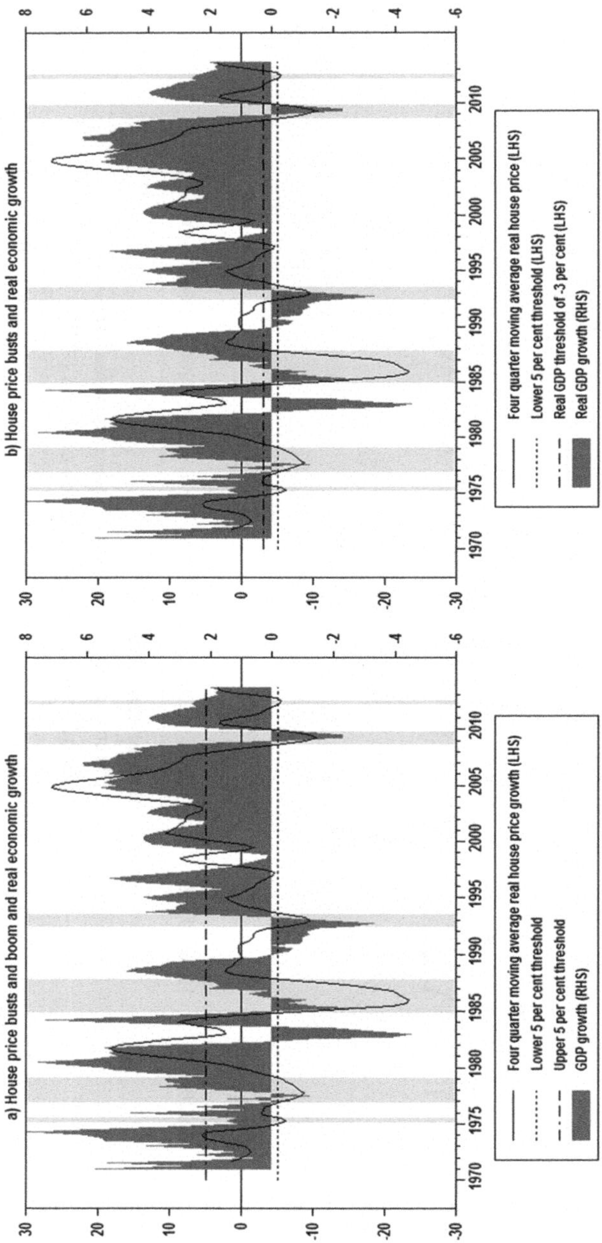

Fig. 7.14 House price booms and busts and economic growth (*Source*: Authors' calculations)

and negative (positive) 5 percent threshold and real economic growth. In Fig. 7.14b during house price busts real economic growth tends to decline by more than 3 percent.

This suggests that house price busts tend to worsen growth prospects, hence they create outsized risk. In the South African case, estimates show that the average house price bust lasts for two and half years, whereas stock price busts last approximately two years.[4] The results are consistent with literature indicating that costly asset price booms with greater output loss are associated with housing booms and busts rather than for stock prices, and they are relatively more persistent.

7.4.1 Credit or Collateral Channel in South Africa Accompanying Costly Booms

For completeness of the analysis of asset price booms and busts and the associated credit booms and busts, we use simple plot analysis to examine the existence of evidence of the credit or collateral channel. This will demonstrate what happens to variables capturing these channels. The variables depicting the credit and the collateral channels are shown in Fig. 7.15, based on the identified costly equity price booms in Fig. 7.13. The purpose is to show the behavior of credit and M3 money supply growth, as well as house prices and residential investment growth prior to, during and after the identified boom periods.

The hypothesis being investigated argues that credit booms or collateral driven asset price boom cycles eventually lead to severe contraction in economic activity, which occurs as the preceding developments are reversed and are propagated via the financial accelerator mechanism. The costly boom periods are shown by the light grey shaded areas. The boom periods, according to the formula used, begin three periods before the start of the periods shown in each graph in Fig. 7.15. House price growth refers to real house prices deflated by the consumer price index.

[4] International evidence shows that the average house price bust lasts for two and a half years, whereas stock price busts last for about one and a half years. The cumulative decline in output below trend is roughly 4.25 percent for the first year after the onset of a house price bust, compared with a 1.25 percent decline after stock price busts. See IMF (2003, 2008), Claessens et al. (2008), Dekten and Smets (2004), Mishkin (2008), Borgy et al. (2009).

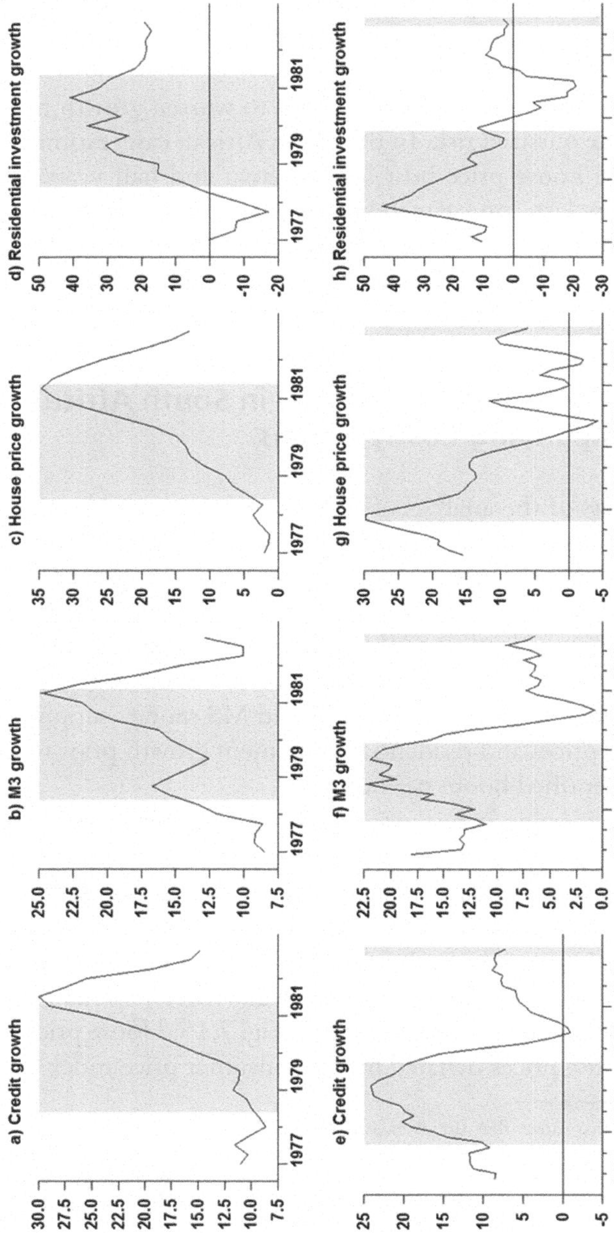

Fig. 7.15 The behavior of selected variables prior to during and after two costly boom episodes (*Source*: Authors' calculations)

The trends in Fig. 7.15 showing the most severe and costly booms during 1982–1983 and 2008 reveal that credit, house price growth and residential investment tend to become negative in costly boom periods identified in the 2000s, compared to the costly booms identified in the early 1980s. The decline in credit and M3 growth confirm that the credit channel is present during costly boom periods while house price growth points to the collateral channel. A similar trend is visible for economic growth, household consumption and gross fixed capital formation in Fig. A7.1 in the Appendix.

These findings suggest that costly equity price booms tend to be associated with credit booms or house price booms, implying that collateral driven asset price boom–bust cycles are followed by severe contractions in economic activity.

7.4.2 Financial Imbalance Build-Ups During the Identified Episodes of Costly Booms

The estimates of the financial imbalance build-ups are captured by the deviations of actual growth rates of these variables from their six-year trailing moving average. This includes showing what happens to these variables before, during and after the identified costly boom episodes. A great deal of the literature suggests that based on deviations from an underlying trend derived using the six-year moving average, this can ring an "alarm."[5] Fig. 7.16a, d and g show the actual growth rates and the six-year trailing moving averages. Fig. 7.16b, e and h show the gaps, capturing imbalances in the first boom periods in the 1980s and Fig. 7.16c, f and i show financial imbalances in the late 2000s.

There is evidence of financial imbalance build-ups during costly boom periods accompanied by massive slowdown—except for residential investment in the 2000s, which began to show weakened build-ups in imbalances before the end of costly boom episodes.

[5] See Kaminsky et al. (1998) and Kaminsky and Reinhart (1999), Borgy et al. (2009), Kannan et al. (2009).

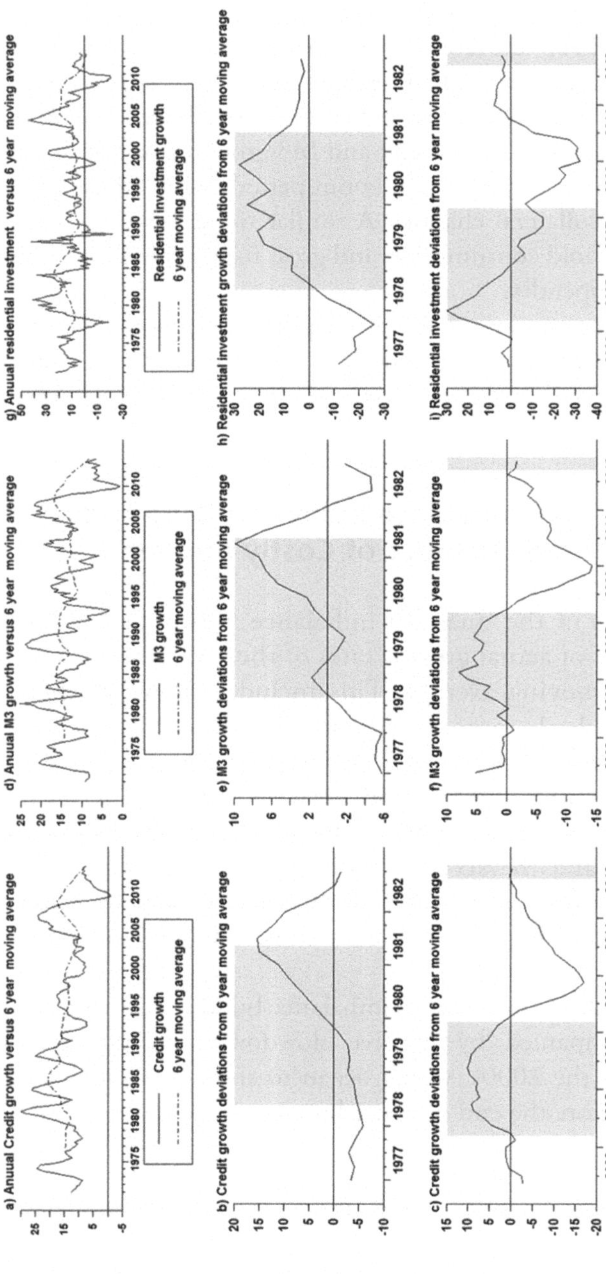

Fig. 7.16 Financial imbalances during two periods of costly booms (*Source*: Authors' calculations)

7.4.3 Inferences From the Role of Monetary Policy Based on Deviations from the Taylor Rule

This section looks at the role of monetary policy in episodes of costly equity price booms. The approach considers the interaction of nominal interest rates, real interest rates, inflation gap and the output gap to assess whether policy was accommodative during these costly boom episodes. The Taylor gap is defined as in Eq. (7.1) to capture whether monetary policy settings were systematically lower than those predicted by the Taylor rule.

$$i_t - \left[r_t * + \pi_t + 0.5\left(\pi_t - \pi_t *\right) + 0.5\left(y_t - y_t *\right) \right] \tag{7.1}$$

Where, r*, π* and y* are the ex-post HP trends derived with λ=1600. A negative gap implies that monetary conditions were accommodative relative to prescriptions of the Taylor rule. The results in Fig. 7.17a show that monetary policy was highly accommodative. However, in Fig. 7.17b this was not necessarily the case in the early part of the booms under the inflation-targeting period.

These results corroborate other studies showing that with inflation typically under control, monetary policy was not the main or systematic

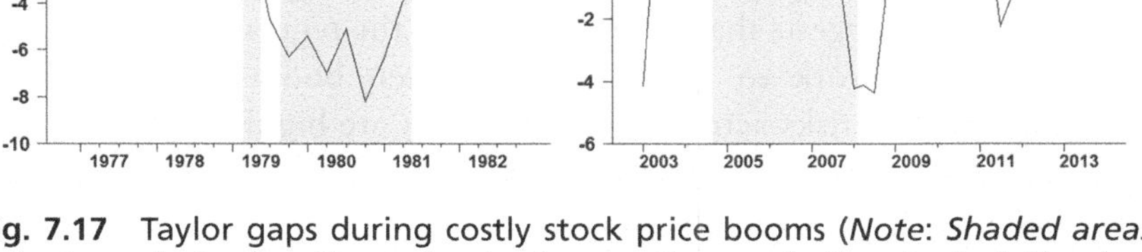

Fig. 7.17 Taylor gaps during costly stock price booms (*Note*: *Shaded areas* refer to periods of costly stock price booms. *Source*: Authors' calculations)

source of the excesses that led to the recent price boom. Rather, monetary policy effectively accommodated these growing imbalances, raising the risk of damaging busts. For ease of reference, the estimated Taylor gaps and four-quarter moving averages for real house prices and real stock price returns are shown in Fig. 7.18.

7.5 Conclusion and Policy Implications

This chapter contrasted the effects of stock price returns and volatility on economic growth. The evidence indicates that the contributions of stock price returns and stock price volatility tend to move in the same direction and reinforce each other. The effects are magnified in the presence of stock price returns. An unexpected positive portfolio outflows shock depresses economic growth significantly for nearly a year and it is transmitted into the economy through volatility and stock returns. Furthermore, evidence shows that the depressing effects of stock price volatility tend to be smaller when compared to those exerted by a positive monetary policy shock. In addition, inflation has depressing effects on GDP growth that are far more severe compared to those of stock price volatility and interest rates.

The findings show that not all booms are followed by costly busts. Costly booms were associated with the build-up of financial imbalances in the form of credit,M3 growth and house price growth. This suggests that policies need to address those asset price booms in which there is feedback between asset prices and credit booms. These credit- and collateral-driven asset price booms may lead to financial instability and damaging effects on the economy.

The Taylor gaps evidence shows that monetary policy did not systematically lead to a build-up in financial imbalances during the pre-2008 asset price bust. This suggests that there is a role for the regulatory and macro-prudential framework to address credit-driven booms. In particular, the monitoring of risks across institutions that are highly correlated and the use of macro-prudential instruments designed specifically to dampen potentially costly credit market cycles.

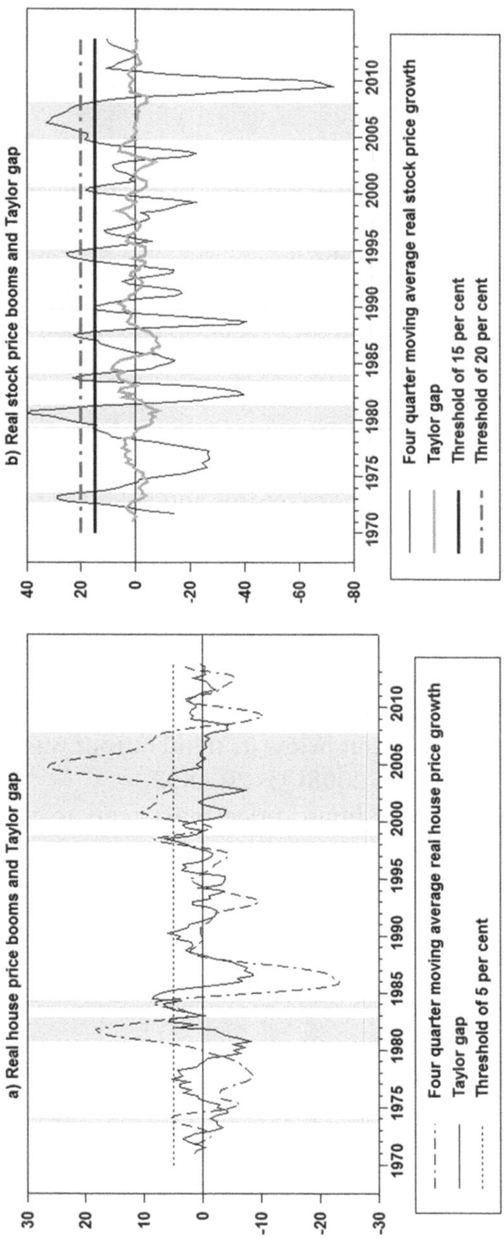

Fig. 7.18 Taylor gaps and real house and stock price booms (*Source*: Authors' calculations)

Summary of Main Findings

- Stock price returns and volatility have different impacts on macroeconomic variables.
- Stock price returns are positively related to economic growth while stock price volatility is negatively related to economic growth.
- GDP growth declines due to unexpected stock price volatility and monetary policy tightening shocks.
- The negative effects of stock price volatility shocks tend to be smaller when compared to those exerted by a positive monetary policy shock.
- Unexpected stock returns shock increases inflation more than it raises economic growth
- Inflation depresses economic growth significantly, to the extent that it neutralizes the stimulating effects of stock returns on GDP growth.
- The contributions of stock price returns and volatility tend to move in the same direction and reinforce each other.
- An unexpected positive portfolio outflows shock depresses economic growth significantly for nearly a year and it is transmitted into economy through volatility and stock returns.
- The findings show that not all booms are followed by costly busts. However, costly stock price busts last approximately two years and the cumulative decline in output below its trend output was the severest at 1.6 percent for the period 2008Q3–2010Q2.
- In addition we find that house price busts tend to worsen growth prospects as they create outsized risks. Average house price busts last for two and half years, whereas stock price busts last nearly seven quarters.

Appendix A7.1

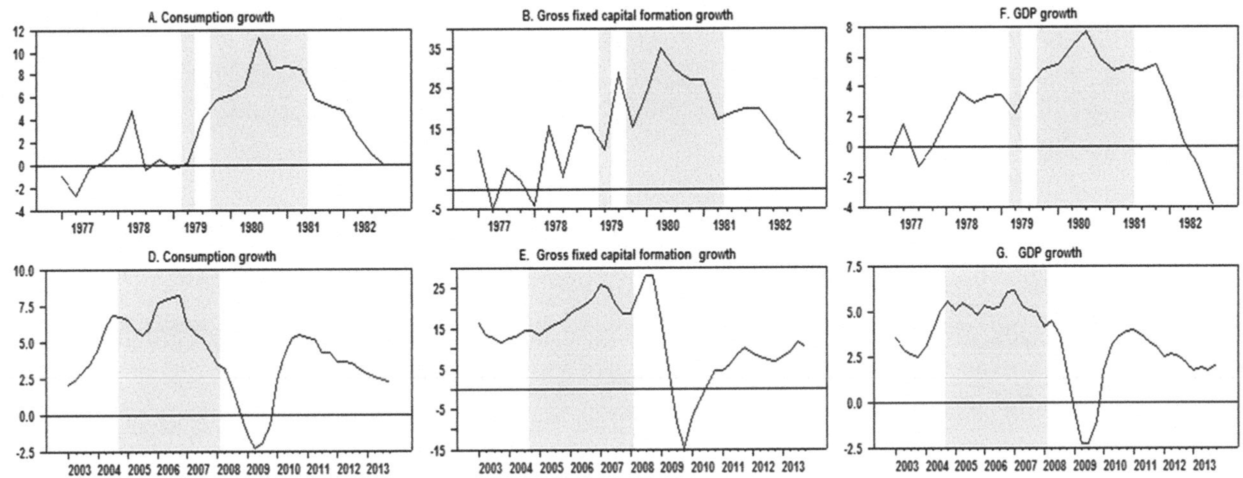

Fig. A7.1 The behavior of selected real variables before, during and after two costly boom episodes (*Source*: Authors' calculations)

8

The Interaction Between Credit Conditions, Monetary Policy and Economic Activity

Learning Objectives

- Understand the construction of the credit conditions index and its importance for policy inferences
- Examine the extent to which accommodative monetary policy post-2009 impacted credit conditions
- Disentangle the effects of credit conditions and those of other adverse business cycles shocks, adverse business confidence and equity price shocks and other bank lending standards
- Asses the different impact of credit conditions on manufacturing production, property market and business confidence
- Establish the interaction between tight credit conditions and monetary policy, the contributions of the monetary policy stance to credit conditions and the amplifying role of credit conditions to repo rate responses to inflationary pressures

N. Gumata, E. Ndou, *Bank Credit Extension and Real Economic Activity in South Africa*, DOI 10.1007/978-3-319-43551-0_8

8.1 Introduction

This chapter extends the preceding analysis by looking at the interaction between credit conditions, monetary policy and real economic activity. Theoretically, the financial accelerator mechanism amplifies the effects of financial cycles on the real economy. This works by affecting borrowers' values of collateral and to a large extent the willingness of the financial system to provide credit to the economy. The literature postulates that shocks that affect the creditworthiness of borrowers tend to accentuate swings in output. The bank capital channel suggests that when bank capital is eroded, banks become more reluctant to lend and may be forced to deleverage, thus leading to even sharper economic downturns.

The events subsequent to the financial crisis demonstrated such conditions and policymakers have come to understand that credit conditions play an important role as sources of shocks and propagators of other shocks. Furthermore, recent empirical evidence has shown that the impact of financial shocks on the real economy and the business cycles heightens the persistence of these shocks. This chapter contributes to policy and academic research by constructing a credit condition index (CCI) for South Africa. Thereafter, the constructed CCI is used in a VAR analysis to examine the extent to which tighter credit conditions (1) impact real economic activity, (2) interact with tight monetary policy conditions and (3) propagate the adverse effects of other shocks.

8.2 Construction of Credit Conditions Index

The CCI differs from the financial conditions index (FCI) and the monetary conditions index (MCI) mainly due to the variables included in the construction of the index. Table 8.1 shows the variables included in the CCI. The wide range of the included variables facilitates the identification of the fundamental characteristics linked to credit conditions emanating from large shifts in asset prices, abrupt shifts in liquidity and the health of the banking system. In addition, the variables provide a comprehensive view of the channels and mechanisms through which credit conditions affect economic cycles. The data is monthly

Table 8.1 Components of the credit conditions index

Debt market indicators	Banking indicators
5-year spread between SA and US government bond	Non-performing loans
Spread between 10-year government bond and 28-days SARB debentures	Return on equity
Spread between corporate and government bonds	Tier 1 capital adequacy ratio
Bond market liquidity ratio	Spread between banks and government bonds
5-year SA banks credit default swap	Spread between bank lending and deposit rate

Source: SARB and authors' calculations

observations from January 2001 to December 2015. The data is grouped into two components: (1) debt market indicators and (2) banking indicators as shown in Table 8.1.

The debt market indicators consist of yields from various asset classes such as bonds, money market and credit derivative instruments issued by the corporate sector entities, national and foreign governments. Credit spreads are then derived from these instruments. Widening credit spreads show deteriorating conditions in credit markets as investors require a high premium to safeguard against risk of default. By contrast, narrow spreads indicate positive investor confidence and improving credit conditions.

Movements in credit spreads contain important signals regarding the evolution of the real economy and risks to the economic outlook. For instance, Gilchrist and Zakrajsek (2012) show that deterioration in the capital position of financial intermediaries leads to a slowdown in credit extension and rising debt financing costs. This has adverse impacts on spending and production decisions.

Liquidity in the bond market also forms an important component of the CCI, while banking sector indicators are also taken into consideration in the construction of the CCI. Banking sector indicators play an important role as banks are integral in the provision of credit. When operating in the loan market, banks have to manage a variety of risks such as credit and interest rate risks, bearing in mind the need to maximize shareholder returns. For instance, rising levels of defaults might induce banks to reduce their lending or tighten their lending conditions.

Simultaneously, without adequate capital positions and higher funding costs, banks might be forced to curtail the extension of credit or tighten their lending conditions.

8.2.1 The Credit Conditions Index

The variables used in CCI are standardized and the equal weighting approach is applied to derive a common factor and construct the index. The constructed CCI is shown in Fig. 8.1. Positive values indicate that prevailing credit conditions are tighter while negative values indicate looser credit conditions.

Based on the CCI, credit conditions were tighter prior 2004 and during 2008 to 2010. Thereafter, credit conditions have more or less fluctuated around the zero level, suggesting neutral conditions with a loose bias.

8.2.2 Credit Conditions Index and Business Cycle and Bank Lending Standard Indicators

Is the constructed CCI a suitable measure of credit conditions in the economy? How does it compare with various business cycle indicators,

Fig. 8.1 The credit conditions index (*Source*: Authors' calculations)

consumer and business confidence and the Bureau of Economics Research (BER) Ernst and Young (EY) lending standards? To establish the nature of the relationship with other business cycle indicators and bank credit lending standards, Figs. 8.2 and 8.3 show the bilateral relationships between the CCI and the BER EY bank credit lending standards. The BER EY bank credit lending standard is a quarterly opinion survey on bank credit standards for approving applications for loans and credit lines. It is a qualitative measure by construction but is also aimed at measuring credit conditions in the banking sector.

From Fig. 8.2a it is evident that the CCI and the coincident business cycle indicator (CBC) move in opposite directions. This is especially the case from 2004 and onwards. The observed relationship is consistent with theoretical assertions that looser credit conditions tend to be associated with the period of an expansionary business cycle phase. On the other hand, tighter credit conditions tend to correspond to contractionary or subdued business cycle phases.

The slope and R-squared in the scatter plots are bigger in Fig. 8.2b than in 8.2d, indicating that the relationship between the CCI and the CBC is much stronger than that between the CCI and the leading indicator (LBC). In addition, the negative relationships suggest that an improvement in changes in the CBC and the LBC leads to loosening of credit conditions. Similarly, consumer (CCI) and business confidence (BCI) are needed for looser credit conditions as shown Fig. 8.2f, h.

The lead relationships show that worsening in credit conditions leads to a transitory deterioration in the LBC and CBC in Fig. 8.3a. However, the negative association is more pronounced in relation to the CBC than the LBC indicator.

What happens when improvement in the LBC and CBC indicators precede the credit conditions index? Fig. 8.3b shows that an improvement in the LBC and CBC indicators leads to the loosening of credit conditions. However, the credit conditions are loosened more to the improvement in the CBC indicators than the LBC indicators. The scatter plots in Fig. 8.4 reveal that the BER/EY bank credit lending standards for retail and investment banks explains about 14 and 18 percent of the changes in the CCI, respectively.

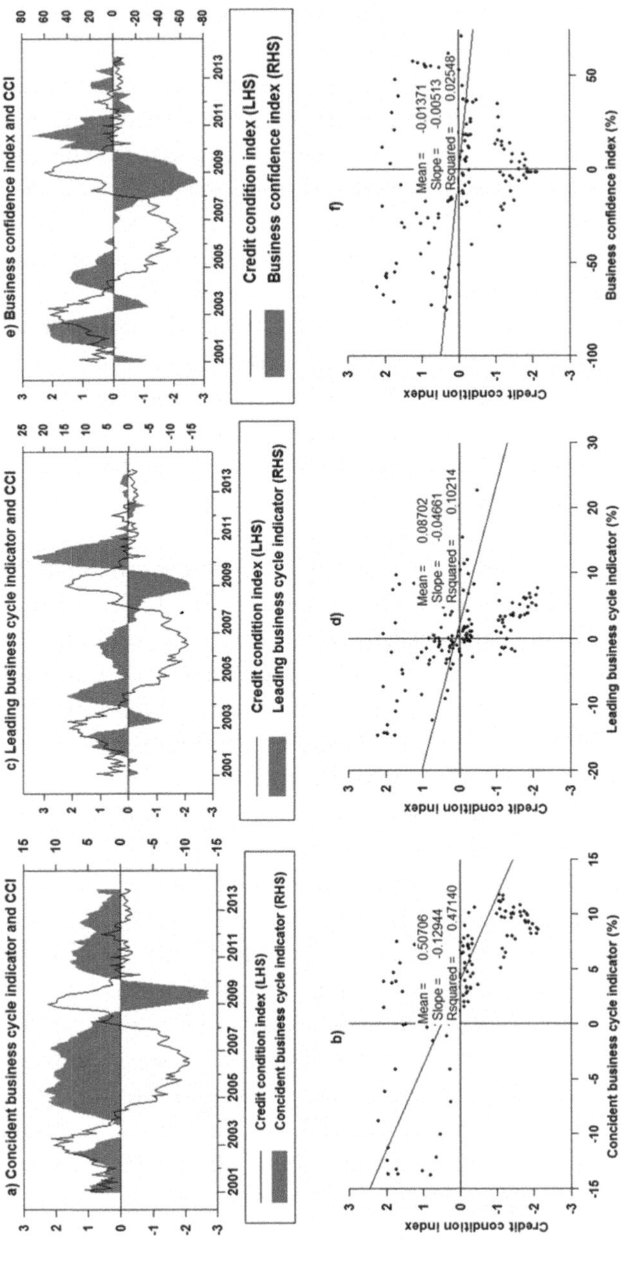

Fig. 8.2 The credit conditions index and other business cycle indicators (*Source*: Authors' calculations)

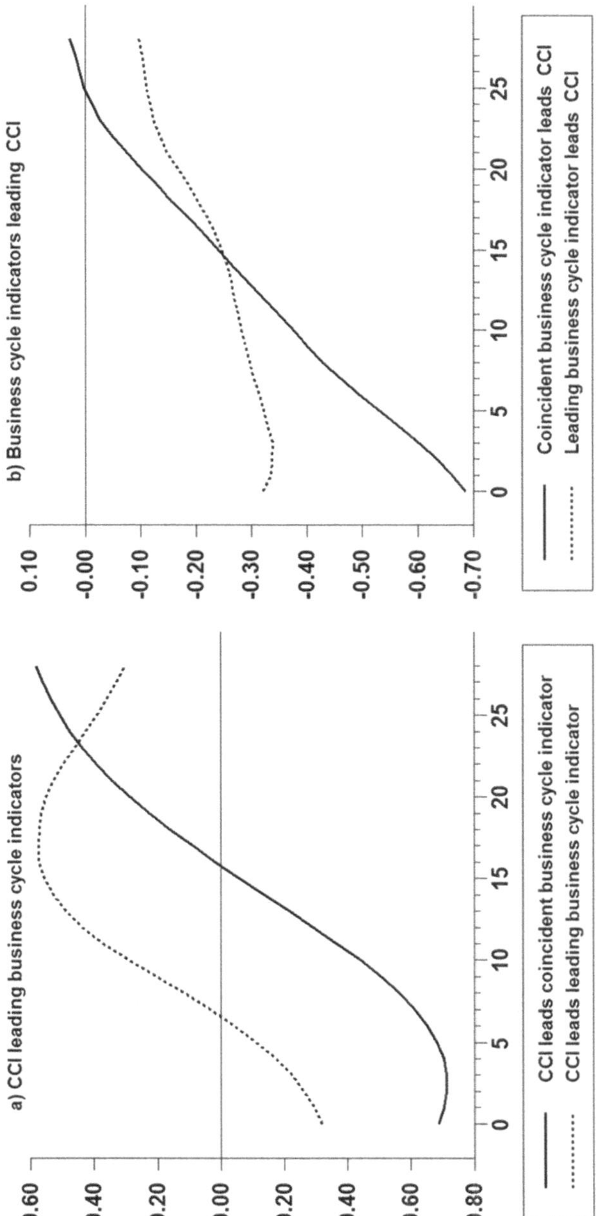

Fig. 8.3 Plot of cross correlations between the CCI and business cycle indicators (*Source*: Authors' calculations)

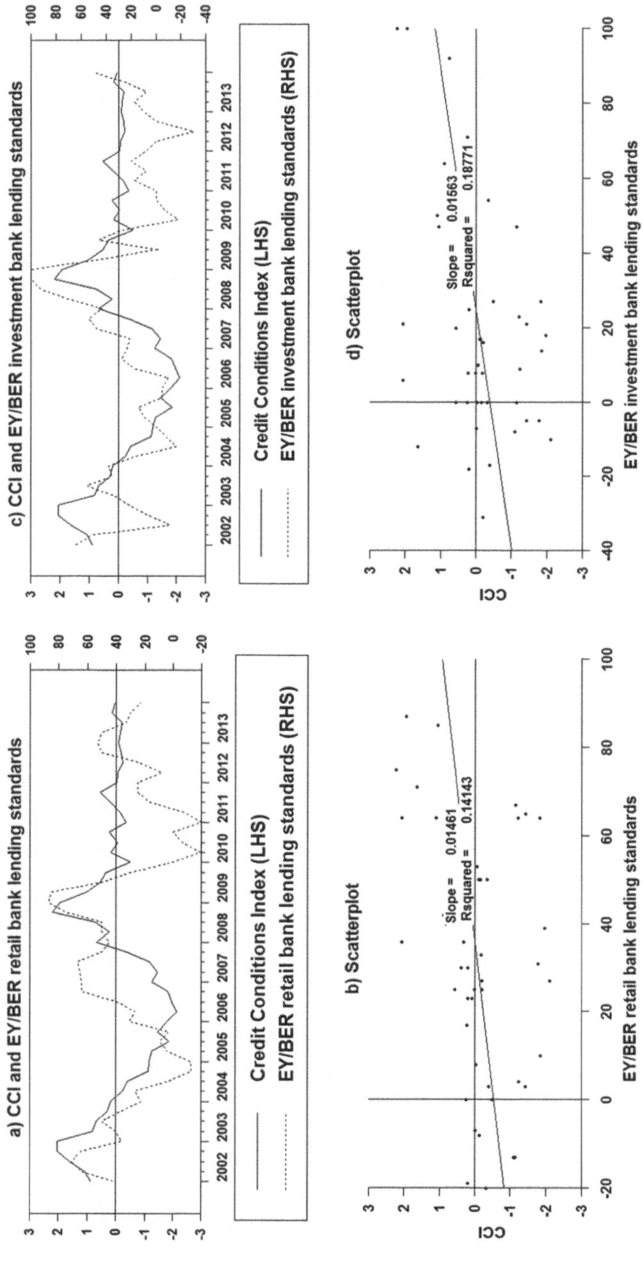

Fig. 8.4 The credit conditions index and bank credit lending standards (*Source*: SARB, BER and authors' calculations)

For instance, as banks started to loosen their lending standards during 2003 to 2006, credit conditions were also loose. Similarly, when banks applied stricter lending criteria between 2006 and 2008, credit conditions were tight.

8.2.3 The Relationships Between Credit Conditions, Repo Rate and Economic Activity

What is the macroeconomic and policy significance of the CCI? The relationships between (1) the CCI and manufacturing production growth and (2) the CCI and the repo rate in Fig. 8.5 show that there is a negative relationship between manufacturing growth and the CCI. For instance, the decline in manufacturing growth in 2009 coincided with severe tightening in the CCI. This evidence suggests that tighter credit conditions tend to be accompanied by a decline in or weakness of manufacturing production. Overall, the bilateral relationships establish that there is a negative relationship between manufacturing production growth and the CCI.

Fig. 8.5c shows that although the relationship between the monetary policy stance and the credit conditions is positive, there are lags in the reaction of the CCI to the repo rate. This is especially evident around 2006 and 2008 when credit conditions were still tighter. Similarly, when the repo rate began declining at the end of 2008, credit conditions only started to loosen with a delay. Fig. 8.5d indicates a negative relationship between the CCI and manufacturing production and a positive relationship with the repo rate. Is this conclusion robust in light of different techniques? Yes, Fig. 8.6 shows the bilateral cross correlations between (1) manufacturing growth and the CCI and (2) the repo rate and the CCI.

Fig. 8.6a shows a negative relationship between manufacturing growth and the CCI. This suggests that when credit conditions tighten, growth in manufacturing production declines. The reverse suggests that an improvement in growth in manufacturing production leads to loosening in credit conditions. In Fig. 8.6b there is a positive relationship when the repo rate leads the CCI. This suggests that a tightening in the monetary policy stance is accompanied by tighter credit conditions.

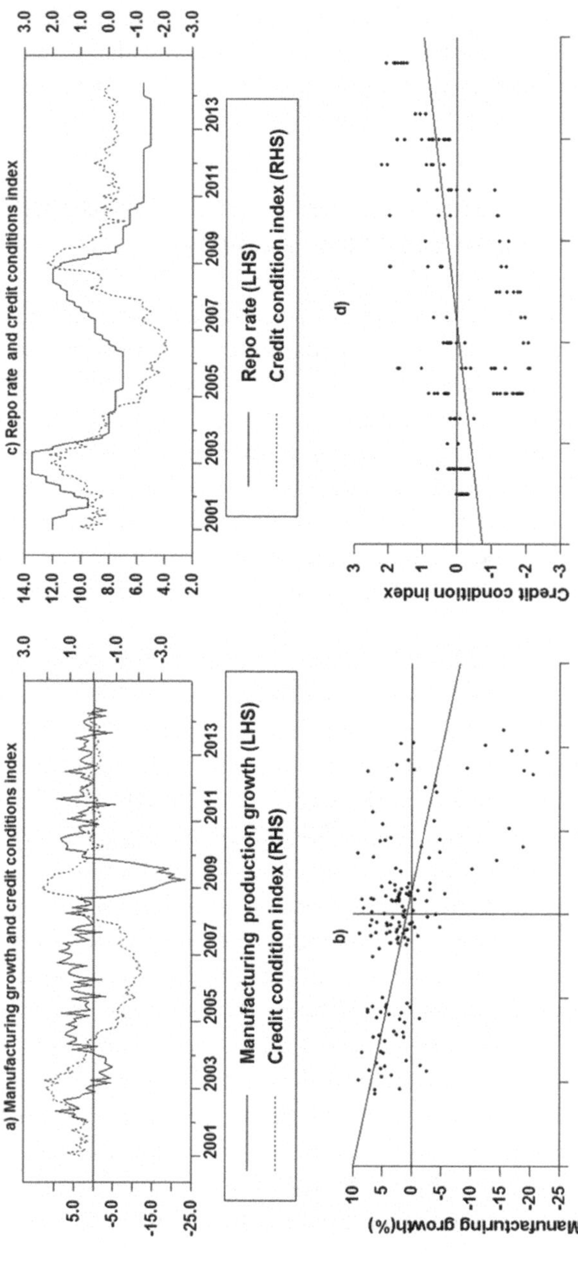

Fig. 8.5 The CCI, manufacturing production and the repo rate (*Source*: SARB and authors' calculations)

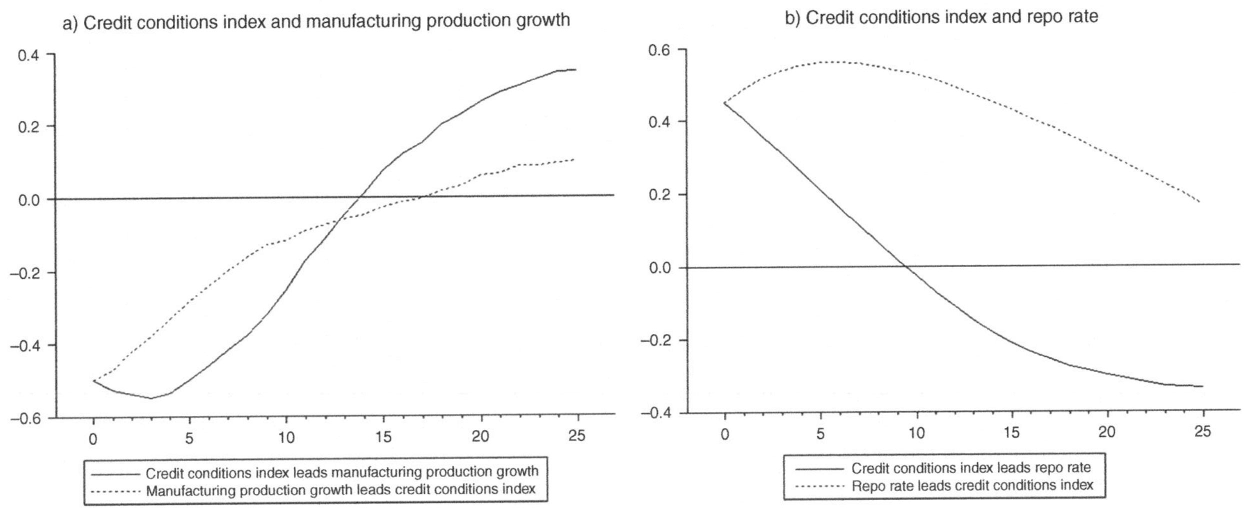

Fig. 8.6 Cross correlation between the CCI, manufacturing production and the repo rate (*Source*: Authors' calculations)

The lagged responses of the credit conditions to the loosening monetary policy stance are confirmed.

8.3 The Empirical Methodology

For the empirical analysis this chapter estimates a vector autoregression (VAR) model including growth in economic activity proxied by manufacturing production growth, the repo rate and the CCI. The data is monthly (M) data from January 2001 to June 2014. The repo rate captures the stance of monetary policy and the CCI captures the state of banking financing conditions. In the estimations, the variables are ordered such that economic activity is exogenous to the model and the policy rate is placed second, suggesting that it responds contemporaneously to manufacturing production. The CCI is placed last, suggesting that this variable reacts contemporaneously to the current state of economic activity and the policy stance.

The model is estimated using three lags as selected by the Akaike Information Criterion (AIC) and includes a dummy variable for the recession in 2009. The dummy variable equals one for period 2009M1 to 2009M9 and zero otherwise. The battery of tests conducted include (1) testing for robustness to ordering, (2) sensitivity of the model to size by adding more variables such as the repo rate gap which is calculated as the difference between the repo rate and the trend of the repo rate extracted using the Hodrick–Prescott (HP) filter, and (3) sensitivity to sample size by extending the model. The shaded areas in the impulse responses denote the 16th and 84th percentiles for confidence bands. The impulses are responses to one standard deviation shock.

8.3.1 Empirical Results and Discussion

How does economic activity respond to tight credit conditions shocks? Fig. 8.7 shows that a tighter CCI shock leads to economically and statistically significant decline in economic activity. In turn, monetary policy is eased in response to the adverse economic developments. Both tighter

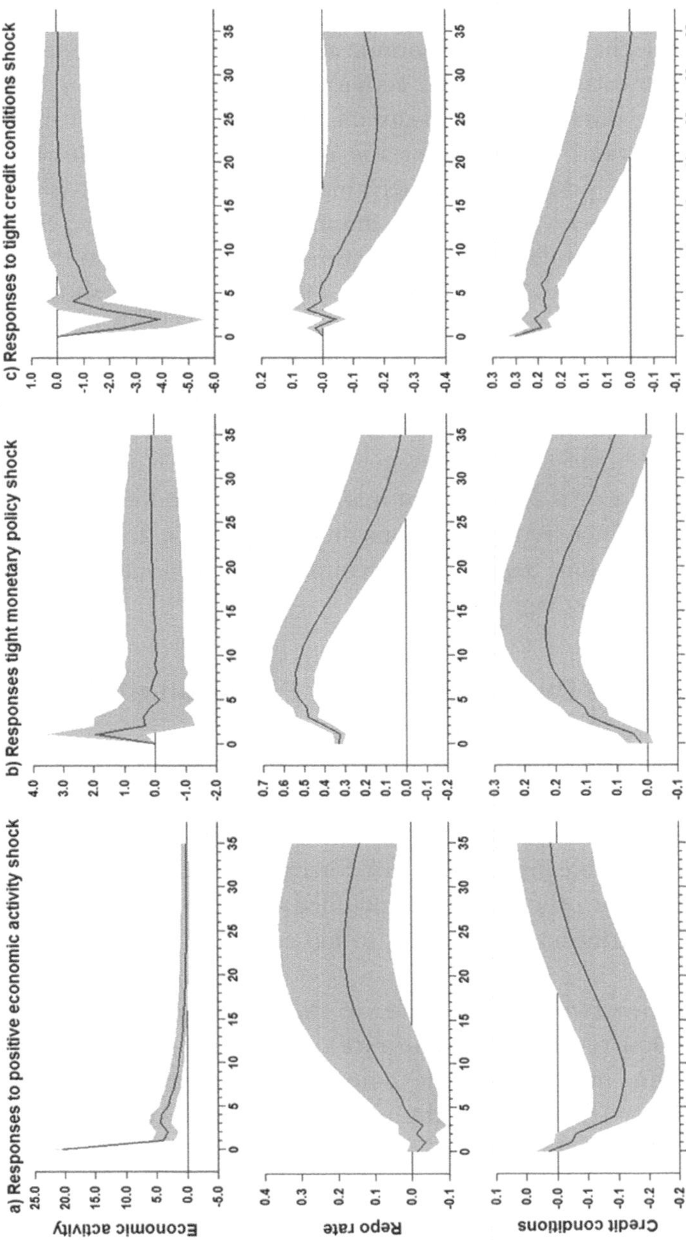

Fig. 8.7 The effects of tight credit conditions and monetary policy shocks (*Source*: Authors' calculations)

monetary policy and credit conditions shocks lower economic activity significantly, but the decline in economic activity is not permanent.

Would the effects of economic activity on credit conditions index vary when using durable and non-durable components of total manufacturing production? To assess for the differential credit conditions, responses to three positive manufacturing production growth shocks were examined, namely: (1) aggregate manufacturing production shock, (2) durable goods manufacturing production shock and (3) non-durable goods manufacturing production shocks. Fig. 8.8a, c and e show that unexpected positive manufacturing production growth leads to loosening in credit conditions. Positive total manufacturing production growth shocks loosen credit conditions for nearly 16 months, which is double the duration exerted by positive shocks in the durable and non-durable components.

What happens to the responses of manufacturing production and its components to tighter credit conditions shock? Fig. 8.8b, d, f shows that tighter credit conditions depress total manufacturing production and its component for at most eight months.

8.3.2 Repo Rate Dynamics and the Evolution of the Credit Conditions Index

The contributions of the repo rate to changes in the CCI are assessed using a historical decomposition approach. The historical contributions break down the variable into its own base forecast, own contributions and the contributions of other variables included in the model. Therefore, the repo rate contributions can result in looser as well as tighter credit conditions.

Fig. 8.9b shows two distinct cycles of the repo rate contributions. (1) Around 2004 to 2007 the repo rate contributed to looser credit conditions. This means that the counterfactual credit conditions would have been less loose in the absence of the lower policy rate environment. And (2), around 2011 to mid-2014, suggesting that the prolonged period of easier monetary policy helped in loosening credit conditions.

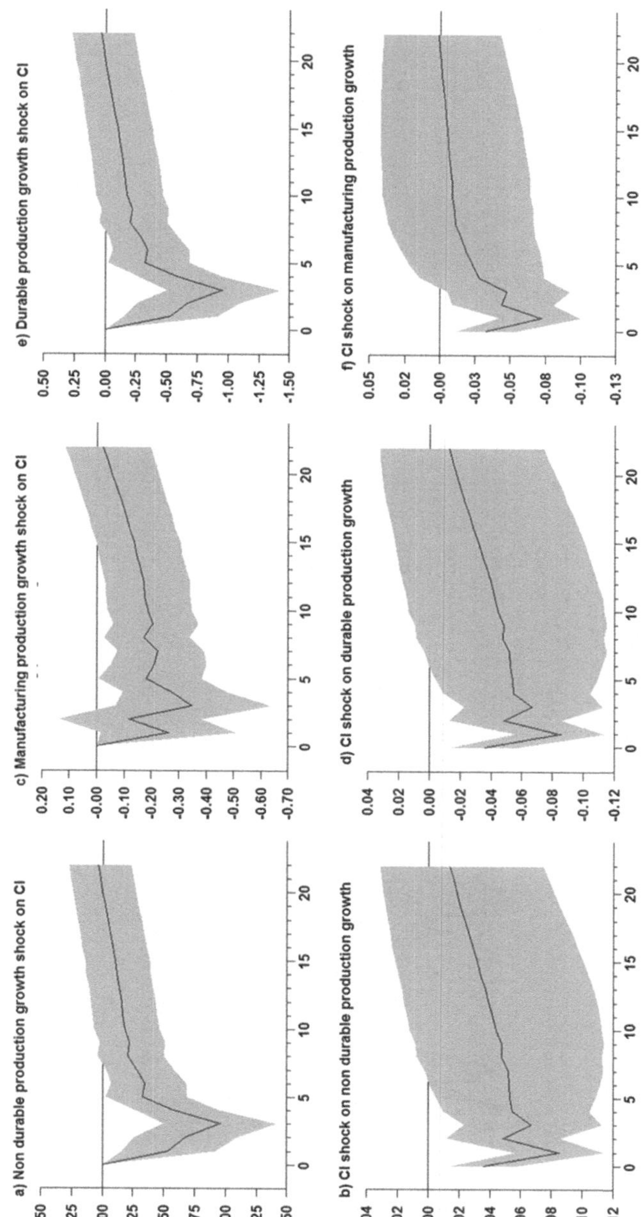

Fig. 8.8 Responses to positive economic activity shocks and tight credit conditions (*Source*: Authors' calculations)

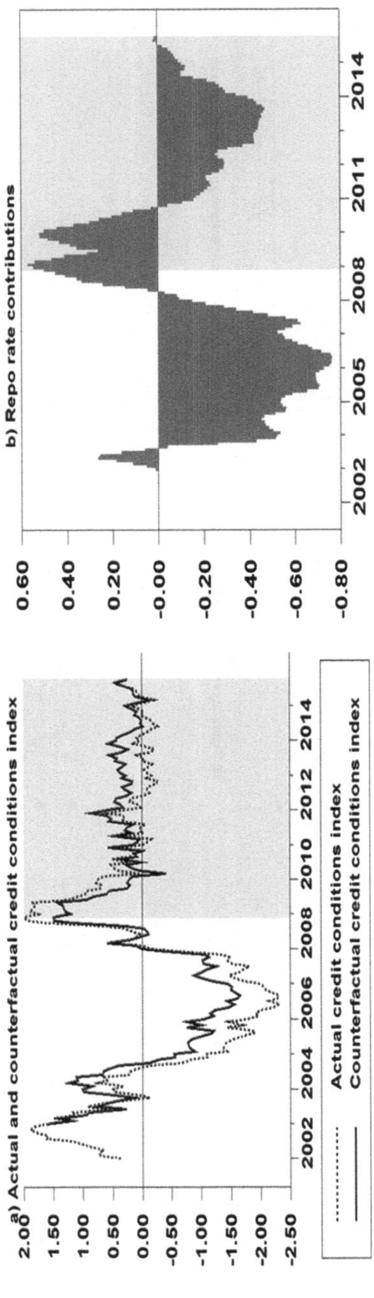

Fig. 8.9 Actual and counterfactual CCI and repo rate contributions (*Source*: Authors' calculations)

8.3.3 Impact of Credit Conditions on Residential and Non-residential Sector Activity

The residential sector is important in the transmission of credit conditions and monetary policy shocks. It is possible that residential sector activity can remain subdued for a prolonged period, even when the policy rate declines if credit conditions are still tight. To assess the role of the residential sector, this section shows the extent to which improvements in this sector's impact on credit conditions.

Fig. 8.10 shows that a positive shock in nominal house prices, residential and non-residential building plans passed results in looser credit conditions. This suggests that credit conditions are loosened. However, improvements in non-residential building plans passed has a weaker effect in stimulating credit conditions.

Fig. 8.11 shows that tightening in credit conditions impacts residential and non-residential sectors. House price growth contracts but insignificantly, non-residential building plans growth falls significantly for 14 months, which is longer than the 7 months in residential building plans growth. Thus, the property sector variables respond in a heterogeneous way to tighter credit conditions.

8.4 Tight Credit Conditions Versus Contractionary Monetary Policy and Negative Equity Price Shock

This section conducts robustness analysis by increasing the number of variables in the model. The effects of unexpected equity price index decline are included in the model. Fig. 8.12 shows that tighter monetary policy shocks and credit conditions significantly lower economic activity. These findings are similar to those established using a three variable model. Evidence indicates that tighter monetary policy shock

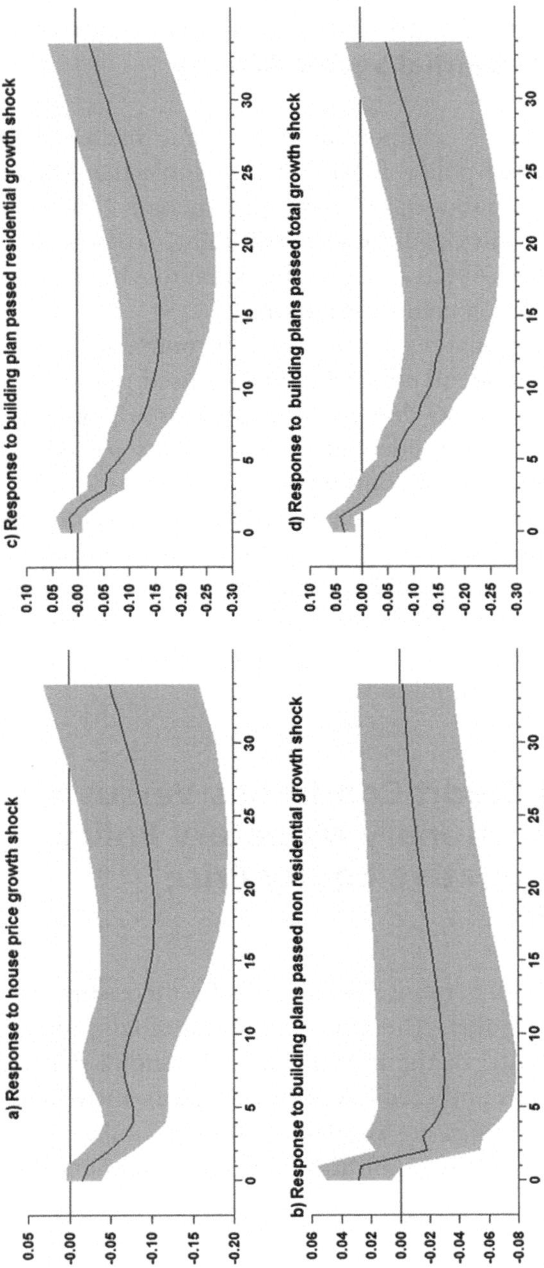

Fig. 8.10 Credit conditions responses to property market indicators (*Source:* Authors' calculations)

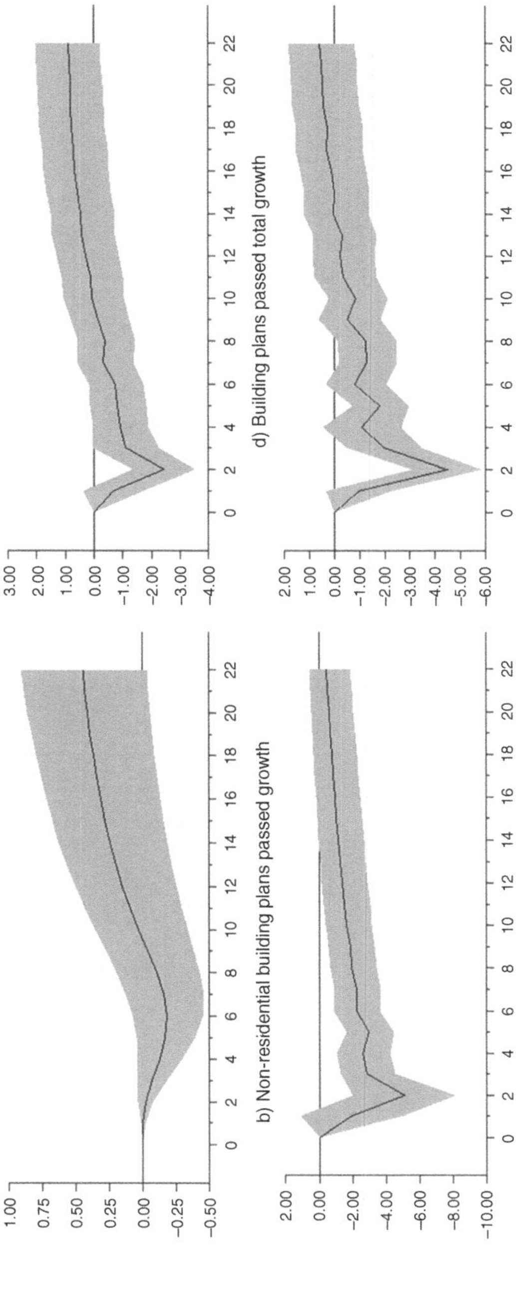

Fig. 8.11 Responses of property sector variables to tight credit condition shock (*Source*: Authors' calculations)

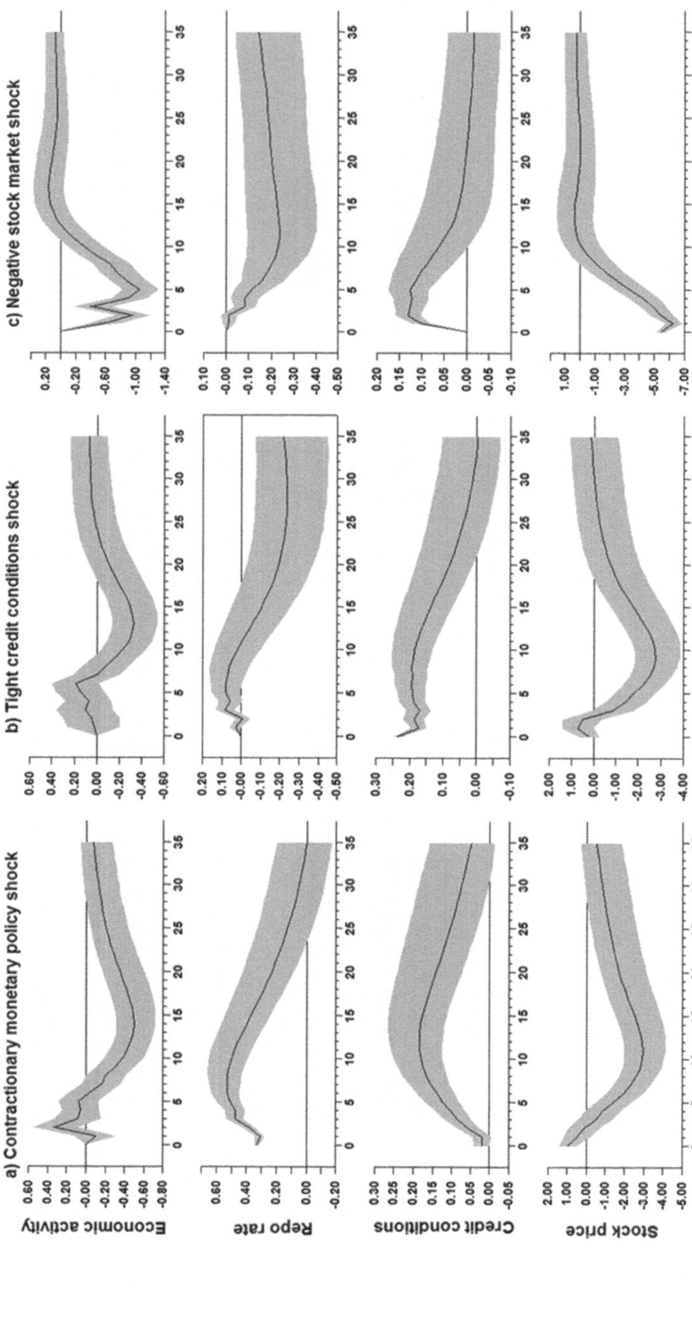

Fig. 8.12 The responses to negative stock price and tight credit condition shocks (*Source*: Authors' calculations)

leads to tighter credit conditions. These effects are robust to the inclusion of changes in equity price growth.

8.4.1 Tight Credit Conditions Versus Contractionary Monetary Policy and Negative Business Confidence Shock Effects

Further robustness analysis uses variables in levels and includes the business confidence index. For this exercise the variables are ordered as follows: total manufacturing production, business confidence index, the repo rate and the credit condition index. Fig. 8.13a shows that the deterioration of the business conditions index weakens economic activity with a delay of about 10 months and credit conditions tighten significantly between 3 and 25 months.

A tighter credit conditions shock in Fig. 8.13c leads to a quick deterioration between 2 and 13 months in economic growth. It is evident that the business confidence index does not decline significantly in response to negative credit conditions. Hence, the effects associated with a negative business confidence shock differ from those of a tighter credit conditions shock.

8.4.2 Tight Credit Conditions Versus Negative Coincident and Leading Business Cycle Shocks

For further robustness analysis the role of the coincident and leading business cycles indicators are assessed. It is possible that the results shown so far may be capturing the effects of the deterioration in the leading and coincident business cycle indicators. In the estimations here, the BCI and the LBC and CBC indicators are replaced and included separately. Fig. 8.14a shows that the deterioration in the CBC indicator lowers economic activity for nearly 15 months. This is similar to the duration exerted by the deterioration in the LBC indicator in Fig. 8.14b.

The tighter credit conditions significantly depress economic activity for nearly 25 months, which is relatively longer than the effects

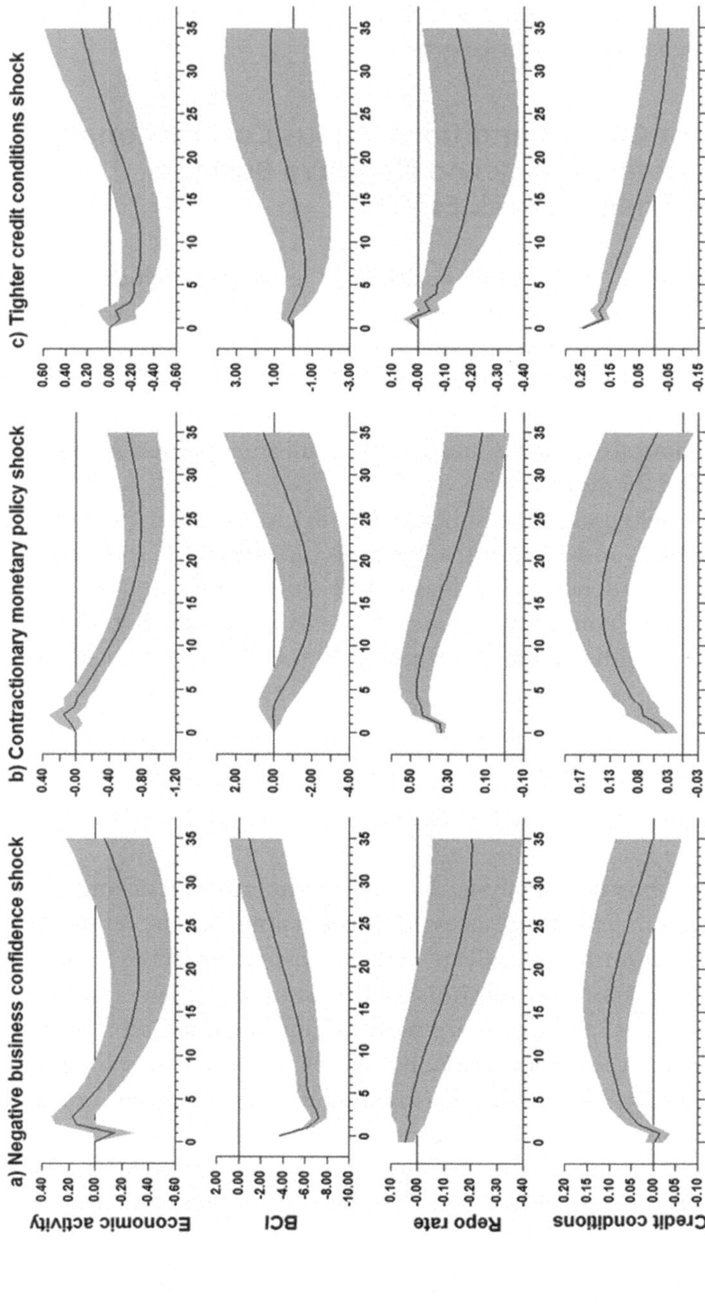

Fig. 8.13 Responses to business confidence index and tighter credit condition shock (*Source:* Authors' calculations)

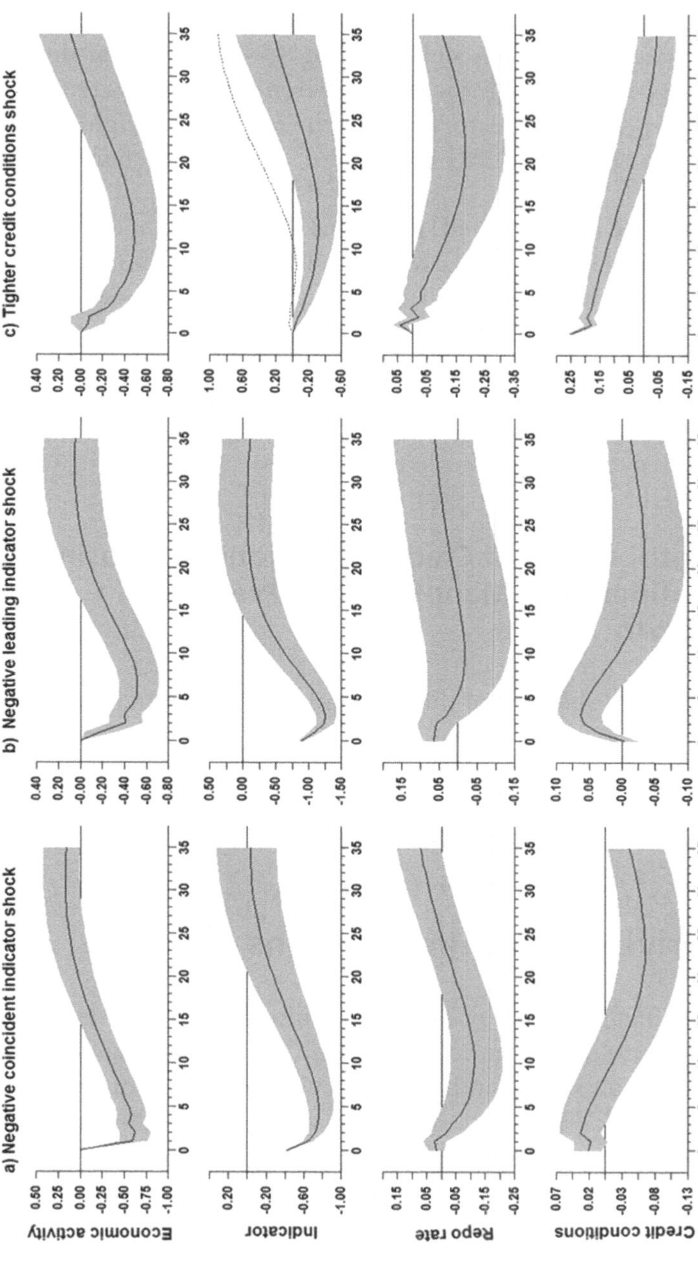

Fig. 8.14 Effects of negative business cycles indicators and tighter credit conditions shocks (*Source:* Authors' calculations)

due to the deterioration in the CBC and LBC indicators, respectively. The tighter credit conditions shock in Fig. 8.14c shows that the LBC indicator responds in a significantly different way compared to the CBC indicator. Both indicators decline in response to tighter credit conditions. However, the CBC indicator declines more than the leading indicator.

In addition, the repo rate tends to decline significantly in response to a tight credit conditions shock relative to the deterioration in the LBC and CBC indicators. Furthermore, there are some interdependencies such that the deterioration in the leading and coincident business cycles indicators lead to transitory tighter credit conditions. Overall, the robustness analysis shows that indeed the effects of tighter credit conditions differ from those of the deterioration in business confidence, LBC and CBC indicators.

8.4.3 Contributions of Credit Conditions and Business Confidence to Manufacturing Production Growth

The historical contributions of the BCI and CCI to manufacturing production since 2003 are shown in Fig. 8.15. The evidence reveals that the contributions of these two variables tend to be in the same direction, although the magnitudes are large with respect to the BCI. However, the contributions of the CCI fluctuate less relative to those of the BCI.

8.5 Deriving Policy Implications

This chapter concludes by looking at the counterfactual analysis to determine the extent to which the CCI amplifies (1) the policy rate responses to positive inflation shocks and (2) economic activity responses to positive repo rate shock. The counterfactual analysis involves shutting off the effects of the CCI to determine the counterfactual responses. The VAR model used to generate the counterfactual responses includes inflation,

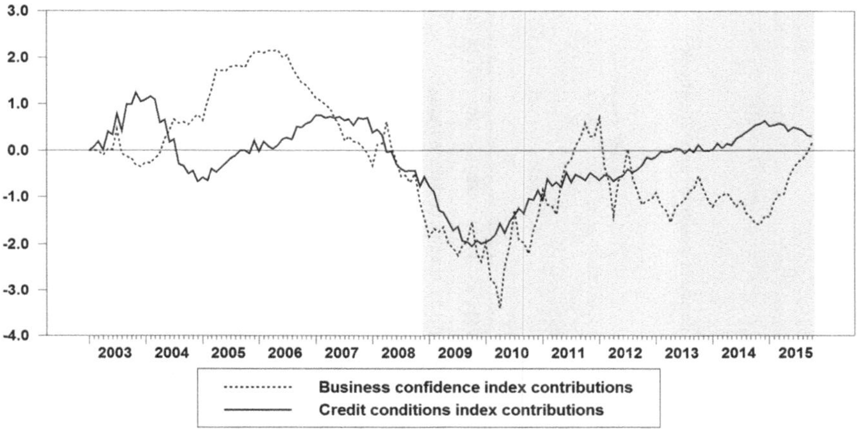

Fig. 8.15 Historical contributions of BCI and CCI to total manufacturing production (*Source*: Authors' calculations)

manufacturing production growth, changes in the BCI, repo rate and CCI. In the estimations, the BCI and the CCI are introduced separately to assess the individual responses.

Fig. 8.16 shows that the repo rate is tightened due to positive inflation shocks whether CCI is included or not. This implies that monetary policy has a primary mandate of enforcing price stability. However, the evidence indicates that the magnitudes of the repo rate tightening differ. The repo is tightened less in the presence of tight credit conditions than what the counterfactual suggests. The repo rate adjustments are less aggressive in responding to inflationary pressures when credit conditions are tight. The estimations suggest that in the long term the repo rate may be nearly 35 basis points lower, as shown in Fig. 8.16b.

In addition, Fig. 8.16c shows that the monetary policy tightening shocks lowers output growth more in the presence of tight credit conditions than when these are shut off. Output growth declines by as much as 0.5 percentage points and policy rate is less tightened in the presence of tight credit conditions.

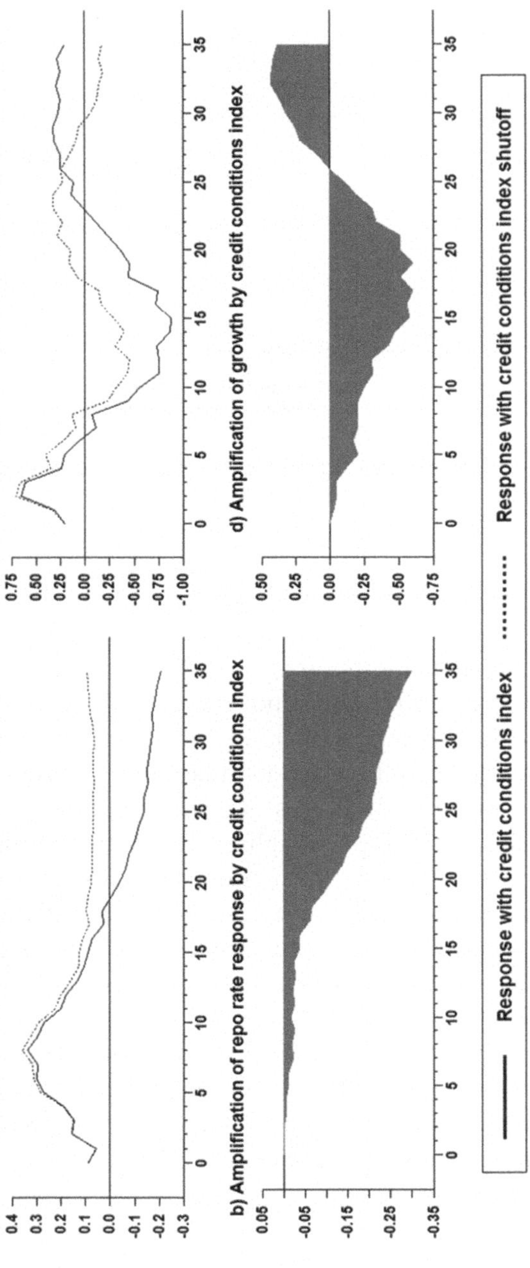

Fig. 8.16 Actual and counterfactual repo rate and economic activity responses (*Source*: Authors' calculations)

8.6 Conclusion and Policy Implications

The effects of negative shocks to credit conditions on real economic activity are similar to those of negative shocks to business confidence, the leading and coincident business cycle indicators. This suggests that policymakers should be cognizant that tight credit conditions can accentuate worsening economic conditions and the vice versa. Hence it is important for policymakers to diagnose the cause of both worsening indicators of business conditions and credit conditions. In addition, policymakers should be aware that monetary policy should be loosened during periods of exogenous tightening in credit conditions. This is because tightening monetary policy will just reinforce the feedback effects.

The repo rate tightening relative to positive inflation shocks shows that whether the credit conditions index is included or not, monetary policy has a mandate to enforce price stability. But evidence indicates the magnitudes of tightening differ. These findings have implications for monetary policy conduct. The repo is tightened less in the presence of tight credit conditions than what the counterfactual suggests. This shows that monetary policymakers should be less aggressive in tightening the repo rate when curbing inflationary pressures when credit markets conditions are tight.

Summary of Findings

- The chapter constructed a credit conditions index based on bank and debt market variables
- The credit conditions index suggests that credit conditions were tighter prior to 2004 and 2008–2010
- Credit conditions index fluctuated around the zero level around since 2014 suggesting neutral credit conditions
- Tighter credit conditions index shocks lead to significant declines in economic activity; the monetary policy stance is eased in response to adverse credit conditions
- Residential and non-residential building plans passed decline significantly for a short period in response to tighter credit conditions

- Historical decomposition shows the repo rate contributed to looser credit conditions in the 2004 to 2007 cycle and mid-2010–2013
- The effects of tight credit conditions shocks differ to those of negative shocks to business confidence, the leading and coincident business cycle indicators
- The tightening in the repo rate is less aggressive in the presence of tight credit conditions.

9

Credit Conditions and the Amplification of Exchange Rate Depreciation and Other Unexpected Macroeconomic Shocks

Learning Objectives

- See the different impacts of CCI on credit to households and companies.
- Examine the fluctuations and nonlinearities induced by the CCI on GDP growth and repo rate responses to inflation before, during and after the global financial crisis.
- Look at the impact of tight credit conditions on credit driven demand shocks and propagation of rand depreciation shocks on inflation and the exchange rate pass-through.

9.1 Introduction

Developments in credit markets can lead to tighter conditions independent of changes in the policy stance. This means that conditions in the banking sector, capital and debt markets become sources of shocks. In addition, it has become evident that despite the uncertainty involved in the measurement of the output gap, the negative output gap conveys

N. Gumata, E. Ndou, *Bank Credit Extension and Real Economic Activity in South Africa*, DOI 10.1007/978-3-319-43551-0_9

limited information about the inflationary pressures post-2009, hence suggestions that the Philips curve has flattened. This chapter determines the size of the amplifications induced by credit conditions on the responses of GDP growth to positive repo rate and inflation shocks. In addition, inflation would respond differently to rand–US dollar depreciation shocks in the absence of the credit conditions index (CCI). Positive inflation shocks lead the repo rate to increase but remain lower that the level reached when credit conditions index is shut off in the model.

9.2 How Do Credit Conditions and Lending Standards Impact GDP Growth?

The analysis begins by showing the effects of the CCI and the Bureau of Economics Research (BER) Ernst and Young (EY) lending standards on GDP growth. The relationships shown in Fig. 9.1b, d show that the CCI is positively related to the BER/EY lending standards, meaning that tight credit conditions also capture the tightening of lending criteria by banks.

On the other hand, the negative relationships between GDP, CCI and the BER/EY lending standards suggests that improved GDP growth results in the loosening of the lending standards and credit conditions. However, credit extension has displayed diverging trends with credit growth to companies growing faster than that to households. Is it possible that the tightening in credit conditions tells us more about the household sector conditions? In Fig. 9.2b the bigger slope magnitude than in Fig. 9.2d suggests that household credit growth seems to be more sensitive to changes in the CCI compared to credit to companies.

In addition, because the housing sector constitutes a larger share of household finances and credit to the household sector, Fig. 9.3 shows the relationship between the CCI, repo rate, nominal house prices and the average mortgage repayments on an 80 percent mortgage bond. The relationship shows that tight credit conditions are positively related to mortgage repayments. However, in Fig. 9.3 the R-squares suggest that mortgage repayments are highly responsive to changes in the repo rate compared to house prices.vvIn addition, Fig. 9.4 shows that house prices

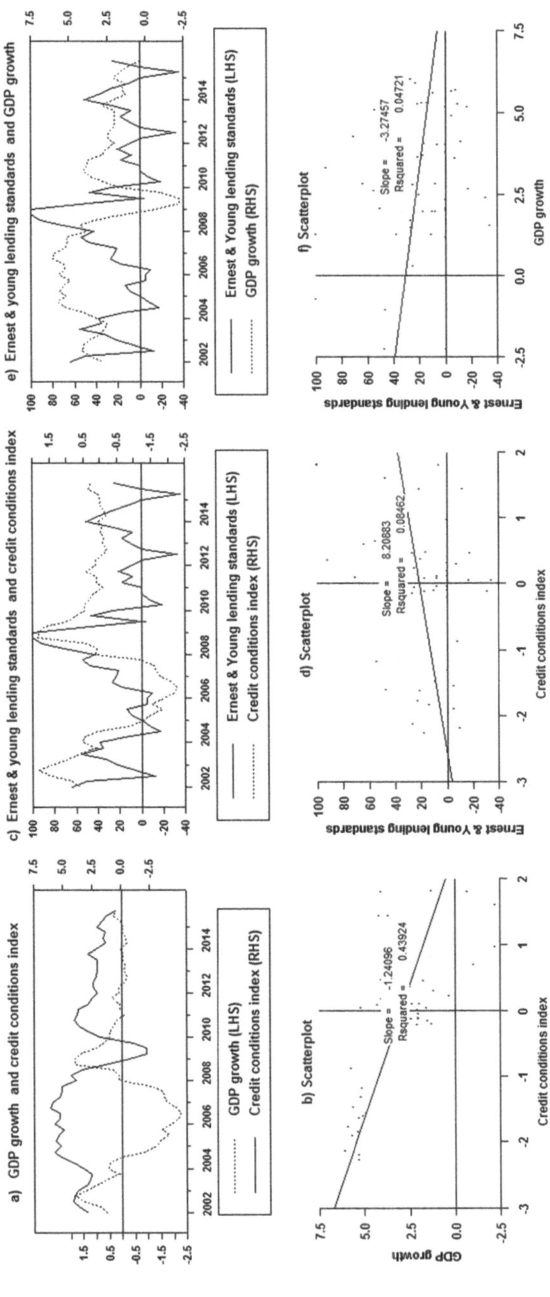

Fig. 9.1 Credit conditions, GDP and lending standards (*Source*: SARB, BER and authors' calculations)

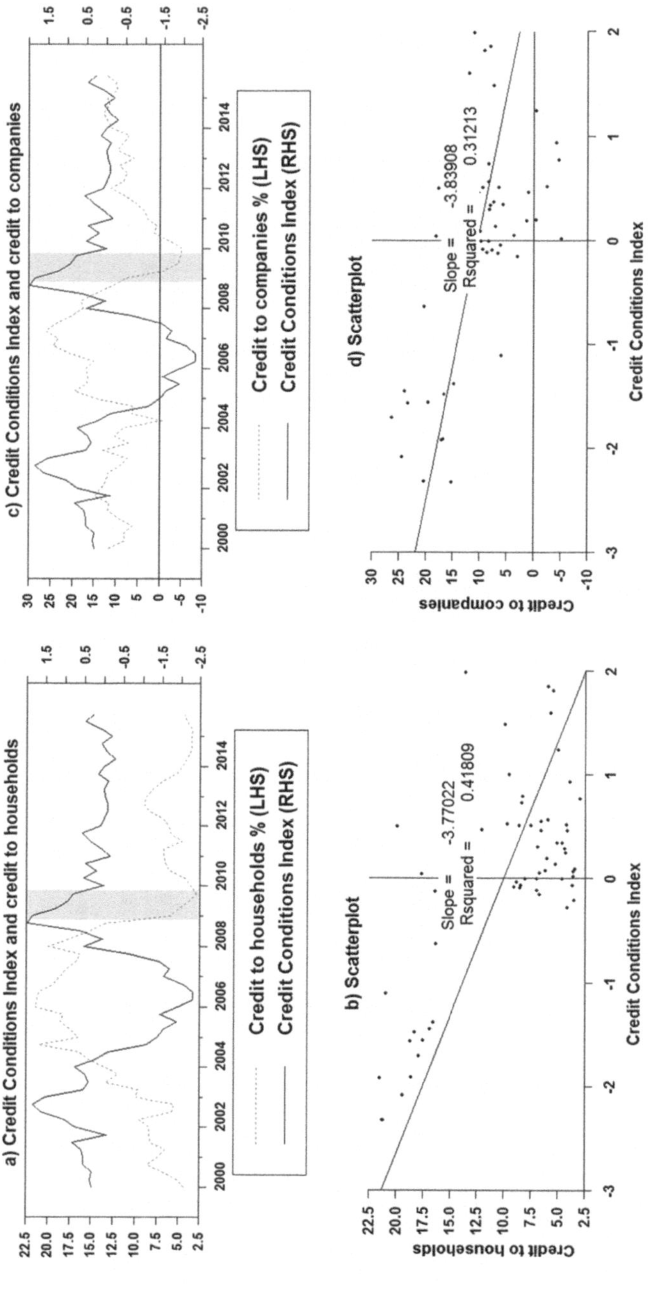

Fig. 9.2 Relationship between the credit conditions index and sectorial credit (*Source*: SARB, BER and authors' calculations)

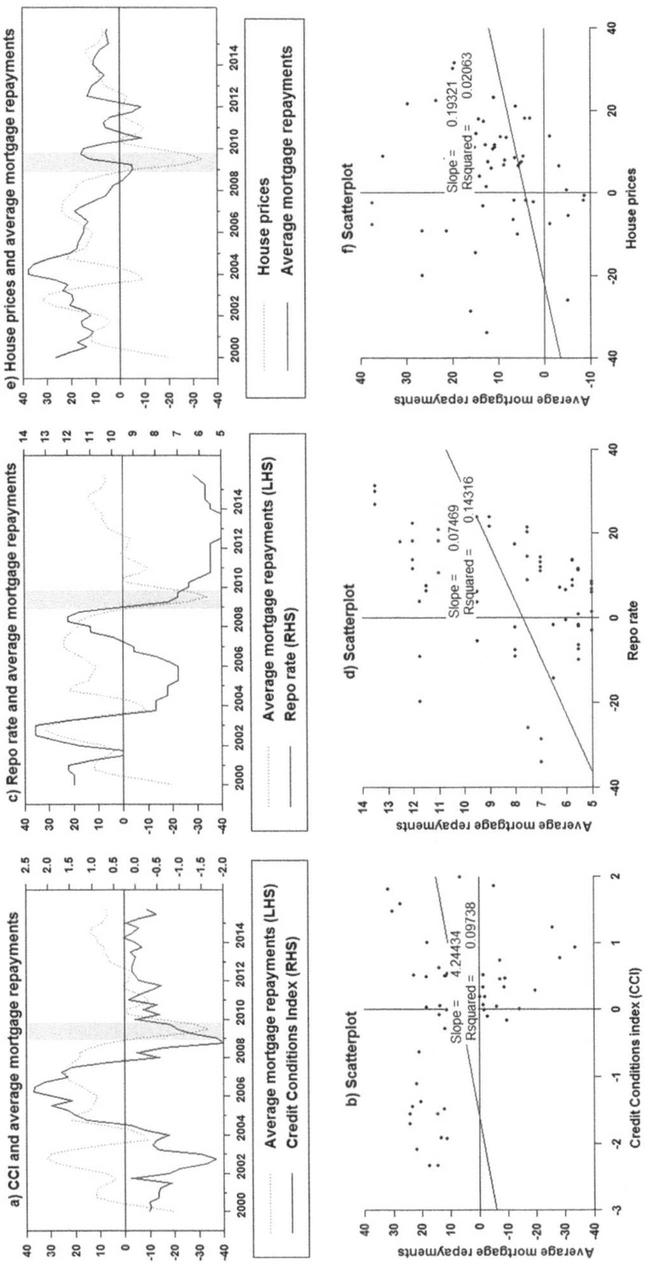

Fig. 9.3 Repo rate, house prices and average mortgage repayments (*Source*: SARB and authors' calculations)

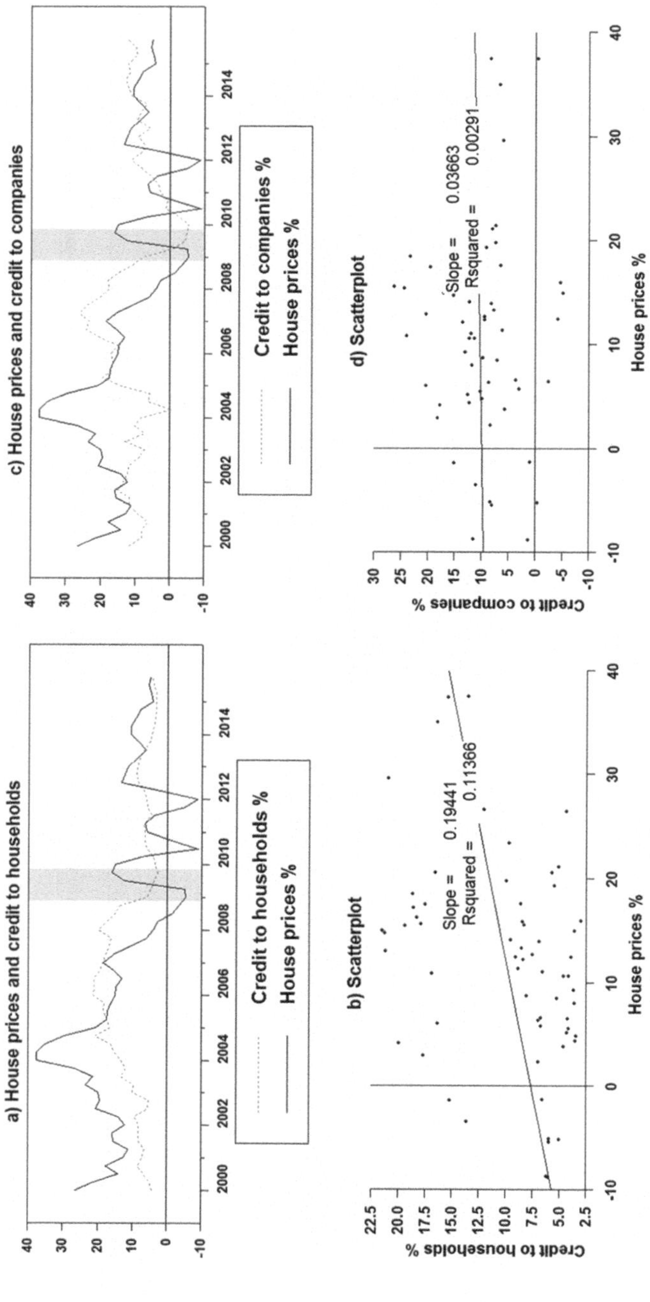

Fig. 9.4 Credit to households, companies and nominal house prices (*Source*: Authors' calculations)

matter more for household credit. The relationship is positive for the corporate sector credit but flat.

9.3 Fluctuations and Nonlinearities Induced by the CCI

Some studies in the literature indicate that credit and financial conditions exert nonlinear effects on GDP, with implications for potential GDP and the output gap trajectories. This also means that credit conditions have implications for inflationary pressures. Therefore, how much fluctuations are induced by the CCI shock on inflation and GDP growth is relative to those induced by the repo rate.

9.3.1 Fluctuations Induced by Credit Conditions on GDP and Inflation

To examine if the CCI amplifies the responses of macroeconomic variables to various economic shocks, a four-variable vector autoregression (VAR) model is estimated. The model includes headline Consumer Price Index (CPI) inflation, GDP growth, repo rate and CCI. The sample spans 2000Q1–2015Q4. The model is estimated using two lags selected by the Akaike Information Criterion (AIC). A shock refers to a standard deviation shock. Fig. 9.5a shows that credit conditions explain about 8 percent of fluctuations in inflation after eight quarters. This is less than 10 percent explained by the repo rate shocks.

In contrast, credit conditions induce more fluctuations in GDP than the repo rate. Thus, evidence points to the ability of credit conditions to induce large movements and amplification in macroeconomic responses.

9.3.2 Is There a Nonlinear Effect of Credit Conditions on GDP Growth?

To determine the nonlinear effects of tight credit conditions CCI_t on GDP growth, a nonlinear equation (9.1) is estimated. The equation

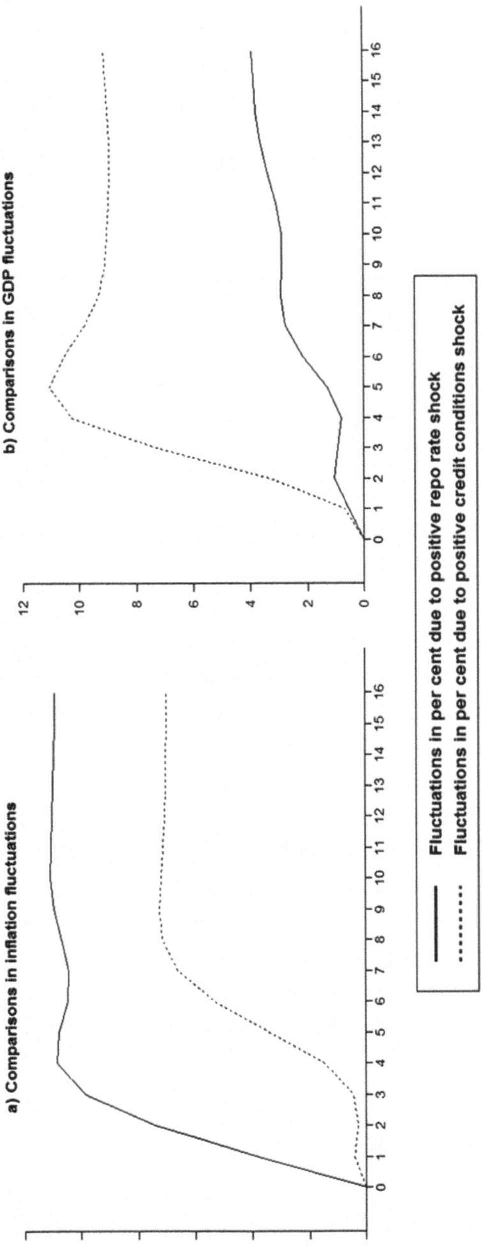

Fig. 9.5 Fluctuations induced by the CCI and repo rate (*Source*: Authors' calculations)

includes the squared CCI_t^2, X_t, which is the set of variables that include the inflation rate, current GDP growth, lagged GDP growth; the crisis dummy D is equal to one after 2008Q4 and zero otherwise. The interaction of the dummy variable for the crisis with the credit conditions $D * CCI_t$ *and* $D * CCI_t^2$ variables is used to distinguish the effects pre-, during and post the financial crisis through t.

Equation (9.1) is estimated with instrumental variables techniques to deal with possible endogeneity between credit conditions and GDP growth. The instruments include four to five lags of each variable.

$$GDP_{growth} = Constant + \alpha_i CCI_t + \gamma_i CCI_t^2 + \partial_i D * CCI_t + \omega_i D * CCI_t^2 + \rho_i X_t + \varepsilon_t \quad (9.1)$$

The negative sign on current GDP levels indicates convergence. Evidence in Table 9.1 suggests that tighter credit conditions have adverse effects on GDP growth and the effects are accentuated post-2008Q4. Overall, the results suggest that credit conditions affect GDP growth in a nonlinear way.

9.4 Amplification Due to Credit Conditions: A Counterfactual VAR Approach

Do the credit conditions amplify responses of GDP growth to positive repo rate and inflation shocks? Fig. 9.5a shows that GDP growth declines very much more in the presence of the CCI than when the credit conditions are shut off in the inflation equation. This suggests that tight credit conditions worsen the GDP growth decline due to positive inflation shocks. The amplification magnitudes shown in Fig. 9.6b indicate that the peak effect occurs during the sixth quarter.

The amplification abilities of the CCI are not only restricted to positive inflation shock effects. The effects are evident in the response to positive repo rate shocks, as shown in Fig. 9.7. Similarly, GDP growth rate declines

Table 9.1 Results from Eq. (9.1)

	Model 1		Model 2		Model 3		Model 4	
Variable	Coefficient	P-value	Coefficient	P-value	Coefficient	P-value	Coefficient	P-value
Initial GDP	–	–	−0.03	(0.01)	−0.03	(0.01)	−0.06	(0.00)
CCI	−0.35	(0.01)	−0.47	(0.00)	−0.61	(0.00)	−0.69	(0.00)
D*CCI	–	–	−0.93	(0.01)	–	–	**1.42**	**(0.17)**
CCI^2	−0.12	(0.18)	–	–	−0.25	(0.01)	−0.27	(0.05)
$D*CCI^2$	–	–	–	–	–	–	−1.07	(0.09)

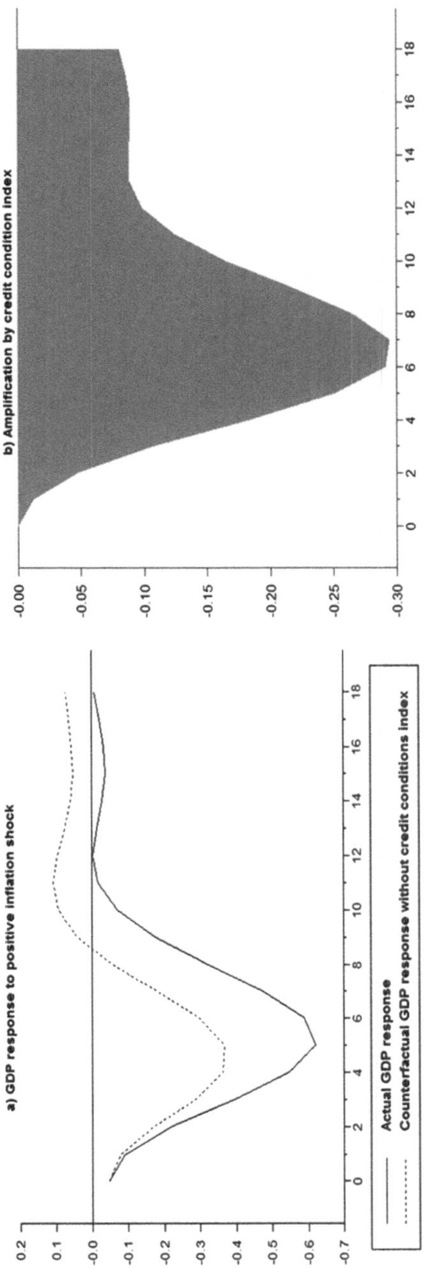

Fig. 9.6 GDP responses to inflation shocks and amplification by the CCI (*Source*: SARB and authors' calculations)

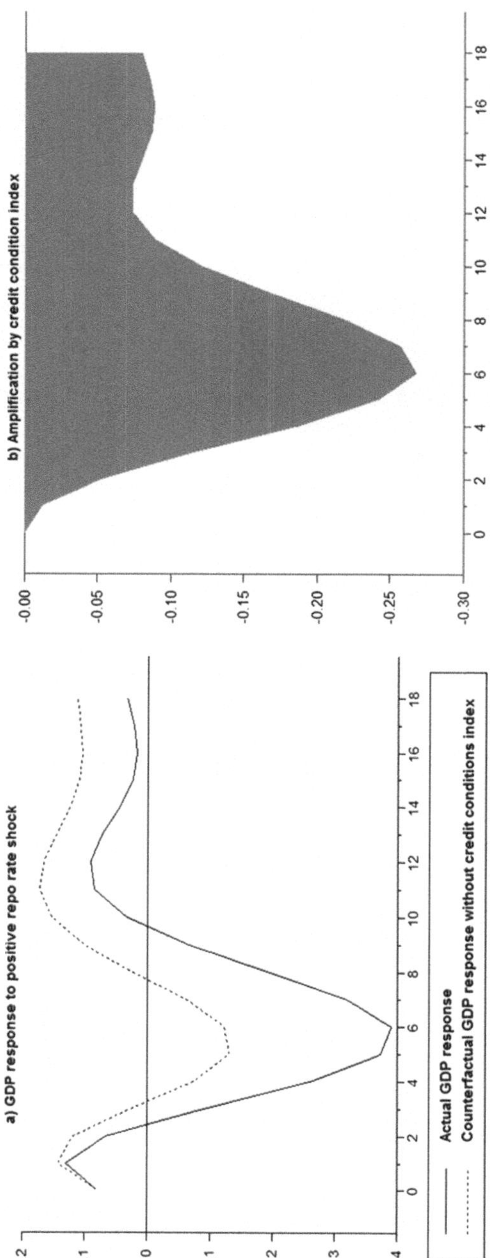

Fig. 9.7 GDP responses to repo rate shocks and amplification by credit condition index (*Source*: SARB and authors' calculations)

much more in the presence of tight credit conditions than when these are shut off.

This evidence shows that credit conditions play a big role in GDP growth dynamics as a transmitter of positive inflation and repo rate shocks.

9.4.1 Inflation Response to Rand Depreciation Shocks in the Absence of the CCI

Does the CCI propagate the rand depreciation shocks effects? Fig. 9.8a shows evidence that inflation is much lower in the presence of tight credit conditions than in their absence due to rand depreciation shock.

In cumulative terms, inflation would rise by a peak of 5 percentage points when credit conditions are shut off compared to 2 percentage points when credit conditions are included in the models. Fig. 9.8b shows that tight credit conditions dampen the inflationary pressures associated with rand depreciation effects.

9.5 The Role of Tight Credit Conditions and GDP Growth in the Repo Rate Reactions to Positive Inflation Shocks

The preceding sections showed that credit conditions amplify as well dampen macroeconomic responses to unexpected shocks. These effects have implications for monetary policy. So, what are the effects of credit conditions on the repo rate responses to inflationary pressures? Does the presence or absence of the CCI make a difference? The counterfactual analysis in Fig. 9.9b shows that the repo rate is tightened to inflation shock. But the tightening differs when the CCI is included and when it is shut off. The repo rate is aggressively tightened to positive inflation shocks when credit conditions are shut off. This evidence suggests that tight credit conditions lead to less aggressive policy tightening towards inflationary pressures. Fig. 9.9b shows the dampening

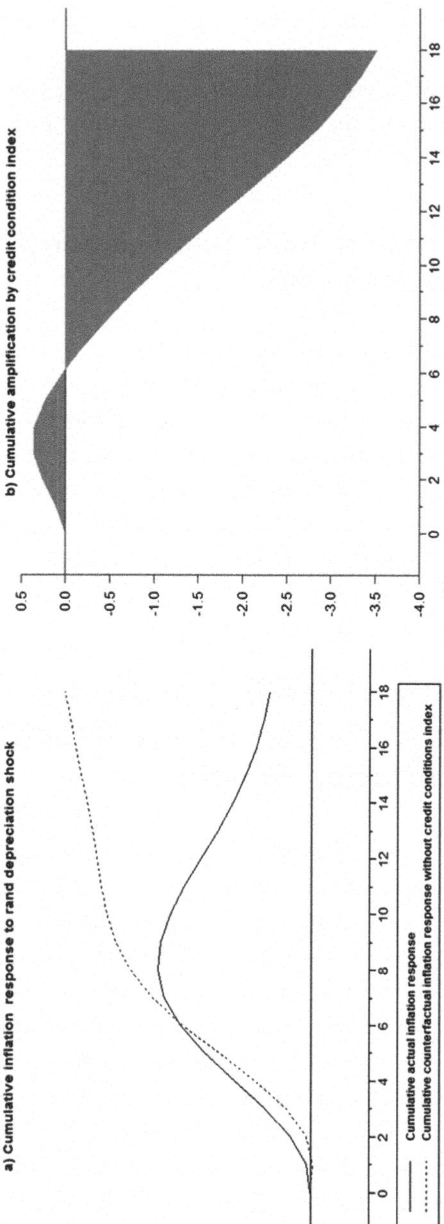

Fig. 9.8 Inflation responses to rand depreciation shocks and amplification by the CCI (*Source*: SARB and authors' calculations)

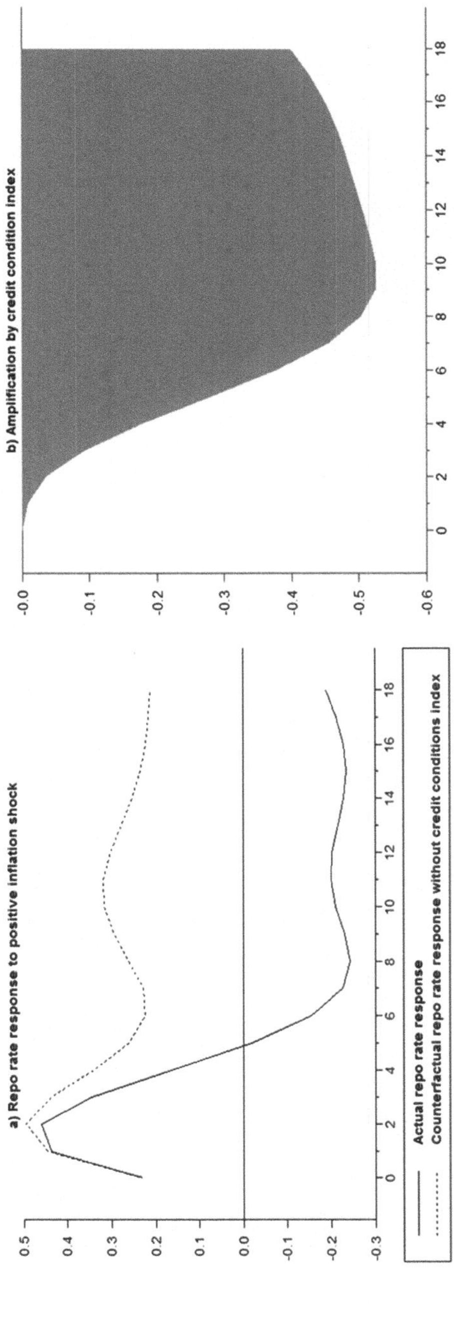

Fig. 9.9 Repo rate responses to inflation shocks and the amplification by the CCI (*Source*: SARB and authors' calculations)

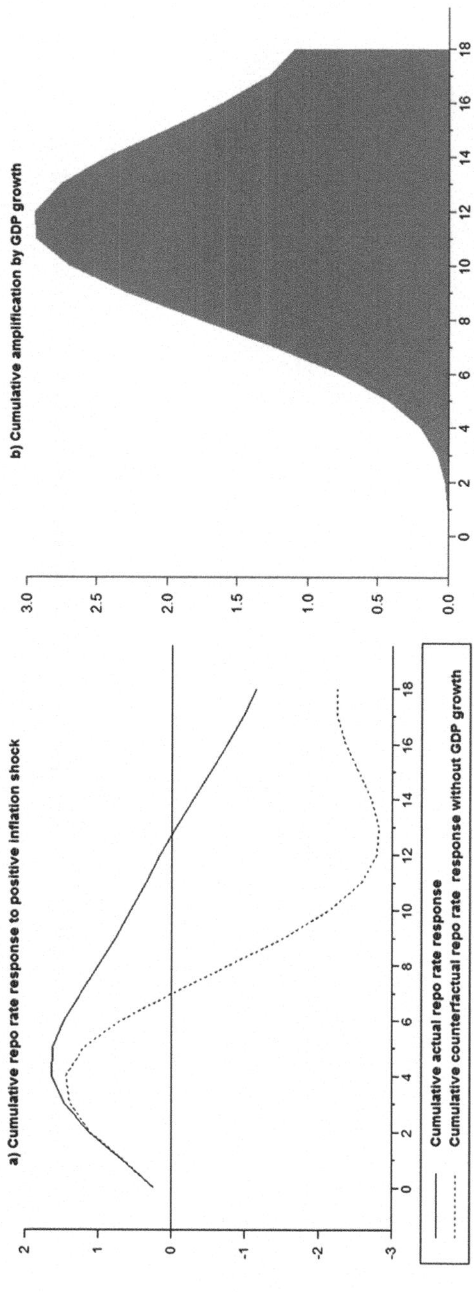

Fig. 9.10 Repo rate responses to inflation shocks and amplification by GDP growth (*Source*: SARB and authors' calculations)

effects of a tight credit conditions index on the repo rate in response to inflation shocks.

Due to the subdued GDP growth conditions post-2009, how does the repo rate respond to positive inflationary shocks in the presence and absence of GDP growth? Evidence indicates that the repo rate is tightened to positive inflationary shocks. The repo rate is tightened more due to positive inflation shocks in the presence of GDP growth in Fig. 9.10 than when GDP growth is shut off. As shown in Fig. 9.10b, higher GDP growth leads to aggressive repo rate tightening to positive inflation shocks.

9.5.1 Historical Decomposition and Counterfactual Approaches

The historical decomposition approach decomposes GDP growth, inflation and repo rate, respectively into their own trend, own contributions and contributions from other variables. The counterfactual inflation and repo rate values are calculated by purging the contributions of the CCI from inflation and repo rate, respectively. For GDP growth, the counterfactual value is purged of the combined contributions of the repo rate and the CCI. This is to isolate the effects of financial variables on GDP growth evolution.

Actual GDP growth rate tends to be lower than the counterfactual in Fig. 9.11, suggesting that tight credit conditions possibly mitigated the

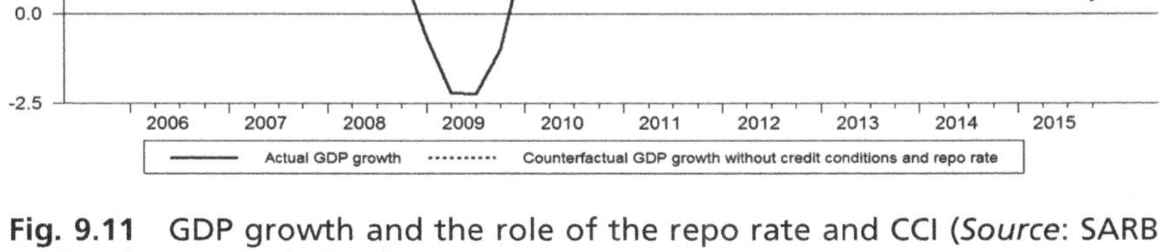

Fig. 9.11 GDP growth and the role of the repo rate and CCI (*Source*: SARB and authors' calculations)

expansionary effects of policy rate. However, the gap between actual and counterfactual GDP is smaller in 2015, implying that the GDP growth phenomenon post-2009 recession period may explain the persistently negative output gap.

Fig. 9.12 compares the actual and counterfactual inflation rate post-2009 recession period. Between 2011 and 2015Q2 actual inflation was lower than the counterfactual value, suggesting that tight credit conditions lead to lower inflation than that would prevail in their absence. This could be another explanation for a low or muted exchange rate pass-through to inflation. The low credit driven demand pressures are exerting a downward pressure on inflation. However, the actual inflation exceeding counterfactual in last two quarters of 2015 may be reflective of the persistent effects of exchange rate depreciation as opposed to demand pressures.

The repo rate changes in the presence and absence of credit conditions are shown in Fig. 9.13 and suggest that tight credit conditions lead to a lower repo rate level than would prevail in the absence of tight credit conditions.

9.6 Conclusions and Policy Implications

This chapter investigated the extent to which credit conditions amplify macroeconomic responses to various unexpected macroeconomic shocks. First, evidence shows that tight credit conditions have a disproportionate effect on credit to households relative to companies. This could be on account of the role of the direct effects of inflation and the policy rate and indirectly the effects of GDP growth. Second, credit conditions exacerbate the negative effects of GDP growth responses to positive repo rate and inflation shocks.

However, inflation rises by a lesser magnitude to rand depreciation shocks in the absence of the credit conditions index. In addition, the actual inflation has been much lower than the counterfactual between 2011 and 2014, suggesting that the low pass-through can be partly attributed to tighter credit conditions. This means that muted credit driven demand results in muted inflation and exchange rate pass-through. For

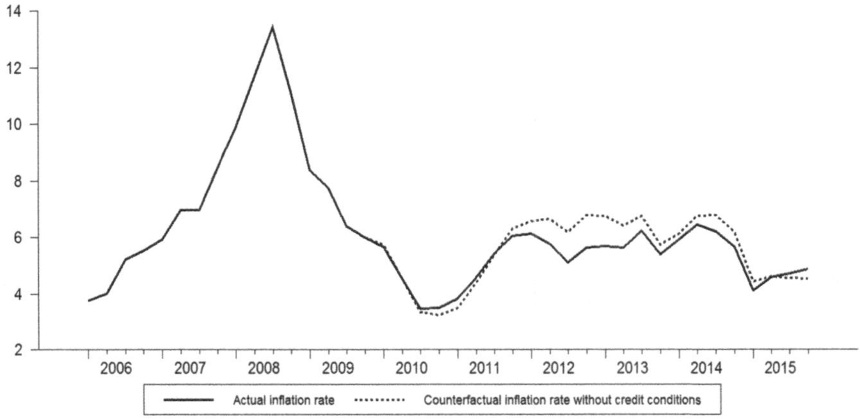

Fig. 9.12 The evolution of inflation and role of the CCI (*Source*: SARB and authors' calculations)

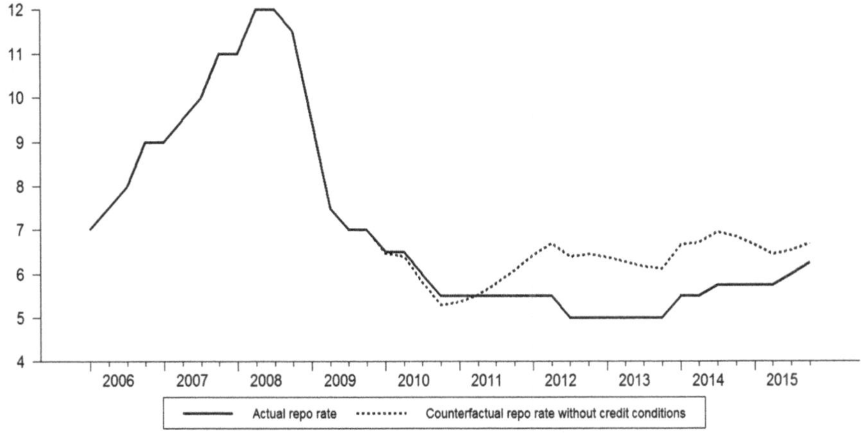

Fig. 9.13 The repo rate and role of the CCI (*Source*: SARB and authors' calculations)

policy implications, the evidence shows that the counterfactual of repo rate is higher when credit conditions indexes are shut off. The implication is that tighter credit conditions have assisted the policy rate in neutralizing inflationary pressures.

Summary of Findings

- Credit conditions have a disproportionate effect on households relative to companies. The direct effects of inflation and the policy rate and indirectly the effects of GDP growth contribute to the disproportionate effects.
- Tight credit conditions exert nonlinear adverse effects on GDP growth. The adverse effects are accentuated post-2008Q4.
- Tight credit conditions have assisted the policy rate in neutralizing inflationary pressures.
- Tight credit conditions are partly responsible for the low pass-through. Muted credit driven demand contributes to muted inflation and the exchange rate pass-through of rand depreciation shocks.

Part II

Credit Supply Dynamics and the Economy

10

The Lending-Deposit Rate Spread and the Bank Pricing Behavior

Learning Objectives

- Determining the thresholds of the lending-deposit spread, the asymmetry and the momentum in change in spread towards the equilibrium level
- The direction of momentum in the lending-deposit spread adjustment when the policy rate is adjusted
- The prevalence of the asymmetric adjustment of the lending-deposit rate spread
- Insight on the transmission mechanism of adjustments in the policy rate
- Testing for collusive pricing and transaction costs theory in the setting of the deposit and lending rates spread
- Testing for adverse customer reaction in banks' behavior

10.1 Introduction

The price setting behavior of banks for deposit and lending rates influences the effectiveness of monetary policy. The lending-deposit spread is a reflection of a number of factors, such as (1) the micro-structure

N. Gumata, E. Ndou, *Bank Credit Extension and Real Economic Activity in South Africa*, DOI 10.1007/978-3-319-43551-0_10

of the banking sector, (2) intermediation (intermediary) costs and (3) macroeconomic factors.[1] Furthermore, despite the policymakers reducing the policy rate to historically low levels, lending rate margins widened. This chapter assesses the prevalence of the asymmetric adjustment of the lending-deposit rate spread. This will give insights regarding the transmission mechanism of adjustments in the policy rate.

The lending-deposit rate spread reflects the premium or mark-up over banks' deposit rates. This premium is market driven and stable if markets function well. In cases when the premium is perceived to be misaligned, financial markets will discipline banks and force an adjustment to some equilibrium spread (Thompson 2006). So, which economic hypothesis best describe banks' price setting behavior for deposits and loans? In which direction is there a momentum in the lending-deposit spread adjustment when the policy rate is adjusted?

Why does the analysis of lending-deposit rates spread matter for policymaking? First, the literature shows that the two-sided nature of the banking problem has to be recognized and therefore empirical analysis has to look at both sides on the banks' balance sheets. This is because banks can use a cross-subsidizing approach of lending rates via the deposit margin to attract new customers (Gropp et al. 2007). Second, the increase in the lending-deposit spread happened at the time the policy rate was declining, hence concerns that the benefits of the monetary policy easing were not passed-through to the real economy.

Why is it important to assess the direction of momentum in the adjustment of spread? First, the presence of asymmetries, for instance the downward stickiness of lending rates, could minimize the effect of expansionary monetary policy leading to the asymmetric effects of monetary policy on output. Furthermore, this means that monetary policy aimed at lowering lending rates could take longer to achieve the desired results than monetary policy tightening if banks are reluctant to reduce lending rates when deposits are decreasing (Lee et al. 2013). Second, this chapter is more interested in the message that such adjustments in

[1] Intermediation costs, for example, include costs of funding, intermediation services, default and other operational costs. Macroeconomic factors include regulatory policies, monetary policy and fiscal policy, amongst others.

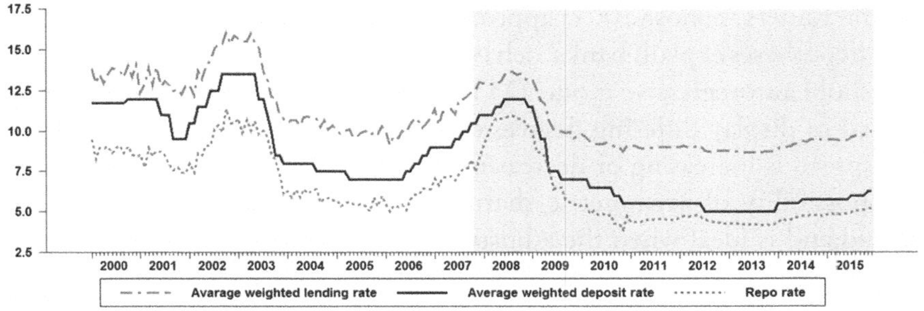

Fig. 10.1 Banks' deposit and lending rates and the policy rate (*Source*: SARB and authors' calculations)

the lending spread tell policymakers about the behavior of banks. As a result, the empirical analysis focuses on the direction of the momentum in the spread by testing the existence of the following hypotheses since 2007M11.

Hypothesis 1 *The lending-deposit rate spread will adjust quickly when the spread is narrowing (decreasing) below a threshold level than when the spread is widening (increasing) above this limit.* In essence, Hypothesis 1 tests for the collusive pricing and transaction costs theory.

Hypothesis 2 *The lending-deposit rate spread will adjust more quickly when the spread is widening (increasing) above a threshold level than when the spread is narrowing (decreasing) below this limit.* Thus, Hypothesis 2 tests for adverse customer reaction in banks' behavior

The assessment of the lending-deposit rate spread captures aspects of the cross-subsidizing approach. Fig. 10.1 shows bank-weighted average lending, deposit rates and the repo rate. It is evident that deposits and lending rates form a corridor for the policy rate. Deposit rates in general are priced at a discount below the repo rate, whereas the lending rates are at a premium or mark-up above the deposit and repo rate.

The Enders–Siklos (2001) approach is used to determine which of the two hypotheses explain banks' behavior in South Africa.[2] The momentum threshold autoregressive model (MTAR) enables the lending-deposit rate spread to display differing degrees of adjustment depending on whether the spread is increasing or decreasing. Furthermore, the MTAR captures the possibility of asymmetric sharp movements in the lending-deposit spread and is ideal when the adjustment exhibits some form of momentum more in one direction than the other.

10.2 Dynamics of Lending and Deposits Rates

The repo rate is not the only rate at which banks fund themselves when raising funds from deposits. Banks fund themselves at negotiable certificate deposits (NCD) rates and retail deposit rates at different maturities and the repo rate. These rates are priced at varying margins relative to the repo rate depending on maturity reflecting the opportunity cost involved.

Fig. 10.2a shows that the spread between lending-deposit rates was for most of the period before November 2007 below the deposit rate, but adjusted to the same level as the deposit rate. The lending-deposit rate spread can be characterized by Eq. (10.1) and the components are shown in Fig. 10.2b.

$$\begin{aligned} \textit{Lending rate} - \textit{Deposit rate} = (\textit{lending rate} - \textit{repo rate}) + \\ (\textit{repo rate} - \textit{deposit rate}) \end{aligned} \tag{10.1}$$

Fig. 10.1 showed that the main driver of the convergence is the steep increase in the lending–repo rate spread. Furthermore, it is evident in Fig. 10.1 that the repo–deposit rate spread varies more, possibly reflecting that it is part of the cost of funds and the main component of the marginal cost of lending. The repo–deposits spread capture the opportunity cost of deposits for depositors and profitability of deposits to bank

[2] Enders and Siklos (2001) did not assess the spread in the banking sector but applied the approach to the bond market.

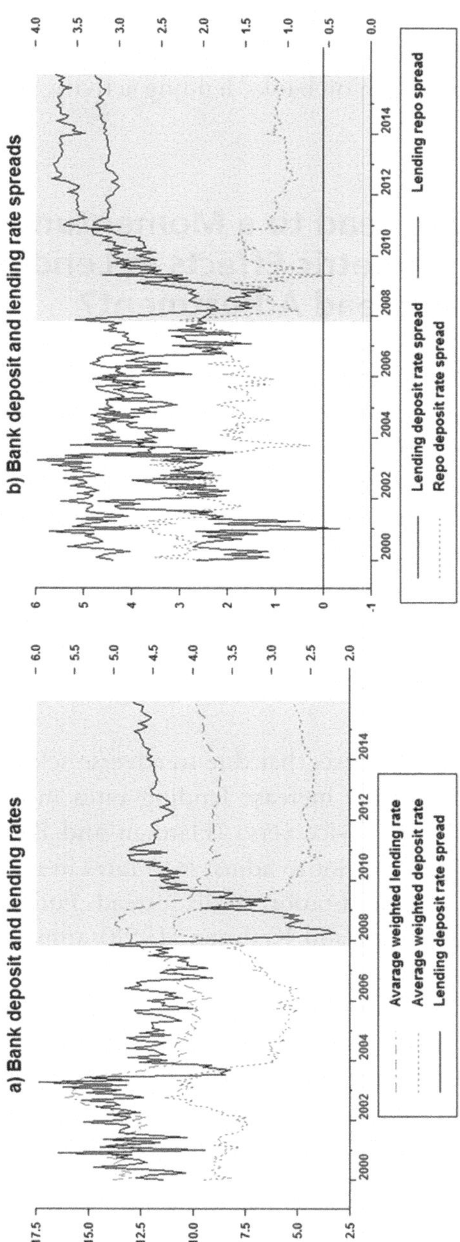

Fig. 10.2 Banks' deposit and lending rates spreads (*Source*: SARB and authors' calculations)

(Gropp et al. 2007). Overall, the implication of the trends shown in Fig. 10.1 is that the lending-deposit rate spread post-2008 widened on account of a larger premium on banks' lending activity, as opposed to the return on deposit funding.

10.3 What Can Lead to a Momentum and Asymmetric Effects in Lending-Deposit Spread Adjustment?

Theoretically, asymmetries in the spread can manifest in many forms. First, based on the bank concentration (competition) and the depositor base of banks hypothesis, the adjustment of lending and deposit rates occurs at different speeds and determines the surplus a bank can extract from consumers. Hannan and Berger (1991) as well as Neumark and Sharpe (1992) postulated that collusive pricing arrangements or market power could lead banks to raise lending rates more quickly when deposit rates are rising than vice versa. Thus banks in concentrated markets are slower to adjust deposit rates upwards and are faster to adjust them downwards while exhibiting the opposite behavior regarding lending rates.

A second hypothesis suggests that due to adverse selection and moral hazard problems banks may increase lending rates more slowly when deposit rates are rising and vice versa (Hannan and Berger 1991).[3] In addition, banks may choose not to adjust loan rates in response to a policy rate change (increase) and ration credit instead. Furthermore, Berger and Udell (1992) and Elsas and Krahnen (1998) argue that banks can offer long-term borrowers implicit interest rate insurance. This means that banks smooth bank loan rates over the business cycle. Banks can offer rates below the market rates during policy tightening and compensate for this behavior during policy easing. The third hypothesis about fixed search and switching costs, from Rajan (1992), suggests that once customers establish a working relationship with their lending institutions,

[3] See also Neumark and Sharpe (1992) and Rajan (1992).

costs of shopping for a loan will make customers less likely to shop elsewhere if lending rates fall slowly when deposits are decreasing.

10.4 Is There an Asymmetric Adjustment in the Spread Between Lending Rates and Deposit Rate Since 2008?

The MTAR approach requires analysis to be made in two steps. First, the Enders and Siklos (2001) momentum threshold approach is applied and the relationship between the lending and deposits rates is estimated and the residuals (the spread) from Eq. (10.2) are extracted. We express the lending and deposit rate in logarithmic form. This introduces the concept of elasticity in the interpretation of the results in Eq. (10.2). The estimated coefficients show that despite the deposit rate explaining nearly 97 percent of the lending rate developments, the elasticity coefficient is 0.46, which suggests an inelastic relationship between deposit and lending rates.

$$lending\ rate_t = 1.5072 + 0.4602 * Deposit\ rate_t + Spread_t, \bar{R}^2 = 96.88\% \quad (10.2)$$

The results of the inelastic relationship imply that the spreads are not necessarily adversely affected by substitutes to banking products. The inelastic demand for loans and supply of deposits allows for higher premiums, and this is characteristic of the banks' ability to exercise market power. Empirical studies establish this kind of bank behavior for cases where there is less competition from non-bank financial products. In particular, this applies in cases where households and non-financial corporations' access the bulk of funding from banks and very little from other sources. The absence of competition from other sources of funding and investment vehicles does not pressure banks to narrow their spread. There are no market forces applying pressure on banks to price their lending and deposit rates more competitively (Gropp et al. 2002).

10.4.1 Second Step: Is There Evidence of the Momentum Change in Lending Deposit Spread?

The results of two versions of a MTAR model, using the residuals derived in Eq. (10.2), are shown. Thereafter, a determination of whether there is evidence of momentum in the spread in one direction and whether this depends on the zero and non-zero threshold is made.

10.4.2 Evidence from the Model-Estimated Threshold

The threshold is determined endogenously using the consistent Chan (1993) approach. The approach sorts potential thresholds in an ascending order and excludes values within the lowest and highest 15th percentiles. According to Chan's approach, the consistent estimate of the threshold is the one that yields the smallest residual sum of squares over the remaining 70 percent. Based on this approach we find a threshold value of −0.0137 percent.

$$\Delta Spread_t = -0.1910 * I_t * Spread_{t-1} - 0.5616 * \left(1 - I_t\right) * Spread_{t-1} + \sum_{i=1}^{l} \beta_i \Delta Spread_{t-i} + \varepsilon_t$$

$$\text{Where, } I_t = \begin{cases} 1 & if\, \Delta Spread_{t-1} \geq -0.0137 \\ 0 & if\, \Delta Spread_{t-1} \leq -0.0137 \end{cases}$$

The point estimate suggests that spread tends to decay faster at an absolute rate of 0.5616 for changes in the spread below the threshold. The rate of decay is smaller at an absolute pace of 0.1910 for change in spread above the threshold value.

In Table 10.1 the evidence of symmetric adjustment around the threshold is rejected. This means that both versions of the MTAR model indicate the existence of a cointegration relationship and convergence in the speed of adjustment.[4] The negative sign on the speed of adjustment indicates

[4] The T-max exceeds the statistics given by Enders and Granger (1998). In addition, the Phi value allows us to reject the null hypothesis of no cointegration.

Table 10.1 Cointegration and asymmetry tests

	MTAR consistent threshold model Coefficient (p-value)		MTAR zero threshold model Coefficient (p-value)		Decision
Direction of adjustment in change in spreads					
Impact when $\Delta Spread_{t-1}$ ≥threshold ($\rho 1$)	−0.19	(0.086)*	−0.221	(0.115)	
Impact when $\Delta Spread_{t-1}$ ≤threshold (ρ_2)	−0.56	(0.127)	−0.351	(0.095)**	
Threshold of $\Delta Spread_{t-1}$	−0.014		0.0		
Null hypothesis of no cointegration					
[a]T-Max	−2.22		−1.921		There is cointegration
[b]Phi ... $\rho_1 = \rho_2 = 0$	11.27		7.995		There is cointegration
Testing null hypothesis of no symmetry					
[c]$\rho_1 = \rho_2$	6.48		4.841		There is asymmetric adjustment

[a]T-max exceeds EG statistics at 5 %
[b]Phi exceeds EG statistics at 10 %
[c]Testing equality which implies symmetric adjustment
*Implies significance at 5 % level
**implies significance at 10 % level

that the spread converges towards equilibrium point. This means that after deviating from the equilibrium, the spread returns to the long-term equilibrium. This indicates that adjustment towards the −0.0137 percent threshold tends to persist more when the lending-deposit spread is narrowing than when it is widening.

This means that the lending-deposit spread will adjust more quickly when the spread is narrowing (decreasing) below a threshold level than when it is widening (increasing) above the threshold hold level. This is consistent with the collusive and transactions hypothesis. Thus the evidence suggests that banks adjust their lending rates differently to rising versus declining market rates and this behavior is consistent with collusive pricing and transaction costs theory. This supports Hypothesis 1, regarding the existence of elements of collusiveness and transactions costs in the behavior of South African banks.

10.4.3 Evidence from a Zero Threshold

Would these conclusions differ if a zero threshold is used? This is assessed by using a zero threshold.

$$\Delta Spread_t = -0.2212 * I_t * Spread_{t-1} - 0.3505 * \left(1 - I_t\right) * Spread_{t-1} + \sum_{i=1}^{l} \beta_i \Delta Spread_{t-i} + \varepsilon_t$$

$$\text{Where, } I_t = \begin{cases} 1 & if\, \Delta Spread_{t-1} \geq 0 \\ 0 & if\, \Delta Spread_{t-1} \leq 0 \end{cases}$$

The adjustment is faster (that is, −0.3505 percent) for changes in the spread below the threshold. The rate of decay is smaller and occurs at the rate of −0.2212 percent correction per month for change in spread above the threshold value.

10.4.4 So How Does the Lending-Deposit Spread Adjust Based on a Different Technique Such as the Asymmetric Error Correction Approach?

The asymmetric error correction approach confirms the results of the MTAR model on the speed of adjustment. The equation shows that the lending-deposit spread adjusts slowly above the threshold and more when it is below the threshold. This finding suggests that lending-deposit spread adjusts faster when the spread is narrowing than when the spread is widening. This evidence is consistent with collusive pricing and transaction costs theory.

Size of adjustment above threshold **Size of adjustment below threshold**

$$\Delta lendingrate_t = -0.00078 - \mathbf{0.1429} * I_t Spread_{t-1} - \mathbf{0.4691} * (1 - I_t)\rho_2 Spread_{t-1} + \boldsymbol{A_i(L)}\Delta lendingrate_{t-i} + \boldsymbol{B_i(L)}\Delta depositrate_{t-i} + \varepsilon_t$$

$$\bar{R}^2 = 50.4\%, \qquad Durbin\ Watson\ test\ statictic = 2.14$$

Note: *The bold letters indicates the values are high and significant at conventional statistically significance level.* $A_i(L)\Delta \mathbf{Lending\_rate}_{t-i}$ *refers to lags 1 and 2.* $B_i(L)\Delta \mathbf{Deposit\_rate}_{t-i}$ *refers to lags 0, 1 and 2*

The transactions cost aspect of the hypothesis may arise from the level of bank capital, credit risk and the state of the economy (business cycle). These factors play a role in the price setting behavior of banks and can affect the lending-deposit spread. In later chapters, banks' holdings of excess capital and other regulatory instruments for compliance with various aspects of Basel III are explored. Literature shows that holding excess regulatory equity capital is a more expensive source of funding liabilities and banks can therefore seek to cover some of the increase in the average cost of capital via higher interest rate spreads. Furthermore, later chapters on macro-prudential tools explore the use of other tools such as the application of the National Credit Act, loan-to-value ratios and repayment-to-income ratios to manage credit risk. This therefore means that changes in credit risk will positively affect the lending-deposit spread.

10.5 Conclusion and Policy Implications

This chapter analyzed factors influencing the deposit and lending rates by assessing the behavioral aspects of the adjustment of the lendingdeposit spread. Three approaches were used to determine the thresholds of the spread, the asymmetry and the momentum in change in spread towards the equilibrium level. The results establish that the deposit rate explains almost 97 percent of the lending rate developments but the elasticity coefficient is less than one. This value means that the relationship between deposit and lending rates is inelastic. This implies that spreads are not necessarily adversely affected by substitutes to banking products. The results in the study indicate that the absence of competition from other bank funding sources does not exert pressure on banks to narrow their lending spreads. There are no market forces applying pressure on banks to price their lending and deposit rates more competitively.

The rate of adjustment of the deviations from the equilibrium rate shows that the lending-deposit spread adjusts asymmetrically towards the equilibrium. The spread is faster to adjust to both zero and non-zero estimated thresholds when the spread is narrowing (decreasing) below a threshold level than when the spread is widening (increasing) above the threshold level. The results collectively confirm collusive and transaction theories behavior in South African banks' lending-deposit spread.

Summary of Findings

- The deposit rate explains almost 97 percent of the lending rate developments. The elasticity coefficient is less than one, meaning that the relationship between deposit and lending rates is inelastic.
- There is absence of competition from other sources of funding and investment vehicles. This contributes to lack of pressure on banks to narrow spreads.
- The rate of adjustment of the deviations from the equilibrium rate suggests that the lending-deposit spread adjusts asymmetrically towards the equilibrium.
- The spread adjusts more quickly to both zero and non-zero thresholds when the spread is narrowing (decreasing) below a threshold level than when the spread is widening (increasing) above the threshold level.
- Evidence confirms collusive and transaction theories behavior in South African banks' lending-deposit spread.

11

Adverse Credit Supply Shocks and Weak Economic Growth

Learning Objectives

- Know the benefits of using the pure sign restriction and penalty function sign restriction approaches in VAR.
- Distinguish between adverse credit supply effects, tighter monetary policy and adverse credit demand shocks on lending spreads, GDP and credit growth.
- Show that adverse credit supply shock is partly responsible for the weak economic growth recovery and elevated loan spreads.
- Determine the role of global economic uncertainty shocks on elevated lending spreads.

11.1 Introduction

Bank lending contracted sharply during the financial crisis and has not recovered consistently to robust levels. The credit slowdown coincided with a significant decline in the policy rate and sluggish economic growth. It is possible that credit supply effects were reinforced by credit demand

N. Gumata, E. Ndou, *Bank Credit Extension and Real Economic Activity in South Africa*, DOI 10.1007/978-3-319-43551-0_11

dynamics and the widening of the lending rate spreads. Hence, it is necessary to disentangle the role of credit supply and demand shocks during this period. The separation of supply and demand factors will reveal whether an adverse credit demand and credit supply shock reinforce or mitigate the effects of monetary policy. This chapter explores the extent to which adverse credit supply shocks contribute to weak economic growth recovery and elevated credit interest rate spreads. The separation is relevant to policy discussions as it enables policymakers to design appropriate intervention tools in dealing with credit market developments.

Funding and financial intermediation is crucial for transmitting policy rate changes into the economy and this may be impeded by adverse credit market developments. To ascertain the extent to which banks played a role during the economic downturn, the effects of the adverse credit supply shock on the economy are examined. First, the adverse credit supply effects are disentangled from those of tighter monetary policy and adverse credit demand shocks. Second, the extent to which an adverse credit supply shock could be responsible for the weak economic growth recovery and elevated loan spreads simultaneously is established. How do these effects differ from those of a tighter monetary policy shock? Third, the effects emanating from a global economic uncertainty shock are determined and compared to those of an adverse credit supply, tighter monetary policy shocks on economic growth, credit growth and loan spreads. In this regard: can the rise in the loan spreads be linked to global economic uncertainty shock?

11.2 The Importance of Proper Identification of Loan Demand and Supply Shocks

Why should policymakers be concerned about adverse loan supply shocks? It is well established in the literature that the financial accelerator can amplify the effects of financial cycles on the real economy. This operates through changes in the values of collateral and on the willingness of financial intermediaries to provide credit to the economy.[1] This sug-

[1] See Bernanke and Gertler (1995), Bernanke et al. (1999), Kiyotaki and Moore (1997).

gests that shocks that affect creditworthiness tend to accentuate swings in output. It is not only the borrower's side that is impacted, lenders are also affected. In this regard, the bank capital channel argues that the deterioration in bank capital makes banks reluctant to lend. Banks may deleverage to some extent, leading to sharper economic downturns.

Why is a proper identification of an adverse loan supply shock important? Hristov et al. (2012) argue that shocks caused by banks trigger economic disturbances due to credit frictions which emanate from different sources. These include rising loan losses, an unexpected destruction of bank capital and changes in banks' willingness to lend, which can manifest itself through the rejection of more loan applications or higher interest rates. This suggests that the economic effects of such shocks can be huge. If so, is there evidence that be attributed to this shock in South Africa? If loan spreads are already exerting adverse economic effects, could it be the case that the policy tightening has exacerbated these effects? As a consequence, the analysis shows the contributions of tighter loan spreads and monetary policy on economic growth evolution, which includes the recent policy tightening episode. The analysis shows the contributions of tighter loans spreads and monetary policy on economic growth evolution, which includes the recent policy tightening episode.

Furthermore, the analysis assesses whether there is a threshold level of loan spreads which can anchor the policy debate and discussions on the levels of lending rates that are potentially excessive and detrimental to financial stability. Is it possible that above a certain threshold of margins the increase in the repo rate, growth in credit and inflation exert differential effects on economic growth? Levels at or above this estimated threshold level will indicate whether lending margins affect the manner in which monetary policy tightening, credit growth and inflation impact economic growth.

Discussions in empirical literature highlight the difficulty in disentangling movements of bank loans to supply and demand shocks. When does the difficulty arise? For instance, an economy can be hit by a negative shock which makes it difficult to distinguish whether the deceleration in bank lending is due to shifts in loan demand or supply. It is possible that the decline in credit growth is on account of a shift in loan supply, which may reflect fewer investment opportunities. In addition, it may be an indication that banks are less inclined to lend and reject more loan applications or may charge a higher interest rate (Hristov et al. 2012).

The recent techniques make it feasible to separate these adverse credit shocks, given that there is less clear differentiation of these shock effects on the economy. Disentangling the adverse credit demand and supply shock is challenging but the separation is very relevant for the monetary policy decision-making process. In this regard, we use the latest techniques, which rely on sign restrictions predicted by theoretical models to separate the two adverse shocks.[2] To disentangle the shocks, the chapter uses a modified sign-restricted vector autoregression (VAR) model corresponding to specifications in Hristov et al. (2012) and Eickmeier et al. (2014). The signs imposed to identify the structural shocks are based on theoretical predictions. For robustness analysis the results derived from the sign restriction approach are compared with those from a Cholesky ordering approach, which is motivated by how the economy works based on theoretical models.

Why is it a unique approach to disentangle the credit demand and supply shocks? This is because the imposed sign restrictions to identify a loan supply shock suggest that an adverse loan supply shock leads to a reduction in loans extended. This leads to an increase in the lending rate, which also raises the loan margins.[3] In contrast, theoretical models suggest that an adverse credit demand shock lowers both credit extended and the lending rate; if policy rates are sticky the spreads decline.

11.3 Theoretical Relationship Between Loan Spreads and Adverse Credit Supply and Demand Shocks

The analysis begins by reviewing and showing simple theoretical models that highlight the role of the elasticity of the credit supply curve. References to the elasticity of credit supply have not featured much in policy discussions. Does this mean it is irrelevant? Theory suggests that

[2] Micro-data on banks' balance sheets and lending criteria as reported by banks can be used to distinguish between demand and supply shocks.

[3] See Hristov et al. (2012), Gertler and Karadi (2011), Curdia and Woodford (2010).

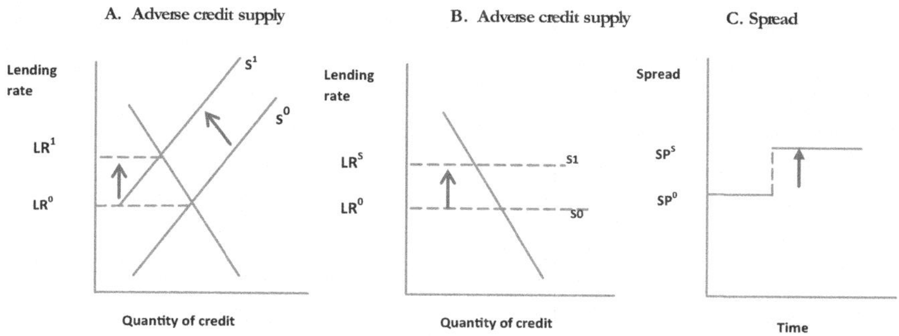

Fig. 11.1 Credit supply, lending rates and spreads (*Note*: The spread (SP) refers to margins above the policy rate. In both situations, we assume the policy rate has not changed. Credit supply curve is less elastic in (**a**) and perfectly elastic in (**b**). *Source*: Author's drawing)

credit supply depends on the nature of credit markets. If the credit supply curve is upward sloping this suggests that an increase in the supply of credit should be accompanied by rising lending rates.[4] In contrast, if the supply curve depicts a flat slope, then the lending rate is dependent on the policy rate and the mark-up. In contrast, a downward sloping credit demand curve suggests that lower lending rates should lead to an increase in the quantity of credit extended.

Fig. 11.1 illustrates the effects of an adverse credit supply shock and distinguishes the slopes of the credit supply curve. However, the objective is to show that under certain assumptions about the elasticity of the credit supply curve, there is concurrence of a decline in credit supply and an increase in lending rates and margins. Elasticity can be categorized as inelastic, perfectly elastic and less elastic. These elasticity categories have implications for credit dynamics. The analysis of an inelastic credit supply curve is excluded because it suggests that credit volumes do not change at all and that the lending rate does all the necessary adjustment. Clearly, this was not the case, as we know that credit volumes declined during the recession and the recent crisis.

[4] This section does not engage in an in-depth discussion of determining the South African micro-credit market structure. Instead, a distinction between the effects of the (price?) elasticity the credit loan supply curve is demonstrated.

A credit supply shock leads to a sudden decline in credit extension in Fig. 11.1a. This leads to an upward shift (decline) in credit supply from S^0 to S^1, leading to higher lending rates through rising from LR^0 to LR^1. The decline in the volume of credit and an increase in the lending rate happen irrespective of the elasticity of the loan supply curve as shown in Fig. 11.1b and the loan margins rise as shown in Fig. 11.1c. This reveals that irrespective of the elasticity of the credit supply curve, an adverse credit supply shock raises lending rates and margins even if the policy rate remains constant or is reduced.

Fact 1 This establishes that lending spreads rise due to a credit supply shock, irrespective of the elasticity of credit supply curve. The adverse credit supply shock raises the lending spreads. This is consistent with the sign restriction identification scheme we adopt later as well as much of the literature.

Fig. 11.2a shows the effects of an adverse credit demand shock, which lowers the quantity of credit irrespective of whether the supply curve is perfectly elastic or less elastic. However, in this case the lending rate can either decline as shown in Fig. 11.2a or it can remain constant but the quantity of credit demanded declines as shown in Fig. 11.2b.

This means that, depending on the elasticity of the credit supply curve as shown in Fig. 11.2a, b, lending spreads can decline or they can

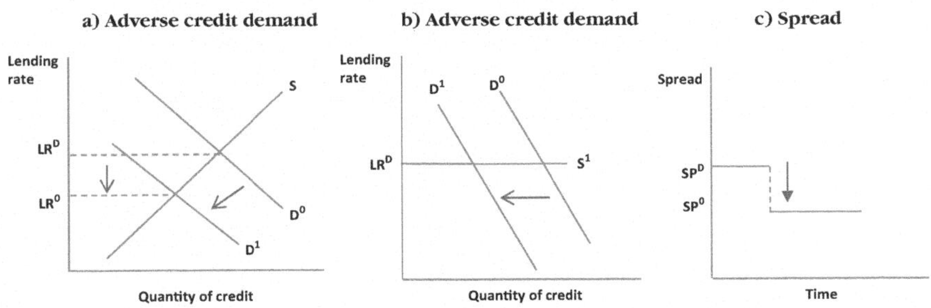

Fig. 11.2 Credit demand, lending rates and spreads (*Note*: The spread (SP) refers to margins above the policy rate. In both situations, we assume the policy rate has not changed. Credit supply curve is less elastic in (**a**) and perfectly elastic in (**b**). *Source*: Author's drawing)

remain constant as shown in Fig. 8.2f. Fig. 11.2 demonstrates that even in the absence of the adjustment to the policy rate, the spreads should decline in response to lower demand. Therefore, the diverging effects of the credit supply shock and the credit demand shock have consequences for the direction of lending spreads in the absence of policy adjustments.

Fact 2 Depending on the elasticity of the credit supply curve, an adverse credit demand shock may lower lending spreads or they can remain unchanged.

11.3.1 Margins on Credit, the Repo Rate and Growth in Credit

Fig. 11.3a, b shows the developments in the policy rate, margins and growth in credit. It is evident in Fig. 11.3a that the increase in margins occurred during the tightening in 2006 and at the height (or peak) of the growth in credit. However, it is also evident that the margins did not respond to the decline in the policy rate as they stayed constant (with an upward bias) at elevated levels. In addition, Fig. 11.3b shows it is evident that the increase in spreads coincided with a steep deceleration in credit growth. Therefore, the slowing credit extension was accompanied by a rise in loan spreads at the same time as the policy rate was reduced to historically low levels, and this is consistent with the predictions of a credit supply shock.

As demonstrated earlier, even in the absence of the adjustment to the policy rate, the spreads should decline in response to lower demand. So what is evident in Fig. 11.3 is that there was a decline in the quantity of credit accompanied by an increase in margins at the same time as there was a massive decline in the policy rate. As shown earlier, this period coincided with an increase in banks' net interest income. This further suggests that there is preliminary evidence pointing to the dominance of a supply shock impacting developments in the quantity of loans.

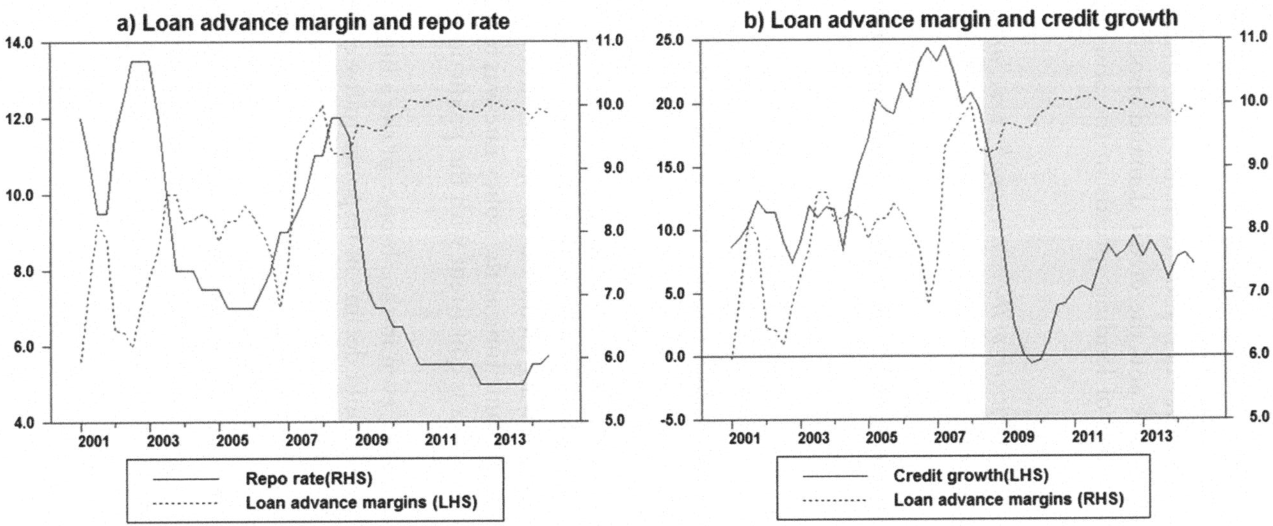

Fig. 11.3 The repo rate, margins and credit growth (*Note*: The shaded portion shows the period when the repo rate started to decline until the recent policy tightening phase. *Source*: SARB and authors' calculations)

11.3.2 Financial Regulatory Uncertainty Contribution to an Increase in Margins

This chapter does not focus on the role of regulatory uncertainty that characterized the financial landscape following the financial crisis. Nonetheless, it is useful to bring aspects of its contributions to the fore. As a result the chapter investigates: Did financial regulatory Policy uncertainty contribute to the rise in lending margins? It did not, based on evidence in determining if the rise in the spread was due to financial regulatory uncertainty or was it driven by own movements. Fig. 11.4b shows that the rise in margins was mainly due to own movements.

The own factors are captured by how much own movements in margins contribute to the evolution of spreads based on the historical decompositions approach. Own changes in lending spreads may be due to changes in risk aversion or bearing, repricing, changes in banking products and other bank or credit market-specific factors such as profit motives and maintaining market share.[5] Similar to predictions in the theoretical sections, the preliminary evidence concludes that an adverse credit supply shock resulted in an increase in spreads. This would have been the case even in the absence of additional regulatory burden. Regulatory reform may just have exacerbated the situation.

11.3.3 Facts Between Margins and Selected Macroeconomic Variables

Yes, it is possible not only based on data trends but based on the theoretical model discussed earlier. The theoretical sections showed the relationship between credit dynamics and spreads and the policy rate in the case of both an adverse credit supply and demand shocks. To determine

[5] See Walentin (2014).

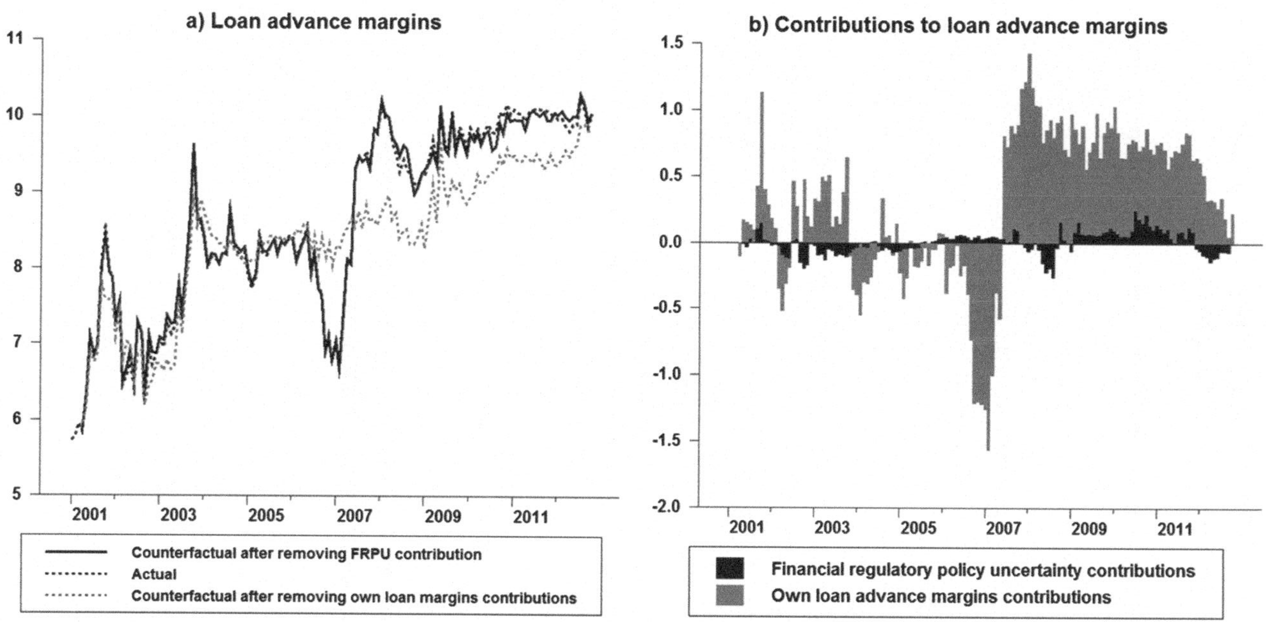

Fig. 11.4 Comparison of regulatory uncertainty and own loan margins contributions on the margins' movements (*Source*: SARB and authors' calculations)

the stylized facts, GDP growth, repo rate, credit growth and margins are plotted together to assess the bilateral relationships.

Both the scatter plots and cross correlations are applied to determine the relationship. The scatter plots suggest a negative bilateral relationship. That is, when GDP growth accelerates the loan spreads decline. This possibly reflects a decline in risk perceptions linked to improved economic activity and the outlook.

Which economic variable is more sensitive to loan spreads increases as measured by the slope of the bilateral relationships in Fig. 11.5? The sensitivity of the relationship is determined by the size of the slopes. The magnitudes of the slopes are depicted in Fig. 11.6.

The biggest magnitude of slope indicates that growth in credit is highly sensitive to spreads increases. Credit growth is nearly three times more sensitive than GDP growth and nearly five times the repo rate responses. This suggests that an abrupt rise in spreads can have adverse effects on credit growth.

11.3.4 Cross Correlations and Macroeconomic Bilateral Interdependencies

The analysis is extended to determine the lead relationships within a bilateral framework. We assess what happens when economic growth leads margins and vice versa. And also what happens when margins lead the credit growth and the vice versa. Finally, what happens when margins leads the repo rate and vice versa? We examine these questions to determine if they converge with findings based on the scatter plots in Fig. 8.5. We show the cross correlations in Fig. 11.7a–c.

The negative cross correlations suggest that an increase in one variable is accompanied by a movement in another variable in a different direction. The results show that when the increase in spread precedes economic growth, the repo rate and growth in credit, these variables tend to decline. However, when economic growth, the repo rate and growth in credit precede the spreads, the latter tends to fall.

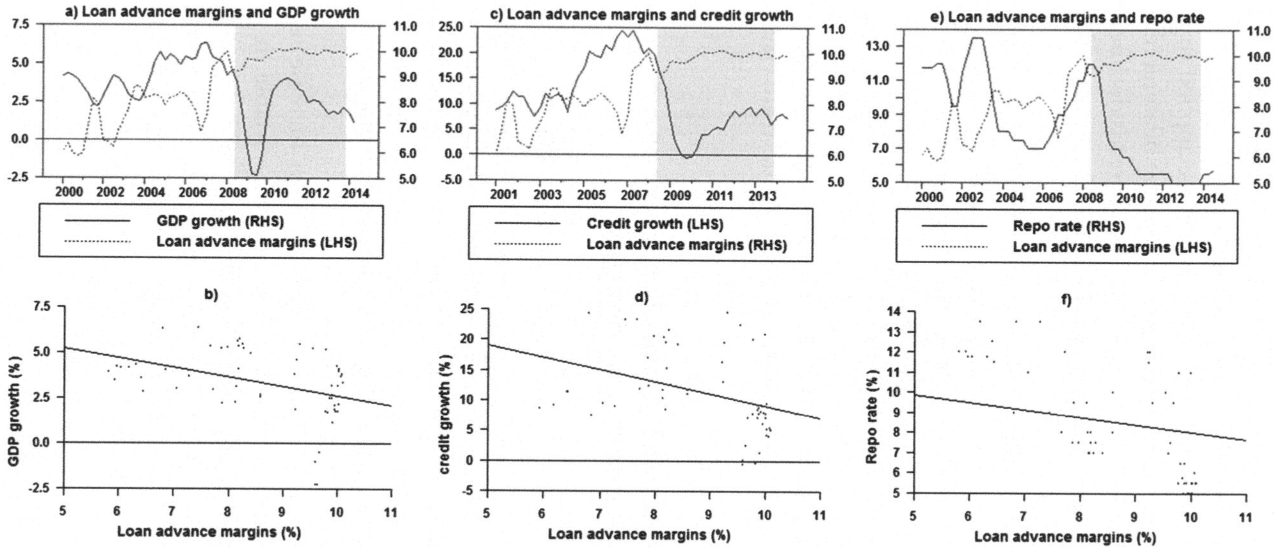

Fig. 11.5 Relationships between loan advance margins and selected macroeconomic variables (*Note*: The *shaded portion* shows the period when repo rate started to fall until the recent policy tightening. The data is on a quarterly (Q) basis from 2000Q1 to 2014Q3. *Source*: SARB and authors' calculations)

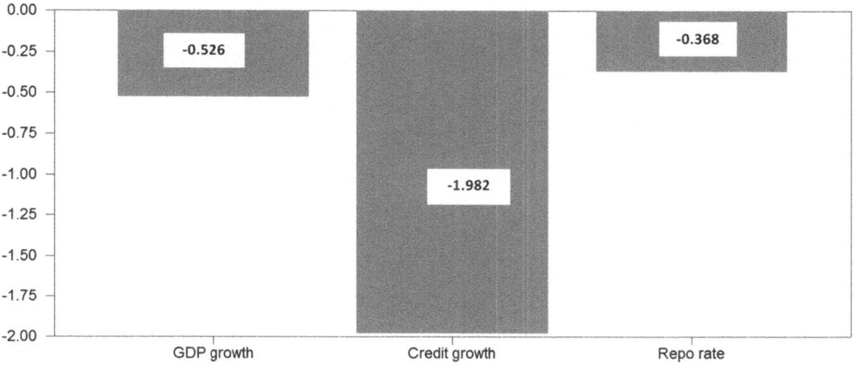

Fig. 11.6 Responses of economic variables to loan spreads (*Note*: These refer to slope of relationship shown in Fig. 8.5. *Source*: Authors' calculations)

11.4 Effects of an Adverse Credit Shock, Tight Monetary Shock and Spreads and Elevated Global Economic Uncertainty Shock

The empirical analysis is conducted via estimating a VAR model using quarterly (Q) data from 2000Q1 to 2014Q2. The variables include GDP growth, repo rate, margins or spreads and growth in credit.[6] This enables us to determine the effects of: (1) a tight monetary policy shock, (2) tight loan spreads shock, (3) an adverse credit supply shock and (4) effects of global economic uncertainty. The ordering of the variables assumes that economic growth is determined by factors outside the model but it is affected after a lag by other variables. However, economic growth affects other variables contemporaneously, including the policy rate. Loan spreads depend on the policy stance and economic growth. Credit

[6] We use two lags selected by AIC. The variables are estimated using the ordering stated. However, we used different ordering to assess for robustness and the results were robust to different ordering. The results were also robust to various lags. We used Monte Carlo simulation with 10,000 draws. We also controlled for the effects of the recession in 2009Q1 to 2009Q3.

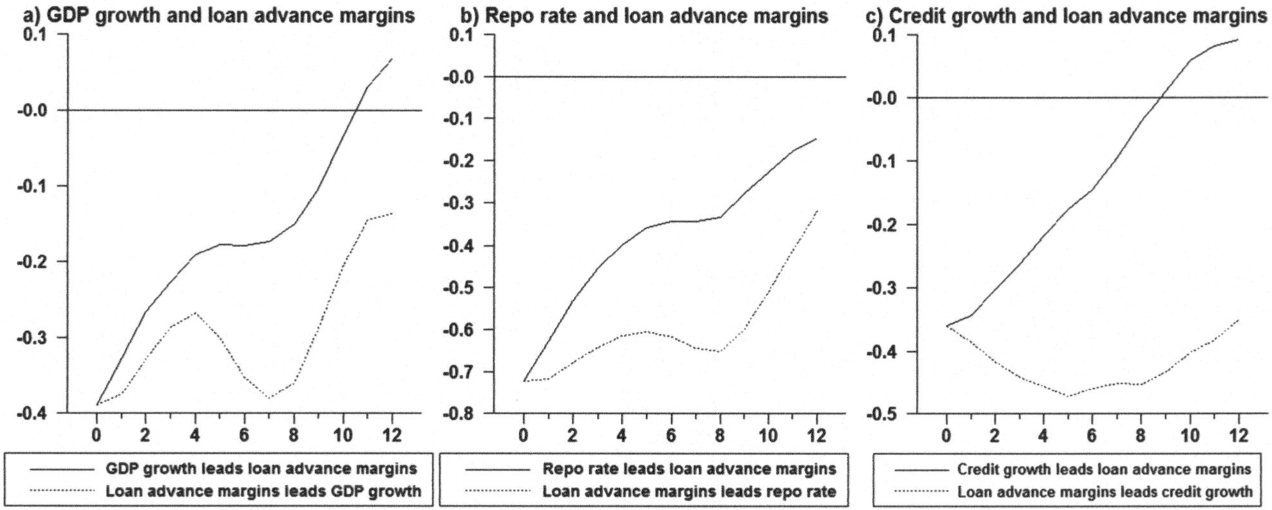

Fig. 11.7 Bilateral cross correlations (*Note*: The value on the vertical axis refers to strength of correlation and negative value, meaning this variable moves in the opposite direction while positive values mean these values move in the same direction. *Source*: Authors' calculations)

growth is impacted contemporaneously by economic growth, repo rate and loan spreads.

To capture the influence of global developments, the model includes the dummy variable for global economic uncertainty as an exogenous variable. Thereafter, we assess the effects of this variable on economic growth, repo rate, spreads and credit growth. Is it possible to obtain impulse responses from an exogenous variable in the model? Yes, modeling techniques allow us to determine the responses of the endogenous variables in the model to an exogenous dummy variable shock. The responses to tight monetary policy, tight loan spreads, adverse credit shocks and effects of positive global economic uncertainty shock are shown in Fig. 11.8.

An adverse credit supply shock lasts for nearly ten quarters, raise spreads within the first three quarters and spreads remain significantly positive for nearly five quarters. The shock to spreads also depresses economic growth for nearly ten quarters and credit growth remains significantly subdued for nearly 15 quarters. Thus, loan spreads shock depressed credit growth and economic growth more than effects exerted by tighter monetary policy. It is evident that monetary policy has to be loosened for a longer period to deal with the adverse effects of the loan spreads shock and an adverse credit supply shock.

To show the severity of the shocks, Fig. 11.9 depicts a comparison of the responses of economic growth to tighter monetary policy, tighter loan spreads and tighter credit supply shocks. It is evident that tighter loan spreads lead to larger declines in economic growth relative to the effects exerted by both tighter monetary policy and credit spreads. In addition, economic growth remains depressed for a longer period following an adverse loan supply shock.

So, what did the global economic uncertainty shock do to loan spreads, economic growth and credit growth? How did monetary policymakers respond to global economic uncertainty shock? The policy discourse has pointed out the role of the financial crisis and the ensuing period of policy uncertainty in the evolution of the protracted and subdued economic recovery. Apart from just pointing to the downward trend in economic growth and the subsequent sluggish economic growth recovery, the anal-

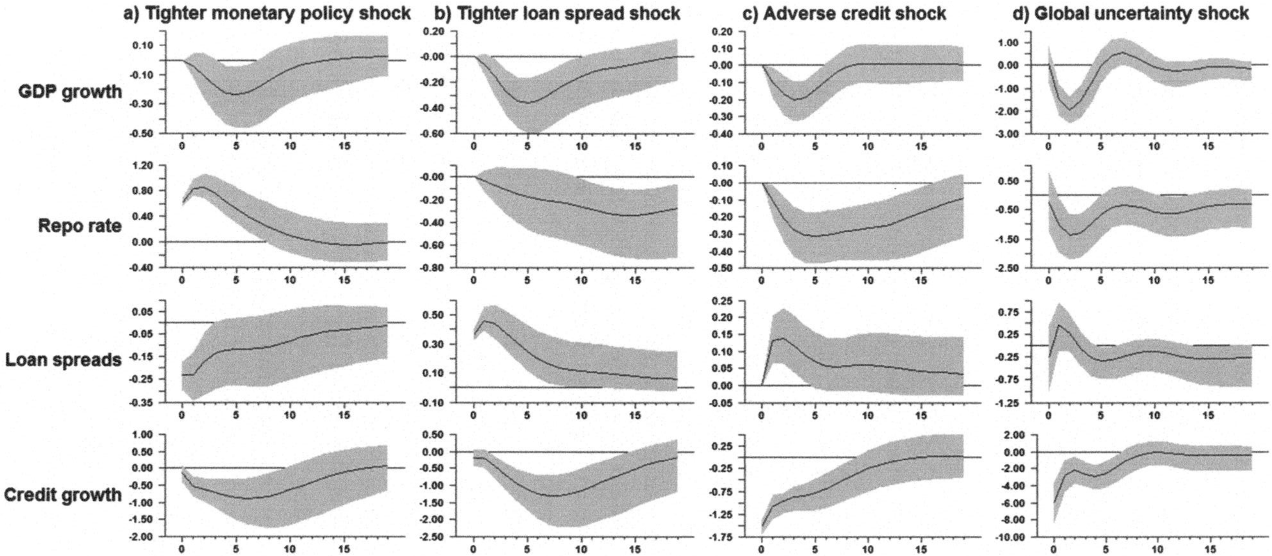

Fig. 11.8 Effects of a contractionary monetary policy, spreads and adverse credit supply shock (*Note*: The global economic uncertainty dummy is an exogenous dummy variable in the model. The dummy equals one from 2007Q3 to 2014Q3 when USA ended tapering of asset purchases and zero otherwise. The *solid line* denotes the impulse responses. The *grey shaded area* refers to the confidence bands of each shock. We conclude that the shock has significant effects if the bands do not include the zero line. We estimate the VAR using Monte Carlo estimation with 10,000 draws. *Source*: Authors' calculations)

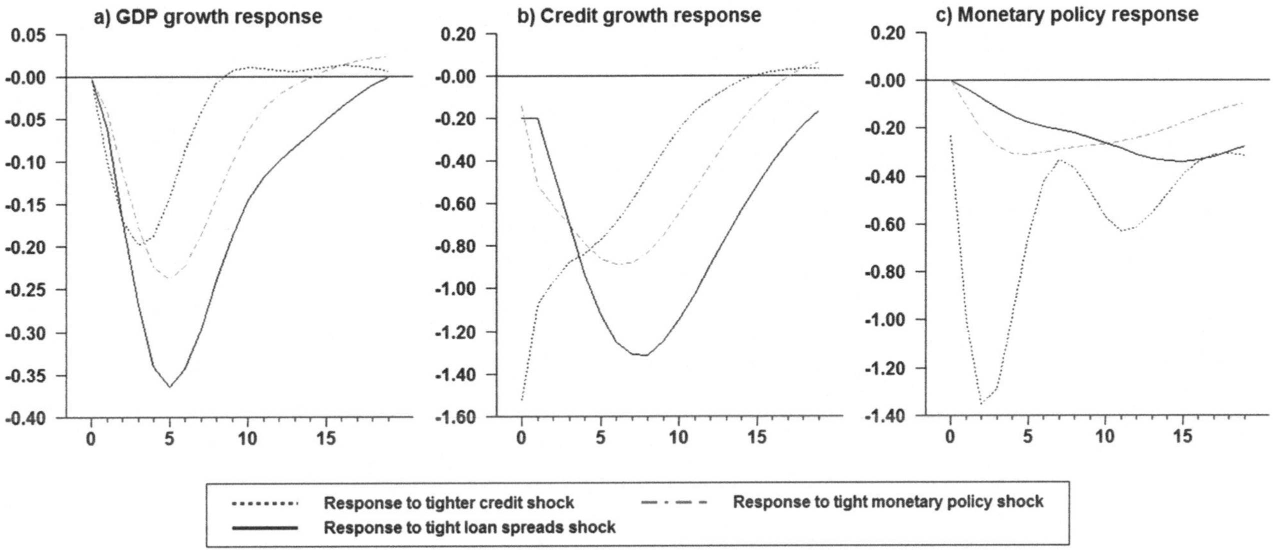

Fig. 11.9 Comparison of repo rate, economic and credit growth responses to one positive standard deviation shock (*Source*: Authors' calculations)

ysis demonstrates the impact of global economic uncertainty shock on economic growth, loan margins, credit growth and the policy response.[7]

Responses in Fig. 11.8d reveal that positive global economic uncertainty shock depresses economic growth for nearly a year. The recovery thereafter is very weak and wobbles around the no growth region. In addition, the policymakers respond aggressively by significantly lowering the policy rate for nearly five quarters. In fact, the policy rate remains expansionary for a prolonged period. Similar to observed trends during the global financial crisis, the evidence indicates that global economic uncertainty shock results in a severe contraction in credit growth for a prolonged period.

Is it possible to allude to the spike in loan spreads as being exogenously determined by the global financial crisis? Regarding the extent to which global uncertainty shock lead to structural breaks in loan spreads to higher levels, the evidence could not convincingly point to global economic uncertainty shock as a main source. In this context, the global economic uncertainty shock did not have a significant upward impact on the rise in loan spreads. The loan spreads responses are rather weak and transitory in response to this shock.

Do increases in loan spreads revert to their levels after experiencing an unexpected shock to their level? Evidence indicates this return takes longer, particularly if it is a loan spread shock only. Spreads remain significantly elevated for long periods, in this case twelve quarters. Therefore, evidence indicates that loans spreads tend to be slightly persistent in response to their own shocks and this is a similar reaction to the adverse credit supply shock. This poses a question to policymakers regarding whether they should leave spreads unattended to and rather use macro-prudential tools that impact credit volumes, rather than monetary policy as a tool for the altering price of credit to rapidly lower spreads.

What has happened to loan spreads now after the policy tightening in 2014? Based on data up to 2014Q2, the loan spreads declined minimally

[7] The approach used in the estimations follows the work that used dummy variables to determine the impact of wars and other shocks on economic growth.

in January 2014 and thereafter increased and have remained at a higher level. So what does the presence of high loan spreads and tight monetary policy do to the evolution of economic growth? A historical decomposition approach is applied to extract the contributions of these shocks to economic growth. Positive contributions imply that each specific shock made positive contributions to economic growth. In contrast, negative contributions imply the specific shock made negative contributions and was a drag on economic growth.

The contributions depicted in Fig. 11.10, show that a combination of (1) tight monetary policy shock, (2) loan spreads shock and (3) an adverse credit supply can have a devastating effect on the economy, particularly when they occur concurrently.

11.4.1 Can Economic Growth Mitigate Higher Spreads?

Apart from monetary policy initiatives, is it possible that improved economic growth can compress loan spreads? Yes, as shown in Fig. 11.11, a positive economic growth shock raises GDP growth by about 0.6 percentage points but leads to a transitory decline in loan spreads. However, it seems that spreads return to pre-shock levels in less than three quarters. Credit growth also rises significantly for nearly thirteen quarters, implying that the credit quantity effects can also be achieved via robust economic growth.

11.4.2 Evidence Based on the Penalty Function Sign Restriction Approach

The severity of an adverse credit supply shock is identified through comparing its effect to those of a tighter monetary policy shock and an adverse credit demand shock. The monetary policy, adverse credit supply shock and the adverse demand shock are identified via the sign restriction approach, in particular through applying the loss or penalty function

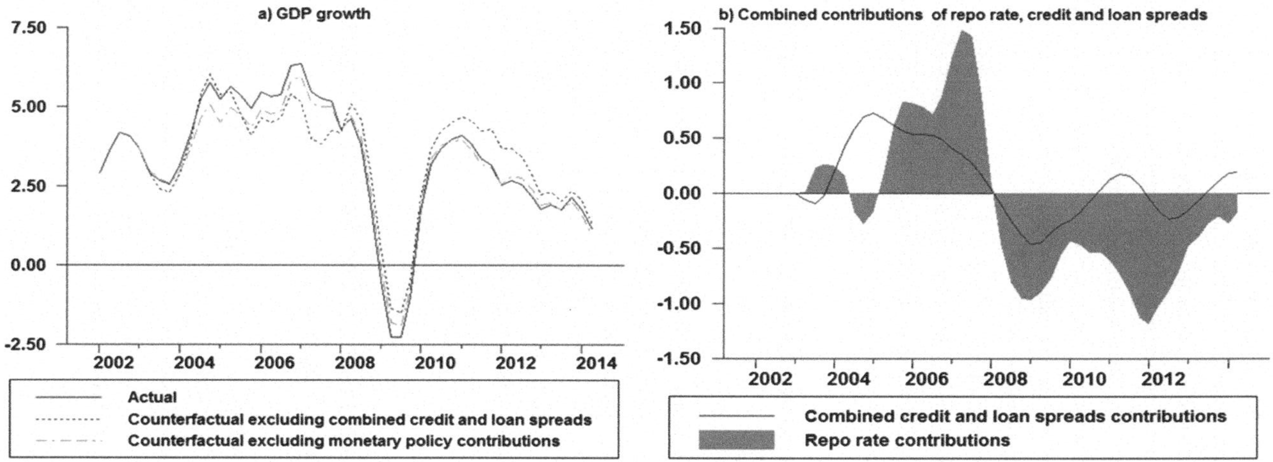

Fig. 11.10 Combined contributions of credit, loan spreads and repo rate on economic growth (*Source*: Authors' calculations)

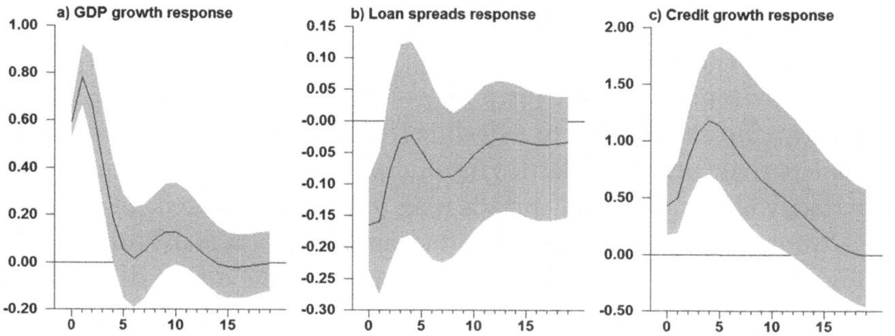

Fig. 11.11 Responses to unexpected positive standard deviation economic growth shocks (*Note*: The *solid lines* denote the impulse responses. The *grey shaded area* refers to confidence bands. We conclude the shock has significant effects if bands do not include the zero line. We estimate the VAR using Monte Carlo estimation with 10,000 draws *Source*: Authors' calculations)

approach as tools to sharpen the analysis.[8] This approach heavily penalizes those responses which violate the signs imposed based on the theoretical predictions. In turn, the approach rewards those responses which obey the imposed restrictions.

A tight monetary policy shock is a shock which raises the repo rate, lowers spreads and lowers growth in credit. In addition, an adverse credit supply shock is a shock which lowers growth in credit and raises spreads, whereas the repo rate declines.[9] These shock effects are restricted to last for at least two quarters. At the same time, the identification is agnostic about the response of economic growth to both shocks. Subsequently, this variable is left unrestricted to allow the data to tell us the responses.

How then does the modeling approach disentangle the adverse loan supply shock from the adverse credit demand shocks? To disentangle the credit shocks between adverse credit supply and demand shocks, we use a pure sign restriction approach to the identification of structural shocks. The pure sign restriction approach uses theoretical signs to identify the structural shocks based on theoretical considerations in the modelling exercises. Both of these two shocks lower volume (quantities) of credit but have opposing (different) effects on the price of credit. Therefore, an

[8] For further details see Uhlig (2005), Mountford and Uhlig (2005), Rafiq and Mallick (2008), amongst others.

[9] For further details see Hristov et al. (2012).

adverse credit demand shock should lower the volume of credit and the price of credit (lending rate).

In an environment where the policy rate is left unchanged, the adverse credit demand shocks lead to a decline (fall) in loan spreads, if loan supply is less than perfectly elastic. As alluded to earlier on, if loan supply is perfectly elastic, the loan spreads may remain unchanged. In contrast, the adverse credit supply shocks lead to an increase in loan spreads. This is how the effects of an adverse credit supply and the demand shocks are distinguished using a sign restriction penalty function approach.

What does a tighter monetary policy shock do? In Fig. 11.12a the evidence shows that a tight monetary policy shock depresses growth in credit and spreads for longer periods. Since economic growth was unrestricted, evidence indicates that this shock depresses growth significantly between four and eight quarters. Do these responses differ from those of an adverse credit supply shock? As shown in Fig. 11.12b, the adverse credit supply shock leads to a significant contraction in economic growth and this lasts up to seven quarters. This suggests that economic growth is very responsive to a financial shock. The results also show that a one-standard deviation shock in credit supply lowers credit by nearly 2 percentage points on impact and results in a significant increase in the spreads. The adverse credit supply shock leads to a persistent contraction in credit growth and a rise in loan spreads.

If lending spreads capture risk taking by banks, the fact that spreads tend to fall when the policy rate tightens augers well for the impact of policy in reducing risk behavior. Moreover, to some extent this alleviates the burden on macro-prudential tools. These findings are consistent with other empirically established results, suggesting that monetary policy is non-neutral from a financial stability perspective. It is not exactly the right tool for the task of financial stability. Nonetheless, it does possess an advantage relative to financial supervision and regulation, in that "it gets in all of the cracks."[10] This finding is robust to using the penalty function sign restriction approach and the Cholesky ordering approach.

Fig. 11.13, compares the responses of economic growth and credit growth to (1) tighter credit shock, (2) tight monetary policy shock

[10] For further reading, see Stein (2014) and Altunbas et al. (2014).

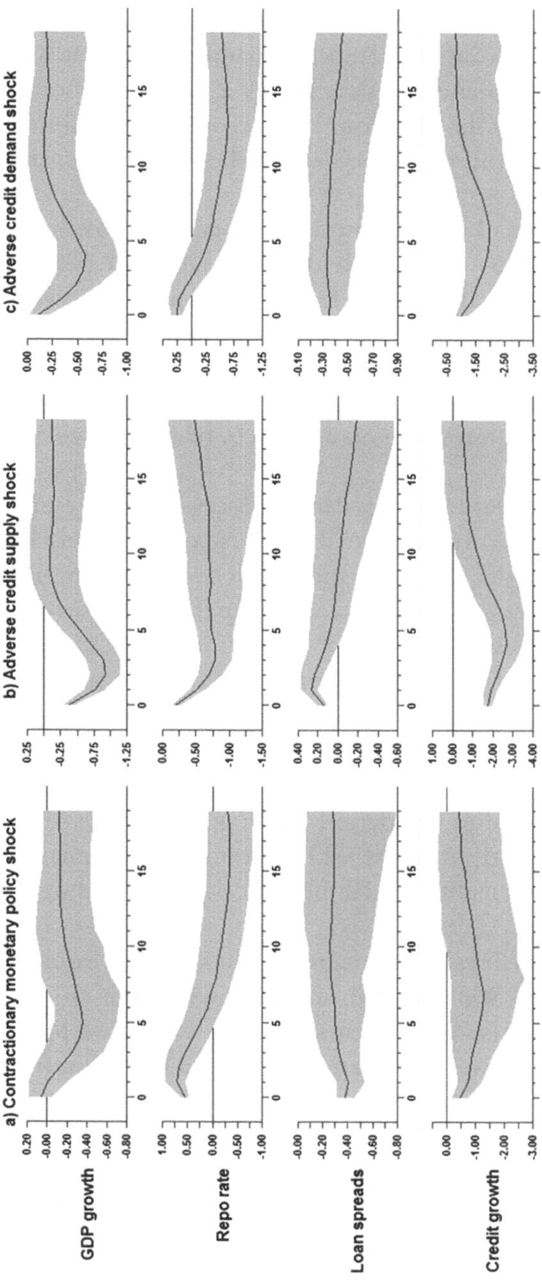

Fig. 11.12 Responses to tighter monetary policy shock and adverse credit supply and demand shocks (*Note*: The vertical shows the variables responding and the shocks are shown at the *top* of each graph. We estimate the VAR using Monte Carlo estimation with 10,000 draws *Source*: Authors' calculations)

and (3) shock to tighter loan spreads shock. The same figure shows the impulses derived from different models, namely, one that assumes the Cholseky ordering and the one that adopts a sign restriction approach. This approach answers the question: If the economy is assumed to operate as predicted by economic theory, would the results be sensitive to this assumption?

The results in Fig. 11.13a show that economic growth declines in response to all shocks, albeit with different lags and peak responses. Evidence indicates that the largest decline in economic growth is due to an adverse credit supply based on sign restrictions. This is followed by responses to tighter spreads shock. Evidence indicates very little difference in the responses of economic growth to a tighter monetary policy shock based on the sign restrictions approach, relative to when the shock is exogenous.

In Fig. 11.13b similar responses can be observed. The volume of credit declines significantly in response to an adverse credit supply shock. It is evident from the results that the responses derived from the shocks with signs imposed in the model tend to accentuate the responses of economic growth and credit growth.

The comparison of the credit demand and credit supply shocks is shown in Fig. 11.14a, b. Evidence indicates that both adverse credit shocks lower credit growth and economic growth. In Fig. 11.14a economic growth declines significantly due to an adverse credit supply shock in first two quarters. After this period, GDP growth falls within the confidence bands. This indicates that GDP responds in a similar manner to both shocks, despite the differential theoretically predicted signs imposed on these shocks.

Credit growth declines and remains subdued for an extended period due to both shocks. We find that credit growth tends to decline very much due to an adverse credit demand shock compared to credit supply induced shock. However, evidence indicates a lack of statistically significant differences in Fig. 11.14b, implying that credit growth decline induced by demand shock is different from that induced by credit supply shock. Therefore, the evidence concludes that the evolution of credit growth would not be statistically different to a demand shock relative to a supply shock.

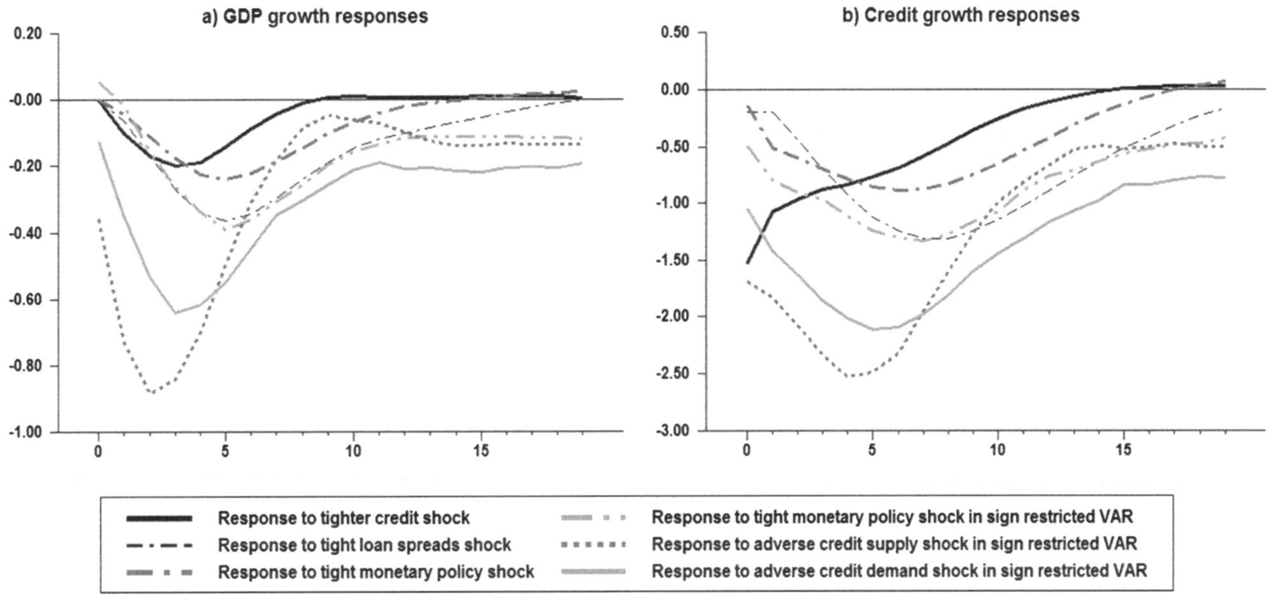

Fig. 11.13 Comparison of economic growth responses and credit growth responses to various shocks (*Note*: The other shocks are based on Cholesky decomposition, which suggests that economic growth is exogenous, that monetary policy responds to economic growth and that loans respond to both economic growth and policy rate, and that credit growth responds to economic growth, repo rate and loans spreads. The shocks based on sign-restricted VAR uses signs predicted by economic theory. *Source*: Authors' calculations)

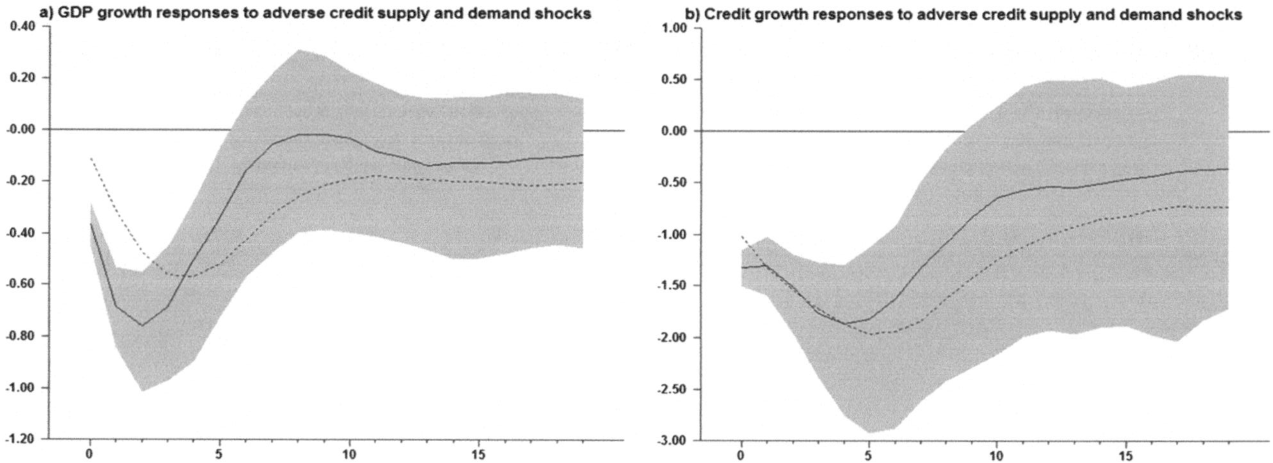

Fig. 11.14 Comparison of GDP and credit growth responses to adverse credit supply and demand shocks (*Note*: The responses are in percentage points. The *dotted line* refers to responses to adverse credit demand shocks and the *solid lines* denote responses to adverse credit supply shocks. The *light shaded area* denotes the confidence from adverse credit supply shock. *Source*: Authors' calculations)

11.5 Adverse Credit Supply Shock and the Conduct of Monetary Policy and Loan Rate Margins

The analysis now extends to examining the role of an adverse credit supply shock on the evolution of GDP growth and the repo rate. The analysis is based on the counterfactual approach, which enables comparisons between the actual and counterfactual values of these variables.[11] Evidence indicates a clear and distinct contribution of the adverse credit supply shock on repo rate in Fig. 11.15a, b. The adverse credit supply shock made positive contributions to the repo rate for the most part, prior to the recession in 2009. Since then, the negative credit supply shock has contributed to a lower repo rate. This includes the two repo rate increases in 2014, which were still lower than the counterfactual suggests. Overall, the adverse credit supply shock contributed in the prevailing lower repo rate than that would have been the case in the absence of the shock.

Did the adverse credit supply shock lead to worsening of economic growth? Undoubtedly it did; the adverse credit supply shock in Fig. 11.15c, d exacerbated the economic growth decline in 2009. However, the contributions post-recession have been briefly positive in 2010 and negative thereafter.

Fig. 11.16b, shows that the credit supply shock contributed positively to the elevated levels of margins. The contributions have been persistently positive, albeit with varying magnitudes since the beginning of 2009. In Fig. 11.16d, it is evident that the adverse credit supply shock contributed much of the contraction in credit growth in 2007. The contributions have since remained negative. All the evidence based on repo rate and credit growth trajectories beginning in 2009 suggests that indeed policy-makers' decisions impacted the price of credit. The repo rate was lower

[11] The counterfactual values refer to values that we get after removing (shutting off) the contributions of the credit supply shock to the variables of interest. When the actual exceeds the counterfactual it implies that adverse credit supply shock made positive contributions to the variable of interest.

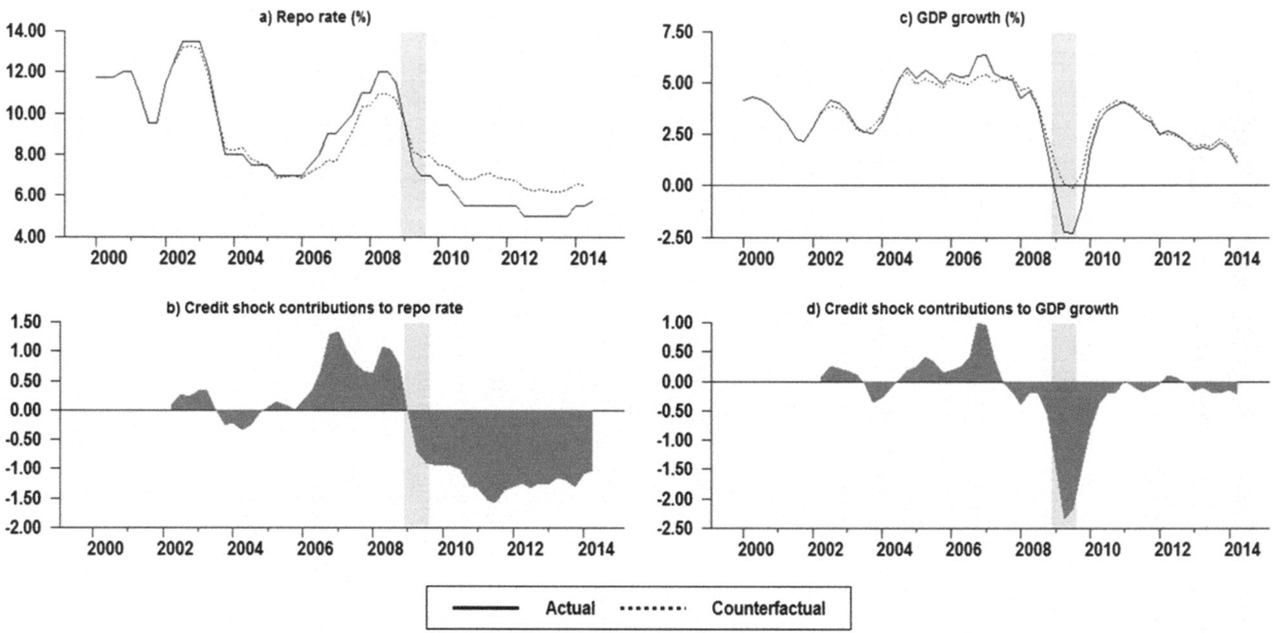

Fig. 11.15 Actual and counterfactual economic variables and the contributions of adverse credit supply shock to repo rate and GDP growth (*Note*: The contributions are in percentages. The *light grey shaded area* denotes the recession period in 2009. *Source*: Authors' calculations)

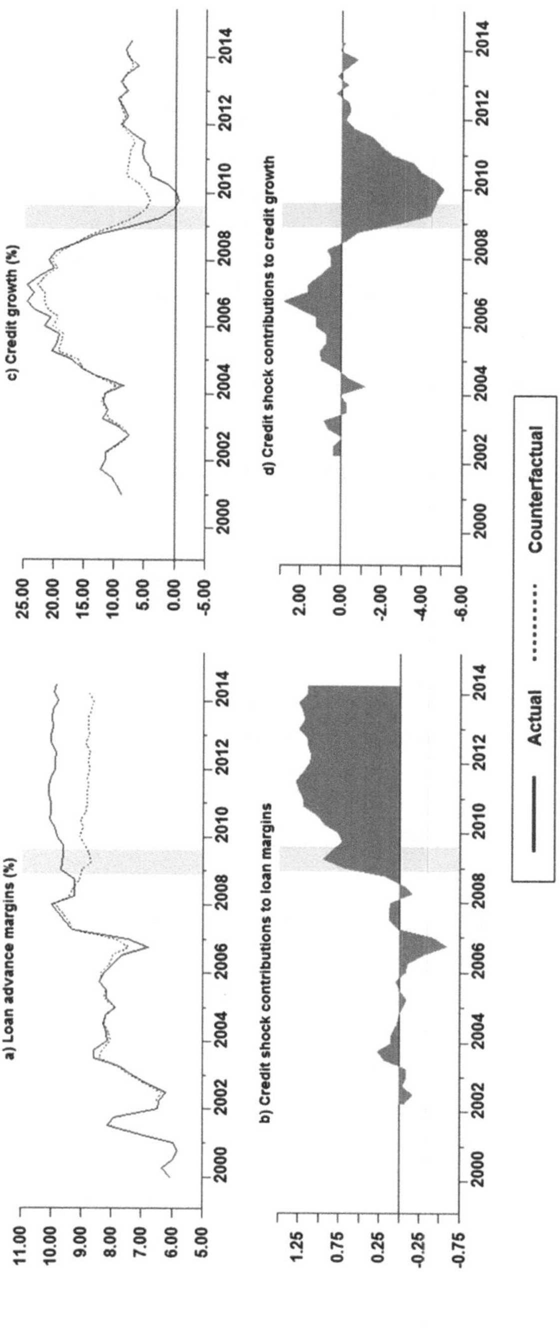

Fig. 11.16 Actual and counterfactual loan advance margins and GDP growth (*Note*: The contributions of adverse credit supply shocks are in percentage points. The *light grey shaded area* denotes the recession period in 2009. *Source*: Authors' calculations)

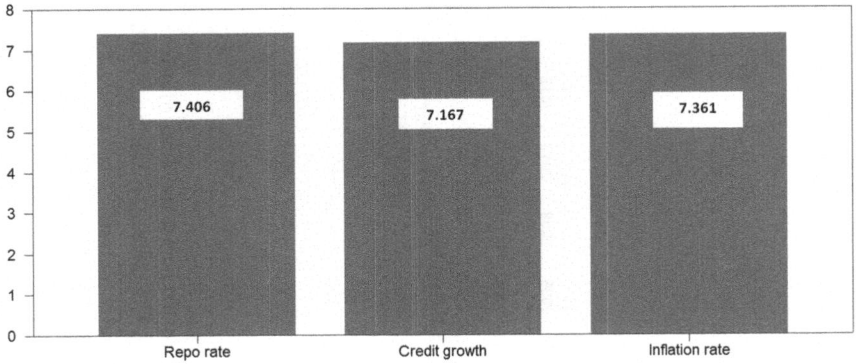

Fig. 11.17 Lending margins' threshold levels at which the repo rate, credit and inflation have differential effects on economic growth (*Note*: The magnitudes are the thresholds for the loan margins based on the variables that are included in the both the linear and nonlinear parts of the model. *Source*: Authors' calculations)

than its counterfactual rate. The latter is the repo rate that would prevail in the absence of an adverse credit shock.

What about the impact on credit volumes? The credit volume remained depressed, suggesting that credit growth was still below what would have prevailed in the absence of adverse credit supply shock. This implies that the quantity component was not stimulated enough and they should have risen this much had additional measures been taken to stimulate the credit quantities rather than price of credit.

11.5.1 Is There a Threshold Level Beyond Which Loan Spreads Have Adverse Effects on Economic Growth?

In earlier sections, evidence indicated that an unexpected increase in spreads directly reduces economic growth. This therefore propels us to ask whether there is an indirect channel operating through some threshold level of margins. The threshold is determined by estimating a nonlinear logistic model. The specification of the threshold model suggests that economic growth depends on the repo rate, lagged GDP growth,

Table 11.1 The effects of the repo rate, credit growth and inflation on economic growth when margins exceed threshold

Loan margin (%)	Effect of repo rate when loan margins exceed 7.406 percent	Effects of credit when loan margins exceed 7.167 percent	Effect of inflation when loan margins exceed 7.361 percent
8	−0.2076	−0.8034	−0.8097
9	−0.2193	−0.8326	−0.8409
10	−0.2193	−0.8331	−0.8411
11	−0.2193	−0.8331	−0.8411

Source: Authors' calculations

inflation and credit growth. However, above the threshold for margins (or the nonlinear regime) economic growth depends on either the repo rate or credit growth or inflation.[12]

Is it possible that above a certain threshold of margins the increase in the repo rate, growth in credit and inflation exert differential effects on economic growth? Yes, this seems to be the case. The estimated thresholds for margins are shown in Fig. 11.17.[13] The threshold levels for margins as shown in Fig. 11.17 vary but are below 7.5 percent. Thus, at or above this estimated threshold level, lending margins affect the manner in which monetary policy tightening, credit growth and inflation impact economic growth.

In Table 11.1 we show the estimated long-run effects exerted by the increase in the repo rate, credit growth and inflation when the various levels of lending margins thresholds are exceeded.[14] There is clear worsening of the differential effects when loan margins increase from 8 percent to 10 percent. For example, the long-run values in Table 8.1 show that when the loan margin is at 10 percent, an increase in the repo rate lowers economic growth by 0.22 percentage points. Similarly, credit extension

[12] We conclude similarly when replacing the repo rate with repo rate gap calculated based on the HP filtered gap.

[13] We present the results in Table A8.1 below. It is evident that the signs and the significance of the impact of the repo rate, credit growth and inflation vary significantly below and above the thresholds for margins. The transition functions are shown in Fig. A8.1.

[14] We say the margins are in high state if margins exceed the threshold values given in Table A8.2. To calculate the long-run effects on economic growth we only use the values that are significant, as shown in Table A8.1.

lowers economic growth by 0.83 percentage points and inflation lowers growth by 0.84 percentage points. Moreover, the evidence establishes that larger output losses are associated with increases in inflation and credit when margins exceed the estimated margins threshold level.

This evidence shows that there is a threshold level beyond which higher margins become detrimental to economic growth via their impact on the repo rate and inflation.

11.6 Conclusion and Policy Implications

In policy terms, the findings suggest that monetary policy and initiatives to bolster economic growth are necessary but are insufficient policy interventions in dealing with the negative consequences of lending margins and attempts to compress them. This is particularly the case if policymakers have a view on the levels of spreads that are potentially excessive, thereby weakening the desired effects of monetary policy easing, and which are detrimental to financial stability. To anchor the policy debate and discussions, we estimated threshold levels of loan spreads above which they exert negative effects on economic growth. Evidence indicates that beyond a lending margins' threshold level of 7.17 to 7.5 percent, higher margins become detrimental to economic growth via their impact on the repo rate and inflation.

Furthermore, for financial stability purposes, if lending spreads capture risk taking by banks, the fact that spreads tend to fall when the policy rate tightens augers well for the impact of policy in reducing risk behavior. Despite monetary policy not being the right tool for the task of financial stability, to some extent these findings identify monetary policy as a potential tool that can alleviate the burden on macro-prudential tools. This finding is robust to the using the penalty function sign restriction approach and the Cholesky ordering approach.

All the evidence based on repo rate trajectories and credit growth trajectories beginning in 2009 suggests that indeed policymakers had an impact on the price of credit, because the actual repo rate was lower than the counterfactual. However, growth in credit volumes remained depressed relative to that would have prevailed in the absence of an adverse credit supply shock. This suggests that the quantity component was not stimulated enough and that additional policy measures were possibly needed to stimulate the credit quantities and to complement the policy effects on the price of credit. The adverse effects of an unexpected positive loan spreads shock suggests that policymakers should determine that the threshold levels of loan spreads are less harmful to economic growth and credit growth.

Overall, the findings point to a policy lesson that while monetary policy can lower the policy rate to mitigate the adverse effects of loan spreads there is a need for supplementary tools, possibly from the macroprudential tools, to deal with the quantity aspect which may also lower spreads. In addition, if spreads are sticky to downward adjustments to the policy rate but highly responsive to repo rate hikes, then a forecasted path of the future interest rates might lead to a faster mark-up and pricing of the projected interest rate hike. This will further raise spreads and have damaging effects, particularly on new loans, even if the rate hikes do not materialize. Experience has taught us that the pricing of loans occurs instantaneously. Such a policy initiative being used as a communication tool to the extent that it guides the pricing of loans can have a detrimental effect on the quantities (new loans).

Summary of Main Findings

- An adverse credit supply shock raises loan spreads for a prolonged period.
- Loan spreads shocks depress growth in credit and GDP more than tighter monetary policy shock.
- Monetary policy is not the only policy intervention that can deal with the adverse credit supply shock and compress spreads.
- Improved economic growth can compress loan spreads, raise growth of credit.
- The estimated lending margins threshold levels are less than 7.5 percent.
- Above the thresholds, higher margins become detrimental to economic growth.

Appendix

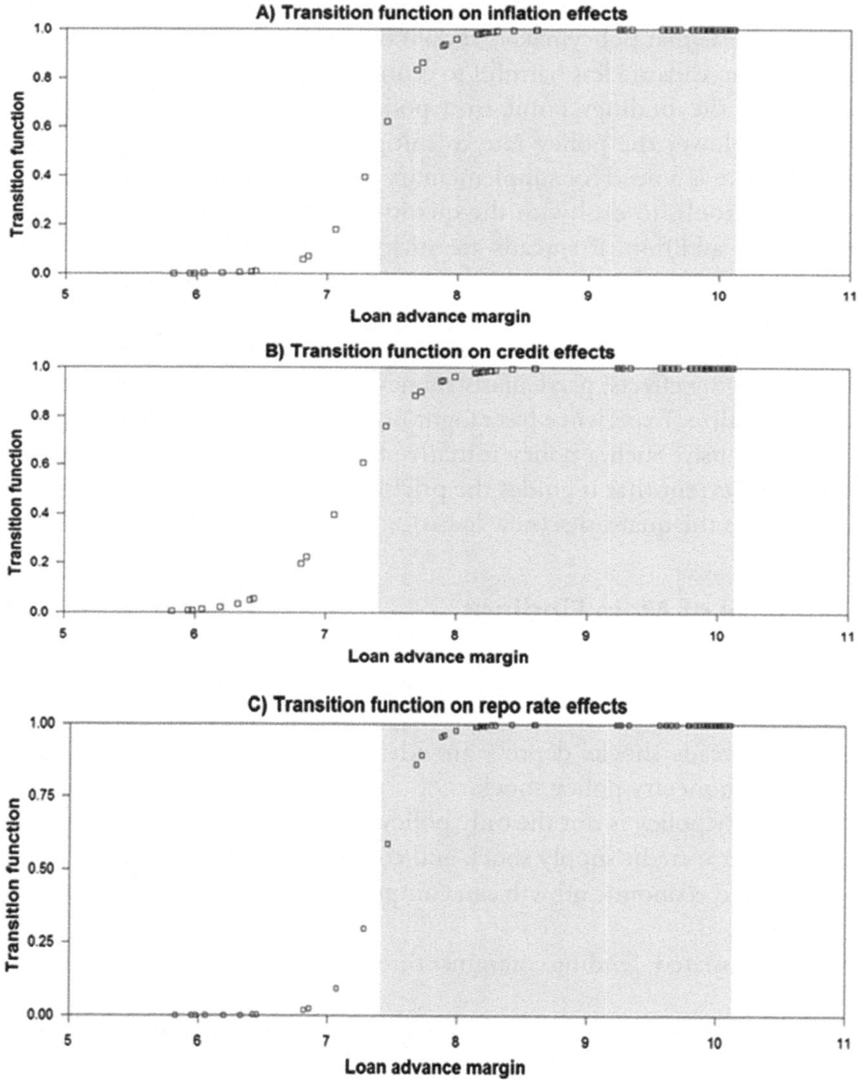

Fig. A11.1 The transition functions (*Source*: Authors' calculations)

Table A11.1 Nonlinear threshold model

Variable	Model with repo		Model with credit		Model with inflation	
	Coefficient		Coefficient		Coefficient	
			Linear regime			
Constant	1.158	(0.00)*	0.919	(0.01)*	1.267	(0.00)*
Repo rate	0.059	(0.05)**	0.012	(0.73)	−0.042	(0.40)
GDP $_{t-1}$	0.853	(0.00)*	0.905	(0.00)*	0.824	(0.00)*
Inflation	−0.140	(0.00)*	−0.133	(0.00)*	−0.003	(0.96)
Credit	0.012	(0.54)	0.065	(0.15)	0.021	(0.29)
			Nonlinear regime			
Repo rate	−0.091	(0.00)*				
Credit			−0.079	(0.08)*		
Inflation					−0.15	(0.00)*
Value of transition	6.65		3.96		5.09	
Lending margin threshold	7.41		7.17		7.36	

Source: Authors' calculations
*Implies significance at 5% level
**implies significance at 10 % level

12

Credit Supply Shocks and Real Economic Activity

Learning Objectives

- See how credit supply shock drives real economic activity cycles
- Credit market dynamics explain slowing growth of GDP, credit and capital formation
- Adverse credit demand contributions slow economic activity
- Credit demand shocks contributions elevate and depress credit growth and capital formation
- Sovereign bond yields impact credit supply shock contributions to GDP
- High government bond yields impact credit supply conditions

12.1 Introduction

The South African economy has been buffeted by multiple supply side shocks at the same time. For a better understanding of which shocks dominate developments, here we group shocks into aggregate supply, credit supply and aggregate demand. In this chapter, shocks that drive sluggish growth

N. Gumata, E. Ndou, *Bank Credit Extension and Real Economic Activity in South Africa*, DOI 10.1007/978-3-319-43551-0_12

in credit and GDP are assessed. To what extent have credit supply shock contributions been the driver of real economic activity cycles? Within the credit market dynamics, which shock between credit supply and demand is slowing GDP growth, credit growth and gross fixed capital formation?

The relative role of credit supply and demand shocks has different implications for macroeconomic conditions. For instance, Bijsterbosch et al. (2015) argue that if sluggish bank lending reflects bottlenecks in the supply of credit rather than the lack of demand, weak lending is likely to dampen economic activity. If credit demand is not met by adequate credit supply, investment projects cannot be undertaken and this drags economic recovery. Since demand and supply shocks often occur at the same time, they need to be correctly identified to better inform policymakers. Furthermore, US policy tightening raises the possibility that bond yields will rise over and above the adjustment that has already occurred. Hence, this chapter determines the relationship between government bond yields and credit risk[1] on credit supply contributions to growth in (1) GDP and (2) gross fixed capital formation.

12.2 Credit Supply Shock and Economic Activity

A credit supply shock is not merely the release of large credit volumes but should also have desired effects on the real economy. A graphical illustration in Fig. 12.1 is used to show the differences of the effects of a credit supply and demand shock on economic activity. The chapter separates credit supply effects from those of aggregate supply shocks which may arise from technology or productivity shocks, oil price shocks and labor supply shocks (Gambetti and Muso 2012). In addition, the chapter also separates credit supply shocks from aggregate demand or credit demand shocks which may emanate from consumption and investment demand shocks, fiscal policy and monetary policy independent of credit conditions.

In order to properly capture the shock effects, the analysis uses the economic fundamentals which suggest that aggregate supply shock moves

[1] As proxied by non-performing loans (NPLs).

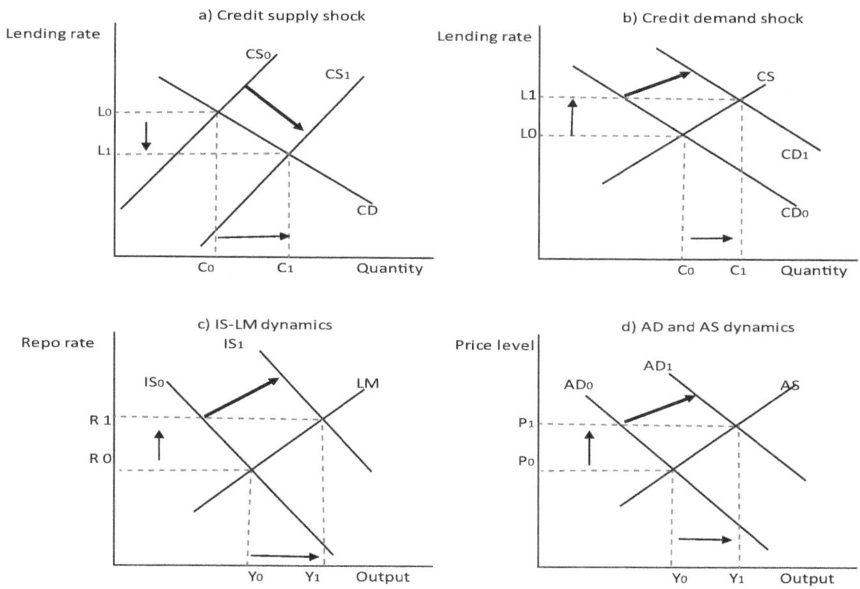

Fig. 12.1 Linkages between credit markets, aggregate demand and supply, and IS-LM dynamics (*Note*: CS_0 and CS_1 denote credit supply at the initial point and after the credit supply shock. CD_0 and CD_1 denote credit supply at the initial point and after the credit supply shock. C_0 and C_1 denote initial and new credit quantity after impact. L_0 and L_l refers to the initial and new lending rate. AD_0 and AD_1 denote the aggregate demand curves at the initial point and after the credit supply shock. P_0 and P_1 denote the old and new price levels. Y_0 and Y_l refer to old and new output levels. IS_0 and IS_1 denote the investment saving curves at the initial point and after the credit supply shock. R_0 and R_1 denote the old and new repo rate levels. Y_0 and Y_l refer to old and new output levels. *Source*: Author's drawing.

output and prices in different directions. The aggregate demand shock moves output and prices in the same direction. Why is it important to assess these shocks simultaneously? Because expansionary shocks, such as aggregate supply and aggregate demand shocks, raise GDP and credit and also raise lending rates. Therefore, they need to be correctly identified. However, in a later section we let data determine if lending rates rise to aggregate demand shocks. In contrast, credit supply shocks lower lending rates)

Credit supply shocks encompass various events, such as unexpected changes in bank capital available for loans, regulatory changes, changes in funding, changes in risk perception of potential borrowers and changes in the degree of competition in the banking sector (Gambetti and Musso 2012). Consistent with the theoretical predictions in Fig. 12.1, a credit supply shock is a shock which lowers (1) the lending rate and the quantity of available credit in Fig. 12.1a, (2) raises inflation in Fig. 12.1d and (3) increase the repo rate in Fig. 12.1c. An increase in credit supply will lead to increased consumption and investment which shifts the investment saving curve upward from IS_0 to IS_1 in Fig. 12.1c, lifting the policy rate. Increased consumption and investment will raise aggregate demand from AD_0 to AD_1 and raise the price level. The preceding adjustments still hold in the case of a credit demand shock except that the lending rate rises in Fig. 12.1b.[2]

A Bayesian sign restricted vector autoregression (VAR) model is estimated. The model includes the lending rate, repo rate, CPI inflation, credit growth, GDP growth and growth in gross fixed capital formation. A credit supply shock suggests that the lending rates should decline, whereas the policy rate, growth in GDP, inflation and growth in credit growth should be positive. However, we left growth in capital formation unrestricted to all shocks. All shock effects are restricted to last for two quarters.

The model is estimated using quarterly (Q) data spanning 1990Q1–2014Q2 and the four shocks are estimated for the same time. These shocks are credit supply shock, credit demand shock, aggregate demand shock and aggregate supply shock. The aggregate demand, aggregate supply and credit supply shocks are defined as in Bijsterbosch et al. (2015). The credit demand differs from credit supply shock as lending rate increases. Aggregate demand differs from credit demand through raising the lending rates in the latter. The responses of lending rates to aggregate demand shocks are left unrestricted. The responses to credit supply shock are illustrated in Fig. 12.2, which shows that the model obeys the restric-

[2] The credit supply shock based on Fig. 12.1 differs from a monetary policy shock. The monetary policy shock leads to a decrease in interest rates in the short run. Aggregate demand and supply will induce increased demand for loans leading to an increase in loan quantities and lending rates.

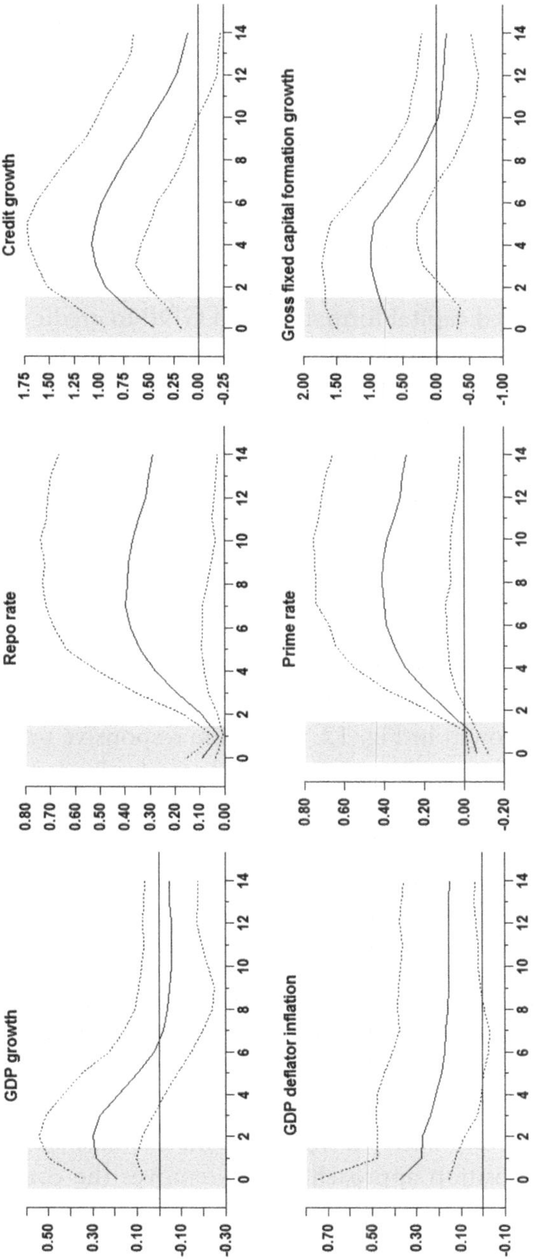

Fig. 12.2 Responses to expansionary credit supply shocks (*Source*: Authors' calculations)

tions imposed, while the evidence indicates that growth in gross fixed capital formation increases significantly even though it was left unrestricted.

12.2.1 Effects of These Shocks on Growth in GDP and Investment

The aggregate demand, aggregate supply and credit supply shocks are as defined as in Bijsterbosch et al. (2015). Fig. 12.3 shows the responses of growth in gross fixed capital formation and GDP to credit supply shock, aggregate demand shock and aggregate supply shock. In Fig. 12.3 these three shocks have a more delayed effect on growth of fixed capital formation than on GDP growth. In addition, the aggregate supply shock raises growth in gross fixed capital formation for three quarters, which is relatively shorter than the six quarters of GDP growth.

In Fig. 12.4 the credit supply shock significantly raises growth in gross fixed capital formation, more than other shocks in Fig. 12.4a. Aggregate supply shock raises GDP growth significantly for longer periods than other shocks in Fig. 12.4b.

Fig. 12.5 compares the responses of credit growth, GDP and gross fixed capital formation to the three shocks, respectively. Evidence indicates that credit growth in Fig. 12.5a is more responsive to credit supply shocks than to both aggregate demand and supply shocks. GDP growth in Fig. 12.5b rises to an aggregate demand shock much more than to both credit supply and aggregate supply shocks. Gross fixed capital formation in Fig. 12.5c rises much more in response to aggregate supply shock than the other two shocks.

12.2.2 The Influence of Credit Supply Shocks on Economic Growth, Credit and Investment

Fig. 12.6 shows the actual and counterfactual growth in credit, gross fixed capital formation and GDP. The counterfactuals are based on the historical decomposition approach which removes the contributions of

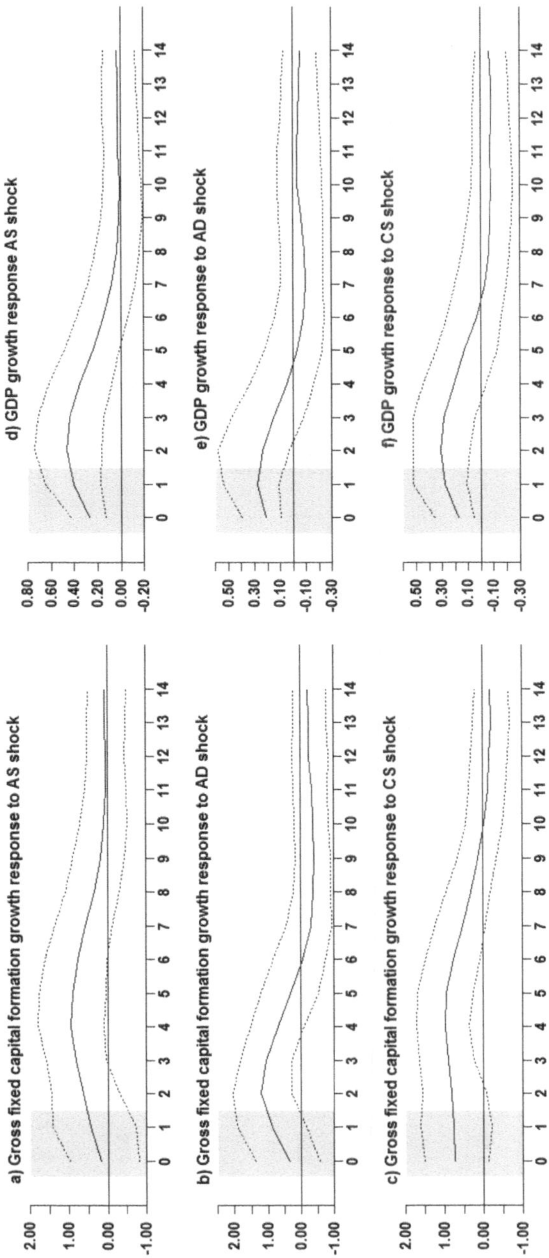

Fig. 12.3 Responses of GDP and capital formation growth responses to expansionary credit supply (CS), aggregate demand (AD) and supply shocks (SS) (*Source*: Authors' calculations)

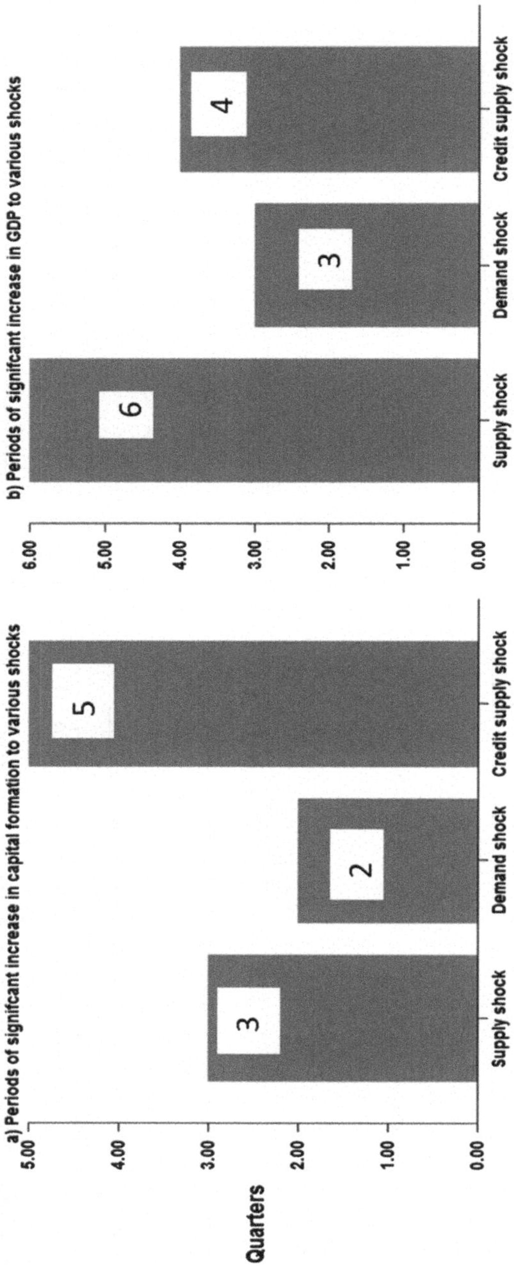

Fig. 12.4 Periods of elevated responses to expansionary credit supply, aggregate demand and supply shocks (*Source*: Authors' calculations)

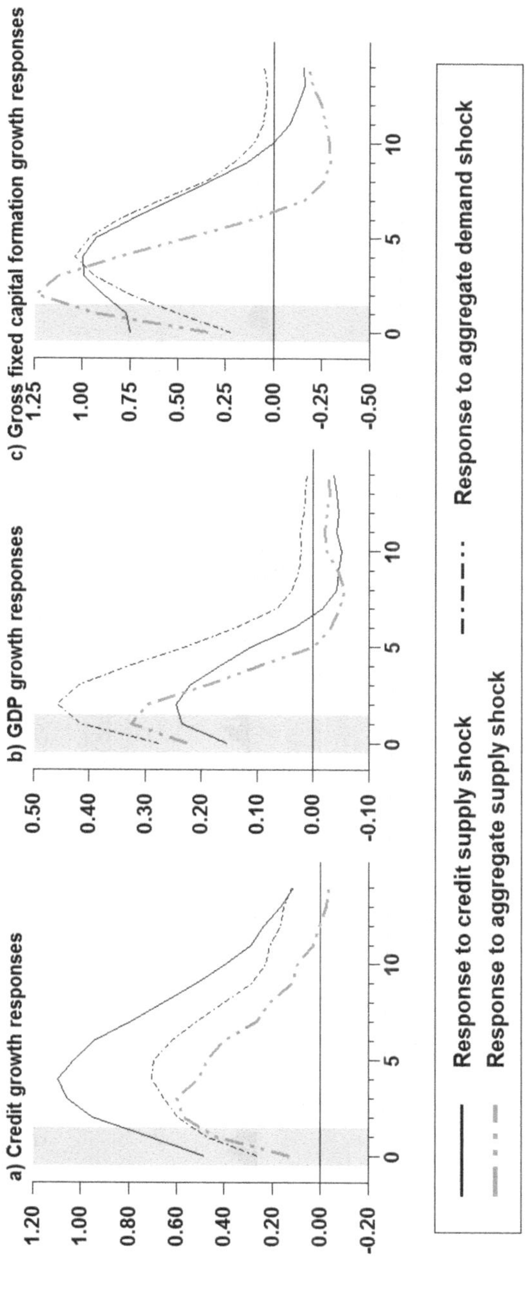

Fig. 12.5 Comparisons of responses to credit supply, aggregate demand and aggregate supply shocks (*Source:* Authors' calculations)

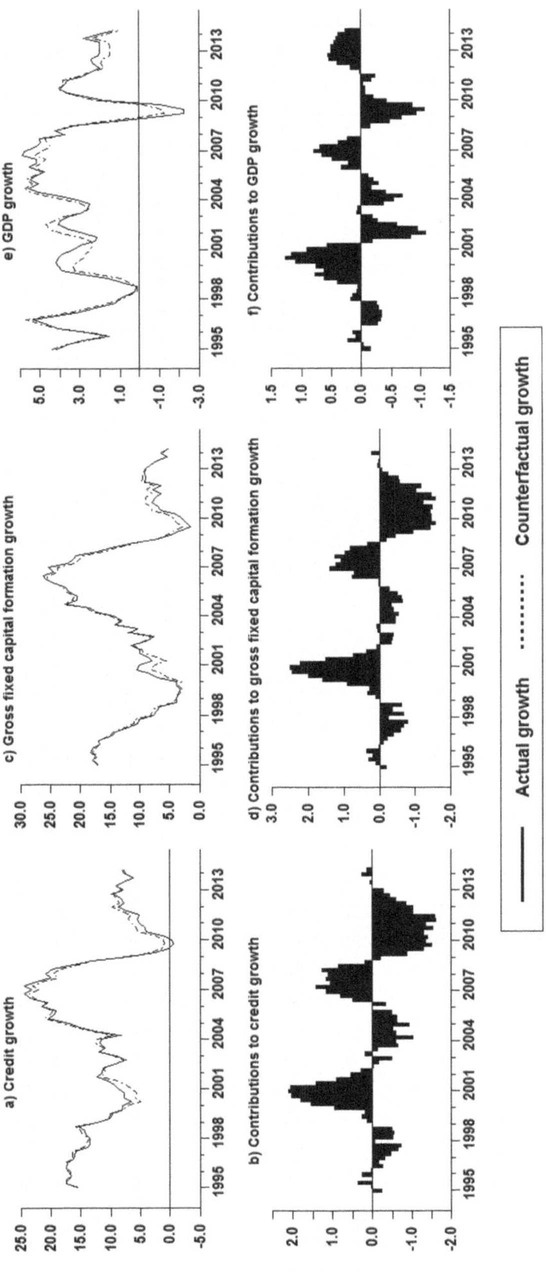

Fig. 12.6 Actual and counterfactual variables (*Source*: Authors' calculations)

credit supply shocks on growth in credit, gross fixed capital formation and GDP. The credit supply contributions to each variable are shown in Fig. 12.6b, d, f. A contribution above zero shows that it raised growth while negative values indicate a drag on growth.

Evidence indicates well-defined cyclical movements in the credit supply contributions. The cyclical contributions are visible in Fig. 12.6b, d, f for credit, gross fixed capital formation and GDP, respectively. The credit supply shock raised growth in (1) credit, (2) gross fixed capital formation and (3) GDP in the periods 2000–2002 and 2006–2008. However, between 2009 and 2012 the credit supply shock contributed to contraction in growth in credit, GDP and gross fixed capital formation.

So in which periods since 2009Q1 did the credit supply shock contributions uplift and drag real economic activity recovery? It is evident that sluggish growth in credit and weak growth in gross capital formation is largely due to the depressing contributions of the credit supply shocks (Fig. 12.7).

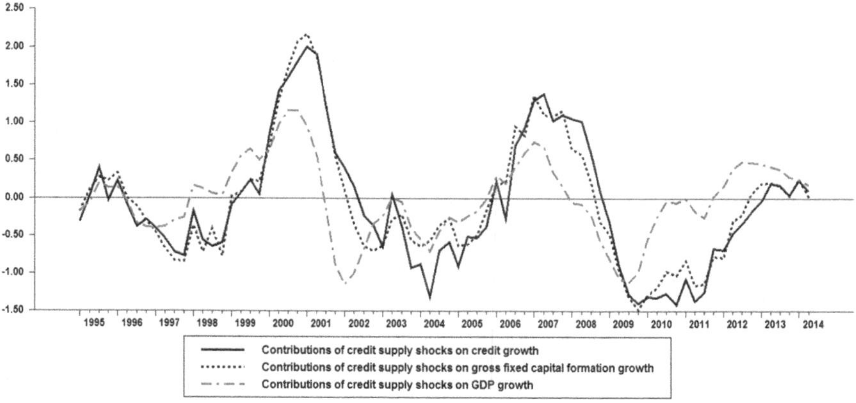

Fig. 12.7 Comparisons of contributions of credit supply shock on selected economic variables (*Source*: Authors' calculations)

12.3 Relationship Between Bond Yields and Credit Supply Shock Contributions to GDP Growth Post 2007Q2

This chapter now examines whether there is a strong link in the evolution of credit supply shocks and government bond yields. In addition, it assesses the two relationships between (1) credit supply shocks contributions to GDP growth and sovereign bond yields, and (2) credit supply shock contributions to gross capital formation and sovereign bond yields.

Evidence in Fig. 12.8b indicates that government bond yields had a positive relationship with credit supply shock contributions to GDP before the financial crisis in 2007Q2. The relationship became negative in 2007Q3–2008Q4 in Fig. 12.8c. The large negative effects during the recession in 2009Q1–2014Q2 period in Fig. 12.8d suggest a worsened relationship during that time.

Bijsterbosch et al. (2015) argue that high sovereign bond yields are likely to have an impact on credit supply conditions as they reflect increased risk of funding for governments. This happens when banks include large amounts of government bonds on their balance sheets. Cantero-Saiz et al. (2014) find that sovereign risk in Europe influenced bank credit supply via the bank lending channel. It is possible that this may be the case in South Africa too.

We now further assess whether government bond yields impacted the credit supply contributions to gross fixed capital formation. The negative relationship before 2007Q2 is exhibited in Fig. 12.9b. Although the relationship in Fig. 12.8c is negative, it is smaller in magnitude compared to that observed in the beginning of recession in 2009Q1 until 2014Q2 in Fig. 12.8d. This suggests that high bond yields during the euro sovereign debt crisis reduced the contribution of credit supply shocks to growth in fixed capital formation.

Thus, credit supply shocks are an important factor in the evolution of credit supply dynamics. Evidence indicates that the financial crisis changed the relationship between government bond yields and credit

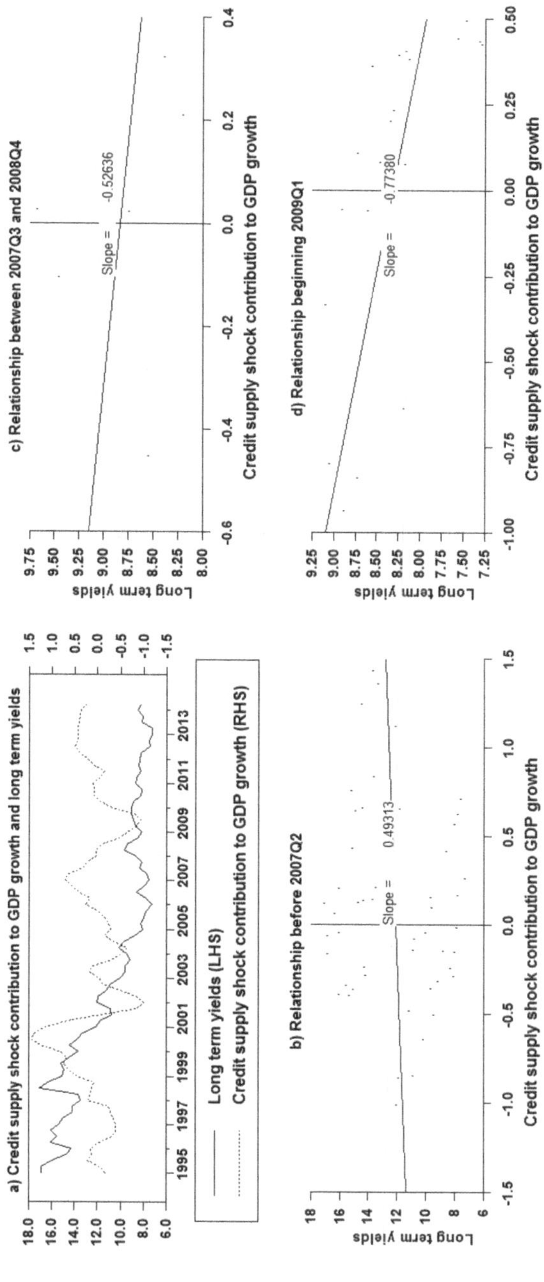

Fig. 12.8 Relationship between bond yields and credit supply shock contributions to GDP growth (*Source*: Authors' calculations)

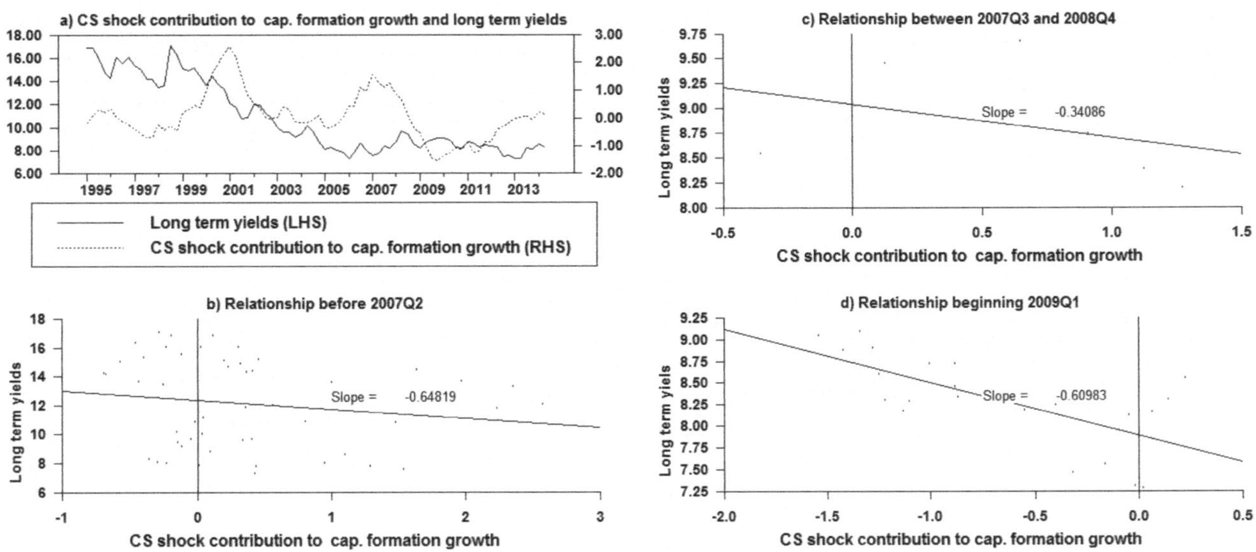

Fig. 12.9 Relationship between bond yields and credit supply shock (CS) contributions to capital formation growth (*Source*: Authors' calculations)

supply contributions to growth in GDP and gross fixed capital formation. However, the relationship changed drastically beginning with the recession in 2009.

12.3.1 Relationship Between Credit Risk, Credit Supply and Demand Contributions to GDP Growth Post 2000

The analysis examines further whether the quality of banks' balance sheets via non-performing loans impacted credit supply contributions to real economic activity. Non-performing loans (NPLs) may restrain the supply of bank credit by reducing banks' income and capital. Reduced capital lowers the banks' capacity to lend and raises uncertainty about the banks capitalization. This is reflected in high provisioning for loan losses and higher risk premiums on bank funding, curtailing banks' access to financing. Costs of managing NPLs may reduce banks' efficiency, potentially raising lending rates and reducing the credit supply.

Fig. 12.10 shows that NPLs were elevated during the crisis. The contributions of credit supply shocks on GDP growth were negative during the crisis and very small around 2010. In addition, the evidence indicates a positive relationship between credit supply contributions to GDP growth before 2007Q2 in Fig. 12.10d. In contrast, during the prolonged increase in NPLs between 2007Q3 and 2009Q3 in Fig. 12.10a the contributions of credit supply shocks to GDP growth were negative. Fig. 12.10c confirms a negative relationship between credit supply contributions to GDP and NPLs.

Did credit risk impact credit demand contributions to GDP growth? Yes, there are differences in the relationship between the credit risk and credit demand contributions to GDP growth in Fig. 12.11. There is a positive relationship between the NPLs and credit demand contributions to GDP growth when NPLs were very low, especially prior to 2007Q2 in Fig. 12.11d.

Moreover, evidence shows that credit risk negatively impacted the credit demand contribution to GDP growth after 2007Q2. The adverse relationship is bigger in the 2009Q4–2014Q2 period in Fig. 12.11b. This is possibly due to elevated macroeconomic uncertainty after 2009Q4.

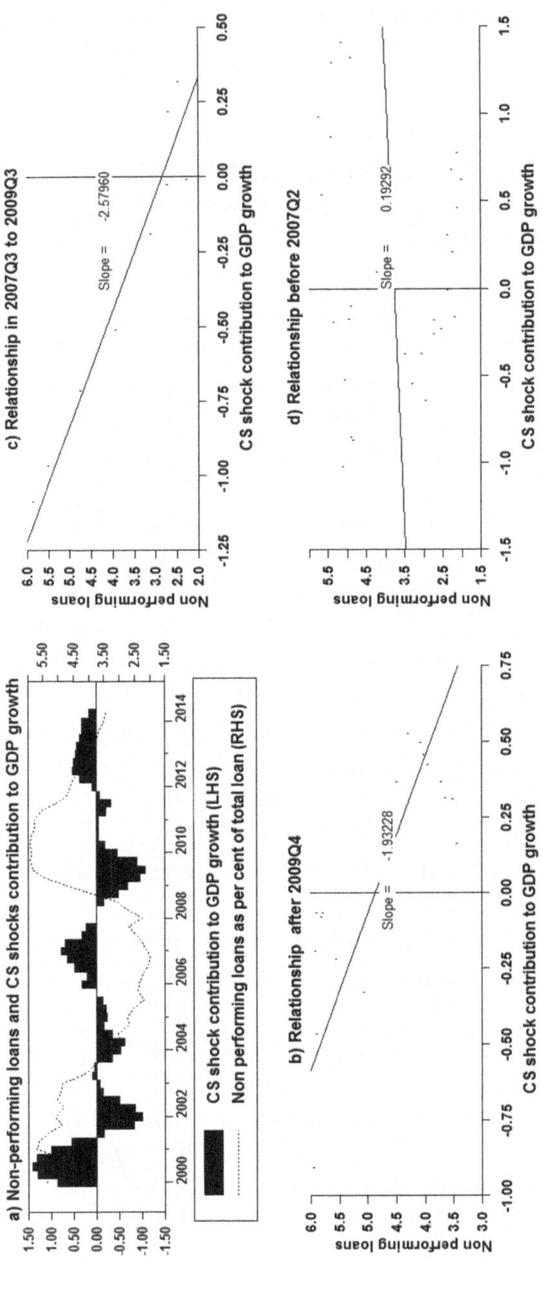

Fig. 12.10 Relationship between NPLs and credit supply shock (CS) contributions to GDP growth (*Source*: Authors' calculations)

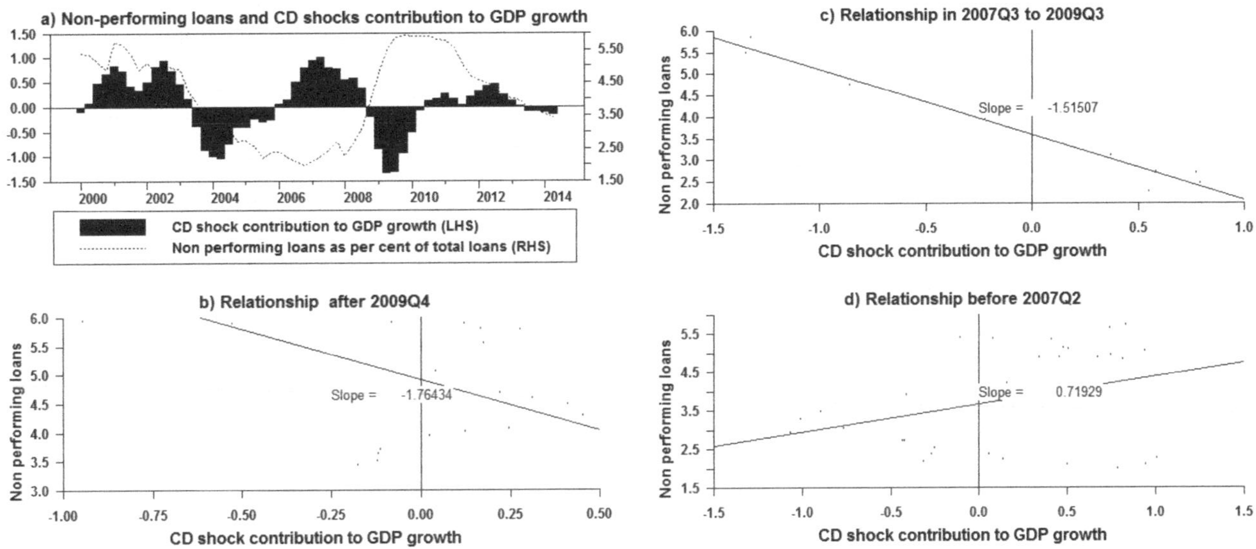

Fig. 12.11 Relationship between NPLs and credit demand shocks (CS) contributions to GDP growth (*Source*: Authors' calculations)

Indeed, the relationship changed from being positive to negative during the financial crisis.

12.3.2 Do Aggregate Supply Shocks Explain Sluggish Growth in Credit and GDP?

Fig. 12.12 compares the contributions from aggregate demand shock, aggregate supply shock and credit supply shock on the evolution of growth in credit and GDP beginning in 2009Q1. It shows that all shocks contributed to declines in growth in credit during the recession in 2009. Aggregate demand shocks contributed positively to credit growth since 2011, which happened earlier than those from credit supply contributions. Overall, the evidence indicates that aggregate supply is the most significant drag on the recovery of credit growth, as opposed to credit supply effects.

Fig. 12.12b shows that both credit supply and aggregate demand shocks contributed to a quick recovery in GDP growth after the recession in 2009. In contrast, the evidence further indicates that aggregate supply shocks contributed negatively, indicating that these are a drag on GDP recovery. These results are consistent with findings of a positive but transitory relationship when credit growth leads GDP growth. We conclude that the lead lag results between credit and GDP growth indicate that interdependency and a strong positive feedback loop are dependent on a high growth regime. High credit growth on its own does not lead to prolonged high GDP growth.

12.3.3 Credit Supply and Credit Demand Shocks and Subdued GDP, Credit and Investment Growth

The chapter concludes by comparing the contributions of credit supply shock and credit demand shock on growth in (1) credit, (2) GDP and (3) capital formation in Fig. 12.13. Since 2002, the contributions of these shocks tend to move in the same direction, suggesting they reinforce each

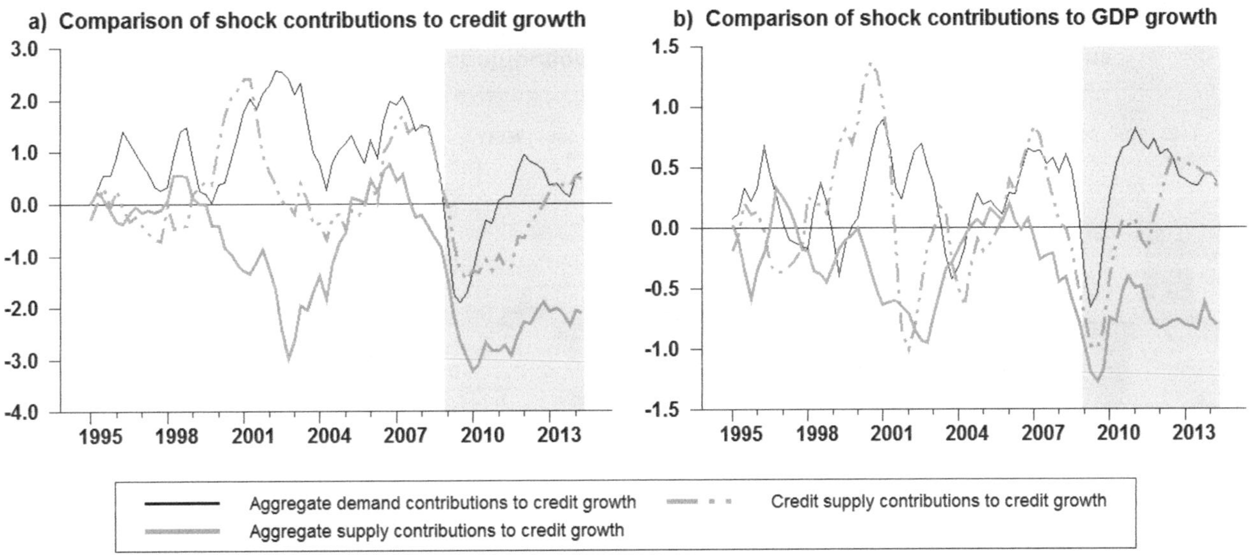

Fig. 12.12 Comparison of shock contribution to credit and GDP growth (*Source*: Authors' calculations)

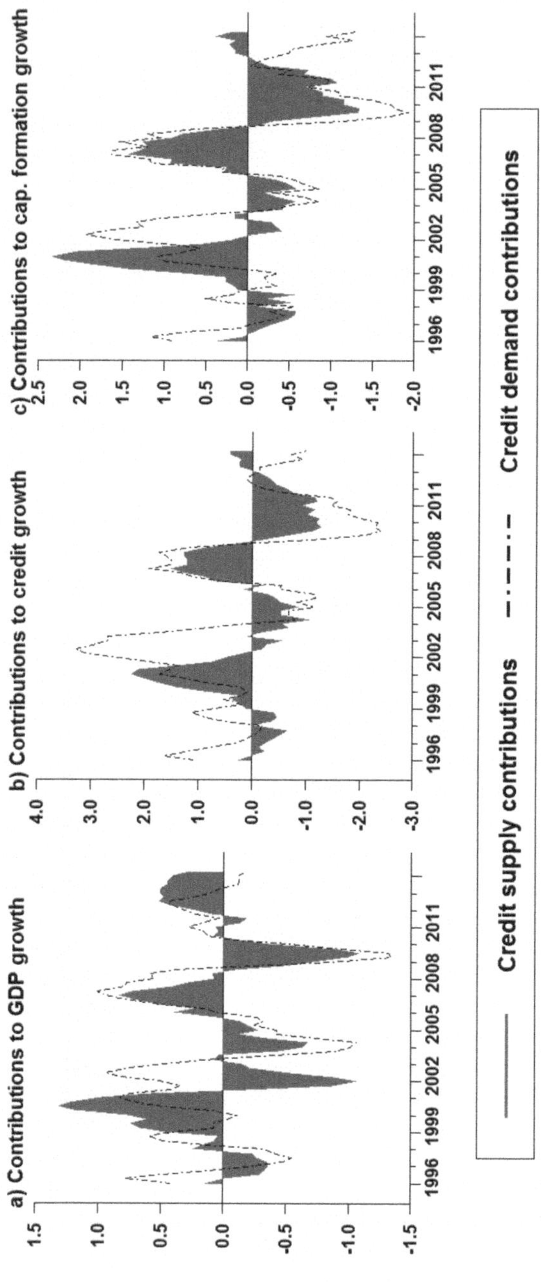

Fig. 12.13 Comparison of shock contribution to credit and GDP growth (*Source*: Authors' calculations)

other. However, at the turning points the contributions of credit demand shocks exceed those of the credit supply shock contributions. From 2013, these contributions show diverging trends. Credit supply shocks contribute positively to credit, GDP and capital formation. In contrast, the credit demand shock contributions are negative—suggesting they drag growth in economic activity. The negative contributions are big with respect to credit growth and capital formation growth. Therefore, credit demand shock rather than credit supply shock is a drag on economic activity.

12.4 Conclusion and Policy Implications

The evidence finds that aggregate supply shocks contribute negatively to GDP growth and are a worse drag on GDP recovery than credit supply shocks. Conversely, the credit demand contributions are negative suggesting that they also slow economic activity. The contributions of credit demand shocks are negative and major with respect to credit growth and capital formation. In addition, sovereign bond yields had a positive relationship with credit supply shock contributions to GDP before the financial crisis but the relationship became negative thereafter. The evidence leads us to conclude that high government bond yields possibly had an impact on credit supply conditions. It is possible that they increased risk and funding costs. Furthermore, credit risk had a negative impact on credit demand shock contributions to GDP after the financial crisis.

Summary of Main Findings

- The credit supply shock significantly raises growth in gross fixed capital formation, more so than other shocks.
- GDP growth rises due to an aggregate demand shock much more than due to both credit supply and aggregate supply shocks.
- The relationship between sovereign bond yields and credit supply shock contributions to GDP changed after the financial crisis and became negative.
- High government bond yields possibly had an impact on credit supply conditions and increased risk and funding costs.

13

Credit Growth Threshold and the Nonlinear Transmission of Credit Shocks

Learning Objectives

- The growth rate at which the credit growth rate threshold occurs
- The credit regimes and their nonlinear and asymmetric effects in transmitting shocks
- The threshold effects on the pace and magnitudes of the policy rate adjustments in curbing inflationary pressures
- The asymmetric effects of the threshold on inflation shocks and economic growth
- Consideration of nonlinearity effects induced by the thresholds and by policy

13.1 Introduction

Credit and GDP growth following the global financial crisis and recession in 2009 has remained subdued. In Fig. 13.1 credit and GDP levels are shown to have not returned to the pre-crisis and recession trends. These trends mean that the domestic economy has been plagued by two

N. Gumata, E. Ndou, *Bank Credit Extension and Real Economic Activity in South Africa*, DOI 10.1007/978-3-319-43551-0_13

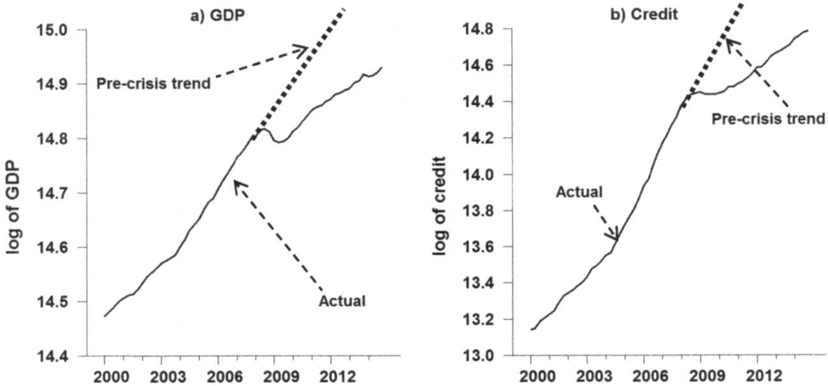

Fig. 13.1 Credit and GDP trends pre- and post-global financial crisis and recession (*Source*: SARB and authors' calculations)

negative gaps: in the credit markets and the real economy. But the trends shown in Fig. 13.1 assume linearity and yet the period after the global financial crisis is characterized by unconventional policy interventions and zero (even negative) policy rates which represent nonlinearity.

This chapter assesses the nonlinear and asymmetric transmission of credit shocks subject to credit regimes in South Africa. So, does a threshold value exist for credit growth? Furthermore, does it lead to nonlinear and asymmetric effects of economic shocks? Are there differential effects of an inflation shock on economic growth based on the credit threshold? If so, what is the threshold level of the growth in credit that introduces a nonlinear impact on the policy rate and inflation responses? Does the threshold lead to different paths and magnitudes of policy rate adjustments that work in any way towards the primary mandate of curbing inflationary pressures?

The role of credit and how it propagates policy and growth shocks as subject to the credit growth threshold is an unexplored research policy issue in South Africa. Here we contribute to filling this gap. Establishing credit growth thresholds and nonlinearities in credit market dynamics, as well as their relevance for monetary policy and financial stability, is an under researched area.

This chapter directly assesses the role of credit markets as sources and propagators of shocks. The analysis shows that credit market frictions introduce nonlinear effects and these effects have implications for the direction and magnitude of the repo rate adjustment and inflation dynamics. However, this analysis by no means implies that policymakers should go back to the long-gone days of targeting some particular level of credit and money growth. Rather, the focus is merely on giving context and perspective to the role of credit growth by estimating the credit growth threshold level. Knowledge of the credit threshold can assist in thinking about growth in credit within the policy space of the interaction of monetary policy and financial stability.

It is common knowledge that the global financial crisis once again showed that a rapid increase in (or excessive) credit is a reliable leading indicator of financial instability. As a result, one of the main policy responses has been a focus on the credit-to-GDP ratio as a benchmark of the sustainable credit growth. Significant deviations between the actual and long-run trends of the credit-to-GDP ratio (i.e. the credit gaps) are used as signals of the state of the credit markets by policymakers and regulators.

Credit gaps are some of the indicators proposed to be used to calibrate a countercyclical capital buffer for regulatory purposes. The main aim in calibrating an early warning indicator is to identify credit growth that is most aligned to economic fundamentals relative to that which is viewed as excessive. For this task, the Basel Committee on Banking Supervision (2010b) uses the Hodrick–Prescott (HP) filter to set a threshold level. However, there are a number of drawbacks associated with the HP approach. It is for this reason that we think that the estimation of the threshold for credit growth as discussed in this chapter contributes to efforts that use different quantitative techniques in this area.

13.2 Why May the Nonlinear Response of Economic Activity to Various Shocks Depend on Credit Regimes?

Why are credit frictions a pertinent policy concern? Credit market frictions significantly amplify real and nominal shocks to the economy and lie at the center of the intersection of macroeconomics and finance

(Bernanke et al. 1995).[1] Furthermore, Choi et al. (1996) argue that in the presence of information asymmetry, inflation harms economic growth by accentuating financial market frictions and these then have an adverse impact on the supply of credit and funding of investment ventures.

The literature also points out that elevated levels of inflation can have adverse consequences for the long-run growth rate and the level of real activity. Hence, increases in inflation tend to interfere with the ability of the financial sector to allocate resources efficiently (Boyd et al. 2001). In addition, Huybens and Smith (1998, 1999) emphasize the importance of informational asymmetries in credit markets. They demonstrate how increases in the rate of inflation adversely affect credit market frictions with negative repercussions for both banks and equity market performance and long-run real economic activity.

Why is it important and useful to determine the impact of economic shocks subject to the state of credit regimes? Avdjiev and Zeng (2014) argue that financial institutions tend to be highly leveraged during economic booms, such that small adverse credit risk shocks can trigger vicious deleveraging spirals, which can have a considerable negative impact on real economic activity. In addition, theory suggests that if economic agents are constrained in their access to credit, credit supply shocks have relatively larger effects on consumer and business spending decisions than in the case of abundant credit availability. Furthermore, Bernanke and Gertler (1989) and Kiyotaki and Moore (1997) argue that the effects of agency costs of financial intermediation in the presence of information asymmetry in financial markets make agents behave as if they are financially constrained. The financing constraints are more binding in recessionary times rather than in expansionary ones.

These conditions are different to those observed in high credit growth regimes. For instance, in high credit environments firms are likely to be less dependent on the availability of bank credit. They can adjust more easily to shocks to bank lending by substituting it with other means of financing, such as internal finance or the issuance of debt securities (Calza and Sousa 2006).

[1] Swathes of literature subsequent to the global financial crisis established that financial factors are the key determinants of economic fluctuations. They were critical triggers and propagators in the global financial crisis. See also, Halvorsen and Jacobsen (2009) and Christiano et al. (2010).

13.3 Descriptive Statistics

The analysis uses quarterly (Q) data from 1990Q1 to 2014Q4 to show selected bilateral relationships. Fig. 13.2a shows that in many instances pronounced peaks in inflation tend to precede a slowdown in economic growth. Fig. 13.2b shows a negative relationship, suggesting that higher inflation leads to a slowdown in economic growth. Evidence indicates a positive relationship in Fig. 13.2d, suggesting that higher credit growth is accompanied by higher inflation. Fig. 13.2f shows that rising inflation is accompanied by an increase in the repo rate.

Furthermore, the bilateral relationships shown in Fig. 13.3a reveal that in some instances the high repo rate levels coincide with economic slowdown. The negative relationship depicted in Fig. 13.3b shows that the elevated repo rate levels lead to a slowdown in economic growth. In Fig. 13.3c the economic growth tends to co-move with credit growth. This is particularly the case since the beginning of 2004. Fig. 13.3d shows a positive relationship, suggesting that higher credit growth stimulates economic growth.

13.3.1 Cross Correlations Between Macroeconomic Variables

Fig. 13.4 further shows the bilateral relationships in order to assess the lead relationships using the cross-correlation approach. Similar to the conclusions reached based on trends established earlier, Fig. 13.4a shows that increases in inflation precede increases in the repo rate.

However, Fig. 13.4b shows a negative relationship between inflation and economic growth. These results indicate that an increase in inflation is accompanied by a slowdown in economic growth. In Fig. 13.4c an increase in credit growth is associated with rising inflation. In contrast, higher inflation leads to a decline in credit growth between the 2nd and 13th quarters. Fig. 13.4d shows a positive but transitory relationship when credit growth leads to GDP growth. But a positive relationship arises for long periods when the increase in economic growth precedes credit growth. The lead relationship between credit and GDP growth

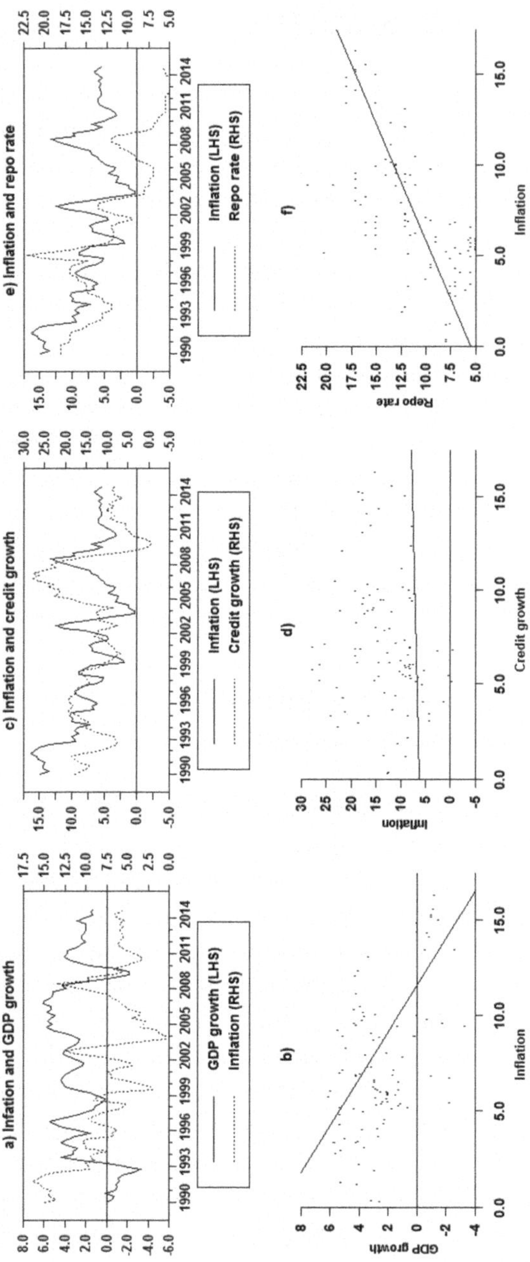

Fig. 13.2 Relationships between economic variables (*Source*: SARB and authors' calculations)

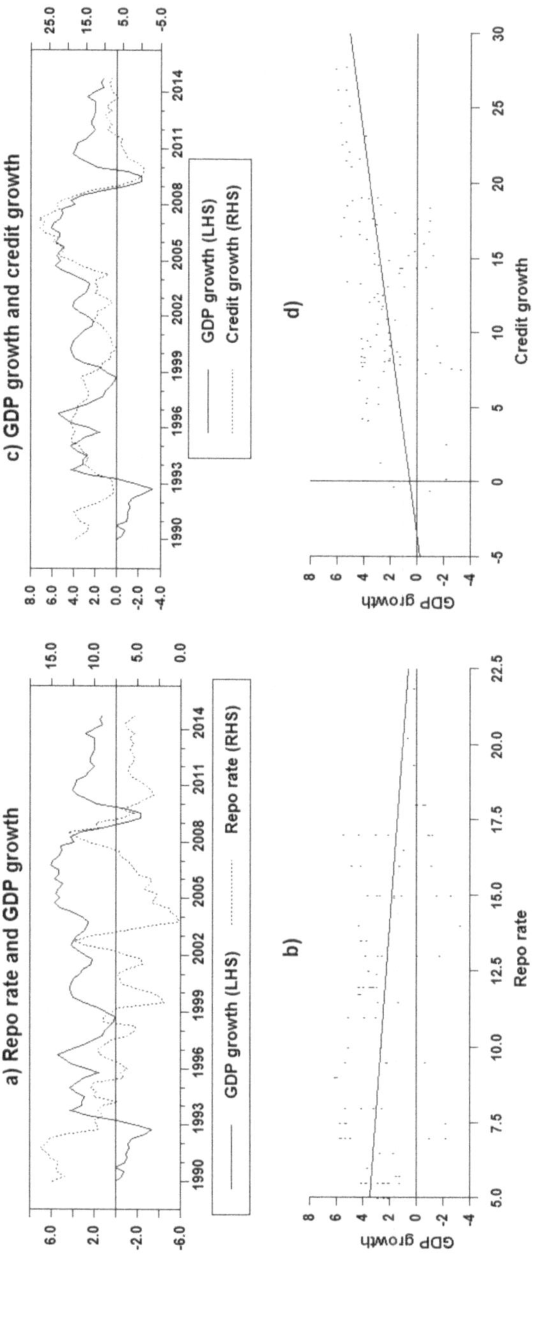

Fig. 13.3 Relationships between economic variables (*Source*: SARB and authors' calculations)

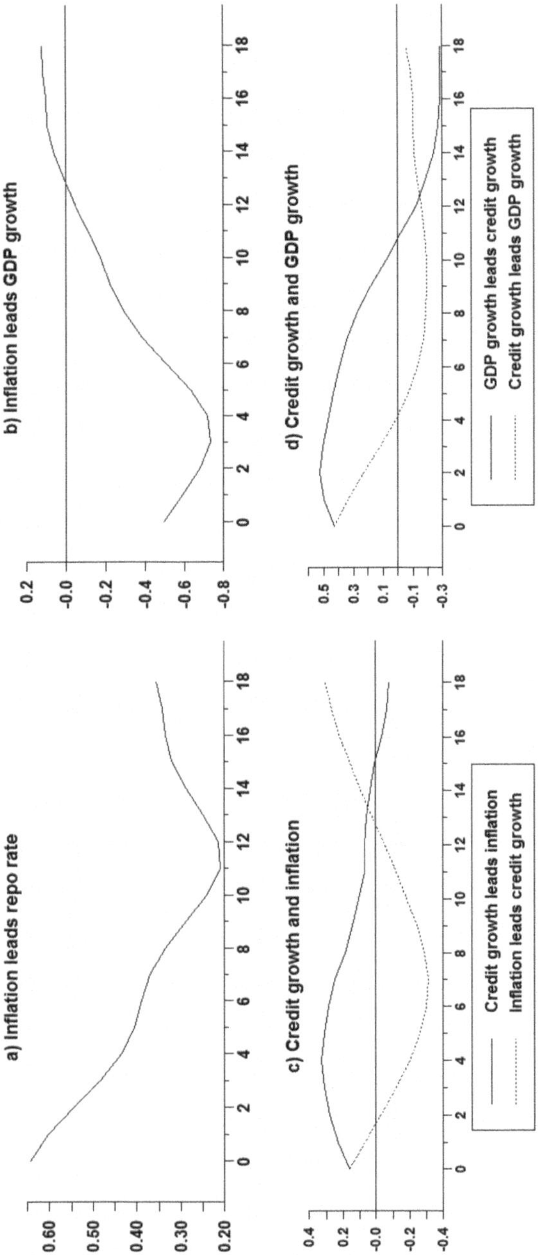

Fig. 13.4 Cross correlations (*Source*: Authors' calculations)

indicates that the interdependency and the strong positive feedback loop is possibly dependent on a high growth regime. A high credit regime on its own does not lead to a prolonged high growth regime.

13.4 Dynamics Between Credit Growth, Inflation and Economic Activity

This chapter uses a vector autoregression (VAR) approach with quarterly (Q) data spanning 1990Q1 to 2014Q4, to examine a number of empirical relationships in this section. The variables include economic growth, inflation, the repo rate and credit growth.[2] The real sector variables are placed before those related to the credit market, as done in Calza and Sousa (2006). This means that shocks to economic growth affect other variables contemporaneously. In contrast, economic growth reacts slowly to shocks to inflation, the repo rate and credit growth. In addition, the ordering suggests that inflation reacts contemporaneously to economic growth shocks. The policy rate responds contemporaneously to economic growth and inflation. Credit growth responds contemporaneously to all variables and it affects other variables with a quarter lag.

The responses of economic growth to a positive one percent unexpected rise in inflation are shown in Fig. 13.5. An unexpected rise in inflation lowers economic growth, but the effects are not permanent, as in Fig. 13.5a, and a positive credit growth shock raises inflation for a longer period in Fig. 13.5b

In Fig. 13.6a economic growth declines significantly due to a positive inflationary shock relative to a policy rate shock. Inflation depresses economic growth for a relatively longer period relative to a repo rate shock of a similar magnitude. Inflation increases more than the repo rate in Fig. 13.6b due to an unexpected positive credit growth shock.

[2] The VAR models were estimated using one and two lags based on the regime-dependent impulses. We use two lags as selected by AIC when estimating asymmetric effects in the later sections.

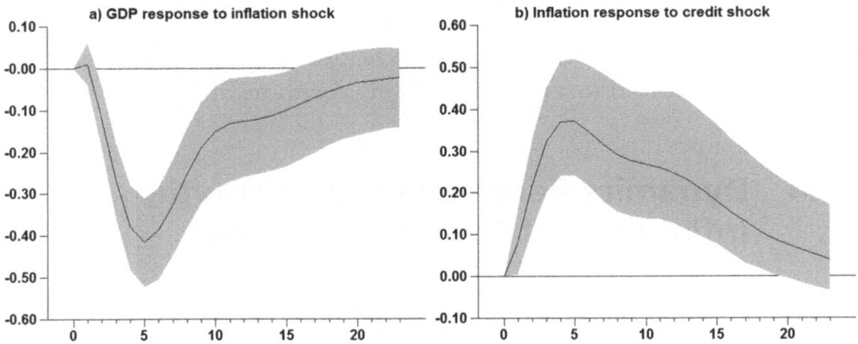

Fig. 13.5 Selected macroeconomic responses in a linear VAR (*Note*: The responses denote percentage points. These are responses to a one percent positive shock. *Source*: Authors' calculations)

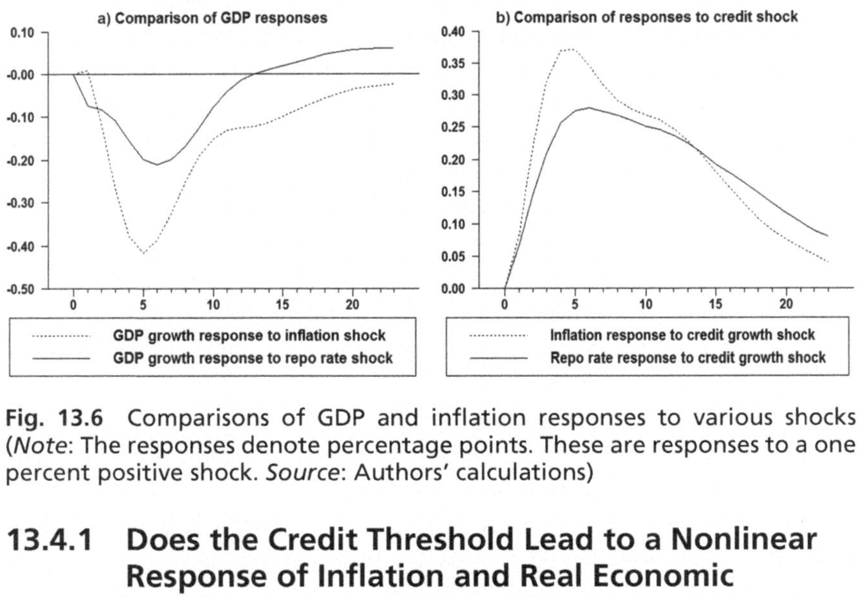

Fig. 13.6 Comparisons of GDP and inflation responses to various shocks (*Note*: The responses denote percentage points. These are responses to a one percent positive shock. *Source*: Authors' calculations)

13.4.1 Does the Credit Threshold Lead to a Nonlinear Response of Inflation and Real Economic Activity to an Unexpected GDP Growth Shock?

Indeed, empirical evidence in other countries suggests that the credit threshold leads to a nonlinear transmission of unexpected GDP growth shocks. Balke (2000) empirically examined whether credit plays a role as a nonlinear propagator of shocks. The nonlinear effects arise from the Bernanke and Gertler (1989) model which shows that the balance sheet conditions of firms can amplify fluctuations in output. In these conditions, negative shocks are likely to have a greater impact relative to positive shocks.

The next subsection determines whether credit regimes are an important source of shocks as well as an important nonlinear propagator of GDP growth shocks. First, the subsection determines a credit growth threshold and shows the nonlinear effects of an unexpected shock to credit growth in a low and high credit regime on inflation and the adjustments in the policy rate.

13.4.2 What Is the Threshold Value for Credit Growth?

To establish the credit growth threshold, the analysis begins by testing the null hypothesis of no threshold versus the alternative that a threshold exists. This involves applying three tests, namely the arranged autoregression test based on Tsay (1989), the Hansen threshold test and the smooth transition autoregression test (STAR), to determine whether there is a break in the credit series. The use of different test statistics is to ascertain whether these tests converge and arrive at the same conclusion. The credit equation used to test for the existence of a break point is specified such that the credit growth rate depends on a constant and its two lags required for estimation by the Akaike Information Criterion (AIC). The results are shown in Table 13.1.

All the tests reject the null of no threshold in favor of the existence of a threshold and nonlinearity in the growth of credit. However, these techniques do not establish the threshold value for credit growth. Hence the threshold value is established via the modified Balke (2000) threshold technique. The model identifies the threshold value based on a lowest likelihood ratio test. This approach differs from the transition models that determine the threshold above or below which credit growth exerts positive or negative differential effects on GDP growth or inflation. Rather, the Balke (2000) approach establishes the sensitivity or the responsiveness of inflation and GDP growth subject to the established threshold. The modified Balke (2000) threshold technique establishes a threshold value around 9.5 percent for credit growth. Fig. 13.7 shows the estimated threshold credit growth.

Table 13.1 Tests for nonlinearity in the credit growth series

Test	Null hypothesis	F-value		Decision
Arranged autoregression test (Tsay1998)	No break point in the series	35.00	(0.00)**	Break point in the series
Hansen threshold test	No threshold in the series	53.81	(0.00)**	Threshold in the series
Smooth transition autoregressions (STAR)	Linearity in the series	18.0	(0.00)*	Nonlinearity in the series

Note: The numbers in (.) denote the p-value
Source: Authors' calculations
*denotes significance at 1 percent; ** denotes significance at 10 percent

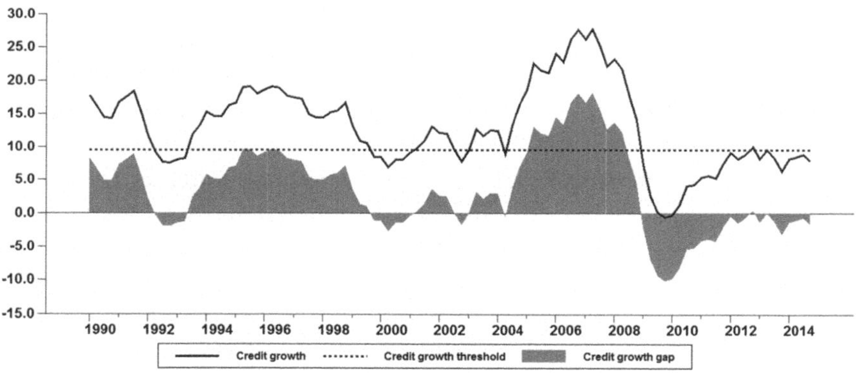

Fig. 13.7 Credit growth, credit gap and the estimated threshold (*Source*: Authors' calculations)

It is evident from Fig. 13.7 that credit growth has remained much closer to the thresholds subsequent to the steep decline and negative growth just after the global financial crisis and the recession in 2009.

13.4.3 Nonlinear Threshold Responses of Inflation and Repo Rate

In this section we estimate impulse responses using the regime-dependent approach following Atanasova (2003) and Balke (2000). According to

Calza and Sousa (2006) the regime-dependent approach is ideal and is an effective tool to characterize the behavior of a system within each regime. In addition, the conditional nonlinearity approach is important in determining the signs, size and persistence of impulse responses across regimes.

The estimated impulse responses are conditional to the system remaining in the prevailing regime at the time of the shock throughout the horizons of the responses. The analysis of the responses will reveal the extent of nonlinearities and whether credit shocks have differential effects on GDP growth, inflation and the repo rate in the lower and higher credit regimes. Fig. 13.8 shows the regime-dependent impulse responses.

The results in Fig. 13.8 show that in both higher and lower credit regimes a positive credit shock does not lead to a persistent rise in GDP growth (Fig. 13.8a). This suggests that additional aggregate demand created by the expansion in credit volumes leads to higher inflation as shown in Fig. 13.8b rather than to higher output growth.[3] However, inflation rises significantly in the higher credit regime and remains elevated relative to the lower credit regime. The trajectory of the inflation response in the high credit regime is similar to that observed in a model that does not distinguish between credit regimes after five quarters.

However, in Fig. 13.8c the repo rate remains elevated in the higher credit regime, which is supportive of the policy stance that curbs persistent inflationary pressures in the higher credit regimes. It is clear that the repo rate shocks are much elevated and persistent in the model without regimes and the model with the high credit regime, relative to the low credit regime model. In addition, the credit growth responses differ between the higher and lower credit regimes in Fig. 13.8d. The credit shock is slightly persistent in the higher regime and in the model without credit regimes. Overall, the results presented in Fig. 13.8 provide evidence that the inability to distinguish between credit regimes implies a much more aggressive policy stance relative to when considering regimes.

For further comparisons and analysis of the repo rate effects across regimes, Fig. 13.9 shows the peak responses. It is evident in Fig. 13.9a that the repo rate lowers GDP growth significantly in the higher credit regime relative to the lower credit regime. The decline in GDP growth

[3] See, for example, Avdjiev and Zeng (2014).

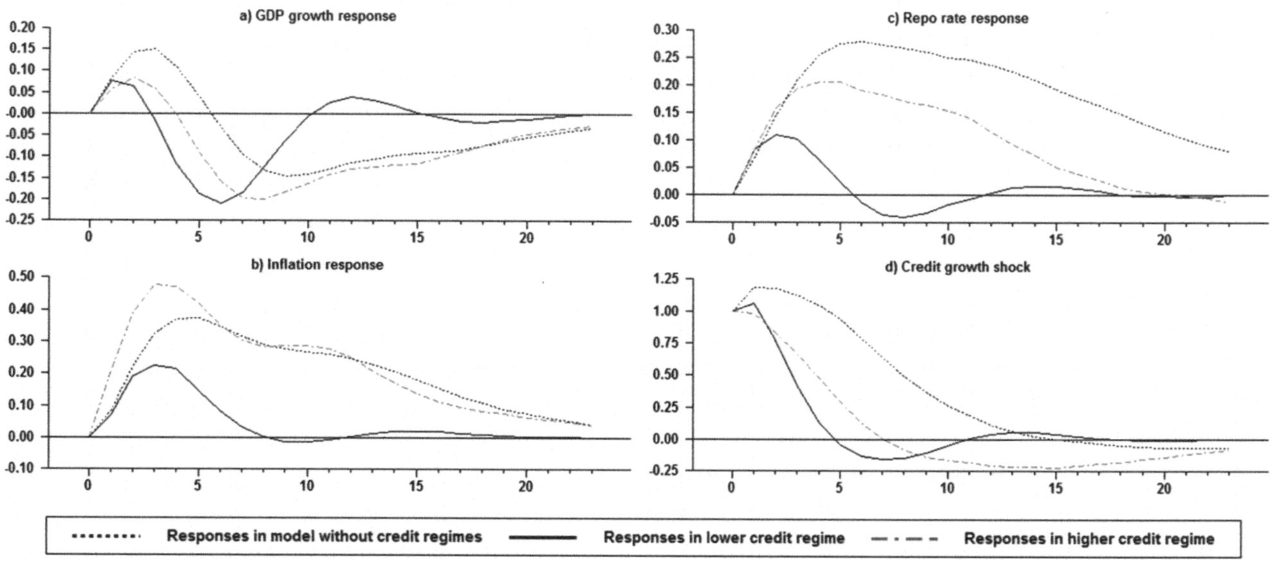

Fig. 13.8 Effects of unexpected positive credit shocks on GDP growth, inflation and repo rate in different credit growth regimes (*Note*: The responses denote percentage points to unexpected one percent positive credit shock. The error bands that illustrate the significance of different impulse responses over the horizon are not shown here. *Source*: Authors' calculations)

in the higher credit regime is nearly twice the size of the decline in the lower credit regime. The peak decline in economic growth occurs in five quarters in the higher credit regime, which is a much quicker impact compared to eight quarters observed in the lower credit regime.

The different responses to the repo rate shown in this section suggest that the policy rate exerts a nonlinear impact on economic growth subject to credit regimes. Furthermore, the trajectory of inflation differs across credit regimes. Therefore, evidence indicates that credit shocks subject to credit regimes exert nonlinear effects on the macroeconomy via GDP growth, inflation and the repo rate responses.

13.4.4 Inflation Shocks and Economic Growth Effects

Evidence indicates the differential responses of inflation and the repo rate to a positive credit growth shock within credit regimes. So, what are the implications of credit regimes for the reaction of economic growth to positive inflation shocks? Vast amounts of literature have established that positive inflation shock has adverse effects on economic growth. However, do these effects depend on credit regimes? Evidence illustrated in Fig. 13.10 fails to refute the hypothesis that the effects of inflation on growth are independent of the existing credit regime across horizons.

Evidence in Fig. 13.10a suggests that inflation reduces economic growth significantly. There are no discernible statistically significant differences in the responses of the decline in GDP growth in first six quarters between the credit regimes. The differences only become statistically important between the 9th and 14th quarters. The constant decline in economic growth over longer horizons in the higher credit regime seems to be due to a persistently high inflation shock therein, as shown in Fig. 13.10b. Therefore, the evidence indicates that inflation is bad for economic growth, irrespective of credit regimes. It indicates that the negative effects of inflation are not constrained by credit regimes—meaning that even in low credit regimes, high inflation exerts disproportionately negative effects on growth.

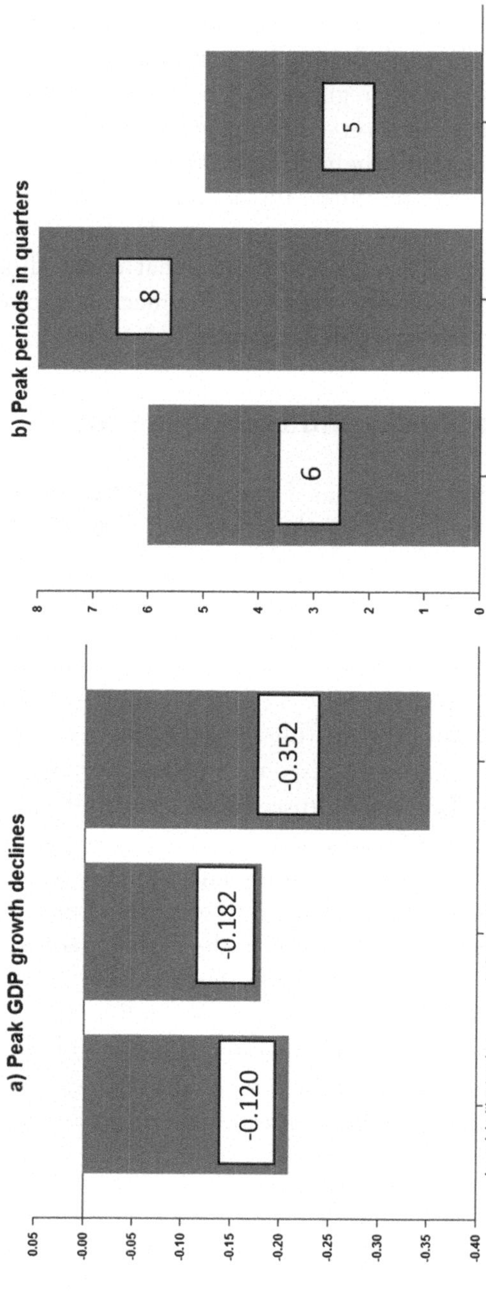

Fig. 13.9 Economic growth responses to repo rate shocks (*Note*: The responses denote percentage points. *Source*: Authors' calculations)

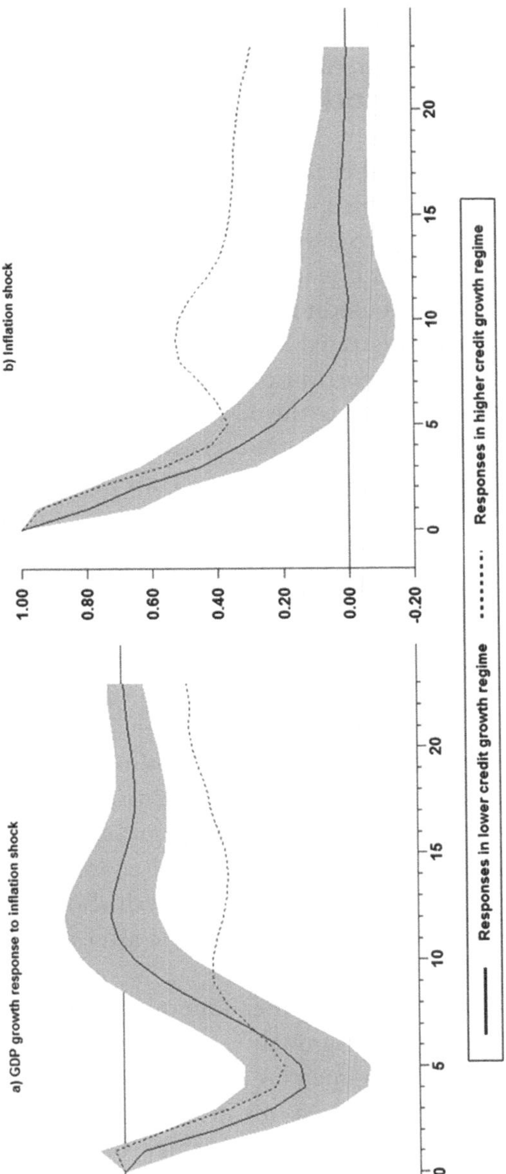

Fig. 13.10 GDP growth and inflation responses to inflation shocks (*Note*: The responses denote percentage points. *Source*: Authors' calculations)

13.4.5 Are the Prevailing Credit Market Conditions an Important Nonlinear Propagator of Economic Shocks?

This chapter has determined that credit conditions are an important source of nonlinear shocks. This section assesses whether credit conditions are important propagators of economic growth shocks. The variance decomposition approach is used to show the variability induced by credit shocks in different credit regimes with regard to GDP growth and inflation. Evidence illustrated in Fig. 13.11a indicates that credit shocks explain a higher proportion of fluctuations in inflation in the higher credit regime relative to the lower credit regime. Thus, this evidence supports the assertions that credit shocks are important drivers of inflation in high credit regimes. Policymakers should take note of the differential influences exerted by low and high credit regimes.

In addition, Fig. 13.11b, using the variance decomposition approach, corroborates the evidence established in the previous section that inflation shocks explain higher fluctuations in economic growth in the higher credit regime between the 4th and 19th quarters relative to fluctuations in the lower credit regime. These findings are in line with large amounts of empirical evidence showing that in periods of high credit and GDP growth regimes, additional accommodative monetary policy simply adds to inflationary pressures. Furthermore, Fig. 13.12a, c establish that the proportion of economic growth and repo rate fluctuations explained by credit growth shocks are larger in the high credit regime than in the lower regime after the 11th and 5th quarters, respectively.

Results presented in Fig. 13.12b offer support to the hypothesis that repo rate shocks drive economic growth much more in the higher credit regime than in low credit regime. Fig. 13.12d reveals that economic growth shocks induce more fluctuations in credit growth in the higher credit regime after ten quarters relative to three quarters in the lower credit regime.

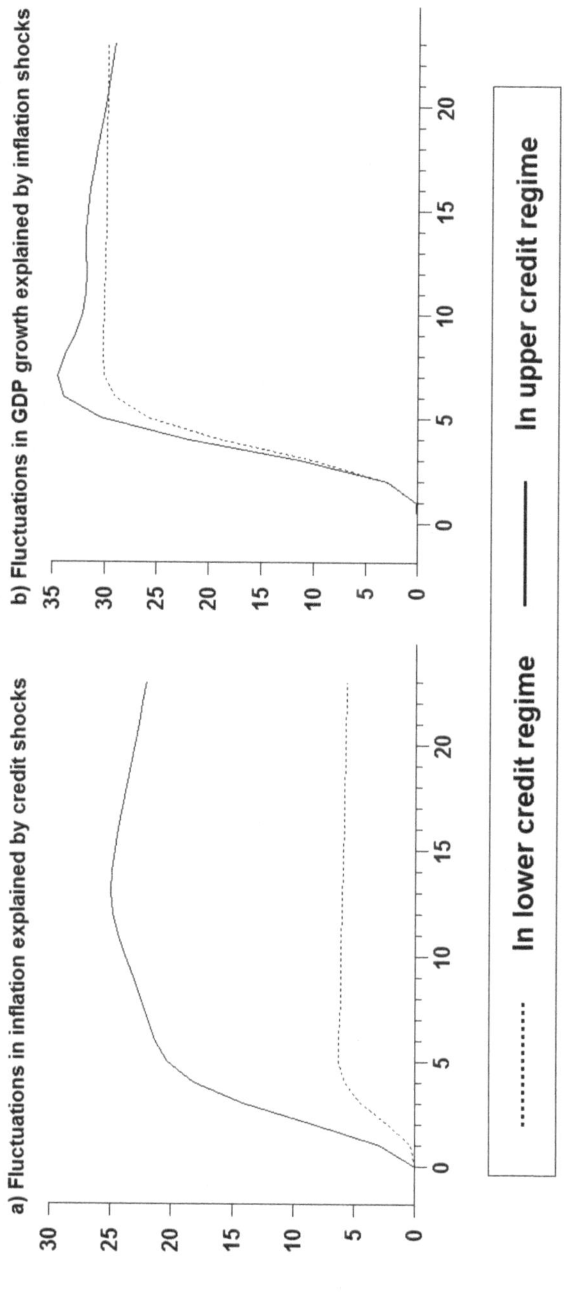

Fig. 13.11 Fluctuations in inflation and GDP growth in different credit regimes (*Source*: Authors' calculations)

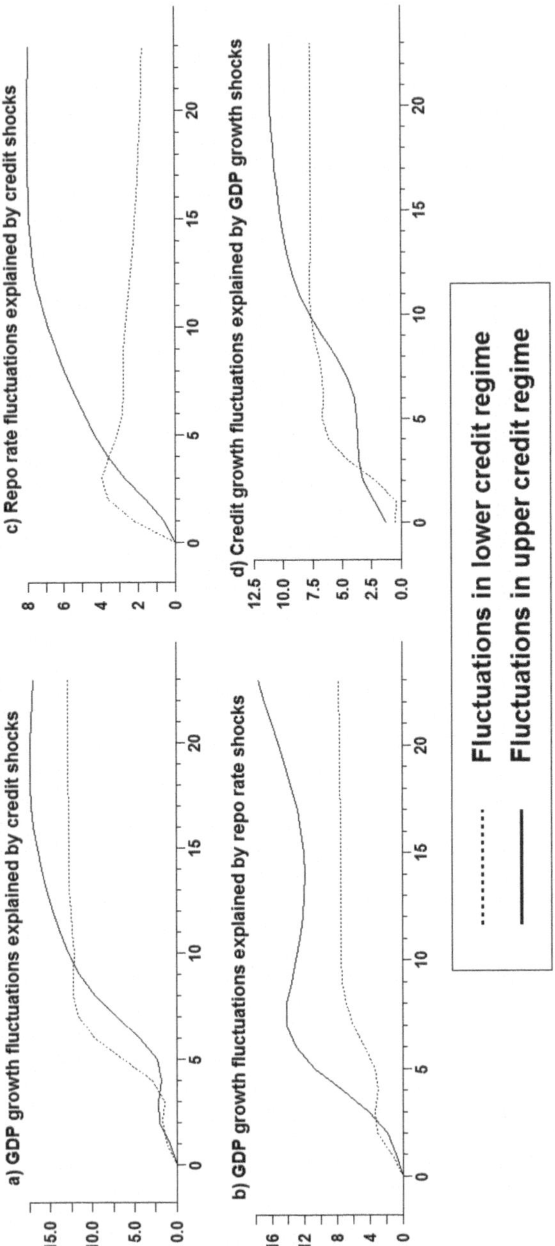

Fig. 13.12 Fluctuations in selected variables explained by credit, inflation and economic shocks (*Source*: Authors' calculations)

13.5 Do Inflation Shocks Have Asymmetric Effects on Economic Growth Dependent on Credit Regimes?

This section assesses the inflation effects subject to credit regimes. The asymmetry is determined via applying the Balke (2000) nonlinear approach. This approach estimates a vector autoregression model that changes the economic structure when the credit conditions cross the credit growth threshold of 9.5 percent. In addition, this approach enables us to determine the asymmetric effects of inflation shocks on economic growth. The generalized impulse response functions are used to avoid econometric estimations in which results will be dependent on the ordering of the variables. Fig. 13.13 shows the responses of economic growth to inflation shocks in the low and high credit regimes.

In Fig. 13.13c, d the evidence shows that positive inflationary shocks have bigger effects than negative inflationary trends, suggesting asymmetric responses of economic growth in the lower and higher credit regime.

First, evidence establishes that the peak magnitude of GDP growth decline is larger due to an unexpected positive inflation shock in both credit regimes. Comparative analysis reveals the magnitude of decline is bigger in the higher credit regime relative to a lower credit regime. Therefore, we can conclude that higher inflation lowers long-run economic growth and the effects are more severe in the higher credit regime relative to lower credit regime.

This result is not surprising, as Boyd et al. (2001) found that during high inflation intermediaries lend less and allocate capital less effectively. In addition, banking and stock market developments exhibit a strong negative correlation and a nonlinear relationship with inflation. Fig. 13.13b shows a positive uptick in economic growth due to a positive inflation shock. This might reflect that the economy has not fully adjusted to a new inflation rate and the associated relative price distortions effects. In addition, uncertainty about future rates of inflation may still be weak in the first two quarters following the inflation shock.

In light of preceding evidence on the effects of high inflation we now explore two questions. Are unexpected declines in the inflation rate ben-

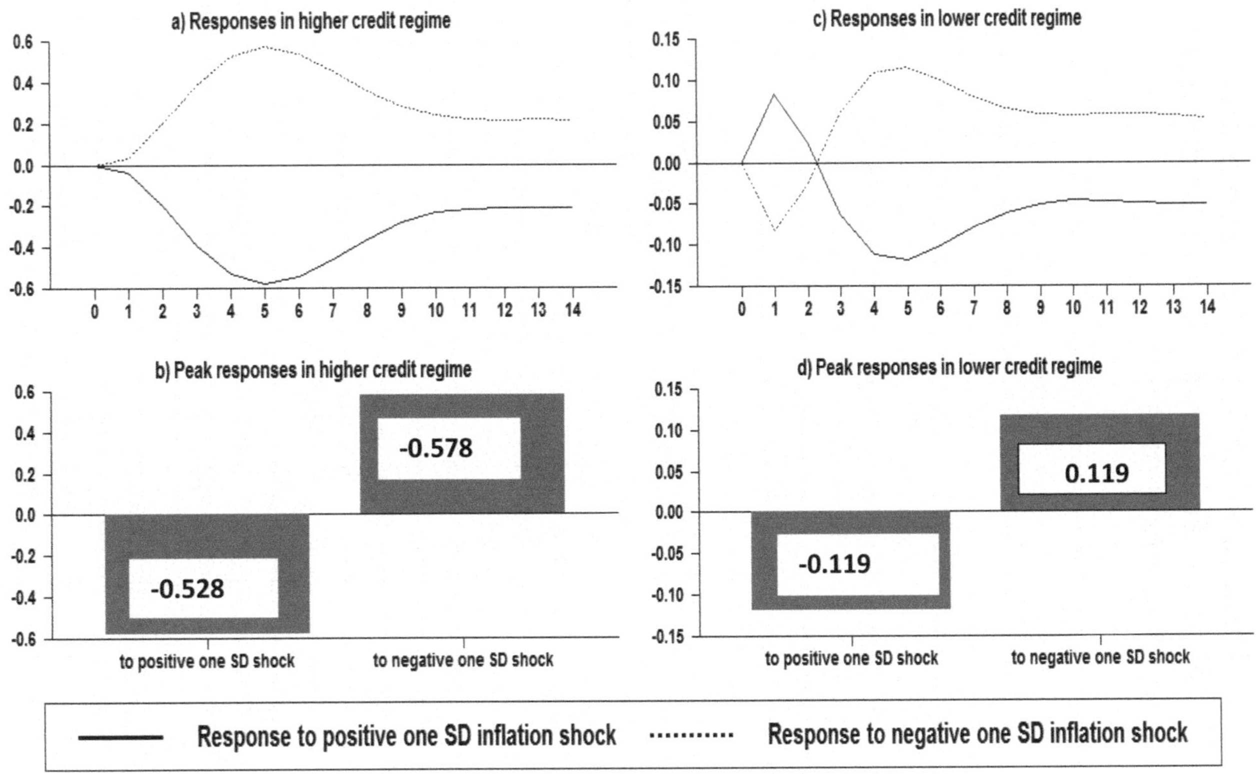

Fig. 13.13 Growth responses to inflation shocks in high and low credit regimes (*Note*: The responses denote percentage points. The inflation shock refers to one positive standard deviation increase in inflation rate. *Source*: Authors' calculations)

eficial to economic growth? Do their effects differ between the higher and lower credit regimes? Yes, based on Fig. 13.14c, d, an unexpected decline in inflation raises economic growth in the long run and the effects are much bigger when the unexpected decline in inflation occurs in a higher credit regime. Thus, an unexpected decline in inflation has asymmetric effects on economic growth depending on the existing credit regime.

These findings are not unique to this study. Azariadas and Smith (1996) and Boyd et al. (1997) explain that when inflation is very low in a high growth regime, credit market frictions are non-binding. In such cases, inflation does not distort the flow of information or interfere with resource allocation and growth. However, once the rate of inflation exceeds some threshold level credit market frictions become a binding constraint, leading to a discrete drop in financial sector performance as credit rationing intensifies. This does not imply that there is credit rationing in South Africa; instead, lenders may be using other tools, such as lending standards, to contain credit growth.

Along this line of thought, Choi et al. (1996) suggested that during periods of great macroeconomic stability associated with low inflation, credit market frictions are potentially harmless. This is because in a low inflationary environment, credit rationing might not emerge at all and the negative link between inflation and capital accumulation disappears. However, this does not mean that there are no risks that can emerge in low inflation environments. The recent global financial crisis demonstrated that periods of robust growth and well-contained inflation can mask significantly large financial excesses and imbalances, undermining financial stability. Hence, there is a role for regulatory, supervisory and macro-prudential policies.

13.5.1 Do Credit Regimes Impact the Repo Rate Reaction to Positive Inflation Shocks?

In the earlier sections we established that inflation is bad for economic growth in both higher and lower credit regimes. Is it possible then that the speed of policy rate adjustment aimed at curbing inflationary pressures is dependent on the existing credit regime? In Fig. 13.14 it is shown

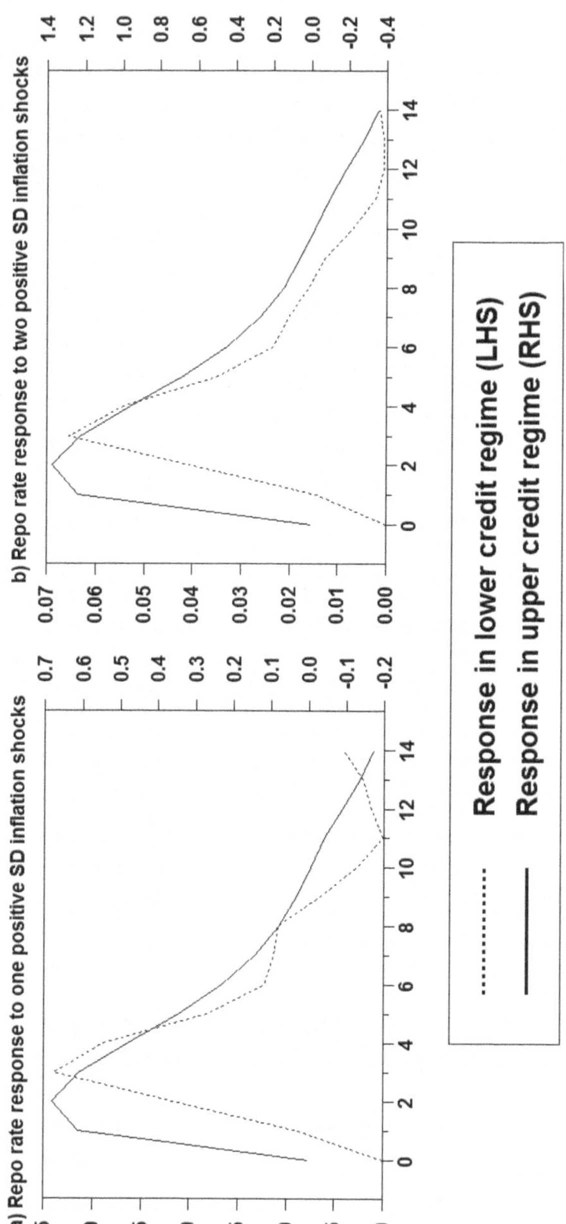

Fig. 13.14 Response of repo rate to inflation shocks according to credit regimes (*Note*: To avoid ordering issues, generalized impulse responses functions are estimated. The responses denote percentage points. The inflation shock refers to one (or two) positive standard deviation(s) (SD) increase in inflation rate. *Source*: Authors' calculations)

that a contractionary policy stance to curb inflation pressures tends to be more aggressive in the higher credit growth regime than in the lower credit growth regime.

13.6 Conclusion and Policy Implications

For monetary policy, the findings provide evidence that the inability to distinguish between credit regimes implies a much more aggressive policy stance relative to when credit regimes are considered. Therefore, the evidence indicates that inflation is bad for economic growth, irrespective of credit regimes. It indicates that the negative effects of inflation are not constrained by credit regimes. This means than even in low credit regimes, high inflation exerts disproportionately negative effects on growth.

The evidence therefore brings us to conclude that higher inflation lowers long-run economic growth and the effects are more severe in a higher credit regime relative to a lower credit regime. These findings imply that monetary policy has a duty to enforce price stability. For financial stability considerations, the estimated credit gap based on the credit threshold is marginally negative or just zero. The credit gap is not as negative or as wide as other measures estimate. Credit conditions are neutral.

Summary of Findings

- The credit growth threshold occurs at 9.5 percent.
- Cross correlation indicates a positive but transitory relationship when credit growth leads GDP growth.
- A positive and longer-lasting association arises when GDP growth precedes credit growth.
- A high credit regime on its own does not lead to prolonged credit growth.
- The repo rate increases steeply and persists at elevated levels in the higher rather than in the lower credit regime apropos inflationary shock.

- The repo rate shock lowers GDP growth significantly in the higher credit regime relative to the lower credit regime.
- The decline in GDP growth in the higher credit regime is much faster and nearly twice the size of the decline in the lower credit regime.
- An unexpected decline in inflation in the high credit regime has greater positive effects on GDP growth relative to the lower credit regime.
- An unexpected decline in inflation has asymmetric effects on economic growth depending on the existing credit regime.

14

Credit Regimes and Balance Sheet Effects

Learning Objectives

- Show the credit growth threshold and its influence in constraining economic responses in different credit regimes
- Distinguish the credit shocks effects on output in low and high credit growth regimes

14.1 Introduction

The preceding chapter established a threshold of 9.5 percent for credit growth. In addition, the analysis revealed that credit regimes exert non-linear effects in the transmission of shocks to GDP growth, inflation and the repo. Theory and empirical evidence attest to the amplification role of credit frictions on the real economic activity. Bernanke et al. (1995) and Kiyotaki and Moore (1997) explain that temporary shocks to the economy affect the balance sheets of economic agents by lowering the value of existing collateral, which increases the external finance premium, tightens the borrowing constraints and propagates the shock to the economy.

N. Gumata, E. Ndou, *Bank Credit Extension and Real Economic Activity in South Africa*, DOI 10.1007/978-3-319-43551-0_14

So how does the established credit threshold square up to the two theoretical hypotheses on balance sheet effects? This chapter conducts further robustness analysis on the estimated credit threshold. It mainly focuses on testing the relevance of two hypotheses postulated in the literature regarding the role of the credit threshold and its ability to exert asymmetric effects. The two hypotheses are:

Hypothesis 1 Negative credit shocks lead to larger declines in output under a low credit regime relative to a high credit regime.

Hypothesis 2 Positive economic growth shocks lead to higher credit growth in a lower credit regime relative to a higher credit regime.

The two hypotheses are tested using Balke's (2000) threshold vector autoregression (VAR) approach. This approach estimates nonlinear impulse responses that do not bind the system to remain within the prevailing regime at the time of initial shock. This system allows the economy to sufficiently switch away from the starting regime once the direct impact and effects feed through. Over time, the responses may potentially switch repeatedly between the two regimes (Calza and Sousa 2006).

The estimations use quarterly (Q) data from 1990Q1 to 2014Q4 for GDP growth, inflation, repo rate and credit growth. The model is estimated using two lags and 10,000 draws and the credit growth threshold of 9.5 percent.

14.2 Do Negative Credit Shocks Lead to Larger Declines in Output in the Low Credit Regime Relative to the High Credit Regime?

Essentially, the first hypothesis argues that a low credit regime may signal a situation where firms and households are generally restricted in their access to finance and cannot substitute sources of funding. Therefore, a negative bank lending shock should impact firms' and households'

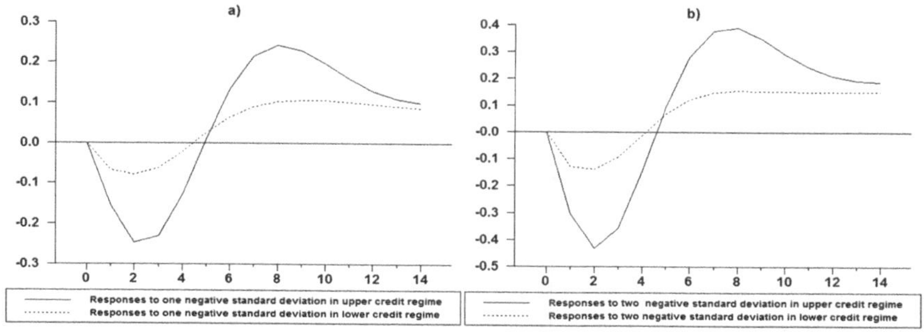

Fig. 14.1 Responses of economic growth to a negative credit supply shock (*Note*: To avoid ordering issues, we estimate generalized impulse responses functions. The responses denote percentages. *Source*: Authors' calculations)

financing ability of investments and expenditure. This will have a stronger impact on economic growth. In contrast, the higher credit regime is associated with conditions in which firms and households may adjust easily to bank lending shocks by substituting bank funding with other means of financing, such as internal finance or the issuance of debt securities.

Evidence does not support this hypothesis. In Fig. 14.1 a negative credit shock leads to a pronounced decline in economic growth in the higher credit regime relative to a lower credit regime.

This may be due to the sensitivity of firms and households to negative credit developments in the higher credit regime relative to the lower credit regime. The changing outlook may also play an important role. The decline in GDP growth in the high credit regime leads to pessimism and lowers confidence levels, spending and investment patterns and plans.

14.2.1 Do Positive Economic Growth Shocks Lead to Higher Credit Growth in the Lower Credit Regime Relative to the Higher Credit Regime?

Basically, the second hypothesis suggests that a positive economic growth shock improves labor markets and asset prices, with positive effects on the balance sheets of households and firms. The improved state of the economy alleviates financial constraints on households and firms.

So, increases in the net worth of consumers and businesses due to the improved economic outlook will increase their creditworthiness and credit supply (volumes). A positive economic growth shock also raises the profitability of lending institutions, hence this allows them to expand their balance sheets through new lending. This boosts total credit growth and lowers credit spreads.

Figure 14.2 shows the responses of credit growth to economic growth shocks in the low and high credit regimes. Evidence supports the existence of the second hypothesis. A positive economic growth shock, irrespective of the magnitude of the shock, raises credit growth by a big magnitude in the lower credit regime more than in the higher credit regime, as seen in Fig. 14.2a, b, d. This result is robust to the size of the economic growth shock.

What about the responses of credit supply (quantities)? Do negative output shocks have larger effects on credit quantities relative to positive shocks? The comparison of peak responses extracted from Fig. 14.2a, b are shown in Fig. 14.3. Based on absolute values, negative output shocks do not lead to larger effects on credit quantities than the positive ones.

According to Avdjiev and Zeng (2014) this finding may arise when positive economic growth shocks improve firms' and households' net worth, moving them away from the point of insolvency. This raises the incentive for financial institutions to increase the supply of credit. For debt contracts and debt portfolios, this implies that lenders gain when borrowers' net worth rises.

14.3 Conclusion and Policy Implications

The main policy implication, therefore, is that positive economic growth shocks matter more for credit constraints, balance sheets and the transmission of policy adjustments in the lower credit regime.

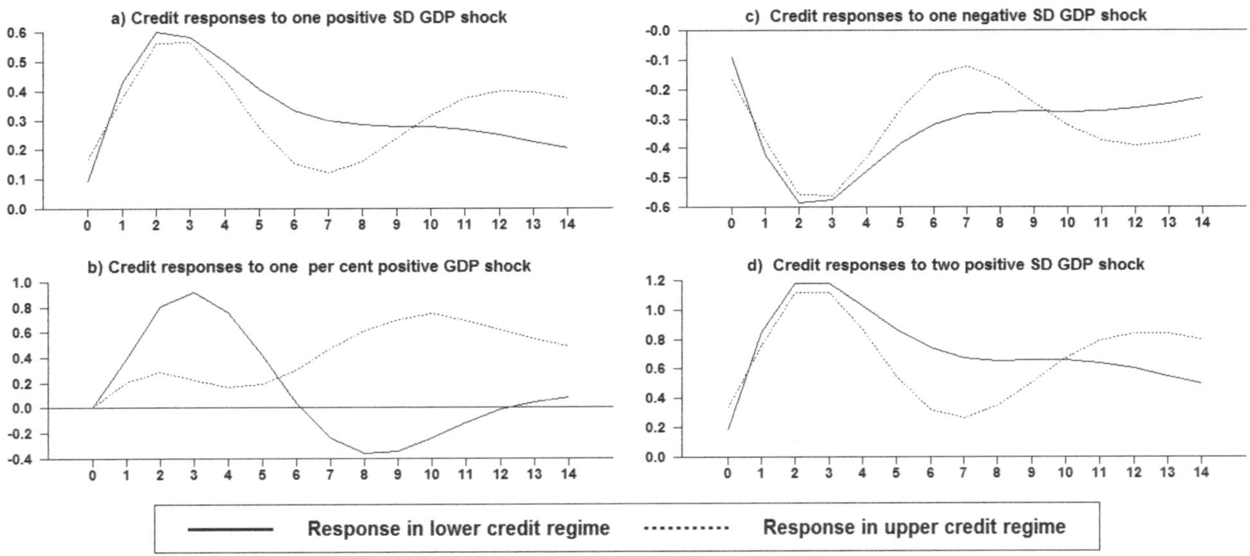

Fig. 14.2 Credit responses to various economic growth shocks of different standerd deviations (SD) (*Note*: Parts (**a**), (**c**) and (**d**) use the Balke (2000) approach while part (**b**) uses the regime dependent or conditional impulse according to the credit regime. To avoid ordering issues, generalized impulse responses functions are estimated. The responses denote percentages. *Source*: Authors' calculations)

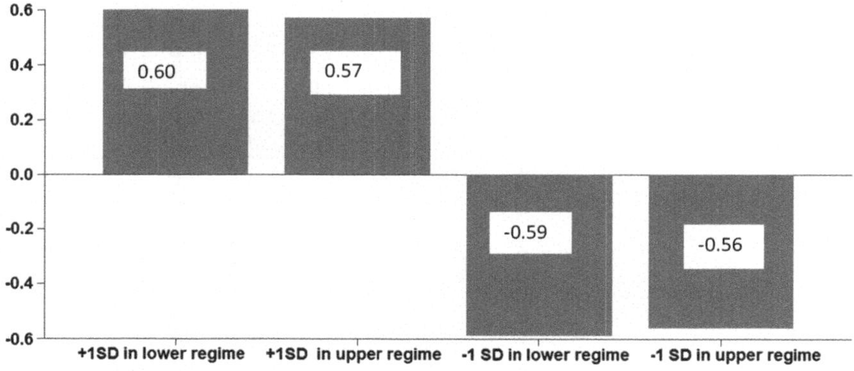

Fig. 14.3 Peak responses of credit to various magnitudes of GDP growth shocks (*Note*: The responses denote percentages. To avoid ordering issues, we estimate generalized impulse responses functions. *Source*: Authors' calculations)

Summary of Main Findings

- No evidence found supporting the idea that negative credit shocks lead to larger declines in output under a low credit regime relative to a high credit regime.
- Established evidence that an unexpected positive economic growth shock raises credit growth significantly in a low credit regime relative to a high credit regime.

Part III

Financial Regulatory Uncertainty and Bank Risk Taking

15

The Banking Risk-Taking Channel of Monetary Policy in South Africa

Learning Objectives

- Determine if there is a banking risk-taking channel of monetary policy in South Africa.
- Provide empirical evidence on the link between monetary policy and bank risk taking; and that high interest rates reduce risk-taking behavior.
- Quantify and demonstrate the extent to which contractionary monetary policy affects the bank risk-taking channel and the implications for macroeconomic performance.
- Show the implications of the monetary policy tightening cycle.

15.1 Introduction

The debate around prolonged periods of low interest rates and expansionary monetary policy is premised on the effects of bank risk-taking behavior. If interest rates are low for protracted periods and encourage risk taking, then high interest rates should reduce risk-taking behavior.

N. Gumata, E. Ndou, *Bank Credit Extension and Real Economic Activity in South Africa*, DOI 10.1007/978-3-319-43551-0_15

We quantify and demonstrate the extent to which a contractionary policy shock affects the bank risk-taking channel and the implications for macroeconomic performance. Is there a banking risk-taking channel of monetary policy in South Africa? What are the implications for the monetary policy tightening cycle? The purpose of this chapter is to explore these issues and provide empirical evidence on the link between monetary policy and bank risk taking.

Interest rates influence bank balance sheet risks in different ways with varying time lags, is it possible that risk taking and interest rates move in the same direction? Not necessarily. Angeloni et al. (2013) show that in the short run, risk is likely to be positively correlated with interest rates. This relationship is likely to be reversed in the long run and become negative as the risk-taking channel dominates, particularly through changes in the funding side. In Fig. 15.1 we show that GDP growth and funding risk are negatively correlated. Meaning that bank funding risk has a negative impact on economic activity. We explore this channel in detail in this chapter.

15.2 What Is the Bank Risk-Taking Channel of Monetary Policy?

In essence, the bank risk-taking channel largely extends the bank-lending channel. The bank-lending channel assumes that banks' conditions are not neutral for the transmission of monetary policy. The bank risk-taking channel goes further and assumes that the direction of causality possibly runs from monetary policy to bank risk (Altunbas et al. 2010; Gaggl and Valderrama 2010). The risk-taking channel occurs when expansionary monetary policy lasts for extended periods, therefore impacting risk perceptions, attitudes and incentives of banks to take on more risk in their portfolios.

In this case, the channels of transmission involved are no longer the increase in the volume of loans in line with the traditional transmission mechanisms, but also an increase in the risk aspect of lending aligned with the deterioration in the quality of portfolios (Angeloni et al. 2013). This channel implies that interest rates affect the quality and not just the

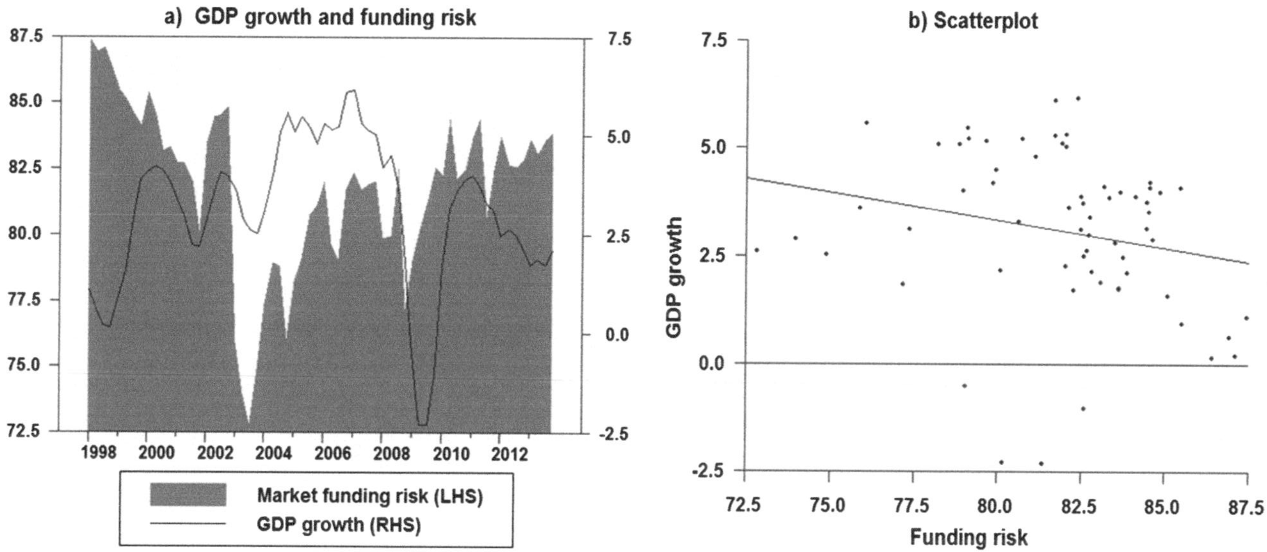

Fig. 15.1 GDP growth and funding risk (*Source*: SARB and authors' calculations)

quantity of bank credit.[1] Hence, it is argued that in such cases monetary policy actions can contribute to the build-up of financial imbalances. This occurs through a change in risk attitudes and these can ultimately result in boom and bust episodes.

Why is the focus on bank risk as a channel for the monetary policy risk-taking channel? It is because banks play an important role in the key channels of transmission involved: (1) the credit channel and (2) the risk-taking channel of monetary transmission. In the credit channel, a decrease in interest rates leads to a rise in asset values, as well as collateral or net worth of the borrowers, and improves the repayment abilities. Under such circumstances banks are willing to increase the supply of loans given that there is less risk involved in lending. In this situation there is no change in banks' risk tolerance and their risk position can even be enhanced.

In the empirical analysis we differentiate between funding risk and lending risk. For funding risk, we use all customer funding (i.e. deposits for the household, companies and government and other sources) as ratios of total bank assets. The analysis uses the realized volatility of the bank stock price index calculated as the absolute return of the index over each quarter as a proxy for total bank risk. For the asset side and lending risk we use non-performing loans.[2]

Is there a risk-taking channel working through non-performing loans via an unexpected rise in house price growth shocks? This channel suggests that an increase in house prices leads to a higher value of collateral, which encourages over-borrowing. This impacts the capacity of borrowers to repay and ultimately leads to high non-performing loans. The assessment of this channel is also meant to capture (1) the basic mechanism of leverage and (2) credit constraints that depend on the value of collateral and the amplification of monetary policy shocks. These propagating effects occur due to the deterioration in the asset quality of the banking

[1] Specifically, the view is that interest rates were held low for too long in the run-up to the recent financial crisis and that this helped to fuel an asset price boom, spurring financial intermediaries to increase leverage and take on excessive risks. More recently, a related debate has ensued on whether continued expectations of exceptionally low interest rates are setting the stage for the next financial crisis. See, Rajan (2010), Farhi and Tirole (2012), Borio and Zhu (2008), Adrian and Shin (2009), Taylor (2009), Giovanni et al. (2013), amongst others.

[2] Credit lending standards as a proxy for lending risk and perceptions of borrowers' risk are not used due to the short sample available for the times series.

sector as non-performing loans rise and result in a contraction of the supply of bank lending.

The empirical approach used in this chapter is based on the modified vector autoregression (VAR) framework by Angeloni et al. (2013). The chapter establishes the macroeconomic effects of the risk-taking behavior on GDP growth by performing a historical decomposition. The counterfactual analysis helps to explore how economic growth would have evolved if risk taking was not prevalent. Hence, we examine the estimates of economic growth in the absence of or having removed the contributions of non-performing loans, bank and funding risk—as well as the combined effects of the two shocks.

To evaluate the interactions between the policy rate, real economic activity and bank risk taking, we evaluate how bank risk impacts economic growth relative to a contractionary monetary policy shock. The contributions of the repo rate are also considered and compared to those of bank risk. This facilitates the assessment of whether the effects moved in same the direction or diverged over time.

15.3 Relationship Between Funding Risk and Economic Growth

The analysis begins by looking at the relationship between funding risk and economic growth shown in Fig. 15.2. The data used is quarterly spanning 1995Q1–2013Q4. The scatter plots show a negative relationship between funding risk measures and economic growth, with the exception of Fig. 15.2f for household deposits.

15.4 Can the Model Capture the Stylized Effects of an Unexpected Repo Rate Hike?

This section assesses the effects of an unexpected repo rate on real variables and examines if their responses are consistent with conventional views. The analysis relies on the VAR approach to get the trajectories of selected

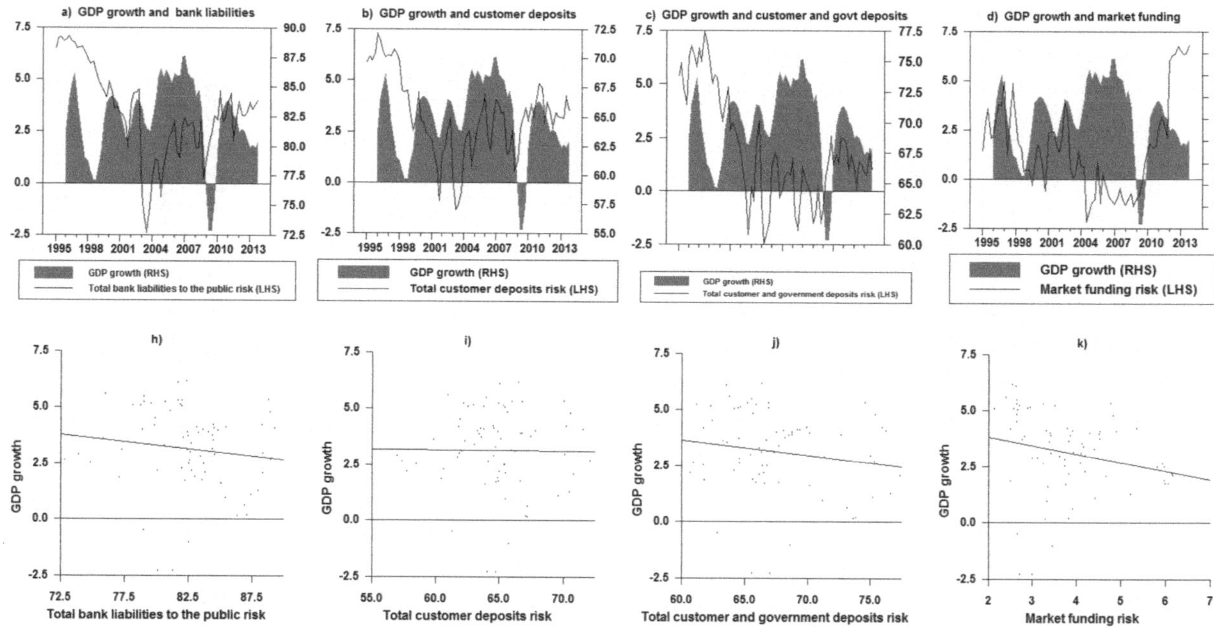

Fig. 15.2a The relationship between the components of funding risk and GDP growth (*Note*: Funding risk refers to the ratio of the funding variables to total assets expressed in percentage terms, govt refers to government. *Source*: SARB and authors' calculations)

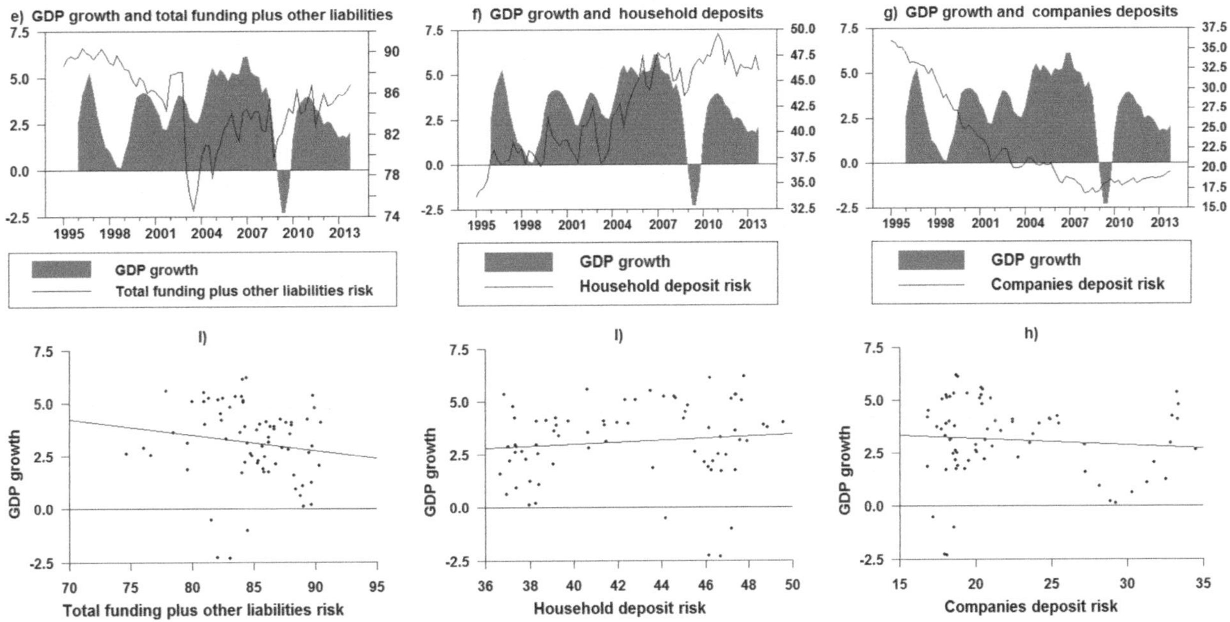

Fig. 15.2b The relationship between the components of funding risk and GDP growth (*Note*: Funding risk refers to the ratio of the funding variables to total assets expressed in percentage terms, govt refers to government. *Source*: SARB and authors' calculations)

variables to investigate the effects of an unexpected repo rate hike, a rise in funding and bank credit risk shocks. The model uses GDP growth, the GDP deflator inflation (as a proxy for inflation), the detrended repo rate, macroeconomic uncertainty (proxied by bank stock uncertainty), house price inflation, non-performing loans, credit growth, funding risk and bank risk. The funding and bank risk variables are measured as defined in Angeloni et al. (2013).

The variables are also ordered as in Angeloni et al. (2013). Different model sizes with three to eight variables are used, and come to the same findings. The results reported here are based on two lags. The results are also robust to using four lags as a default lag for quarterly data. A dummy for the adoption of inflation targeting is used which equals one beginning in 2000Q1 to end of sample and zero otherwise. The dummy for the recession equals one in 2009Q1–2009Q3 and zero otherwise.

The analysis starts by presenting the responses of economic growth, GDP deflator inflation, house prices and credit extension to test how well they reflect conventional evidence reported in the literature. In Fig. 15.3 an unexpected repo rate hike has a contractionary effect on all variables but non-performing loans respond with a lag. The reaction of these macroeconomic variables is consistent with theoretical predictions that monetary policy has an adverse effect on them. Table 15.1 shows a summary of the responses in Fig. 15.3 and concludes that the responses of the variables do capture the effects of the repo rate.

15.1.1 Is There Evidence of the Bank Risk-Taking Channel of Monetary Policy?

The analysis goes a step further and assesses the transmission of monetary policy to bank funding risk via (1) the liability side of the banks' balance sheets and (2) the asset side of the balance sheet (i.e. bank risk). This analysis will determine if the risk-taking channel of monetary policy operating via the liability and asset sides of funding and bank risks declines significantly due to a contractionary monetary policy shock. If the results fail to show a significant decline in the funding and bank risks this will indicate that there exists no statistically significant evidence of monetary

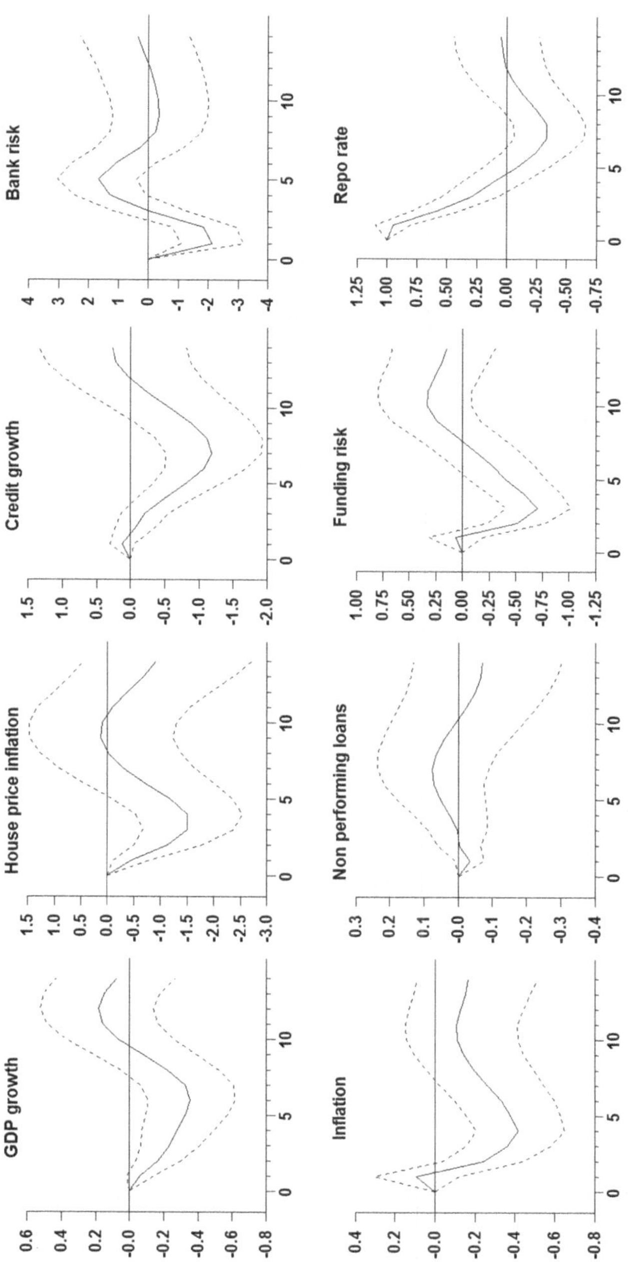

Fig. 15.3 Responses to a 1 percent unexpected rise in the repo rate (*Source*: Authors' calculations)

Table 15.1 Summary of variables' responses

Variable	Response			Peak	Duration (quarters)	
	Theoretical	Observed	Decision	Decline/rise	Period	
GDP growth	–	–	Significant	−0.36	6	8
Inflation	–	–	Significant	−0.41	4	8
House prices	–	–	Significant	−1.52	3	6
NPLs	+	+	Insignificant	0.08	7	0
Credit growth	–	–	Significant	−1.19	7	10
Funding risk	–	–	Significant	−0.70	3	6
Bank risk	–	–	Significant	−2.13	1	3

Note: – means negative and + means positive
Source: Authors' calculations

policy bank risk-taking channels. The results in Fig. 15.3 confirm the bank risk-taking channel of monetary policy, since contractionary monetary policy significantly reduces funding and bank risk.

The rise in funding risk in the short run indicates that the short end of the yield curve responds much quicker to policy tightening since funding instruments priced off the short end of the yield curve adjust more quickly to changes in policy rate shocks. The evidence concludes that responses of bank risk are largely driven by what happens on the liability side, especially the share of market-based sources of funding. However, the non-performing loans respond with a lag to an unexpected repo rate hike.

Since the focus of this chapter is also on the impact of economic growth and monetary policy on bank risk taking, we show fluctuations these variables induce on bank risk taking in Fig. 15.4. Economic growth explains relatively higher variability in the movements of non-performing loans but accounts for less than 10 percent of the variation in funding and bank risk in Fig. 15.4a. In Fig. 15.4b the repo rate induces more fluctuations in funding risk and they exceed those of both non-performing loans and bank risk.

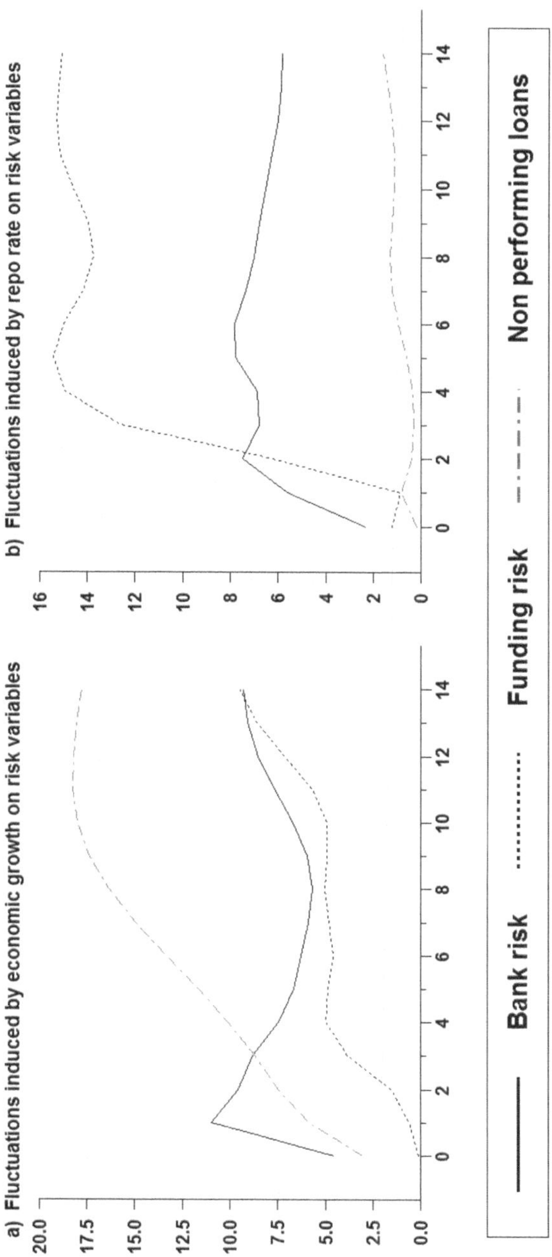

Fig. 15.4 The variability in bank risk variables due to economic growth and repo rate shocks (percent) (*Source:* Authors' calculations)

15.1.2 Are the Direction and Significance of the Results Sensitive to Sample Size?

The preceding results are based on data that includes the recession in 2009Q1–Q3 and later periods associated with the quantitative easing effects from advanced economies. For the inference of strong policy implications, this chapter examines if the impact would have been different if we used data up to 2008Q4 only. The results examining the two impulse responses estimated using data that spans 1995Q1–2013Q4 and 1995Q1–2008Q4 are shown in Fig. 15.5.

Evidence shows that the impulse responses for the subsamples are bounded within the error band. This suggests that we could have arrived at similar conclusions with respect to the effects of an unexpected repo rate shock on economic growth and the bank risk variables. Apart from the funding risk in Fig. 15.5c1, which transitorily moves outside the error bands at peak decline, the response is as expected.

Irrespective of the period under review, evidence in Fig. 15.5 reveals that an unexpected increase in the repo rate impacts funding and bank risk negatively, confirming the presence of the bank risk-taking channel. This is independent of whether the data includes or excludes the recession period. These findings agree with conventional views that an unexpected rise in the repo rate depresses economic growth and risk variables.

The preceding results reveal that an unexpected rise in the repo rate significantly lowers the funding and bank risk. What about the reactions of other categories of funding risks? Is there evidence of the bank risk-taking channel being dependent on a measure of the funding risk shock? In Fig. 15.6 all categories of funding risks decline significantly in response to a monetary policy tightening shock.

15.1.3 Is There a Risk-Taking Channel via Non-performing Loans and House Prices?

The analysis assesses the bank risk-taking channel in conjunction with house prices. Houses can be used as collateral to access credit, and fluctuations in collateral are an important driver of credit booms and busts.

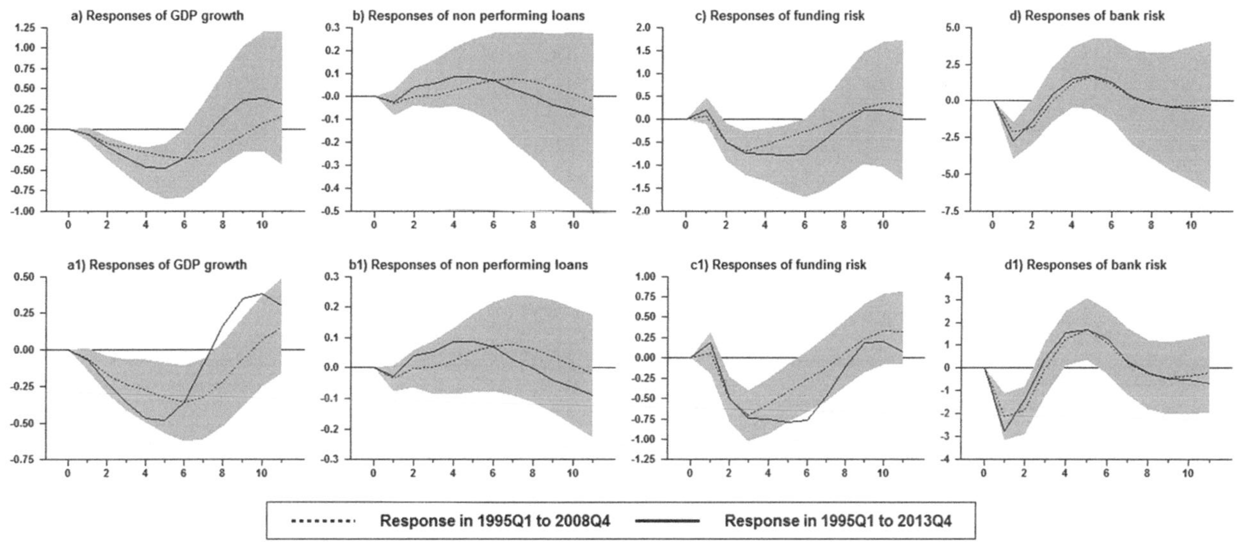

Fig. 15.5 Responses to repo rate shocks for two subsamples (*Note*: The *light shaded* error bands in first row are calculated using the data spanning 1995Q1–2008Q4. The *grey* error bands in second row are calculated using data spanning 1995Q1–2013Q4. *Source*: Authors' calculations)

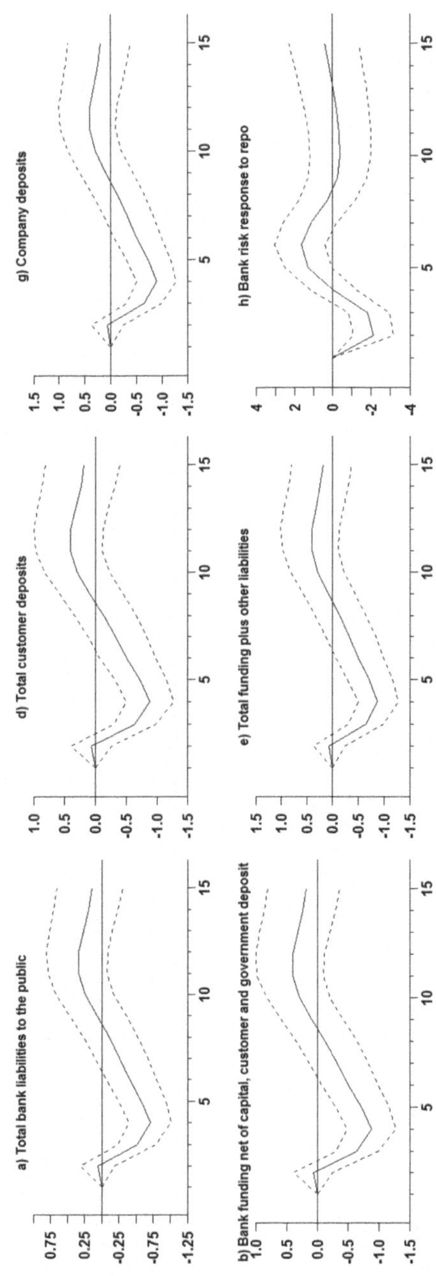

Fig. 15.6 Responses of various funding risk measures to repo rate shock (*Source*: Authors' calculations)

Higher house prices can lead to higher credit supply, over-borrowing and large scale defaults. This feedback loop suggests a positive relationship between higher house prices and non-performing loans as well as a positive relationship between house prices and credit supply. By increasing collateral values for loans, house price increases improve the creditworthiness and debt capacity of borrowers. The trends between non-performing loans and house price growth are shown in Fig. 15.7a and the relationship between economic growth and non-performing loans are shown in (b).

The linear relationship shown by scatter plots suggests that a 1 percent increase in non-performing loans lowers house prices by 2.9 percent. Moreover, a 1 percent rise in non-performing loans reduces economic activity by about 0.81 percentage points.

So, to what extent do house prices, GDP growth and non-performing loans drive credit extension? The responses of credit to the three shocks are presented in Fig. 15.8a–c. An unexpected rise in non-performing loans depresses credit extension for a year, while an unexpected rise in economic and house price growth leads to a significant rise in credit extension.

An unexpected increase in economic growth in Fig. 15.8d and house price growth in Fig. 15.8e depress non-performing loans. Non-performing loans tend to rise following a shock to credit growth in Fig. 15.8f, although these rises are insignificant. There is lack of evidence that a credit extension shock leads to significantly high non-performing loans. Hence, the findings conclude that there is limited evidence of weak or lax supervisory practices. The decline in non-performing loans due to an unexpected house price inflation shock does not support the collateral effects of the risk-taking channel, which implies that house price increases can facilitate borrowers to take on more debt as the high collateral value enhances the supply of further loans.

Since the primary mandate of the bank is price stability, what do impulse responses reveal about policy responses and inflationary developments linked to credit markets? In Fig. 15.8g the repo rate rises significantly after three quarters, and returns to pre-shock levels after six quarters. Consistent with economic predictions, credit extension has inflationary consequences in Fig. 15.8h.

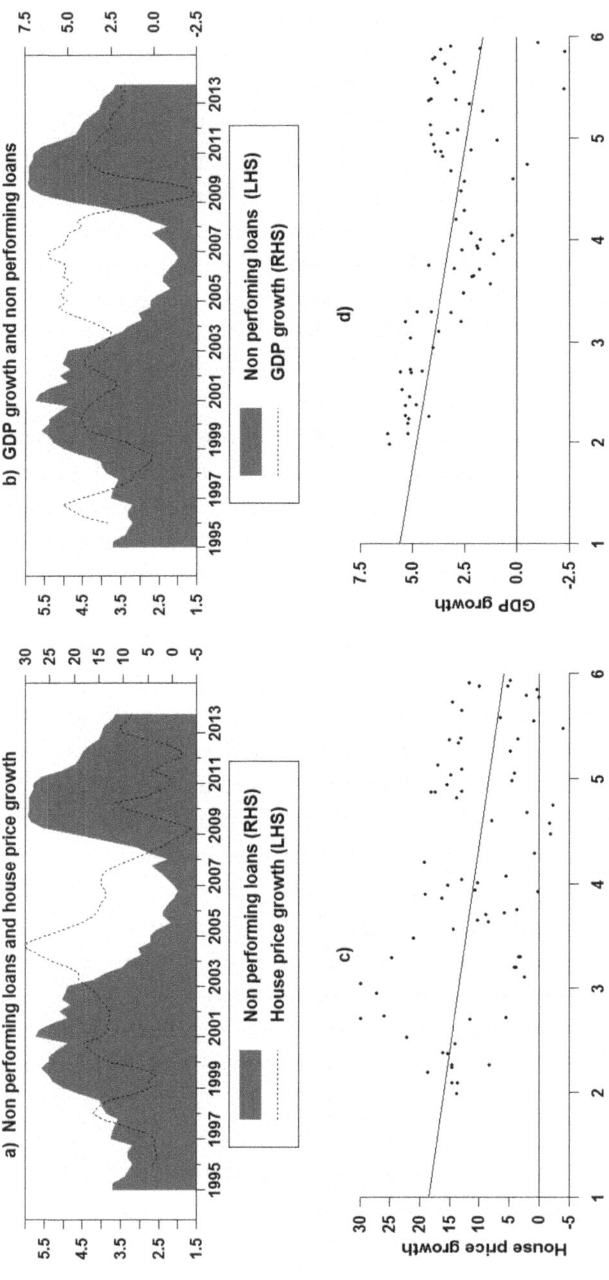

Fig. 15.7 Relationship between non-performing loans and real variables (*Source*: Authors' calculations)

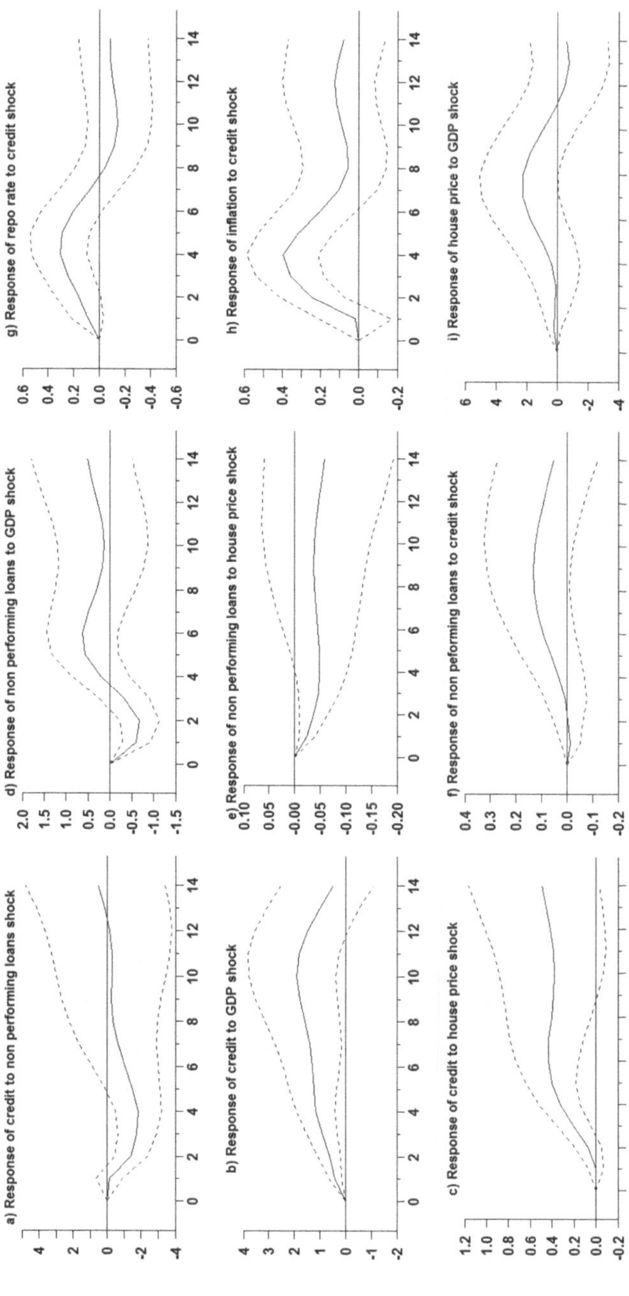

Fig. 15.8 The relationship between non-performing loans, credit extension, house prices and economic growth (*Source*: Authors' calculations)

So, to what extent do the domestic factors, namely, economic growth, house price growth and the repo rate, explain movements in credit and non-performing loans over time? Do they explain sluggish credit extension developments post-2009? Credit growth and non-performing loans due to three domestic factors are shown in Fig. 15.9a, b, respectively.

It is evident in Fig. 15.9 that house prices, economic growth and the repo rate give contrasting contributions on the evolution of credit and non-performing loans. House prices have had significantly higher positive contributions to credit, compared to both the repo rate and economic growth between late 2003 and mid-2008. However, they have since dragged credit extension downwards since 2009 and it is evident that the contributions have not recovered.

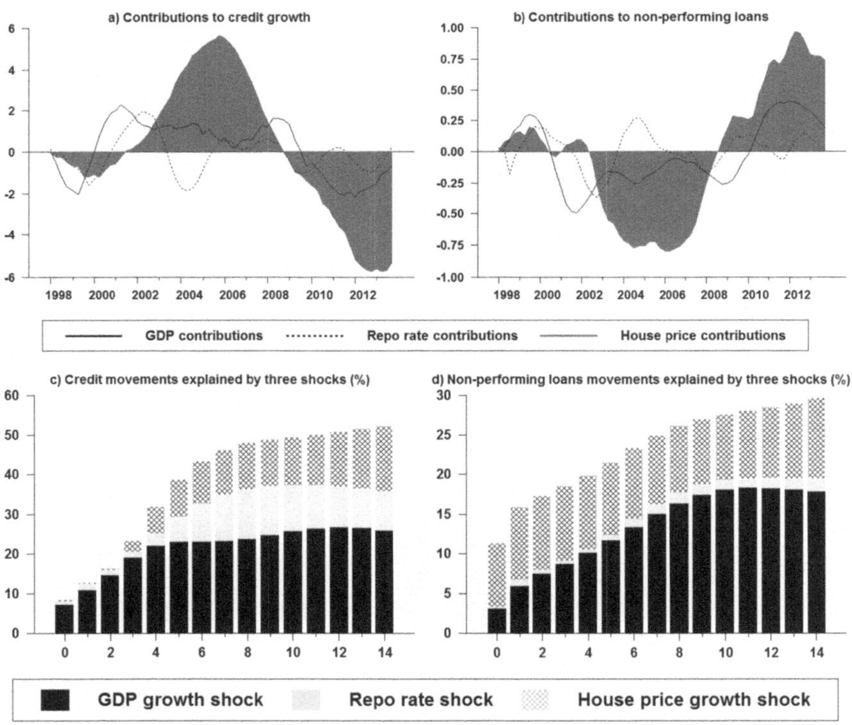

Fig. 15.9 Contributions and fluctuations induced by macroeconomic variables to credit and non-performing loans (*Note*: In (**a**) and (**b**) the *lightly shaded portions* denote the recession in 2009. *Source*: Authors' calculations)

Despite the repo rate, economic growth and house prices contributing negatively to credit extension, it is evident that the effect tends to be magnified in relation to house prices. This effect of house prices possibly indicates the role of collateral in credit extension. Between economic growth and the repo rate, it is clear that before the financial crisis and during the recession in 2009, economic growth played a more significant role in developments in credit extension relative to those of the repo rate. Thus, economic growth played a bigger role in stimulating credit growth but has since contributed more in dragging credit extension downwards following the recession. Thus economic growth and house price growth remain to a larger extent the main factors that are still slowing (dragging) down credit extension since 2009.

With regards to non-performing loans, we find an inverse relationship between non-performing loans and macroeconomic variables (i.e. house prices, economic growth and repo rate). House prices contributed negatively to non-performing loans in the period 2002–2009. This coincides with the house price boom period. The economic developments post-2009, which include slow economic growth and the sluggish housing recovery relative to the pre-crisis level explain these factors' positive contributions to increased non-performing loans. In addition, economic growth developments contributed positively to non-performing loans and far exceed the repo rate contributions. This suggests that the state of the macroeconomic environment, in the form of robust economic growth and house prices, plays a significant role in non-performing loans dynamics. In Fig. 15.9c, d economic growth, house price growth and the repo rate tend to propagate movements in the credit growth and non-performing loans, respectively.

A question arises: Which shock dominates the propagation effects in credit growth and non-performing loans? It is evident that economic growth dominates house price growth and the repo rate in propagating movements in credit extension and non-performing loans. In the order of contributions, house price growth comes second, whereas the repo rate comes third. As concluded earlier, the repo rate propagates movements in non-performing loans to a limited extent compared to inducing credit growth.

15.1.4 Which Risk Shocks Depress Economic Growth as Well as Propagating Fluctuations in Economic Growth?

Given that policymakers also care about economic growth in their decision-making process, to what extent do unexpected banking risk shocks (i.e. non-performing loans, funding risks and bank risk) on economic growth tell policymakers what to do? Fig. 15.10 examines the impact of an unexpected rise in non-performing loans, funding and bank risk shocks on economic growth and compares the effects to those of the repo rate.

Both the unexpected rise in various banking risk variables and the repo rate tend to depress economic growth but the peaks and the duration of the effects vary. The magnitudes of peak economic growth declines and the period at which these occur in response to the unexpected shocks are shown in Fig. 15.11a.

The biggest economic growth decline of 0.7 percentage points occurred due to non-performing loans, followed by the repo rate shock, funding risk and lastly, bank risk. With respect to the lag effects of the shocks, Fig. 15.11 shows that (1) the biggest economic growth decline of 0.7 percentage points occurred due to non-performing loans in the second quarter, (2) bank risk in the fourth quarter, (3) followed by the repo shock in the sixth quarter and (4) funding risk in the seventh quarter.

To give more insight into the role played by the repo rate, funding risk, bank risk and non-performing loans given the differing peak effects and their timing, we show the peak effects in Fig. 15.11b. The propagation effects are very small with respect to non-performing loans. Earlier on, the evidence found non-performing loans to significantly depress economic growth in less than a year. After five quarters, the repo rate explains more fluctuations in economic growth than the other risk measures. Amongst the banking risk variables, the bank risk measure induces more fluctuations in economic growth followed by funding risk and non-performing loans.

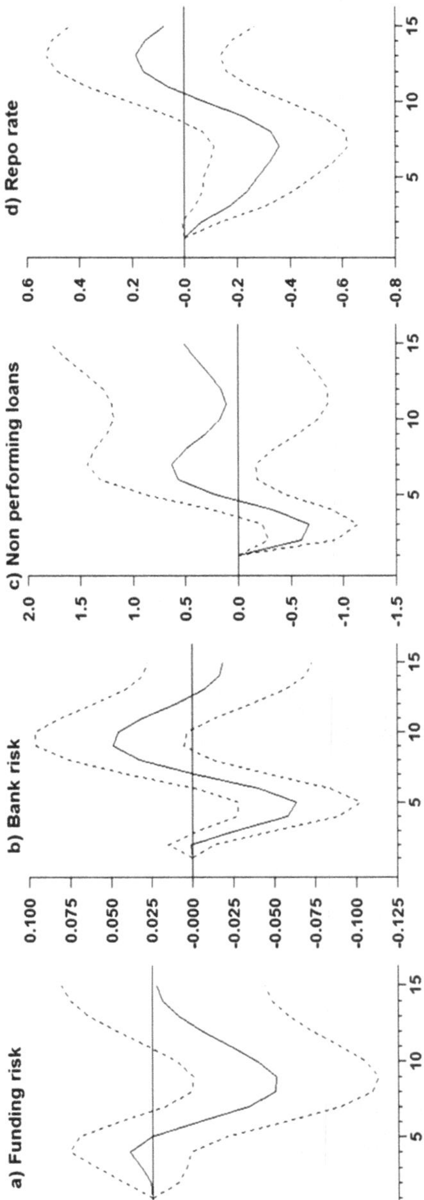

Fig. 15.10 Responses of economic growth to positive banking risk and repo rate shocks (*Source*: Authors' calculations)

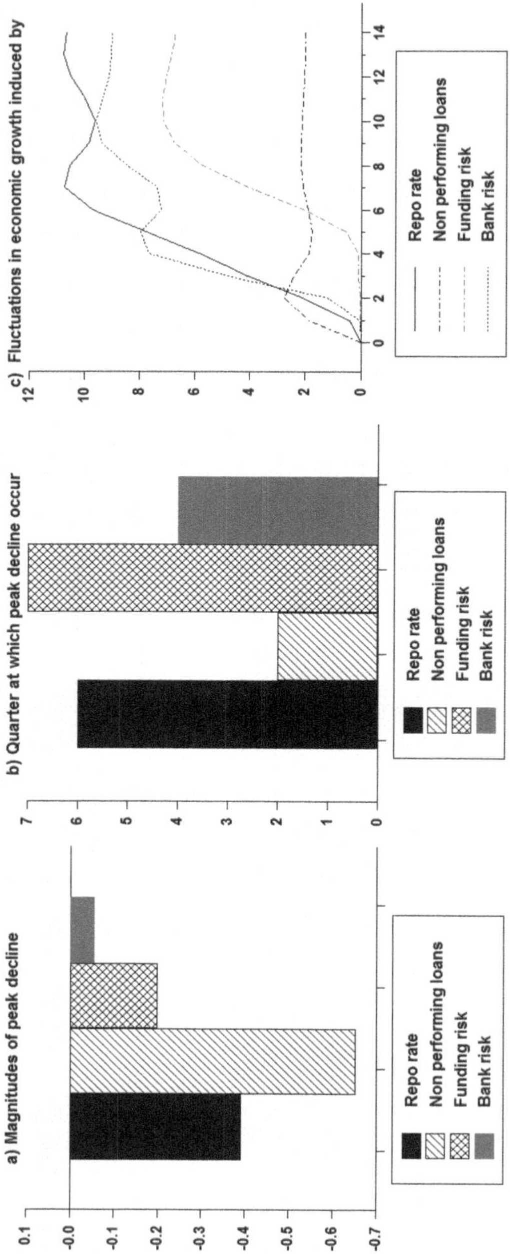

Fig. 15.11 The peak GDP decline to various shocks and periods of peak impact (*Source*: Authors' calculations)

15.1.5 What Would Economic Growth Be Like in the Absence of Various Banking Risk Shocks?

The preceding sections focused on the reaction of economic growth to unexpected funding and bank risk shocks; this was an initial step in the analysis. However, the analysis is unable to show historically the effects of these risk variables over the business cycle. Did these risk variables contribute in different ways to economic growth? If so, then what can policymakers infer about the role of these risk variables on economic growth following the 2009 recession? The first question is answered by applying the counterfactual approach and assessing how economic growth would have evolved historically when excluding the contributions of risk variables (non-performing loans, bank risk and funding risk) to overall economic growth.

The results in Fig. 15.12a show the actual economic growth rate compared to counterfactual growth rate. The gap between actual and the counterfactual growth in Fig. 15.12b measures the contributions made by the risk variables to economic growth. If actual growth lies above (below) counterfactual growth, it implies that the risk variable uplifted (retarded) economic growth. In 2009, the combined risk variables contributed to the contraction in economic growth as shown in Fig. 15.12b. Fig. 15.12c shows which risk variable's contribution dominates in the combined risk effects displayed in Fig. 15.12b, regarding the evolution of economic growth. In addition, we compare the magnitudes of their contributions to economic growth.

Based on the peaks and troughs in Fig. 15.12c bank risk contributions tend to exceed those of the other two risk factors. For instance, between 2006 and 2008 bank risk contributions dominated the funding risk contribution. However, post-2012 the bank risk variable dominated both the non-performing loans and funding risk in dragging down economic growth.

Amongst the risk variables analyzed in this chapter, bank risk contributes relatively higher than funding risk measures and non-performing loans in Fig. 15.12c. Hence, Fig. 15.12d shows a negative relationship between bank risk contributions to GDP and bank risk. This is supported by a relatively steeper negative relationship between bank risk

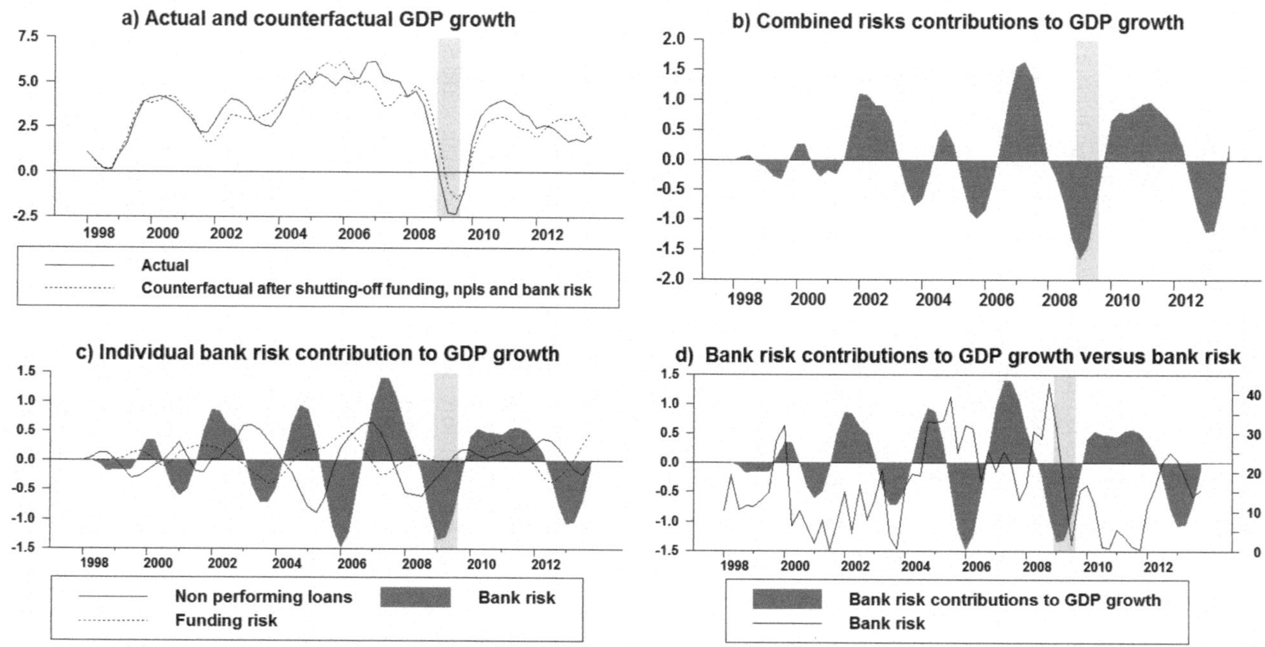

Fig. 15.12 The effects of individual and combined risk variables on economic growth (*Source*: Authors' calculations)

and its contributions to economic growth in the scatter plot (not presented here). This suggests that the higher bank risk becomes, the more its contributions to economic growth pull down economic growth. This implies that stability in the banking sector is necessary to sustain economic growth.

15.1.6 Do Contributions from the Repo Rate Reinforce Those of Combined Banking?

In order to give more insight to policymakers, the contributions of the repo rate to economic growth are compared to those of combined risk variables. Fig. 15.13 plots the contributions to economic growth from combined risk and the repo rate to assess both their direction and magnitudes in paying attention to periods before, during and post-recession in 2009. We do this to ascertain the sensitivity of aggregated banking risk to the inclusion of the funding risk.

Evidence in all parts of Fig. 15.13 shows that before the recession the repo rate contributed positively to economic growth and during the recession period its contributions were negative until 2010Q1. This finding is robust to definition of the different funding risk measures.

Did the inclusion of separate funding risk measures impact the turning point of the repo rate contributions to economic growth? The magnitudes

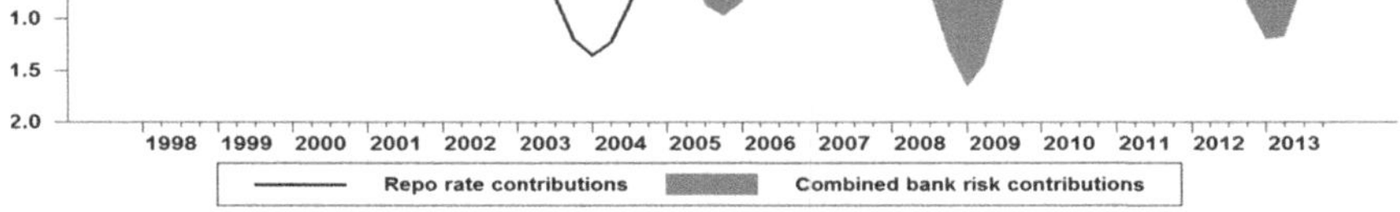

Fig. 15.13 Combined bank risk versus repo rate contributions to economic growth (*Source*: Authors' calculations)

of the repo rate contributions in the presence of various bank funding risks show that they moved in the same direction and there are no significant divergences, other than the variation of the magnitudes of contributions at the different turning points.

15.5 Conclusion and Policy Implications

This chapter has examined the existence of the bank risk-taking channel in South Africa by considering both sides of the banks' balance sheets. To test for the existence of the bank risk-taking channel of monetary policy, we assessed the responses of three bank risk-taking indicators—namely, bank funding risk, bank risk and bank lending risk—to a contractionary monetary policy shock. We find evidence of the bank risk-taking channel of monetary policy through the funding risk channel and weak evidence of the lending risk channel. Findings confirm that a rise in both funding and bank risk lowers output significantly.

The analysis searched for evidence of the existence of a bank risk-taking channel working through non-performing loans via an unexpected rise in a house price growth shock. Non-performing loans tend to rise (although they are insignificant) following a shock to credit extension. There is no evidence that a credit extension shock leads to significantly high non-performing loans. Moreover, these results can also be interpreted to suggest that there is limited evidence of weak or lax supervisory practices. The decline in non-performing loans due to an unexpected house price inflation shock does not support the collateral effects of the risk taking channel, which implies that house price increases can facilitate borrowers to take on more debt as the high collateral value enhances the supply of further loans.

Overall, the findings in this chapter contribute to the ongoing debate about the role of monetary policy on financial stability. They suggest that monetary policy has a bearing on bank risk attitudes and risk taking. All funding risk measures respond negatively to tightening in monetary policy. This implies that monetary policy is not neutral from a financial stability perspective. Monetary policy is not exactly the right tool for the task of financial stability. Stein (2014) asserts that monetary policy possesses an important advantage relative to financial supervision and regulation—it gets in all the cracks.[3] At the same time, we established a strong feedback loop between macroeconomic performance and lending risk. Thus, economic growth matters for the lending or asset side of the bank risk-taking channel.

Summary of Evidence

- There is evidence of the bank risk-taking channel of monetary policy through the funding-risk channel.
- Bank lending risk as proxied by non-performing loans suggests weak evidence of the lending risk channel.
- Evidence confirms that a rise in both funding and bank risk lowers output significantly.
- Non-performing loans tend to rise following a shock to credit extension.
- There is no evidence that a credit extension shock leads to significantly high non-performing loans.
- Evidence does not support the collateral effects of the risk-taking channel. This implies that house price increases can facilitate borrowers to take on more debt as the high collateral value enhances the supply of further loans.
- GDP growth, house price growth and the repo rate explain large movements in credit and non-performing loans.
- House prices had significantly higher positive contributions to credit, compared to both the repo rate and economic growth between late 2003 and mid-2008.
- Monetary policy has a bearing on bank risk attitudes and risk taking. All funding risk measures respond negatively to tightening in monetary policy.

[3] See Altunbas et al. (2014).

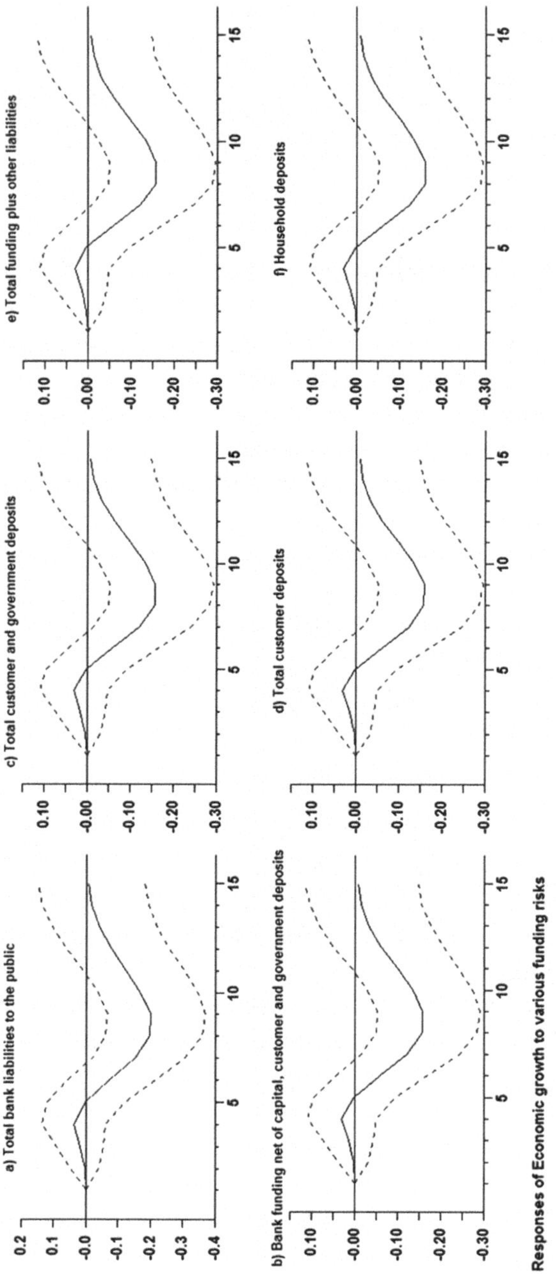

Fig. A.15.1 Response of economic growth to various funding risks measures (*Source*: Authors' calculations)

16

Financial Regulation Policy Uncertainty and the Sluggish Recovery in Credit Growth

Learning Objectives

- Interaction between elevated financial regulation policy uncertainty, lending rate margins, credit risk and the sluggish recovery in credit growth in South Africa
- The extent to which lending spreads are driven by financial regulatory policy uncertainty
- Whether the impact of financial regulatory policy uncertainty complements or neutralizes monetary policy effects
- The impact of financial regulatory policy uncertainty on funding margins, lending spreads and provisions for credit losses

16.1 Introduction

Can elevated financial regulation policy uncertainty explain the lending rate margins, credit risk and the sluggish recovery in credit growth in South Africa? The rise in lending margins remains a topical policy concern, despite the reduction of policy rates to historic low levels and

N. Gumata, E. Ndou, *Bank Credit Extension and Real Economic Activity in South Africa*, DOI 10.1007/978-3-319-43551-0_16

unconventional monetary policy interventions. This chapter extends the exploration of factors contributing to lending margins. The chapter explores the extent to which lending spreads are driven by financial regulatory policy uncertainty (FRPU).[1]

Does financial regulatory policy uncertainty complement or neutralize monetary policy effects? How does it affect funding margins, lending spreads and provisions for credit losses? Walentin (2014) states that an unexpected rise in interest rate margins can be due to factors ranging from changes in the prepayment risk premium, changes in the ability of the financial system to bear risk, regulatory reforms and financial innovation. Informed by such changes, the business cycle literature and models have relaxed the assumption of one interest rate as sufficient to characterize the economy.

The concern that low policy rates have not been fully transmitted to lending rates has been raised and investigated in most advanced economies. The thrust of the investigation is whether there is disconnect between policy rates and both funding and lending rates. In particular, the assessment of the effectiveness of the transmission of policy has focused on interest rates charged on new lending to households. The model specifications considered the effects of policy uncertainty and risk factors in interest rate setting behavior.

It is shown in the earlier chapters that lending rate margins on all credit categories to the household sector have increased despite historic low levels in the policy rate. This chapter extends analysis and quantifies the role of funding rate margins and credit risk, determining the macroeconomic effects of lending spreads and the extent to which lending spreads and credit risk contributed to credit growth. This kind of analysis will convey information on whether the expansionary monetary policy was neutralized or propagated.

To capture the asset and liability side of bank balance sheets, we examine the effects of regulatory uncertainty on funding rates and credit risk. The chapter further examines the extent to which credit risk is driven by the FRPU and house prices. Bloom (2014) asserts

[1] See Nodari (2014) and Baker et al. (2013).

that uncertainty shocks are not different to demand shocks and then compares the responses of real variables to the FRPU, the repo rate and interest rate margins shocks. The analyses here examine scenarios of what would have happened to credit extension in the absence of (1) FRPU shock, (2) lending rate margins shock, (3) repo rate shocks and (4) the combined contributions. This will show the extent to which the repo rate, FRPU and interest rate margins reinforced or neutralized each other's effects on credit growth.

16.2 Why Should Policymakers Be Concerned About Regulatory Uncertainty Shocks?

For monetary policy, a complete and symmetrical pass-through supports the authorities' policy objective. Whereas, from a financial stability and regulatory perspective, the way banks set lending rates affects their margins, profitability and the soundness of the financial system. Thus, an understanding of the interaction of the two mandates is important. Because if lending spreads are driven by regulatory motives they may impede the benefits of a looser monetary policy stance.

Regulatory reforms are not bad and are in part aimed at re-establishing trust in the financial system and to make financial markets and institutions more transparent. Reforms are also motivated by restoring appropriate and prudent levels of credit growth to limit future episodes of costly credit and asset price booms and busts. Nodari (2014) states that although financial regulatory reforms are desirable, the uncertainty surrounding these reforms can result in adverse economic effects. This is particularly of concern when the policymaking process regarding the agreements and their implementation is surrounded by high uncertainty. This uncertainty can increase the risk associated with lending activities, raise the borrowing costs and depress investment and spending plans. In addition, the higher safety margins may add to operating costs for lenders and these costs will be passed in full or partially to the real economy.

16.3 To What Extent Have Banks' Balance Sheet Items Changed in the Period Pre- and Post-recession in 2009?

This section presents highlights of the main developments regarding the liability and asset sides of the banking sector and shows the evolution in (1) funding spreads, (2) lending spread; and (3) banks' interest income and expenses. The dynamics of these variables are linked to trends in monetary policy settings.

16.3.1 Is There Evidence of a Systematic Shift in Bank Funding Sources?

We assess whether there have been significant changes in the balance sheets items of banks that can at least give us an indication of the changes in liabilities and assets for the period 2000–2008 and 2009–September 2014. The trends in Fig. 16.1 suggest that there are no significant changes in the balance sheet items of banks. Banks still rely on deposits as their main source of funding for total loans and advances. Interbank bank liabilities have declined relative to the period 2000–2008.

16.3.2 Studies in Other Countries Indicated Rising Funding Cost Margins Post-2009, How Did Funding Margins in South Africa Evolve?

Earlier chapters showed a significant structural shift in lending interest spreads. Fig. 16.2 assesses whether there are any discernible changes that can convey more information about the pricing of funding that is not immediately evident from the balance sheet items shown in Fig. 16.1. In Fig. 16.2 the funding rate margins have changed relative to the repo rate. For instance, the money market interest rate margins based on the three-month Johannesburg Interbank Agreed Rate (JIBAR) and the Negotiable Certificates of Deposit (NCDs) have become marginally positive. The weighted deposit rates have moved up to levels around zero.

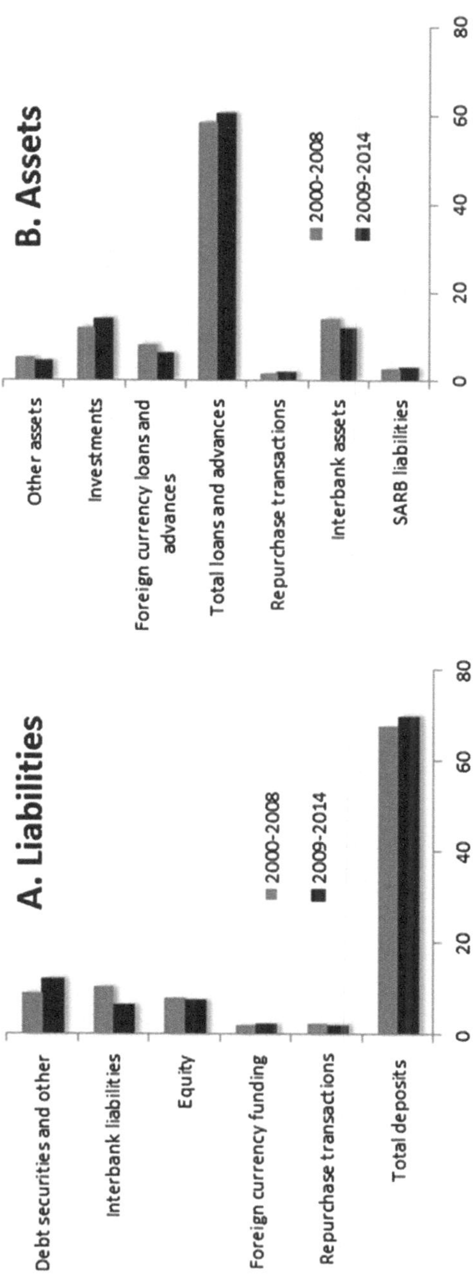

Fig. 16.1 Banks' balance sheet developments before and after 2008 (as a share of total assets and liabilities) (*Source:* SARB and authors' calculations)

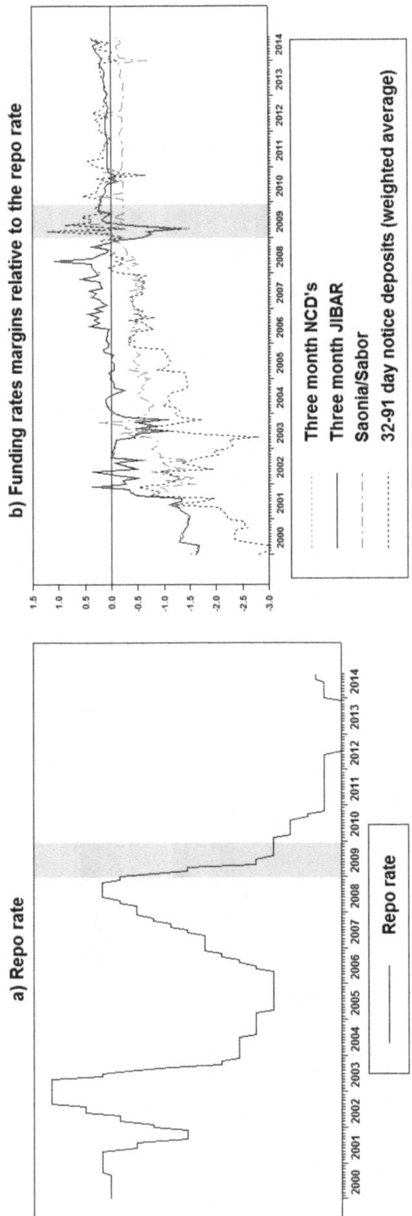

Fig. 16.2 Repo rate and funding rate margins (*Source*: SARB and authors' calculations)

These increases in the funding rate margins happened at a time when the repurchase rate was declining and was at historically low levels.

16.3.3 Did Lending Spreads Widen as Postulated by Theory During Episodes of Low Interest Rates?

In Fig. 16.3 the lending rate margins widened. There have been significant shifts in lending rate margins relative to the repo rate. The lending rate margins have in the past mirrored changes in the repo rate.

It is also evident that there has been a permanent structural level shift in the other loans and advances interest rate margins and that this occurred between February and July 2007 and was closely aligned to increases in the repo rate. However, the increase in the installment sales interest rate margin occurred in November 2008, much later relative to the increase in the repo rate. In fact it seems to coincide with the period of sharp declines in the repo rate. The mortgage rate margins have also increased from 1.69 percent in April 2008 to 2.79 percent during the latest observed point in 2014, which is almost double.

From Fig. 16.3 for the period 2001–2002, when the repurchase rate increased and subsequently declined, lending margins displayed similar movements. This suggests a well-functioning pass-through

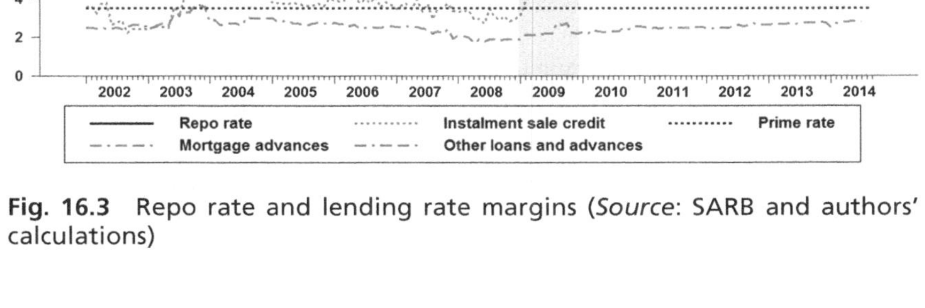

Fig. 16.3 Repo rate and lending rate margins (*Source*: SARB and authors' calculations)

and transmission of the monetary policy rate changes to lending rates. However, post-2007 this has changed and lending rate margins have not declined even though the repo rate declined massively. The next sections show how two core aspects of bank balance sheets, (1) the interest rate earned and (2) interest expense dynamics, have evolved relative to the monetary policy stance.

16.3.4 Liability and Asset Sides of Bank Balance Sheets

The funding and asset components of banks' balance sheets have not changed much and yet funding and lending rate margins display permanent upward shifts of varying magnitudes. What does this mean for banks' interest income and expenses? Fig. 16.4 shows the relationship between the policy rate, interest received and interest paid by banks. How have these evolved and what can they tell us about interest rate margins and credit risk?

Fig. 16.4a, b present the levels of interest income, expense and the net interest income as a percentage of interest earning assets of banks. These variables display trends aligned to changes in the repo rate. It is also clear that post-2009 the gap between interest income and expense has widened and interest income has increased. At the same time, interest expenses have moved sideways at a time when the repo rate declined to historic low levels. As a result, net interest income as a percentage of interest earning assets of banks has increased since 2011 and is currently at levels above those recorded in 2008. This level is comparable to those recorded in 2003 when the economy showed robust growth rates. The gap between interest income and expense, having flattened between 2009 and 2010, has widened and increased steeply since 2011.

In Fig. 16.4d the widening gap at a time when the repo rate was declining suggests the significant role played by lending margins and credit risk post-2009. There is a clear disconnect with the movements in the repo rate. Such developments in profitability may reflect that risk margins on loans have risen to neutralize the adverse effects linked to higher expected losses.

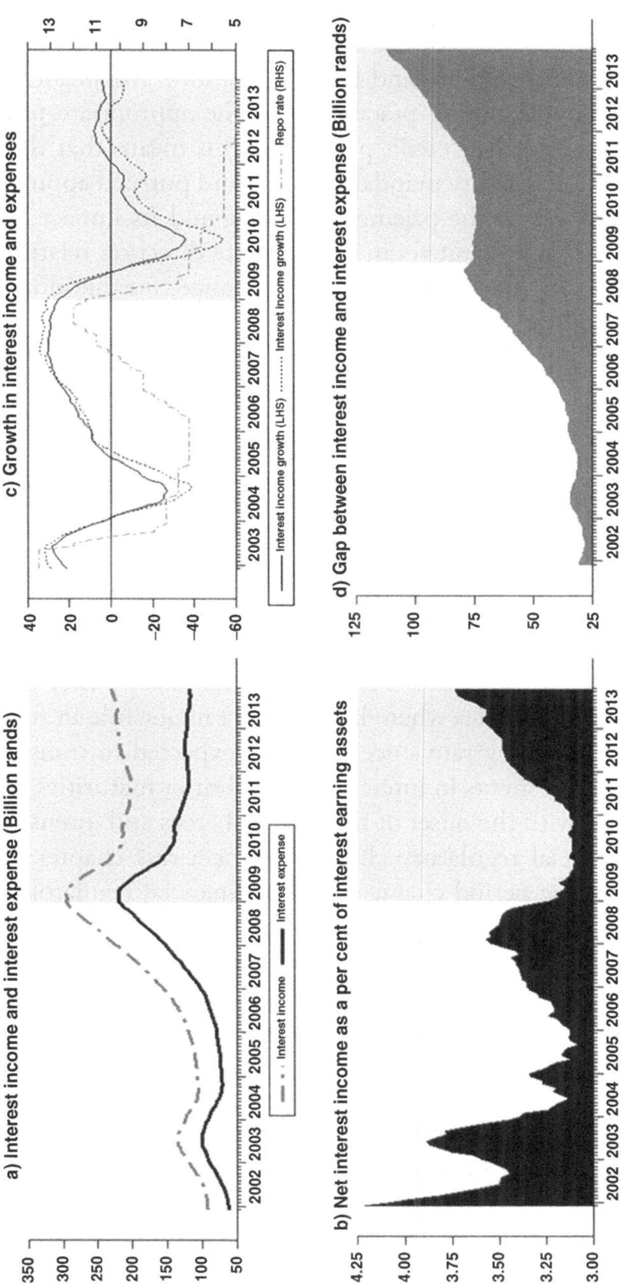

Fig. 16.4 Interest rate income streams of banks and the policy rate (*Source*: South African Reserve Bank and authors' calculations)

These developments convey conflicting messages on Monetary Policy Committee, financial stability and bank regulation. The profitability of banks reflects sound banking practices, and the appropriate pricing of risk is reflective of prudent credit provision. This means that the objectives of the financial stability mandate are met and pursued appropriately. However, the impact of the pricing of lending and its impact on lending rate margins certainly moves in the opposite direction relative to the desirable effects of a loose monetary policy stance. Furthermore, if the pricing of risk and the mark-up proves to be excessive, it ends up defeating the intended purpose and can also put financial stability at risk.

16.4 What Can the Lessons Be About the Funding Rate Reactions to the FRPU Shocks?

It is not surprising to witness a heightened interest in exploring the dynamics of the interest rate pass-through to other short-term rates. The interest rate channel constitutes a key part of monetary policy transmission, especially in countries where banks play a major role in financing. Reductions in the policy rate since 2008 are expected to translate into broadly similar movements in interest rates at shorter maturities. But this period coincided with the onset of the financial crisis and intense discussions about financial regulatory changes. Hence, this chapter explores whether the ensuing period characterized by financial regulatory uncertainties had any meaningful impact on funding rates.

Why funding rates? Because money markets constitute an important part of banks' funding cost, thus affecting lending and deposit rates offered to firms and households, with an ultimate impact on savings and investment decisions and real economic activity. Moreover, an assessment of the dynamics in funding rates can shed some light on the role of the FRPU and the extent of liquidity risk involved in funding long-term assets with short-term liabilities.

Given the limited changes in the funding side of the banks' balance sheets and the evolution of funding rates and their margins to the repo

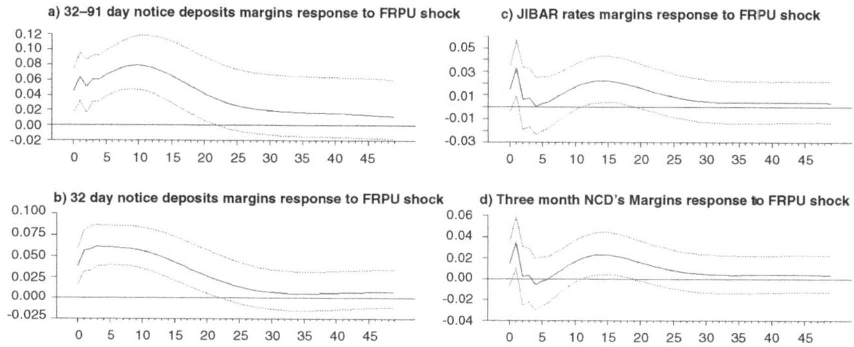

Fig. 16.5 The responses of funding rate margins to the FRPU shock (*Note*: These are responses to a one standard deviation increase in the FRPU. *Source*: Authors' calculations)

rate, we limit the empirical analysis of funding rates to their responses to an unexpected FRPU shock only. The results of the responses of three categories of funding rate margins to the FRPU shock are shown in Fig. 16.5.

Fig. 16.5a, d show the response of the different measures of funding rate margins to the FRPU shock. The 31–91-day notice deposit margin rises significantly on initial impact by nearly four basis points and reaches a peak of eight basis points in eight months, with the impact lasting 21 months. Both the JIBAR and the three-month NCDs margins display a similar trajectory and rise significantly only between 11 and 18 months, with a peak of nearly two basis points in 15 months.

16.5 Stylized Effects of Interest Rate Margins, the FRPU and Key Macroeconomic Variables

The empirical section begins by examining the basic relationships between the FRPU and various macroeconomic variables for both SA and the USA using monthly (M) data from 2000M1 to 2012M10 based on the regulatory uncertainty index we received from Nodari (2014).[2] The

[2] See Nodari (2014).

financial regulatory policy uncertainty in South Africa is approximated by using the index constructed in Nodari (2014). It is an appropriate benchmark because financial regulation measures tend to be coordinated across the globe and there are spill-overs of such regulatory changes. For this reason data ends in 2012M10.

In this section, we apply simple scatter plots and cross correlations between the FRPU and selected macroeconomic variables. The use of cross correlations enables us to assess what happens to other variables of interest when the FRPU rises before them. The main purpose of using these techniques is to identify the effects on bilateral relationships. However, the reader should be cognizant that the purpose is not to test for the presence of asymmetric effects or nonlinear threshold effects. It is possible that the effects may vary and differ after some particular level.

The bilateral relationships are shown in Fig. 16.6a–d. There is a negative relationship between the FRPU and SA manufacturing production growth in Fig. 16.6a, house price growth in Fig. 16.6b, credit growth in Fig. 16.6c and US industrial growth in Fig. 16.6d. The interpretation of the relationships based on this simple preliminary statistical analysis is that elevated levels of regulatory uncertainty have adverse effects on SA and US economic growth, and SA house prices and credit extension.

Fig. 16.7 shows further bilateral relationships and tests for the nature of the relationship between the FRPU and lending rate margins.

There is a negative relationship between the FRPU and retail sales growth in Fig. 16.7a. However, the relationship is positive between the FRPU and the interest rate margins (see installment sale rate margin in Fig. 16.7b and other loans and advances rate margins in Fig. 16.7c. In addition, there is a negative relationship between the FRPU and the US federal funds rate in Fig. 16.7d. The established positive relationship between the FRPU and the lending rates margins suggests that elevated regulatory uncertainty tends to be associated with an increase in these margins. The results of the scatter plots for the FRPU and selected macroeconomic variables are shown in Fig. 16.7. The results of the preliminary and bilateral relationships further confirm the direct impact of the FRPU on various macroeconomic variables.

The analysis concludes by looking at the cross correlations when FRPU rises before (that is, leads) selected macroeconomic variables. This is assessed via investigating: What happens to various macroeconomic

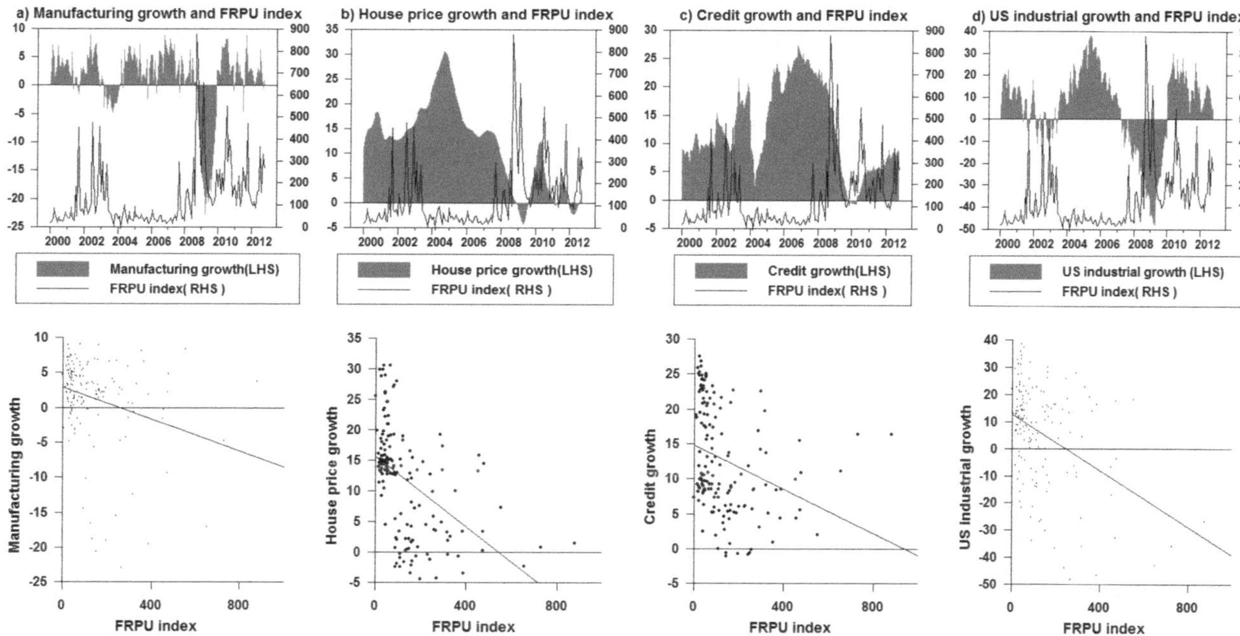

Fig. 16.6 Bilateral relationships between FRPU and selected macroeconomic variables (*Note*: The *light shaded portion* denotes the recession in 2009. The FRPU is calculated as monthly number of articles containing jointly references to financial regulation policies, uncertainty and the economy (Nodari 2014). Baker et al. (2013) divide the raw counts in each newspaper by total number of articles in same newspaper for same month and thereafter normalize each index to have a unit standard deviation. *Source*: Authors' calculations)

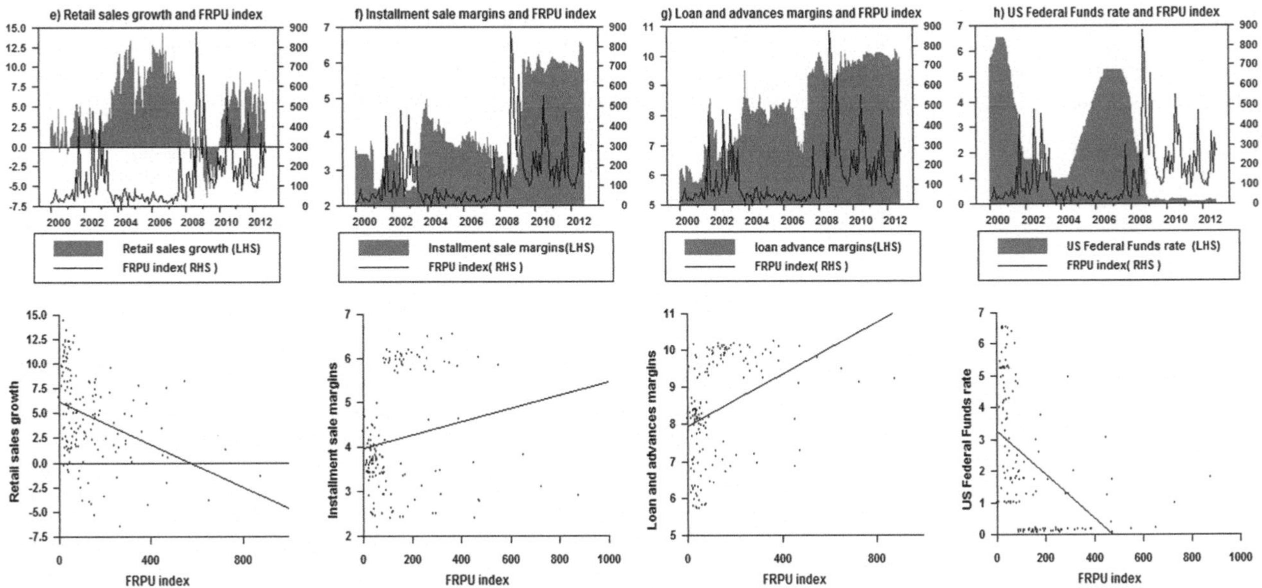

Fig. 16.7 Bilateral relationships between the FRPU and selected macroeconomic variables (*Note*: The *light shaded portion* denotes the recession in 2009. This FRPU is calculated as monthly number of articles containing jointly references to financial regulation policies, uncertainty and the economy (Nodari 2014). Baker et al. (2013) divide the raw counts in each newspaper by total number of articles in same newspaper for same month and thereafter normalize each index to have a unit standard deviation. *Source*: Authors' calculations)

variables when elevated FRPU rises before them? In this regard, a cross-correlation approach is used to examine what happens to the relationship, initially on impact and then at peak. The results from the cross-correlation approach shown in Fig. 16.8 reveal a positive relationship when FRPU leads lending margins in Fig. 16.8f, g, and the correlation is higher on impact with regard to other loans and advances lending rate margins. Its cross-correlation peak occurs in a year for the installment sale lending rate margins. The correlations are negative throughout the horizons in Fig. 16.8b–d, h, when the FRPU leads house price growth, credit growth, the US federal funds rate and the repo rate, respectively.

The peak negative correlation (i) between the FRPU and credit in Fig. 16.8c occurs after a year (ii) and it is within six months between the FRPU and US federal funds rate in Fig. 16.8d. This is comparable to the effects observed between the FRPU and house prices in Fig. 16.8b. The manufacturing growth and retail sales growth are negatively correlated with the FRPU and the peak effects occur at around six months as shown in Fig. 16.8a, e. Based on these results, evidence indicates there is convergence in the findings from scatter plots and cross-correlation approaches.

Both the scatter plots and cross-correlation analysis suggests that, to a large extent, the FRPU is negatively associated with selected macroeconomic variables. However, the FRPU is positively associated with both measures of the lending rate margins, namely the installment sale and loan and advances interest rate margins. The results highlight (1) the sign of the cross correlation on impact, (2) peak correlation values and (3) the month in which the peak response of other macroeconomic variables to the FRPU shock when it leads other macroeconomic variables occurs. The results are presented in Table 16.1.

16.6 What Can the Policymaker Learn About the Effects of FRPU on the South African Economy?

Similar to other measures of uncertainty, financial regulatory uncertainty is a latent variable—in other words a variable that cannot be directly observed but is rather deduced from others (Bloom et al. 2014). This

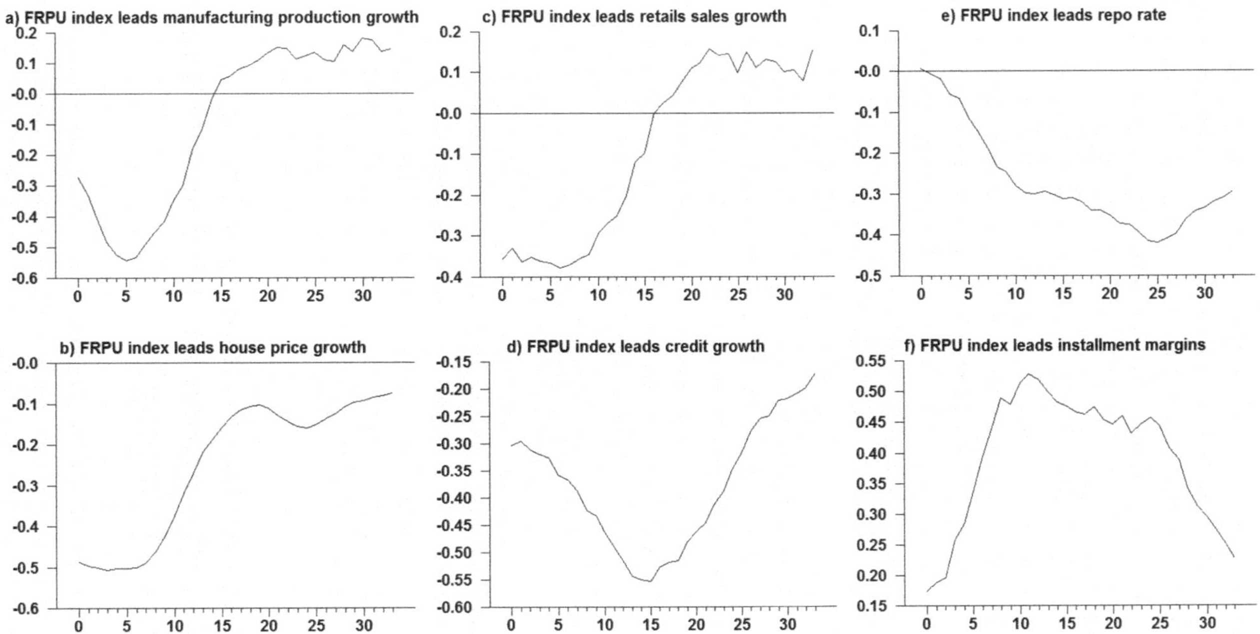

Fig. 16.8 Cross correlations when the FRPU leads other variables (*Note*: The horizontal axis in each graph shows the months and the vertical axis shows the values of the cross correlations. *Source*: Authors' calculations)

Table 16.1 Cross correlations between the FRPU and various macroeconomic variables

	Sign of correlation value on impact	Peak correlation values	Months FRPU leads indicated variable
Manufacturing production growth	Negative	−0.54	5
House price growth	Negative	−0.51	3
Credit growth	Negative	−0.55	15
Retail sales growth	Negative	−0.38	3
OLA margins	Positive	0.37	0
Installment sale margins	Positive	0.53	11
Repo rate	Negative	−0.42	25
US Federal Funds rate	Negative	−0.50	3

NB: OLA means other loans and advances lending margins
Source: Authors' calculations

chapter applies a modified vector autoregression (VAR) framework proposed by Nodari (2014) to quantify the extent of FRPU shocks on macroeconomic effects to enable us to derive policy implications that will be informative and of value to policymakers.

This section relies on a model that includes the FRPU, US growth and the federal funds rate; as well as SA economic growth, repo rate, growth in house prices, retail sales, total loans and advances and lending rate margins.[3] Prior to proceeding with the discussion on the results, we highlight the economic assumptions we make in the model. The FRPU is placed first, suggesting that it is determined outside the model, possibly by external factors. External conditions in the model include variables that capture the evolution of the US economy and the policy reaction by the US Federal Reserve Bank matter. These variables are (1) determined outside the model and (2) cannot be influenced by SA variables. This is consistent with the limited effect possible for a small open economy to impact a large economy.

[3] A VAR with two lags chosen by the Akaike Information Criterion AIC is used. The results were robust to using a model without two US variables, the result also remain unchanged even when using small number of variables such as five and six variables.

Second, to what extent does our model capture the direction and significance of the FRPU on US economic growth and the US policy rate?[4] This is a necessary condition, alternatively a pre-requirement that our model should pass. Finding similarities in the responses of US economic growth and the federal funds rate, as found in Nodari (2014), enables us to proceed and assess the effects of the FRPU on SA variables. The economic impact of an unexpected one-standard deviation increase in the FRPU is presented in Fig. 16.9.

The preliminary analysis starts by assessing the extent to which our model captures the direction of the responses of US economic growth and the federal funds rate. Fig. 16.9a, b confirm that both US industrial production growth and the federal funds rate decline significantly. The specification does capture the adverse effects of the FRPU on US variables and this permits us to proceed with the analysis. However, the ability to go back to the initial levels suggests that FRPU has temporary effects on economic growth and policy rate response. What do these results tell us about the stance of US monetary policy? The 0.1 percentage points decline in US federal funds rate at its peak in the fifth month is an indication of easing of US monetary policy to impede the adverse FRPU effects (Nodari 2014).

What can policymakers learn about the impact of an unexpected rise in the FRPU on various SA macroeconomic variables? The results are presented in Fig. 16.9d, c, e, f, g. The repo rate and the real economic activity variables decline significantly. What about the reactions of the lending rate margins? These rise, although at different horizons. The increase in margins indicates the presence of financial frictions in the credit markets. For instance, the installment sales margins in Fig. 16.9h rise by as much as 11 basis points at its peak response in the 11th month. In contrast, the other loans and advances interest rate margin in Fig. 16.9i rises significantly on impact for two months. Table 16.2 summarizes the information on the impulse responses shown in Fig. 16.9 by reporting the signs of impact, the peak response and the duration of the responses of these variables to an unexpected increase in the FRPU.

[4] See Nodari (2014).

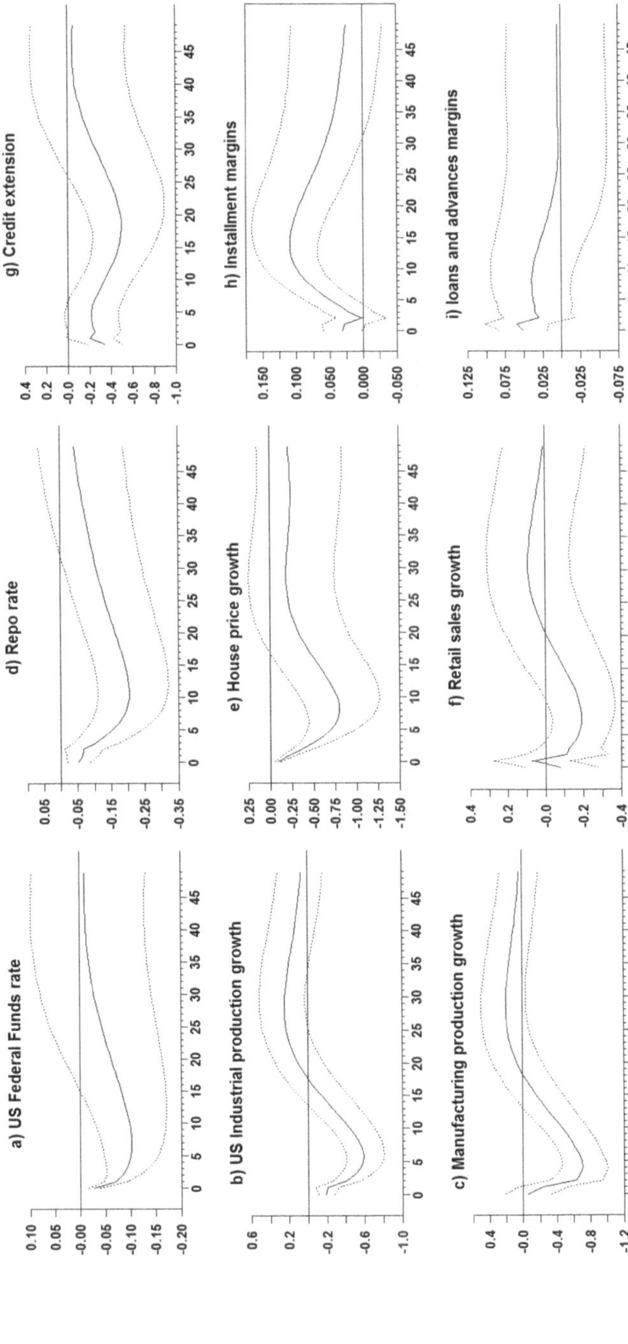

Fig. 16.9 Responses to an unexpected FRPU shocks (*Source*: Authors' calculations)

Table 16.2 Response of variables to FRPU shocks

Variable	Sign of responding variable on impact	Peak value in percentage points	Peak period (months)	Duration of effects
US variables				
Federal Funds rate	Negative	−0.101	7	14
Industrial production growth	Negative	−0.584	6	13
SA variables				
Manufacturing production growth	Negative	−0.709	4	12
Repo rate	Negative	−0.205	11	32
House price growth	Negative	−0.798	8	16
Retail sales growth	Negative	−0.186	8	10
Credit extension	Negative	−0.501	18	25
SA interest rate margins				
Installment sale credit	Positive	0.110	14	4
Other loans and advances	Positive	0.059	1	2

Source: Authors' calculations

The results show that growth in manufacturing production and house price growth slow down for nearly 12 and 16 months, respectively. In addition, at their peak, effects growth in manufacturing production declines by nearly 0.7 percentage points in the fourth quarter and house price growth falls by nearly 0.8 percentage points in the eight month. In addition, retail sales growth slows down significantly for nearly 10 months, whereas credit extension to the private sector remains depressed for 25 months.

How sensitive are SA economic growth and monetary policy responses to FRPU shock compared to their US counterparts? While the direction of the reaction is similar for economic growth and policy reaction, there are, however, visible differences in the peak magnitudes and durations within which the peak occurs. Based on the peak response evidence, we conclude that both SA economic growth and monetary policy are marginally more responsive to the FRPU relative to US responses. This may be due to structural differences in the economies and the allowing of SA real economic variables to react to other US variables.

To what extent does the FRPU impact the interest rate margins? Fig. 16.10 shows a comparison of the responses of both lending interest rate margins, namely, installment sale and the other loans and advances margins to the FRPU shocks. The results show that, apart from the initial reactions, the installment sales interest rate margins are highly responsive to the FRPU shocks as opposed to loans and advances.

16.6.1 Do the Macroeconomic Effects of an Unexpected Increase in the FRPU Vary from Those of an Unexpected Rise in the Repo and Installment Sales Interest Rate Margins Shocks?

The efficacy of the transmission mechanism of the policy rate changes is inferred through comparing the effects of an unexpected one-standard deviation increase in the FRPU, the repo and the installment sales interest rate margins shocks. That is, are the effects of high lending rate margins similar to those of monetary policy tightening? If so, does it mean that high lending rate margins worked against the expected effects of an expansionary policy stance? The installment sale credit margin is considered only in this section because it is highly responsive to FRPU and

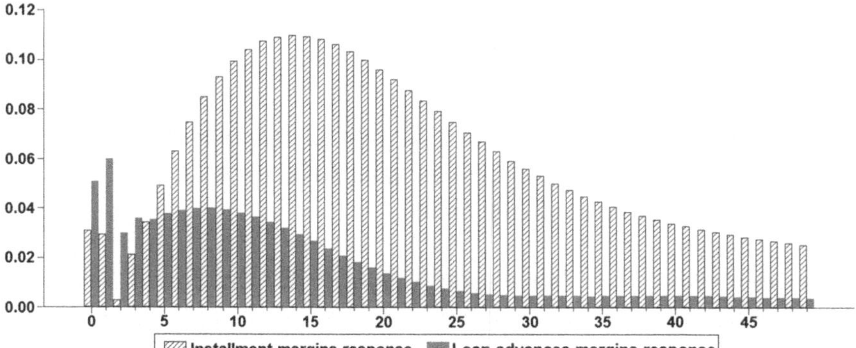

Fig. 16.10 Comparing the response of interest rate margins to one standard deviation FRPU shock (*Source*: Authors' calculations)

remains significant over longer periods than the other loans and advances rate margins. However, comparison of the responses of selected macroeconomic variables is done in later sections. We assess the impact of these shocks on manufacturing production, retail sales, credit extension and house prices.

The results presented in Fig. 16.11 show that there is no ambiguous or unclear initial impact of the FRPU, the repo rate and the installment sales credit interest rate margins shocks on house price growth in Fig. 16.11b.

However, it is also evident that their peak effects vary in both magnitudes and peak period. The FRPU depresses both house price growth by −0.8 percentage points and credit extension by −0.5 percentage points, which is more than the depressing effects of the repo rate and the installment sale margins shocks. It is possible that this is due to the fact that in anticipation of the implementation of tougher minimum regulatory capital requirements and additional capital buffers, the strategies of banks change with regards to balance sheets positioning and capital planning decisions.

The impulse responses of growth in manufacturing production (used here as a proxy for economic activity) and retail sales growth (used here as proxy for consumption expenditure) do decline. However, they decline more in response to the repo rate than the FRPU and the installment margins shocks. Amongst these three shocks, the FRPU exerted the least depressing impact on retail sales growth, whereas the FRPU depresses manufacturing production growth more than the repo rate and the installment sales interest rate margins shocks.

16.6.2 Does It Matter if the Shock Originates from the Other Loans and Advances or Installments Sale Side?

It has been shown in earlier sections that both the installment sales and the other loans and advances interest rate margins increased in different months. Additionally, the structural permanent level shift in the other loans and advances interest rate margins occurred between February and July 2007. In contrast, the level shift in installment margins occurred

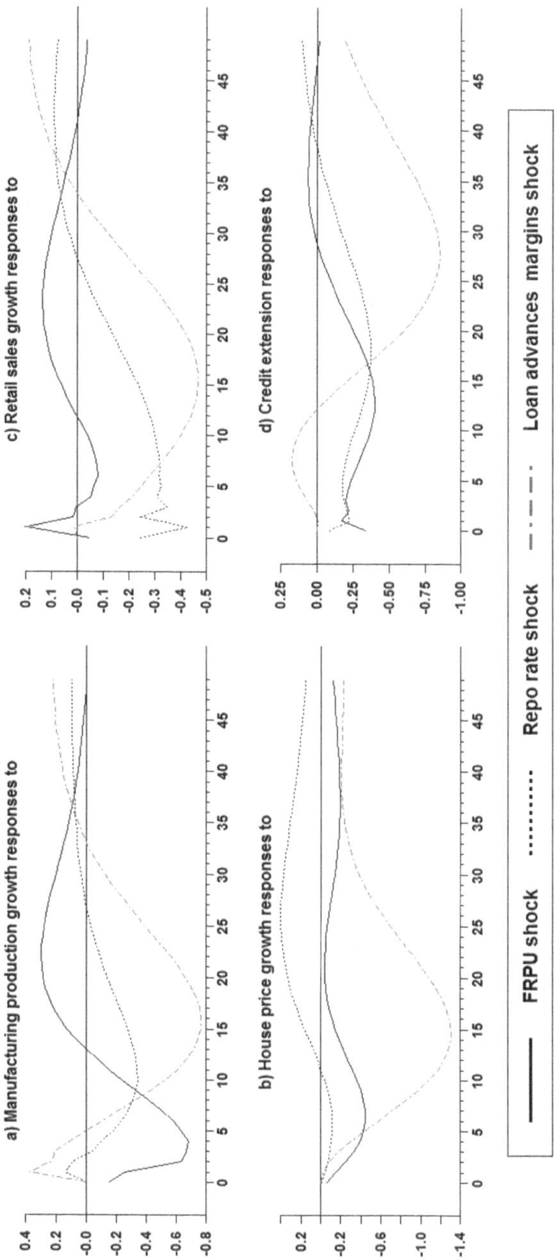

Fig. 16.11 Responses to FRPU, repo rate and installment margins shocks (*Source:* Authors' calculations)

between November 2008 and May 2009. The magnitude of changes is bigger in the installment sale credit margins as shown in Fig. 16.12.

Can the magnitude of the changes in interest rate margins indicate the potency of the specific lending rate margins shocks? Fig. 16.13 compares the macroeconomic variables' responses to an unexpected rise in both lending rate margins shocks. Although both shocks depressed these variables over long periods, the installment sales margins shock resulted in much depressed effects on the macro-variables relative to the other loans and advances interest rate margins shock. This suggests that shocks to lending interest rate margins tend to move in the same direction or tend to reinforce each other, such that if these shocks occur simultaneously or concurrently they can lead to significantly adverse effects on the economy.

In addition, when we focus on the magnitudes of the peak declines, we find that the contraction is larger in house price growth in Fig. 16.13a, followed by manufacturing production in Fig. 16.13c, then followed by credit extension in Fig. 16.13b and retail sales growth in Fig. 16.13d. What role can monetary policy play to dissipate the negative effects of these lending spreads, if any? In an attempt to answer this question, we present the scatter plots in Fig. 16.14 to show the relationship between the repo rate and the lending rate margins.

The scatter plots in Fig. 16.14c, d show a negative relationship between the repo rate and lending rate margins, which suggests that when the

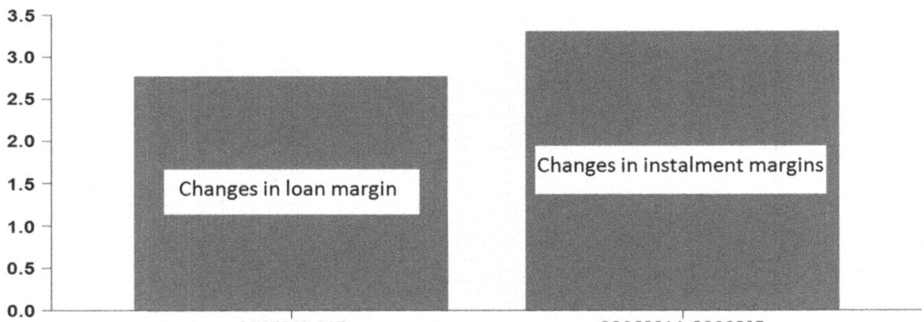

Fig. 16.12 Increase in margins during identified structural breaks (*Source*: South African Reserve Bank and authors' calculations)

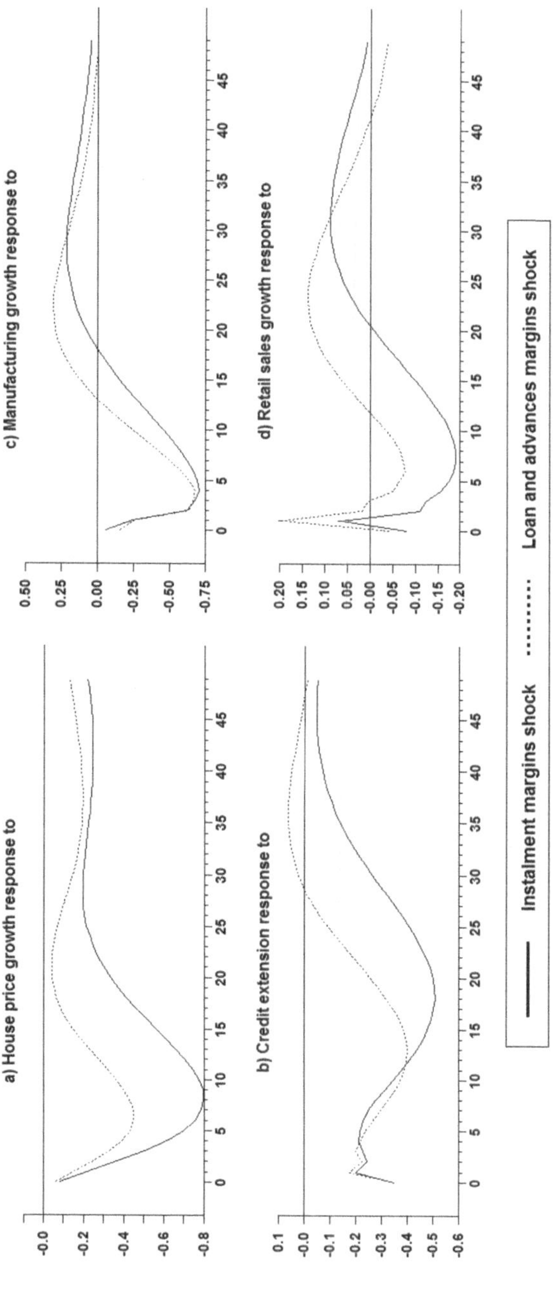

Fig. 16.13 Comparisons of responses of selected variables to unexpected increase in installment sale and other loans and advances margins shocks (*Source*: Authors' calculations)

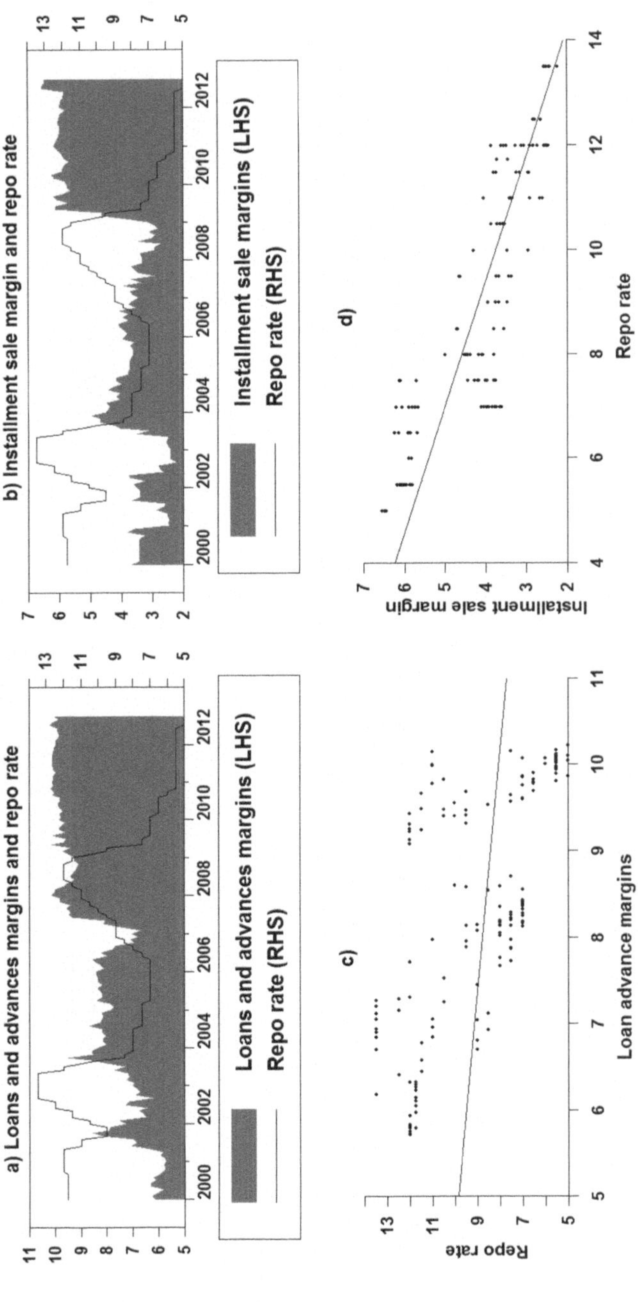

Fig. 16.14 The relationship between lending spreads and repo rate (*Source*: Authors' calculations)

policy rate tightens the spreads should fall. If lending spreads capture risk taking by banks, this means raising rates reduces risk taking and this may lessen the burden on the use of macro-prudential tools. Nonetheless, it has been empirically established that monetary policy is not neutral from a financial stability perspective; it is not exactly the right tool for the task of ensuring financial stability. However, it possesses an important advantage relative to financial supervision and regulation, in that "it gets in all of the cracks."[5]

16.6.3 To What Extent Is It Possible to Attribute the Evolution of Both Margins to Own and FRPU Contributions?

Can the variables used in this model explain what led to sharp increases in margins, albeit in different years? The ability to know which variables played a role in increasing or widening the margins will enable us to infer proper policy implications and recommendations pertaining to the regulatory and supervisory institutions dealing with the inherent inefficiencies or uncompetitive practices in financial institutions.

Is it possible that such an unexpected rise in margins perhaps compromised the monetary policy transmission mechanism process? Yes; Chami and Cosimano (2010) articulate that binding capital constraints can frustrate the goals of a more accommodating monetary policy. This arises as capital-constrained banks decide to reduce deposit rates and increase loan margins in order to enhance their profitability instead of increasing lending quantities.

The rise in the other loans and advances interest rate margins around 2007M2 preceded the rise in installment sales interest rate margins around 2009M1. What can explain the spike in these lending rates margins? This is a pertinent policy question requiring anecdotal explanations to be supplemented by empirical estimations and quantification. Regarding the anecdotal approach, Walentin (2014) noted that interest rate margins are susceptible to changes in prepayment risk premiums,

[5] See Stein (2014) and Altunbas et al. (2014).

changes in both risk aversion and the ability of the financial system to bear risk, regulatory reforms and changes in financial practices such as the degree of financial innovation.

Rather than focusing on all these factors, here we examine only two factors in detail, namely: (1) financial regulatory policy uncertainty and (2) own changes in lending spreads, which may be due to changes in risk aversion or risk bearing, risk repricing, changes that arise from within banking products themselves and other bank or credit market-specific factors. The own factors are captured by how much own movements in lending rate margins contribute to the evolution of spreads based on the historical decompositions approach.

Fig. 16.15a, b compare the actual to the counterfactual lending rate margins. The counterfactual refers to the lending rate margins that would occur after removing the FRPU contributions. The results show that the actual margins exceed the counterfactual margin in Fig. 16.15a. This suggests that the FRPU contributed to a higher level of the interest rate margins for the installments sales credit interest rate margins; otherwise these margins would have been lower.

Fig. 16.15b shows that the gap between the actual and the counterfactual other loans and advances rate margins is very small, suggesting that the FRPU played a fairly insignificant role in influencing these lending margins. Fig. 16.15c, d examines the role of own movements in these lending rate margins and their evolution. The results presented in (d) indicate a persistent wider gap, showing that an increase in the other loans and advances rate margins was due to own movements. This possibly suggests the effects of the repricing of risk and products consistent with the realignment of banks' internal strategies as postulated by Walentin (2014).

How do these contributions compare to the overall contributions of the remaining variables in the model? The comparisons of the FRPU contributions to the combined contributions from other variables in the model are shown in Fig. 16.16a. The results show evidence that post-2009 the FRPU contributions exceeded the installments sales rate margins' own contributions. This suggests that own movements in installment sale credit margins played a much smaller role than FRPU and other macroeconomic factors.

In contrast, Fig. 16.16b reveals that the other loans and advances interest rate margins' contributions played a bigger role in their own evolution

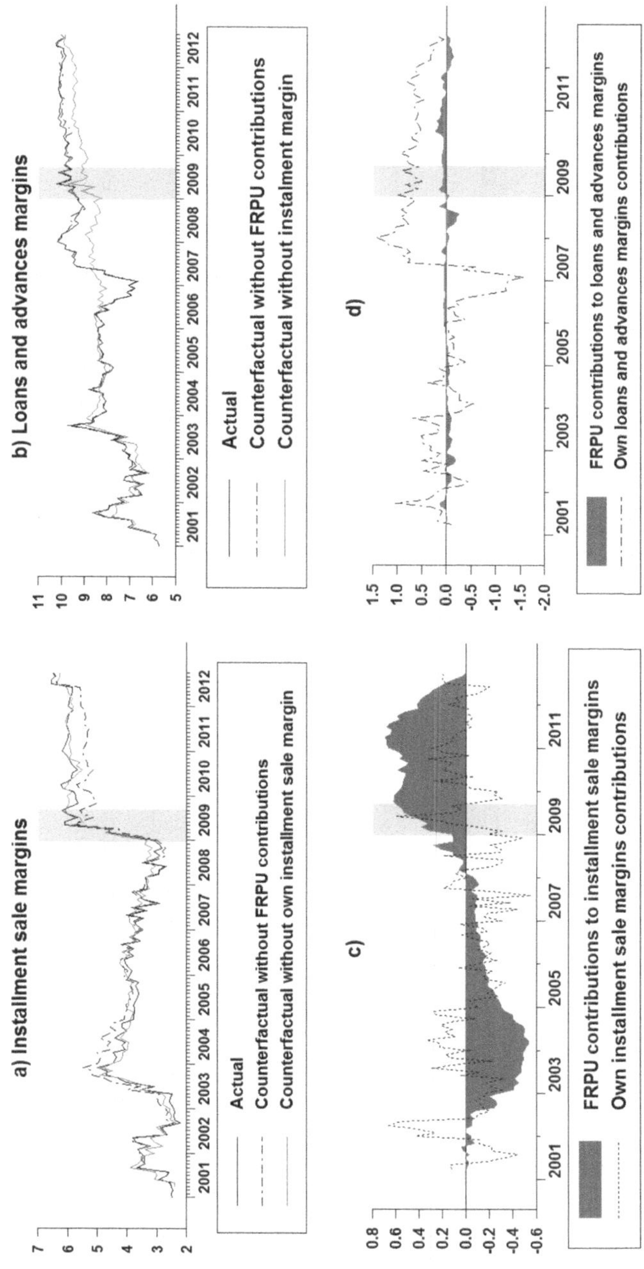

Fig. 16.15 The roles of the FRPU and own margins in the evolution of spreads (*Note*: The *light shaded parts* denote the recession in 2009. *Source*: Authors' calculations)

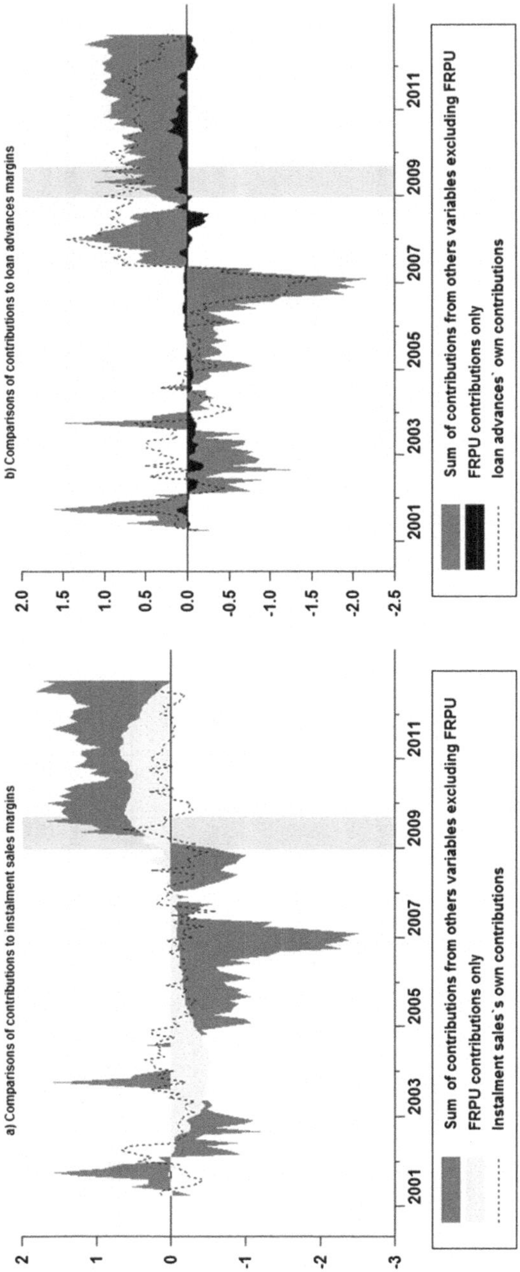

Fig. 16.16 Comparing total contributions without the FRPU, own and FRPU contributions on the evolution of rate margins (*Note*: The *light shaded portion* denotes the recession in 2009. *Source*: Authors' calculations)

post-2007, relative to the contributions of the other factors. These own other loans and advances contributions are almost equal to the combined contributions from all the other variables. Therefore, if changes in the other loans and advance spreads are driven by the banks' internal pricing strategies, it may be that these factors played a bigger role in the structural level shift of the lending rate margins. There is very limited evidence that the FRPU played a bigger role.

16.6.4 To What Extent Did the Margins Impact the Evolution of Credit Extension?

How does the FRPU impact interest rate margins and subsequently the supply of credit? To investigate this matter we rely on Bassett and Covas' (2013) arguments stating that capital adequacy will impact the banks' ability and willingness to extend credit. This arises due to the risk of introducing tougher capital and liquidity requirements over the short term. Hastiness in implementation can cause financial institutions to maintain and even enforce new restraining credit practices for longer periods than they otherwise would, thus impeding expansionary monetary policy actions and economic activity recovery.

As suggested in empirical studies, such as Bassett et al. (2014), increases in interest rate margins and fluctuations to credit supply and demand are perhaps due to the fundamental reassessment of the inherent riskiness of bank lending lines, changes in the industry's business strategies and more so changes in the structure or the intensity of bank supervision and regulation.

This section assesses the combined roles of the FRPU and the lending rate margins based on the counterfactual approach to assess what would have happened to credit growth in the absence of (1) the lending rate margins, (2) the FRPU contributions and (3) their combined influence. Fig. 16.17 displays what happened to these contributions prior to and after 2009. We find that the lending rate margins' movements vary according to the type of margin used in the estimation. To expand on this, the analysis shows the contributions from each lending rate margin as well as the sum of both the FRPU and the lending rate margin used.

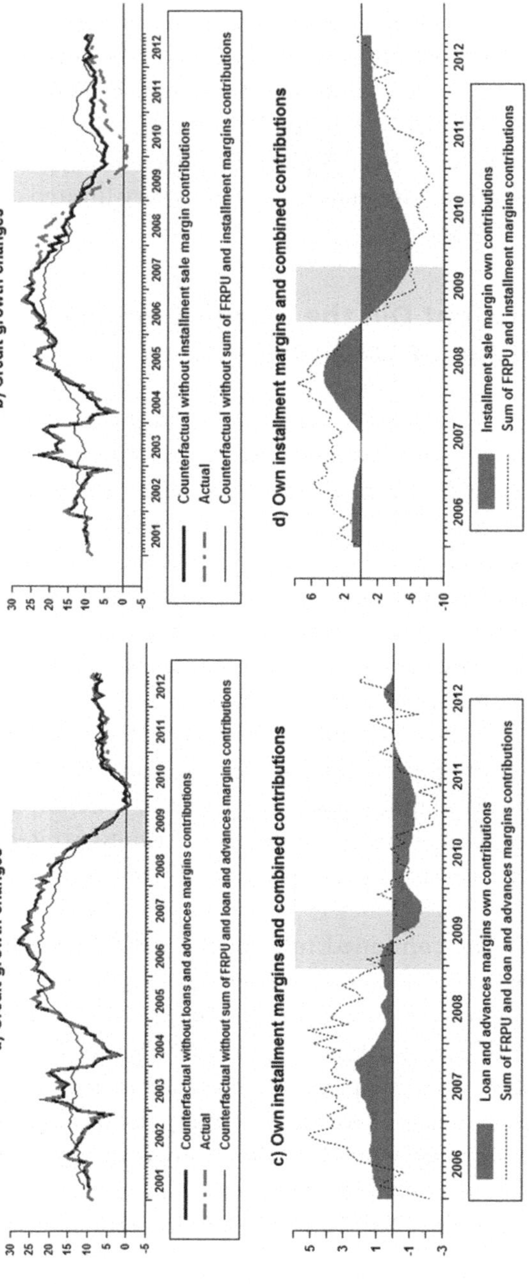

Fig. 16.17 The role of lending margins and the FRPU on credit growth (*Note*: The *light shaded portion* denotes the recession in 2009. *Source*: Authors' calculations)

The decline in credit growth in Fig. 16.17 is much pronounced when controlling for the role of the installment sale interest rate margins, as credit fell by as much as 5 percentage points in late 2009 and early 2010. This suggests that financial frictions during the period of heightened uncertainty and volatile economic conditions depressed credit supply and demand. A similar conclusion is arrived at based on the combined contributions of the FRPU and the installment sales interest rate margins in Fig. 16.17d. The net effect on credit growth in Fig. 16.17c suggests that the sluggish growth in credit extension between 2009 and 2012 can be attributed to the unexpected rise in the installment sale margins and the FRPU. Their combined effects tended to drag down growth in credit extension by more than 6 percentage points between 2009 and early 2011. So, there is a role played by the interest rate margins in the demand and supply for credit.

Fig. 16.17a, b shows the comparison of the FRPU and the other loans and advances interest rate margins' contributions on credit growth. The FRPU and lending rate margins variables' contributions reinforce each other. This supports the earlier findings which showed that both the FRPU and the margins reinforce each other's effects on credit as they both depress growth in credit extension. However, credit growth is severely depressed when assessing the combined effects of the FRPU and the installment sales credit interest rate margins.

High margins may be undesirable and inefficient for the conduct of monetary policy when policy settings are loosened, hence the following question is posited: How were the repo rate contributions related to credit growth since the recession in 2009, when it reached its historic lowest levels in 30 years? The counterfactual in Fig. 16.18a lies above the actual credit line, suggesting that the prevailing conditions in 2009 impeded the stimulatory effects of the repo rate changes on credit growth. The green line in (a) lies above the red line suggesting that credit extension fell significantly due to the combined contribution from the repo, the FRPU and installment sale credit margins shocks.

How do the repo rate contributions compare to those from the FRPU and the installment margin rate contributions to credit? Fig. 16.18b shows: (1) the repo rate level, to capture the monetary policy stance; and (2) the contributions of the FRPU, repo rate and installment margins to credit growth. It is evident in Fig. 16.18b that both the repo rate and

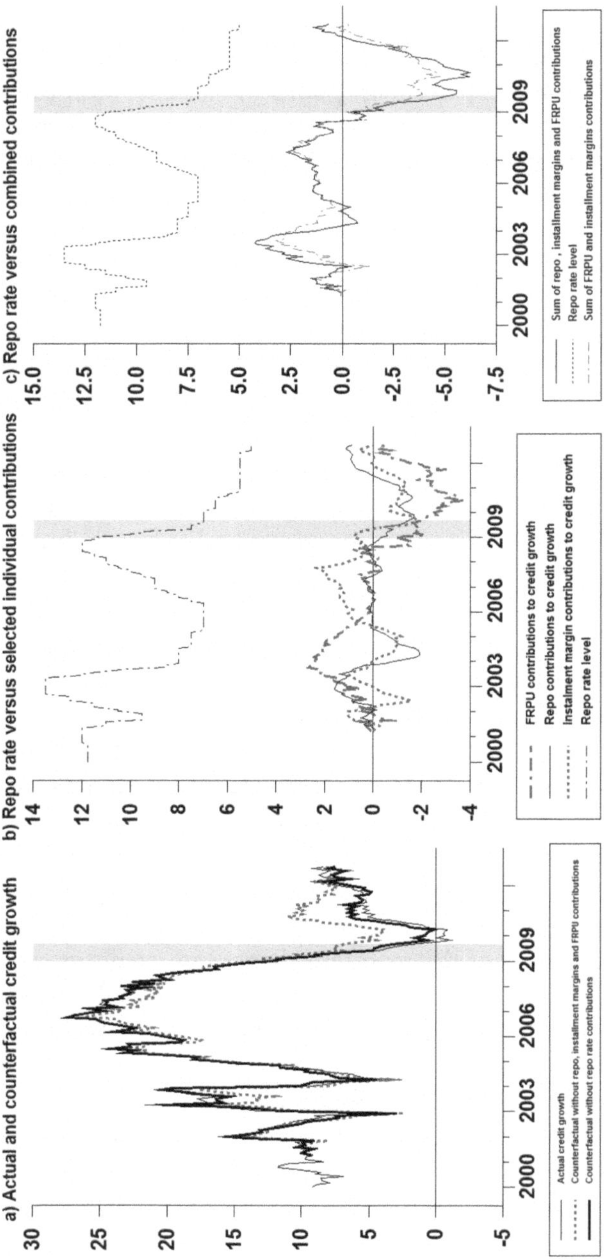

Fig. 16.18 The role of repo rate, FRPU and installment sale credit contributions on credit growth (*Note*: The *light shaded portion* denotes the recession in 2009. *Source*: Authors' calculations)

the FRPU started contributing negatively to credit extension prior 2009, and these adverse effects were accentuated after the recession, coinciding with a period of global economic uncertainty. The repo rate continued to drag down credit extension until mid-2011. Since 2009, the FRPU contributions were still dragging down credit extension. Moreover, even installment rate margins contributed to a slowdown of credit extension.

Collectively, as shown in Fig. 16.18c the three combined contributions dragged down growth in credit extension by more than 6 percentage points around 2010. This happened despite the repo rate being lowered to historically low levels.

What can explain why the repo, instead of stimulating credit extension, contributed to its slowdown between 2009 and the early part of 2011? Over and above the lagged effects, Chami and Cosimano (2010) offer a possible explanation which arises when capital regulations introduce asymmetries, thereby impacting on monetary policy influences on the supply and cost of loans. Capital binding constraints hamper the desired impact of monetary policy easing, such that the resulting reduction in the marginal cost of loans fails to generate the desired increase in the quantity of loans or a fall-off in loan rates. Thus, easing only achieves reduced loan rates (in particular for existing loans) without the desired impact on the quantity, as banks increase loan spreads in order to boost their profitability rather than expand lending. Can this irregularity occur during the monetary policy tightening cycle? According to Chami and Cosimano (2010) this is unlikely, as the increase in the marginal cost of lending following a tightening of monetary policy generates the desired quantity and price effects.

16.6.5 Growth in House Prices and Retail Sales and Regulatory Uncertainty Shocks

To what extent is the evolution of growth in house prices and retail sales influenced by the spill-overs of regulatory uncertainty and directly by the repo rate and installment sale credit margins shocks? The FRPU has real effects which resemble those of a demand shock; hence, this section compares its contributions to those of the repo rate and installment sale rate margins on growth on house prices and retail sales. This requires identifying both growth in house prices and retail sales channels as drivers of growth in credit. Any adverse disturbances to these factors may also lead to undesirable credit growth fluctuations. So, can sluggish growth in house prices and retail sales be attributed to the FRPU, lending rate margins and the monetary policy stance? How can this capture the extent to which growth in these variables was impacted by these shocks?

The historical contributions are used to visualize the influence of these shocks on growth in house prices and retail sales, respectively. This is shown in Fig. 16.19. To get magnitudes of the extent to which monetary policy played a role, we add the repo rate contributions in Fig. 16.19a, c. The FRPU shown in Fig. 16.19a contributed significantly to sluggish growth in house prices for prolonged periods. The effects of the FRPU are much more significant than both the repo rate and the lending rate margins. Between 2010 and early 2011 both the lending rate margins and the repo rate seem to have transitorily uplifted the growth in house prices.

Were the repo rate contributions dominating or neutralized by the FRPU and the installment sale credit lending rate margins? Fig. 16.19b, d Show the combined effects of the FRPU, the installment sales credit lending rate margins and the repo rate. Post-2009, despite the repo contributions being positive, in Fig. 16.19b, the FRPU neutralized the repo rate contributions, thereby pulling down growth in house prices. In contrast, in Fig. 16.19c since 2010 the repo rate dominated both the FRPU and installment sale credit margins to support the recovery in retail sales growth relative to what it did during the recession period. It is also evident in Fig. 16.19c that all shocks contributed to retarding retail sales growth during the crisis in 2009 but the retail sales recovery since 2010 is mainly due to the stimulatory monetary policy stance.

16.6.6 How Does Credit Risk React to the FRPU, House Prices and Installment Sale Credit Rate Margins Shocks?

As stated earlier, the way banks set lending rates can be unrelated to the monetary policy settings, and some drivers include (1) the risk premia

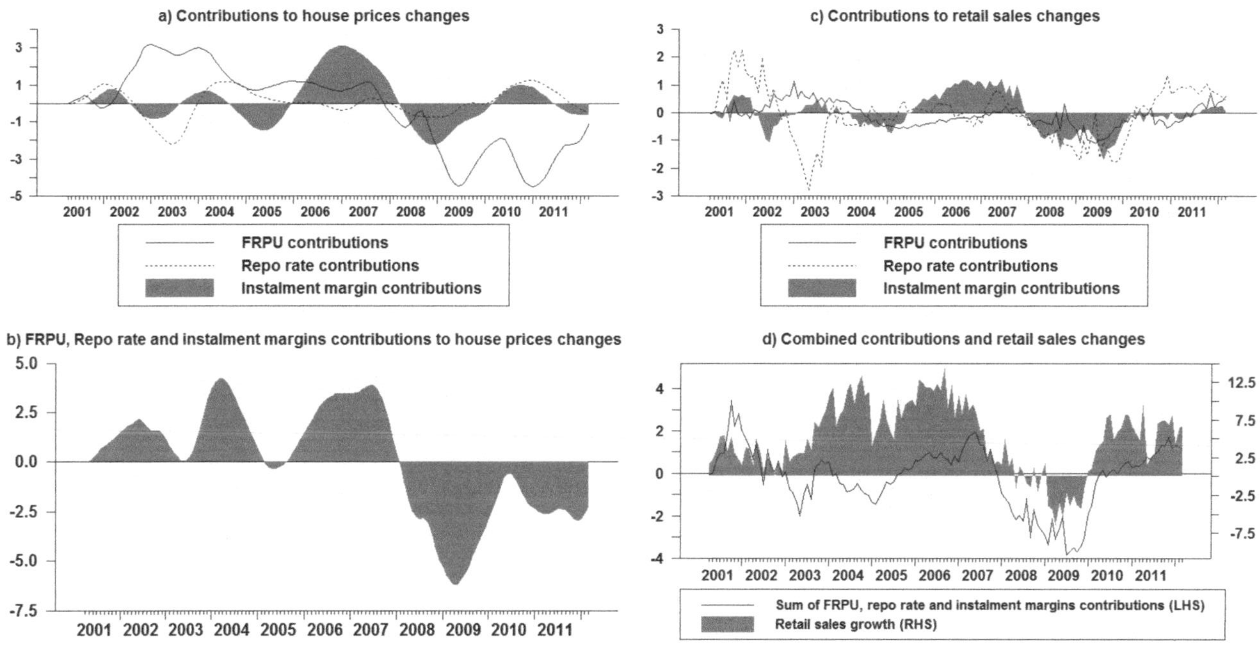

Fig. 16.19 Contributions of the FRPU, lending rate margins and the repo rate on growth in house prices and retail sales (*Note*: The *light shaded portion* denotes the recession in 2009. *Source*: Authors' calculations)

associated with different types of risk peculiar to the institution; and the (2) losses that banks expect to incur on their lending activities, such as the credit risk associated with loans. To bring the aspect of credit risk into the analysis we assess the responses of the credit risk to shocks from the FRPU, house prices and the installment sale credit and other loans and advances lending rate margins. The results are shown in Fig. 16.20.

It is clear in Fig. 16.20d, e that credit provisions increase significantly for nearly 40 months to both the installment sale credit and the other loans and advances lending rate margins shocks, reaching a peak of 4–7 percentage points in nearly 25 of the months. In Fig. 16.20f we show that a positive house price shock results in lower credit provisions. The positive impact of house prices is significant and lowers the provision for credit losses for about 36 months, by magnitude of nearly 7 percentage points at its peak in 25 months.

16.6.7 What Would Have Happened to Credit Loss Provisions as a Measure of Risk Pre- and Post-recession in 2009?

This section disentangles the extent to which the FRPU, installment sale credit lending rate margins and growth in house prices influenced credit risk. The actual and counterfactual credit provisions and the measure of risk are shown in Fig. 16.21. The counterfactual refers to credit provisions excluding (1) house price contribution, which measures deterioration in collateral, and (2) installment sale credit margins and (3) FRPU contributions.

In Fig. 16.21c, d the impact of the FRPU contributions and the combined role of house prices, the FRPU and installment sale credit lending rate margins are shown. It is evident that the installment sale credit margins pulled down the credit risk levels prior to the crisis more than growth in house prices and the FRPU in Fig. 16.21c. However, the increase in credit risk post-recession in 2009 is largely due to house prices followed by the installment sales credit lending rate margins and, lastly, the FRPU. These results confirm that the role of collateral in the form of house price growth is a very important driver of credit risk. Collectively, in Fig. 16.21d these three factors are revealed to have raised credit provisions since 2009.

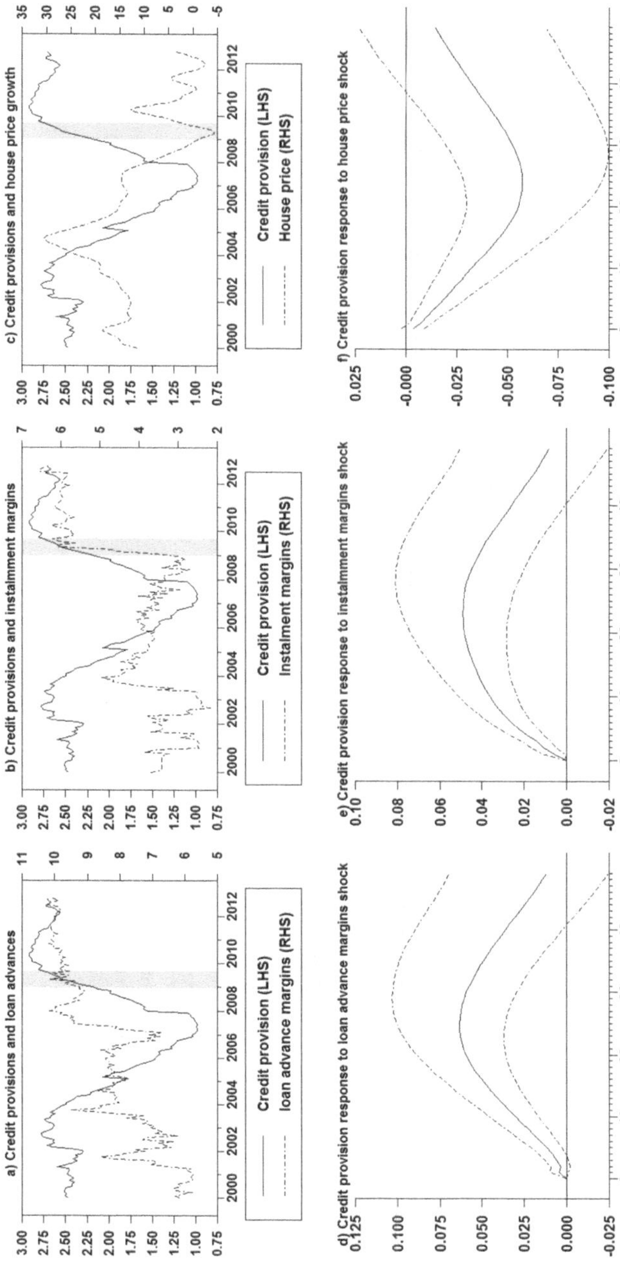

Fig. 16.20 Credit provisions responses to various shocks (*Source*: Authors' calculations)

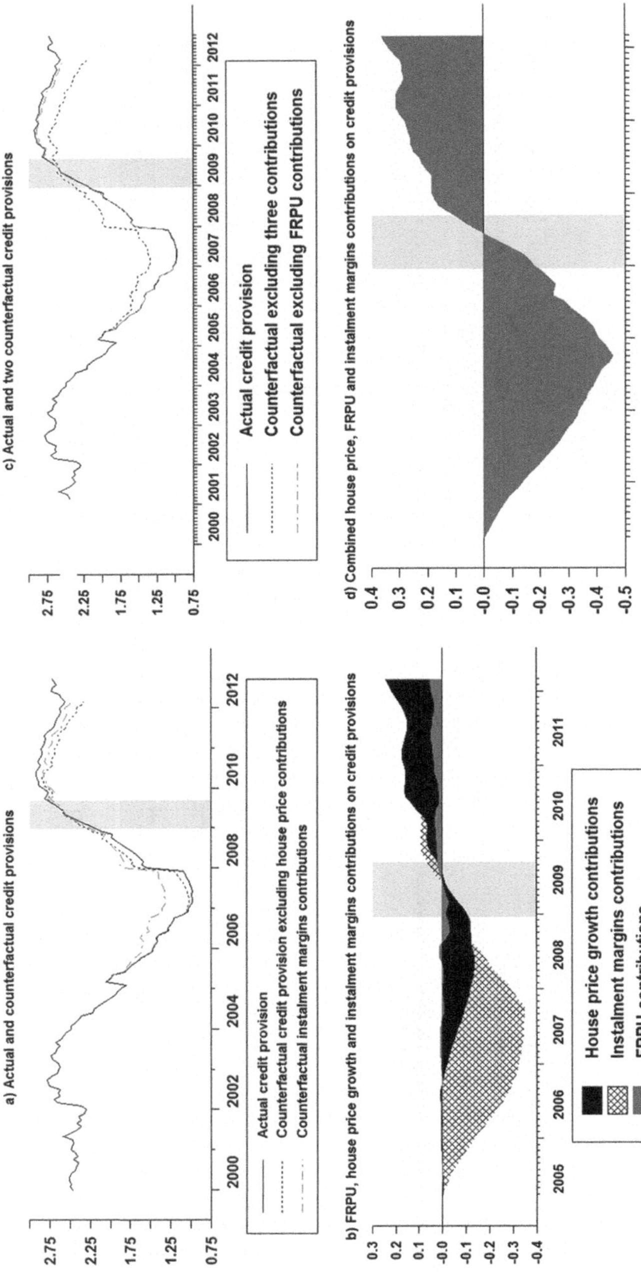

Fig. 16.21 Actual and counterfactual credit provisions and the role of house prices (*Source*: Authors' calculations)

16.7 Conclusion and Policy Implications

The findings in this chapter reveal that banking sector financial frictions as measured by the FRPU and lending rate interest rate margins affect the business cycle fluctuations and the transmission of monetary policy settings. Evidence indicates that the other loans and advances interest rate margins' self-induced fluctuations contributed significantly to own evolution. This is consistent with banks' internal reassessment of the riskiness of certain types of bank lending and clients, as well as changes in banks' business strategies. Such practices can affect the intermediation of credit and also impede the desired easing effects of the monetary policy on quantities or volume of new loans.

Financial regulation policy uncertainty shocks are similar to demand shocks. They exert depressing effects on output and other macroeconomic variables. Nodari (2014) suggests that the FRPU's adverse effects imply that policymakers should pay considerable attention to the design of financial regulation from both credibility and policy management perspectives because lack of transparency in this policy design can have adverse macroeconomic effects. Hence, it is recommended that, while the trade-off exists between policy correctness and decisiveness, there should be no ambiguity in policies on which many economic agents require engage in purposeful production and spending decisions.

Summary of Findings

- Evidence indicates that banking sector financial frictions as measured by the FRPU and lending rate interest rate margins affect business cycle fluctuations and the transmission of monetary policy settings
- FRPU, which captures uncertainty about regulation and supervisory issues, contributed significantly to the reduction in credit extension.
- Other loans and advances interest rate margins' self-induced fluctuations contributed significantly to own evolution.

Part IV

Macro-prudential Tools and Monetary Policy

17

Excess Capital Adequacy and Liquid Asset Holdings and Credit

Learning Objectives

- Establish the impact of the LCR on banks' assets and risk
- Analyze the costs involved in the LCR requirements
- Understand the impact of regulations on bank credit supply and pricing of loans
- Assess the impact of excess CAR and LAH on credit developments
- Examine whether excess CAR and LAH induce any frictions in credit markets by raising lending spreads
- Distinguish between the effects of excess CAR and LAH and those associated with the National Credit Act (NCA) and the Basel III shocks
- Consider the responses of inflation and the repo rate to tight bank regulatory shocks

17.1 Introduction

This chapter extend the analysis of the interaction of monetary policy and various macro-prudential tools. In this case, we assess the macroeconomic effects of excess capital adequacy ratio (CAR) and liquid asset

N. Gumata, E. Ndou, *Bank Credit Extension and Real Economic Activity in South Africa*, DOI 10.1007/978-3-319-43551-0_17

holdings (LAH) of banks. It is an undisputable fact, as Fig. 17.1 shows, that CAR has exceeded the minimum required ratio over long horizons. The LAH of banks have exceeded the minimum required levels since 2009. Hence, we ask: To what extent do the excess CAR and LAH exert adverse macroeconomic effects? How have excess capital adequacy and liquid asset holdings impacted credit dynamics? Do their effects differ from other tight regulatory shocks?

Bank capital and liquidity are two fundamentally linked concepts. Both tools play an important role in moderating risks in the core business of banking, namely "borrow short and lend long" (Bonner and Hilbers 2015). Capital is part of banks' liabilities; it is a source of funding and can absorb losses. It is a key indicator of a bank's solvency and resilience (Le Lesle and Avramova 2012). On the other hand, liquid assets are part of banks' assets and are used to absorb the risk of bank runs or of other funding sources drying up.

The Basel III regulatory framework introduced the liquidity coverage ratio (LCR) and the net stable funding ratio (NSFR).[1] Under these regulations banks are required to hold sufficient liquid assets to accommodate the withdrawal of deposits at different horizons. These regulations also interact with previously existing regulations such as CAR. Hence, similar to Covas and Driscoll (2011), we assess the macroeconomic impact of the excess holdings of CAR and LAH.

In essence, the LCR compels banks to hold a higher fraction of their assets as low risk and highly liquid securities.[2] Even though such liquidity requirements are meant to reduce the likelihood of bank runs and financial crises, they come at a cost. Furthermore, these regulations may exert adverse effects on bank credit supply and pricing of loans.

So to what extent did the holding of excess CAR and LAH impact credit dynamics? In view of the costs involved, did these excesses induce any frictions in credit markets by raising lending spreads? How do the effects of these excesses differ from those associated with the National

[1] See banks' liabilities to the public and required reserves in Fig. A.17.1. Although the trend in the required reserves and liabilities to the public have been on a steep upward trend, on average banks still hold around the required 2.5 percent.

[2] In Fig. A.17.2, we show that banks hold the bulk of the required securities under the LCR in the form of government securities.

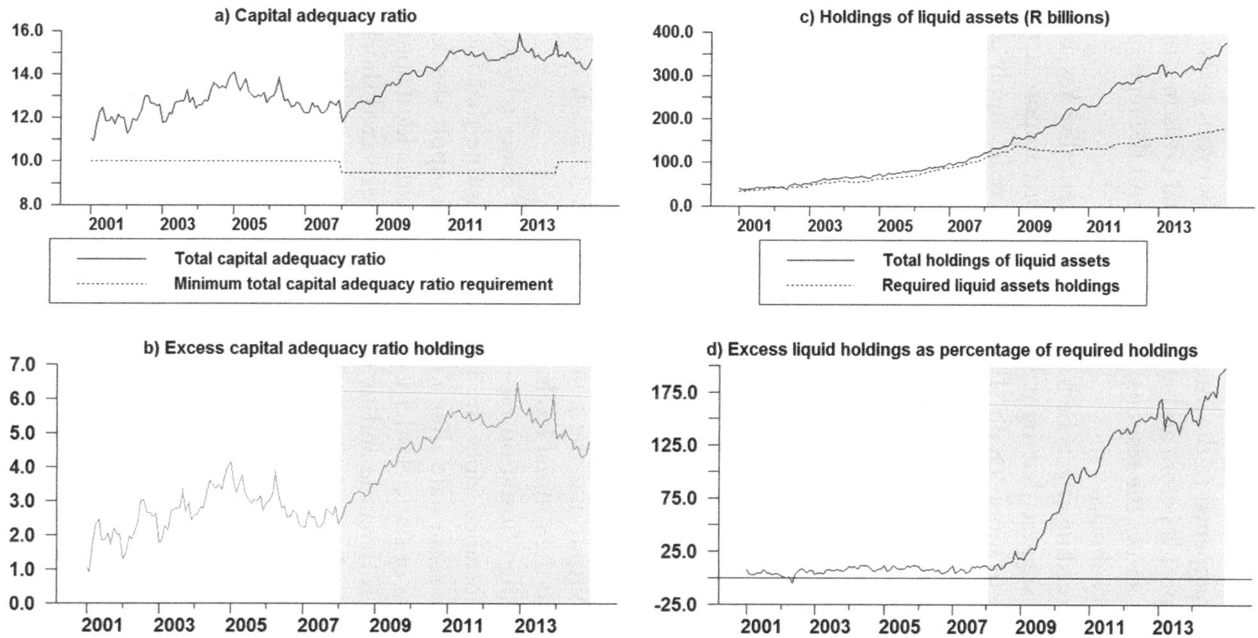

Fig.17.1 Total capital adequacy ratio and the holding of liquid assets (*Source*: South African Reserve Bank (SARB) and authors' calculations)

Credit Act (NCA) and the Basel III shocks? The analysis show policymakers what happened to the interdependence between growth in credit and lending spreads before and after the financial crisis in August 2007. In addition, it shows the responses of inflation and the repo rate to tight bank regulatory shocks.

Can the preceding effects be backed up theoretically? Yes, in line with literature, we suggest that tight bank regulations impose a tax on the lenders' ability to supply credit. This rotates the credit supply curve to the left in Fig. 17.2a, leading to a higher lending rate and reduced quantity of credit. These effects are not limited to credit markets; they spill-over into real economic activity via the Investment Saving – Liquidity Preference Money Supply (IS–LM) relationship in Fig. 17.2b.

Theoretically, the reduced credit supply lowers consumption and investment, which are components of the IS curve in Fig. 17.2b, compressing output and lowering the policy rate. While,the direction of the responses of macroeconomic variables seems unambiguous theoretically, they may be permanent or transitory displacements. Given that economies do recover after being hit by unexpected shocks, in Fig. 17.2d, g lending rates and spreads will rise and return to pre-shock levels. In contrast, credit, output and the policy rate in Fig. 17.2c, f, e decline and slowly revert to their initial levels.

The preceding illustration raises a number of issues related to policymaking. For instance, does the policymaker assume that the economy remains in the same state after a negative credit supply shock, such that point estimates or static elasticity coefficients are the ideal approach? The real economy is dynamic and its reaction to unexpected shocks leads to cyclical episodes in the form of (1) economic booms and busts, (2) low and high growth and (3) credit regimes. The prevalence of such cyclical adjustments weakens the reliance on approaches that quantify point estimates in measuring long-run effects.

A model vector autoregression (VAR) is estimated to derive impulse responses, capturing the extent to which these shock effects persist. This enables us to distinguish the contemporaneous and the lagged effects of an adverse shock. In short, this approach enables us to determine whether economic activity contractions are followed by significant expansions and what happens in the long run.

17.2 What Does Preliminary Data Analysis Suggest Is the Link Between Excess CAR, LAH and Credit Growth?

We examine whether the relationships illustrated above can be validated by the data. We apply techniques that reveal the signs of the relationship. All the scatter plots in Fig. 17.3b, d, f depict a negative relationship.

Therefore, a rise in bank lending spreads, excess CAR and LAH lead to a decrease in credit growth. This is consistent with theoretical suggestions that higher lending spreads can discourage potential borrowers from accessing bank credit.[3] This possibly restrains investment and economic growth. However, in Fig. 17.3c, it is evident that the relationship between excess CAR and credit growth varies. In 2004, lower excess CAR coincided with unprecedented growth in credit. In contrast, rising excess CAR in late 2007 coincided with a decline in credit growth. Fig. 17.3e shows that credit growth reached its peak when excess CAR was very low. This is in stark contrast to weak growth in credit post-2009 in the presence of even higher levels of excess CAR.

Fact 1 There is a negative relationship between credit growth and an increase in lending spreads, excess CAR and LAH. Widening lending spreads is an alternative direct strategy for banks to boost profits but it can have adverse effect on credit growth, investment and growth.

How is this possible? In view of the fact that the regulatory capital framework remains heavily dependent on risk-weighted assets (RWAs), this chapter looks at the components of bank capital for possible answers. Le Lesle and Avramova (2012) indicate that RWAs form an important part of the micro- and macro-prudential toolkit. They form part of the regulatory framework in ensuring that bank capital allocation to assets is

[3] Furthermore, literature shows that another strategy and direct channel of adjustment to higher capital ratios available to banks is increasing the spread between interest rates charged on loans relative to that paid on funding. This scenario becomes prevalent if all banks follow a similar strategy at the time when alternative funding channels do not offer competitive and attractive rates (Cohen 2013).

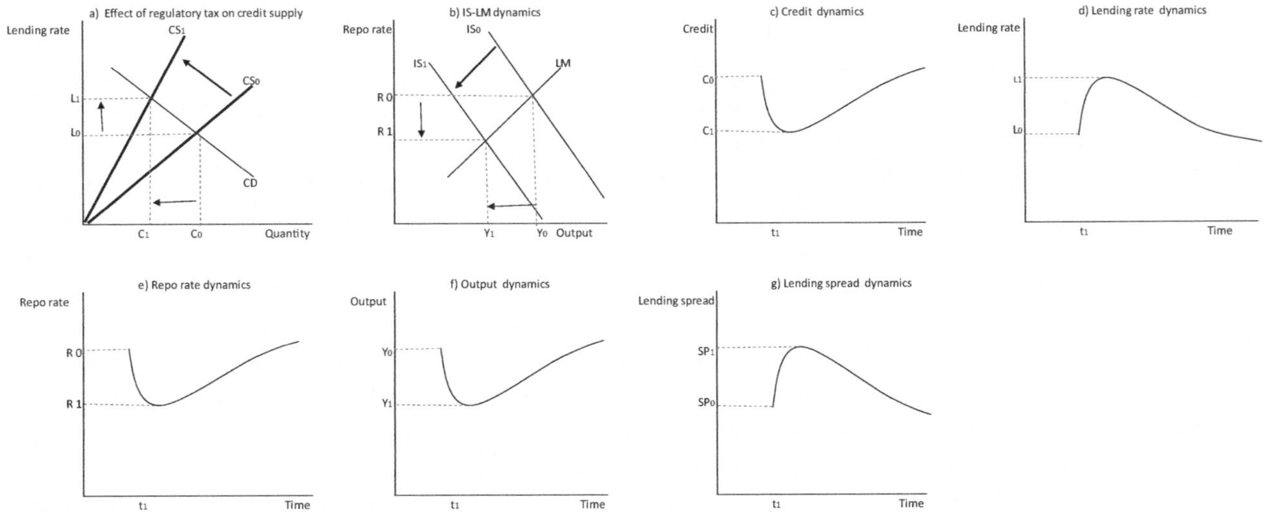

Fig. 17.2 The effect of excess CAR and LAH and other tight bank regulatory shocks on credit supply and real economic activity (*Note*: CS_0 and CS_1 refer to credit supply curves before and after the shock, respectively. C_0 and C_1 are initial and new quantities of credit. CD refers to the credit demand curve. L_0 and L_1 are old and new lending rate, respectively. R_0 and R_1 refer to initial and new repo rate following the shock, respectively. IS_0 and IS_1 refer to investment and saving curves before and after the shock, respectively. Y_0 and Y_1 refer to initial and new output following the shock, respectively. SP_0 and SP_1 refer to old and new lending spread, respectively. *Source*: Author's drawing)

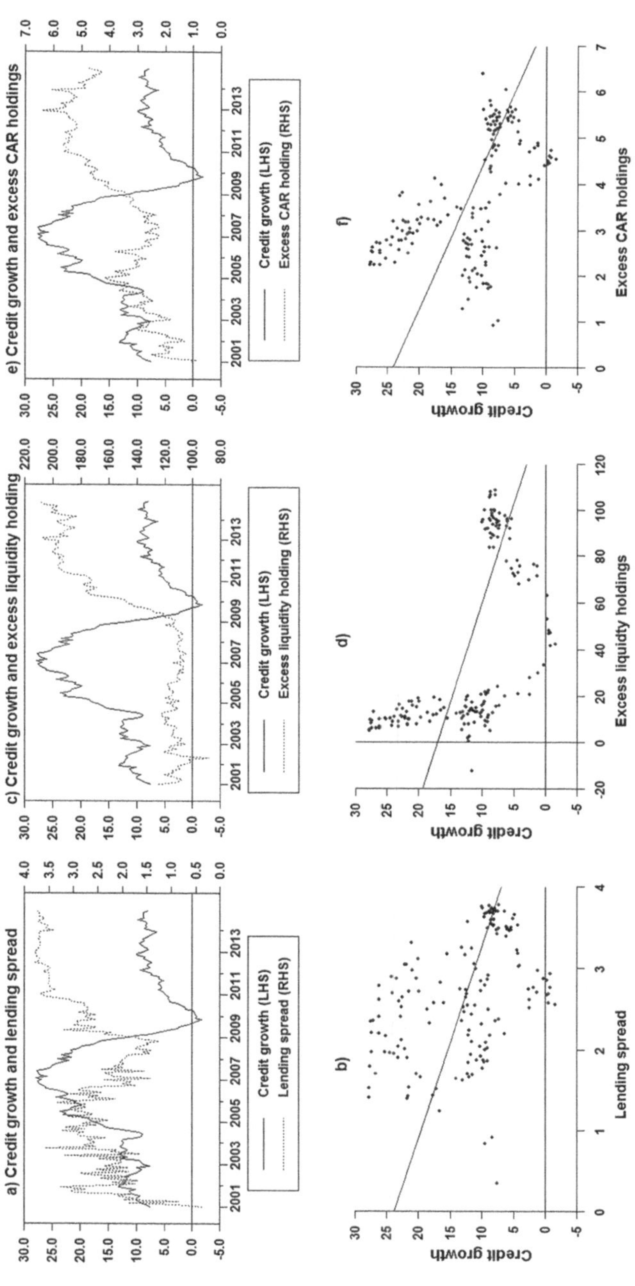

Fig. 17.3 Credit growth, lending spreads and excess CAR and LAH (*Source*: SARB and authors' calculation)

commensurate with the risk profiles. Moreover, RWAs are able to point to asset classes or credit categories where there are potentially destabilizing financial imbalances. Evidence indicates that indeed when excess CAR declines, RWAs and credit growth increase at unprecedented levels, as in Fig. 17.4a, b.

A closer look at the composition of total loans and advances in Fig. 17.5 shows that during this period all credit categories were growing at levels above 10 percent. However, post-2009 the trend has remained subdued, with the exception of other loans and advances and installment sale and leasing credit.

The trend in RWAs is highly procyclical, although this is not immediately evident in the trend displayed by CAR and excess CAR. Assessing headline CAR and highlighting the fact that banks hold excess CAR hides a lot of cyclicality, and, which is more informative about the credit cycles, potential risks in bank lending conditions. The cross correlations in Fig. 17.6 confirm the negative relationships observed in Fig. 17.3. For instance, Fig. 17.6a reveals that growth in credit should decline when preceded by elevated lending spreads, excess LCAR and LAH.

Fact 2 Periods of an increase in excess CAR coincide with a decline in RWAs and growth in credit. It is also evident that in 2009 lending rate spreads, excess CAR and LAH increased at the same time, and credit growth declined significantly. Lending spreads, excess CAR and LAH have remained at elevated levels since 2009 and credit growth has not recovered meaningfully.

17.3 How Has the Interdependence Between Credit Growth and Lending Changed?

To answer this question, this section estimates a small VAR model with three variables for various reasons, including for easing of comparability of results, parsimonious modeling and to have enough degrees of freedom in estimation after 2007M8. The model includes the policy rate, growth in credit and lending spreads. The variables used in this section

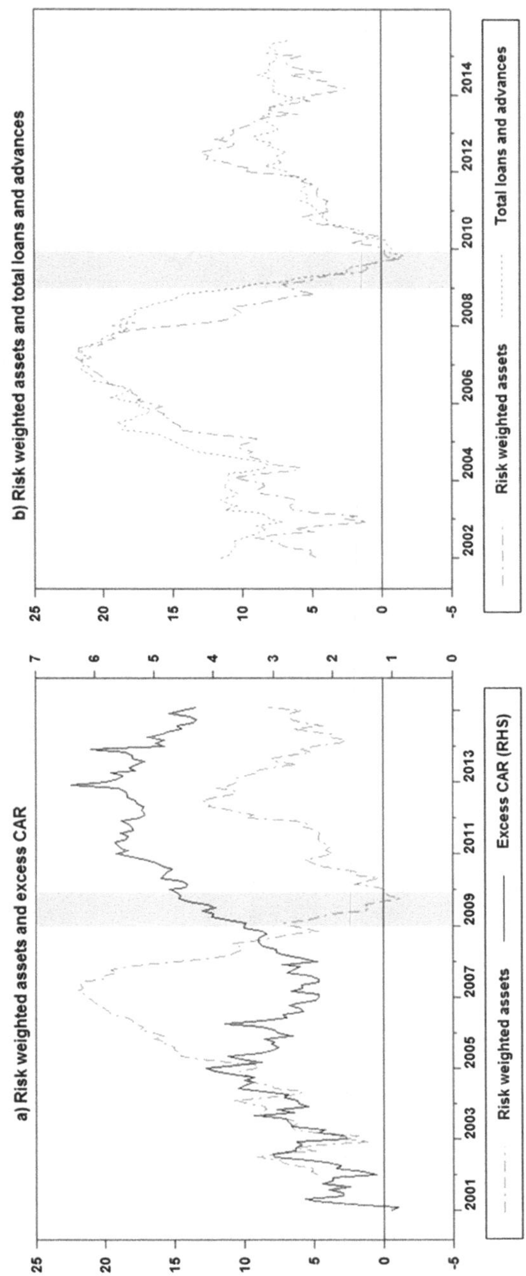

Fig. 17.4 Excess CAR, RWA and total loans and advances (*Source*: SARB and authors' calculation)

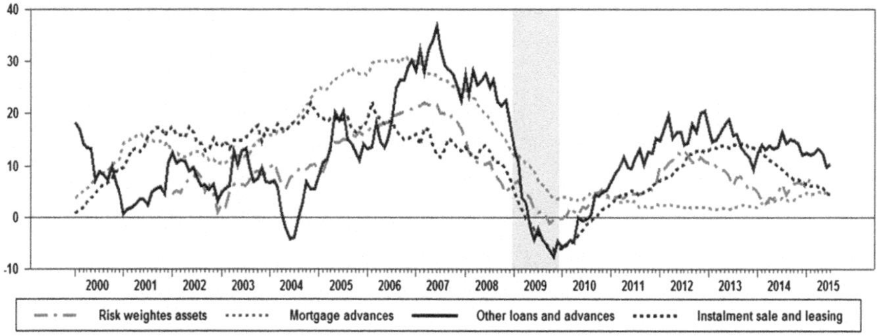

Fig. 17.5 RWA and credit categories (*Source*: SARB and authors' calculation)

are consistent with the theoretical model in Fig. 17.1a, b. Growth in credit reacts contemporaneously to its own shock and to the repo rate, but reacts with a lag to lending spreads. The lending spreads depend on the policy rate, the credit and lending spreads shocks. The two periods under review represent the periods of economic stability before the financial crisis in 2007M7 and the period characterized by elevated economic uncertainty. The analysis compares the responses for the three periods (1) 2001M1–2007M7, (2) 2007M8–2014M12 and (3) 2001M1–2014M12.

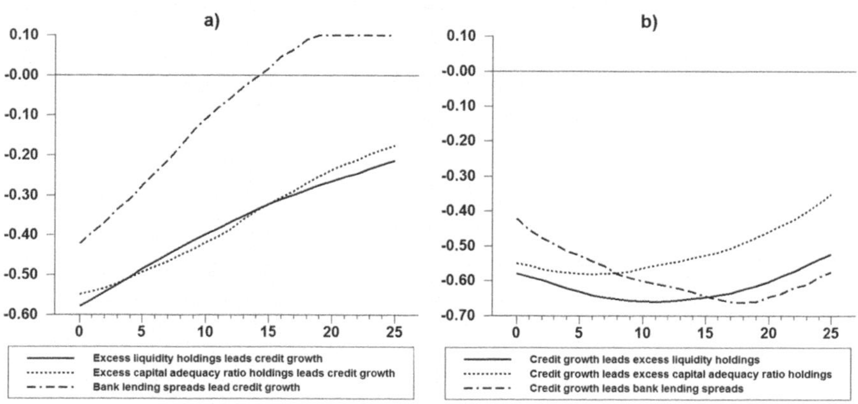

Fig. 17.6 Bilateral cross correlations (*Source*: Authors' calculation)

17.3.1 Impact of an Unexpected 25 Basis Points Increase in the Lending Spread on Credit Growth

Theory suggests that there exists a negative relationship between the quantity of credit and its price. Sometimes empirical analysis can reveal contrasting results, leading to puzzles. So, what is the nature of this relationship in South Africa? We find in Fig. 17.7 that the relationship has changed between 2001M1–2007M7 and 2007M8–2014M12. An unexpected positive lending spread shock exerts pronounced adverse effects on credit.

The effects are significantly severe in 2007M8–2014M12, like those in both 2001M1–2007M7 and 2001M1–2014M12. This implies that a lending spread shock that hits economic activity during periods of heightened financial and economic uncertainty leads to severe credit contraction. In addition, failure to separate the periods may lead to underestimating the effects of lending spread shock on credit dynamics.

At the same time, the difference in the sensitivities can be attributed to the high persistence of lending spreads in 2007M8–2014M12 relative to other periods. This indicates that the more persistent the shock the more long-lasting are its adverse effects on growth in credit.

17.3.2 The Evolution of Lending Spreads and Unexpected Negative Growth in Credit Shock

Fig. 17.8 examines the impact of an unexpected negative 1 percent growth in credit on lending spreads. Overall, all lending spreads in different periods rise for prolonged periods with differing magnitudes. In contrast, the lending spreads remained elevated in 2007M8–2014M12, while spreads in other periods returned towards their pre-shock levels. In policy terms this suggests that unexpected negative credit shock in 2007M8–2014M12 accelerated the negative effects of lending spreads on real economic activity.

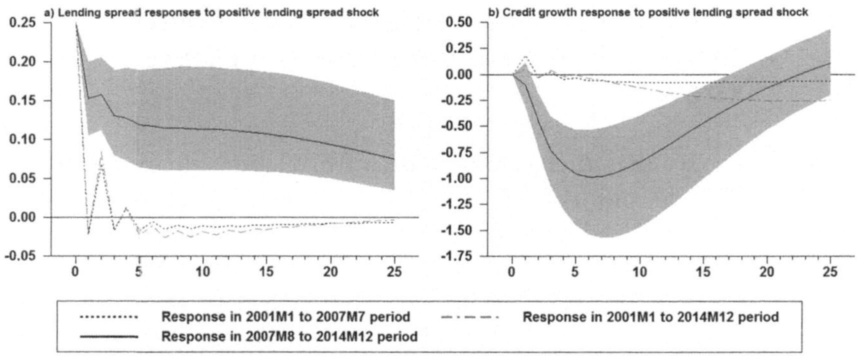

Fig. 17.7 Responses of credit growth to a 25 basis points increase in lending spreads (*Note*: The *grey shaded area* denotes the 16th and 84th percentile which measures the confidence bands. *Source*: Authors' calculation)

How quickly does an unexpected credit shock dissipate? Despite credit shocks moving in the same direction the negative credit shocks lose their half-life between 13 and 15 months. This suggests that credit shocks tend to be slightly persistent.

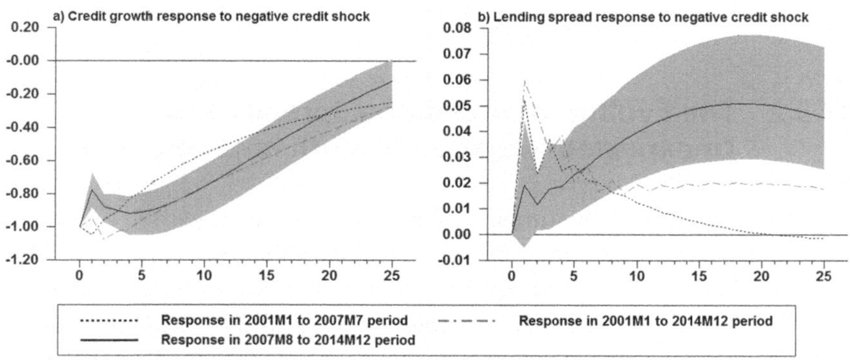

Fig. 17.8 Responses of lending spreads to negative credit growth shock (*Note*: The *grey shaded areas* refer to the 16th and 84th percentile bands. The responses represent percentage point changes. *Source*: Authors' calculation)

Fig. 17.9 examines whether there are differences in proportion of fluctuations in growth in credit induced by lending spread shocks in the three periods. This further explains the existence of the differential growth in credit responses to the positive lending spread shock. A lending spread shock induces more fluctuations after two months in growth in credit in the 2007M8–2014M12 relative to other periods. This explains why lending spreads reduced growth in credit very much after 2007M7, more so than in other periods.

Fact 3 Failure to identify the role of the financial crisis and regulatory changes leads to understating of the magnified role of lending spreads on growth in credit.

17.4 Tight Credit Regulation Shocks on Economic and Credit Growth

To what extent do tight credit regulation shocks impact growth in credit? The previous VAR model is extended by adding growth in manufacturing and growth in retail sales as part of endogenous variables. The NCA is defined as a dummy equal to one for 2007M6–2014M12 and zero otherwise. We define the Basel III shocks as dummy equal to one from 2012M1 to 2014M12 and zero otherwise.[4] This analysis will reveal whether tight bank regulation shocks exert any macroeconomic effect. If so, are the impacts transitory or permanent?

Fig. 17.10 shows the responses to one unit of positive shock in excess CAR, LAH, NCA and Basel III shocks on the credit growth. This equivalent to 1 percent in excess CAR and LAH. We assume these shocks are exogenous to the model and are independent of each other. First, we find that credit growth shrinks significantly over different months, suggesting that regulation has an adverse effect on growth in credit.

We therefore conclude that tight regulatory shocks have adverse effects on growth in credit. However, these effects depend on the regulatory shock. Nonetheless, evidence refutes the hypothesis that regulation leads to a per-

[4] This period includes Basel 2.5.

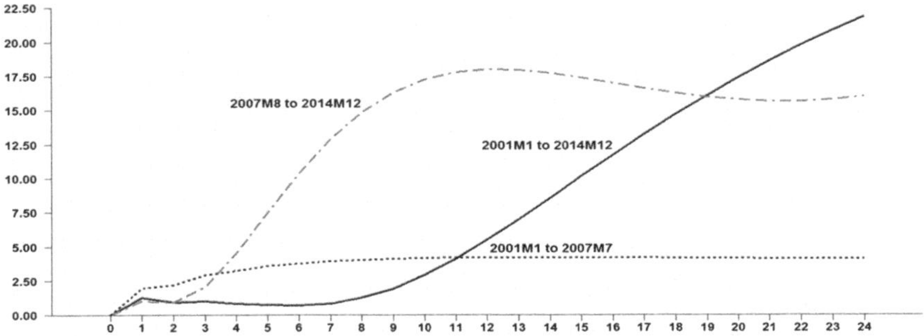

Fig. 17.9 Proportions of fluctuations in growth in credit due to lending spread shock (*Source*: Authors' calculation)

manent decline in credit extension. Furthermore, despite credit growth recovering, it does not increase significantly. This confirms that all these regulatory tools will probably minimize the recurrence of credit booms.

Fact 4 Evidence refutes the hypothesis that tight credit regulation shocks lead to a permanent decline in credit extension. However, subsequent to regulatory shocks the recovery in credit is low.

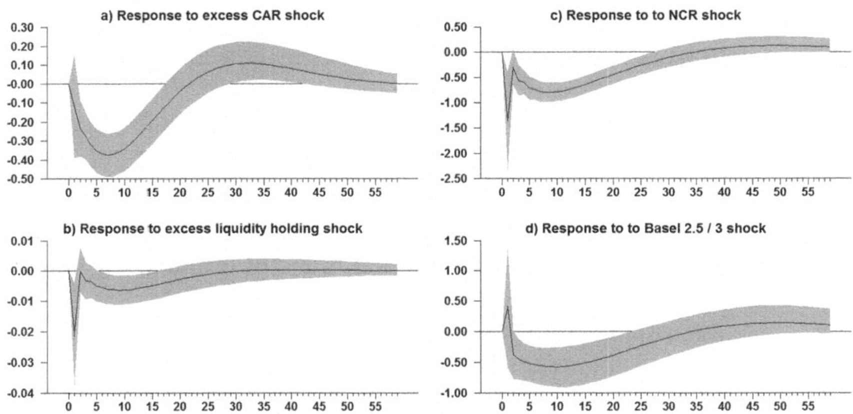

Fig. 17.10 Responses in growth in credit to tight credit regulatory shocks (*Note*: The *grey shaded area* denotes the 16th and 84th percentile, which measures the confidence bands. *Source*: Authors' calculation)

So which tight credit regulatory shocks have more adverse effects on credit? Which ones result in a prolonged recovery in credit? The peak effects on growth in credit in Fig. 17.11a reveal that the biggest contraction in growth in credit is due to the NCA shock followed by Basel III shock. Amongst the shocks related to excesses above minimum regulatory requirements, the excess CAR shock has a bigger effect and the excess LAH shock has the least effect. The peak effects of excess CAR occur in the seventh month, which is longer than the one month due to excess LAH shocks. These effects probably attest to the fact that they are directed at different aspects of the banks' balance sheets.

The biggest peak decline in Fig. 17.11b occurs in the ninth month due to a Basel III shock. The effects last longer than the seven months due to excess CAR shocks. In contrast, the effects due to the NCA and LAH shocks are felt fairly quickly, within one month.

How long do these effects take to die? Fig. 17.11c shows the duration of contraction in credit growth due to various shocks. We find that growth in credit takes the longest time in following an NCA shock at 27 months. This is followed by shocks due to Basel III shock at 22 months. However, growth in credit takes nearly the same amount of time, needing one and half years to recover following excess LAH and excess CAR shocks. It is surprising that the Basel III shock has pronounced effects before its full implementation.

17.4.1 Spill-Over Effects of Regulatory Shocks to Real Economic Activity

We illustrated in Fig. 17.2 that regulation is a market distortion intervention and it acts like tax on economic activity, and we suggested that there may be spill-over to real economic activity via the IS–LM link. Fig. 17.12 shows that tight regulation shocks have adverse effects on real economic activity but with varied significance. The effects are adverse in period subsequent to the shock and not in the long run. In addition, the effects depend on the regulatory shock. Manufacturing reacts more significantly to excess CAR and NCR shocks than other shocks. These shocks lower growth in manufacturing significantly in the first

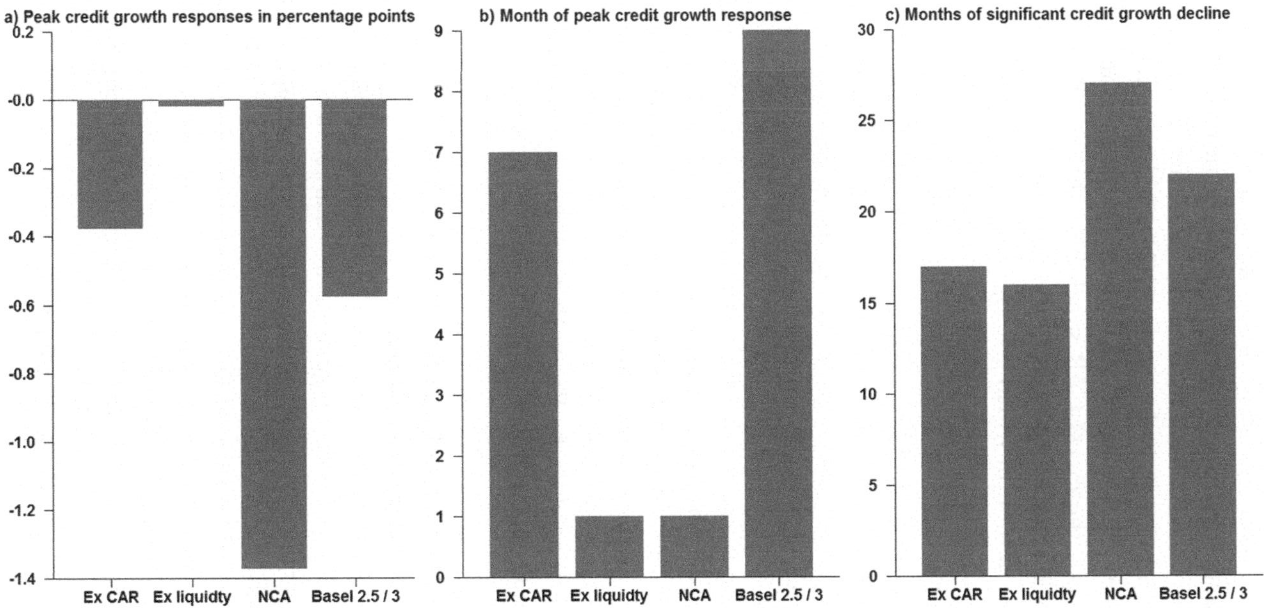

Fig. 17.11 Comparison of responses in growth in credit to various regulatory shocks (*Note*: EX CAR refers to excess CAR, Ex liquidity refers to excess liquid excet holdings. *Source*: Authors' calculation)

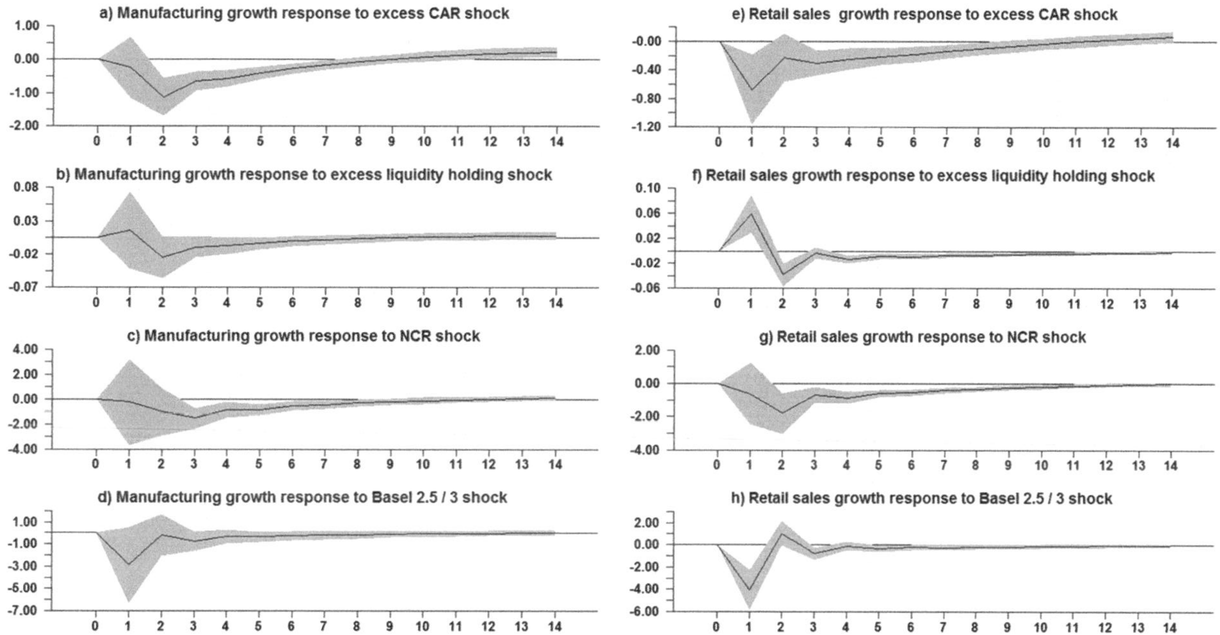

Fig. 17.12 Responses of manufacturing growth to tight credit regulatory shock (*Note*: The *grey shaded areas* denote the 16th and 84th percentile which measures the confidence bands. *Source*: Authors' calculation)

ten months, followed by a weak but significant recovery which vanishes in the long run. Despite Basel III and excess LAH shocks adversely affecting manufacturing, the effects are insignificant over all horizons.

Do tight credit regulatory shocks have selective effects on growth in retail sales? In contrast, all four regulatory shocks have adverse effects on retail sales growth which is a proxy for consumption. Therefore, regulatory shocks are not neutral on retail sales growth. The Basel III shock has a big effect on growth in retail sales, although the effects are highly transitory relative to those exerted by other shocks.

17.4.2 Is Monetary Policy Neutral to Unexpected Credit Regulatory Shocks?

We showed in Fig. 17.2 that monetary policy is impacted by a negative credit supply shock and the introduction of credit regulations. We proceed to test the applicability of this theoretical prediction on South African data. Despite varying responses, we established that unexpected tight credit regulatory changes exert adverse effects on growth in credit, manufacturing production and retail sales. What are the implications for monetary policy? Despite differing effects, the repo rate is lowered with varying magnitudes and durations in Fig. 17.13 to all four unexpected tight credit regulatory shocks.

Fact 5 Monetary policy is slightly but not permanently loosened in response to regulatory shocks. This indicates that monetary policy is not neutral to unexpected tight credit regulatory shocks.

Does monetary policy respond in a similar fashion to all four regulatory shocks? No, the repo rate responses vary according to shocks. A comparison of the duration and peak effects of the reductions in the repo rate reduction in Fig. 17.14 indicates that the repo rate responses differ very much with regulatory shock. The peak reduction in the repo rate in Fig. 17.14a is smallest in response to the excess LAH shock amongst all four regulatory shocks. In Fig. 17.14c it is revealed that the repo rate significantly declines for the longest period of 30 months due to unexpected NCA shock. We

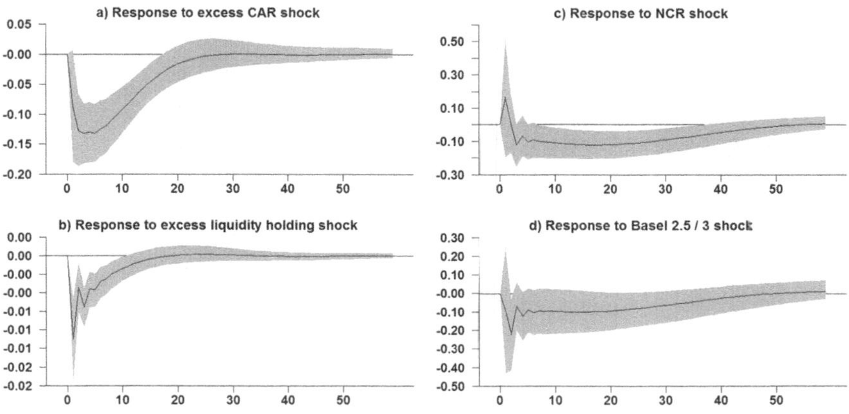

Fig. 17.13 Response of the repo rate to tight credit regulatory shocks (*Note*: The *grey shaded area* denotes the 16th and 84th percentile which measures the confidence bands. *Source*: Authors' calculation)

also find that the repo rate declines for 16 months due to unexpected excess CAR shock. This exceeds the 10 months due to the excess LAH shock.

Is the finding that the repo rate declines due to unexpected tight credit regulatory shocks counterintuitive? Theoretically, it is not counterintuitive at all. Because in Fig. 17.15 a decline in credit supply in Fig. 17.15a leads to reduced aggregate demand in the economy and lowers output, the depressed state of the economy exerts downward pressures on price levels in Fig. 17.15b. Hence, a forward-looking monetary policymaker should reduce policy rate as inflationary pressures are likely to be subdued.

Fig. 17.1 shows that inflation tends to decline with varied magnitudes and durations. Inflation declines significantly within a year of an excess LAH and Basel III shocks. However, the decline in inflation is not significant with regards to an excess CAR shock. In contrast, inflation increases significantly for eight months due to the NCA shock and then declines transitorily between 15 and 33 months after the shock. Thus, evidence confirms tight regulatory shocks do impact inflation despite not being a determinant of inflationary processes.

In light of the responses in inflation, we show the of evolution of inflation during the two periods of NCA and Basel III shocks. Fig. 17.17a

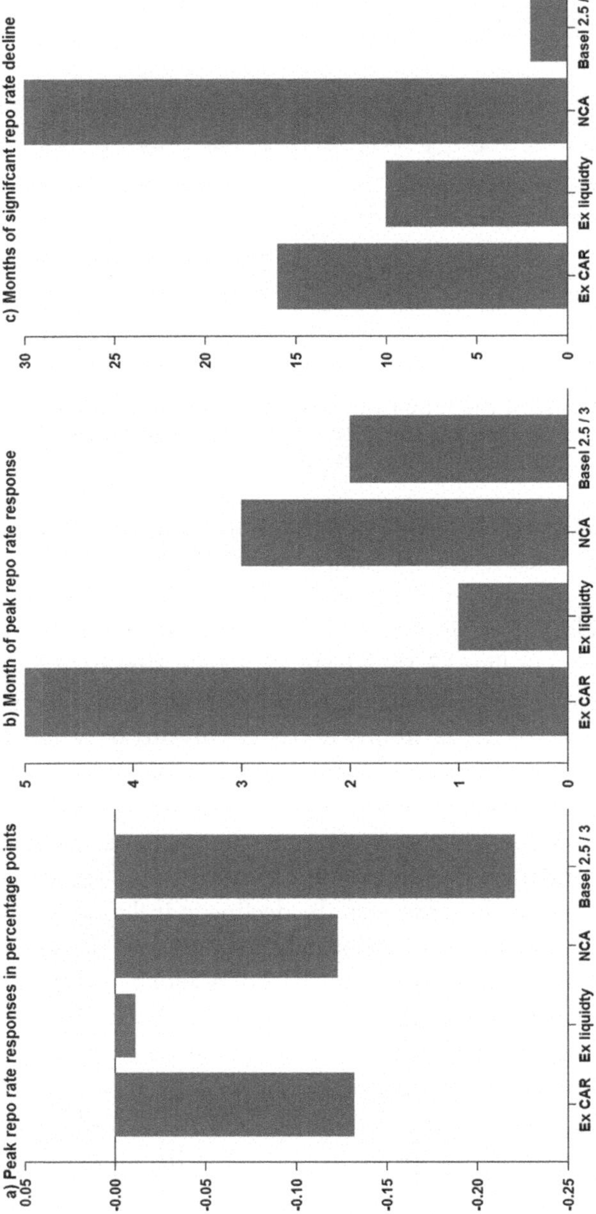

Fig. 17.14 Different aspects of the repo rate responses to tight regulatory shocks (*Note*: EX CAR refers to excess CAR, Ex liquidity refers to excess liquid excet holdings. *Source*: Authors' calculation)

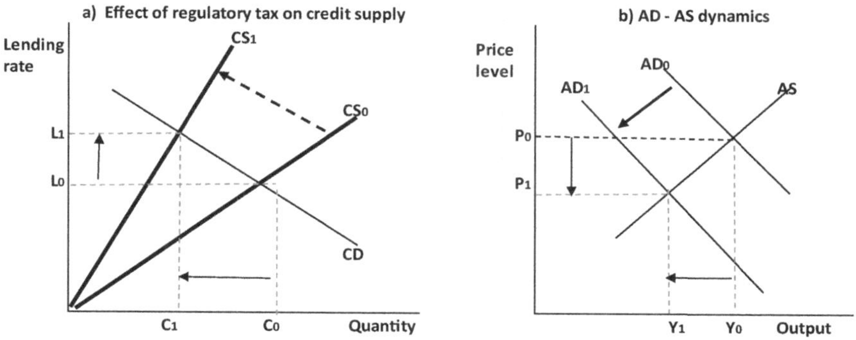

Fig. 17.15 Linking regulation to aggregate demand–aggregate supply model (AD–AS) relationship (*Note*: CS_0 and CS_1 refer to credit supply curves before and after the shock, respectively. C_0 and C_1 are initial and new quantities of credit. CD refers to credit demand curve. L_0 and L_1 are old and new lending rate, respectively. P_0 and P_1 refer to initial and new price level following the shock, respectively. AD_0 and AD_1 refer to aggregate demand curves before and after the shock, respectively. AS refers to the aggregate supply curve. Y_0 and Y_1 refer to initial and new output following the shock, respectively. *Source*: Author's drawing)

shows that during the NCA implementation, inflation increased aggressively before declining over long horizons.

So, What economic factors could explain the link between inflation and the NCA? The inflationary pressures could reflect the lagged impact of credit during the famous frontloading of credit extension prior to the adoption of the NCA. In addition, the adoption of Basel III coincides with muted periods of inflation. This offers support that can be linked to the NCA and Basel III's tight lending criteria as measured by the loan-to-value ratios and muted house price growth. Nonetheless, this does not imply that these regulatory tools are on their own the major drivers of inflation.

17.4.3 Cumulative Effects of Unexpected Regulatory Shocks on Growth in Credit and Lending Spreads

The empirical analysis concludes by showing the combined effects of tight credit regulatory shocks on growth in credit in Fig. 17.18a, b,

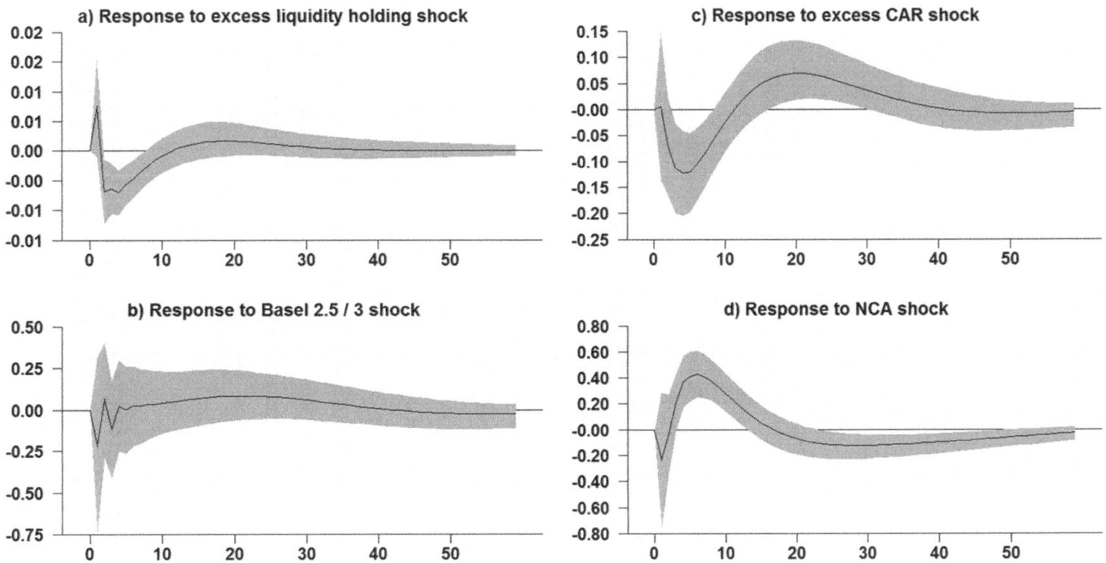

Fig. 17.16 Inflation response to tight credit regulation shocks (*Note*. The *grey shaded areas* denote the 16th and 84th percentile, which measures the confidence bands. *Source*: Authors' calculation)

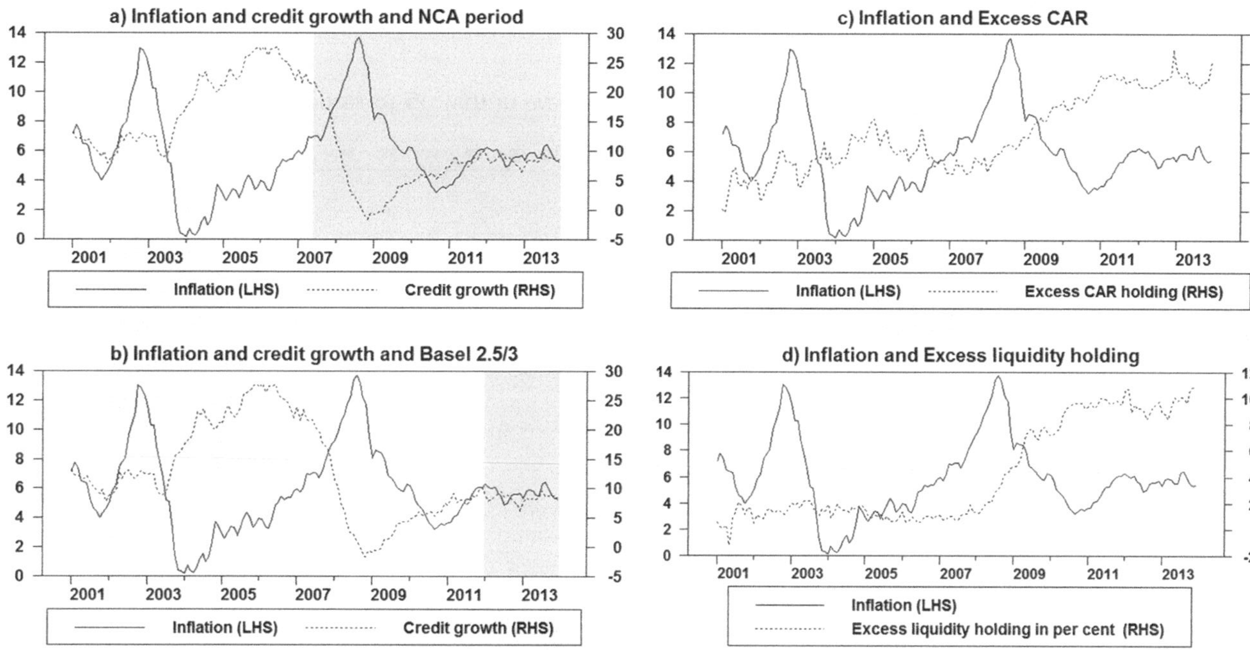

Fig. 17.17 CPI inflation, growth in credit and regulation (*Note*: The *shaded portion* in part (**a**) refers to the period of NCA while in part (**b**) it shows period of Basel III. *Source*: South African Reserve Bank and authors' calculation)

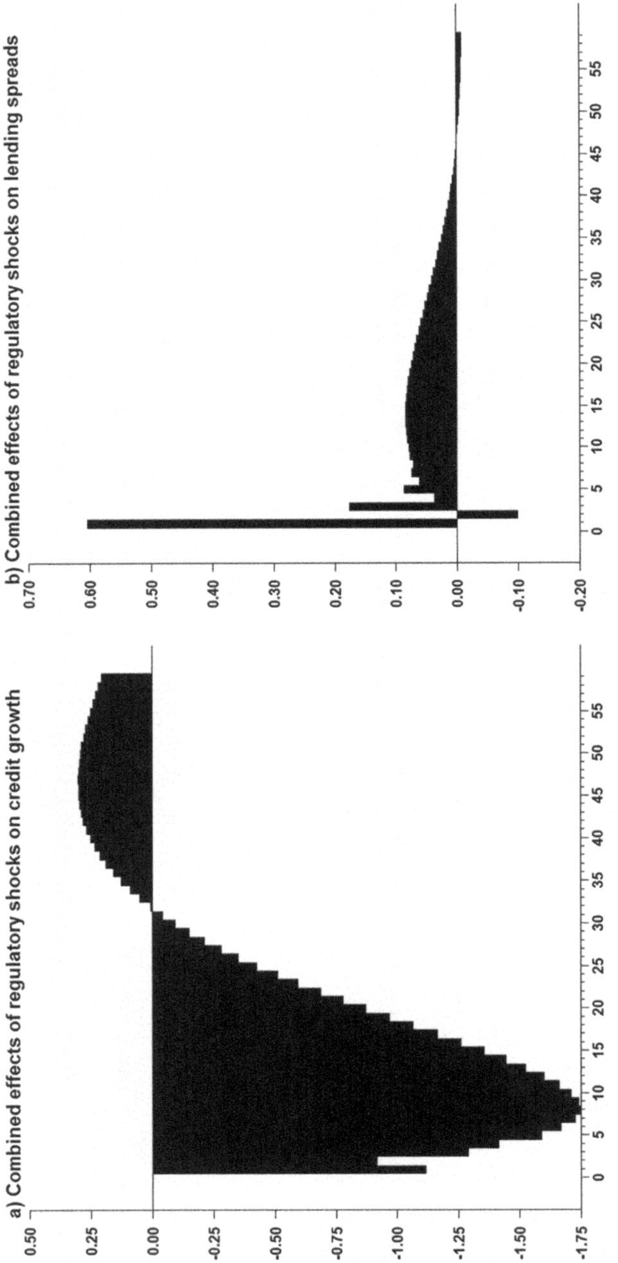

Fig. 17.18 Combined responses of growth in credit and lending spreads to regulatory shocks (*Source*: Authors' calculation)

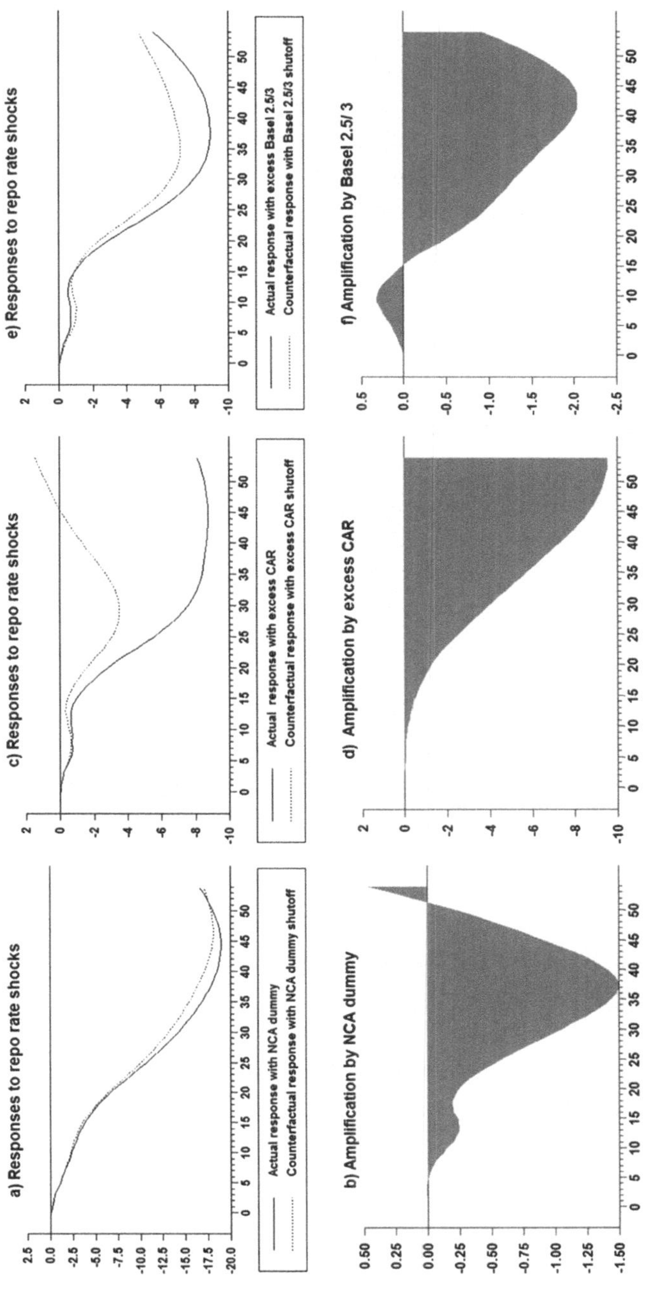

Fig. 17.19 Accumulated credit growth responses and amplification by excess car and Basel 2.5/III

and the lending spreads. The main assumption is that the implementation of these shocks is independent. These tight regulatory shocks lead to a big reduction in growth in credit in Fig. 17.18a for a nearly 30 months. The reduction in growth in credit is accompanied by a rise in lending spreads which remain elevated for nearly 40 months. This confirms that regulatory shocks move credit and lending spreads in different directions.

Fact 6 Tight credit regulatory shocks move quantity of credit and lending spreads in different directions for long periods of time.

17.4.4 Counterfactual Responses

The analysis concludes by performing a counterfactual analysis to see the extent to which NCA, excess CAR and Basel 2.5/III affect things. These regulatory-related variables are shut off in the repo rate equations to determine the effects of policy rate shock on credit growth. The gaps between the actual and counterfactual responses measure the amplifying effects due to these regulatory variables. The positive repo rate shocks depress credit growth, irrespective of whether these regulatory variables are shut off or not. However, the credit growth decline is bigger when these regulatory variables are not shut off than when they are shut off. This suggests that regulatory variables worsen the credit growth decline to positive repo rate shocks (Fig. 17.19).

17.5 Conclusions and Policy Recommendations

This chapter examined the extent to which positive excess CAR and LAH shocks impact credit dynamics and whether the effects differ from other tight credit regulatory shocks. Evidence indicates a negative relationship between credit growth and excess CAR and LAH above the minimum regulatory level. There is a negative relationship between the quantity of credit and its price measured by lending spreads consistent with theoretical models. There is a feedback effect between lending spreads and growth in credit which intensifies the adverse effects of lending spreads on real economic activity. Furthermore, excess LAH is more aligned to the increase in funding costs, but we caution that this is a partial view of bank funding costs. There are other aspects that need to be thoroughly reviewed to come to a comprehensive measure of bank funding costs.

The chapter further examines the extent to which the relationship between lending spreads and credit growth changed between 2001M1–2007M7 and 2007M8–2014M12. Evidence indicates that an unexpected 25 basis point increase in the lending spreads has nonlinear effects on macroeconomic activity. Moreover, the nonlinear effects tend to be more pronounced during periods of financial and economic instability. Furthermore, we established that the differential effects can be linked to the persistence effects in trajectories of lending spread shocks. Failure to identify the role of financial crisis leads to an understatement of the magnified role of lending spreads on credit.

Evidence refutes the hypothesis that a tight credit regulation shock leads to permanent decline in credit extension but the subsequent credit recovery is not followed by credit booms. Monetary policy is slightly, but not permanently, loosened. This indicates that monetary policy is not neutral to unexpected tight credit regulatory shocks. Tight credit regulatory shocks move the quantity of credit and lending spreads in different directions for long periods of time. This may mean that policies need to be coordinated, especially during periods of inflationary pressure.

Summary of Findings

- There is a negative relationship between credit growth and excess CAR and LAH above the minimum regulatory level.
- There is negative relationship between the quantity of credit and its price measured by lending spreads consistent with theoretical models.
- There is feedback effect between lending spreads and growth in credit which intensifies the adverse effects of lending spreads on real economic activity.

- Excess LAH is more aligned to the increase in funding costs, but we caution that this is a partial view of bank funding costs.
- There are other aspects that need to be thoroughly reviewed to come to a comprehensive measure of bank funding costs.
- Evidence indicates that an unexpected 25 basis point increase in the lending spreads has nonlinear effects on macroeconomic activity.
- The nonlinear effects tend to be more pronounced during periods of financial and economic instability.
- There are differential effects that can be linked to the persistence effects in trajectories of lending spread shocks.
- Failure to identify the role of financial crisis leads to an understatement of the magnified role of lending spreads on credit.

Appendix

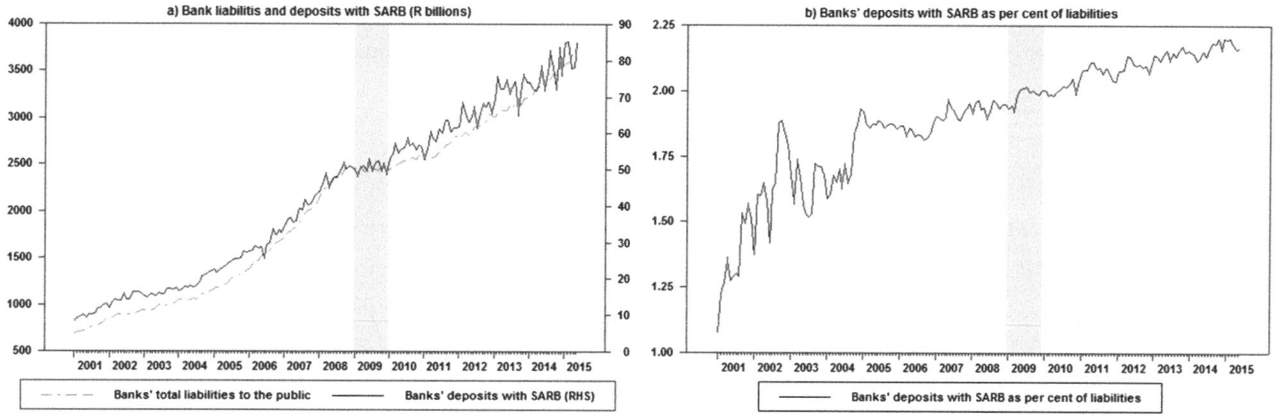

AU7 **Fig. A.17.1** Banks deposits with the SARB (*Source*: SARB and authors' calculations)

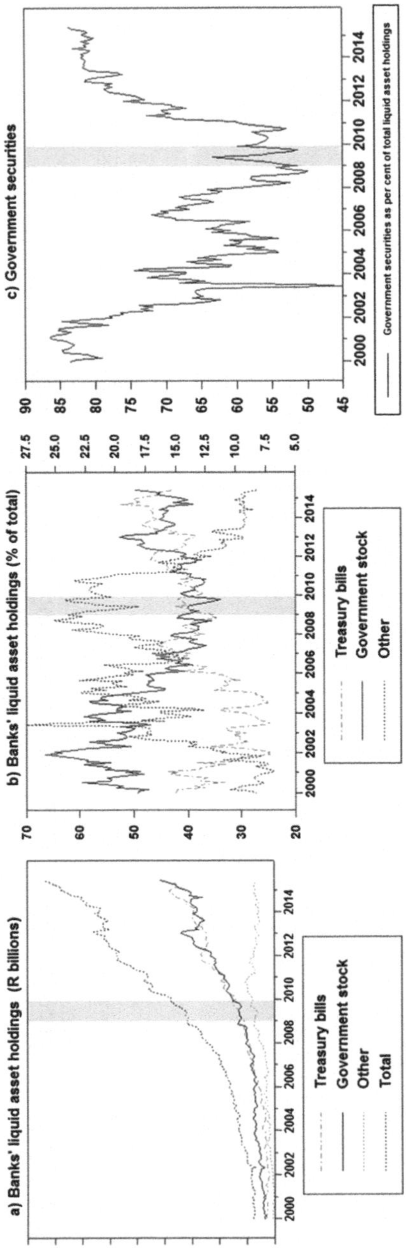

Fig. A.17.2 The instrument breakdown of securities held by banks (*Source*: SARB and authors' calculation)

18

Credit Loss Provisions as a Macro-prudential Tool

Learning Objectives

- Assess how weak growth in credit can be linked to elevated credit loss provisions as macro-prudential tool
- Understand the extent to which provisions have been a driver of business cycle fluctuations in South Africa
- Distinguish how credit provisions can be classified into low and high regimes
- Consider how credit provisions shocks impact real economic activity in a nonlinear way
- Assess how tighter provisioning for credit losses makes monetary policy adjustments need to be less aggressive to curb positive inflation surprises
- Understand how elevated policy rates accentuate the adverse effects of tighter credit loan loss provisions on credit contractions

N. Gumata, E. Ndou, *Bank Credit Extension and Real Economic Activity in South Africa*, DOI 10.1007/978-3-319-43551-0_18

18.1 Introduction

Chapter 14 pinpointed that literature shows that there is no single tool that influences all financial behavior and stability consistently; rather, a variety of tools is used. The macro-prudential toolkit contains a wide range of prudential instruments related to liquidity[1] and capital.[2] Credit loss provisions are part of this macro-prudential toolkit. This chapter assesses whether the weak growth in credit can be in any way linked to credit loss provisions as a macro-prudential tool. To what extent have provisions been a driver of business cycle fluctuations in South Africa? Are there nonlinear effects? The chapter embarks on counterfactual analysis to determine the extent to which the credit loss provisions interact with monetary policy shock. This will reveal if monetary policy's ability to enforce price stability is influenced by the state of credit loss provisions and vice versa.

How does a prudential tool in the form of tighter provisioning for credit losses impact monetary policy? To what extent have credit provisions shock as a macro-prudential tool driven the business cycle fluctuations? Did these shocks have an effect on the real economy? To contextualize these research questions, we plot credit loss provisions and the repo rate in Fig. 18.1.

It is evident that between 2000 and early 2006, as well as between the second quarter of 2007 and early 2008, the two variables moved together in the same direction. At the beginning of the last quarter of 2008 the relationship diverged, as the repo rate continued to decline and credit loss provisions increased have remained elevated at high levels. From looking at the data it is clear that these policy tools were moving in different directions.

Some aspects explored include the following issues: Can the diverging trends of credit provisions and the repo rate be another source of muted credit growth? Do the credit loss provisions drive business cycle fluctuations and possibly explain what happened to credit growth since 2009?

---

[1] This includes limits on net open currency positions and limits on maturity mismatch.

[2] This includes countercyclical or time-varying capital requirements and time-varying or dynamic provisioning.

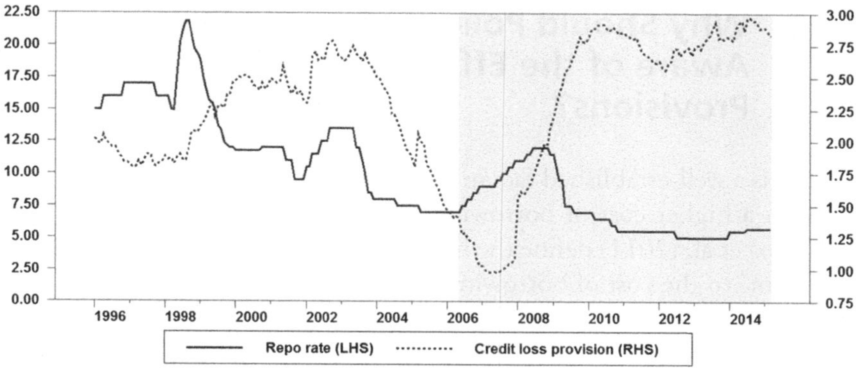

Fig. 18.1 Credit loss provisions as a percentage of total loans and advances and the repo rate (*Note*: The variables are expressed in percentages. *Source*: South African Reserve Bank and authors' calculations)

Do credit loss provisions lead to a reduction in growth in consumer expenditure, for example, as measured by retail sales and credit growth? To what extent does a positive shock in provisions constrain growth in various sector categories of credit? Continuing on the theme of thresholds, is there any nonlinear response to credit provisions shock?

This chapter fills the policy research gaps in the space of the interaction of monetary policy and macro-prudential tools, in this case loan loss provisions. Second, the chapter fills the policy gaps regarding the role of nonlinearities introduced by credit provisions in credit markets and the real economy. Third, it fills the policy gaps by quantifying the real effects of the implementation of the proposed regulatory changes from the incurred loss model to the expected loss model.[3] The incurred loss model has been criticized for recognizing impairment losses too little and too late and therefore promoting cyclicality. It is possible that the observed trend in loan loss provision shown in Fig. 18.1 is due to the front-loading in anticipation of such changes.

[3] The changeover is expected to be effective in 2018 (Pool et al. 2015.

18.2 Why Should Policymakers Be Made Aware of the Effects of Credit Provisions?

First, it is a well-established fact in literature that macro-prudential policy imposes a higher cost of borrowing for economic agents. For instance, Columba et al. (2011) define the higher costs as an additional "regulation premium" to the cost of borrowing. In addition, Blanchard et al. (2010) assert that financial regulation is not macroeconomic neutral—macro-prudential policies and tools affect the level of output and prices, constrain borrowing and expenditure and ultimately overall output.

The second issue relates to assertions by Pool et al. (2015) that the potential weakness in backward provisioning is procyclicality. This suggests that expected credit losses are under-provisioned during business upswings when few credit problems are identified, leading to low credit provisioning. In contrast, during downturns provisioning increases due to high credit defaults. Furthermore, studies such as Bouvatier and Lepetit (2012), show that forward-looking provisions can eliminate procyclicality in lending standards linked to backward-looking provisions, and can reduce volatility in both financial and real variables.

The third issue articulated in Zilberman and Tayler (2014) and Pool et al. (2015) relates to the fact that the forward-looking provisioning approach in conjunction with accounting rules for credit loss provisions are expected to alter the transmission mechanism of monetary policy.

Nonetheless, the chapter notes that policymakers do not target a certain level of credit or GDP growth. They are neither tasked with a mandate to do so, nor do they have intentions of driving credit and GDP growth to levels recorded prior to the global financial crisis. However, in pursuing their primary mandate they are expected to not unduly exert negative effects on GDP growth. Credit and banking sector developments play an important role in the regulatory, supervisory and financial stability assessment as well as in the deliberations on the setting of monetary policy.

18.3 What Is an Unexpected Positive Credit Loss Provisioning Shock and Its Expected Impact on Credit and the Real Economy?

This chapter defines and illustrates the effects of a loan provisioning shock to various economic variables. Pool et al. (2015) show that credit risk impacts credit growth through two channels. If the realized number of credit defaults exceeds the expected defaults this would lead to reduced credit due to expected decreases in future interest rate earnings. In addition, banks update their beliefs through raising risk premiums and the anticipated loss weakens their capital. This weakening of bank capital exerts upward pressure on lending rates.

The chapter shows the dynamics of the effects of a credit provision shock by introducing and illustrating the dynamic path of selected variables in Fig. 18.2. Unlike Pool et al. (2015), Fig. 18.2 distinguishes

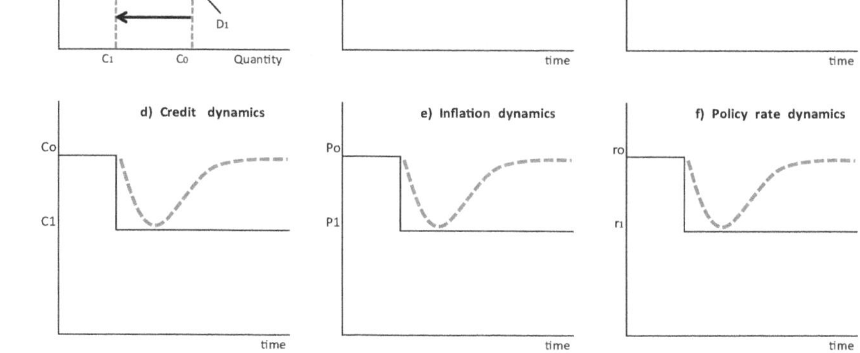

Fig. 18.2 Dynamics of credit loss provisioning shock (*Source*: Author's drawing)

between an impulse showing a quick adjustment and those showing a slow adjustment and the feedback effects.

Fig. 18.2 extends the framework in Pool et al. (2015) and shows the effects of a positive credit provisioning shock. The positive credit loss provisioning shock is due to an increase in the banks' expectation of a reduced credit repayment rate. What do banks do to credit extension in light of this shock? In order to minimize the expected loss, banks will reduce credit supply, shifting the supply curve from S_0 to S_1. This leads to an increase in the lending rate from i_0 to i_1 as shown in Fig. 18.2a, b. Credit extension contracts following an increase in credit loss provisioning. The increased lending rate should reduce economic growth in part (d) as reduced credit lowers aggregate demand. In addition, reduced aggregate demand lowers the inflation rate in Fig. 18.2e. Weak credit growth affects cash available for consumption and purchases of various goods.

Is there a feedback effect? Reduced economic growth lowers credit demand and shifts the credit demand curve in Fig. 18.2a from D_0 to D_1. What should monetary policy do when faced with such a situation? This depends on whether the policymakers are guided by some form of a Taylor rule in adjusting policy rates, such that a wider negative output gap and lower inflation will lead to a reduced policy rate following a positive provisioning shock.

Whether the lending rates decline or rise, this depends on the elasticities of the credit supply and demand. However, credit quantities will decline in either circumstance. The solid continuous lines show a quick adjustment that is accompanied by permanent effects, which do not return to pre-shock levels following a permanent positive provisioning shock. However, if the shock is temporarily characterized by rigidities, the effects on the variables will exhibit responses shown by the dotted line in each panel in Fig. 18.2.

18.4 Stylized Facts

The preliminary analysis begins by looking at the bilateral relationships between annual credit provisions changes and real economic variables using data spanning 1995Q1–2014Q4. Fig. 18.3 shows the trends and

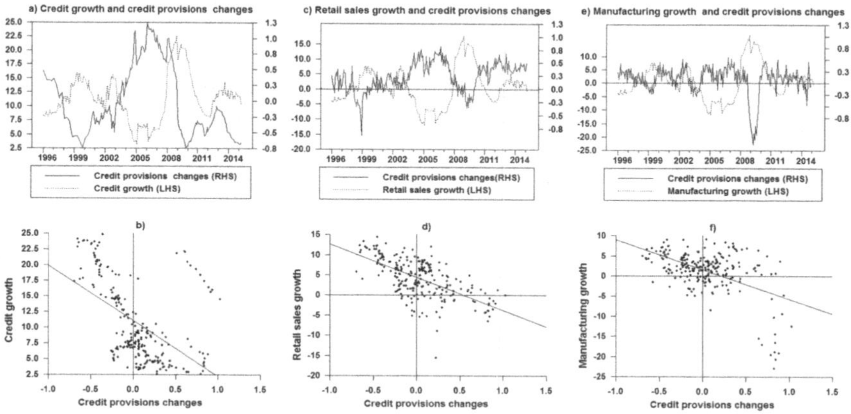

Fig. 18.3 Trend analysis and scatter plots (*Source*: South African Reserve Bank and authors' calculations)

scatter plots to determine the relationships. Trend analysis reveals an inverse relationship between economic activity and changes in credit provisions. That is increases (decreases) in credit growth, retail sales growth and manufacturing production growth are accompanied by lower (higher) changes in credit provisions in parts in Fig. 18.3a, c, e. The scatter plots in Fig. 18.3b, d, f show a negative relationship, which suggests that increases in credit loss provisions are detrimental to credit growth, retail sales growth and manufacturing production growth.

In relation to the effects of macro-prudential tools and their effects on cyclicality between GDP and credit growth, international evidence has shown that macro-prudential instruments seem to have been effective in reducing the correlation between credit and GDP growth. Literature indicates that in countries where ceilings on credit growth or dynamic provisioning were introduced, the correlation between credit growth and GDP growth became negative. On the other hand, countries where caps on loan to value, debt to income and reserve requirements were introduced, the correlation became positive and much smaller relative to countries without (Columba 2011).

The negative bilateral cross correlations in Fig. 18.4a reveal that elevated levels of credit provisions lead to a reduction in both credit growth and retail sales growth. However, the correlation remains negative throughout all horizons with regards to credit growth. The elevated credit provisions are positively associated with rising interest rate margins on loans and advances as well those on installments sales in part (b).

18.5 How Well Does the Estimated Model Capture the Established Responses of Selected Variables in Literature?

The chapter estimates a five variable vector autoregression (VAR) model using monthly (M) data spanning 1995M1–2015M3. The variables are annual credit provisions changes, indicators of real economic activity proxied by manufacturing production and retail sales growth, inflation, the repo rate and credit growth. The model is estimated using variables in this sequence. This suggests that credit provision is affected contemporaneously by provisioning shocks and all other shocks have an impact after one period. Pool et al. (2015) suggest this assumption reflects backward-looking provisioning behavior.

In addition, the ordering suggests that economic activity growth leads to a positive output gap and that this responds to credit provisions developments. Inflation is placed third, indicating it is contemporaneously affected by provisioning and economic activity. This is in line with the assumption that prices respond very sluggishly to shocks in other variables, as in Christiano et al. (1999) and other studies. The repo rate is placed fourth and is affected by provisioning, economic activity and inflation. Credit is placed last as we assume that it is affected by credit provisioning, economic activity, inflation and policy rates. This is consistent with banks assessing the state of the economy to determine credit supply.

Fig. 18.5 shows the selected impulse responses. The positive repo rate shock significantly depresses retail sales growth in Fig. 18.5a. In Fig. 18.5f there is an upward but insignificant pressure on annual credit provisions

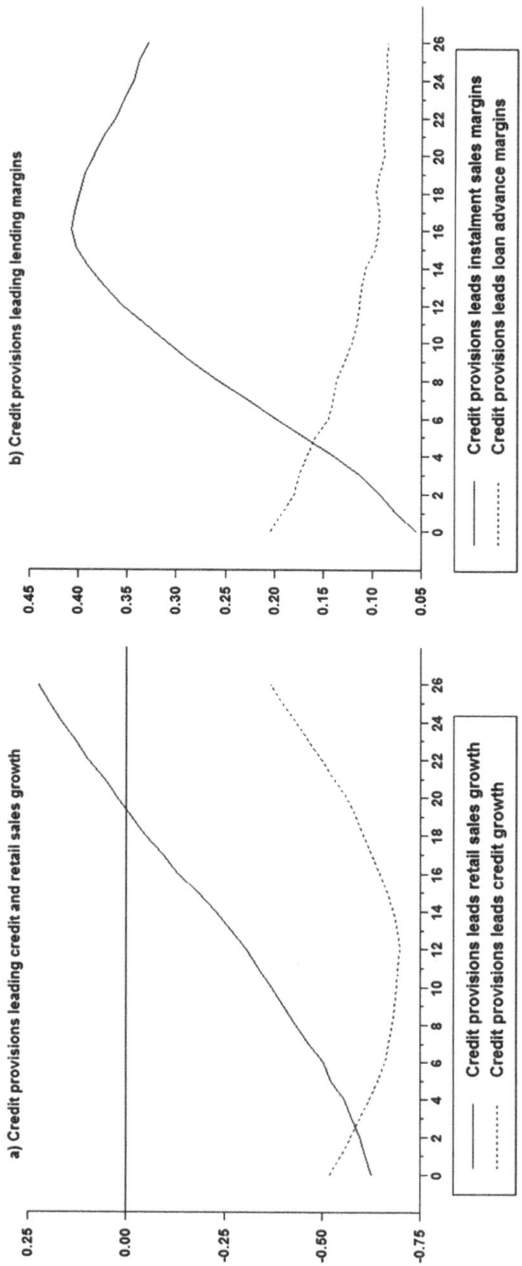

Fig. 18.4 Cross correlations (*Source*: Authors' calculations)

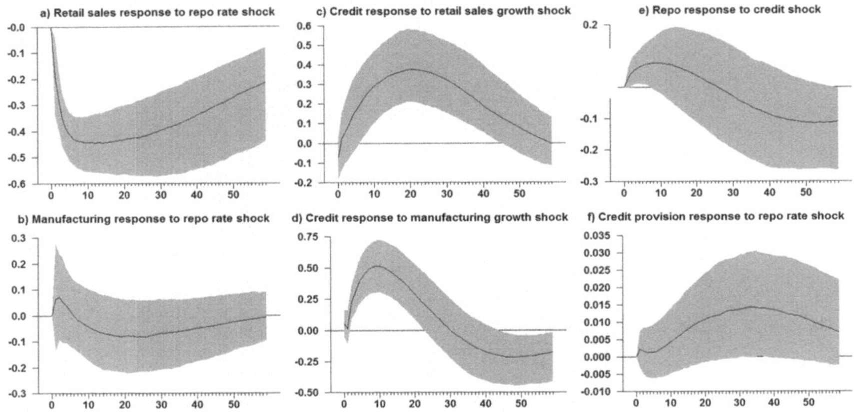

Fig. 18.5 Selected impulse responses (*Source*: Authors' calculations)

from an unexpected repo rate shock. The repo rate rises significantly in a transitory way in response to unexpected credit growth in Fig. 18.5e.

Evidence indicates that both unexpected positive manufacturing production and retail sales growth shocks raise credit growth in Fig. 18.5c, d but the peak in credit growth does not exceed 0.5 percentage points. Based on these responses, evidence indicates that the model captures some of the stylized effects reported in the literature.

18.5.1 What Are the Effects of Credit Provisioning on the Real Economy?

As stated earlier, the focus is not identifying the determinants of credit loss provisioning or income smoothing. Rather, the focus is in assessing the effects of credit loss provisions on the macroeconomy. Fig. 18.6 shows the responses to a positive one-standard deviation credit provisions shock. A credit loss provisions shock leads to a reduction in credit growth and retail sales growth in parts Fig. 18.6a, c, respectively. Retail sales growth declines for nearly 15 months and credit growth remains significantly depressed for nearly 40 months. This is a first result which confirms that credit loss provisions impact business cycle fluctuations.

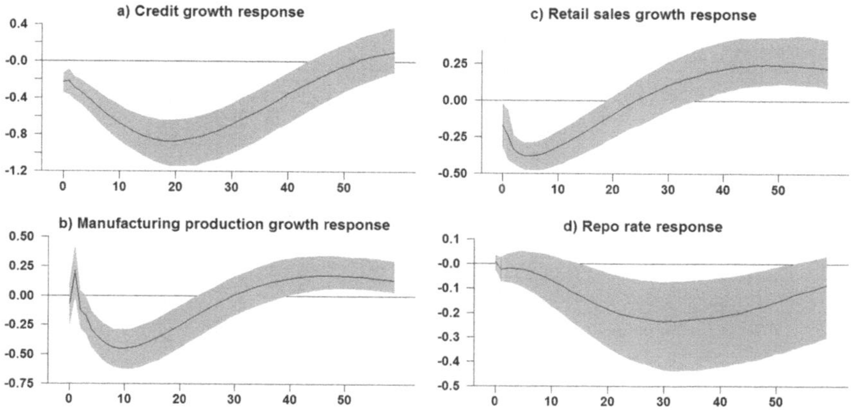

Fig. 18.6 Responses to unexpected credit provisions shocks (*Source*: Authors' calculations)

Fig. 18.5b shows that manufacturing growth significantly declines for nearly 25 months. These responses are consistent with the trajectories shown in Fig. 18.3. How does monetary policy respond under these circumstances? Fig. 18.6d shows that the repo rate is lowered significantly after 15 months and returns to pre-shock levels at around 48 months.

Does it mean all credit categories react in the same way? Fig. 18.7 shows the effects of positive credit provisions shocks on various total credit and sector categories. Fig. 18.7a, b show that sector categories decline but reach peaks in different periods. In Fig. 18.7a the total credit declines move relative to corporate and household credit.[4]

18.5.2 To What Extent Does the Annual Change in Credit Provisions Influence the Business Cycle?

Fig. 18.8 depicts the contributions of annual credit provisions changes to the evolution of retail sales growth, manufacturing production growth and credit growth from January 2000 to February 2015. Fig. 18.8 plots

[4] The significance of these responses to one positive standard deviation credit provisioning shock is shown in Fig. A.18.1.

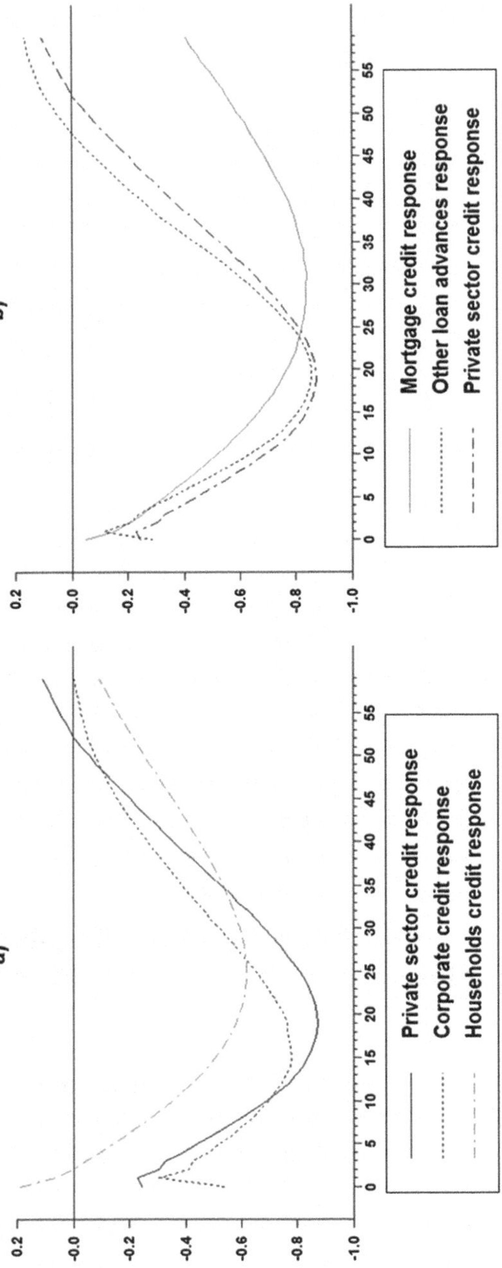

Fig. 18.7 Reactions of total and sector categories of credit to a positive credit provisions shock (*Source:* Authors' calculations)

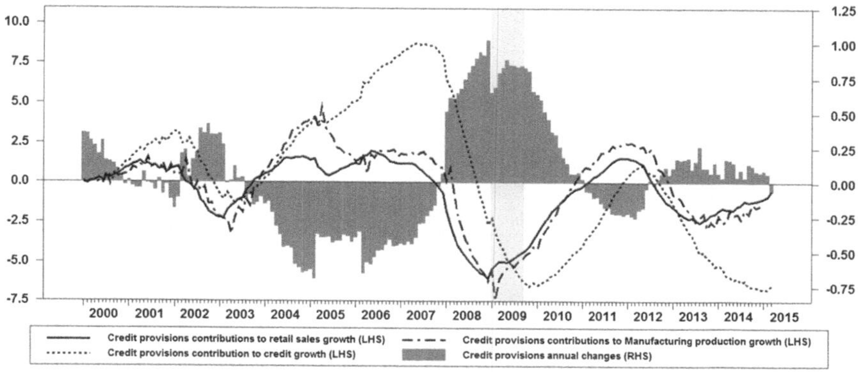

Fig. 18.8 Credit provision contributions to real economic activity (*Source*: Authors' calculations)

together the contributions of credit provisions to retail sales growth and manufacturing production growth to visualize the interactions in the results. This shows what happens to contributions when annual credit provision changes are negative and when these changes are positive.

Evidence indicates a negative relationship between credit provisions contributions and real economic changes. When annual credit provisions are negative (decline), proxies for real economic activity growth rise and they slowdown when annual credit provisions changes are positive (increase). In addition, the large credit growth pre-2008 was linked to negative (decline) changes in annual credit provision changes. This suggests that elevated levels of annual credit provisions changes since 2008 have been a drag on proxies for real economic activity. Therefore, evidence indicates that credit provisions influence business cycle fluctuations. In addition, it tends to accentuate the adverse effects during the recession, as shown by light grey shaded portion in the Fig. 18.9. The positive changes since 2012 are also contributing to low levels of proxies for real economic activity.

What about credit and its sector categories? Do the effects of credit provisions differ based on the sector category of credit? Figs. 18.9 and 18.10 show the actual and counterfactual credit growth for each component. In addition, both figs plot the contributions of annual credit provisions changes and credit provisions changes. Both Figs. 18.9 and 18.10

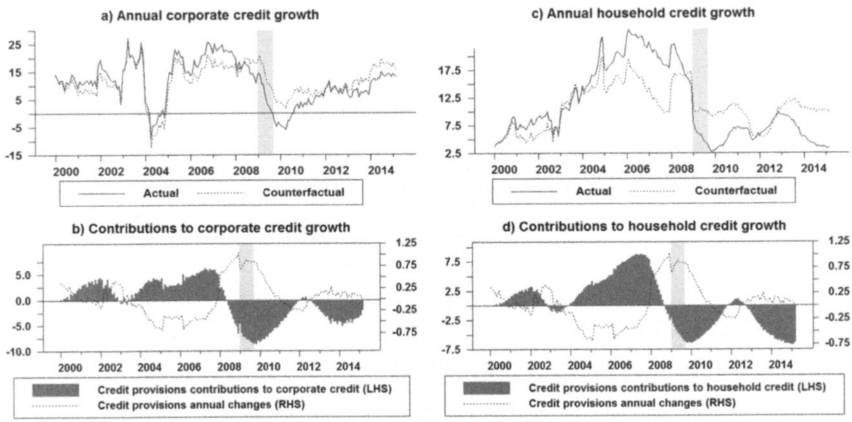

Fig. 18.9 Actual and counterfactual household and corporate credit growth and contributions from changes in credit provisions (*Note*: The contributions are percentage points. *Source*: Authors' calculations)

exhibit similar patterns as those found between aggregate credit growth and annual credit provisions changes.

Evidence indicates that the severely protracted decline in credit growth after 2007 coincided with a prolonged rise in changes in credit provisions. This finding is robust to all credit categories. The counterfactual

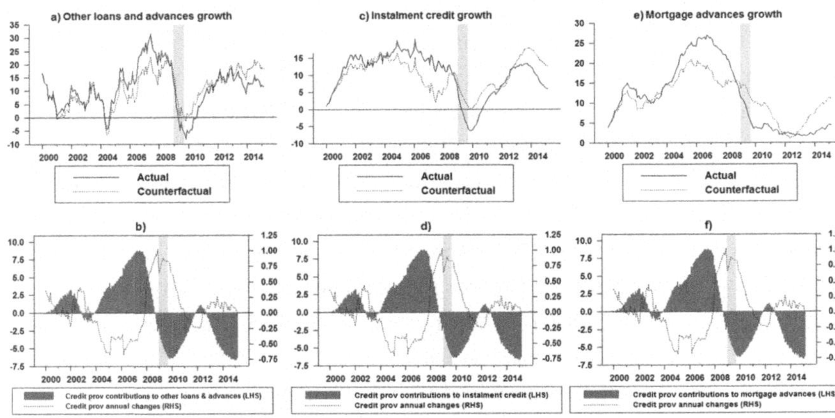

Fig. 18.10 Actual and counterfactual credit growth and contributions from changes in credit provisions (*Note*: The contributions are percentage point. *Source*: Authors' calculations)

scenarios show that indeed the provisions for loan losses have been a drag on credit growth, possibly pointing to the role of the deterioration in the balance sheets of households and firms.

It is important to show how the household and corporate credit growth all impacted by annual changes in credit provisions shock. Fig. 18.11 shows a comparison of credit provisions contributions to the household and corporate credit categories. Thus, between 2003 and 2009, household credit growth was mostly supported by a slowdown (negative) in annual credit provisions changes, more than by corporate credit growth. However, during the recession in 2009, corporate credit growth declined more than household credit growth, suggesting that highly elevated changes in credit provisions were very detrimental to credit extension to the corporate. The household sector growth is possibly explained by the increase in unsecured lending that dominated lending to households during this period.

18.5.3 What Does Nonlinearity in the Credit Loss Provisioning Mean for Economic Activity and Credit Growth Shock?

Extensive recent literature shows that the effects of macro-prudential tools vary depending on a tool being used during a particular phase of the finan-

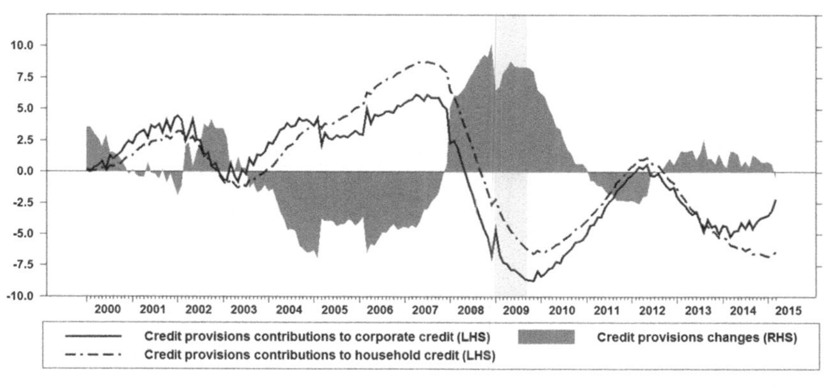

Fig. 18.11 Comparisons of contributions of changes in credit provisions to corporate and household credit growth (*Note*: These are percentage contributions. *Source*: Authors' calculations)

cial and economic cycle. As shown in the earlier chapters, there are different approaches to determining nonlinearity and threshold values. The Tsay arranged test is used in this section to investigate the presence of nonlinearity in annual changes in credit provisions. The test concluded that existence of a threshold cannot be rejected. However, this test did not determine the value of threshold. Thereafter, the Hansen test is used to establish a threshold of 0.36 percentage points of annual credit provision change.

To further ascertain the prior conclusion, the chapter applied the smooth transition model test for nonlinearity. The test rejected the linear model in favor of the nonlinear model but failed to establish the ideal model to estimate the impact of the annual credit provisions threshold. Hence, this model is not used in this chapter.

The annual changes in provisions are shown in Fig. 18.12. The periods in which the level of provisions exceeds the identified threshold are shown in the light shaded area. Hence, periods that exceed 0.36 percentage points denote high a credit provisioning regime and those that lie below show a low regime. It is visible that the high provisions regime was the longest between 2008 and 2009 relative to other periods in the late 1990s and early 2000s.

The trends of the provisions over the grey shaded areas indeed show that there has been high procyclicality between this macro-prudential tool

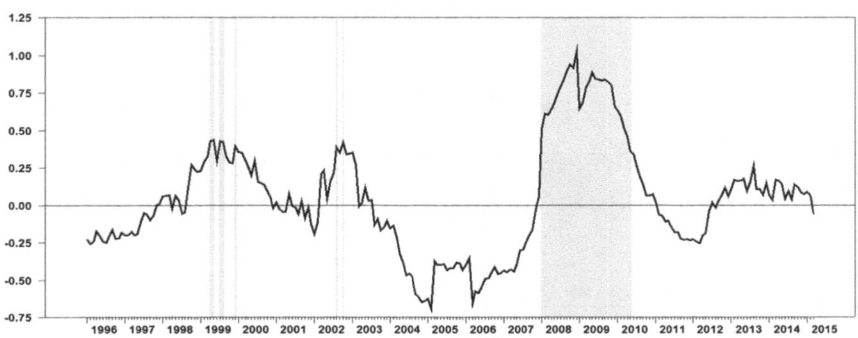

Fig. 18.12 Annual changes in specific credit provisions (*Note*: *Shaded areas* denote the periods which exceed 0.36 percentage points. *Source*: Authors' calculations)

and the business cycles prior to 2012. This has been reduced post-2012, as provisions have been countercyclical, although still below the threshold.

18.5.4 Do Nonlinear Effects Matter?

This section estimates a VAR model with three variables to assess the effects of nonlinearity of unexpected positive credit provisions shock using a threshold of annual change of 0.36 percent in credit provision.

What do the results reveal about how banks use the economic outlook? Fig. 18.13b, c show the responses of annual credit provisions changes to unexpected real economic activity shock in the form of positive retail sales and credit growth shocks. However, Fig. 18.13b shows that an improved outlook in the form of increased retail sales lowers credit provisions more in the low credit provisioning regime than in the higher credit provisioning regime.

Fig. 18.13c shows that banks decrease provisioning when credit extension is in the low credit provisions regime, which coincides with improved economic outlook. In contrast, banks increase provision in the higher credit loss regime which often coincides with periods of economic slowdown. This suggests that during upswings banks take on more risk by building up relatively low provisions while in downswings banks build up more loan loss provisions.

This evidence is supported by the relationships between retail sales growth and credit provisions conditioned on the threshold of credit provisions in Fig. 18.14a. Fig. 18.14b shows the relationships between credit growth and credit provisions, considering the threshold of credit provisions.

Fig. 18.15 compares the proportions of fluctuations explained by selected variables depending on the credit provision threshold. Fig. 18.15a, b shows that a credit provisions shock explains more movements in credit and retail sales growth over all horizons in the higher credit provisions regime than in the lower regime. This confirms why the credit growth declines more significantly in the higher credit regime than in the lower credit provisions regime.

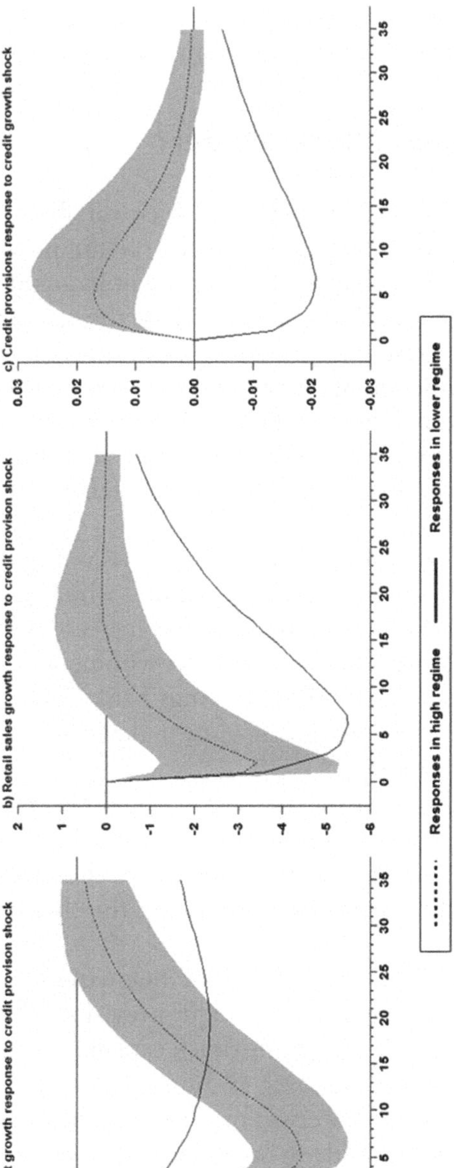

Fig. 18.13 Effects of nonlinearity in credit provisions shock (*Note*: The models consist of the following variables: annual credit provisions changes, annual retail sales growth and annual credit growth. These are percentage contributions. *Source*: Authors' calculations)

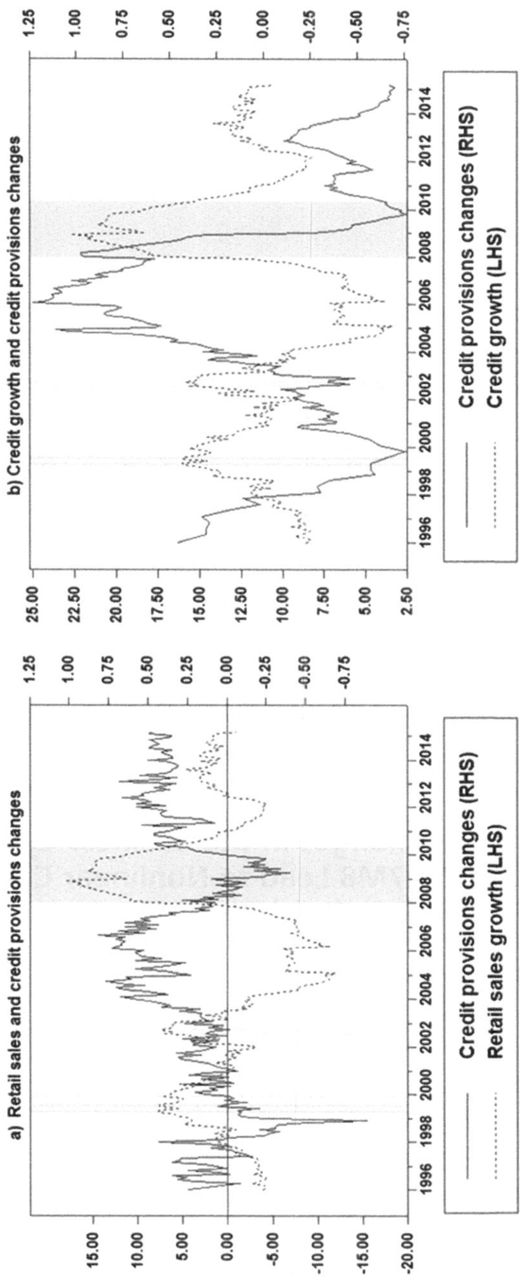

Fig. 18.14 Measures of economic activity, credit provisions and thresholds (*Source*: Authors' calculations)

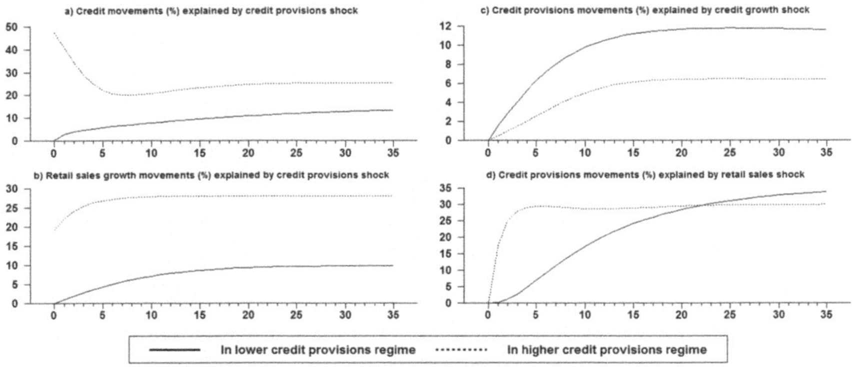

Fig. 18.15 Fluctuations in various variables (*Source*: Authors' calculations)

Fig. 18.15d shows that fluctuations in credit provisions are induced by retail sales in higher credit provision in the first four months and thereafter the fluctuations converge to 30 percent. This explains why credit provision in the higher credit provisions regime decline and reach a peak decline in the third month after the shocks and thereafter quickly return to pre-shock levels. Fig. 18.15c shows that credit growth explains higher fluctuations in the low credit provisions regime. This supports observations that during periods of positive economic outlook banks take on more risk by building up relatively low provisions.

18.5.5 Did the Changes in the Business Cycle After 2007M8 Lead to Nonlinear Credit Provisioning Shocks Effects?

This section looks further at the fluctuations explained by credit provisions shock and retails sales shock and shows the differences in the impulse responses in the 2007M8–2015M3 and 1995–2007M7 periods. It also determines the effects of credit provisioning shocks on credit growth and retails sales growth and shows whether there are any differential effects between the period before and after the financial crisis post-2007.

Fig. 18.16a shows that positive provisioning shock had severe depressing effects on credit growth between 2007M8–2015M3 relative to

1995–2007M7 periods. This suggests that a positive provisioning shock has more adverse effects on credit growth during periods characterized by economic instability and macroeconomic uncertainties.

Similarly, in Fig. 18.16 credit provisions tend to decline much more when retail sales growth increased prior to the 2007M7 period, which was characterized by stable economic growth and no recession. This suggests an improved outlook made banks engage in risk provisions and that they under-provisioned for credit losses. Fig. 18.16b shows that the retail sales shock is elevated and slightly more persistent in 1995–2007M7 than in 2007M8–2015M3. These effects are statistically different as they are not within the same error bands.

It appears in Fig. 18.17 that banks decreased provisioning when retail sales growth increases as an indicator of improved economic outlook during 1995–2007M7 relative to 2007M8–2015M3 period. This suggests that during upswings banks take on more risk by building up relatively low provisions whereas in downswings banks build up more credit loss provisions.

Fig. 18.18 looks at the fluctuations in credit growth induced by provisions shocks in 1995–2007M7 and 2007M8–2015M3. Provisions shocks induce more variations after 11 months in the credit growth in 2007M8–2015M3 relative to 1995–2007M7.

This supports the fact that the pronounced decline in credit growth was related to elevated provision between 2007M8 and 2015M3, as shown in Fig. 18.18. In addition, provisions shocks induced more fluctuations in the retail sales growth in 1995–2007M7, consistent with a significant decline in provisions due to positive retail sales.

18.5.6 Counterfactual Analysis

The analysis concludes by assessing the interaction between credit provisions and the repo rate using a counterfactual analysis similar to that explained in earlier chapters. These are based on the VAR described above. The counterfactual responses refer to responses when the repo rate is shut off in the credit provisions equations. The amplification effect is measured by the gap between actual and counterfactual responses.

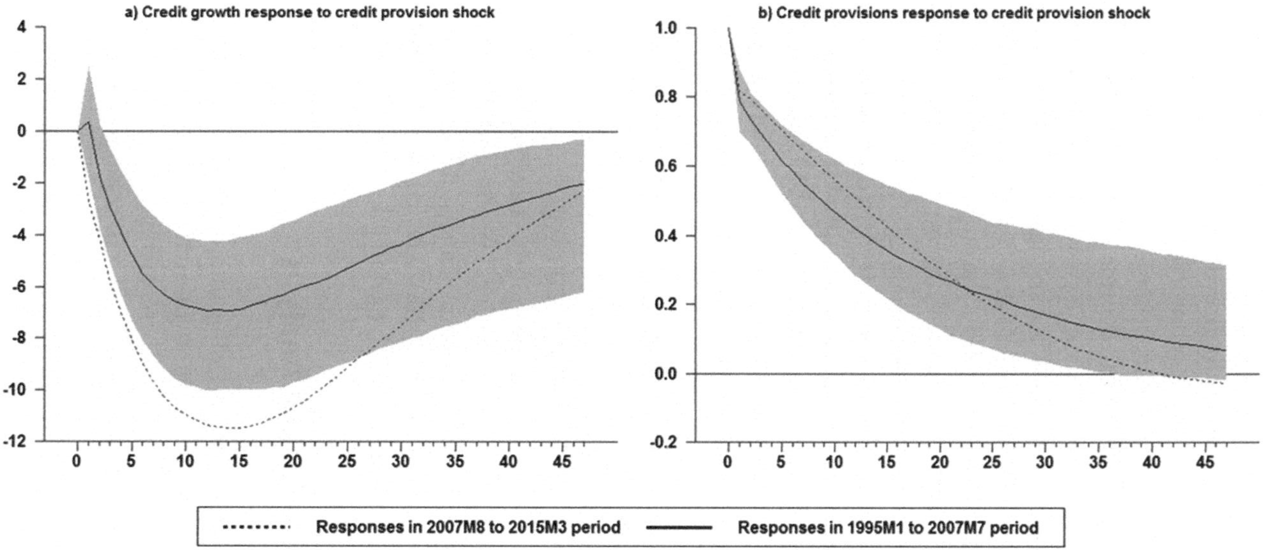

Fig. 18.16 Effects of provisions shocks in 2007M8–2015M3 and 1995–2007M7 (*Note*: The contributions are percentage points. *Source*: Authors' calculations)

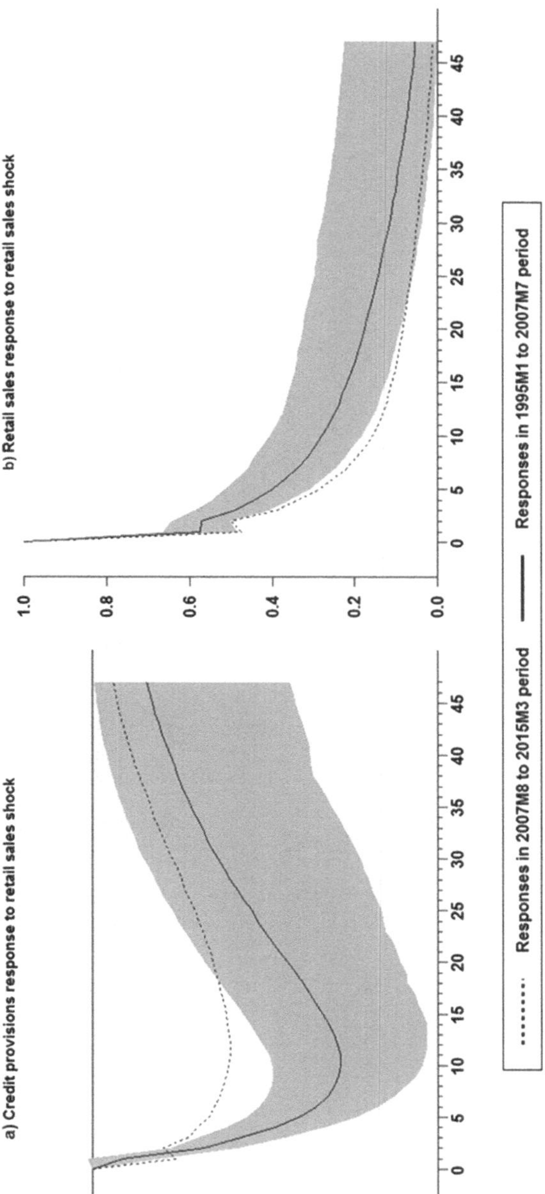

Fig. 18.17 Effects of retail sales growth shocks in 2007M8–2015M3 and 1995–2007M7 (*Note*: The contributions are percentages. *Source*: Authors' calculations)

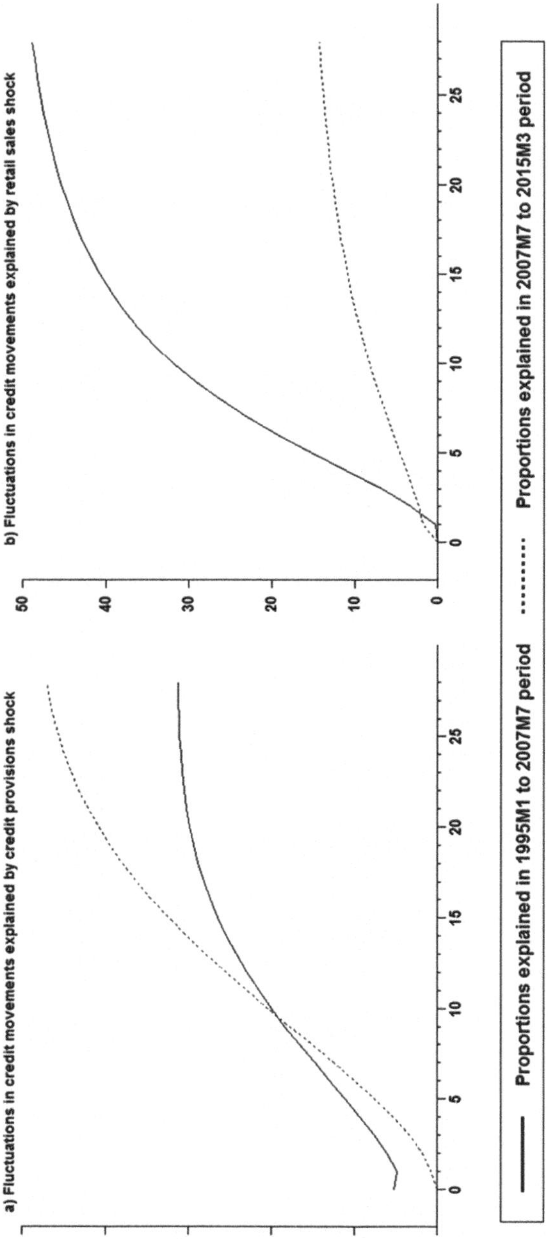

Fig. 18.18 Fluctuations due to selected shocks in 1995–2007M7 and 2007M8–2015M3 periods (*Source*: Authors' calculations)

So, does the repo rate magnify or worsen the credit growth responses to credit provisions shocks? The positive credit provisions shocks in Fig. 18.19 depress credit growth and loans and advances growth more when the repo rate is not shut off than when it is shut off. This indicates that elevated repo rate magnitudes lead to worsening of credit contraction to positive credit provisions shock.

Are the responses of the repo rate to impact inflation influenced by credit provisions and financial regulatory policy uncertainty (FRPU)? The FRPU replaced credit provisions variables in the model described above. The amplifications and dampening effects are shown by the gap between the actual and counterfactual repo rate responses in Fig. 18.20. Evidence indicates that the repo rate would be higher when credit provisions and FRPU are shut off in the model. This suggests that elevated credit provisions and FRPU respectively make the repo rate rise less aggressively compared to when these are not included.

18.6 Conclusion and Policy Implications

The chapter set out to establish the effects of provisions as a macro-prudential tool on the business cycle and their interaction with the policy rate. We found that credit loss provisions play an important role in influencing business cycle fluctuations. We established that there is a procyclical relationship between provisions, credit growth and the proxies of real economic activity.

A similar pattern of inverse relationships and responses is found when using the provisions threshold to distinguish between high and low provisions regimes. These results imply that banks take up more risk during upswings and provide less. In contrast, banks increase provisions during growth downswings. Historical decompositions confirm that this backward-looking approach to provisions amplifies fluctuations in credit growth, retail sales and manufacturing production.

The findings in this chapter show that this provisions model has adverse real economic effects as it counteracts the accommodative effects of monetary policy actions during downturns and recessions. However, the results show that since 2012 provisions have been countercyclical

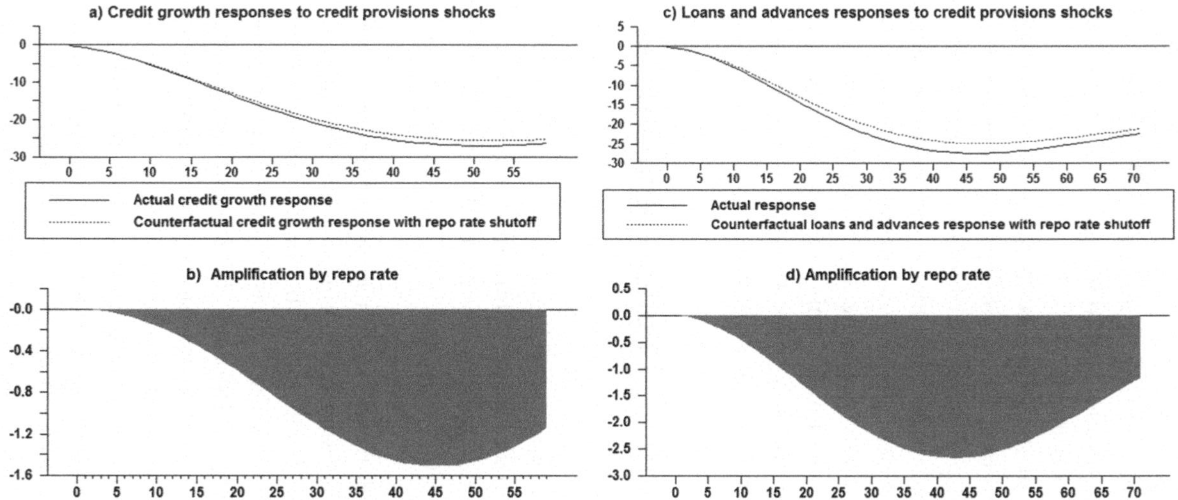

Fig. 18.19 Cumulative responses of credit growth to positive credit provision shock and amplification by repo rate (*Source*: Authors' calculations)

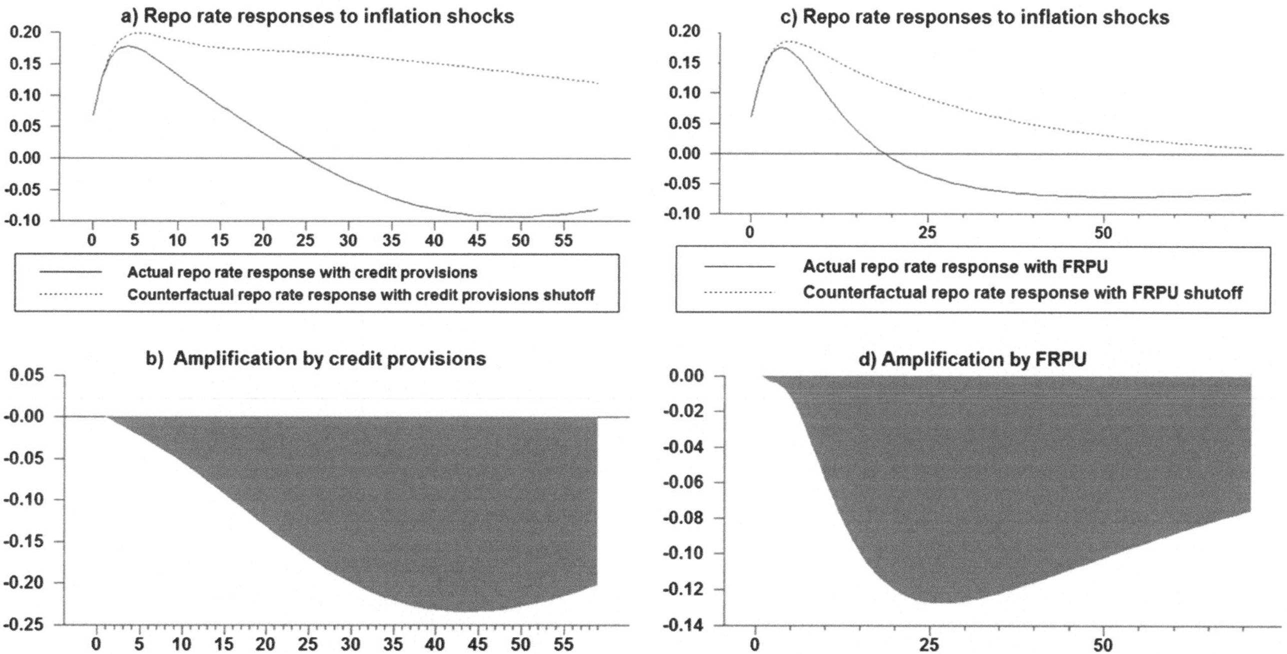

Fig. 18.20 Repo rate responses to positive inflation shocks and amplifications by credit provisions and FRPU (*Source*: Authors' calculations)

and a drag on credit and economic activity. They have counteracted the effects of accommodative monetary policy to some degree, as shown by the counterfactual scenarios.

The policy implication is that the provisions support tight monetary policy as they restrain credit growth. Furthermore, the non-performing loans remain fairly elevated by historical standards possibly explaining the reluctance to lend. Trends observed in other macro-prudential tools also pull in the same tightening direction as provisions.

The positive credit provisions shock depresses credit growth and loans and advances growth more when the repo rate is not shut off than when it is shut off. This indicates that elevated repo rate magnitudes lead to worsening of credit contraction to positive credit provisions shock. Evidence implies that the repo rate would rise much more in response to positive inflation shocks when credit provisions and FRPU variables are shut off in the model than when allowed to operate in the model. This suggests that elevated credit provisions and FRPU respectively make the repo rate rise less aggressively compared to when these are not included. This evidence suggests that policymakers should consider the interaction of these policy tools in the policy decision-making process.

Summary of Findings

- Evidence indicates that credit loss provisions play an important role in influencing business cycle fluctuations.
- An unexpected increase in provisions significantly lowers credit growth, retail sales and manufacturing production growth; whereas, banks decrease provisions when the economic outlook is positive, leading to growth in credit.
- There is a procyclical relationship between provisions, credit growth and the proxies of real economic activity. Banks take up more risk during upswings and provide less.
- Banks increase provisions during growth downswings.
- Historical decompositions confirm backward looking approach to provisions amplifies fluctuations in credit growth, retail sales and manufacturing production.

- The backward-looking approach to provisions model has adverse real economic effects as it counteracts the accommodative effects of monetary policy actions during downturns and recessions.
- Elevated provisions counteracted the effects of accommodative monetary policy to some degree as shown by the counterfactual scenarios

Appendix

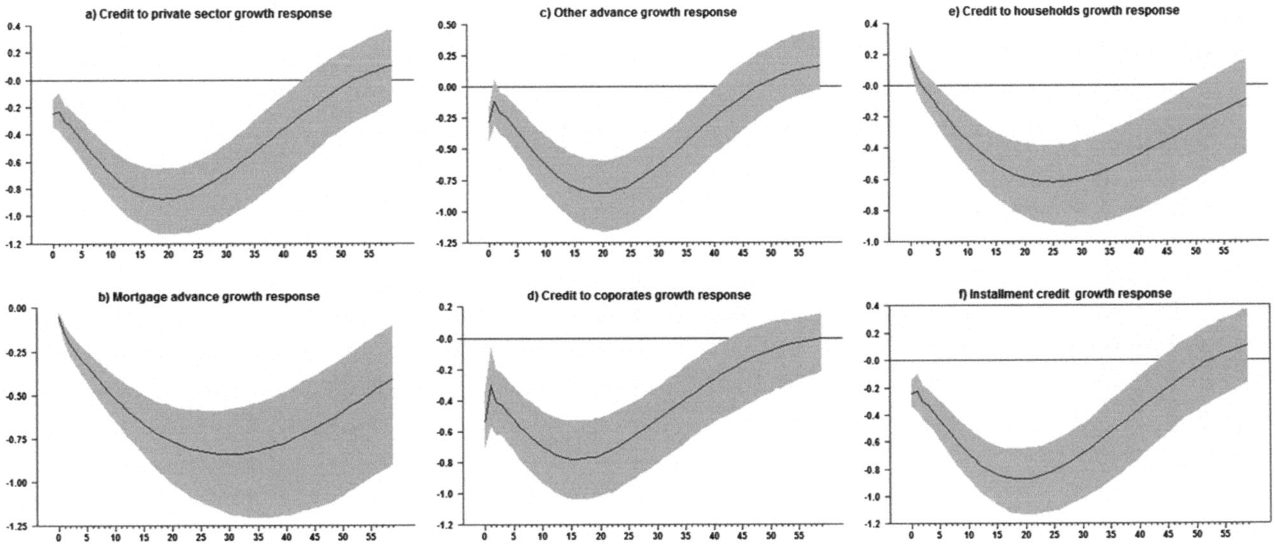

Fig. A.18.1 Positive annual credit provisions shocks and growth in the various credit categories (*Source*: Authors' calculations)

19

The National Credit Act, Monetary Policy and Credit Growth

Learning Objectives

- Analyze how the National Credit Act (NCA) propagates the effects of monetary policy on credit and output
- Determine the interaction and effectiveness of monetary policy and the NCA as part of the macro-prudential toolkit
- Determine whether there is an economic case for these tools to be coordinated
- Establish the degree to which the NCA and the repo rate reinforce each other

19.1 Introduction

Central bank mandates explicitly attend to financial stability as well as price stability. Studies show that the policy rate is a poor tool to deal with excess leverage, risk taking or the apparent deviations of asset prices from fundamentals. Furthermore, the policy rate is a blunt tool. A higher policy rate does reduce some excessively high asset prices but it comes at a cost of a larger output gap (IMF 2013). In addition, the literature

N. Gumata, E. Ndou, *Bank Credit Extension and Real Economic Activity in South Africa*, DOI 10.1007/978-3-319-43551-0_19

shows that as there is no single tool that influences all financial behavior and stability consistently, a variety of tools is used. In the banking sector, tools range from countercyclical capital buffers, dynamic provisioning, reserve requirements and levies on short-term borrowing. Whereas in the household sector, loan-to-value (LTV) caps for mortgage loans and debt-to-income (DTI) limits or lending standards are employed. It is, however, also true that none of these tools is a silver bullet. All can be circumvented to some degree. This chapter introduces a comprehensive coverage of active macro-prudential tools in South Africa.

The chapter starts with the analysis of the National Credit Act (NCA). To be specific, this chapter asks: Does the National Credit Act propagate the effects of monetary policy on credit and output? Thus, the chapter explores the interaction and effectiveness of monetary policy and the NCA as part of the macro-prudential toolkit. This is motivated by the fact that the repurchase rate and the NCA at a given point interact with each other to the extent that they have a common effect on the cost and availability of credit. These policy tools affect lending standards and conditions for the supply and demand of credit. The chapter conducts a counterfactual analysis to show the reinforcing abilities via determining the size of amplifications.

The NCA affects the loan supply and lending standards. On the other hand, the repurchase rate has effects on both the demand and supply of credit. It is possible that as these tools interact they neutralize or propagate each other's shocks, as well as external ones. Therefore, the analysis will reveal if there is an economic case for these tools to be coordinated. The data will reveal the relationship between the two instruments in three ways. First, the directions of the responses of the real variables to these tools are determined. Second, we investigate the extent to which these tools react to each other and not only on real variables. Third, we determine the historical contributions of these tools to the evolution of credit. In a nutshell, what are the properties and characteristics of these tools over time? Did the contributions of these tools diverge from (neutralize) each other or move in the same direction (propagate) each other.

Based on the results and the direction of the responses of the affected variables, if the reaction of these variables is similar, this may require policymakers to make decisions on how these tools can be coordinated so as to minimize the adverse effects which are exacerbated when the other policy tool is not taken into account when making a policy decision. Related to the facts raised above, Blanchard et al. (2010) argue that financial regulation is not macroeconomically neutral and that macro-prudential policies and tools affect the level of output and prices, constraining borrowing and expenditure and ultimately overall output. The effects vary with each particular macro-prudential tool being used, as well as the stage of the financial and economic cycle (IMF 2013).

The interactions of these tools can be mutually reinforcing and amplify each other's effects on the financial sector, real economy and the business cycle, hence their effects and interactions warrant appropriate investigation. In this context, the chapter adopts the Tovar et al. (2012) approach, and uses the NCA as a macro-prudential tool to deal with credit conditions, but its effects are not only restricted to credit as they can spill-over into economic activity. The NCA was passed into legislation in 2005 and implemented in June 2007.[1] Despite the NCA having been implemented for some time now, empirically little is known about this macro-prudential tool's effectiveness and how it interacts with monetary policy. It is therefore important to assess the macroeconomic performance of these instruments.

19.2 Effects of Unexpected Policy Shocks on Economic Activity

Prior to identifying the characteristics related to the substitutability or complementarity between the NCA and the repo rate, the analysis begins by demonstrating whether both policy tools exert similar effects on selected macro-variables. In so doing, the analysis examines their effects on credit extension and economic activity, given that, for instance, an unexpected positive (increase) monetary policy shock may have its effects

[1] For further information and details on the Financial Sector Charter that predates the implementation of the NCA and on the NCA see http://www.banking.org.za/index.php/consumer-centre/national-credit-act and http://www.banking.org.za/index.php/consumer-centre/financial-sector-charter-code/

exacerbated by the NCA if these reinforce each other, and the NCA will magnify the policy rate effects in the same direction and lead to a greater impact on financial and real variables.[2]

The distinction of the response to unexpected policy shocks is crucial in the analysis of the interaction of monetary policy and macro-prudential tools. This chapter applies a methodology which enables us to identify and map the credit growth and economic activity trajectories following an unexpected shock on monetary policy and the NCA shock. In addition, this methodology also maps trajectories (impulse responses) of the NCA to monetary policy shocks and vice versa.

The chapter uses a vector autoregression approach (VAR) and the shocks refer to the same unit shocks. The approach imposes an assumption that the macro-prudential policy variable is exogenous. In the estimations, the repo rate is placed second and followed by economic activity and finally, bank credit extension.[3] Specifically, our analysis relies on impulse response functions where the NCA is captured by the dummy variable defined to equal one for the period beginning in June 2007, including later periods, and zero prior to its implementation.[4] The modeling approach enables making conclusions which validate the inferences about the importance of the impact of two shocks by including confidence bands around the trajectories' paths into the future.[5]

The analysis begins by looking at the responses of economic activity measured by manufacturing production.[6] In addition, the analysis examines whether the effects of these two policy shocks differ according to the data sample. To address the criticism that the results may be dependent on and significantly influenced by the start of the sample, we

[2] For example, a 50 basis point change in the repo rate.

[3] A Cholesky decomposition is used. In addition, the results were also evaluated using an alternative ordering of variables. We place the repo rate before the NCA, suggesting the repo rate has contemporaneous impact on the NCA, and not vice versa, and we found the results to be robust. The Generalised Impulse Responses Function (GIRF) is used and the results are also robust.

[4] A cumulative dummy as a dummy for number of months since the implementation of the NCA is used, see Tovar et al. (2012).

[5] The standard errors for the confidence intervals are calculated using Monte Carlo simulations.

[6] Similarly to various other studies, we approximate economic activity by using manufacturing production or industrial production.

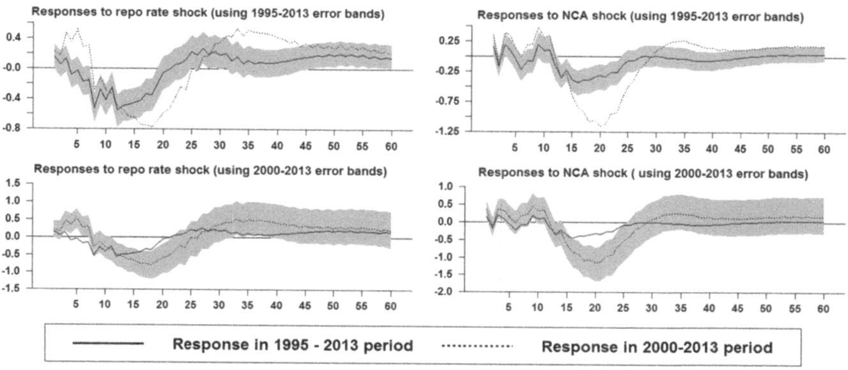

Fig. 19.1 Responses of economic activity to repo rate and NCA shocks (*Source*: Authors' calculations)

report results for two periods: 1995–2013 and 2000–2013. As shown in Fig. 16.1, the trajectories in both graphs confirm that both policy shocks affect economic activity significantly, although with some delay.

To assess the extent to which both policy shocks affect economic growth for the two sample periods, we compare two impulse responses represented by the continuous and dotted lines in Fig. 19.1. Since the dotted lines are not within the continuous lines for some months after the shock, this shows that the repo and NCA impact economic activity differently for the two sample periods. The evidence indicates there are significant differences in the response of economic activity to both shocks, which is influenced by the sample. However, the evidence also indicates that both shocks tend to depress economic activity.

19.3 How Resilient Is Credit Growth to the Repo Rate and NCA Shocks?

The analysis examines the effects of unexpected tightening in the NCA and repo rate on the trajectories of growth in credit extension in the months ahead following the two shocks. The confidence bands are used to interpret the economic significance of economic activity responses.

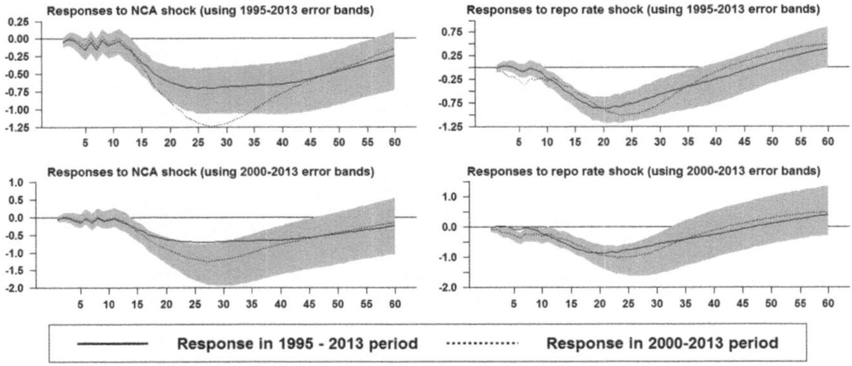

Fig. 19.2 Responses of credit growth to repo rate and NCA shocks (*Source*: Authors' calculations)

The results in Fig. 19.2 show that both the unexpected tightening in the repo rate and the NCA depresses growth in credit. The maximum impact occurs between 20 and 30 months after the shock, and effects depend on the shock and period under review. Evidence indicates that growth in credit declines significantly due to the NCA shock and the maximum impacts significantly vary between the two sample periods. Consistent with economic predictions, growth in credit falls significantly to a positive repo rate shock but the trajectories do not differ between both periods.

The evidence established that both the unexpected repo rate and NCA shocks have depressing effects on economic growth and loan advances growth across different samples. Fig. 19.3 compares the effects of these two shocks simultaneously on economic activity and growth in credit for 2000–2013.

The results show that the NCA shock tends to have a larger depressing effect on growth in credit and economic activity relative to the impact of the repo rate shock. These results concur with much empirical evidence that shows that changes in bank lending standards have significant effects on both credit growth and economic activity (see for instance, Ciccarelli et al. 2010 and 2013).

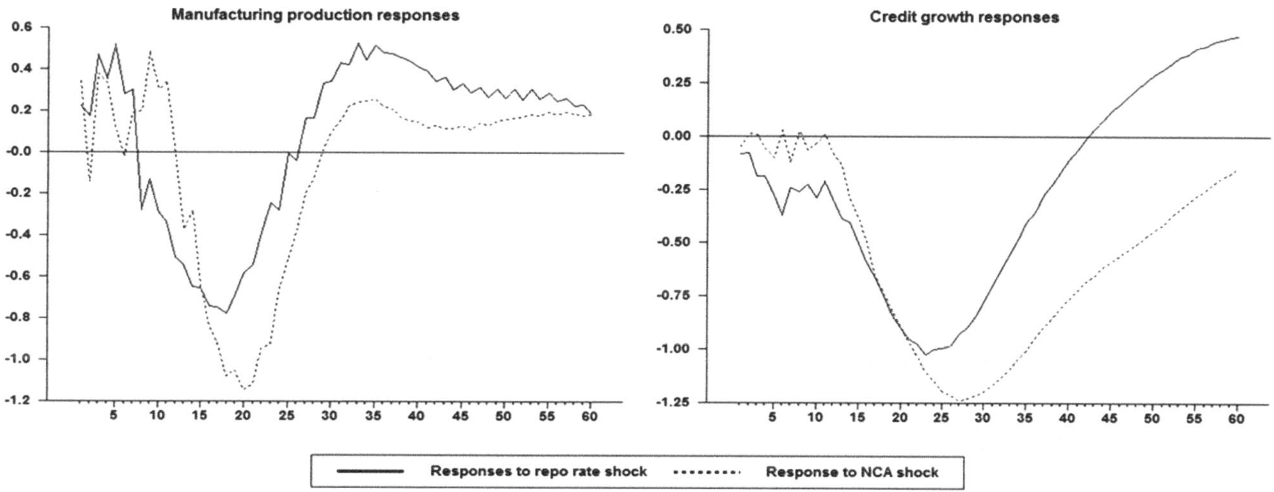

Fig. 19.3 Comparison of the impact of the repo and NCA shocks on economic activity and growth in credit (*Source*: Authors' calculations)

19.4 Is There Evidence That the Monetary Policy and NCA Shocks Complement Each Other?

Evidence shows that the effects of monetary policy and the NCA shocks result in a significant decline of growth in credit and economic activity. So, does a tit-for-tat exchange exist between the NCA and monetary policy shocks? This interaction is assessed using impulse responses. Alternatively, do these tools have complementary effects on the selected financial and real variables? The historical decompositions approach is used to assess for contributions of these policy tools over time, whether they were complementing or conflicting with each other.

Policy-oriented discussions generally assume that both policies will be counter cyclical most of the time, but there have been concerns raised by policymakers and certain commentators as to scenarios that may place the two policies at odds with each other over the business cycle. The results presented in Fig. 19.4 show that the two tools reinforce each other's effects in very modest magnitudes. The reinforcement is significantly pronounced when using data in levels for manufacturing production, a proxy for economic activity, and credit, as shown in Fig. 19.4, rather than with estimations using growth rates (the results are not show here, but can be availed to the reader upon request).

Having established that the repo rate and the NCA shocks tend to reinforce each other, how would growth in credit have evolved in the absence of these shocks? To gain insights with respect to growth in credit, we look at three scenarios based on the decomposition of growth in credit into own contributions and base forecast (i.e. credit growth trends), contributions from the repo rate, contributions from the NCA and lastly contributions from economic activity. Based on these contributions, somehow it is possible to reconstruct growth in credit from 2003 to 2013 as follows: (1) isolate the contributions of the NCA; (2) isolate the contributions of the repo rate; and (3) isolate the contributions of the combined effects of both the repo rate and the NCA.

The effects of the repo rate and the NCA based on the three scenarios above are presented in Fig. 19.5. The results show that the NCA contrib-

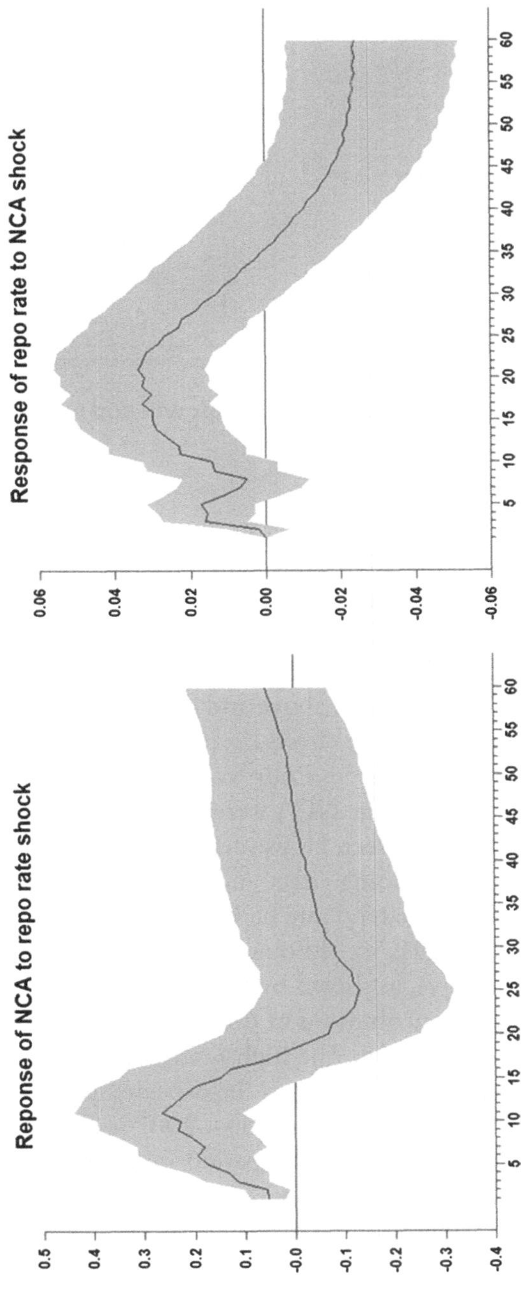

Fig. 19.4 Responses of policy tools to each other in model data levels (*Source*: Authors' calculations)

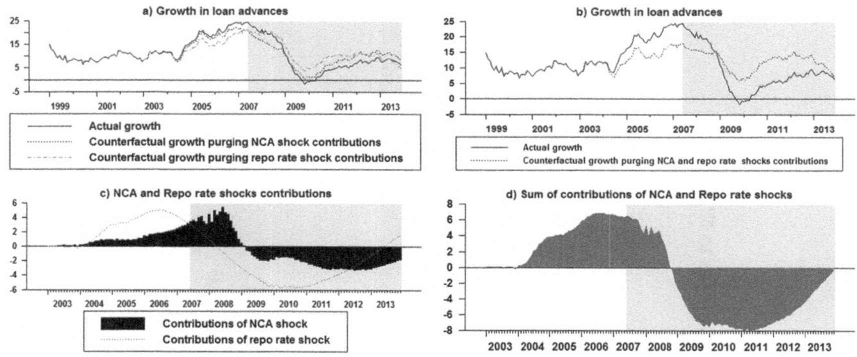

Fig. 19.5 Counterfactual scenarios of credit growth and policy contributions (*Source*: Authors' calculations)

utes positively until a few months after its implementation in 2007. This probably indicates the much-reported and anecdotal evidence pointing to the role of front-loading and the splurge in credit provision by banks in anticipation of the actual implementation.

However, a much clearer picture of the policy contributions made according to each scenario stated above and further evidence of the reinforcing effects of the two policy effects, in particular following crisis and recession, is shown in Fig. 19.5c. Prior to the financial crisis and recession, both the repo rate and the NCA were stimulating growth in credit, and they have a similar net effect. However, following crisis and recession, both policies had a constraining effect and dragged down the growth in credit, as in Fig. 19.5d. The repo rate had a stimulating effect in the later part of 2013, as in Fig. 19.5c, although the net contributions of both policies were still negative, as shown by Figs. 19.5d and 19.6.

Fig. 19.6 shows the contributions of the repo rate since 1997 and contributions of NCA since 2004. The high interest rate episodes of 1999, 2001 and 2008 are clearly visible, with the expected lag period. The easing period associated with the period 2004–2007 is also clearly evident. It is, however, interesting that for the period mid-2008–mid-2013, the repo rate was contributing to the downward growth of credit despite the steep lowering of the policy rate to historic lows.

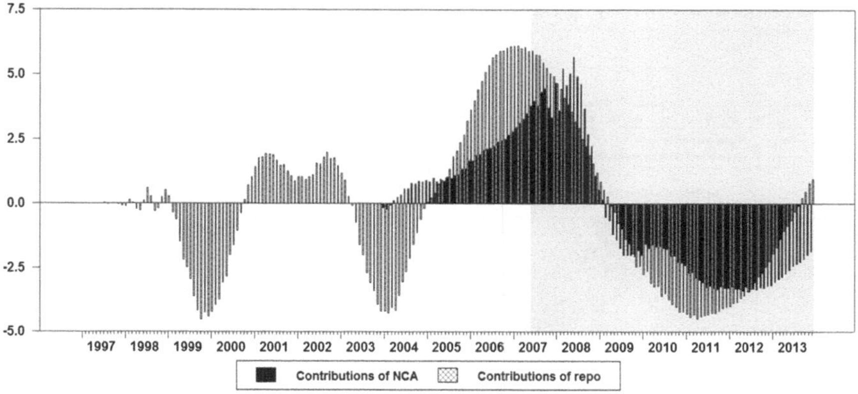

Fig. 19.6 Contributions from NCA and repo rate on credit growth (*Source*: Authors' calculations)

19.5 Counterfactual Responses

The chapter concludes by determining the amplifying or stifling abilities of (1) repo rate on NCA and (2) NCA and repo rate. Thus, would the loan advances impulse responses have been different in regard to repo rate (NCA) shocks when NCA (repo rate) is shut off? The counterfactual refers to loan advances responses when one channel is shut off. A model with four variables using policy rate, manufacturing productions, loans and advances and an NCA dummy is estimated. The manufacturing production and loan advances are estimated in levels. The gap between actual and counterfactual shows the size of amplification of the loan and advances responses by repo rate.

Fig. 19.7a and c show that actual loans and advance impulses decline more than the counterfactual responses to both repo rate and NCA shocks. The amplifications in Fig. 19.7b show that the NCA makes loan advances decline very much when related to a repo rate shock. In addition, in Fig. 19.7d the repo rate makes the loan advance decline very much when related to NCA shock.

Furthermore, the effects of these shocks on manufacturing production are assessed, with the NCA dummy and repo rate shut off respec-

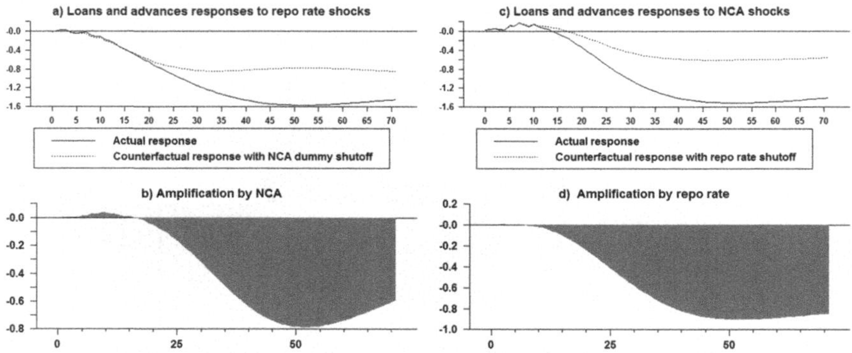

Fig. 19.7 Amplification effects on loan and advances (*Source*: Authors' calculations)

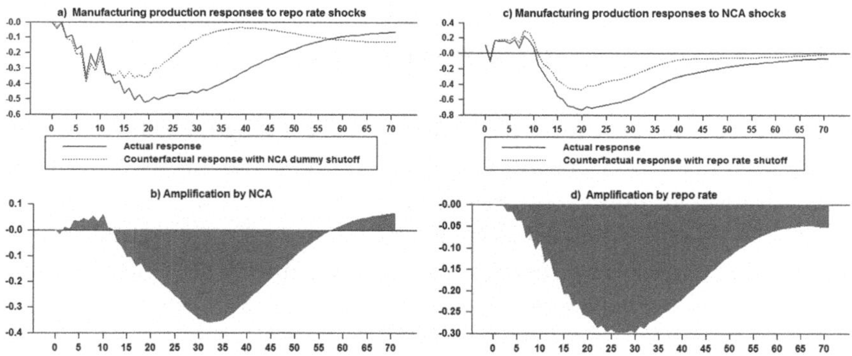

Fig. 19.8 Amplification effects on manufacturing production (*Source*: Authors' calculations)

tively. Using the above methodology, the evidence indicates that actual manufacturing production responses decline more than counterfactual responses to NCA shock. In addition, the actual manufacturing production declines more than the counterfactual to repo rate shock. This suggests that both the NCA and the repo rate amplifies the manufacturing production responses.

19.6 Policy Implications

This chapter set out to explore the effectiveness of these two policy tools, namely the NCA and the repo rate, and to assess whether they exert similar effects on the selected real economic variables; and therefore to contribute towards the analytical framework for the interaction of the NCA as a macro-prudential policy tool within monetary policy. Based on the estimated credit trend, the findings also contribute towards other measures of the credit gap that can be considered as possible indicators.

The empirical results presented in the chapter suggest that there has been a mutually reinforcing interaction between monetary policy and the NCA as a macro-prudential tool with little evidence of the existence of substitution effects. From both monetary and financial stability policy perspectives, evidence that the NCA and the repo rate have reinforcing effects calls for the coordination of the tools. From a monetary policy perspective, the evidence suggests that policymakers should be cognizant that the NCA reinforces the impact of the repo rate, possibly indicating that the repo rate should not be adjusted aggressively. Reinforcing the abilities of the NCA may lead to more adverse effects on real economic activity than expected.

Summary of Findings

- Evidence suggests that there has been a mutually reinforcing interaction between monetary policy and the NCA as a macro-prudential tool, with little evidence of the existence of substitution effects.
- The analysis shows that both unexpected NCA and repo rate shocks have depressing effects on both economic activity and growth in credit extension
- Evidence shows that the NCA tends to depress both growth in credit and economic activity to a larger degree when compared to the repo rate shock effects.
- The counterfactual analysis shows that actual manufacturing production responses decline more than counterfactual responses to NCA shock when repo rate is shut off relative to when it is not shut off.

20

Loan-to-Value Ratios, Contractionary Monetary Policy and Inflation Expectations

Learning Objectives

- Discern the nature of the interaction between LTVs and the repo rate since 2001
- Assess the extent to which the tight (loose) LTVs reinforce (neutralize) the contractionary (accommodative) monetary policy stance
- Analyze whether the transmission of the LTV shocks occur through the same channels that are impacted by a tight (accommodative) monetary policy shock
- Examine the impact of the repo rate and LTV shocks on household balance sheets
- Assess the response of LTVs to an unexpected positive current inflation expectations shock and inflation
- Assess how deterioration in the inflation outlook leads to the LTV tightening
- Understand the impact of LTV tightening shocks on price stability

N. Gumata, E. Ndou, *Bank Credit Extension and Real Economic Activity in South Africa*, DOI 10.1007/978-3-319-43551-0_20

20.1 Introduction

The literature on the interaction of monetary and financial policy argues that some features of the housing market explain that differences in the transmission of monetary policy can amplify swings in the real economy and can be sources of financial instability. The interaction of macro-prudential policies for residential mortgage lending and monetary policy can induce macroeconomic fluctuations, particularly if they move in the same direction as other shocks that amplify or dampen collateral constraints.

The chapter takes its cue from the ongoing international debates that when it comes to macro-prudential tools "Take nothing on its looks–take everything on evidence." This chapter asks: What does the data tell us about the nature of the interaction between loan-to-value ratios LTVs and the repo rate since 2001? To what extent do tight (loose) LTVs reinforce (neutralize) the contractionary (accommodative) monetary policy stance? Does the transmission of the LTV shock occur through the same channels that are impacted by a tight (accommodative) monetary policy shock?

Fig. 20.1 shows the repo rate, LTVs and headline inflation. Between 2011 and 2013 the tightening in LTVs was accompanied by the historically low policy rate. This is in stark contrast to the massive loosening in LTVs prior to 2007, which coincided with the repo rate tightening. Furthermore, Fig. 20.1 shows that inflation has moved in the same direction as LTVs before 2011. However, after 2011 the decline in LTVs was not accompanied by a similar declining trend in the inflation rate. Price stability is the primary mandate of the monetary policy authorities, hence we raise the question: Is there a spill-over impact of a macro-prudential tool such as the LTV tightening shock on inflation and inflation expectations? Inflation expectations impact economic activity and inflation outcomes.

Fig. 20.2a and b show the plot between LTVs and the Bureau of Economic Research (BER) regarding all current inflation expectations. The cross correlations reveal that when LTVs lead current inflation expec-

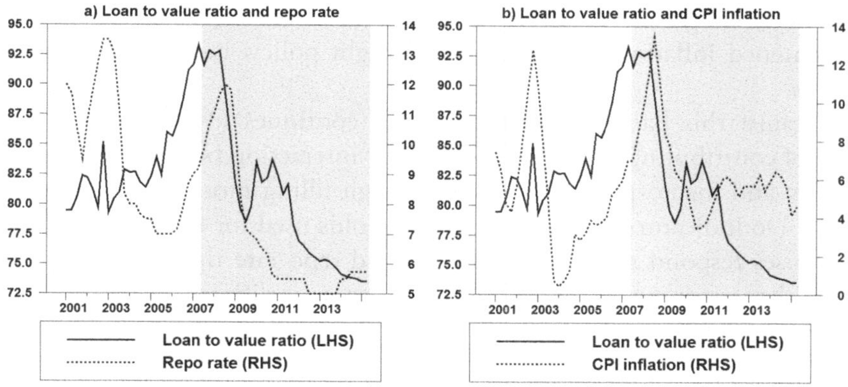

Fig. 20.1 Repo rate, LTV ratio and headline inflation (*Note*: The *grey* highlighted area in all the graphs shows the period of the National Credit Act and the National Credit Act Amendments. *Source*: SARB and authors' calculations)

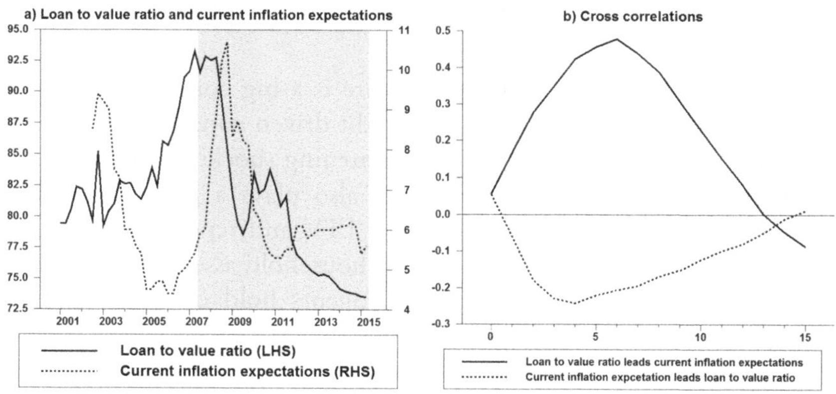

Fig. 20.2 Relationship between LTV and inflation expectation (*Note*: The *grey* highlighted area in all the graphs shows the period of the National Credit Act and the National Credit Act Amendments. *Source*: SARB and authors' calculations)

tations, the latter tends to rise for a prolonged period—meaning that periods of loose LTVs tend to be associated with inflationary episodes. On the other hand, when current inflation expectations lead the LTVs, the latter is tightened. The implication is that banks associate periods of heightened inflationary pressures with tight policy, hence they tighten LTVs.

Against this background, the chapter continues towards the objective of contributing to the research on the interaction between monetary policy and macro-prudential tools through filling more policy research gaps. Do indicators of wellness of households used for financial stability purposes respond to unexpected LTV and repo rate tightening shocks? This chapter shows policymakers that there exist differential sensitivities of household disposable income, debt and financing costs, as well as the ratios of household financial wellness indicators to both repo rate and LTV tightening shocks.

Given that most indicators of household financial wellness are expressed as ratios, we determine whether it is numerators or denominators that drive the sensitivities of these ratios to LTV and repo rate shocks. Based on the evidence of household financial wellness ratios as indicators of financial stability, we derive policy implications and offer recommendations.

Credit-driven consumption expenditure is a big contributor to economic growth. So how potent is the credit driven consumption spending channel in transmitting the LTV tightening shock? Over and above disposable income, the wealth channel also plays a meaningful role. Therefore, we ask: Is there evidence that LTV and repo rate tightening shocks reinforce each other in impacting household assets?

The literature asserts that economic agents hold certain subjective beliefs about price behavior. The updating of these beliefs can propagate economic shocks in either direction. After all, it is a fact that if inflation expectations are stable, low nominal interest rates translate into low real rates which are conducive to loose lending conditions, the build-up of financial excesses and risks. So, if that is the case, what is the nature of the link between LTVs and inflation expectations? Do high inflation expectations pose risks to financial stability via the LTV channel? If so, when did the LTV tightening shock uplift and drag inflation outcomes and expectations?

20.2 How Are the LTVs and RTIs Determined in South Africa? [1]

Currently, in South Africa LTVs and repayment-to-income ratio (RTIs) limits are the outcome of banks' management of the credit decision processes reinforced by the implementation of the National Credit Act (NCA) and the National Credit Act Amendments. As an outcome of the internal credit affordability score-cards and background checks, banks use their discretion on what limits to apply on LTVs and RTIs.

Given banks have been using these tools for some time, the analysis asks: What can the regulator and policymakers learn for the past cycles? Are there any benefits regarding the role of limits on LTVs and RTIs used together on all or as a proportion of new lending? What regulatory policy inferences can be made with regards to the coordinations of these tools with monetary policy?

First, these residential macro-prudential tools can strengthen the resilience of the banking sector by reducing the likelihood of mortgage defaults and losses, if the defaults materialize. Second, emerging literature largely based on cross-country experiences shows that LTVs and RTIs should be put in place early on to help prevent problems emerging. They should not be deferred until corrective action is necessary. They are a first line of defence against the build-up of financial excesses and risks, and constraining credit and or financial booms (Mester 2014).

Third, banks' lending standards as captured by LTVs, RTIs and debt-to-income ratio (DTIs) are amongst the best indicators of credit market conditions in particular, the residential housing market and house prices. Last but not least is that together these tools can be progressively used to relax (or tighten) borrowing constraints that can generate a strong negative (or positive) correlation with house prices, consumption expenditure

[1] Regulations on LTVs and RTIs are essentially macro-prudential policy measures targeted at lending standards on the system as a whole throughout the credit cycle. They aim to enhance the stability of the financial system to future shocks. They are complementary tools to existing micro-prudential supervision and to banks' own internal risk management practices, such as credit assessment policies and procedures dealing with different aspects of credit risk associated with the borrower. Other countries also intensify the rate and duration of amortization as a tool aimed at reducing indebtedness (Central Bank of Ireland and Sveriges Riksbank 2015).

and economic activity.[2] In a nutshell, lower collateral and income repayment requirements ease credit constraints; facilitate access to external funding and drive up house prices (Ferrero, 2012).

20.3 How Have RTIs and LTVs Evolved in South Africa?

In the empirical sections of the study we use the weighted LTVs, being aware that banks adopt an approach that distributes LTVs and RTIs across the house price and income spectrum. For instance, they can allocate a 100 percent LTV on low income houses ranges relative to other house price categories. The results of such a strategy can be a heterogeneous growth in different segments of the housing market and target group.

Why do banks use LTVs and RTIs together on all or as a proportion of new lending? LTV caps on their own might be an insufficient tool due to the fact that the level of indebtedness still rises when housing prices increase. So, does this mean LTVs and RTIs can work together? It turns out that LTVs and RTIs tend to be complementary tools used in dampening the cyclicality of lending to the property sector. As complementary tools, the LTV is used to mainly address the wealth or the degree of the potential loss to the bank in the event of default. On the other hand, the RTI is aimed at dealing with the income aspects or the affordability for the borrower. In this respect, RTIs may be more effective in markets where house prices are rising faster than incomes. It is generally used as an indicator of mortgage market repayment stress. Overall, these tools are used to mitigate credit risks via both the collateral channel and the repayment channel (McCarthy and McQuinn, 2013).

---

[2] IMF (2013) shows that of the macro-prudential instruments to address real estate booms, the most widely used tool is the limit on LTV ratios, followed by sectoral capital requirements and RTI caps or a combination of LTV and RTI limits. Furthermore, evidence shows that although these instruments are not typically aimed at house price growth, they have modest and lagged effects on house price growth.

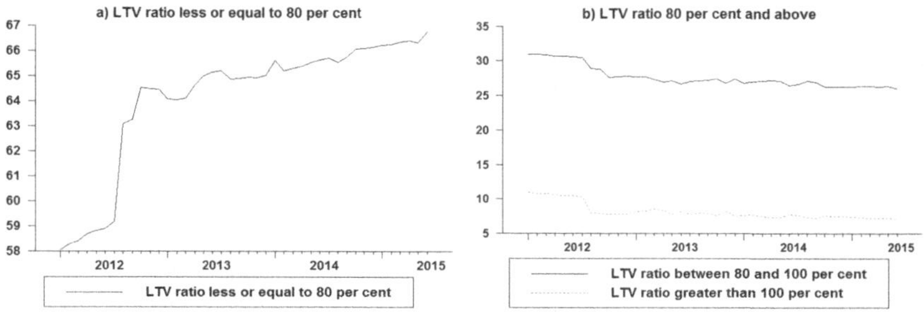

Fig. 20.3 The distribution of LTVs (*Source*: SARB and authors' calculations)

20.3.1 Are Households Deleveraging or Have LTVs and RTIs Shifted the Scales?

To contribute to the ongoing debate on whether households have deleveraged and, if so, to what degree, we look to the housing market for clues. We show residential mortgage loans granted in each of the three LTV segments in Fig. 20.3a.[3] It is evident that the proportion of residential mortgages paid-out at LTV less or equal to 80 percent has increased since 2012. This proportion has increased from nearly 58 percent of the total mortgage pay-outs in 2012 to nearly 68 percent in 2015—this still suggests that indeed banks have tightened LTVs.

Has there been a shift in the mortgage shares according to the distribution of LTVs? Yes, in Fig. 20.4b the percentage of residential mortgages with LTVs greater than 100 percent declined from 10 to around 8 percent of the total. Similarly, the proportion of mortgages with LTVs between 80 and 100 percent declined from around 31 percent in January 2013 to an average of 27 percent of the total since January 2014.

What does this mean for policymakers? Most home buyers have to put down payment of at least 20 percent of the loan value requested when buying a house. This seems more a case of tightening of lending conditions as opposed to households deleveraging.

[3] The distribution of the LTVs has an impact on the sensitivity of households to changes in interests. As the LTV thresholds progressively increase, the interest rate costs and sensitivities increase.

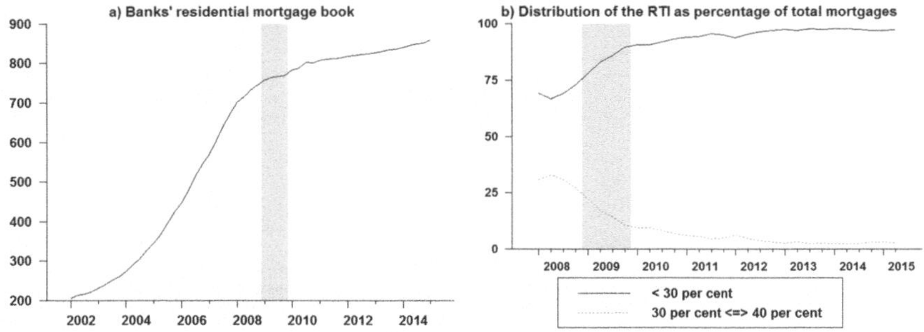

Fig. 20.4 Banks' residential mortgage book and distribution of mortgage loan repayment to income ratio (*Source*: SARB and authors' calculations)

20.3.2 Are Households Making Excessive Repayments Relative to Their Income?

To answer this question, we show the evolution of the weighted RTI in Fig. 20.4a, starting in 2004. Similar to LTVs, banks distribute RTIs across their mortgage book. However, the data on the distribution of the RTI is only available from 2008Q1. We show the relative sizes of loans in each RTI category as a percentage of the total mortgage book in Fig. 20.4b.

Fig. 20.4a shows that the weighted RTIs increased from 15 to just above 30 percent for the period 2004Q3 to 2008Q2. RTIs have since declined and stabilized around 20 percent. This decline means banks did not want to overburden their clients with excessive repayments relative to their income, which is consistent with prudent lending decisions.

How has this shifted the distribution of RTIs as percentage of total mortgage advances paid out? The share of mortgage advances in less than or equal to 30 percent of the RTI category increased to almost 100 percent of total mortgage advances paid out. Alternatively, the share of mortgage advances in the 30–40 percent RTI category decreased to almost 0 percent of the total since 2012 until the present. This evidence implies that banks have improved the standard they use to assess for the affordability of granting mortgage advances and this possibly contributes to lessening the household repayment burdens and debt levels.

Is the application of the RTIs without condemnation? Not so, because the effectiveness of RTIs in fully capturing indebtedness and comprehensive guide of creditworthiness has its own disapprovals. As an alternative to RTIs, households' total DTI ratio and limits is the ultimate tool in helping to restrict the borrower debt servicing cost relative to the income. Why is this the case? This is based on the recognition that over-indebtedness of households emanates from additional secured or unsecured borrowings from multiple sources.

So, is this still an ideal tool to control the over-indebtedness? Yes, it is. But it has its own fair share of weaknesses. It is noted that operationally it will be difficult to impose the limits on the DTI ratio as it requires net income and a comprehensive view of the debt service cost, including all the borrower's loans. This extends to stress tests under different interest rate and income scenarios.[4]

Will the countercyclical capital buffer (CCB) help in dealing with household resilience to indebtedness? It seems not. Research notes that while the CCB increases the banks' capacity to absorb losses in a downturn, it does not specifically target households' resilience or indebtedness. Moreover, even though an increase in sectorial capital requirements could lead to an increase in banks' lending spreads, which could moderate lending volumes to that sector, it falls short of directly addressing household demand for credit, or the household sector's financial resilience and indebtedness (Bank of Ireland 2014).

20.3.3 Is the Ratio of Residential Non-performing Loans Still Inhibiting Credit Extension?

For further evidence on the extent or degree of household deleveraging, we look at the value and number of residential non-performing loans (NPLs). Similarly, the value and number of NPLs as a percentage of mortgage advances has declined from peak levels recorded in 2010 and are now at low levels, comparable to those recorded in 2004. The trends in the NPLs of banks' mortgage books support the possibility that it is

---

[4] Nonetheless, it is possible that such aspects fall within the remit of the National Credit Regulator.

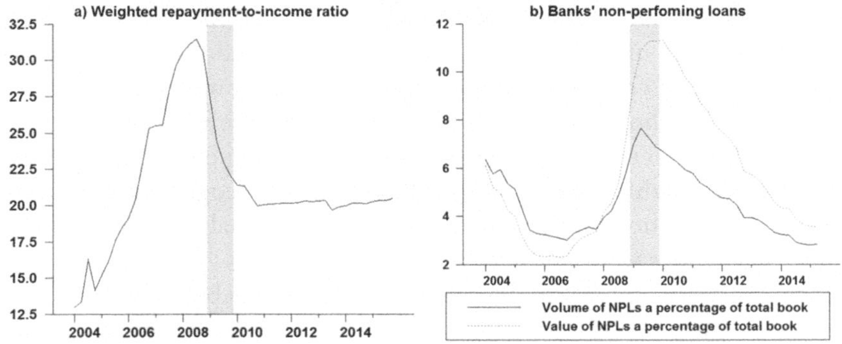

Fig. 20.5 Weighted repayment-to-income ratio and non-performing loans (*Source*: SARB and authors' calculations)

more a case of prudent management or credit quality of the residential mortgage books than the deleveraging of households per se.

It is very possible that the high levels of NPLs were on account of the earlier loose LTVs and high RTIs. Literature shows that borrowers with high LTVs and RTIs are more likely to default on their debt. This likelihood is mostly the case for borrowers who suffered the most when the unemployment rates increased.

Nonetheless, the implication of the current low levels in NPLs is that they will probably afford banks' space to grow their mortgage books, which have been fairly stagnant, as shown in Fig. 20.5a.

20.4 To What Extent Did the LTV Tightening Shock Reinforce or Offset the Effects of the Repo Rate Tightening Shock?

The empirical analysis begins by primarily investigating the channel through which the LTV and repo rate tightening shocks are transmitted using a small vector autoregression (VAR) model with quarterly data from 2001Q1 to 2015Q2. However, in the latter section when we use inflation expectations data, we change the sample size to 2002Q3–2015Q2 to accommodate the starting date of inflation expectations. The model comprises of GDP, the repo rate, LTVs and either total loans and advances or mortgage advances or household balance sheet variables. The last variables are used interchangeably in the model. Apart from the repo rate, LTV and other ratios which are in percentages, we estimate the model in levels rather than in differenced form.

The GDP is log transformed and multiplied by 100, hence its response should be interpreted as percentage deviation from the trend. In addition, other variables that measure the quantities are similarly transformed. The model is estimated using two lags as selected by the Akaike Information Criterion and 2,000 draws. The analysis is based on one positive standard deviation shocks. To overcome ordering problems related to the Cholesky econometric estimation issues, we test if the results are robust to placing the LTV before repo rate. Indeed, the results are robust.

Does an LTV tightening shock exert different effects compared to the repo rate tightening shock? Not based on the direction of the responses exhibited in Fig. 20.6.

Both the LTVs and the repo rate tightening shocks lead to significant contractions in GDP, total loan advances and mortgage advances. Despite the similar directional responses, the positive repo rate shock leads to bigger contractions in GDP, mortgage advances and total loan advances than the LTV tightening shock. This is preliminary evidence indicating that the repo rate and LTV tightening shock effects reinforce each other. Furthermore, in line with expectations of targeted tools, it seems that LTVs exert limited responses on growth.

How does this finding relate to current policy discussions? This chapter is cognizant of the current ongoing heated debate on whether monetary policy should "lean against" or "clean up after" the credit cycle or asset (house) price booms. Without getting into a detailed discussion of the pros and cons of either approach or their alternatives, we simply show evidence. This evidence reveals that when the policymaker is mandated with maintaining price and financial stability, the interaction of available policy tools has to be thoroughly understood. Such an understanding may enhance policy coordination, leading to either optimal or desired outcomes.

Based on the direction of the responses, we argue that the model we used in this analysis does capture some stylized effects of the policy on macroeconomic variables. However, it is important to understand how

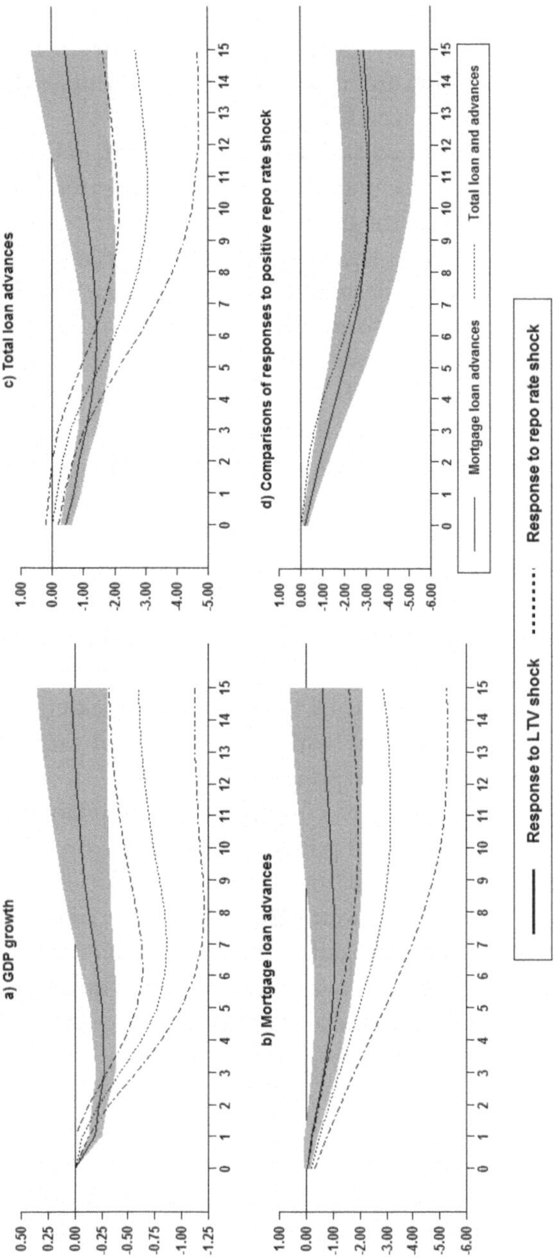

Fig. 20.6 Responses of GDP, total loans and advances and mortgage advances (*Source*: Authors calculations)

residential macro-prudential tools targeted at the housing market, such as the LTVs, interact with monetary policy.

Does the LTV shock as a regulatory rule work in the same direction as monetary policy? If so, does this depend on which shock preceded the other shock? Or is it evident that the LTV shock as a regulatory tool might work against the repo rate? Fig. 20.7a shows that the LTVs decline significantly and return to pre-shock level after 11 quarters following a positive repo rate shock. The tightening of LTVs suggests that lending standards are also tightened, following the tightening of the repo rate. Furthermore, the repo rate effects on economic variables may be compounded by further tightening of LTVs as a lending standard.

This evidence concurs with well-established facts that financial frictions in financial intermediation matter for monetary policy transmission. In this context, models using Taylor type rules augmented with financial stress indicators, asset prices, credit and or some indicator that best captures developments in the financial variables of interest, have been shown to improve macroeconomic stabilization.

What should monetary policy do if it is preceded by an unexpected LTV tightening shock? Evidence shows that if the shock originates in LTVs as tightening in lending standards, the repo rate is loosened significantly, as in Fig. 20.7b. This reveals that efforts to gradually integrate financial stability into monetary policy decisions should be accompanied

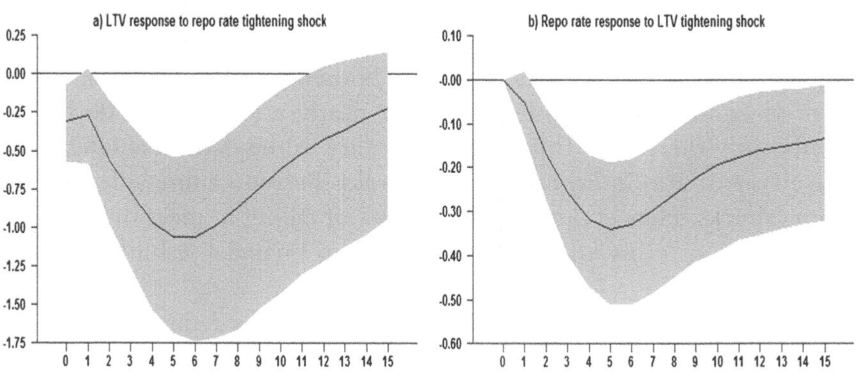

Fig. 20.7 Responses of the LTV and repo rate (*Source*: Authors calculations)

by the recognition of the potential "trade-offs" in instruments, so that they have the desired effects on their own targets, and identifying the source of shock in real estate markets.

20.4.1 Sensitivity of Household Disposable Income, Debt and Financing Costs to Repo Rate and LTV Tightening Shocks

This section investigates whether the tightening of LTVs reduces the expansion in household debt, thus mitigating rising household leverage and financial system vulnerabilities. In essence, we attempt to capture the role of shocks to the repo rate and LTVs to household liabilities and disposable income. Fig. 20.8a, b and e show that a repo rate shock leads to a bigger contraction in household debt-to-disposable income and the constituents of this ratio, namely, household debt and disposable income. The contraction of these variables suggests both shocks reinforce each other. Thus, debt is highly responsive to the policy rate changes relative to adjustments in the LTVs. This evidence confirms the existence of spillovers when decisions on these two policy tools are under the influence of different and independent institutions.

What happens to the ratio of debt servicing costs-to-disposable income and household debt financing costs? This ratio measures households' debt servicing costs as percentage of household disposable income and it is argued that it is a better indicator of financial stress than the aggregate DTI ratio. A positive repo rate shock raises the ratio of debt service costs-to-disposable income. In addition, the household debt financing costs increase significantly on impact and for nearly a year, before declining significantly thereafter. This shows cyclicality in the debt financing cost. The elevated ratio indicates that households become vulnerable to economic shocks. Hence, they are at high risk of failing to meet their financial obligations. This, therefore, poses risks to financial stability and the economy.

In contrast, the LTV tightening shock leads to a reduction in both debt serving costs-to-disposable income and the debt financing costs.

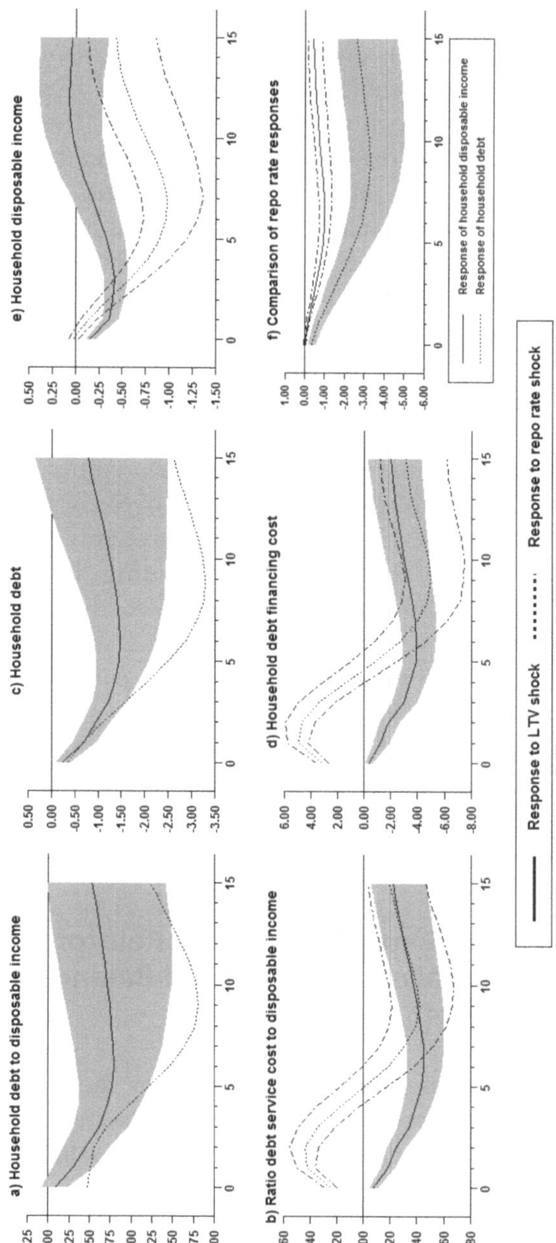

Fig. 20.8 Responses of household debt, debt servicing costs and disposable income (*Source*: Authors calculations)

The decline in the ratio indicates a decrease in the number of vulnerable households which may find it difficult to make their debt repayments. Fig. 20.8d reveals that household debt financing cost is more sensitive to a repo rate tightening shock than the LTV shock. This is a sensible outcome due to the fact that the repo rate changes affect the cost of debt, whereas the LTVs reduce the initial debt commitments and may therefore reduce the sensitivity to interest rate changes. As mentioned earlier, LTVs at their core reduce initial debt and therefore limit the degree of the potential losses to the bank in the event of default.

Which policy shock can lead to a big reduction in household debt? We find that repo rate tightening has larger effect than an LTV tightening shock in dampening household debt and household disposable income. In addition, a tight monetary policy shock's big reduction in household disposable income and household debt comes at the cost of larger spill-over effects to output. Is large spill-over always a desirable outcome? Not so, because if the policy objective was not to significantly slow down output, then the LTV tightening shock is effective because it is a tool well-targeted at the source of financial stability vulnerability.

Overall, the results in this section suggest that a contractionary monetary policy by lowering LTVs result in its tightening. LTV tightening as a borrowing constraint leads to the amplification of the economic responses which spill-over to the rest of the economy. Furthermore, LTVs turn out to be less blunt on output relative to the repo rate. This presents a case for coordination of the tools.

20.4.2 Do LTV and Repo Rate Shocks Reinforce Each Other in Impacting Household Balance Sheet Assets?

The financial health of the household matters for the transmission of monetary policy and the stability of the financial system. Why should this matter? Households with liquid assets, such as cash, may draw on these assets to service their debt and ease the financial strain in the event of severe economic shocks. To get more insight that enables us to recommend appropriate policy responses, we determine the reaction of the ratio of household net wealth to disposable income and household total assets or capital gearing to both LTV and repo rate tightening shock. Figure 20.9 reveals that repo rate tightening leads to bigger declines in the indicators of the financial health of household assets than the effects exerted by the LTV tightening shock.

Is it possible to rank the pronounced peak contraction from highest to lowest? Fig. 20.9f shows that the repo rate has a bigger effect on household net wealth than household disposable income. The least peak decline is in household disposable income. The biggest peak contraction is on household net wealth over all horizons. These findings suggest that the repo rate and LTV tightening shocks have significant effects on households' assets. This is in line with earlier assertions that the main objective of LTVs is to address housing market aspects through the wealth and collateral channels. Nonetheless, this has implications for inflation dynamics, which is the primary mandate of the monetary authorities. For example, a decline in wealth and disposable income together with collateral constraints should lead to a reduction in inflationary pressures, *ceteris paribus.*

It is possible to conclude that in view of the fact that the repo rate leads to a bigger decline in household disposable income, households' assets and net wealth than those exerted by LTV tightening shock, this evidence possibly presents yet another encouragement for the coordination of these tools.

Exactly how could these policy tools be coordinated? It seems that when the economy is hit by a financial shock which alters and leads to revaluation of collateral, a countercyclical LTV policy could be a more effective tool for stabilization. Evidence shows that LTVs induce fewer fluctuations in other economic variables compared to monetary policy. Such coordination of the policy tools can loosen the financial and collateral borrowing constraints of households.

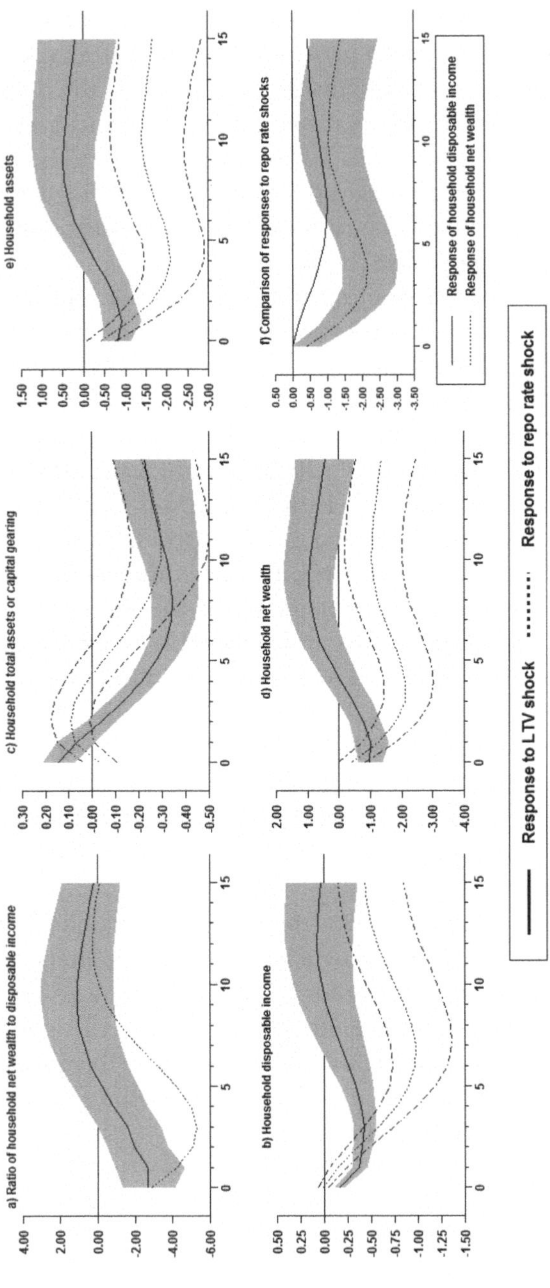

Fig. 20.9 Responses of household net wealth, asset and disposable income (*Source*: Authors calculations)

20.4.3 What Moves the Ratios Due to a Positive Repo Rate Shock and LTV Tightening Shock? Is It the Numerator or the Denominator?

This discussion begins by disentangling the movements in the ratio of net household wealth to disposable income. The household net wealth declines more than disposable income due to an unexpected positive repo rate shock in Fig. 20.10a. Why should the ratio of household net wealth to disposable income decline? It might be because household net wealth is a big driver in pulling down the ratio of the household net wealth to disposable income.

Fig. 20.10b shows that household net wealth declines more than household disposable income in the first three months, which explains the decline in the ratio of household net wealth in Fig. 20.10 due to LTV tightening shock. In addition, the improvement in the ratio of household net wealth after four quarters is due to a large recovery in household net wealth following an LTV tightening shock.

Second, the analysis disentangles movements in the ratio of household debt-to-disposable income. What leads to a decline in the ratio of household debt-to-disposable income due to both the repo rate and LTV tightening shocks? It is evident that household debt shrinks more than the decline in disposable income due to both shocks in Fig. 20.11c and d. In addition, Fig. 20.11f shows that debt costs fall more due to the LTV tightening shock than disposable income. Fig. 20.11e shows that financing costs are more responsive to repo rate tightening than disposable income. All the evidence in this section has implications for the aggregate consumption and its components.

20.4.4 Consumption Spending Channel: What are the Policy Implications Regarding the Inflation Outlook and Inflation Expectations?

One channel that impacts inflation and possible inflation expectations is the consumption channel, in particular credit driven consumption expenditure. Fig. 20.12 shows the responses of total PCE (consumption)

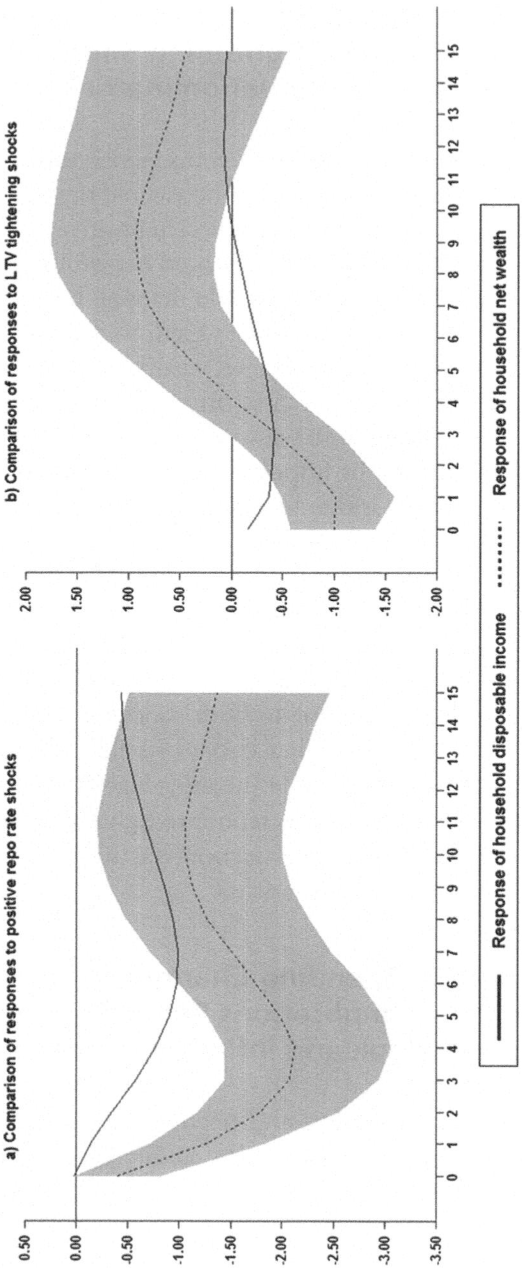

Fig. 20.10 Responses of the components of ratios of household net wealth to disposable income (*Source*: Authors calculations)

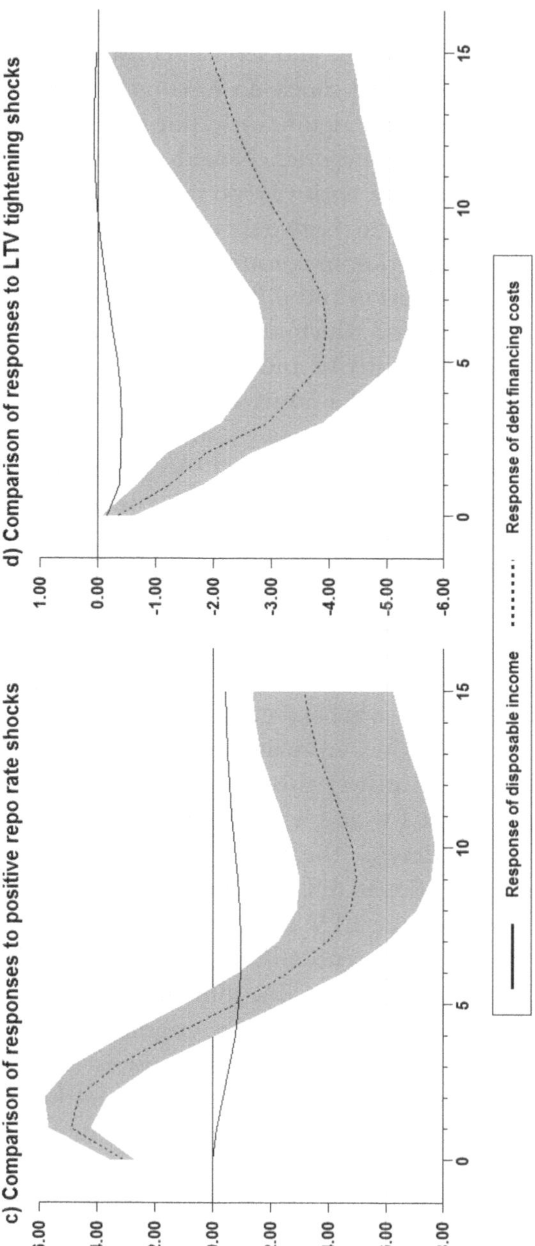

Fig. 20.11 Responses of the components of ratios of household debt to disposable income (*Source*: Authors calculations)

and its components. Total consumption expenditure is decomposed into non-durable, semi-durable, durable and services consumption goods.

What does an LTV tightening shock do to consumption? Fig. 20.12 shows that consumption declines significantly, but not permanently. This trajectory is evident across all categories. Nonetheless, Fig. 20.12f shows that PCE declines more due to a positive repo rate shock than to the LTV tightening shock. The responses to the two shocks are significantly different.

Is it possible that the reduction in consumption due to the LTV tightening shock could affect inflation and inflation expectations? The scatter plots can have a regression line which shows the mean or intercept and slope which measure the sensitivity and signs of the relationship. The scatter plots in Fig. 20.13b reveal a positive bilateral relationship, which suggests that increased consumption raises inflation. In addition, Fig. 20.13a reveals that inflation increases as the LTVs are loosened.

So what would be the mean inflation rate in the absence of credit-driven consumption pressures and LTV loosening? In the absence of any shocks that drive the inflation rate, the mean inflation rates are well below 6 percent. In fact, they are firmly inside the inflation target band. In both a) and b) the mean which is the intercept of the regression are both between 4 and 6 percent.

In light of this evidence, to what extent can the LTV tightening shock help monetary policy authorities in maintaining price stability through its impact on inflation? To answer this question, we use a model that includes GDP, repo rate, LTV and a measure of inflation expectation using two lags and 2,000 draws.[5] The results using this model are robust to different orderings. We use the different measures of inflation expectations interchangeably. Can the LTV tightening shock impact inflation expectations? Yes, the LTV tightening shock in Fig. 20.14 significantly lowers inflation expectations and headline inflation.

Despite inflation expectations declining significantly with varying durations and magnitudes, what matters most is that they imply an improvement in the inflation outlook and therefore the outlook for monetary policy. So which inflation expectations are highly responsive and how do they compare with actual inflation responses? Fig. 20.15a

---

[5] To determine the response of the inflation rate, we use a model that includes GDP, inflation rate, repo rate and LTV. The model has two lags and 2,000 draws. The results were robust to different orderings.

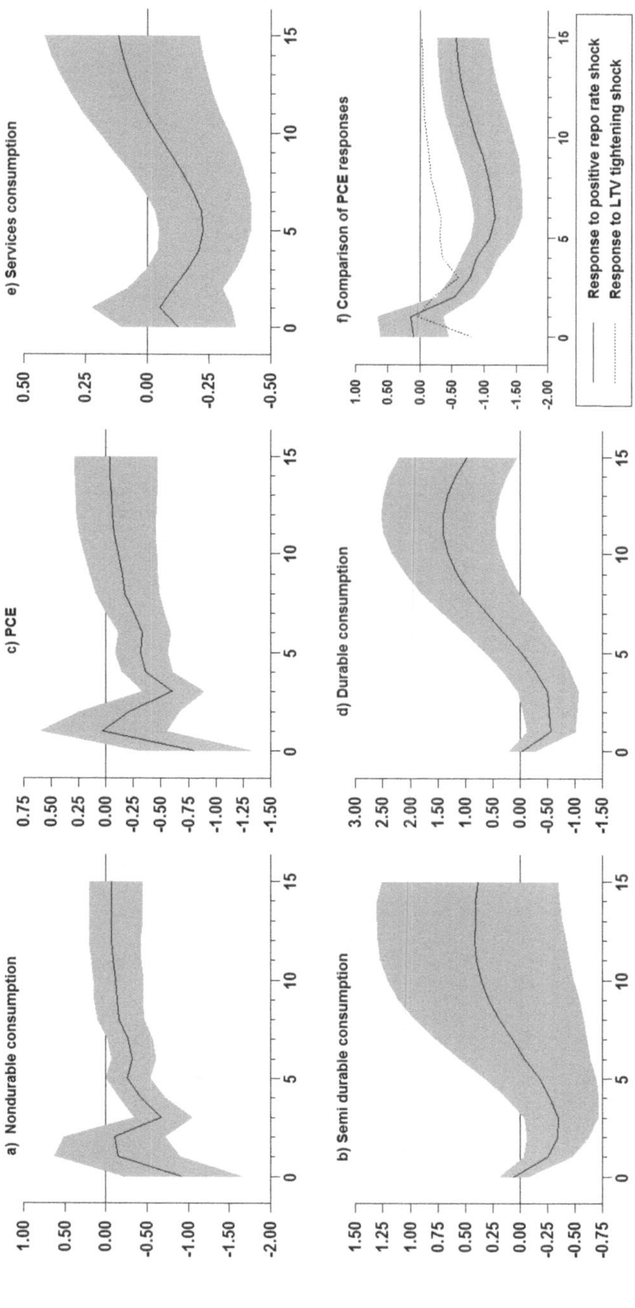

Fig. 20.12 Sensitivities of aggregate consumption and various categories (*Source*: Authors calculations)

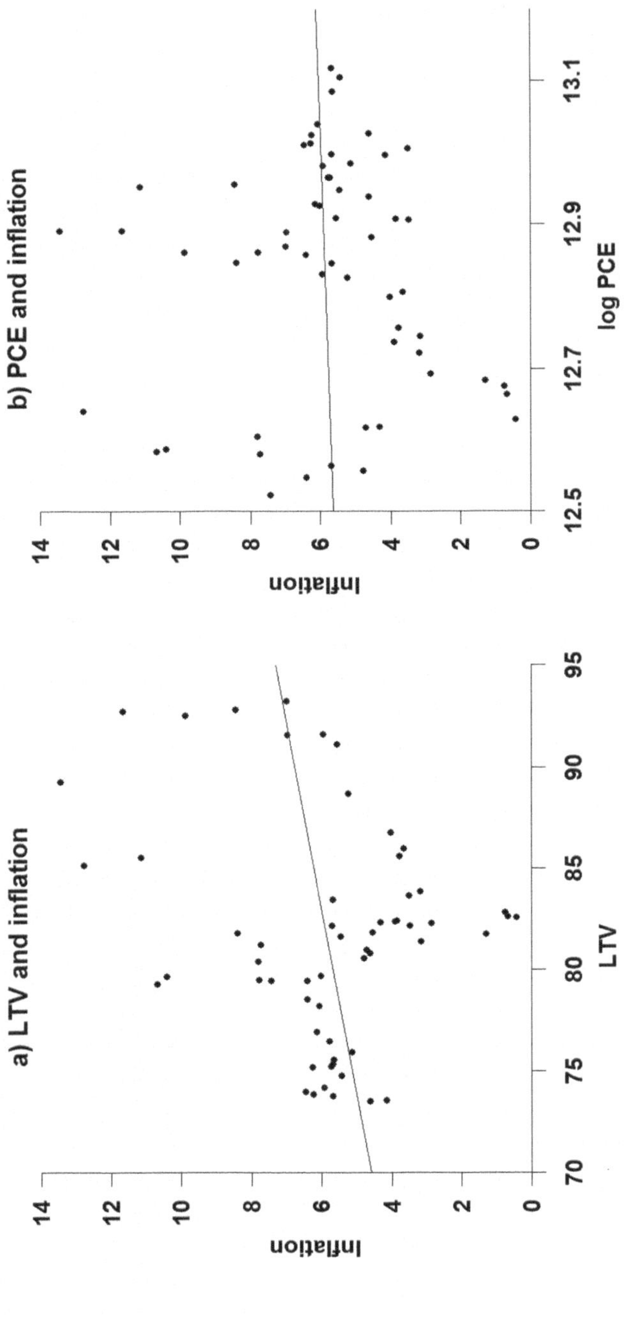

Fig. 20.13 Bilateral relationships between inflation, expenditure and LTVs (*Source*: Authors calculations)

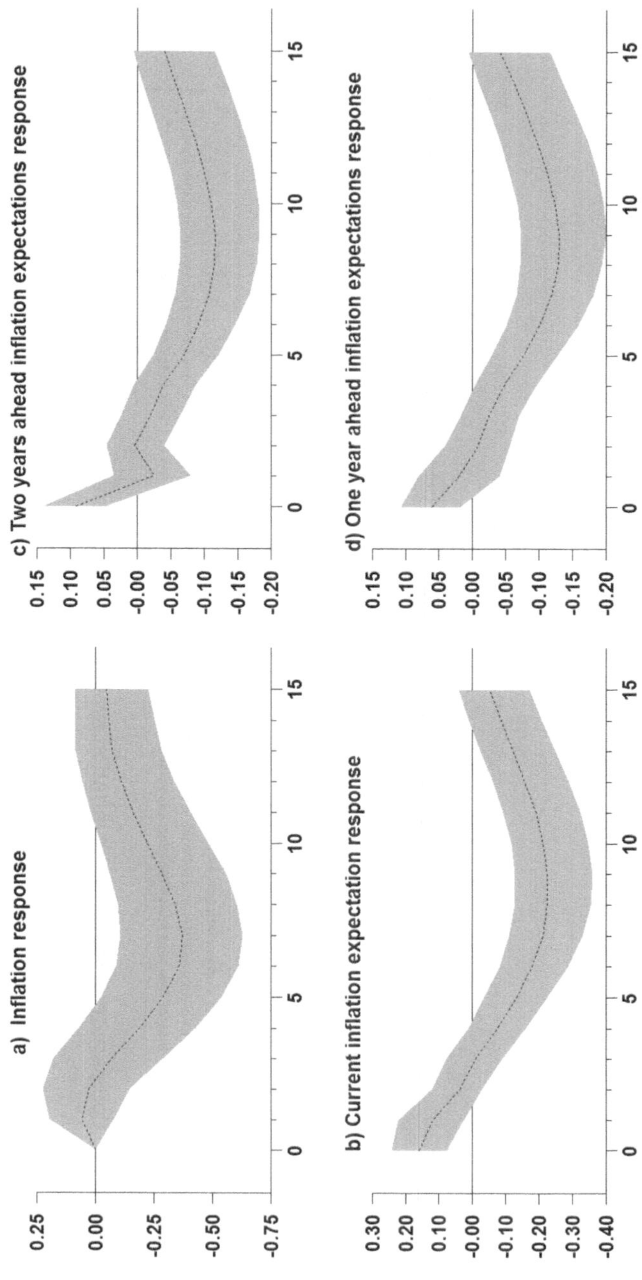

Fig. 20.14 Responses of inflation and inflation expectations to LTV tightening shock (*Source*: Authors calculations)

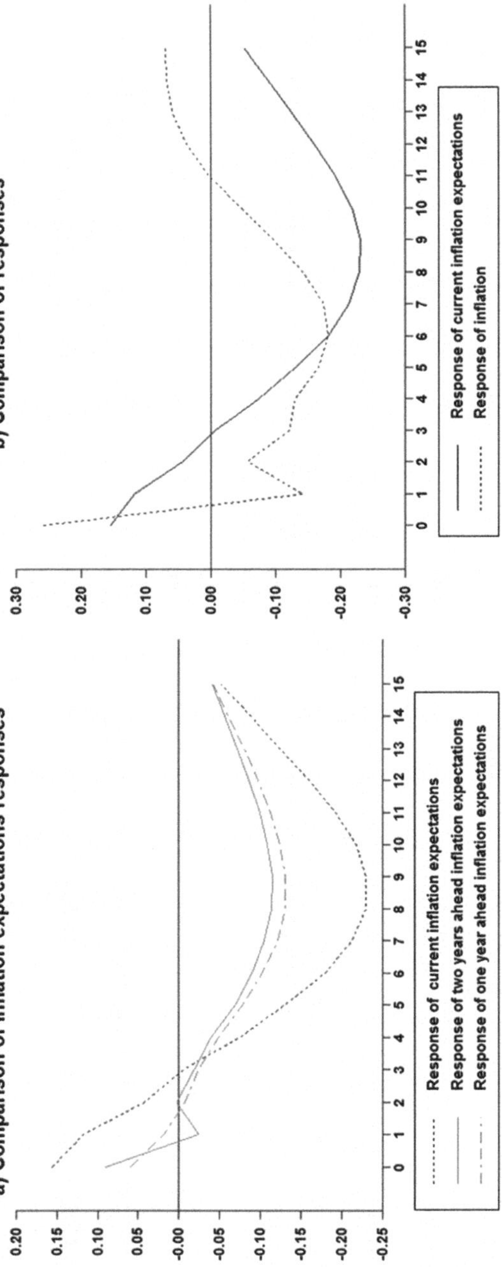

Fig. 20.15 Comparison of responses of inflation expectations and inflation to LTV tightening shock (*Source:* Authors calculations)

shows that current inflation expectations are the most affected by the LTV tightening shock. The current inflation expectations peak decline is nearly twice that of the other inflation expectations.

In addition, Fig. 20.15b shows that current inflation expectations decline much more than inflation at peak responses. This confirms that the LTV tightening shock—if operating efficiently—can reinforce monetary policy intentions to significantly lower inflation expectations for a prolonged period. Overall, it seems that the coordination of the two policy instruments could work well. In the event that these tools are adjusted simultaneously there could be spill-over effects via the inflation and inflation expectation channels.

20.4.5 LTV Tightening Shock and the Evolution of Inflation Outcomes and Expectations

During which periods did the LTV tightening shock uplift and dampen inflation and inflation expectation dynamics? The historical decomposition approach is applied to decompose inflation and inflation expectation respectively into their trends, own contributions and contributions from other variables. The counterfactual refers to inflation and inflation expectation variables that exclude the contributions of the LTV tightening shocks.

What did the LTV shock do to inflation and inflation expectation dynamics in recent times? In most cases since 2013 actual inflation and inflation expectations were lower than what the counterfactual variables suggest in Fig. 20.16. This implies that the LTV tightening dampened inflation and inflation expectations shocks.

The contributions showed in Fig. 20.17 indicate that the LTV tightening shocks reduced inflation expectations very much. In the absence of tighter LTVs, inflation expectations would have been higher than the observed values. This evidence possibly underlies the absence of credit-driven demand pressures.

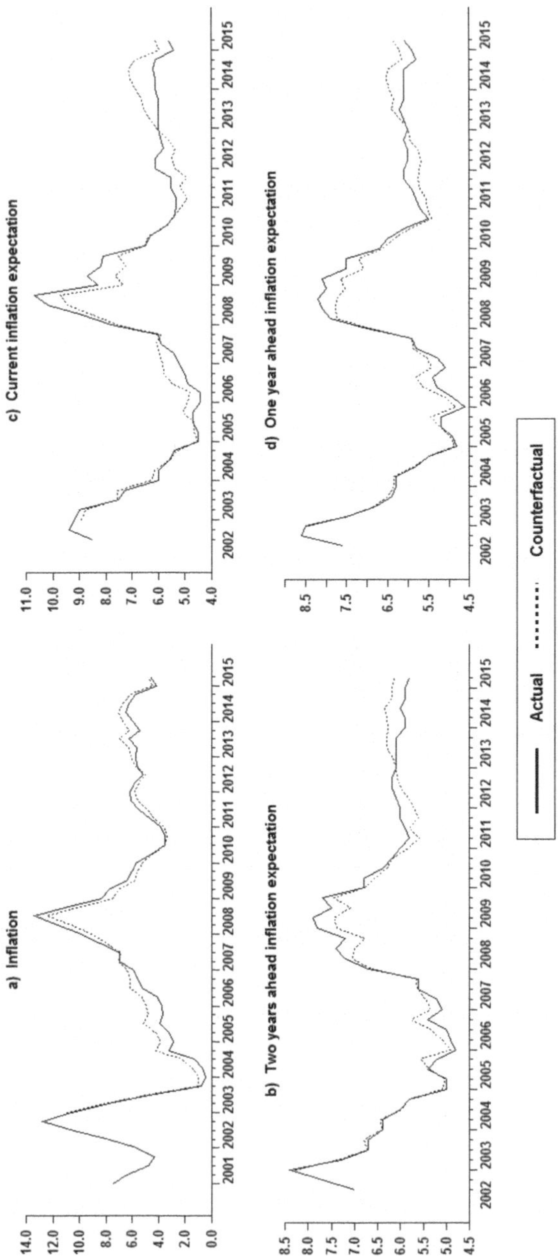

Fig. 20.16 Actual and counterfactual inflation and inflation expectations (*Source*: Authors calculations)

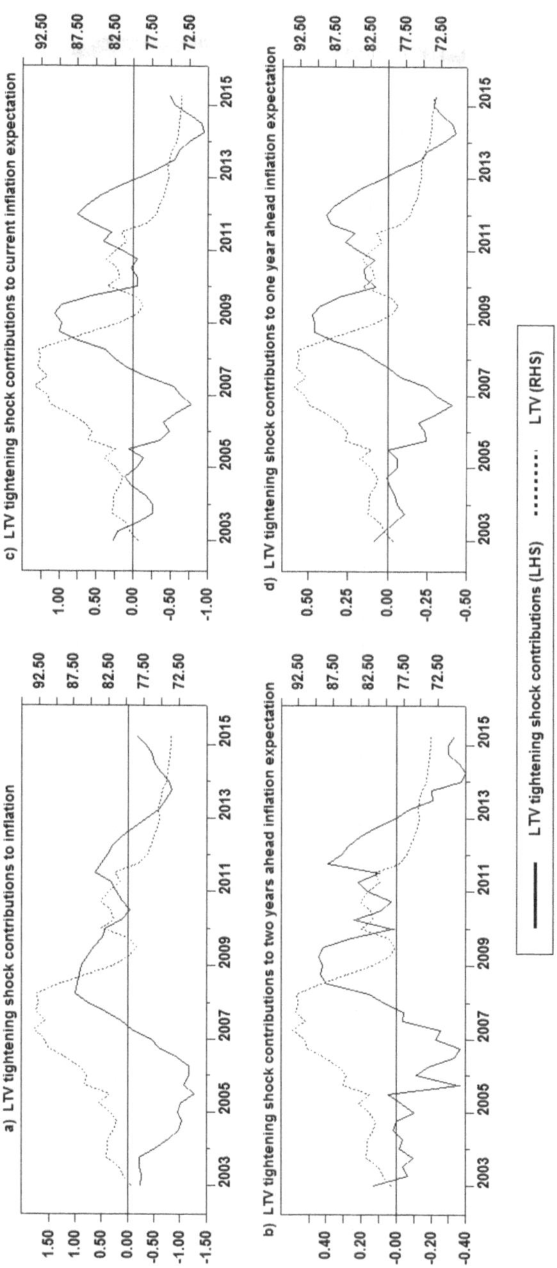

Fig. 20.17 Contributions of the LTV tightening shock to inflation expectations (*Source*: Authors calculations)

20.4.6 Do High Inflation Expectations Pose Risks to Financial Stability Via the LTV Channel?

The analysis examined the extent to which unexpected positive inflation expectations shocks impact the LTV in two ways. First, by determining the direction of the reaction, significance and size of the impulse response functions approach. This assists us to determine whether an unexpected positive inflation expectations shock lead to the LTV tightening or not. Second, to identify periods in which positive inflation expectations shocks lead to the LTV tightening and loosening by applying the historical decomposition approach. This enables the identification of periods during which inflation expectations shocks amongst the current, one year ahead and two years ahead triggered the LTV loosening and tightening. So, the data analysis will reveal if these are permanent or transitory effects.

Fig. 20.18a–c reveals that an unexpected positive inflation expectation shock lowers the LTV significantly for nearly ten quarters. The decline in the LTV suggests that it is tightened very much at the peak due to an unexpected positive current inflation expectation shock. This development has profound policy implications and it implies that the deterioration in the inflation outlook leads to the tightening of LTVs.

This tightening in LTVs reinforces the transmission of policy rates decisions in the case of tightening. In the cases of loosening of monetary policy, the tightening of LTVs may neutralize the intended purposes via the effects in the residential property sector. These conflicting effects again speak to the necessity of coordinating these tools to mitigate unnecessary economic costs.

As stated earlier, the analysis gives further insights into how a positive inflation expectations shock contributes to the LTV dynamics by plotting the actual and counterfactual LTVs (excluding the effects of the inflation expectations shocks). The evidence in Fig. 20.19 shows that inflation expectations categories have an impact on the trajectory of LTVs.

Of great significance to the policymaking process is what has happened recently. The fact that the counterfactual LTV exceeds the actual LTV at the end of sample suggests that the presence of inflation expectation leads to LTV tightening.

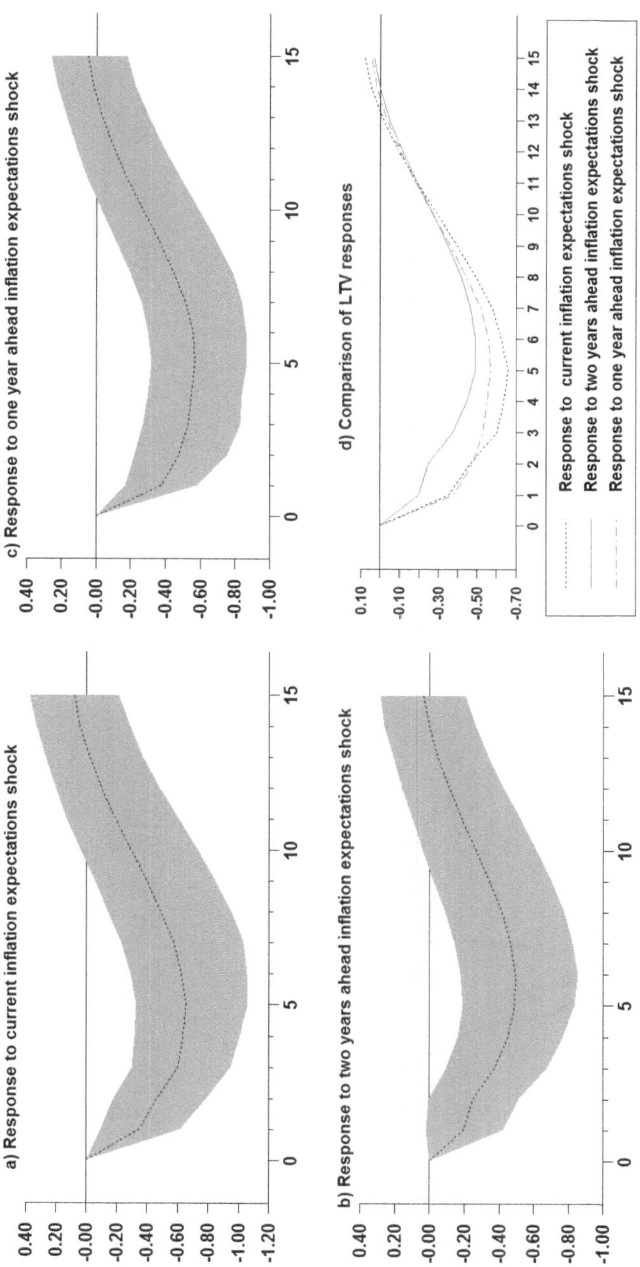

Fig. 20.18 LTV responses to a positive inflation expectations shock (*Source*: Authors' calculations)

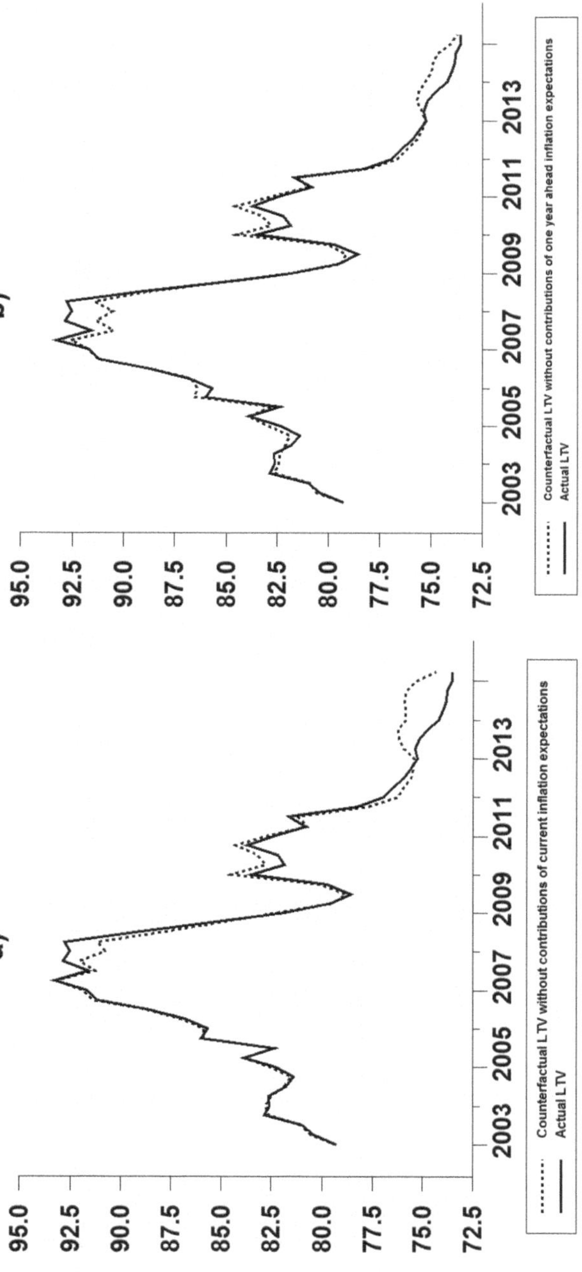

Fig. 20.19 Actual and counterfactual LTV (*Source*: Authors calculations)

To show the magnitude of inflation expectation contributions to LTV dynamics, we plot the contributions from three inflation expectations categories in Fig. 20.20. Since 2013, the inflation expectations shocks were pulling down LTVs. This suggests that inflation expectations shocks lead to LTV tightening. In addition, the tightening is more pronounced with respect to current inflation expectations shock.

20.5 Counterfactual Scenarios

The chapter concludes by applying counterfactual analysis to determine the interaction between LTV and the repo rate via responding to positive inflation and inflation shocks. The model includes the current inflation expectation, GDP growth, repo rate and LTV. The model is estimated using two lags. The counterfactual refers to impulse responses when the LTV variables are shut off in the equation specifying the shock.

Evidence shows that monetary policymakers have a mandate to enforce price stability, but the pace of adjustment differs. The evidence reveals that the repo rate would be higher when the LTV are shut off that when they are not shut off in Fig. 20.21. This suggests that tighter LTVs make the policy rate less aggressive when dealing with positive inflation and inflation expectation shocks. The LTV worsen the GDP response to positive repo rate shocks in Fig. 20.22. The results are robust to different categories of inflation expectations.

20.6 Conclusion and Policy Implications

This chapter examined the question: To what extent has tightening in LTVs reinforced the contractionary monetary policy stance? Evidence indicates that the repo rate and LTV tightening shock effects reinforce each other. In addition, the transmission of the LTV shock occurs through the same channels as those that are impacted by tight monetary policy shock. As such, the repo rate effects on economic variables may be compounded by further tightening of LTVs as a lending standard. In policy terms, this implies that efforts to gradually integrate financial

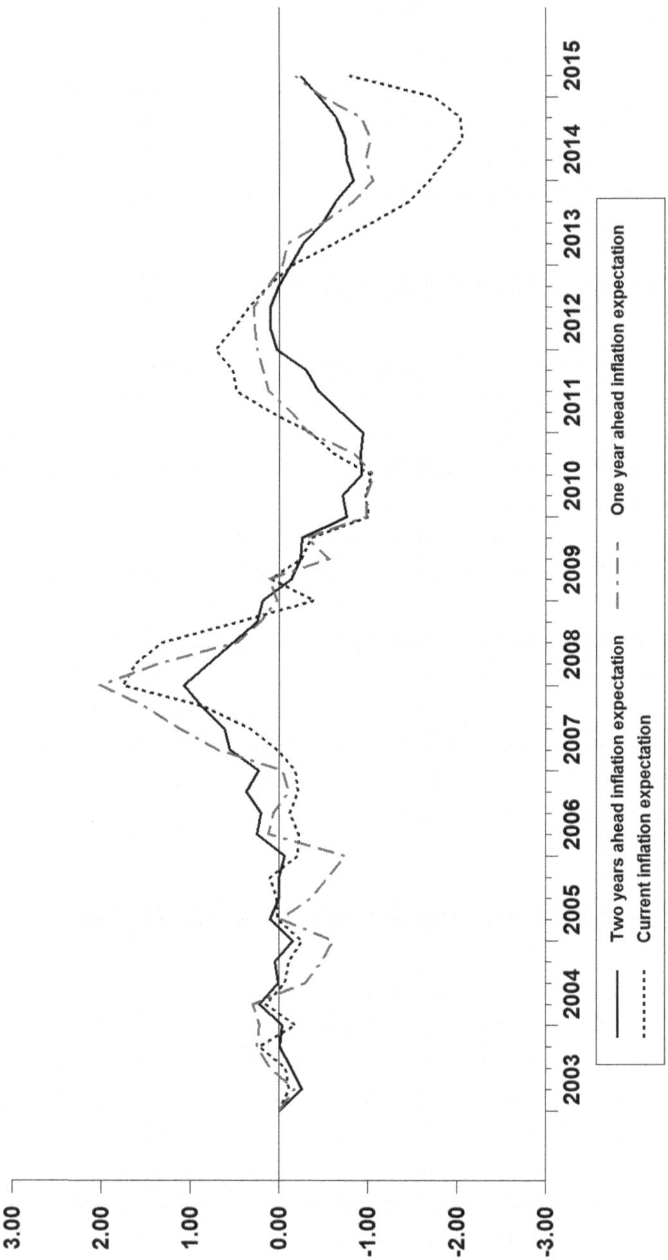

Fig. 20.20 Contributions of positive inflation expectations shock to LTV (*Source*: Authors calculations)

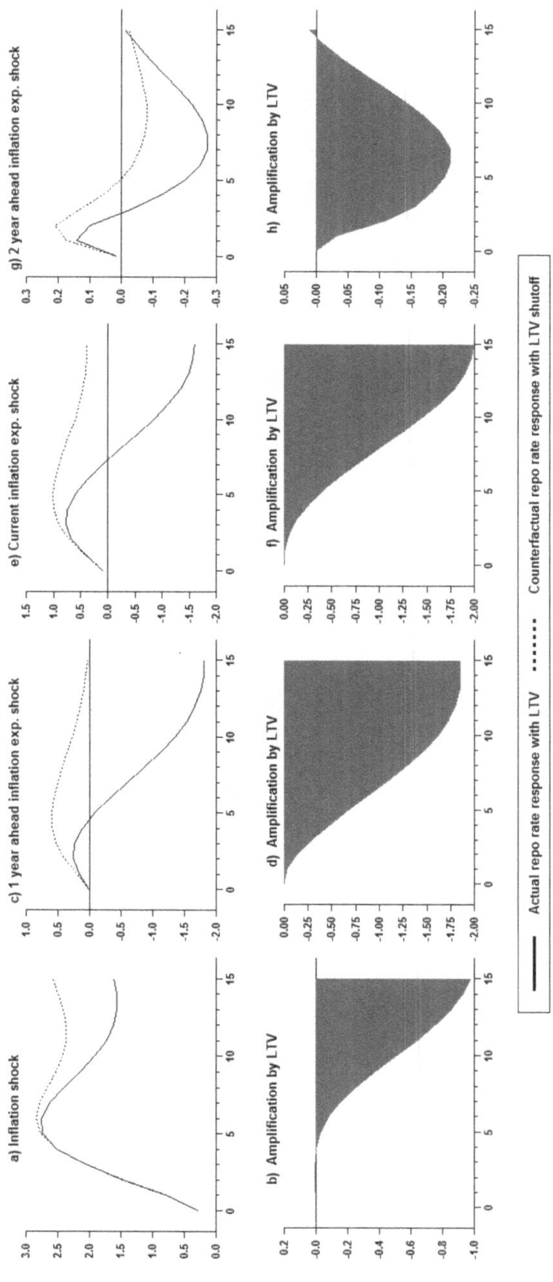

Fig. 20.21 Repo rate responses to positive inflation and inflation expectation shocks and role of LTV (*Source:* Authors calculations)

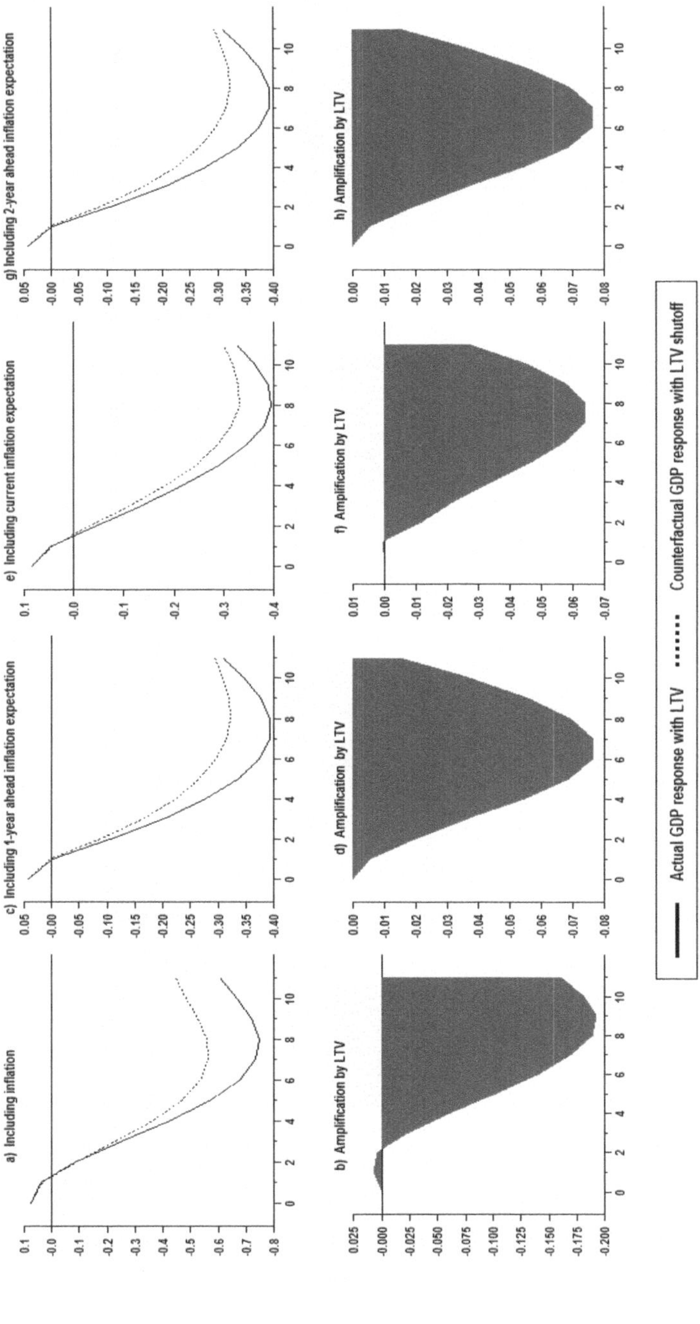

Fig. 20.22 GDP responses to positive repo rate shocks and role of LTV (*Source:* Authors calculations)

stability into monetary policy decisions should be accompanied by the recognition of the potential trade-offs in instruments. This will assist in achieving the desired effects on their own targets.

In addition, a tight monetary policy shock that results in a big reduction in household disposable income and household debt comes at the cost of larger spill-over effects to output. The policy implication therefore is that, largely due to the fact that the large spill-overs are not a desirable policy outcome, the LTV tightening shock is effective as it is a well-targeted tool. In such a scenario, LTVs turn out to be less blunt on output relative to the repo rate. This presents a case for the coordination of tools as they induce fewer fluctuations in other economic variables compared to monetary policy.

The repo rate has a bigger effect on households' net wealth and assets than that exerted by LTV tightening shock over all horizons. This has implications for consumption expenditure, as these tools are transmitted via the wealth and collateral channels. We therefore derive a policy implication that this evidence possibly presents yet another opportunity for the coordination of these tools. It seems very possible that when the economy is hit by a financial shock which alters and leads to revaluation of collateral, a countercyclical LTV policy could be a more effective tool for stabilization. This kind of coordination of the policy tools can loosen the financial and collateral borrowing constraints of households.

We establish that indeed LTVs decline significantly in response to an unexpected positive current inflation expectations shock. The deterioration in the inflation outlook leads to the LTV tightening. In this response LTVs assist in weakening credit-driven inflationary pressures and can help monetary policy to maintain price stability via its impact on inflation. In turn, it is a profound finding that we also establish that the LTV tightening shock significantly lowers inflation expectations and headline inflation. However, the policy implication we derive here is that the tightening in LTVs may conflict with the monetary policy stance if the decision is counter that of the LTVs. This therefore implies that the coordination of these tools is crucial.

The overriding policy implication is that the bank should seriously consider the regulatory aspects allowing the implementation of legal maximum or minimum LTVs. Furthermore, a gradual approach is to properly understand the interaction of LTVs and the repo rate over the monetary transmission mechanism.

Summary of Findings

- Evidence indicates that the repo rate and LTV tightening shock effects reinforce each other.
- The transmission of the LTV shock occurs through the same channels as those that are impacted by tight monetary policy shocks.
- The positive repo rate shock leads to bigger contractions in output and credit aggregates than the LTV tightening shock.
- The repo rate effects on economic variables may be compounded by further tightening of LTVs as a lending standard.
- A repo rate shock leads to a bigger contraction in household debt-to-disposable income and the constituents.
- Household debt is highly responsive to the policy rate changes relative to adjustments in the LTVs.
- A tight monetary policy shock that results in a big reduction in household disposable income and household debt comes at the cost of larger spill-over effects to output.
- The deterioration in the inflation outlook leads to the LTV tightening. In this response LTVs assist in weakening credit-driven inflationary pressures and can help monetary policy to maintain price stability via its impact on inflation.
- The LTV tightening shock significantly lowers inflation expectations and headline inflation.
- Overall, the LTV tightening shocks have some quantitatively important effects on macroeconomic variables such as output, consumption expenditure, household balance sheets, inflation and inflation expectations.

21

Repayment-to-Income and Loan-to-Value Ratios Shocks on the Housing Market

Learning Objectives

- Establish the extent to which positive RTI and LTV tightening shocks impact the economy, inflation and repo rate dynamics
- Analyze whether LTV tightening shocks and the unexpected tightening in the RTI shocks are complementary or supplementary tools
- Understand the role of inflation and inflation expectations in influencing LTV and RTI standards and their spill-over effects into financial stability issues
- Determine whether LTV and RTI tightening shocks benefit price stability
- Establish the influence of the LTV tightening shocks on the level of the repo rate

21.1 Introduction

The analysis continues on the assessment of the interaction of the macroprudential policy for residential mortgage lending tools with the monetary policy tool. However, this chapter focuses on the macroeconomic

N. Gumata, E. Ndou, *Bank Credit Extension and Real Economic Activity in South Africa*, DOI 10.1007/978-3-319-43551-0_21

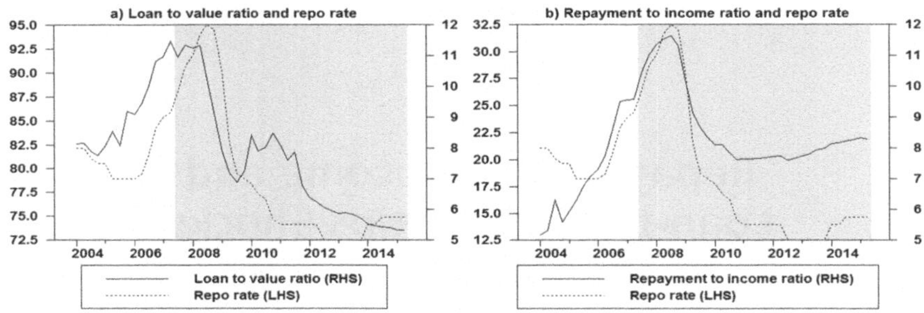

Fig. 21.1 The evolution of the loan-to-value ratio, repayment-to-income and repo rate (*Note*: The *grey* highlighted area in all the graphs shows the period of the National Credit Act and the National Credit Act Amendments. *Source*: SARB and authors' calculations)

effects of an unexpected tightening in the repayment-to-income (RTI)[1] ratio shock and unexpected tightening in loan-to-value (LTV) ratio. Income is a major determinant of housing consumption; hence the RTI as a prudential tool is targeted at risks associated with the debt repayment channel.[2] Thus, RTIs are found to be a more effective tool when house prices are rising faster than incomes.

Nonetheless, these tools do not operate in isolation from the monetary policy framework. As shown in Fig. 21.1, in most instances these tools tend to move with the repo rate, although the relationship is less than perfect. Therefore, the key question explored is: To what extent has the unexpected increase of the RTI and lowering of LTV levels impacted the economy, inflation and the repo rate dynamics?[3]

Is there preliminary evidence which hints at whether the evolution of these two prudential tools indicates already existing coordinated movements? Fig. 21.2 plots the RTI and LTV. Do the signs of relationship between RTI and LTV indicate complementarity between these tools? Indeed, the preliminary evidence suggests these two tools move together

[1] The mortgage repayment-to-income ratio (RTI) is defined as that portion of the households' gross income that is committed to paying interest and principal on mortgage debt.

[2] In addition, LTVs on their own may not be sufficient tools as indebtedness can still increase when house prices increase.

[3] Needless to say, this period is also characterized by the implementation of the National Credit Act (NCA) and the National Credit Act Amendments (NCAA).

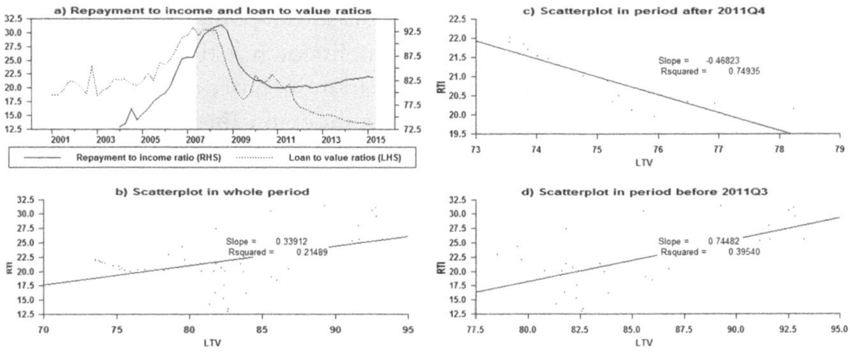

Fig. 21.2 Relationship between RTI and LTV over different periods (*Note*: The *grey* highlighted area in all the graphs shows the period of the National Credit Act and the National Credit Act Amendments. *Source*: SARB and authors' calculations)

but not perfectly. There has been divergence after 2011. Should this then be a concern for policymakers? These developments motivate us to assess how economic shocks affect the LTVs and RTIs and whether these shocks move economic variables in the same direction. The effects are explored in later sections.

This chapter fills various research policy gaps in the area of the interaction of macro-prudential tools and monetary policy. It does so by examining the main question supported by sub-questions. To what extent have the positive RTI and LTV tightening shocks impacted the economy, inflation and repo rate dynamics? In addition, the chapter brings the role of the RTIs into the core of policy discussions on the residential macro-prudential tools. Furthermore, it shows policymakers whether the LTV tightening shocks and the unexpected tightening in the RTI shocks are complementary or supplementary tools.

Is it possible that the LTV tightening was attributed to developments in mortgage advances? Can understanding the interaction between the LTVs and RTIs help in grasping how these tools can be used in attempting to close mortgage advances gap in a prudent way? How did the LTV tightening shock impact non-performing loans?

The role of inflation in influencing LTV and RTI standards has been not clearly articulated in policy circles, nor have its spill-over effects into financial stability issues. Hence, the analysis shows policymakers whether evidence indicates that price stability benefits or not from an LTV and RTI tightening shock. In addition, what can monetary policymakers infer from the influence of the LTV tightening shock on the level of the repo rate? So, how meaningful is the RTI in driving the repo rate dynamics?

21.2 Why Does the Repayment-to-Income Ratio Matter?

The RTI matters for various reasons. First, the implications of the household debt burden for both financial stability and monetary policy are well known. The inability of households to service their debt worsens the credit quality of banks' books as non-performing loans increase. Second, unsustainable debt repayments burden the household sector, dragging consumption expenditure and economic activity in general.

Furthermore, the literature suggests that higher RTIs, which are associated with high mortgage repayment burdens, lead to an increase in the probability of mortgage default rates. Third, the negative income shocks largely emanating from labor market dynamics have an important relationship with mortgage defaults and the household debt burden in general. These issues sit right at the heart of the current debate on the interaction between monetary and macro-prudential tools.[4]

However, there are weaknesses and unintended consequences associated with the RTI as a macro-prudential tool. For instance, some borrowers, in particular first time ones, can be effectively barred for years from entering the housing market as they are unable to meet the higher deposit requirements and lower RTIs at the same time. Furthermore, as the volume of mortgage lending and house prices fall, this will also affect the construction and supply of new housing as the profitability is affected.

However, these aspects fall outside the ambit of the policymakers' financial and price stability mandates. Such unintended consequences

---

[4] See for example Svensson on arguments about using monetary policy as tool to deal with indebtedness in Sweden: http://www.riksbank.se/en/Press-and-published/Speeches/2012/Svensson-Monetary-policy-debt-and-unemployment/andhttp://www.voxeu.org/article/why-leaning-against-wind-wrong-monetary-policy-sweden

will have to be attended to in a coordinated manner by the relevant policy and regulatory institutions. From a financial stability perspective, a positive trade-off that benefits society as whole matters more. The individual welfare costs of a temporary exclusion of some households from the housing market would possibly be outweighed by the aggregate welfare gain if the tightening of LTVs and DTIs are able to prevent or dampen misaligned house prices and costly house price busts. Furthermore, it seems that when well-coordinated, these tools are effective in working to equilibrate demand and supply factors in the housing market, resulting in sustainable house price growth (Igan and Kang 2011). Such an outcome is beneficial to society as a whole.

21.3 Disentangling the Role of the LTV in Housing Market Activity

21.3.1 What Is the Relationship Between the LTV, House Prices and Valuers' Demand and Supply Strength Indices?

Fig. 21.3a shows the relationship between real house price growth and LTV. The positive relationship suggests that LTV loosening leads to an increase in house price growth. However, the relationship is very weak and the LTV explains nearly 1.5 percent of house price growth. So, there are factors in the housing market that have an even greater influence on house prices and are more sensitive to LTVs. Is it possible that the supply and demand factors are more sensitive to LTV loosening?

It is evident in Fig. 21.3b that the steep upward slope suggests that the loosening of LTV leads to an increase in the valuers' demand strength index. The improvement in the valuers' demand index in turn raises house price growth in Fig. 21.3f. In contrast, in Fig.21.3c the loosening of the LTV has a negative effect on the valuers' supply index. This may be due to the fact that increase in the valuers' supply depresses house price growth, as in Fig. 21.3e. These results suggest that the LTV shocks have an impact on the supply and demand factors in the housing market. The

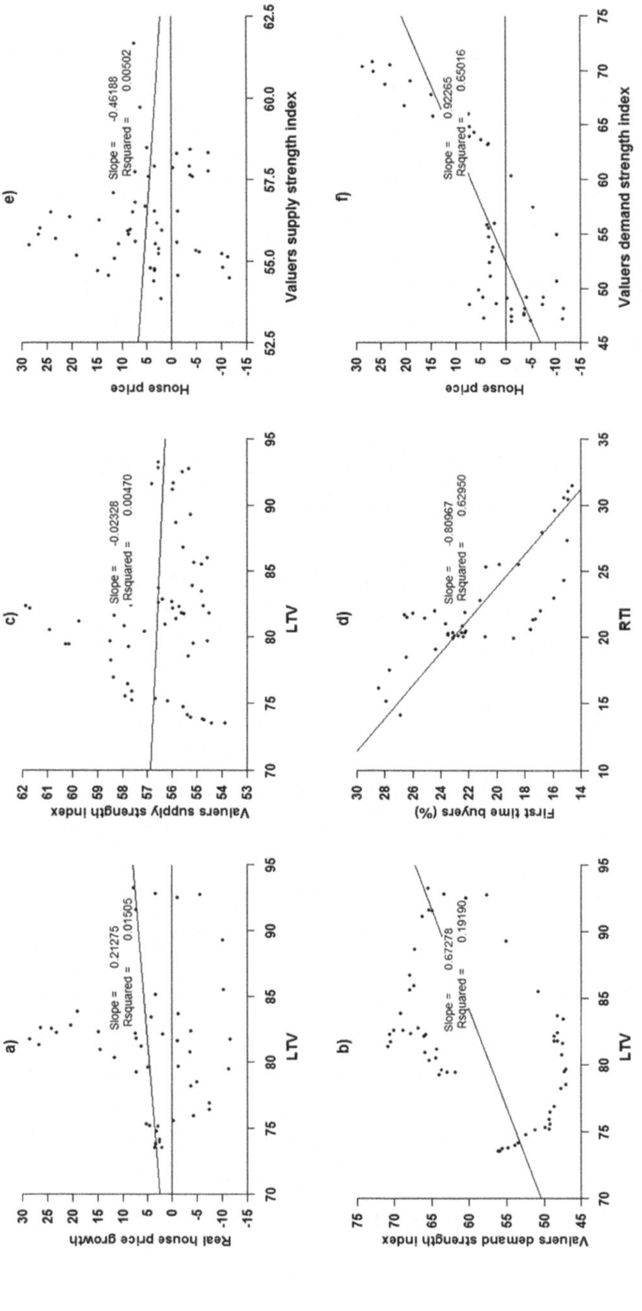

Fig. 21.3 House prices, valuers' demand and supply strength index, LTV and RTI (*Source*: FNB and authors' calculations)

LTV shock moves residential property demand and supply in different directions. In turn, this has implications for house price dynamics and possibly wealth and collateral effects for consumers. This evidence confirms that the LTVs work via different aspects of housing market activity.

What can be inferred about the relationship between first time entrants into property and affordability issues? There is a negative relationship between the proportion of first time property buyers and the RTI in Fig. 21.3d. This speaks to affordability issues. What about other aspects of the housing market and mortgage advances?

Fig. 21.4b shows that there is a negative relationship between first time buyers and LTV. Similarly, when the credit quality of banks' mortgage books deteriorates, as proxied by an increase in non-performing loans (NPLs), mortgage advances and first time entrants decline in Fig. 21.4c and d. Furthermore, the lead–lag relationship between NPLs and first time buyers suggests high cyclicality. As NPLs decline (increase) banks grant more (less) loans to first time buyers. However, in general, NPLs depress house prices in Fig. 21.4e. But it seems that house price growth favors first time entrants in Fig. 21.4a given the positive relationship. This may be related to the demand and supply factors shown in Fig. 21.3.

Fig. 21.3 shows that LTVs via demand and supply forces in the housing market impact house price growth. Is there any further evidence on how the LTVs work via the housing market forces and possibly equilibrate house prices? The effects are assessed through looking at the impact of the LTV on the percentage of properties for sold less than the asking prices, the duration the property stays on the market and the house price-to-income ratio. The relationships based on the scatter plots are shown in Fig. 21.5.

The regression lines in the scatter plots in Fig. 21.5a and c show a negative relationship between the LTV and the percentage of properties sold for less than asking prices as well as the duration properties stay on the market. This suggests that LTV loosening reduces the percentage of properties for sold less than the asking price, as well the duration the property stays on the market. This shows that the LTVs do indeed operate via a number of channels in terms of residential real estate market activity. But

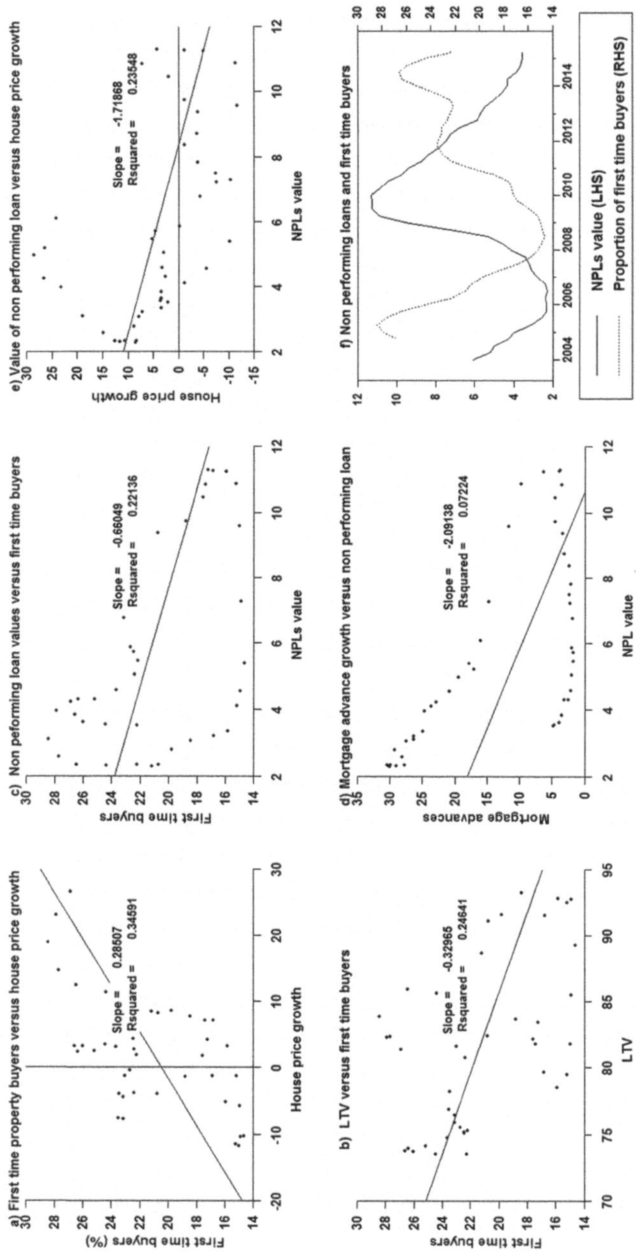

Fig. 21.4 House prices, LTV, non-performing loans, mortgage advances and first time buyers (*Source*: FNB and authors' calculations)

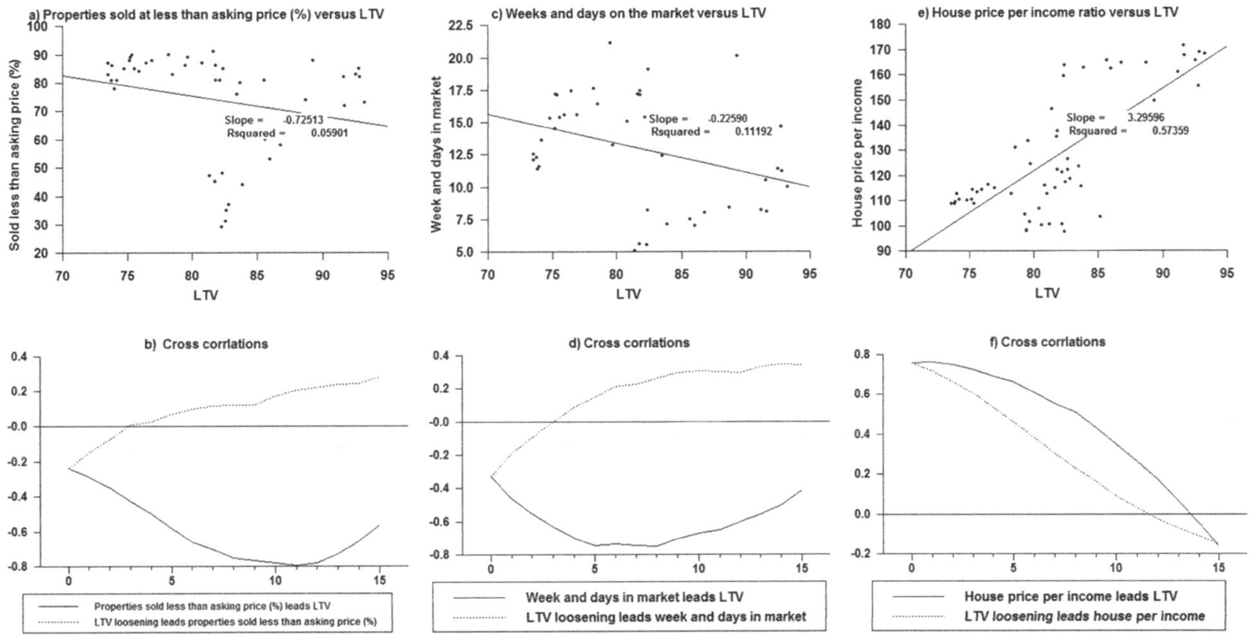

Fig. 21.5 LTV, properties sold less than asking price and duration houses stay on the market (*Source*: FNB and authors' calculations)

this is accompanied by an increase in the house price-to-income ratio and worsens the affordability matrices.

The analyses apply the cross correlations to determine the lead and lag relationships. A negative relationship is in evidence in Fig. 21.5b when the percentage of properties sold for less than asking price leads the LTV. Similarly, a negative relationship is visible in Fig. 21.5d when the duration the house stays on the market leads the LTV. These two findings imply that the LTV is tightened when conditions in the residential real estate market deteriorate.

Does the loosening of the LTV lead to improvements manifested in the few weeks taken to sell property and lead to getting higher than asking prices? Yes, it does. The LTV loosening reduces the percentage of properties for sold less than the asking price but this effect lasts for less than a year in Fig. 21.5b. Thereafter, the proportion of prices sold below asking prices rises. In addition, in Fig. 21.5d the loosening of the LTV reduces the duration the property stays on the market for less than a year, thereafter the period increases. These findings suggest that although LTVs do indeed help in equilibrating demand and supply factors in the housing market, other factors play a role for longer durations. The analysis concludes by looking at the cross correlations between house prices-to-income and LTV in Fig.21.5f. The positive relationship suggests that the loosening of LTVs raises house prices relative to income. The reverse occurs when an improvement in the house prices-to-income leads LTVs.

21.3.2 Do Non-performing Loans Impact LTVs?

The relationship between LTVs and the volume and value of NPLs is depicted in Fig. 21.6a and b. The negative relationship suggests that a deterioration in NPLs leads to the tightening of LTVs. However, which aspect of the NPLs has a pronounced impact on LTVs? The LTV tightens more due to the increase in the value of NPLs in Fig. 21.6a than to the increase in the volumes in Fig. 21.6b.

Is this a robust finding? Yes, it is corroborated by the cross correlations in Fig. 21.6c. The correlations are bigger in Fig. 21.6c when an increase

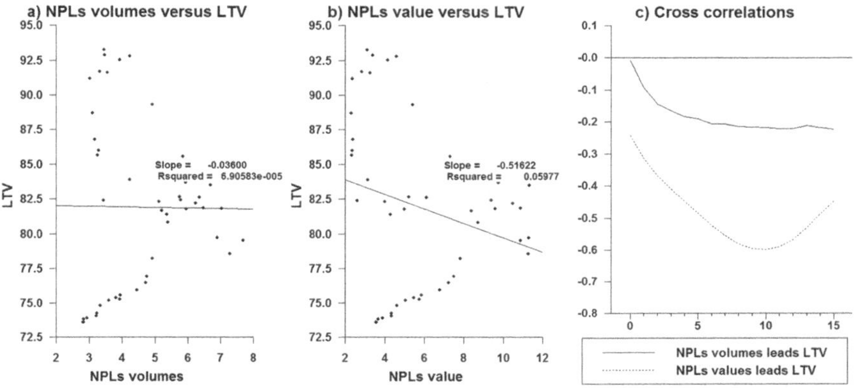

Fig. 21.6 The relationship between NPLs and LTVs (*Source*: SARB and authors' calculations)

in the value of NPLs leads LTVs. As a result, the LTVs are tightened very much as the quality of the mortgage books of banks deteriorates.

21.4 Which Methodology Is Best Used for the Empirical Analysis and to Answer the Relevant Questions?

What approaches does the analysis use to assist in answering these questions? To enable us to answer the preceding questions and appropriately offer policy prescriptions, a bootstrapped VAR approach is used based on 2,500 draws for impulse responses. Quarterly data spans from 2001Q1 to 2015Q2 for GDP, inflation, repo rate, LTV and additional variables. However, the RTI and other variables are available at a later date, so the sample is adjusted to start later than 2001Q1 and to keep the end of sample as 2015Q2. The GDP is log transformed and multiplied by 100. The model uses two lags and the results are robust to using one lag. Additional variables that are not rates were log transformed and multiplied by 100. This enables their impulse responses to shocks to be interpreted as percentage deviation from the trend.

21.4.1 Do Lending Standards Measured by the LTV React to Economic Shocks?

To answer this question, the analysis determines the responses of LTV to various economic shocks in Fig. 21.7. A positive GDP shock in Fig. 21.7a raises the LTV significantly for three quarters; this suggests that improved economic performance leads to loosening of lending standards such as the LTV. A positive total loans and advances and mortgage advances shocks in Fig. 21.7e and f raises the LTV significantly for four and eleven quarters, respectively. This implies credit growth rises very much for a long period via the LTV loosening.

Does a wealth shock matter? Yes, it does. The wealth shock denoted by house prices matters as an unexpected increase in house prices leads to a significant loosening of the LTV over all horizons, as shown in Fig. 21.7d. These results underpin the close relationship between housing prices, LTVs and total credit and mortgage advances. This raises an important question: How does tighter monetary policy and inflation shock affect LTVs?

In Fig. 21.8c and b the LTVs are tightened due to unexpected positive repo rate and inflation shocks. This is consistent with theoretical predictions. In the forward-looking monetary policy conduct the deterioration in the inflation outlook should lead to a tighter policy stance and the latter raises debt financing costs leading to the LTV tightening.

Which shock between inflation and the repo rate has bigger effects on the LTV? Fig. 21.8a, shows that inflationary shocks lead to larger tightening in the LTV relative to a contractionary monetary policy stance. In policy terms, this implies that high inflation accompanied by an increase in the repo rates can lead to very tight LTVs. Hence, it is necessary for policy authorities to lower the inflation rate and anchor inflation expectations within the inflation target band. The role of inflation in influencing LTVs as a lending standard has heretofore not been clearly understood and articulated in policy circles. But it is evident that inflationary pressures and expectations do spill-over to financial stability issues.

Do house prices, mortgage advances and total loans and advances shocks impact the LTV in a similar manner? Yes, these shocks raise the

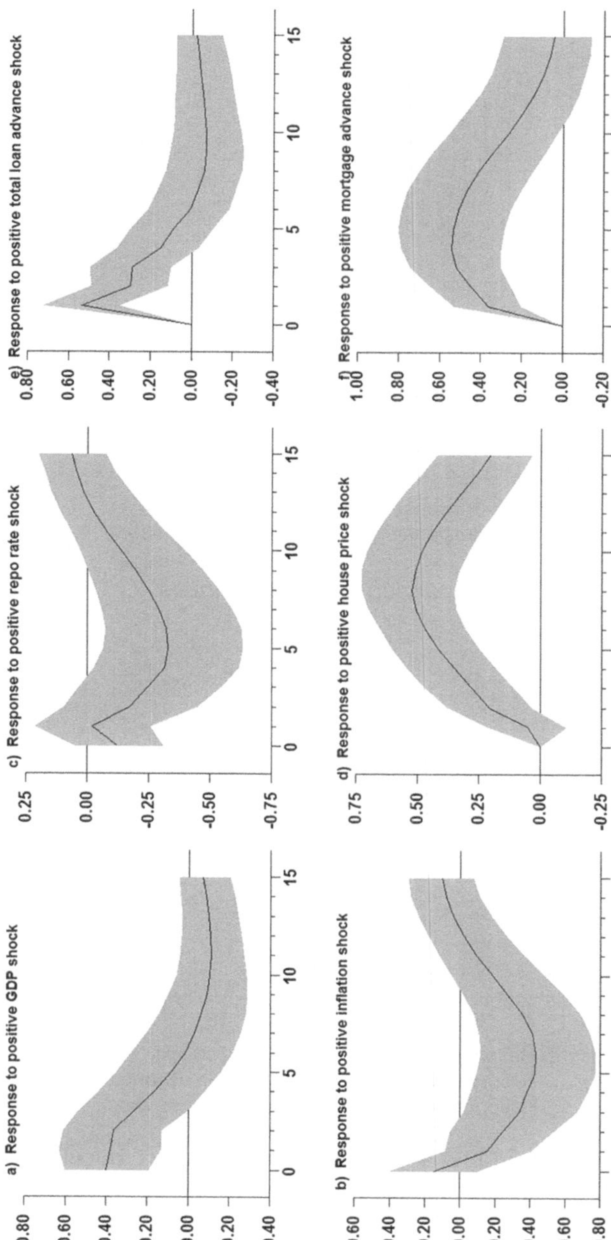

Fig. 21.7 The LTV responses to one positive standard deviation shocks (*Source*: Authors' calculations)

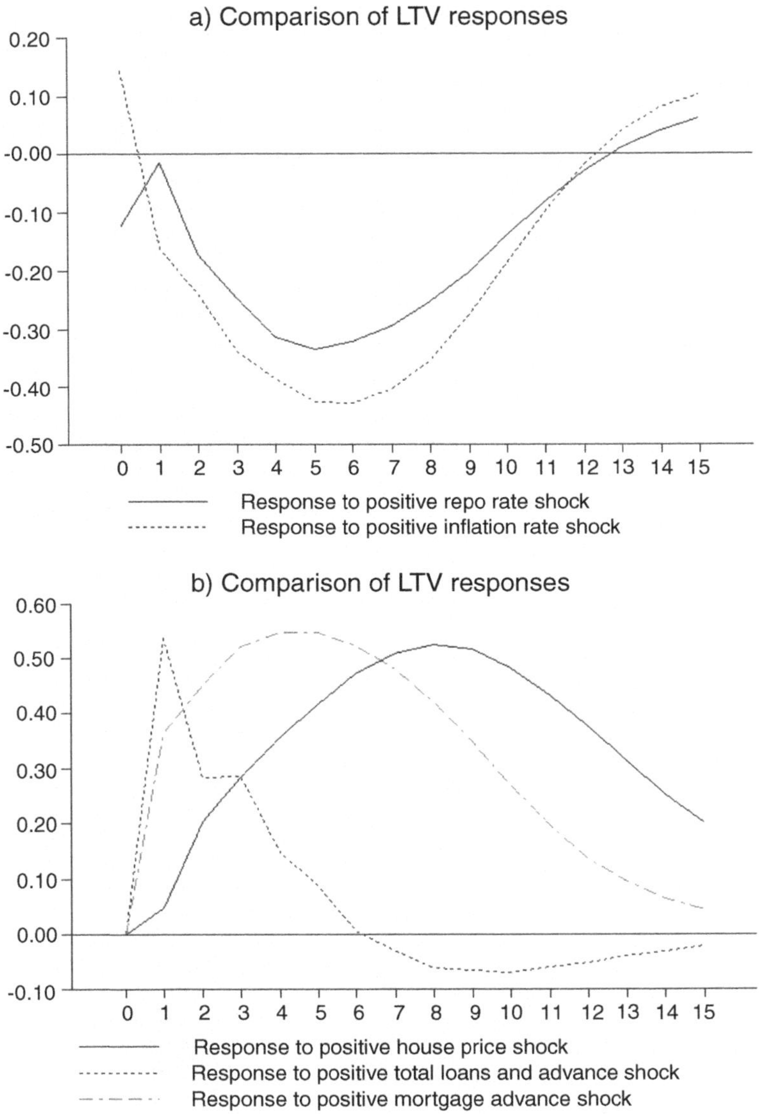

Fig. 21.8 Comparison of LTV responses (*Source*: Authors' calculations)

LTV, but the peak effects are reached in different periods in Fig. 21.8b. The peak LTV increase occurs in first quarter due to total loans and advances shock. This is much shorter than the nine quarters due to a positive house price shock and four quarters due to a positive mortgage advances shock.

21.4.2 To What Extent Do the LTV Responses Differ from Those of the RTI?

Evidence indicates that both RTI and LTV tightening shocks move the variables of interest in the same direction. In Fig. 21.9a, the peak decline in the GDP responses is not different to the RTI and LTV shocks as they are within the same confidence bands. The repo rate and inflation tend to be much lower due to the RTI shock than to the LTV shock in Fig. 21.9b and c within the first year. Thereafter, the responses are not different to each other.

Fig. 21.9d shows that LTVs decline more than the RTI due to an unexpected positive inflation shock. Evidence concludes that both the RTI and LTV shocks impact the variables in the same direction, suggesting that these tools can be used as complementarily.

Fig. 21.10 reveals that the real house prices peak leads the peaks in the LTV based on the cross-correlation approach in Fig. 21.10b. Indeed, in Fig. 21.10b increases in house prices lead to LTV loosening. In addition, Fig. 21.10c indicates a positive relationship.

Fig. 21.11a compares the response of the RTI to those of the LTV to a positive GDP shock. A positive GDP growth shock increases both the RTI and LTV for nearly a year. These responses are not statistically different to each other as they lie within same error bands. Fig. 21.11c shows that a positive house price shock raises the RTI and LTV.

This suggests that an increase in wealth and collateral effects associated with house price appreciation enables the creditors to loosen lending standards based on the LTV. At the same time banks increase the RTI, suggesting that the increase in house prices impacts affordability metrics. This speaks to the interactions of house price increases, LTVs and the RTIs. In order to supply mortgage credit, banks accommodate a positive

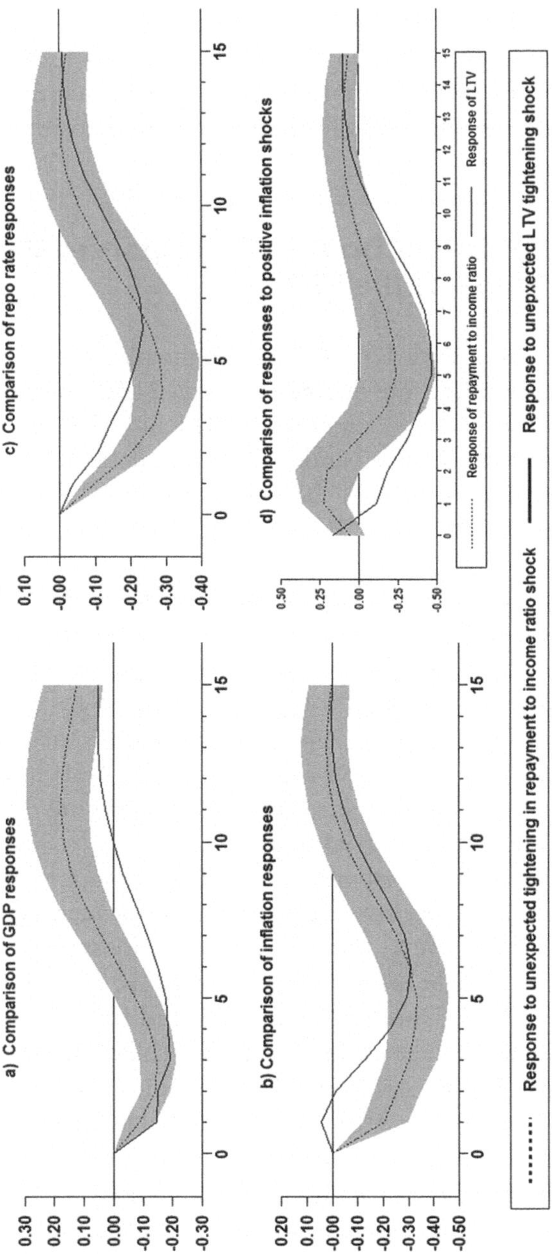

Fig. 21.9 A comparison of the responses of selected variables to the LTV tightening and positive RTI shock (*Source*: Authors' calculations)

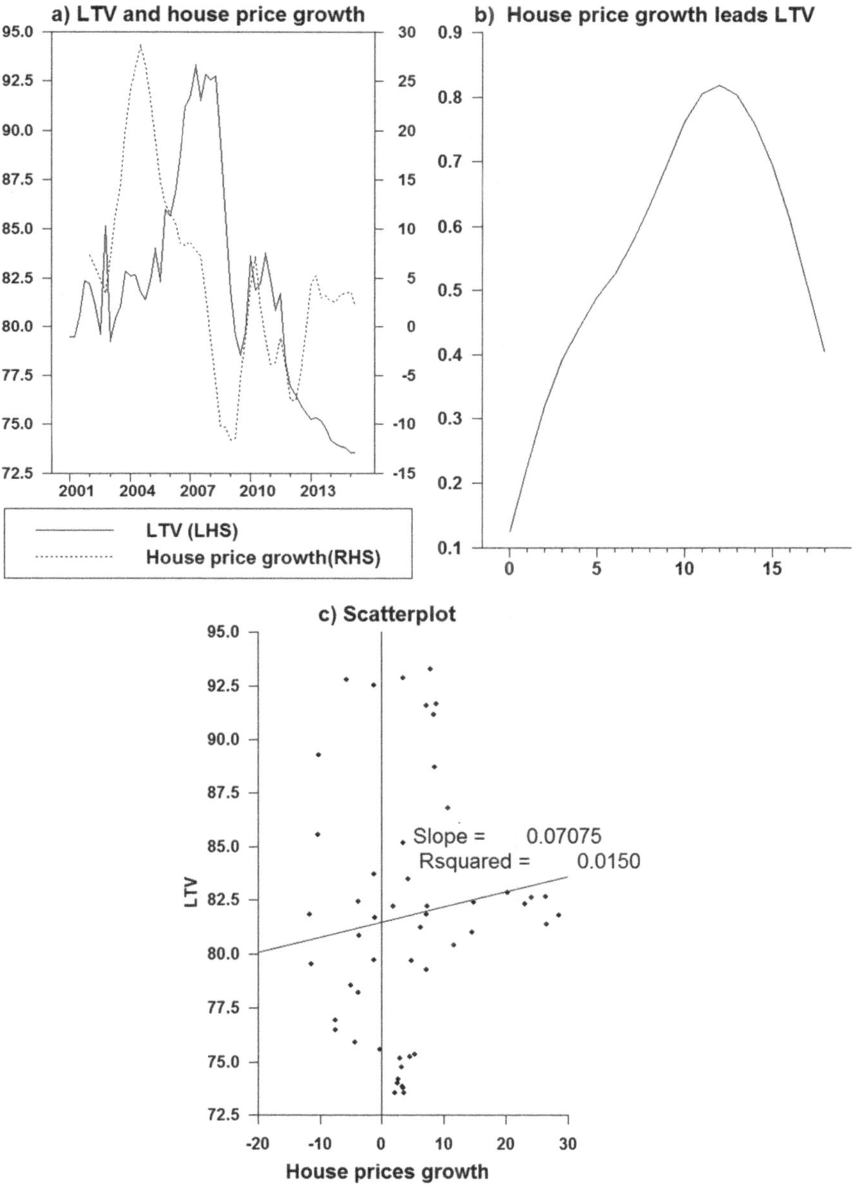

Fig. 21.10 The LTVs and house price dynamics (*Source*: Authors' calculations)

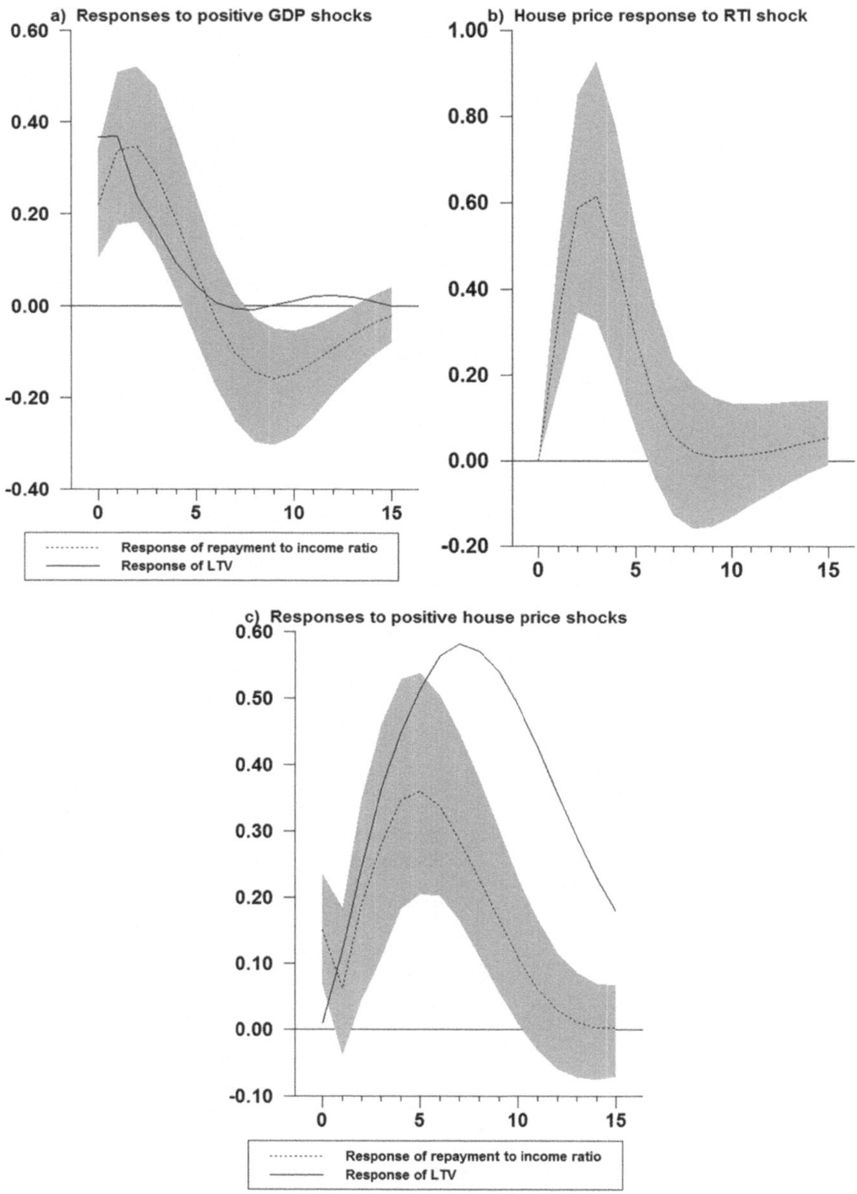

Fig. 21.11 Selected responses to positive economic shocks (*Source*: Authors' calculations)

house price shock by increasing the income gearing or repayment burden and limit of the mandatory down payment.

Furthermore, during the sample period house price increases in most instances preceded the loosening of the LTVs and increase in the RTIs. Implying that as tools at the discretion of banks, LTVs and RTIs help to reinforce the momentum in house prices. As a result, if the intention is to use these tools to avoid overheating or dampen mortgage credit and house price growth, the RTIs and LTVs should be adjusted in a proactive or pre-emptive approach. This approach probably requires a macroprudential regulatory framework. It can potentially exploit the house price link to the LTVs and RTIs via the expectations channel, as agents gradually lower expected house price increases. In addition, through the expectations channel, tighter LTVs and lower RTIs can also dampen speculative activity (Igan and Kang, 2011).

21.4.3 Should Monetary Policy Authorities Be Concerned About Unexpected Developments in LTV Dynamics?

Currently, monetary policy authorities do not set the LTV caps but may implement decisions that directly impact lending standards. In addition, monetary policy authorities may be aware of the pass-through effect of the policy rate changes to lending standards. In turn, banks' tightening of lending standards may have beneficial or adverse effects on the economy. This suggests the need to identify the potency of the transmission channels related to the LTV tightening shock.

Indeed, Fig. 21.12c shows that monetary policy is loosened due to the LTV tightening shock. Credit extension declines in Fig. 21.12e and d. However, the decline in credit is dependent on the credit category. The contraction is larger in total loans and advances than in mortgage advances in Fig. 21.12f. In addition, GDP contracts in Fig. 21.12a and this signifies the potency of changes in lending standards across various categories of credit.

Does price stability benefit from the LTV tightening shock? Yes, it does indeed, as inflation declines in Fig. 21.13b. This suggests that the

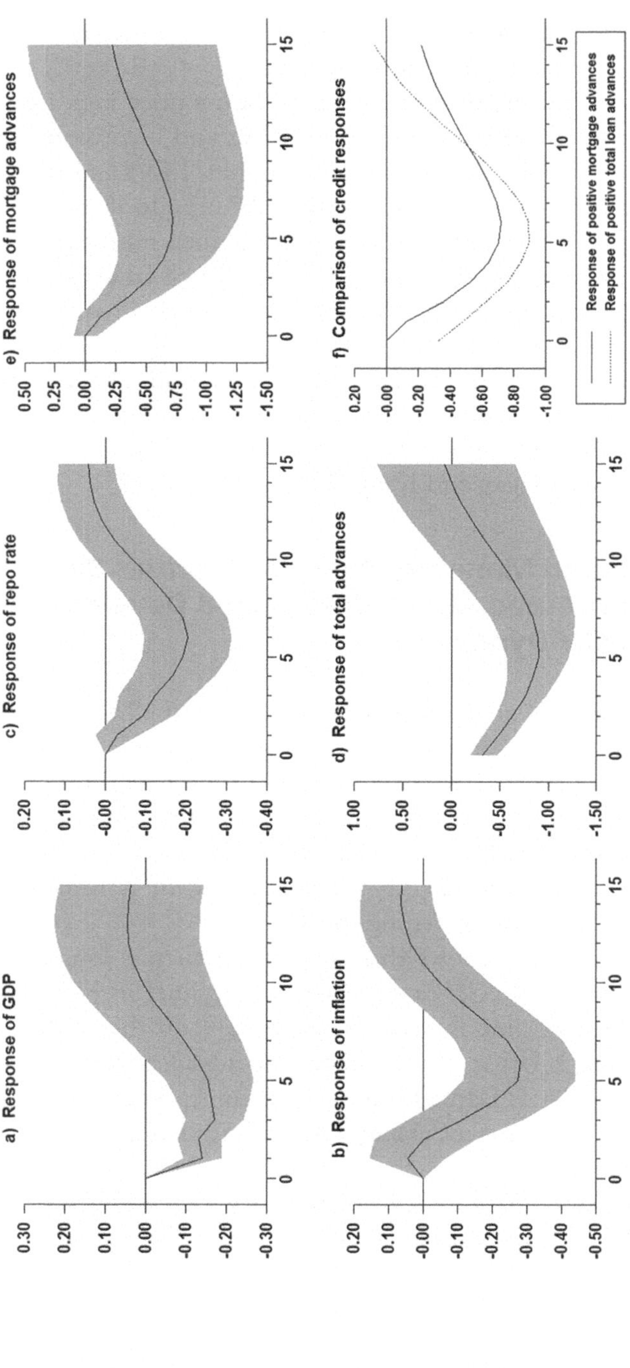

Fig. 21.12 Responses to LTV tightening shocks (*Source*: Authors' calculations)

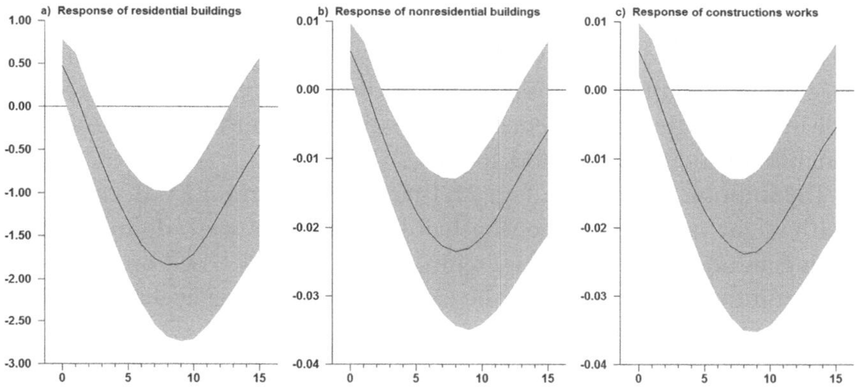

Fig. 21.13 Responses of the residential sector variables (*Source*: Authors' calculations)

absence of credit-driven demand pressures lower inflationary pressures. Furthermore, in the absence of exogenous factors such as oil prices and with a stable currency, an unexpected tightening in lending standards may benefit the price stability mandate. This shows the spill-over benefits from the LTV tightening shocks.

This chapter extends the analysis into activity in the residential and non-residential sectors as they form part of the monetary transmission mechanism, and the responses are shown in Fig. 21.13. Amongst these sectors, evidence indicates that the residential sector in Fig. 21.13a is more highly responsive than both the non-residential and construction works sectors in Fig. 21.13b and e, respectively. Activity in the residential sector declines by about 2 percent at the peak period (around eight quarters) which is larger than nearly 0.03 percent in the non-residential and construction works sector.

21.4.4 When Did the LTV Tightening Shock Series Exhibit both Loosening and Tightening Phases?

The approach adopted in this chapter enables us to extract the estimates of the LTV tightening shock series over time, which includes the influence of variables included in the model. The LTV dynamics may not be wholly indicative of the extent to which it is loosened unless it is purged of the influence of other variables because some prevailing conditions may make it tighter or looser. Plotting the estimated LTV shock series will indicate when it tightened and loosened given the influence of the variables included in the model.

The impulse response in Fig. 21.14a shows that the LTV declined for nearly eight quarters, suggesting lending standards were tightened following an unexpected LTV tightening shock. Hence, based on this eight quarter duration, we calculate the eight-quarter moving average to minimize noise in the estimated shock series as shown in Fig. 21.14b.

Values below zero of this LTV shock series imply tightening, while positive values mean loosening. So, what happened to the LTV shock since 2011–2015Q2? Both the eight and twelve quarters' moving averages show that the LTV shocks have tightened very much relative to periods around 2006 and 2008.

21.4.5 Is It Possible That the LTV Tightening Can Be Attributed to Adverse Developments in Mortgage Advances?

The analysis does not embark on exhaustive assessment of the determinants of what could drive the LTV tightening shock. Rather, we examine whether mortgage advances are partially responsible. The historical decomposition approach is applied to decompose the LTV variable into its trend and its own contributions and contributions from other variables. Thereafter, we determine the counterfactual LTV by shutting off the contributions of the positive mortgage advances shock. This helps us to ascertain the level of LTVs that would prevail. Fig. 21.15 shows that the counterfactual exceeds the actual LTV, which suggests that developments in mortgage advances lead to LTV tightening.

As suggested in the earlier section, it seems that in light of the increase in mortgage defaults, banks adopted prudent management of mortgage books and one of the tools they use is the LTV. Hence, this section examines whether LTV changes relative to a threshold of 80 percent have an impact the value of NPLs. So this means that 80 percent LTVs are the

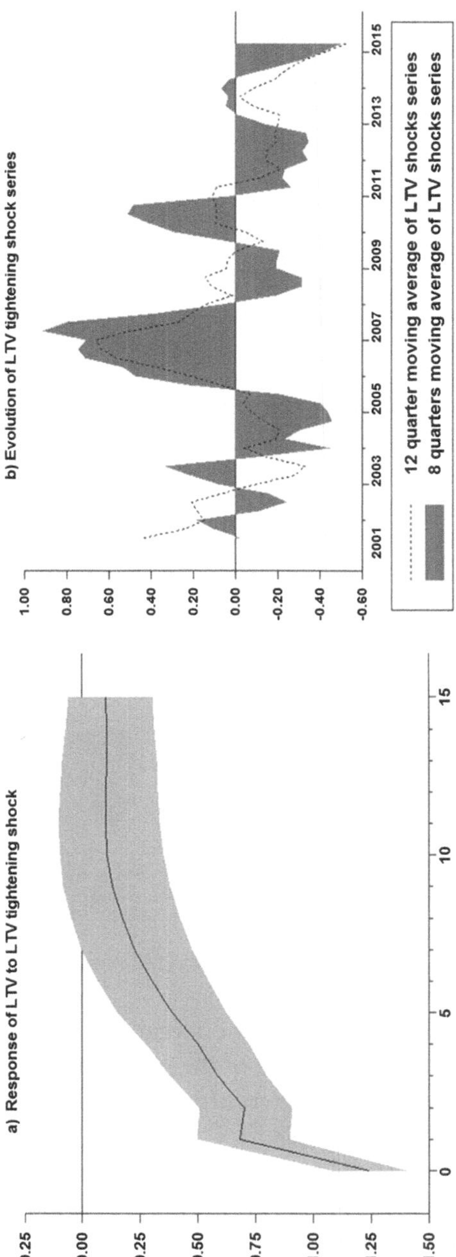

Fig. 21.14 The evolution of the LTV tightening shock (*Source*: Authors' calculations)

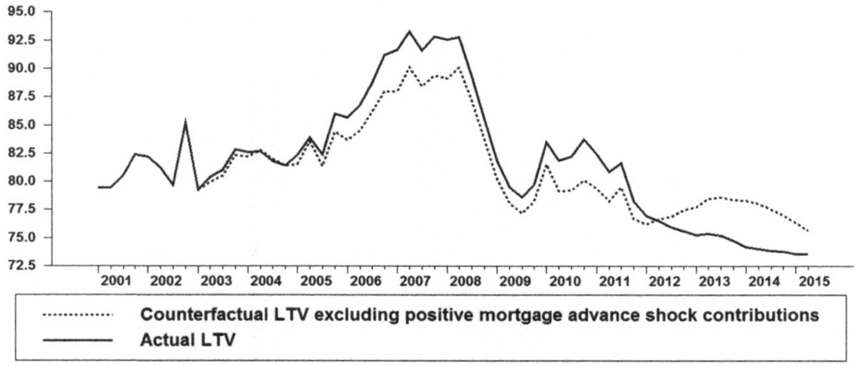

Fig. 21.15 The role of a positive mortgage shock on LTV dynamics (*Source*: Authors' calculations)

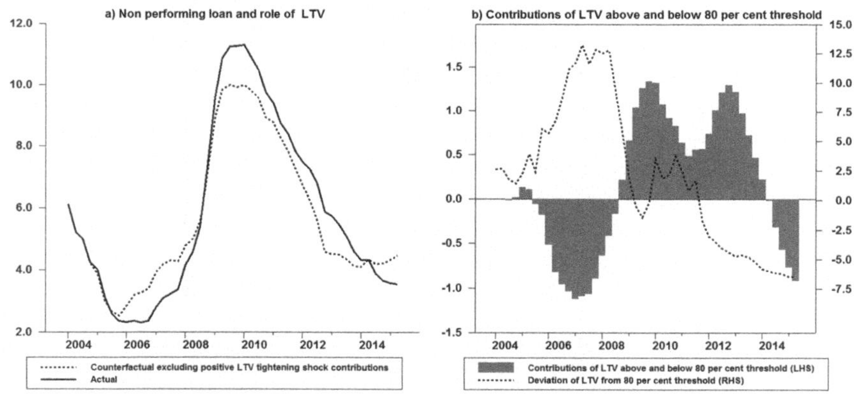

Fig. 21.16 The role of LTVs on NPL dynamics (*Source*: Authors' calculations)

maximum allowed. Fig. 21.16 shows the actual and counterfactual NPLs. The counterfactual NPLs are purged of the effects of the LTV tightening shocks. Fig. 21.16b shows that the continued reduction in NPLs later in 2014 may be attributed to tighter LTVs, which is consistent with prudent lending practices by banks.

Furthermore, it is evident in Fig. 21.17a that NPLs decline significantly in reaction to an unexpected LTV tightening shock. This is in contrast

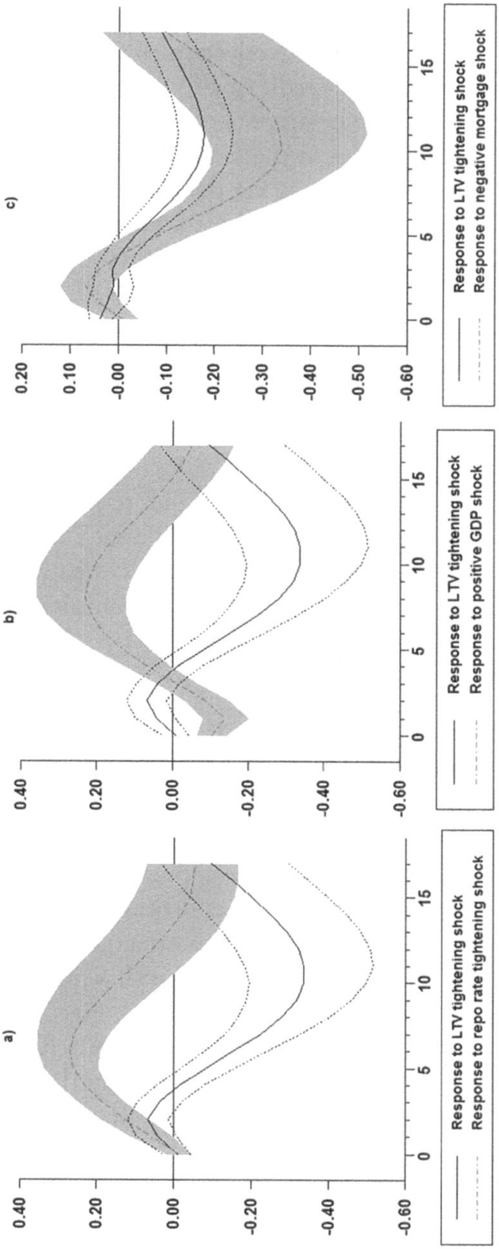

Fig. 21.17 The comparisons of NPL responses (*Source*: Authors' calculations)

to the increase observed in NPLs in response to the repo rate tightening. This probably hints at the relative effectiveness of the tools. Tighter LTVs perform better at managing the credit quality of banks' mortgage books. This is another set of evidence in support of the benefits of the coordination of the tools. It may be due to the fact that because LTVs lower the initial indebtedness, the result in a lower debt burden when interest rates rise and the probability of default is reduced. Hence, by limiting household leverage, they can help potentially reduce the probability of defaults.

This chapter further shows the responses of the NPLs to an unexpected rise in GDP in Fig. 21.17b. Indeed, economic growth does benefit NPLs as they decline, although this is transitory, further implying that the regulation of prudent lending standards via LTVs yields better outcomes for banks' mortgage books. If used well, they can dampen procyclicality in defaults.

In Fig. 21.17c the impact of unexpected reduction in mortgage advances reduces NPLs but not as much as the LTV tightening shock. This means this as part of prudent lending practices banks can lower the supply of mortgage credit by lowering LTVs and enforcing stricter lending standards.

21.4.6 Is There Further Evidence That LTV Tightening Shocks Have Beneficial Spill-Overs to Price Stability?

The historical decomposition approach is applied to decompose the inflation variable into its trend and its own contribution and contributions from other variables. Thereafter, the counterfactual inflation is determined by shutting off the contributions of the LTV tightening shock to determine the level of inflation that would prevail. Fig. 21.18a shows the counterfactual inflation and actual inflation rate. When the counterfactual exceeds the actual inflation rate this suggests that the LTV tightening shock contributed to lowering inflation to less than it would be otherwise. Are there such episodes and what has the LTV tightening shock done to inflation recently?

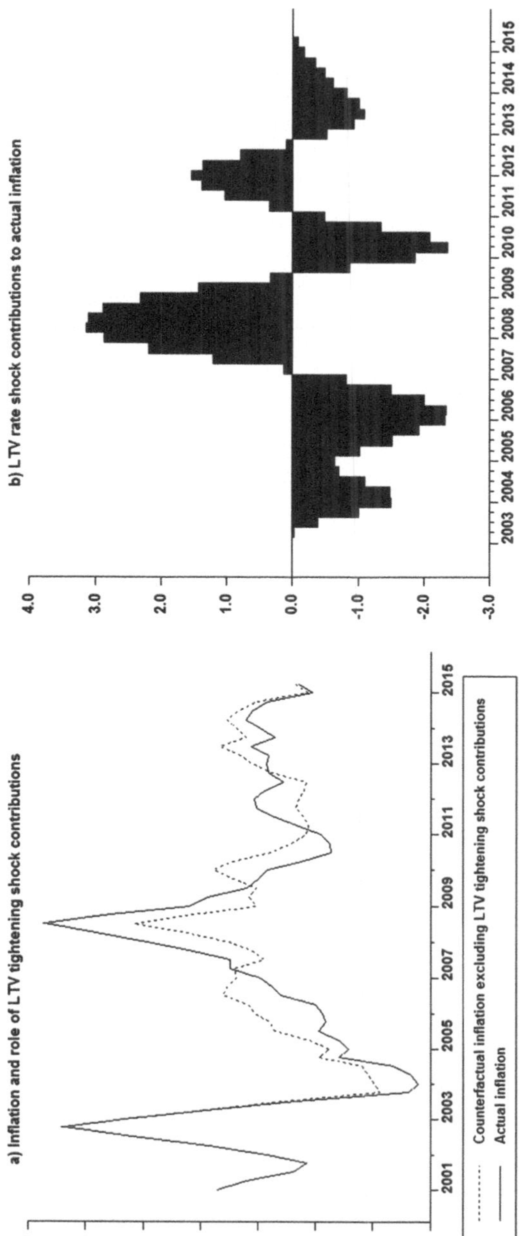

Fig. 21.18 The influence of the LTV tightening shock on inflation dynamics (*Source*: Authors' calculations)

Yes, there are, and since 2013, the LTV tightening shock has contributed to keeping actual inflation lower than what the counterfactual approach suggests it would have been. Fig. 21.18b shows the magnitudes of the contributions. In certain periods the actual inflation is lower by at least 1 percentage point, around 2003–2004, 2005–2007, 2009–2010 and 2013. Thus, the evidence shows that the LTV tightening shock does help to alleviate inflation pressures as it dampens credit-driven demand pressures. This suggests that policymakers can benefit from the coordination of the tools and lessening the burden on the repo rate when the trade-off between financial stability and monetary policy is negligible.

21.4.7 What Can Monetary Policymakers Infer from the Influence of the LTV Tightening Shock on the Level of the Repo Rate?

The historical decomposition approach as described above is used to derive the counterfactual repo rate and to determine the extent to which the LTV tightening shock has influenced the repo rate. The counterfactual repo rate exceeds the actual repo rate since 2013 in Fig. 21.19a. This suggests that an LTV tightening shock led to a lower repo rate than what would have been in the absence of this shock.

The contributions of the LTV tightening shocks to the repo rate suggest that the repo rate was still lower than the counterfactual policy rate in 2015. It was about 1 percentage point lower at the beginning of 2014. This suggests that if policymakers coordinate the tools and, therefore, consider the influence of the LTV, the gradual repo rate adjustments may serve the monetary and financial stability objectives fairly well. The LTV tightening shock does play a positive role for price stability as it impacts the inflation rate. At the same time, it also serves financial stability purposes.

These findings are corroborated by recent literature showing that as the prudential approach to financial stability strengthens and matures, it is very well possible that the equilibrium levels of policy rates will be much lower than they are currently (Du and Miles, 2014).

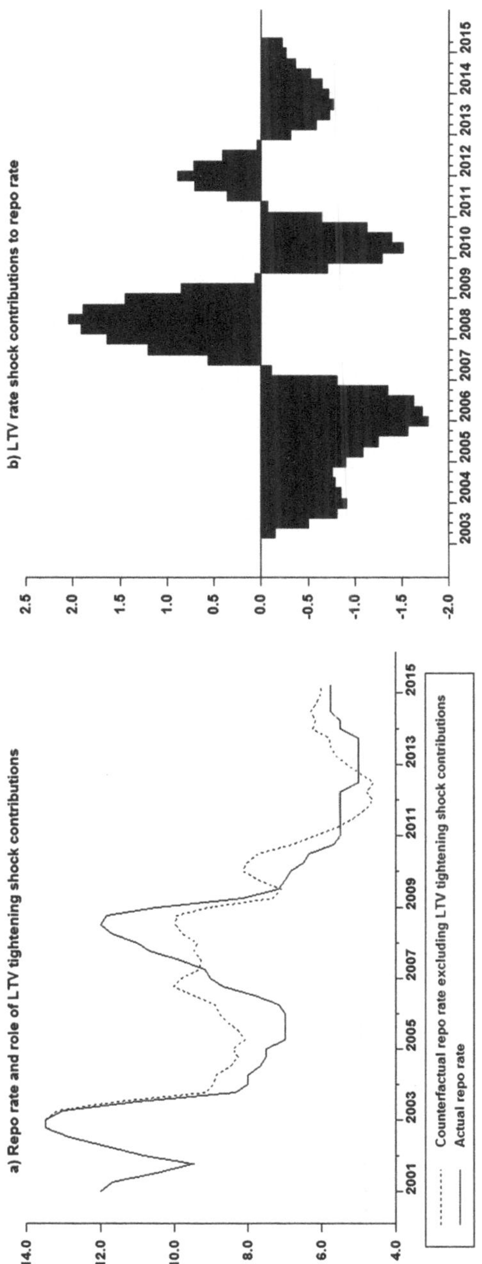

Fig. 21.19 The influence of LTV tightening shock on repo rate (*Source*: Authors' calculations)

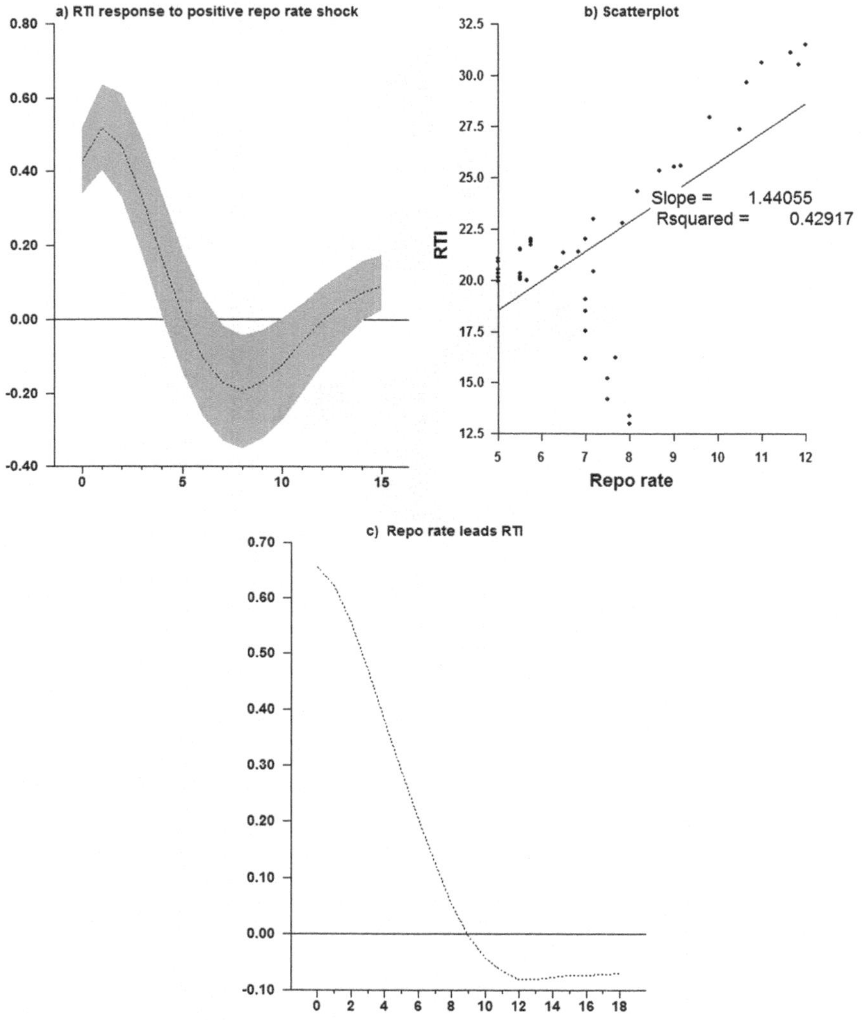

Fig. 21.20 Relationship between repo rate and RTI (*Source*: Authors' calculations)

21.4.8 How Influential Is the RTI Shock in Driving Repo Rate Dynamics?

The analysis is extended to showing the links between the RTI and the repo rate using a variety of techniques. How does the RTI respond to a positive repo rate shock? Fig. 21.20a shows that the RTI rises due to a positive repo rate shock, while the scatter plot in (b) shows a positive relationship. Fig. 21.20c shows that RTI also rises when it is preceded by an increase in the repo rate. All this evidence suggests a positive relationship between the RTI and the repo rate over different horizons and it is more pronounced in the first few quarters in Fig. 21.20a and c.

There is then evidence that the RTI impacted the dynamics of the repo rate based on the historical decomposition approach which shows when the RTI shocks contributed to tighter or looser monetary policy stance. Similarly, the counterfactual repo rate refers to a policy rate that excludes the contribution of RTI shocks.

The decrease in the RTI is visible in Fig. 21.21b and d. Fig. 21.21a shows that since 2013Q1 the actual repo rate exceeded the counterfactual repo rate, suggesting that the gradual decrease in the RTI over this period

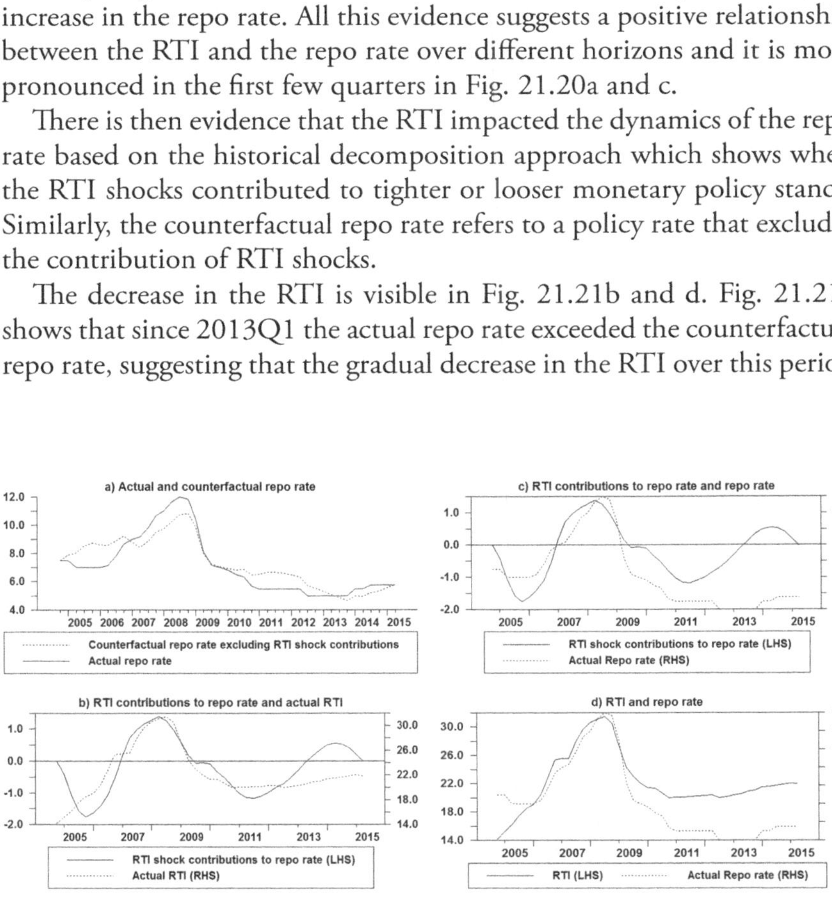

Fig. 21.21 The role of the RTI in the repo rate dynamics (*Source*: Authors' calculations)

implied a tighter repo rate for borrowers. Fig. 21.21c shows that this was the case between 2007 and 2009Q1 and after 2013Q3.

21.5 The Counterfactual Scenarios

The chapter concludes by looking at the interaction between LTV and RTI and repo rate. A particular focus is placed on the amplification by consumer price level, and total loans and advances. Three models are estimated using two lags. The models include the repo rate, GDP, RTI or LTV and consumer price level. The consumer price level is replaced with total loans and advances in the third model. The counterfactual responses are calculated by shutting off the consumer price level, and total loans and advances.

Evidence shows that RTI will rise to a more positive repo rate than what is implied by the counterfactual in the first five quarters, in the presence of the consumer price level. This suggests that elevated consumer price levels amplify the responses. The actual LTV declines much more than the counterfactual in Fig. 21.22c, which suggests that a heightened consumer price level leads to more tightening of LTV in response to positive repo rate shocks. Fig. 21.22e shows that actual LTV is tightened when total loans and advances are not shut off. These findings indicate that consumer price level and total loans and advances amplify RTI and LTV responses to positive repo rate shocks.

21.6 Conclusion and Policy Implications

The chapter assessed the extent to which RTI and LTV shocks impacted macroeconomic housing variables, output, inflation and repo rate dynamics. Evidence suggests that although LTVs do indeed help in equilibrating demand and supply factors in the housing market, other factors play a role for longer durations. An increase in wealth and collateral effects associated with house price appreciation enables the creditors to loosen lend-

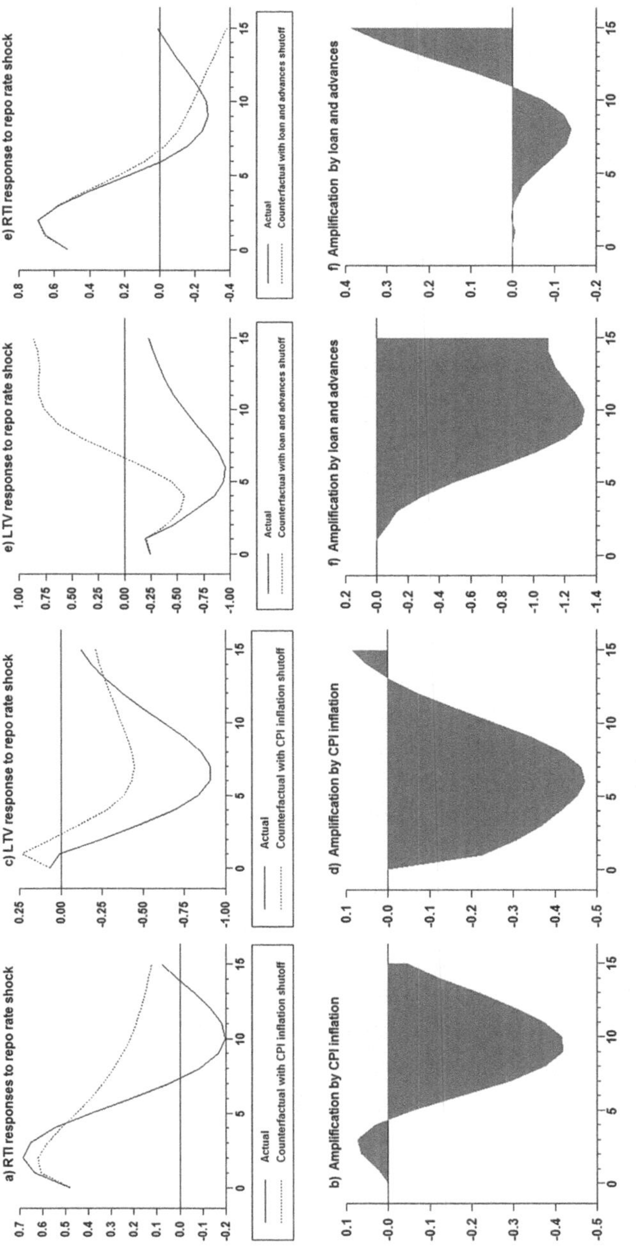

Fig. 21.22 RTI and LTV responses to positive repo rate shocks and amplification by CPI and credit (*Source*: Authors' calculations)

ing standards based on the LTV. At the same time banks increase the RTI, suggesting that the increase in house prices impacts affordability metrics. In order to supply mortgage credit, banks accommodate positive house price shocks by increasing the income gearing or repayment burden and the limit on the mandatory down payment.

Of paramount policy relevance in this relationship is that during the sample period house price increases in most instances preceded the loosening of the LTVs and increase in the RTIs. This implies that as tools at the discretion of banks, LTVs and RTIs help to reinforce the momentum in house prices. As a result, if the intention is to use these tools to avoid overheating or dampen mortgage credit and house price growth, the RTIs and LTVs should be adjusted in a proactive or pre-emptive approach. This approach probably requires a macro-prudential regulatory framework. It can potentially exploit the house price link to the LTVs and RTIs via the expectations channel, as agents gradually lower expected house price increases. In addition, through the expectations channel, tighter LTVs and lower RTIs can also dampen speculative activity. Evidence establishes that between inflation and the repo rate, inflationary shocks lead to larger tightening in the LTV. The policy implication is that high inflation accompanied by an increase in the repo rates can lead to very tight LTVs. It is therefore necessary for policymakers to lower inflation rates and anchor inflation expectations within the inflation target band.

Evidence suggests that the LTV tightening shock does help to alleviate inflation pressures and this suggests that policymakers may benefit from coordination of the tools and lessening the burden on the repo rate. This evidence also points to the fact that if policymakers coordinate the tools and, therefore, consider the influence of the LTV, the gradual repo rate adjustments may serve the monetary and financial stability objectives fairly well. The LTV tightening shock does play a positive role for price stability as it impacts the inflation rate. On the other hand, the RTI shocks suggest that, in recent times, it implied a tighter repo rate for borrowers. There is therefore a need to coordinate all these tools.

Summary of Evidence

- The loosening of LTV leads to an increase in housing demand and raises house prices.
- This is in contrast to the negative effects loose LTVs have on the housing supply.
- The LTV shock moves residential property demand and supply in different directions; this has implications for house price dynamics and possibly wealth and collateral effects for consumers.
- There is a negative relationship between RTIs and first time buyers and the negative relationship holds for LTVs and first time buyers.
- When the credit quality of banks' mortgage books deteriorates as proxied by an increase in NPLs, mortgage advances and first time entrants decline.
- The relationship between NPLs and first time buyers is highly negative and very cyclical.
- An unexpected increase in house prices leads to a significant loosening of the LTV.
- At the same time banks increase the RTI, suggesting that the increase in house prices impacts affordability metrics.
- In order to supply mortgage credit, banks accommodate positive house price shocks by increasing the income gearing or repayment burden and the limit on the mandatory down payment.
- This implies that as tools at the discretion of banks, LTVs and RTIs help to reinforce the momentum in house prices.
- In the absence of exogenous factors inflation declines, suggesting that unexpected tightening in lending standards may benefit the price stability mandate.

References

Acharya, V., & Naqvi, H. (2012). The seeds of a crisis: A theory of bank liquidity and risk-taking over the business cycle. *Journal of Financial Economics, 106*(2), 349–366.

Afonso, G., Kovner, A., & Schoar, A. (2011). *Stressed, not frozen: The federal funds market in the financial crisis* (Staff report No. 437). Federal Reserve Bank of New York Staff Reports. https://www.newyorkfed.org/medialibrary/media/research/staff_reports/sr437.pdf

Agur, I. (2014). *Bank risk within and across equilibria* (IMF working paper WP/14/116). Washington, DC: International Monetary Fund.

Agur, I., & Demertzis, M. (2012). *Excessive bank risk taking and monetary policy* (ECB working paper No. 1457). Frankfurt: European Central Bank.

Akinci, O., & Olmstead-Rumsey, J. (2015). *How effective are macroprudential policies? An empirical investigation* (International Finance discussion papers 1136). https://www.federalreserve.gov/econresdata/ifdp/2015/files/ifdp1136.pdf

Alfelt, G., Lagerwall, B., & Ölcer, D. (2015). *An analysis of the debt-to-income limit as a policy measure* (Riksbank economic commentaries No. 8). http://www.riksbank.se/Documents/Rapporter/Ekonomiska_kommentarer/2015/rap_ek_kom_nr8_150602_eng.pdf

N. Gumata, E. Ndou, *Bank Credit Extension and Real Economic Activity in South Africa*, DOI 10.1007/978-3-319-43551-0

Altunbas, Y., Gambacorta, L., & Marques-Ibanez, D. (2010). *Does monetary policy affect bank risk-taking*? (BIS working papers No 298). Basel: Bank for International Settlements.

Angeloni, I., Faia, E., & Lo Duca, M. (2013). *Monetary policy and risk taking* (SAFE working paper series No. 8). http://bruegel.org/wp-content/uploads/imported/publications/wp_2010_00.pdf

Appleyard, D. R., Field, A., & Cobb, S. L. (2008). *International economics* (6th ed.). Bostan: Macgraw-Hill Irwin.

Atanasova, C. (2003). Credit market imperfections and business cycle dynamics: A non-linear approach. *Studies in Nonlinear Dynamics and Econometrics, 7*(4), 516–536.

Avdjiev, S., & Zeng, Z. (2014). *Credit growth, monetary policy, and economic activity in a three-regime TVAR model* (BIS working papers No. 449). Basel: Bank for International Settlements.

Azariadas, C., & Smith, B. (1996). Private information, money and growth: Indeterminacies, fluctuations and the Mundell-Tobin effect. *Journal of Economic Growth, 1*, 309–322.

Babihuga, R., & Spaltro, M. (2014). *Bank funding costs for international banks* (IMF Working Paper WP/14/71). Washington, DC: International Monetary Fund.

Bacchetta, P., & Caminal, R. (2000). Do capital markets imperfections exacerbate output fluctuations. *European Economic Review, 2*, 449–468.

Balke, N. S. (2000). Credit and economic activity: Credit regimes and nonlinear propagation of shocks. *The Review of Economics and Statistics, 82*(2), 344–349. MIT Press.

Bank capital requirements: Are they costly? http://www.voxeu.org/article/bank-capital-requirements-are-they-costly

Barnett, A., & Thomas, R. (2013). *Has weak lending and activity in the United Kingdom been driven by credit supply shocks*? (Working paper No. 482). London: Bank of England.

Bassett, W. F., & Covas, F. B. (2013). A new look at the relationship between capital constraints and the bank lending. Working Paper Federal Reserve Board. http://www.banque-france.fr/fondation/gb/telechar/pdf/Papier_F_Covas_BankCapital.pdf

Bassett, W. F., Chosak, M. B., Drisoll, J. C., & Zakrajsek, E. (2014). Changes in bank lending standards and the macro economy. *Journal of Monetary Economics, 62*, 23–40.

BCBS. (2010b, December). *Guidance for national authorities operating the countercyclical capital buffer*. Basel: Basel Committee on Banking Supervision.

Beau, E., Hill, J., Hussain, T., & Nixon, D. (2014). Bank funding costs: What are they, what determines them and why do they matter? *Quarterly Bulletin Q4, 54*(4), 370–384. http://www.bankofengland.co.uk/publications/Documents/quarterlybulletin/2014/qb14q4.pdf

Benigno, G., Converse, N., & Fornarox, L. (2015). Large capital inflows, sectoral allocation and economic performance. *Journal of international money and finance* (forthcoming).

Berger, A., De Young, R., Flannery, M., Lee, D., & Oztekin, O. (2008). *How do large banking organizations manage their capital Ratios?* (The Federal Reserve Bank of Kansas City research working papers 08–01). http://citeseerx.ist.psu.edu/viewdoc/download?doi=10.1.1.361.4927&rep=rep1&type=pdf

Berger, A., De Young, R., Flannery, M., Lee, D., & Oztekin, O. (2008). How do large banking organizations manage their capital ratios? *Journal of Financial Services Research, 34*(2), 123–149.

Bergsten, F. (2013). Currency wars, the economy of the United States and reforms of the international monetary system. *12th Stavros Niarchos Foundation Lecture*, Peterson Institute for International Economics.

Berkelmans, L., & Duong, A. (2014, March). Developments in banks' funding costs and lending rates. *Quarterly Bulletin*.

Bernanke, B., & Gertler, M. (1995). Inside the black box: The credit channel of monetary policy transmission. *Journal of Economic Perspectives, 9*(4), 27–48.

Bernanke, B., & Gertler, M. (1999). Monetary policy and asset price volatility. *Federal Reserve Bank of Kansas City Economic Review*, Fourth Quarter.

Bernanke, B. S., Gertler, M., & Gilchrist, S. (1996). The financial accelerator and the flight to quality. *Review of Economics and Statistics, 78*, 1–15.

Bernanke, B. S., Gertler, M., & Gilchrist, S. (1999). The financial accelerator in a quantitative business cycle framework. In M. Woodford & J. Taylor (Eds.), *Handbook of macroeconomics*. Amsterdam: North-Holland.

Bijsterbosch, M., & Falagiarda, M. (2015). Credit supply dynamics and economic activity in euro area countries: A time-varying parameter VAR analysis. *Journal of International Money and Finance* Elsevier, *54*(C), 93–115.

Blanchard, O. (2008). *The crisis: Basic mechanisms, and appropriate policies* (IMF working paper 09-01). Washington, DC: International Monetary Fund.

Blanchard, O., Dell'Ariccia, G., & Mauro, P. (2010). *Rethinking macroeconomic policy* (IMF Staff Position Note. SPN/10/03). https://www.imf.org/external/pubs/ft/spn/2010/spn1003.pdf

Bloom, N. (2009). The impact of uncertainty shocks. *Econometrica, 77*(3), 623–685.

Bordo, M. C., & Jeanne, O. (2002). Monetary policy and asset prices: Does 'benign neglect' make sense? *International Finance, V5*(2,Summer), 139–164.

Bordo, M. D., & Wheelock, D. C. (2006). *When do stock market booms occur? The macroeconomic and policy environments of 20th century booms* (Working paper 2006-051A). St. Louis: Federal Reserve Bank.

Borgy, V., Clerc, L., & Renne, J.-P. (2009). *Asset-price boom-bust cycles and credit: What is the scope of macro-prudential regulation?* Paris: Banque de France.

Borio, C. (2012). *The financial cycle and macroeconomics: What have we learnt?* (BIS working papers No. 395). Basel: Bank for International Settlement.

Bouvatier, V., & Lepetit, L. (2008). Banks' procyclical behaviour: Does provisioning matter? *Journal of International Financial Markets Institutions Money, 18*(5), 513–526.

Bouvatier, V., & Lepetit, L. (2012). Provisioning rules and bank lending: A theoretical model. *Journal of Financial Stability, 8*, 25–31.

Boyd, J. H., Levine, R., & Smith, B. D. (2001). The impact of inflation on financial sector performance. *Journal of Monetary Economics, 47*, 221–248.

Bruno, V. & Shin, H. S. (2013). *Capital flows and the risk-taking channel of monetary policy* (NBER working paper 18942). http://www.nber.org/papers/w18942

Buch, C. M., Eickmeier, S., & Prieto, E. (2011). *In search for yield? Survey-based evidence on bank risk taking* (Discussion paper series No. 10/2011). Deutsche Bundesbank. https://www.bundesbank.de/Redaktion/EN/Downloads/Publications/Discussion_Paper_1/2011/2011_05_13_dkp_10.pdf?__blob=publicationFile

Bushman, R. M., & Williams, C. D. (2012). Accounting discretion, loan loss provisioning, and discipline of banks' risk-taking. *Journal Accounting and Economics, 54*(1), 1–18.

Button, R., Pezzini, S., & Rossiter, N. (2010). Understanding the price of new lending to households. *Bank of England Quarterly Bulletin*, Q3.

Caldara, D., Fuentes-Albero, C., Gilchrist, S., & Zakrajsek, E. (2014). *The macroeconomic impact of financial and uncertainty shocks*. http://www.cepr.org/sites/default/files/Caldara_Fuentes-Albero_Gilchrist_Zakrajsek.pdf

Calza, A., Monacelli, T., & Stracca, L. (2009). *Housing finance and monetary policy* (Working paper 1069). Frankfurt: European Central Bank.

Cantero-Saiz, M., Sanfilippo-Azofra, S., Torre-Olmo, B., & López-Gutiérrez, C. (2014). Sovereign risk and the bank lending channel in Europe. *Journal of International Money and Finance, 47*(C), 1–20.

Cardarelli, R., Elekdag, S., & Lall, S. (2011). Financial stress and economic contractions. *Journal of Financial Stability, 7*, 78–97.

Carstens, A. (2015, April 20). Challenges for emerging economies in the face of unconventional monetary policies in advanced economies. *Stavros Niarchos Foundation Lecture*, Peterson Institute for International Economics.

Cecchetti, S. G. (2006). *Measuring the macroeconomic risks posed by asset price booms* (NBER working paper 12542). Cambridge, MA: National Bureau of Economic Research.

Cesa-Bianchi, A., Cespedes, L. F., & Rebucci, A. (2015). *Global liquidity, house prices, and the macroeconomy: Evidence from advanced and emerging economies* (IMF working paper WP/15/23). Washington, DC: International Monetary Fund.

Chami, R., & Cosimano, T. F. (2010). Monetary policy with a touch of Basel. *Journal of Economics and Business, 62*, 161–175.

Chiarella, C., Flaschel, P., Hartmann, F., Christian, R., & Proaño, C. R. (2011). *Stock market booms, endogenous credit creation and the implications of broad and narrow banking for macroeconomic stability*. University of Kent.

Choi, S., Smith, B., & Boyd, J. (1996). Inflation, financial markets, and capital formation. *Federal Reserve Bank of St. Louis Review, 78*, 9–35.

Christiano, L. J., Eichenbaum, M., & Evans, C. L. (1999). Monetary policy shocks: What have we learned and to what end? In J. B. Taylor, & M. Woodford (Eds.), *Handbook of macroeconomics* (Vol. 1., Chap. 2, pp. 65–148). North-Holland: Elsevier.

Christiano, L., Motto, R., & Rostagno, M. (2009). *Financial factors in economic fluctuations (Preliminary)* (Working paper). Frankfurt: European Central Bank.

Christiano, L., Motto, R., & Rostagno, M. (2010). *Financial factors in economic fluctuations* (ECB working paper series No. 1192). Frankfurt: Main European Central Bank.

Claessens, S. (2014). *An overview of macroprudential policy tools* (IMF working paper WP/14/214). Washington, DC: International Monetary Fund.

Claessens, S., Kose, M. A., & Terrones, M. E. (2011a). *Financial cycles: What? How? When? NBER international seminar on macroeconomics 2010* (L. Reichlin & K. West, Eds., IMF Working Paper No 11/76). National Bureau of Economic Research, forthcoming.

Claessens, S., Kose, M. A., & Terrones, M. E. (2011b). *How do business and financial cycles interact?* (IMF working paper WP/11/88). Washington, DC: International Monetary Fund.

Converse, N. (2014). *Uncertainty, capital flows, and maturity mismatch*. http://personal.lse.ac.uk/converse/Converse_uncertainty&kflows.pdf

Covas, F. B., & Driscoll, J. C. (2011). *The macroeconomic impact of adding liquidity regulations to bank capital regulations.* Federal Reserve Board. http://www.frbsf.org/economic-research/events/2013/january/federal-reserve-day-ahead-financial-markets-institutions/files/Session_2_Paper_2_Covas_Driscoll_regulations.pdf

Deans, C., & Stewart, C. (2012, March). Banks' funding costs and lending rates. *Reserve Bank of Australia Quarterly Bulletin.*

Delis, D. M., Hasan, I., & Mylonidis, N. (2011). *The risk-taking channel of monetary policy in the USA: Evidence from micro-level data* (MPRA paper No. 34084).

Dell'Ariccia, G., Laeven L., & Suarez, G. (2013). *Bank leverage and monetary policy's risk-taking channel: Evidence from the United States* (IMF working paper WP/13/143). Washington, DC: International Monetary Fund.

Detken, C., & Smets, F. (2004). *Asset price booms and monetary policy* (ECB working paper series WP No. 364). Frankfurt: European Central Bank.

Diamond, D. W., & Rajan, R. G. (2009). *Illiquidity and interest rate policy* (NBER working paper No. 15197). Cambridge, MA: National Bureau of Economic Research.

Ehrmann, M., & Fratzscher, M. (2004). *Taking stock: Monetary policy transmission to equity markets* (ECB working paper series No. 354). Frankfurtam: European Central Bank.

Eickmeier, S., Gambacorta, L., & Hofmann, B. (2014). Understanding global liquidity. *European Economic Review, 68*, 1–18.

Enders, W., & Granger, C. W. J. (1998). Unit-root tests and asymmetric adjustment with an example using the term structure of interest rates. *Journal of Business and Economic Statistics, 16*(3), 304–311.

Enders, W., & Siklos, P. L. (2001). Cointegration and threshold adjustment. *Journal of Business & Economic Statistics, 19*, 166–176.

Fabbro, D., & Hack, M. (2011, March). The effects of funding costs and risk on banks' lending rates. *Reserve Bank of Australia Quarterly Bulletin.*

Fatas, A., Kannan, P., Rabanal, P., & Scott, A. (2009, October). *Lessons from asset price fluctuations for monetary policy.* World Economic Outlook.

Forbes, K. J., & Warnock, F. E. (2011). *Capital flow waves: Surges, stops, flight and retrenchments* (Working paper 17351). Cambridge, MA: National Bureau of Economic Research.

Forbes, K. J., & Warnock, F. E. (2012). Capital flow waves: Surges, stops, flight, and retrenchment. *Journal of International Economics, 88*(2), 235–251.

Fratzscher, M. (2011). *Capital flows, push versus pull factors and the global financial crisis* (Working paper series No 1364/JULY 2011). https://www.ecb.europa.eu/pub/pdf/scpwps/ecbwp1364.pdf?49a220a208cf4aeba5f0774b5ae1e7ed

Fukunga, I. (2002). *Financial accelerator effects in Japan's business cycle* (Working paper series 02-6). https://www.boj.or.jp/en/research/wps_rev/wps_2002/data/cwp02e06.pdf

Gabiax, X., Krishnamurthy, A., & Vigneron, O. (2007). Limits of arbitrage: Theory and evidence from the mortgage–backed securities market. *Journal of Finance, 62*, 557–595.

Gambetti, L., & Musso, A. (2012). *Loan supply shocks and the business cycle* (Working paper series 1469). Frankfurt: European Central Bank.

Gelain, P., Lansing, K., & Mendicino, C. (2012), *House prices, credit growth, and excess volatility: Implications for monetary and macroprudential policy* (Norges Bank research working paper 2012/08). http://www.norges-bank.no/pages/89928/Norges_Bank_Working_Paper_2012_08.pdf

Geršl, A., & Seidler, J. (2012). *Credit growth and countercyclical capital buffers: Empirical evidence from central and eastern European countries* (IES working paper 3/2012). Prague: IES FSV. Charles University.

Gertler prescription? Paper prepared for "New perspectives on asset price bubbles: Theory, evidence and policy," Loyola University Chicago.

Gertler, M., & Karadi, P. (2011). A model of unconventional monetary policy. *Journal of Monetary Economics, 58*, 17–34.

Gilchrist, S., & Zakrajsek, E. (2012). Credit spreads and business cycle fluctuations. *American Economic Review, 102*(4), 1692–1720.

Gumata, N., Ndou, E., & Ncube, M. (forthcoming). Capital flows and macroeconomic effects in South Africa.

Gunay, H., & Kilinc, M. (2011). *Credit market imperfections and business cycle asymmetries in Turkey* (Working paper No. 11/07). Central Bank of the Republic of Turkey. http://www.tcmb.gov.tr/wps/wcm/connect/TCMB+EN/TCMB+EN/Main+Menu/PUBLICATIONS/Research/Working+Papers/2011/11-07

Gurkaynak, S. R. (2008). Econometric tests of asset price bubbles: Taking stock. *Journal of Economic Surveys, 22*(1), 166–186.

Hakkio, C. S., & Keeton, W. R. (2009). Financial stress: What is it, how can it be measured, and why does it matter? *Federal Reserve Bank Kansas City Review, 2*, 1–46.

Halvorsen, I. J., & Jacobsen, D. H. (2009). *Are bank lending shocks important for economic fluctuations?* (Working paper No. 27). Oslo: Norges Bank.

Hannan, T. H. (1994). Asymmetric price rigidity and the responsiveness of customers to prices changes: The case of deposit interest rates. *Journal of Financial Services Research, 8*, 257–267.

Hannan, T. H., & Berger, A. N. (1991). The rigidity of prices: Evidence from the banking industry. *American Economic Review, 81*, 938–945.

Harbo Hansen, N., & Welz, P. (2011). *Interest rate pass-through during the global financial crisis: The case of Sweden* (OECD Economics Department working papers No. 855). Paris: OECD Publishing.

Haubrich, J. G. (2015). *How cyclical is bank capital?* (Working paper 15/04). Cleveland: Federal Reserve Bank of Cleveland.

Helbling, T., Huidrom, H., Kose, M. A., & Otrok, C. (2011). Do credit shocks matter? A global perspective. *European Economic Review, 55*, 340–353.

Hristov, N., Huselwig, O., & Wollmershauser, T. (2012). Loan supply shocks during the financial crisis: Evidence for the Euro area. *Journal of International Money and Finance, 31*, 569–592.

Hubrich, R., & Tetlow, R. J. (2015). Financial stress and economic dynamics: The transmission of crises. *Journal of Monetary Economics, 70*, 100–115.

Hull, I. (2015). *Amortization requirements and household indebtedness: An application to Swedish-style mortgages* (Working paper series No. 298). Stockholm: Sveriges Riksbank.

Huybens, E., & Smith, B. (1998). Financial market frictions, monetary policy, and capital accumulation in a small open economy. *Journal of Economic Theory, 81*, 353–400.

Huybens, E., & Smith, B. (1999). Inflation, financial markets, and long-run real activity. *Journal of Monetary Economics, 43*, 283–315.

Igan, D., & Kang, H. (2011). *Do loan-to-value and debt-to-income limits work?* Evidence from Korea (IMF working paper WP/11/297). Washington, DC: International Monetary Fund.

Illes, A., & Lombardi, M. (2013). Interest rate pass-through since the financial crisis. *BIS Quarterly Bulletin*.

IMF. (2013). *The interaction of monetary and macroprudential policies*. IMF.

Ioannidou, V. P., Ongena, S., & Peydro, J. L. (2009). *Monetary policy, risk- taking, and pricing: Evidence from a quasi-natural experiment*. CentER – Tilburg University, mimeo.

Issing, O. (2003). *Monetary and financial stability: Is there a trade-off?* (BIS working paper, 18, 2003). http://www.bis.org/publ/bppdf/bispap18.pdf

Issing, O. (2003). Monetary and financial stability: Is there a trade-off? https://www.ecb.europa.eu/press/key/date/2003/html/sp030329.en.html

Issing, O. (2011). *Lessons for monetary policy: What should the consensus be?* (Working paper 11/97, IMF). Washington, DC: International Monetary Fund.

Jimenez, G., Ongena, S., Peydro, J. L., & Saurina, J. (2008). Hazardous times for monetary policy: What do twenty-three million bank loans say about the effects of monetary policy on credit risk-taking? *Econometrica, 82*(2), 463–505. 03.

Jimenez, G., Ongena, S., Peydro, J. L., & Saurina, J. (2012). *Macroprudential policy, countercyclical bank capital buffers and credit supply: Evidence from the Spanish dynamic provisioning experiments* (Discussion paper 2012–036), Tilburg University, Center for Economic Research. https://pure.uvt.nl/portal/files/1428635/2012-036.pdf

Jones, P., & Enders, W. (2016). The asymmetric effects of uncertainty on macroeconomic activity. *Macroeconomic Dynamics, 20*(5), 1219–1246.

Jordan, T. J. (2015, August 28). *The impact of international spill-overs on inflation dynamics and independent monetary policy: The Swiss experience.* Conference paper presented at Jackson Hole.

Kaminsky, G. L., & Reinhart, C. M. (1999). The twin crises: The causes of banking and balance-of-payments problems. *The American Economic Review, 89*(3), 473–500.

Kannan, P., Rabanal, P., & Scott, A. (2009). *Macroeconomic patterns and monetary policy in the run-up to asset price busts* (Working paper WP/09/252). Washington, DC: International Monetary Fund.

Kara, H. (2013). *Safeguarding macroeconomic and price stability amid capital flow volatility.* Note prepared for the BIS Meeting of Central Bank Chief Economists. Basel: BIS, Central Bank of the Republic of Turkey.

Karras, G. (1996). Are the output effects of monetary policy asymmetric? Evidence from a sample of European countries. *Oxford Bulletin of Economics and Statistics, 58*, 267–278.

Kelly, R., McQuinn, K., & Stuart, R. (2013). *Exploring the steady-state relationship between credit and GDP for a small open economy the case of Ireland* (ECB working paper series No. 1531). Frankfurt: European Central Bank.

Kennedy, G., & Calder T. M. (2011). *The Irish mortgage market stylised facts, negative equity and arrears* (Central Bank of Ireland research technical paper 12/RT/11). http://www.centralbank.ie/publications/documents/12rt11.pdf

Kim, C. (2013, April 16–17). *Macroprudential policies: Korea's experiences.* Paper presented at the Rethinking Macro Policy II: First Steps and Early Lessons conference, hosted by the IMF, Washington, DC.

Kim, S., & Yang, S. Y. (2009). Do capital inflows matter to asset prices? The case of Korea. *Asian Economic Journal, 23*(3), 323–348.

Kiyotaki, N., & Moore, J. (1997). Credit cycles. *The Journal of Political Economy, 105*(2), 211–248.

Kose, M. A., Prasad, E., & Terrones, M. E. (2006). How do trade and financial integration affect relationship between growth and volatility? *Journal of International Economies, 69*(1), 176–202.

Kose, M. A., Prasad, E., Rogoff, K., & Wei, S.-J. (2009). Financial globalization: A reappraisal. *IMF Staff papers, 56*, 8–62.

Kristin, J., Forbes, K. J., & Warnock, F. E. (2011). *Capital flow waves: Surges, stops, flight and retrenchments* (Working paper 17351). Cambridge, MA: National Bureau of Economic Research.

Kuttner, N. K. (2011). Monetary policy and asset price volatility: Should we refill the Bernanke-Gertler prescription?. http://web.williams.edu/Economics/wp/KuttnerMonetaryPolicyAndAssetPriceVolatility.pdf

Laeven, L., & Majnoni, G. (2003). Loan loss provisioning and economic slowdowns: Too much, too late? *Journal of Financial Intermediation, 12*(2), 178–179.

Lavigne, R., Sarker, S., & Vasishtha, G. (2014). *Spillover effects of quantitative easing on emerging market economies*. Ottawa: Bank of Canada.

Le Lesle, V., & Avramova, S. (2012). *Revisiting risk-weighted assets: "Why do RWAs differ across countries and what can be done about it?"* (IMF working paper WP/12/90). Washington, DC: International Monetary Fund.

Lee, J., Strazicich, M. C., & Yu, B. C. (2013). Asymmetric adjustments in the spread of lending and deposit rates: Evidence from extended threshold unit root tests. *Review of Financial Economics, 22*, 187–193.

Li, B. G., O'Connell, S., Adam, C., Berg, A., & Montiel, P. (2016). *VAR meets DSGE: Uncovering the monetary transmission mechanism in low-income countries* (IMF working paper WP/16/90). https://www.imf.org/external/pubs/ft/wp/2016/wp1690.pdf

Lim, C., Columba, F., Costa, A., Kongsamut, P., Otani, A., Saiyid, M., Wezel, T., & Wu, X. (2011). *Macroprudential policy: What instruments and how to use them? Lessons from Country experiences* (IMF working paper 11/238). Washington, DC: International Monetary Fund.

Ludovic Gauvin, L., McLoughlin, C., & Reinhardt, D. (2013). *Policy uncertainty spillovers to emerging markets: Evidence from capital flows* (Document De Travail No. 435). Paris: Banque de France.

Lydon, R., & McCarthy, Y. (2011). *What lies beneath? Understanding recent trends in Irish mortgage arrears* (Bank of Ireland research technical paper 14/RT/11). http://www.centralbank.ie/publications/documents/14rt11.pdf

Macro-prudential policy for residential mortgage lending (Consultation paper CP87). (2014). Dublin: Central Bank of Ireland.

McCarthy, Y. (2014). *Dis-entangling the mortgage arrears crisis: The role of the labour market, income volatility and negative equity*. Dublin: Central Bank of Ireland.

McCarthy, Y., & McQuinn, K. (2013). *Credit conditions in a boom and bust property market* (Central Bank of Ireland Research technical paper 8/RT/13). Dublin: Central Bank of Ireland.

Mendicino, C. (2012). *Collateral requirements: Macroeconomic fluctuations and macro-prudential policy* (Banco de Portugal, working paper 11/2012). https://www.bportugal.pt/en-US/BdP%20Publications%20Research/wp201211.pdf

Meyer, D. (2014). *Household interest rate analysis*. Economic Note presented at the September 2014 MPC.

Mishkin, F. S. (2008, October). *How should we respond to asset price bubbles?* Banque de France, *Financial Stability Review, 12*, Valuation and financial stability.

Neumark, D., & Sharpe, S. (1992). Market structure and the nature of price rigidity. *Quarterly Journal of Economics, 107*, 657–680.

Ng, T. (2011). The predictive content of financial cycle measures for output fluctuations. *BIS Quarterly Review, 1*, 53–65.

Nguyen, C. V., & Islam, A. M. (2010). Asymmetries in the Thai lending-deposit rate spread: An econometric analysis. *Applied Economics Letters, 17*, 1229–1236.

Nodari, G. (2014). Financial regulation policy uncertainty and credits spreads in the US. *Journal of Macroeconomics, 41*, 122–132.

Ozsuca, E. A., & Akbostanci, E. (2012). *An empirical analysis of the risk taking channel of monetary policy in Turkey* (Economic Research Centre working paper 12/08). http://www.erc.metu.edu.tr/menu/series12/1208.pdf

Paligorova, T., & Jimenez, J. A. S. (2012). Monetary Policy and the risk-taking channel: Insight from the Lending Behavior of Banks. *Bank of Canada Review*, Autumn 2012.

Perron, P. (1989). The great crash, the oil price shock, and the unit root hypothesis. *Econometrica, 57*, 1361–1401.

Policy transmission. *Journal of Economic Perspectives, 9*, 27–48.

Pool, S., de Haan, L., & Jacobs, J. P. A. M. (2015). Loan loss provisioning, bank credit and the real economy. *Journal of Macroeconomics, 45*, 124–136.

Rajan, R. (1992). Insiders and outsiders: The choice between informed and arm's length debt. *Journal of Finance, 47*, 1367–1400.

Rhee, W., & Rich, R. (1995). Inflation and the asymmetric effects of money on output fluctuations. *Journal of Macroeconomics, 17*, 683–702.

Robertson, B., & Rush, A. (2013). Developments in banks' funding costs and lending rates. *RBA Bulletin*, pp. 63–70.

Rothenberg, A. D., & Warnock, F. E. (2011). Sudden flight and true sudden stops. *Review of International Economics, 19*(3), 509–524.

Rubio, M., & Carrasco-Gallego, J. (2012). *Macroprudential measures, housing markets and monetary policy* (CEPREMAP Dynare working papers series No. 23). http://www.dynare.org/wp-repo/dynarewp023.pdf

Saborowski. C., & Weber, S. (2013). *Assessing the determinants of interest rate transmission through conditional impulse response functions* (IMF working paper WP/13/23). Washington, DC: International Monetary Fund.

Samarina, A., & Bezemer, D. (2016). Do capital flows change domestic credit allocation? *Journal of International Money and Finance*, forthcoming.

Schembri, L. (2015). *The long-term evolution of house prices: An international perspective*. Remarks at the Canadian Association for Business Economics, Kingston.

Scholnick, B. (1996). Asymmetric adjustment of commercial bank interest rates: Evidence from Malaysia and Singapore. *Journal of International Money and Finance, 15*, 485–496.

Shaw, M., Chang, J., & Chen, H. (2012). *Capital adequacy and the bank lending channel: Macroeconomic implications* (Munich Personal RePEc Archive, MPRA paper No. 41056). https://mpra.ub.uni-muenchen.de/41056/1/MPRA_paper_41056.pdf

Smets, F. (2013, June 3). *Financial stability and monetary policy: How closely interlinked?* European Central Bank. Paper prepared for the Riksbank Conference on "Two decades of inflation targeting: Main lessons and remaining challenges", held in Stockholm.

Smets, F. (2014). Financial stability and monetary policy: How closely interlinked? *International Journal of Central Banking, 10*, 263–300.

Stein, J. (2013). *Overheating in credit markets: Origins, measurement, and policy responses*. Speech at the "Restoring Household Financial Stability after the Great Recession: Why Household Balance Sheets Matter", research symposium sponsored by the Federal Reserve Bank of St. Louis, Missouri.

Svensson, L. (2012a). Comment on Michael Woodford, "Inflation targeting and financial stability". *Sveriges Riksbank Economic Review, 2012*(1), 33–40.

Svensson, L. (2012b). The relation between monetary policy and financial stability policy. *International Journal of Central Banking, 8*(1), 293–295.

Thompson, M. A. (2006). Asymmetric adjustment in the prime lending–deposit rate spread. *Review of Financial Economics, 15*, 323–329.

Tillman, P. (2012). Capital inflows and asset prices: Evidence from emerging Asia. *Journal of Banking & Finance, 37*, 717–729.

Tillman, P. (2013). Capital inflows and asset prices: Evidence from emerging Asia. *Journal of Banking & Finance, 37*(3), 717–729.

Toporowski, J. (2008). *Excess capital and liquidity management* (Working paper No. 549). Annandale-on-Hudson: The Levy Economics Institute.

Tovar, C. E., Garcia-Escribano, M., & Vera Martin, M. (2012). *Credit growth and the effectiveness of reserve requirements and other macroprudential instruments in Latin America* (IMF WP/12/142). Washington, DC: International Monetary Fund.

Van Rixtel, A., & Gasperini, G. (2013). *Financial crises and bank funding: Recent experience in the euro area* (BIS working papers No. 406). Basel: Bank for International Settlements, Monetary and Economic Department.

Walentin, K. (2013). *Housing collateral and the monetary transmission mechanism.* http://www.riksbank.se/Documents/Forskning/Personliga_webbsidor/2013/foe_walentin_housing_130405.pdf

Walentin, K. (2014). Business cycle implications of mortgage spreads. *Journal of Monetary Economics, 67*, 62–77.

Williams, J. C. (2014, June 5). Presentation to the Deutsche Bundesbank Conference Housing Markets and the Macroeconomy: Challenges for Monetary Policy and Financial Stability Eltville am Rhein, Germany.

Wu, P. C., Liu, S. Y., & Pan, S. C. (2012). Non-linear bilateral trade balance-fundamentals nexus: A panel smooth transition regression approach. *International Review of Economics and Finance, 27*, 318–329.

Xiong, W. (2013). Bubbles, crises, and heterogeneous beliefs. In J.-P. Fouque & J. Langsam (Eds.), *Handbook for systemic risk.* Cambridge: Cambridge University Press.

Zilberman, R., & Tayler, W. J. (2014). *Financial shocks, loan loss provisions and macroprudential stability* (Economics working paper series No. 23). Bailrigg: Lancaster University.

Index

Note: Page numbers followed by 'n' denote notes.

N. Gumata, E. Ndou, *Bank Credit Extension and Real Economic Activity in South Africa*, DOI 10.1007/978-3-319-43551-0

The manufacturer's authorised representative in the EU is Springer Nature Customer Service Centre GmbH, Europaplatz 3, 69115 Heidelberg, Germany. If you have any concerns regarding our products, please contact ProductSafety@springernature.com

Printed and bound by CPI Group (UK) Ltd, Croydon, CR0 4YY
25/09/2026
02222881-0010